EXCHANGE RATES AND THE MONETARY SYSTEM

ECONOMISTS OF THE TWENTIETH CENTURY

General Editors: Mark Perlman, *University Professor of Economics, University of Pittsburgh* and Mark Blaug, *Professor Emeritus, University of London; Professor Emeritus, University of Buckingham and Visiting Professor, University of Exeter*

This innovative series comprises specially invited collections of articles and papers by economists whose work has made an important contribution to economics in the late twentieth century.

The proliferation of new journals and the ever-increasing number of new articles make it difficult for even the most assiduous economist to keep track of all the important recent advances. By focusing on those economists whose work is generally recognized to be at the forefront of the discipline, the series will be an essential reference point for the different specialisms included.

A list of published and future titles in this series is printed at the end of this volume.

Exchange Rates and the Monetary System

Selected Essays of Peter B. Kenen

Peter B. Kenen

Walker Professor of Economics and International Finance
Director, International Finance Section
Princeton University, USA

Edward Elgar

332.45
K33e

Published by
Edward Elgar Publishing Limited
Gower House
Croft Road
Aldershot
Hants GU11 3HR
England

Edward Elgar Publishing Company
Old Post Road
Brookfield
Vermont 05036
USA

British Library Cataloguing in Publication Data
Kenen, Peter B.
 Exchange Rates and the Monetary System:
 Selected Essays of Peter B. Kenen. –
 (Economists of the Twentieth Century
 Series)
 I. Title II. Series
 332.4

Library of Congress Cataloguing in Publication Data
Kenen, Peter B., 1932–
  Exchange rates and the monetary system : selected essays of Peter
 B. Kenen / Peter B. Kenen.
    p. cm. — (Economists of the twentieth century)
  1. Foreign exchange rates. I. Title. II. Series.
 HG3851.K46 1994
 332.4'56—dc20   93–38550
                                                                            CIP

Printed and Bound in Great Britain by
Hartnolls Limited, Bodmin, Cornwall.

ISBN 1 85278 943 3

Contents

Acknowledgements

The publishers wish to thank the following who have kindly given permission for the use of copyright material.

American Economic Association for articles: Peter B. Kenen, 'Exchange Rate Management: What Role for Intervention?', *American Economic Review*, May 1987, **77**(2), 194–9; Peter B. Kenen, 'Organizing Debt Relief: The Need for a New Institution', *Journal of Economic Perspectives*, Winter 1990, **4**(1), 7–18.

American Finance Association for the article: Peter B. Kenen, 'The Balance of Payments and Policy Mix: Simulations Based on a U.S. Model', *Journal of Finance*, May 1974, **XXIX**(2), 631–54.

Banco Nazionale del Lavoro for article: Peter B. Kenen, 'The Analytics of a Substitution Account', *Banca Nazionale del Lavoro Quarterly Review*, December 1980, **139**, 403–26.

Blackwell Publishers for excerpt: Peter B. Kenen, 'Exchange Rates and Policy Co-ordination in an Asymmetric Model' in Carlo Carraro et al. (eds), *International Economic Policy Co-ordination*, 1991, 83–107.

Economic Record for article: Peter B. Kenen, 'Forward Rates, Interest Rates, and Expectations under Alternative Exchange-Rate Regimes', *Economic Record*, September 1985, **61**, 654–66.

Elsevier Science Publishers for excerpts: Peter B. Kenen, 'Macroeconomic Theory and Policy: How the Closed Economy Was Opened' in Ronald W. Jones and Peter B. Kenen (eds), *The Handbook of International Economics*, 1985, vol. 2, 625–77; Peter B. Kenen and Elinor B. Yudin, 'The Demand for International Reserves', *Review of Economics and Statistics*, August 1965, **XLVII**(3), 242–50; Peter B. Kenen and Dani Rodrik, 'Measuring and Analyzing the Effects of Short-Term Volatility in Real Exchange Rates', *Review of Economics and Statistics*, Spring 1986, **LXVIII**(2), 311–15; Peter B. Kenen and Kathryn M. Dominguez, 'Intramarginal Intervention in the EMS and the Target-Zone Model of Exchange-Rate Behavior', *European Economic Review*, 1992, **36**, 1523–32.

Group of Thirty for the excerpts: Peter B. Kenen and Clare Pack 'Exchange Rates, Domestic Prices, and the Adjustment Process', *Exchange Rates, Domestic Prices, and the Adjustment Process*, 1980, 1–46; Peter B. Kenen, 'The Role of the Dollar as an International Currency', *The Role of the Dollar as an International Currency*, 1983, 3–31.

HarperCollins Publishers for excerpt: Peter B. Kenen, 'Effects of Intervention and Sterilization in the Short Run and the Long Run' in Richard N. Cooper et al. (eds), *The International Monetary System under Flexible Exchange Rates*, 1981, 51–68.

Helbing & Lichtenhahn Verlag for article: Peter B. Kenen and Constantine S. Voivodas, 'Export Instability and Economic Growth', *Kyklos*, 1972, **XXV**(4), 791–802.

International Economic Journal for article: Peter B. Kenen, 'Debt Buybacks and Forgiveness in a Model with Voluntary Repudiation', *International Economic Journal*, Spring 1991, **5**(1), 1–13.

International Monetary Fund for excerpts: Peter B. Kenen, 'Exchange Rate Arrangements, Seigniorage, and the Provision of Public Goods' in Jacob A. Frenkel and Morris Goldstein (eds), *International Financial Policy*, 1991, 306–44; Peter B. Kenen, 'Use of the SDR to Supplement or Substitute for Other Means of Finance' in George M. von Furstenberg (ed.), *International Money and Credit*, 1983, 327–60; Peter B. Kenen, 'Transitional Arrangements for Trade and Payments among the CMEA Countries', *International Monetary Fund Staff Papers*, June 1991, **38**(2), 235–67.

Organisation for Economic Co-operation and Development for excerpt: Peter B. Kenen, 'Financial Opening and the Exchange Rate Regime' in Helmut Reisen and Bernard Fischer (eds), *Financial Opening: Policy Issues and Experiences in Developing Countries*, 1993, 237–62.

The Overseas Development Council and Transaction Publishers for excerpt: Peter B. Kenen, 'The Use of IMF Credit' in Richard E. Feinberg and Catherine Gwin (eds), *Pulling Together: The International Monetary Fund in a Multipolar World*, 1989, 69–91.

Pergamon Press Ltd, Headington Hill Hall, Oxford OX3 0BW, UK for article: Peter B. Kenen 'What Role for IMF Surveillance?', *World Development*, 1987, **15**(12), 1445–56.

Royal Institute of International Affairs for article: Peter B. Kenen 'The European Central Bank and Monetary Policy in Stage Three of EMU', *International Affairs*, July 1992, **68**(3), 457–74.

University of Chicago Press and University of Chicago for excerpts: Peter B. Kenen, 'The Theory of Optimum Currency Areas: An Eclectic View' in Robert A. Mundell and Alexander K. Swoboda (eds), *Monetary Problems of the International Economy*, 1969, 41–60; Peter B. Kenen, 'The Coordination of Macroeconomic Policies' in William H. Branson, Jacob A. Frenkel, and Morris Goldstein (eds), *International Policy Coordination and Exchange Rate Fluctuations*, 1990, 63–102.

Every effort has been made to trace all the copyright holders, but if any have been inadvertently overlooked, the publishers will be pleased to make the necessary arrangements at the first opportunity.

Introduction

I did not start to think about being an economist until the end of my third year as an undergraduate at Columbia University, and I did not start to consider an academic career until the end of my senior year, when I won a Woodrow Wilson Fellowship for graduate study and had to promise that I would consider it seriously. Before that, I was determined to be an international civil servant. That possibility actually arose much later, but I turned it down to remain an academic.

Like most other children, I had chosen and discarded a number of careers before being old enough to know what they really involved. At one point during the Second World War, I was going to be a naval officer. At another point, I was going to be a surgeon. Both ideas were utterly silly. I could never have met the physical requirements for admission to the US Naval Academy. In fact, I barely passed the swimming test required of Columbia undergraduates. And anyone watching me try to tie a hook to a fishing line would shudder or laugh at my being a surgeon. For a long time, however, I planned to be a biologist, which is why I attended the Bronx High School of Science. It was a remarkable school, not only for the quality of its science courses, but also for its classes in history and the social sciences, where I began to enjoy myself most. I became particularly interested in international politics and, for unusual reasons, the United Nations.

I was born in Cleveland, Ohio, where my father was a journalist. His 'beat' was City Hall, but the talk at our dinner table was about Spain and Munich, aggression, appeasement and isolationism. I can recall very clearly the voices of Adolph Hitler and Franklin Roosevelt coming from the radio in our living room. I can also recall conversations about the plight of Jews in Europe and my father's concern about his own father, who had returned to Poland many years before. We moved to New York in 1943, when my father went to work for the American Jewish Conference, the newly formed alliance of major Jewish organizations concerned to mobilize support for the survivors of the Holocaust and to reopen the doors of Palestine to Jewish immigration. In 1947, he joined the Jewish Agency for Palestine and helped to make its case before the United Nations Special Committee on Palestine. When the State of Israel was established, he became a member of its delegation to the United Nations. He took me to the temporary UN headquarters at Lake Success whenever I had a day off from school.

When I enrolled at Columbia in 1950, I joined the staff of the student radio station and began to broadcast a weekly programme on the United Nations. With help from my father, I obtained my own press card, and would lurk in a corner of the Delegates' Lounge, looking for celebrities to interview. A surprisingly large number of busy people took time to appear on the programme, including Eleanor Roosevelt, who was the was the American representative on the Human Rights Commission. I learned a great deal about the organization, including its early efforts to promote economic development.

I have never worked harder than I did during my four years at Columbia, and have never been rewarded more richly. In my first and second years, I took the required courses in Western civilization, taught entirely in small classes by some of the University's most distinguished faculty. My great debt to those courses leads me to bridle whenever multiculturalists attack them for being provincial and offensive. I am richer for having taken a full-year course on the civilizations of India, China and Japan, but I would be far poorer if the required courses on Western civilization had not introduced me to the ideas, issues and values that have decisively influenced the social and political institutions of my own country and so many other countries.

Undergraduates at Columbia did not have to major in a single subject, but most of us did that in practice, and I took several courses in political science, including a course on American foreign policy with Paul Seabury and one on Soviet foreign policy with Philip Moseley. I took an introductory course in economics, did not excel, and did not plan to take any more. But Paul Seabury changed my plans by saying what we hear far more frequently today. In the course of a conversation about my own plans, he warned me that I would not be able to understand international politics unless I understood international economics. I took his advice and, therefore, another course in economics.

Unfortunately, the Economics Department at Columbia was different from most others there. It was divided sharply between those who taught graduate courses and those who taught undergraduates. There were exceptions. Harold Barger, who taught money and banking, also gave a graduate course on national-income accounting, and C. Lowell Harriss, who taught public finance, gave a graduate course on state and local taxation. But Columbia's most prominent economists, Ragnar Nurkse, Carl Shoup, Arthur Burns and William Vickrey, to name only a few, did not teach undergraduate courses and did not encourage them to take their graduate courses. Furthermore, the undergraduate programme did not greatly emphasize economic theory, because some of its members were overtly hostile to it. The senior seminar, conducted by Horace Taylor, was devoted mainly to the works of Thorstein Veblen, John R. Commons and other institutionalists.

I do not know what I would have done if I had known what economics was really like – that theory was vital and that mathematical skills were helpful, although not absolutely essential, as they are today. I might have stuck to my earlier plan and applied to a graduate programme in international studies. I do know that I would not do graduate work in economics if I were starting today. I don't enjoy mathematics sufficiently, and I am not very good at it. I took a course in calculus at Columbia and was lucky to be in a class taught by Samuel Eilenberg, one of the University's leading mathematicians and a fine teacher. But I got through that course with much coaching from the engineering staff at the student radio station. I have learned more mathematics since, and several of the papers in this volume make use of mathematical methods. But I would not do well if I were starting graduate work today, because mathematics is not my second language.

I cannot remember why I applied to Harvard, Columbia and Cornell, and not other graduate programmes in economics. I was accepted by all three and chose Harvard, partly because it had not accepted me as an undergraduate, and it was a good choice for me. The first-year theory course was taught by Edward Chamberlin, who approached the subject historically, devoting much attention to Mill and Marshall and to his own book on monopolist competition, which has become the basis for the models used most frequently in recent work on trade in differentiated products. Some students skipped Chamberlin's course, going directly into Wassily Leontief's second-year course, which was more rigorous analytically. But Chamberlin's course filled the gap in my knowledge of theory left by the bias against it at Columbia, and it bought me time to learn more mathematics, so that I could survive Leontief's course in my second year. There was no basic course in macroeconomics, but many first-year students took the monetary course given by Alvin Hansen and John Williams, and I also took Gottfried Haberler's course in international economics.

I was equally interested in both branches of international economics – the trade and monetary sides – and worked on both at Harvard. During my second year, while studying for the general examination, I found a way to extend the geometry developed by Robert Baldwin (1952) to depict equilibrium under free trade and under an optimum tariff, and I used it to derive utility possibility curves for the two regimes. It led to my first publication (Kenen, 1957). But I decided to write my thesis on a monetary topic, and looked for one that would give me an excuse to spend a year abroad. At first, I planned to examine the benefits and costs to Britain of being a reserve-currency country. (It did not occur to me or my advisers that the reserve-currency role of the dollar deserved similar study.) But Gottfried Haberler and John Williams urged me to take a different tack – to study the role played by monetary policy in managing the British balance of payments, and the topic served its purpose. It gave me a marvelous year at the London School of Economics.

It was the year in which Lionel Robbins devoted the economics seminar to Don Patinkin's *Money, Interest, and Prices*, and I was allowed to attend, even though my thesis topic classified me as an 'applied' economist. James Meade conducted another seminar, devoted to international economics, and I attended that one too, along with Richard Cooper. Our paths have crossed repeatedly since, to my great benefit. My best days at the LSE, however, were spent with Max Corden, Richard Lipsey and Kelvin Lancaster, who introduced me to the theory of the second best and to Harry Johnson. I was able nonetheless to get on with my thesis, with much help from A.C.L. Day and Richard Sayers at the LSE and from Maurice Allen, the Economic Advisor at the Bank of England, and I brought back a first draft from London. I finished it that summer, just before starting to teach at Columbia.

Before leaving for London, I had talked about teaching positions with Seymour Harris at Harvard, for whom I had worked as a research assistant, and with Harold Barger at Columbia. When I wrote to them from London, applying formally, both of them offered me jobs. I knew that I could not expect to stay at either institution. Harvard exported most of its graduate students, and Columbia did not promote instructors in its undergraduate programme. My wife and I decided, however, that Harvard was riskier, because Seymour Harris would find more work for me to do, and I accepted Columbia's offer, expecting to stay there briefly.

Weeks after defending my thesis at Harvard, however, Harold Barger asked me to assemble my publications – all three of them at that stage – so that the department might decide whether I should be promoted to Assistant Professor. Soon after my promotion, moreover, Schuyler Wallace, the Dean of the School of International

Affairs, invited me to teach a graduate course on US foreign economic policy. (He also told me that my salary would be raised from $5,500 to $6,600, because the new figure had to be divisible by three, in order for the School to pay one-third). Then, in my third year, I was asked to teach the graduate course in international economics, because Ragnar Nurkse would be moving to Princeton, and though the arrangement was meant to be temporary, I taught the course for the next ten years.

In my first year at Columbia, I spent much time revising my thesis for publication. It appeared in 1960, as *British Monetary Policy and the Balance of Payments, 1951–1957*, and it was reviewed in the *Economic Journal* by J.C.R. Dow, who praised my input but not my output. 'Kenen has left no stone unturned in his search for the truth,' he wrote, 'but has told us what he found beneath each one.' He was cruel but quite right.

Two new subjects began to attract my attention as I was revising the thesis. One was the Leontief paradox, the other was the Triffin paradox.

Gary Becker came to Columbia just when I did and had started to develop his ideas on human capital. Donald Keesing arrived soon thereafter and was working on a resolution of the Leontief paradox – the finding that US exports were less capital intensive than US imports, even though the United States was deemed to be a capital-abundant country. Leontief (1956) had already suggested that the paradox might be resolved by taking account of high labour productivity in the United States and thus treating the United States as a labour-abundant country. He had also noted that US exports tend to use skilled labour intensively, and Keesing had begun to develop this theme by examining the skill intensities of various bilateral trade flows (see Keesing, 1966). I took a different tack inspired by work that Becker and Jacob Mincer were doing on the return to human capital. The United States, I suggested, should still be regarded as a capital-abundant country, but one which invests much of its capital in the production of skills. I developed a version of the Heckscher-Ohlin model in which countries are endowed by nature with two basic factors of production – land and labour – that cannot produce commodities until capital has been used to improve them. Each economy has therefore to make two sorts of decisions: how to allocate its stock of capital between land and labour, and how to allocate the resulting flows of land and labour services between land-intensive and labour-intensive activities. I also showed that the United States is indeed a capital-abundant country when allowance is made for the large stock of human capital embodied in its labour. My results appeared in 'Nature, Capital, and Trade' (Kenen, 1965a), which is still my favorite paper; related work by colleagues and students was published in a volume (Kenen and Lawrence, 1968) collecting research conducted in the International Economics Workshop, which I organized soon after coming to Columbia.

My work on the monetary side was influenced heavily by Robert Triffin's *Gold and the Dollar Crisis*, in which he argued that the international monetary system was dangerously unstable because of another paradox. The United States would have to run balance-of-payments deficits to provide dollar reserves to other countries, but the corresponding increase of US liabilities would eventually undermine confidence in the dollar as a reserve asset. Triffin proposed the transformation of the International Monetary Fund into a reserve-creating institution. My first paper on the subject (Kenen, 1960) offered a rigorous formulation of the Triffin paradox. Thereafter, I began empirical work on the reserve-asset preferences of central banks (Kenen, 1963) and, with Elinor Yudin, on the demand for international reserves; the paper reporting our joint work is the earliest one included in this volume. It was advanced for its day, in that it used a first-order autoregressive process to represent the evolution of a country's balance of payments, then took the standard error of each country's balance-of-payments equation to represent the distribution of exogenous shocks and took the autoregressive coefficient to measure the duration of those shocks. These were employed in another regression equation to explain cross-country differences in holdings of reserves.

My work on these matters led to my first involvement in the policy-making process. In November 1960, soon after the election of John F. Kennedy, I was appointed to a task force concerned with the US balance-of-payments problem and the international monetary system. It was chaired by George Ball, soon to become Undersecretary of State, and included Robert Triffin and Edward Bernstein, each of whom had a plan of his own to reform the monetary system. Being the youngest member, I was assigned to work with Meyer Rashish on the first draft of the group's report. We worked through the night but sustained ourselves with the belief that we could greatly influence the form of the group's recommendations. George Ball rewrote our draft completely, however, and President Kennedy set it aside when he was warned that our recommendations might shake confidence in the dollar. During our work, incidentally, we were asked to draft the statement that the President-elect would make on announcing the appointment of Douglas Dillon as Secretary of the Treasury. Our draft reaffirmed the commitment of the United States to defend the dollar price of gold at $35 per ounce, and all but one of us thought that this was the right course to take. Paul Samuelson was the dissenter; he scribbled a note on his copy of the draft, asking whether Kennedy should 'nail his flag to that mast'. Samuelson has said that he was among the first to wonder whether it might be necessary to devalue the dollar. He was – but I have tried without success to find in my files his copy of the first draft, which would support his claim.

Early in 1961, Walter Heller, the incoming Chairman of the Council of Economic Advisers, asked me to do some more drafting, together with Richard Cooper, who would soon join the staff. We were to prepare a first draft of the President's message on the balance of payments and gold. Once again, late-night sessions and frustrations. Our draft was circulated to other agencies, and they mutilated it. (Kenneth Galbraith mentions the episode in *Ambassador's Journal*, where he has some unkind things to say about our prose. When asked if there was anything left of our draft, I said, 'Yes. The prepositions.')

Actually, one sentence did survive, and it gave me another opportunity to learn about the workings of government. The President's message promised to examine the balance-of-payments effects of US direct investment abroad and to ask if investment was being stimulated by inappropriate tax incentives. Stanley Surrey, Assistant Secretary of the Treasury for Tax Policy, asked me to work with Hal Lary on the implementation of that commitment. We wrote a report recommending the elimination of tax deferral on the reinvested profits of the foreign subsidiaries of

US firms. Our recommendation found its way into the first tax bill proposed by the Kennedy administration, but it lost its way in Congress, which adopted provisions limiting the use of foreign tax havens but did not restrict tax deferral *per se*.

My work on the Ball task force had one other consequence. At Robert Triffin's suggestion, I was invited to participate in the first meeting of what came later to be known as the Bellagio group of officials and academics, chaired by Fritz Machlup of Princeton on the academic side and Otmar Emminger of the Bundesbank on the official side. The group met once or twice each year for more than a decade to discuss international monetary issues in an informal setting. The academics included William Fellner, Roy Harrod, Harry Johnson and Robert Mundell; the officials included André de Lattre, Kit MacMahon, Robert Roosa and Emile van Lennep. It was the most successful endeavour of its kind – I have been involved in several since – and contributed greatly to my own education.

My interest in the workings of the monetary system led me away from trade theory and policy. In fact, I wrote only one more paper on trade theory, an analysis of international migration in the context of the Heckscher-Ohlin model, which was published in a volume honouring Charles Kindleberger (Kenen, 1971). But I started to look at new issues on the monetary side. In a paper for a volume honouring Gottfried Haberler, I used mean-variance analysis to analyse the behaviour of forward exchange rates (Kenen, 1965b). In a paper for a conference at the University of Chicago, I sought to reformulate the theory of optimum currency areas developed initially by Robert Mundell and Ronald McKinnon. I paid particular attention to the nature of the exogenous shocks affecting individual economies (now described by the distinction between symmetrical and asymmetrical shocks) and to the relevance of fiscal policies and domains for the delineation and functioning of an optimum currency area. The paper has been cited frequently since the revival of interest in European monetary union, and it is reproduced as the first paper in this book.

I had to curtail my research, however, when I became chairman of the Columbia Department in 1967, and subsequent events forced me to suspend it completely. I became deeply involved in dealing with the aftermath of the student demonstrations of 1968, at the same time that I was voicing my own concerns about the Vietnam War by running for election as a delegate to the Democratic National Convention. I won that election, attended the Chicago Convention, and managed to get myself arrested. Radical students at Columbia saw me as an enemy but greeted me warmly when I joined them in a Chicago jail cell. (My children, however, were less enthusiastic about their father's brief criminal career.) I was charged with being a 'pedestrian obstructing traffic' and gladly paid my fine as a small charge for a very satisfying experience.

My next experience was less satisfying. In the fall of 1969, Andrew Cordier, Columbia's Acting President, asked me to become Provost, and I spent the next year doing that. It was satisfying from one standpoint. Academics cannot learn very much about a large university without venturing out of their own departments. Their colleagues in other disciplines lead lives different from their own, and the problems of the university as a whole are larger than the sum of the problems facing its various schools and departments. I learned a great deal during my year as Provost, but the job was frustrating. I was part of an interim administration in which responsibilities were not clearly allocated, and my time was divided between the demands made by the strident politics of the day and those made by the educational and financial problems of the university. I left the job after a year and left Columbia one year later.

Shortly before becoming Provost at Columbia, I had a call from a colleague at Princeton asking whether I wanted to be considered for the vacancy that would be created by the retirement of Fritz Machlup, who was Walker Professor of Economics and International Finance and Director of the International Finance Section. I said no, because I had just accepted the chairmanship of the Economics Department and felt an obligation to serve out my term. But I called him back three years later to ask whether Princeton might still be interested in me. He said yes, and matters moved quickly thereafter. I joined the faculty at Princeton in the fall of 1971, but took leave right away to spend a year at the Center for Advanced Study in the Behavioral Sciences at Palo Alto, thinking about economics and a new research agenda – which I had not done for three years.

At first, I taught courses similar to those I had taught at Columbia, giving a full-year course in international economics and the lectures in the basic undergraduate course. I also started a research seminar in international economics, in which many colleagues have participated regularly. When Avinash Dixit came to Princeton, however, I ceased to teach the first term of the graduate course on trade theory and policy. I also ceased to lecture in the basic undergraduate course in order to run a workshop on foreign economic policy for graduate students in the Woodrow Wilson School. The subject of the workshop has changed from year to year, but the organization has not. Each year, we examine intensively a single policy problem and study it by holding mock negotiations. We have worked on increasing IMF quotas and allocating Special Drawing Rights, rescheduling the debts of a hypothetical developing country and working out a stabilization programme with the IMF, and planning the implementation of the Maastricht Treaty.

The subjects of the papers in this book describe the range and focus of my research during my 20 years at Princeton, although most of them come from the second half of that period. In my first ten years at Princeton, I worked mainly on the implications of international financial integration for balance-of-payments adjustment, the behaviour of floating exchange rates, and the coordination of national economic policies, but approached those issues in two ways. First, I worked with two graduate students, Peter Dungan and Dennis Warner, to develop a large model of the US balance of payments and used the model to simulate the effects of fiscal and monetary policies. Our results are summarized by a paper in this book; the model itself and more simulations are described in Kenen (1978). Second, I constructed and analysed small theoretical models designed to identify the main effects of asset-market integration.

I had started this work during my year at the Center for Advanced Study in Palo Alto, taking as my point of departure the important paper by Ronald McKinnon and Wallace Oates (1966), which had amended the Fleming-Mundell model by imposing a portfolio-balance constraint and had thus distinguished clearly between stock and flow equilibria, and empirical work by my colleague, William Branson (1968), which pursued the same vital distinction between stocks and flows. My first paper on the subject was published in a volume honouring Jan Tinbergen (Kenen, 1974); it is not reproduced in this book, however, because the model was badly flawed. My next effort was better; it appeared in *Capital Mobility and Financial Integration*, a monograph based on a paper that Fritz Machlup had asked me to write for the Budapest Congress of the International Economic Association. But the model in that monograph could not be used to study exchange-rate behaviour, because it included only one bond, and two bonds are needed to study exchange-rate behaviour in a portfolio-balance framework – one denominated in domestic currency and one denominated in foreign currency. I did not take that next step until I started to work with my colleague, Polly Allen, on a project that began quite modestly but grew far larger. The results appeared in our book, *Asset Markets, Exchange Rates, and Economic Integration*, and the same basic model appears in this volume, in my paper on intervention and sterilization.

Although the work on portfolio-balance models occupied much of my time in the 1970s, I continued to think about policy problems and the international monetary system. During the deliberations of the Committee of Twenty on the reform of the monetary system, the United States had proposed the use of a reserve indicator to signal the need for balance-of-payments adjustment and the possible need for exchange-rate changes. I was worried about using a stock indicator, the level of reserves, to signal the need for a change in a flow variable, the balance of payments, and raised the issue with a colleague. He said that he could handle it analytically and would get back to me shortly. A few days later, I found a note in my mailbox, saying that the problem was intractable. 'Simulate,' it said. I did – and found that the use of a reserve indicator could indeed destabilize the balance of payments (Kenen, 1975). Two years later, I published another paper on the role of reserves in the monetary system, written for a conference in memory of J. Marcus Fleming (Kenen, 1977), and two more papers on the monetary system appear in this volume, one on the analytics of a substitution account designed to replace dollar reserves with SDR-denominated claims on the IMF, and the other on the future of the SDR itself.

In the 1980s, I continued to think about policy coordination and the problems facing the IMF, but my work was influenced by the advent of new issues and analytical innovations. The revival of policy coordination at the 1978 Bonn Summit and the subsequent revival of exchange-rate management under the 1985 Plaza Agreement and 1987 Louvre Accord led many economists to seek ways of modeling policy coordination and to re-examine the effectiveness of official intervention on the foreign-exchange market. The onset of the debt crisis in 1982 led many to look at the nature of sovereign debt, the role of the IMF in managing the crisis, and the case for debt relief. The collapse of the Soviet empire in Eastern Europe and of the Soviet Union itself raised an array of economic issues. The new interest in European monetary union resurrected old questions and posed new ones.

To study the conduct and effects of policy coordination, most economists used the game-theoretic approach introduced earlier by Koichi Hamada (1976). I did, too, but became increasingly sceptical of it. My use of the approach and my doubts about it appeared initially in a paper drafted in 1983–84, while I was visiting the Reserve Bank of Australia. I developed the paper into a book, *Exchange Rates and Policy Coordination*, published in 1988. It used the game-theoretic approach to contrast the need for policy coordination under pegged and floating exchange rates and came to an odd conclusion – that floating exchange rates could increase the need for policy coordination rather than reduce it. I was bothered by the possibility, however, that this result was due to the strongly symmetrical nature of the economies inhabiting my model, and I built another model to show that some of my findings survive when the economies are not symmetrical. This work is described by two papers in this book, one on the coordination of macroeconomic policies, which summarizes the argument of my book, and one that presents the asymmetrical version of my model. The first of those papers also sets out my objections to the game-theoretic approach; it argues that policy coordination should be viewed as a 'regime preserving' process rather than a 'policy optimizing' process.

The huge swing of real and nominal exchange rates for the dollar in the 1980s strengthened my dissatisfaction with floating exchange rates. I was also impressed with the performance of the European Monetary System in its early years – its apparent success in reconciling short-term stability with medium-term flexibility. Like most economists old enough to recall the defects of the Bretton Woods System, I was doubtful initially about the prospects for the EMS. Unlike many others, however, I was not convinced that its subsequent success could be ascribed to the influence of capital controls in limiting speculative pressures; I attached more importance to the elasticity of the reserve-credit arrangements available for financing intervention and thus warding off those pressures. (The 1992 crisis has not caused me to change my mind, because it occurred after the EMS had evolved into a more rigid regime. That crisis, however, has made me wonder whether pegged-rate regimes may be doomed to evolve in that fashion, on account of the nature of the game played between markets and governments.)

These thoughts and my reflections on the implications of the 1987 Louvre Accord led me to ask whether there can be any viable half-way house between freely floating and firmly pegged exchange rates. I raised the question with officials and academics at a meeting of a second Bellagio group, which Richard Cooper and I had organized with the help of Alexander Lamfalussy, the General Manager of the Bank for International Settlements. The question led me to write another book, *Managing Exchange Rates*, drafted in 1987–88, while I was visiting the Royal Institute of International Affairs in London. It urged the major industrial countries to adopt formal target zones for their currencies and to develop a comprehensive framework for macroeconomic coordination. My objections to floating exchange rates were influenced by Paul Krugman's lucid lectures in memory of Lionel Robbins (Krugman, 1989a); my plan for exchange-rate management bore some resemblance to the 'blueprint' developed by John Williamson and Marcus Miller (1987), although it attached much more weight to official intervention.

My work on the debt crisis is represented by two papers in this book. Shortly after the onset of the crisis, I wrote two columns in *The New York Times* suggesting the creation of an International Debt Discount Corporation (IDDC) to buy up the debts of developing countries at a discount and to issue in their place bonds guaranteed indirectly by the developed countries, as sponsors of the IDDC. The proposal was premature analytically and politically. There was as yet little evidence to justify the premise underlying my proposal – that the case-by-case approach to the debt problem would be inadequate, so that debt relief would be needed. At that early stage, moreover, banks were unwilling to contemplate long-term concessions and debtor countries wanted to prove that they could return quickly to creditworthiness. One banker gave me a left-handed compliment; my proposal, he said, was the most sensible of the many silly plans for solving the debt problem. The finance minister of a debtor country was less courteous. 'Be quiet,' he said. 'You are undermining our effort to win credibility.' It took several years for the climate to change, and by the time I published the paper in this book, on organizing debt relief, the Brady plan for debt reduction was being implemented. My analytical paper on debt buybacks provides a rationale for debt reduction that does not depend on the assumption made by Krugman (1989b) and others to obtain the so-called Debt Relief Laffer Curve – the assumption that excessive debt depresses domestic investment, reducing the ability of the debtor country to service its debt in the future. My paper develops a model in which partial debt relief is beneficial to the debtor and its creditors, because it reduces the debtor's incentive to repudiate the whole debt in the future.

My interest in the work of the IMF is represented by two other papers, on IMF surveillance and on the use of IMF credit. My interest in the problems of Central and Eastern Europe is represented by a paper on trade and payments arrangements for that region. It analyses and rejects the case for creating a payments union modeled on the European Payments Union (EPU) of the 1950s. (I have since argued, however, that a clearing union should be created to help revive trade among the republics of the former Soviet Union.)

In 1990–91, I spent the first half of a year's leave from Princeton at the Bank of England and the second half at the IMF. The last two papers in this book reflect my work at those institutions. At the Bank of England, I was fortunate in being able to follow closely the negotiations that led to the plan for Economic and Monetary Union (EMU) embodied in the Maastricht Treaty; as soon as the Treaty was signed, I began work on a monograph, *EMU After Maastricht*, analysing the provisions of the Treaty and the problems likely to arise during the transition. My paper on the European Central Bank draws on that monograph. At the IMF, I studied recent trends in the exchange-rate policies of developing countries, contrasting the older case for using the exchange rate to promote balance-of-payments adjustment with the newer case for pegging the exchange rate to promote price stability. I also examined the challenges posed for exchange-rate and monetary policies by the liberalization of capital market in developing countries and the resulting capital inflows. That work is summarized in my paper on financial opening, prepared for an OECD symposium.

When I started to study economics, I wanted to work for an international organization, and I had an opportunity to do that in 1979, when Jacques de Larosière, Managing Director of the IMF, asked me to be Director of the Research Department and Economic Counsellor. I told him that he was asking me to choose between the most attractive jobs I could hope to hold – my Princeton position and the one at the Fund. After long thought, I decided to stay at Princeton, where I could set my own agenda but could still participate in debate about current policies and the future of the monetary system. This book reflects my agenda in the decade that followed, and I will continue to pursue it, because most of the issues on which I have written are far from being resolved.

References

Baldwin, R.E. (1952), 'The New Welfare Economics and the Gains in International Trade', *Quarterly Journal of Economics*, **66**, 99–101.

Branson, W.H. (1968), *Financial Capital Flows in the U.S. Balance of Payments*, Amsterdam: North-Holland.

Hamada, K. (1976), 'A Strategic Analysis of Monetary Interdependence', *Journal of Political Economy*, **84**, 677–700.

Keesing, D.B. (1966), 'Labor Skills and Comparative Advantage', *American Economic Review: Proceedings*, **56**, 249–58.

Kenen, P.B. (1957), 'On the Geometry of Welfare Economics', *Quarterly Journal of Economics*, **71**, 426–47.

Kenen, P.B. (1960), 'International Liquidity and the Balance of Payments of a Reserve-Currency Country', *Quarterly Journal of Economics*, **74**, 572–86.

Kenen, P.B. (1963), *Reserve-Asset Preferences of Central Banks and Stability of the Gold-Exchange Standard*, Princeton Studies in International Finance 10, Princeton NJ: International Finance Section, Princeton University.

Kenen, P.B. (1965a), 'Nature, Capital, and Trade', *Journal of Political Economy*, **73**, 437–60.

Kenen, P.B. (1965b), 'Trade, Speculation, and the Forward Exchange Rate', in R.E. Baldwin *et al.* (eds), *Trade, Growth and the Balance of Payments*, Chicago: Rand-McNally, 143–69.

Kenen, P.B. (1971), 'Migration, the Terms of Trade, and Economic Welfare in the Source Country', in J.N. Bhagwati *et al.* (eds), *Trade, Balance of Payments and Growth*, Amsterdam: North-Holland, 238–60.

Kenen, P.B. (1974), 'Economic Policy in a Small Economy', in W. Sellekaerts (ed.), *International Trade and Finance*, London: Macmillan, 73–101.

Kenen, P.B. (1975), 'Floats, Glides, and Indicators: A Comparison of Methods for Changing Exchange Rates', *Journal of International Economics*, **5**, 101–51.

Kenen, P.B. (1976), *Capital Mobility and Financial Integration: A Survey*, Princeton Studies in International Finance 39, Princeton NJ: International Finance Section, Princeton University.

Kenen, P.B. (1977), 'Techniques to Control International Reserves', in R.A. Mundell and J.J. Polak (eds), *The New International Monetary System*, New York: Columbia University Press, 202–22.

Kenen, P.B. and R. Lawrence (eds) (1968), *The Open Economy*, New York: Columbia University Press.

Krugman, P. (1989a), *Exchange-Rate Instability*, Cambridge MA: MIT Press.

Krugman, P. (1989b), 'Market-Based Debt Reduction Schemes', in J.A. Frenkel, M.P. Dooley, and P. Wickham (eds), *Analytial Issues in Debt*, Washington: International Monetary Fund.

Leontief, W.W. (1956), 'Factor Proportions and the Structure of American Trade', *Review of Economics and Statistics*, **38**, 386–407.

McKinnon, R. and W. Oates (1966), *The Implications of International Economic Integration for Monetary, Fiscal, and Exchange Rate Policy*, Princeton Studies in International Finance 16, Princeton NJ: International Finance Section, Princeton University.

Williamson, J. and M.H. Miller (1987), *Targets and Indicators: A Blueprint for the International Coordination of Economic Policies*, Policy Analyses in International Economics 22, Washington: Institute for International Economics.

PART I

THEORY

[1]

THE THEORY OF OPTIMUM CURRENCY AREAS: AN ECLECTIC VIEW

Peter B. Kenen

Introduction

When should exchange rates be fixed and when should they fluctuate? What criteria define the optimum currency area, within which the exchange rates should be pegged immutably, but whose rates should fluctuate, or at least be varied, vis-à-vis the outside world? We owe the first explicit formulation of this question to our conference chairman, Robert Mundell, and I shall preface my reply by summarizing his.[1]

In his very terse treatment of the subject, Mundell does not pause to give us many definitions, but two of them emerge inside his argument—a definition of optimality and a definition of an economic region. Optimality relates to the state of the labor market. If the prevailing exchange-rate regime, fixed or flexible, can maintain external balance without causing unemployment (or, on the other side, demand-induced wage inflation), that regime is optimal. If the currency regime within a given area causes unemployment somewhere in that area (or compels some other portion of that same area to accept inflation as the antidote to unemployment), it is not optimal. In Mundell's own words:

> In a currency area comprising different countries with national currencies the pace of employment in deficit countries is set by the willingness of surplus countries to inflate. But in a currency area comprising many regions and a single currency, the pace of inflation is set by the willingness of central authorities to allow unemployment in deficit regions.

> ... But a currency area of either type cannot prevent both unemployment and inflation among its members. The fault lies not with the type of currency area, but with the domain of the currency area. The optimum currency area is not the world.[2]

1. Robert A. Mundell, "A Theory of Optimum Currency Areas," *American Economic Review*, 60, no. 4 (September 1961): 657–65.
2. *ibid.*, p. 659. Mundell's definition of optimality is quite similar to Meade's; see James E. Meade, *The Balance of Payments* (London: Oxford University Press, 1951), pp. 104–7 and 114–24.

One could readily adopt many other points of view. Thus, McKinnon has employed a different definition of optimality

> . . . To describe a single currency area within which mon-
> etary-fiscal policy and flexible external exchange rates can
> be used to give the best resolution of three (sometimes
> conflicting) objectives: (1) the maintenance of full employ-
> ment; (2) the maintenance of balanced international
> payments; (3) the maintenance of a stable internal average
> price level. Objective (3) assumes that any capitalist economy
> requires a stable-valued liquid currency to insure efficient
> resource allocation. . . . The inclusion of objective (3)
> makes the problem as much a part of monetary theory as of
> international trade theory. The idea of optimality, then, is
> complex and difficult to quantify precisely. . . .[3]

I shall have something more to say about McKinnon's third objective, especially his reasons for calling it to our attention. But most of my analysis will make use of the simpler labor-market criterion.

Mundell's other definition, likewise implicit rather than explicit, relates to the delineation of an economic region. It is, again, quite simple and leads his analysis to powerful results. But those same results may not be too helpful from the standpoint of policy and will cause the two of us to part company at an early stage. Mundell's notion of a region is functional not literal. You will not find his regions on an ordinary map but must instead use an input-output table. As I understand the substance of his argument, a region is defined as a homogeneous collection of producers that use the same technology, face the same demand curve, and suffer or prosper together as circumstances change. Thus:

> . . . Suppose that the world consists of two countries,
> Canada and the United States, each of which has separate
> currencies. Also assume that the continent is divided into
> two regions which do not correspond to national boundaries
> —the East, which produces goods like cars, and the West,
> which produces goods like lumber products.[4]

Here, Mundell has used the geographer's language, but solely for expositional convenience. It is, in fact, the difference in the product mix that distinguishes East from West.

Combining his labor-market view of optimality and his rather special

3. Ronald I. McKinnon, "Optimum Currency Areas," *American Economic Review*, 53, no. 4 (September 1963): 717. In McKinnon's model, flexible exchange rates can generate a conflict between (1) and (3) because depreciation will augment the demand for "tradable" output, draw labor away from "non-tradable" output, and cause a general increase in wages and prices.

4. Mundell, "Theory of Optimum Currency Areas," p. 659.

definition of a region, Mundell proceeds to furnish an elegant answer to the question of currency areas. He asks us to suppose that consumers shift their spending from cars to lumber products—from eastern goods to western goods. The East, of course, develops a current-account deficit in its balance of payments and an excess supply of labor. The West develops a current-account surplus and an excess demand for labor.

If workers cannot move from East to West, some way must be found to augment the demand for cars (eastern goods) and diminish the demand for lumber products (western goods). The East has to accept worse terms of trade—a decrease in the price of cars relative to lumber products sufficient to reallocate aggregate demand and thereby to eliminate the disequilibria in both regions' labor markets. And if money wage rates are sticky in both regions, eastern currency must be made cheaper in terms of western currency, whether by depreciation (a free-market change) or devaluation (a calculated alteration in a pegged exchange rate). East and West should not be joined in a monetary union, nor be made to peg their currencies once and for all; they do not comprise an optimum currency area.

What happens, however, if workers can move freely between East and West? The westward migration of unemployed eastern workers will serve to ameliorate the labor-market problems of both regions and, at the same time, will help to solve their payments problem. As workers move from East to West, their purchases of cars will be transformed from home demand into extra eastern exports; their purchases of lumber products will be transformed from western exports into extra home demand. In brief, Mundell contends that interregional factor mobility can substitute for changes in regional exchange rates, and that the entire zone through which labor can move freely delineates the right domain for a monetary union or for fixed exchange rates; with labor mobility, East and West do comprise an optimum currency area.

Peripheral Objections

Aspects of this argument call for further work. What should be done, for instance, when there is a major difference in the labor intensities of eastern and western production? Migration might then leave a residual imbalance in one region's labor market—an enduring excess supply in the East or excess demand in the West. And are we really sure that factor movements can restore a perfect balance in the regions' trade even when it does resolve both of their employment problems? Rather special patterns of consumer demand and methods of production may be needed in each region if a simple labor movement and the corresponding change in the locus of demand are to end an imbalance in two regions' labor markets and also to equilibrate the trade flow between them. Notice, finally, that the increase of demand for lumber products could stimulate additional investment in the West, leading to an increase in its income and imports large enough to open up a current-account deficit in its balance of payments.[5]

But the main lines of the argument are not at issue. Nor can one accuse Mundell of failing to perceive the ultimate, unhappy implication of his argument. When regions are defined by their activities, not geographically or politically, perfect interregional labor mobility requires perfect occupational mobility. And this can only come about when labor is homogeneous (or the several regions belonging to a single currency area display very similar skill requirements). In consequence, Mundell's approach leads to the sad certainty that the optimum currency area has always to be small. It must, indeed, be coextensive with the single-product region. In Mundell's own words:

> ...If, then, the goals of internal stability are to be rigidly pursued, it follows that the greater is the number of separate currency areas in the world, the more successfully will these goals be attained...But this seems to imply that regions ought to be defined so narrowly as to count every minor pocket of unemployment arising from labor immobility as a separate region, each of which should apparently have a separate currency![6]

Mundell and I agree that "such an arrangement hardly appeals to common sense," and we likewise agree on some of the reasons.[7] If every community, however small, could issue its own currency, money would no longer serve to lead us out of barter; and if each region's central bank could run its own printing press with complete autonomy, we would soon have to face the difficult problem that McKinnon posed.

5. See Marina v. N. Whitman, *International and Interregional Payments Adjustment: A Synthetic View. Princeton Studies in International Finance*, No. 19 (Princeton: Princeton Univ. Press, 1967). Mrs. Whitman suggests that this variety of current-account deficit may even be needed to maintain overall balance in interregional payments, for some of the additional investment in the West may be financed by capital imports from the East.

6. Mundell, "Theory of Optimum Currency Areas," p. 662.

7. One of them, in fact, anticipates McKinnon's view, and can best be summarized by quoting Mundell again: "The thesis of those who favor flexible exchange rates is that the community in question is not willing to accept variations in its real income through adjustments in its money wage rate or price level, but that it is willing to accept virtually the same changes...through variations in the rate of exchange.... Now as the currency area grows smaller and the proportion of imports in total consumption grows, this assumption becomes increasingly unlikely." (*Ibid.*, p. 663.)

Investors would be deprived of a "stable-valued liquid currency" to hold as a store of value or use as a standard of value when allocating capital among single-product regions.[8]

It has, of course, been argued that changes in exchange rates, actual or possible, do not much deter international investment and, *in extenso*, might not be barriers to a satisfactory allocation of capital among single-product regions.[9] This argument, however, draws heavily on the very special experience of Canada; it assumes that exchange rates will not wobble much; and, most importantly, it forecasts that forward markets will come into being so that traders and investors can translate uncertainty into calculable costs. Given a multitude of microregions, each with its own currency, the foreign exchange markets might be quite thin; few banks and brokers would be able or willing to deal in the host of currencies that would then abound and might not be capable of taking on net positions, long and short, large enough to guarantee stabilizing speculation. To make matters worse, single-product regions may suffer significant disturbances in their foreign trade and payments, so that exchange rates may fluctuate quite widely. More on this point soon.

I come now to another collection of arguments that Mundell and McKinnon have not explored sufficiently. Economic sovereignty has several dimensions, two of them particularly relevant to the problem of managing aggregate demand and maintaining full employment. Fiscal and monetary policies must go hand in hand, and if there is to be an "optimum policy mix," they should have the same domains.[10] There

8. If there were a single region larger than the rest, or more prudent in managing its money, that region's currency might well come into use as an interregional standard of value. In such a case, however, many debts and claims internal to smaller regions would come to be denominated in that "key currency," driving other currencies out of common use. One wonders if the courts of the other microregions would be willing to enforce contracts of this type. Doing so, after all, they would help to undermine their own regions' currencies, much as the Supreme Court of the United States would have undermined the legal status of the dollar if it had upheld the gold-clause contracts in the 1930's.

9. See, e.g., Egon Sohmen, *Flexible Exchange Rates* (Chicago: University of Chicago Press, 1961), p. 19.

10. This term, another of our chairman's contributions to our jargon, is usually employed to denote the combination of monetary and budgetary policies needed to maintain external and internal balance. If, of course, exchange rates are left free to fluctuate, furnishing external balance, the two internal instruments need not be aligned precisely. Yet an "optimum policy mix" is not unimportant to domestic demand management, taken by itself. Too much reliance on one of the two instruments, monetary or budgetary, can have severe and deplorable consequences for particular sectors of the domestic economy. When, as this is written, interest rates are driven high to make good deficiencies in fiscal policy, construction is hit hard, as is investment in public facilities that have to be financed by bond issues subject to approval by the electorate.

should be a treasury, empowered to tax and spend, opposite each central bank, whether to cooperate with monetary policy or merely to quarrel with it. From other viewpoints, too, the domain of fiscal policy ought to coincide with the currency area or, at least, be no larger than the monetary zone. Otherwise, the treasury will face a host of problems.[11]

How would taxes be collected if a single fiscal system were to span a number of currency areas, each of them entitled to alter its exchange rate? How would a treasury maintain the desired distribution of total tax collections? Suppose that the treasury levied an income tax to be paid in each resident's regional currency and that the West was printing money faster than the East, causing a more rapid rise in prices and incomes. Unless the West's currency were to depreciate *pari passu* with the faster rise in money incomes, the West would come to pay a larger fraction of the tax (and if the tax were graduated, might also have to furnish a larger share of the goods and services absorbed by the government, as its tax payments would rise faster than its prices). The same problem would arise even more dramatically if the treasury relied on property taxation. Property values and property assessments might not keep pace with money incomes, and even if the difference in rates of inflation were exactly matched by the change in the exchange rate, there could be a significant redistribution of the tax burden.[12]

In which currency, moreover, would the central government pay for goods and services? Which one would it use to pay its civil servants?[13] And what may be the thorniest practical problem, in which currency should the central government issue its own debt instruments? None of these difficulties would be insurmountable, but ulcer rates in govern-

---

11. At one point, Meade appears to take a different point of view, arguing for flexible exchange rates within a common market (see James E. Meade, "The Balance-of-Payments Problems of a European Free-Trade Area," *Economic Journal*, 67, no. 3 (September 1957): 379–96. But Meade is not talking of an economic union with a common fiscal system.

12. Analogous problems would arise in respect to transfer payments—and are not hypothetical. Many close observers of the European scene argue that exchange rates can no longer change within the European Economic Community, for any change would undermine the precarious agreement that will govern contributions to the fund financing EEC farm price supports.

13. Notice, in this connection, that a major difference between the currency composition of government receipts and the currency composition of government spending would force the treasury into the exchange market where, willfully or otherwise, it might well become the single speculator capable of altering regional exchange rates. In this case, "the speculative argument against flexible exchange rates would assume weighty dimensions" (Mundell, "Theory of Optimum Currency Areas," p. 663).

ment are already far too high, and ought not to be increased unnecessarily.

In our day, too, government activities may well be subject to important economies of scale. This is surely true in matters of defense and may be true of civil functions. If, then, an optimum currency area should be no smaller than the rather large domain of a least-cost government, it may have to span a great number of single-product regions. If, further, a fiscal system does encompass many such regions, it may actually contribute to internal balance, offsetting the advantage claimed for fragmentation. It is a chief function of fiscal policy, using both sides of the budget, to offset or compensate for regional differences, whether in earned income or in unemployment rates. The large-scale transfer payments built into fiscal systems are interregional, not just interpersonal, and the rules which regulate many of those transfer payments relate to the labor market, just like the criterion Mundell has employed to mark off the optimum currency area. When one looks at fiscal policy in macroeconomic terms, one comes to the unhappy view espoused by Mundell; budgetary policies cannot help but cause inflation in already-prosperous parts of an economy if they are designed to stimulate demand and thereby to eliminate local unemployment. Yet this is not the only way to look at fiscal policy. Given the big numbers, total taxation, and total expenditure, the budget can still combat localized recessions. When a region or community suffers a decline in its external sales, a trade-balance deficit, and internal unemployment,

> ...its federal tax payments diminish at once, slowing the decline in its purchasing power and compressing the cash outflow on its balance of payments. There is also an inflow of federal money—of unemployment benefits. Furthermore, a region can borrow (or sell off securities) in the national capital market more easily than countries can borrow abroad. Finally, regions can...obtain discretionary aid from the central government; special programs of financial and technical assistance to depressed areas have been enacted by a number of countries, including the United States.[14]

On balance, then, a region may come out ahead by foregoing the right to issue its own currency and alter its exchange rate, in order to participate in a major fiscal system.

To sum up, an efficient fiscal system must be made to span many single-product regions and should be coextensive with (or no larger

14. Peter B. Kenen, "Toward a Supranational Monetary System," mimeographed (International Economics Workshop: Columbia University, 1966), pp. 13–14.

than) a single, if non-optimal, currency area. The logic of Mundell's approach, however impeccable, should not cause us to convene another San Francisco conference, there to carve the world up, rather than unite it, so that single-product regions can have their own currencies and can let them fluctuate.

And here, perhaps, Mundell and I are not far apart. The purpose of his argument, he tells us at the end, is not to recommend that there be more currencies, but merely to determine when one ought to recommend that existing currencies be fixed or flexible. He asks us to agree that "the validity of the argument for flexible exchange rates...hinges on the closeness with which nations correspond to regions. The argument works best if each nation (and currency) has internal factor mobility and external factor immobility,"[15] On first reading this last passage, incidentally, I was certain that "regions" had been redefined. Here, it would appear that a region is delineated by factor mobility, not by its principal activity and, therefore, the degree to which its industries suffer the same changes in product demand. Yet when one reads these sentences a little bit differently, the seeming inconsistency vanishes at once. For "regions" let me substitute "optimum currency areas," then paraphrase the argument.[16] Exchange rates should be fixed between single-product regions when labor moves freely between them, for then there is no need to change the terms of trade when a region encounters an external disturbance; and when there is mobility across all the regions making up a nation, that whole nation is an optimum currency area. When, further, workers can move freely between any pair of countries, those two countries jointly form an optimum currency area and can peg their currencies, one to the other. When, contrarily, there is no mobility between the single-product regions of a single nation, it may be very difficult to maintain full employment and price stability throughout its territory; the nation must rely on rather sophisticated internal policies to reallocate demand rather than augment or curb it. When, finally, labor does not move between a pair of countries, their currencies should fluctuate, one against the other, so as to accomplish changes in their terms of trade. Regions, to repeat, are still to be defined by their activities; optimum currency areas are to be defined by the interregional mobility of labor.

15. Mundell, "Theory of Optimum Currency Areas," p. 664.
16. I dwell on this small point in order to be spared another dozen papers by students who believe that they have discovered a fatal flaw in Mundell's analysis and that the whole argument must therefore be wrong.

A Competing Principle

But now it is my task to show that Mundell's approach is not wholly adequate—that marking off zones of perfect labor mobility may not be the best way to delineate optimum currency areas, for perfect mobility rarely prevails. Other criteria will have to be employed when, at the millennium, central bankers come to us and ask if an exchange rate should be fixed or flexible. In my view, diversity in a nation's product mix, the number of single-product regions contained in a single country, may be more relevant than labor mobility. I hope, indeed, to make three points:

> 1) That a well-diversified national economy will not have to undergo changes in its terms of trade as often as a single-product national economy.
> 2) That when, in fact, it does confront a drop in the demand for its principal exports, unemployment will not rise as sharply as it would in a less-diversified national economy.
> 3) That the links between external and domestic demand, especially the link between exports and investment, will be weaker in diversified national economies, so that variations in domestic employment "imported" from abroad will not be greatly aggravated by corresponding variations in capital formation.

The first of these three points can be made most easily. A country that engages in a number of activities is also apt to export a wide range of products. Each individual export may be subject to disturbances, whether due to changes in external demand or in technology. But if those disturbances are independent, consequent on variations in the composition of expenditure or output, rather than massive macro-economic swings affecting the entire export array, the law of large numbers will come into play. At any point in time, a country can expect to suffer significant reversals in export performance, but also to enjoy significant successes. Its aggregate exports, then, are sure to be more stable than those of an economy less thoroughly diversified. From the standpoint of external balance, taken by itself, economic diversification, reflected in export diversification, serves, ex ante, to forestall the need for frequent changes in the terms of trade and, therefore, for frequent changes in national exchange rates.[17]

17. Anyone familiar with random processes knows, of course, that they may not average out quickly or perfectly. That is why the gambler has to have a bankroll and why central banks have to have reserves. If, in fact, one views the balance of payments as a simple sum of stochastic processes, the deficit or surplus, measured by the change in central bank reserves, should obey the central limit

One has at once to qualify this simple proposition. A diversification of output and exports cannot guarantee domestic stability, even when external shocks tend to average out. There must be sufficient occupational mobility to reabsorb the labor and capital idled by adverse disturbances. Here, two possibilities arise. If, on the one hand, external disturbances are truly independent because each export product is quite different from the rest, export earnings will be stable but factor mobility may be very low. Products that differ when classified by final use may differ in their modes of manufacture, so that the factors of production used in making one of them may not be adaptable to making any other. If, on the other hand, the several separate exports of a single country are, in fact, close substitutes when classified by final use, disturbances afflicting external demand will not be fully independent—the law of large numbers will not apply—but there may be more mobility between export industries. Products that are similar in final use are apt to have similar factor requirements, and workers who are idled by an export disturbance may be more readily absorbed in other activities.

My second point is closely related to the first but deals with the consequence of export fluctuations after they appear. A diversification of output will mitigate the damage done by external shocks, not merely diminish the likelihood of major shocks. To make this point, I shall contrast four distinct economies, asking what they have to do to maintain external balances when they are afflicted by exogenous disturbances. These four economies are perfectly competitive and make use of a single variable input, standardized labor, but they differ in two ways.[18] Output is diversified in the first and second countries; each of them produces an export good and an import-competing good. The third and fourth economies, by contrast, are not diversified; they specialize completely in export production. Furthermore, the first and third are small economies, with no influence at all on world prices,[19] while the second

theorem, exhibiting a normal or nearly normal distribution, and a central bank's reserves ought to be an increasing function of the variance or standard deviation of that normal distribution. Surprisingly enough, these things are true; see Peter B. Kenen and Elinor B. Yudin, "The Demand for International Reserves," *Review of Economics and Statistics*, 97, no. 3 (August 1965): 242–50. For a further look at the balance of payments as a somewhat fancier stochastic process, see my *Computer Simulation of the United States Balance of Payments*, mimeographed (International Economics Workshop: Columbia University, 1965).

18. For a more formal representation of these economies, and proofs of the theorems that follow, examine the Appendix.

19. Hence, the first and third resemble the model economies considered in McKinnon's note on optimum currency areas, except that they do not produce "non-tradable" commodities and cannot shift labor (or domestic demand) to and from their local sectors when domestic prices change.

and fourth are large economies, facing a determinate demand for their exports.

Consider, first, a simple exogenous disturbance, an increase in wage rates more rapid than in import prices. Here, all four economies must make the same exchange-rate change to stabilize employment; the requisite devaluation or depreciation must equal the difference between the rates of change of wages and of import prices. Yet the four economies behave rather differently when their central banks opt for fixed exchange rates. In each case, employment is certain to decline, but the changes in employment will not be identical. In the small-country case, the two-product economy will suffer a smaller decline in employment if its export industry has the larger elasticity of demand for labor with respect to real wage rates.[20] In the large-country case, this same condition has to hold, but does not suffice; there is, indeed, a strong presumption that the two-product national economy will suffer the larger change in employment.[21] Facing this type of exogenous disturbance, then, diversified economies may be at a handicap.[22]

Consider, next, a different class of exogenous disturbances, more like the one that figures in Mundell's analysis. Seen by the small countries, this type of shock will appear as an exogenous change in the terms of trade; seen by the large countries, it will appear as an exogenous change in export demand at given terms of trade. Here, there are perceptible differences in the size of the exchange-rate change needed for internal balance, not just in the size of the change in employment occurring when the central banks opt for fixed exchange rates. Whether small or large, the two-product economy is bound to experience the smaller change in its exchange rate.[23] Furthermore, product diversification always serves to shield the labor force from this class of shock. The two-product economy suffers the smaller change in employment under fixed exchange rates, and the larger the fraction of the labor force engaged in import-competing production, the smaller the change in employment occasioned by a change in the terms of trade or demand for exports.[24]

20. See equation (4.5) of the Appendix.
21. See equation (4.6) of the Appendix.
22. Notice, moreover, that this strange result derives from the mere fact of diversification, not from mobility inside an economy. Both parts of the labor force, in export- and import-competing production, are affected the same way by changes in the money wage relative to import prices.
23. See equations (4.7) and (4.8) of the Appendix.
24. See equations (4.9) and (4.10) of the Appendix, and notice once again that the extra stability afforded a diversified economy derives from the mere fact that it has more industries, not from any labor flow inside the country. The two disturbances considered here do not affect employment in the import-competing

52   Kenen

I come now to my third point concerning diversification. Here, I shall combine the first of those three points, concerning the advantages conferred ex ante by export diversity, with my earlier remark, concerning the connection between export demand and the stability of capital formation.

Suppose that an economy is operating at full steam, with no idle capacity in any of its sectors. An increase of demand for that country's exports will introduce damaging inflationary pressures. And those pressures will be amplified in two separate ways—by the familiar Keynesian multiplier and by an increase in capital formation as exporters undertake to satisfy their customers. Exports and investment will increase together, giving a double thrust to aggregate demand. From the standpoint of external balance, this may not be bad. Imports will rise faster and are more apt to offset the initial rise in exports, narrowing the gap in the current-account balance. But from the standpoint of internal balance, the increase of investment induced by the rise in exports will put a larger strain on domestic policy.[25]

Clearly, a country will be least exposed to this compound instability if its exports are thoroughly diversified and the disturbances afflicting

industry. For labor mobility to play a part in stabilizing overall employment, there must be a change in the exchange rate or a decrease of the money wage relative to import prices; these would stimulate production in the import-competing industry and transfer idle workers from the export industry.

25. In the paper cited earlier, Mrs. Whitman has supplied an elegant analysis of these phenomena and, what may be most important, of the complications introduced when some of the investment is financed by foreigners. Here, some simple algebra can illustrate my point. Using the familiar Keynesian relationships:

$$dY = dC + dI + dX - dM,$$
$$dC = (1 - s)\,dY,$$
$$dM = m \cdot dY,$$
$$dB = dX - dM.$$

Introduce a simple link between exports and investment:

$$dI = r \cdot dX.$$

Then:

$$dY = (1 + r)\,dX/(s + m) \qquad \text{and} \qquad dB = (s - rm)\,dX/(s + m).$$

The change in income is an increasing function of the link between exports and investment, while the change in the trade balance is a decreasing function of that same connection, r. Note, in passing, that a diversified economy may have a rather small marginal propensity to import (see Whitman, *International and Interregional Payments*, p. 8), so that dY and dB may be increasing functions of diversification; external disturbances will not spill back out. This may be the chief counterargument to my own contention that diversified economies are the least vulnerable to external shocks and have the least need for flexible rates to maintain internal balance.

those exports are, in consequence, fairly well randomized. The corresponding fluctuations in domestic investment may not average out as well, since an increase of demand for any single export may increase investment in that export industry, while an equal decrease of demand for some other export may not cause a corresponding decrease in investment. Here, much will depend on the capital-intensities of the nation's industries and on investors' judgments regarding the duration of the export disturbance. Yet the asymmetries, if they exist, cannot be large enough to vitiate my basic point. Diversity in exports, protecting the economy from external shocks, will surely help to stabilize capital formation, easing the burden that has to be borne by internal policies.

Again, a major caveat: My argument does not apply when changes in export demand arise from business-cycle swings. When those occur, the whole range of exports will be hit, and export diversification cannot forestall "imported" instability.

This point has been made before and has, indeed, been offered as the principal criterion for choosing a particular exchange-rate regime. Fixed rates, it is said, are much to be preferred if one's own authorities, especially the central bank, are less adept or more prone to err than those of other countries. With fixed rates, the outside world can be made to bear some part of the consequences of one's own mistakes.[26] If, conversely, foreigners are less adept at economic management, flexible exchange rates are much to be preferred, to insulate a stable domestic economy from another country's errors.

These are potent arguments and may even be decisive. They did, in fact, dominate the Canadian debate a few years ago. But surely they do not belong to the theory of optimum currency areas. Optimality has always to be judged from a global point of view,[27] and these defensive arguments are far from cosmopolitan. Countries which adopt fixed

26. This point is the counterpart of another by Mundell: That fiscal policy is more potent under flexible exchange rates "because leakages through foreign trade are closed by changes in the exchange rate," and that the potency of monetary policy is increased even more because of its effects on capital movements; an increase of interest rates, attracting foreign capital, forces an appreciation of the home currency and a concomitant deflationary change in the current-account balance. See Robert Mundell, "Flexible Exchange Rates and Employment Policy," *Canadian Journal of Economics and Political Science*, 27, no. 4 (November 1961): 516; also Sohmen, *Flexible Exchange Rates*, p. 84.

27. If not in other areas of economic thought, certainly in matters pertaining to exchange rates. How many times have we to remind our students—and ourselves as well—that an exchange rate is common to two countries, not the exclusive national property of one or the other? How many times have we heard and ridiculed the remarkable recommendation that "all currencies should fluctuate except the U.S. dollar"?

exchange rates to diffuse their own mistakes inflict those same mistakes on their trading partners; countries which adopt flexible exchange rates compound the consequences of their neighbors' errors.

Conclusion

Where, then, do I wind up? Fixed rates, I believe are most appropriate —or least inappropriate—to well-diversified national economies. *Ex ante*, diversification serves to average out external shocks and, incidentally, to stabilize domestic capital formation. *Ex post*, it serves to minimize the damage done when averaging is incomplete. It is also a prerequisite to the internal factor mobility that Mundell has emphasized, because a continuum of national activities will maximize the number of employment opportunities for each specialized variety of labor.

One more desideratum emerges from my argument. Countries with fixed rates have also to be armed with potent and sophisticated internal policies. Remember that diversified national economies may be particularly vulnerable to the "monetary" shocks represented by a change in money wages relative to import prices. Hence, they must maintain rather close control over money-wage rates, or at least be able to align the rate of change of the money wage with rates of change prevailing abroad. Furthermore, fixed-rate countries must be armed with a wide array of budgetary policies to deal with the stubborn "pockets of unemployment" that are certain to arise from export fluctuations combined with an imperfect mobility of labor.

In brief, I come quite close to endorsing the status quo. The principal developed countries should perhaps adhere to the Bretton Woods regime, rarely resorting to changes in exchange rates.[28] The less-developed countries, being less diversified and less well-equipped with policy instruments, should make more frequent changes or perhaps resort to full flexibility.

Appendix

To sort out the effects of diversification, consider the economies described in the text.

The Small Two-Product Economy

As labor is the only variable input, the two outputs, X_1 and X_2, can be

---

[28] If so, however, they must have large reserves. For a longer argument along these same lines, see my "Toward a Supranational Monetary System," cited above.

written as functions of employment, N_1 and N_2, and those functions will display diminishing returns:

$$X_1 = g_1(N_1), \qquad g_1' > 0, g_1'' < 0 \qquad (1.1)$$
$$X_2 = g_2(N_2), \qquad g_2' > 0, g_2'' < 0 \qquad (1.2)$$

Next, define total employment, N, and real income, Y, using the price of the export product as numeraire:

$$N = N_1 + N_2 \qquad (1.3)$$
$$Y = X_1 + \frac{1}{p} \cdot X_2 \qquad (1.4)$$
$$p = P_1/P_2 \qquad (1.5)$$

Furthermore, labor will be paid a money wage, W, equal to the value of its marginal product, so that:

$$W = P_1 \cdot g_1' \qquad (1.6)$$
$$W = P_2 \cdot g_2' \qquad (1.7)$$

Now define the domestic consumption of X_1 and X_2 on the supposition that there is no net saving, so that expenditure will always equal income:

$$X_1^c = C(Y, p) \qquad (1.8)$$
$$X_2^c = (Y - X_1^c)p \qquad (1.9)$$

Note that (1.8) and (1.9) imply a continuous equality between exports and imports.[29] Finally, define the foreign-currency prices of the two products, P_1^f and P_2^f, and write the exchange rate, R, in units of foreign currency per unit of home currency. Then:

$$RP_1 = P_1^f \qquad (1.10)$$
$$RP_2 = P_2^f \qquad (1.11)$$

If W, R, P_1^f and P_2^f are treated as exogenous, the eleven equations given above uniquely determine X_1, X_2, N_1, N_2, Y, p, P_1, P_2, X_1^c, and X_2^c.

The Large Two-Product Economy

Use (1.1) through (1.9) and (1.11) above, but replace (1.10) with a demand function for exports, X_1^e:

$$X_1^e = X_1 - X_1^c = E(RP_1/P_2^f, t) \qquad (1.10')$$

where t is an exogenous disturbance.

29. Exports will be $(X_1 - X_1^c)$ and imports will be valued at $(X_2^c - X_2)/p$. Invoking (1.9) and (1.4), above, imports can be written as $(Y - X_1^c - X_2/p)$, which is $(X_1 - X_1^c)$.

The Small One-Product Economy

Use (1.1), (1.5), (1.6), and (1.8) through (1.11), but replace (1.3) and (1.4) with:

$$N = N_1 \tag{1.3'}$$
$$Y = X_1 \tag{1.4'}$$

This economy has nine equations and an equal number of endogenous variables; equations (1.2) and (1.7) have dropped out, but so too have X_2 and N_2.

The Large One-Product Economy

Use (1.1), (1.3'), (1.4'), (1.5), (1.6), (1.8), (1.9), (1.10'), and (1.11). This economy, like the one before has nine equations and nine endogenous variables.

To simplify subsequent analysis, rewrite the essential part of each economic model. For the small two-product case:

$$N = N_1 + N_2 \tag{2.1}$$

$$Y = g_1(N_1) + \frac{1}{p} \cdot g_2(N_2) \tag{2.2}$$

$$p = P_1^f / P_2^f \tag{2.3}$$

$$RW = P_1^f \cdot g_1' \tag{2.4}$$

$$RW = P_2^f \cdot g_2'. \tag{2.5}$$

For the large two-product case, use (2.1), (2.2), and (2.5), above, but replace (2.3) and (2.4) with

$$p = P_1 / P_2^f \tag{2.3'}$$

$$W = P_1 \cdot g_1' \tag{2.4'}$$

and combine (1.8) and (1.10') into

$$g_1(N_1) = C(Y, p) + E(p, t). \tag{2.6}$$

For the small one-product case, use (2.3) and (2.4) above, but replace (2.1) and (2.2) with

$$N = N_1 \tag{2.1'}$$

$$Y = g_1(N_1), \tag{2.2'}$$

and for the large one-product case, use (2.1'), (2.2'), (2.3'), (2.4'), and (2.6).

Differentiate (2.1) through (2.5) to furnish four equations for the small two-product country:

$$dN_1 + dN_2 - dN = 0 \tag{3.1}$$

$$g_1' \, dN_1 + g_1' \, dN_2 - dY - (X_2/p)\overset{*}{p} = 0 \tag{3.2}$$

$$\frac{1}{e_1 \cdot N_1} \, dN_1 - \overset{*}{p} = (\overset{*}{P_2^f} - \overset{*}{W} - \overset{*}{R}) \tag{3.3}$$

$$\frac{1}{e_1 \cdot N_1} \, dN_1 - \frac{1}{e_2 \cdot N_2} \, dN_2 - \overset{*}{p} = 0 \tag{3.4}$$

where $\overset{*}{p}$, $\overset{*}{P_2^f}$, $\overset{*}{W}$, and $\overset{*}{R}$ are the percentage rates of change in p, P_2^f, W, and R, and where $e_1 = -(g_1'/g_1'')/N_1$ and $e_2 = -(g_2'/g_2'')/N_2$, the elasticities of N_1 and N_2 with respect to real wage rates. Here, the percentage change in relative prices, $\overset{*}{p}$, is exogenous; the four equations (3.1) through (3.4) suffice merely to solve for dN_1, dN_2, dN, and dY.

Differentiate (2.1), (2.2), (2.3′), (2.4′), (2.5), and (2.6) to obtain five equations for the large two-product country: equations (3.1) through (3.4) and

$$g_1' \, dN_1 - c_1 \cdot dY + (n^c \cdot X_1^c + n^e \cdot X_1^f)\overset{*}{p} = dX_1^{ea} \tag{3.5}$$

where $c_1 = (\partial C/\partial Y)$, the marginal propensity to spend on X_1; where $n^c = -(\partial C/\partial p)(p/X_1^c)$, the price elasticity of home demand for X_1; where $n^e = -(\partial E/\partial p)(p/X_1^c)$, the price elasticity of foreign demand for X_1, and where dX_1^{ea} is the autonomous change in export demand, $(\partial E/\partial t) \, dt$. Here, the percentage change in relative prices, $\overset{*}{p}$, is endogenous; the five equations (3.1) through (3.5) suffice to solve for dN_1, dN_2, dN, dY, and $\overset{*}{p}$.

Differentiate (2.1′), (2.2′), (2.3), and (2.4) to obtain two equations for the small one-product country:

$$g_1' \, dN - dY = 0 \tag{3.6}$$

$$\frac{1}{e_1 \cdot N} \, dN - \overset{*}{p} = (\overset{*}{P_2^f} - \overset{*}{W} - \overset{*}{R}). \tag{3.7}$$

Here, again, $\overset{*}{p}$ is exogenous; equations (3.6) and (3.7) suffice merely to solve for dN and dY.

Finally, differentiate (2.1′), (2.2′), (2.3′), (2.4′), and (2.6) to obtain three equations for the large one-product country: Equations (3.6), (3.7), and (3.5), but with total N replacing N_2 in (3.5). These three equations suffice to solve for dN, dY, and $\overset{*}{p}$.

Now write out the changes in employment, dN, attaching a superscript to each result so as to identify the case from which it comes. In the small one-product country:

$$dN^{1s} = Ne_1(\overset{*}{P_2^f} - \overset{*}{W} - \overset{*}{R} + \overset{*}{p}). \tag{4.1}$$

In the small two-product country

$$dN_1 = N_1 \cdot e_1(\overset{*}{P_2^f} - \overset{*}{W} - \overset{*}{R} + \overset{*}{p}),$$

$$dN_2 = N_2 \cdot e_2(\overset{*}{P_2^f} - \overset{*}{W} - \overset{*}{R}),$$

$$dN^{2s} = [Ne_1 + N_2(e_2 - e_1)](\overset{*}{P_2^f} - \overset{*}{W} - \overset{*}{R}) + (N_1 \cdot e_1)\overset{*}{p}. \tag{4.2}$$

In the large one-product country

$$dN^{1l} = \frac{1}{D_1} [n^\alpha(\overset{*}{P_2^f} - \overset{*}{W} - \overset{*}{R}) + dX_1^{ea}] \tag{4.3}$$

where $n^\alpha = (n^c \cdot X_1^c + n^e \cdot X_1^e)$ and $D_1 = g_1'(1 - c_1) + n^\alpha/Ne_1$ (with $D_1 > 0$ because $c_1 < 1$ when X_2 is not an inferior good). Finally, in the large two-product country

$$dN_1 = \frac{1}{D_2} \{[(n^\alpha + c_1 \cdot X_2/p) + c_1(N_2 \cdot e_2)g_1'](\overset{*}{P_2^f} - \overset{*}{W} - \overset{*}{R}) + dX_1^{ea}\},$$

$$dN_2 = (N_2 \cdot e_2)(\overset{*}{P_2^f} - \overset{*}{W} - \overset{*}{R}),$$

$$dN^{2l} = \frac{1}{D_2} \left\{ \left[\frac{Ne_1 + N_2(e_2 - e_1)}{N_1 \cdot e_1} \right] (n^\alpha + c_1 \cdot X_2/p) + (N_2 \cdot e_2)g_1' \right]$$

$$\times (\overset{*}{P_2^f} - \overset{*}{W} - \overset{*}{R}) + dX_1^{ea} \right\} \tag{4.4}$$

where $D_2 = D_1 + [n^\alpha(N_2/N) + c_1 \cdot X_2/p]/(N_1 \cdot e_1)$. The new arguments figuring in D_2 represent the two effects of product diversification. The term $n^\alpha(N_2/N)$ is the direct effect of splitting the labor force into N_1 and N_2. The term $c_1 \cdot X_2/p$ is an indirect terms-of-trade effect, measuring the change in home spending on X_1 resulting from a change in relative prices that alters the X_1 value of X_2 output and, to that extent, alters the national income. It takes this form because the X_1 value of national income, Y, is used as an argument in the demand function for X_1, equation (1.8), above.

Now let $\overset{*}{p} = 0$ in (4.1) and (4.2), let $dX_1^{ea} = 0$ in (4.3) and (4.4), and let $\overset{*}{R} = 0$ for fixed exchange rates. Pairing off the countries according to size:

$$dN^{1s} - dN^{2s} = N_2(e_1 - e_2)(\overset{*}{P_2^f} - \overset{*}{W}) \tag{4.5}$$

$$dN^{1l} - dN^{2l} = \frac{1}{D_2}\left\{N_2(e_1 - e_2)(n^\alpha + c_1 \cdot X_2/p)/(N_1 \cdot e_1)\right.$$
$$\left. - g_1'\left[N_2 \cdot e_2 + (1 - c_1)Ne_1\left(\frac{D_2 - D_1}{D_1}\right)\right]\right\}$$
$$\times (\overset{*}{P_2^f} - \overset{*}{W}) \tag{4.6}$$

In the small-country case, the condition $e_1 > e_2$ is sufficient to diminish variations in employment arising from disparities between $\overset{*}{P_2^f}$ and $\overset{*}{W}$. In the large-country case, $e_1 > e_2$ is needed but does not suffice; the other argument of (4.6) is unambiguously positive. When $\overset{*}{P_2^f} \neq \overset{*}{W}$, then, the diversified economy may suffer larger changes in employment.[30]

Next, let $\overset{*}{P_2^f} = \overset{*}{W}$ to study the external shocks $\overset{*}{p}$ and dX_1^{ea}. Whereas, before, all four economies had to make the very same changes in exchange rates for internal balance ($dN = 0$), here, each economy must make a different change. Using (4.1) through (4.4), compute the requisite changes in exchange rates and the pairwise differences. As:

$$\overset{*}{R}^{1s} = \overset{*}{p},$$
$$\overset{*}{R}^{2s} = (1 - \overset{*}{V})p,$$
$$\overset{*}{R}^{1l} = \frac{dX_1^{ea}}{n^\alpha},$$
$$\overset{*}{R}^{2l} = \frac{(1 - V)\,dX_1^{ea}}{n^\alpha + c_1 \cdot X_2/p + N_2 \cdot e_2(1 - V)g_1'},$$

where $V = (N_1 \cdot e_1)/[(N_1 \cdot e_1) + (N_2 \cdot e_2)]$, then:

$$\overset{*}{R}^{1s} - \overset{*}{R}^{2s} = (1 - V)\overset{*}{p} \tag{4.7}$$

$$\overset{*}{R}^{1l} - \overset{*}{R}^{2l} = \frac{Vn^\alpha + c_1 \cdot X_2/p + N_2 \cdot e_2(1 - V)g_1'}{n^\alpha[n^\alpha + c_1 \cdot X_2/p + N_2 \cdot e_2(1 - V)g_1']}\,dX_1^{ea}. \tag{4.8}$$

The one-product economy is bound to experience the larger change in its exchange rate.

30. Mere size, however, is advantageous. In the one-product case, for example: $dN^{1s} - dN^{1l} = \frac{1}{D_1} Ne_1(1 - c_1)g_1'(\overset{*}{P_2^f} - \overset{*}{W})$. The small country will experience the larger change in aggregate employment.

60   Kenen

If, now, $\overset{*}{R} = 0$, $\overset{*}{p}$ and dX_1^{ea} lead to different changes in aggregate employment:

$$dN^{1s} - dN^{2s} = (N_2 \cdot e_2)\overset{*}{p} \tag{4.9}$$

$$dN^{1l} - dN^{2l} = \left(\frac{D_2 - D_1}{D_1 \cdot D_2}\right) dX_1^{ea}$$

$$= \left[\frac{n^\alpha(N_2/N) + c_1 \cdot X_2/p}{(N_1 \cdot e_1)D_1 \cdot D_2}\right] dX^{ea} \tag{4.10}$$

In each case, the diversified national economy suffers the smaller change in employment.

4 EFFECTS OF INTERVENTION AND STERILIZATION IN THE SHORT RUN AND THE LONG RUN

Peter B. Kenen

INTRODUCTION

Academic views about flexible exchange rates are even more volatile than the rates themselves. At the start of the current float, in 1973, there was much criticism of official intervention. What we want, said the critics, is a "clean" float rather than a "dirty" float. Five years later, in 1978, there was much criticism of the United States because of its reluctance to intervene in the support of the dollar.

The recent move toward more management and, therefore, more intervention should not surprise or disappoint Robert Triffin. "On balance," he wrote, "stabilizing interventions by the Central Bank itself, with their implicit bias toward internal monetary adjustments, would often present advantages over private stabilizing interventions with their implicit bias toward neutralization" (Triffin 1960:85). This brief passage is especially interesting today, because it anticipates the debate that has begun concerning the effects of sterilized and nonsterilized intervention.

In a thoughtful paper on official intervention under floating exchange rates, Mussa (1980) weighs the several arguments for intervention and finds some of them persuasive. But he comes down strongly on the side of nonsterilized intervention. Intervention will not have long-lasting influence, he says, if central banks sterilize its money supply effects.

This chapter was written while I was Ford Visiting Research Professor at the University of California, Berkeley. I am grateful to Polly Allen, Jeffrey Frankel, Jorge de Macedo, and Jerry Stein for comments on an earlier version.

Intervention can affect exchange rates temporarily by changing expectations about economic policies:

> The argument that official intervention is required to correct for the defects of private speculation, specifically excessive variation caused by "bandwagon effects," is not especially convincing, particularly in view of the possibility that official intervention may itself be responsible for the purported defects of private speculation. There is, however, a valid case for official intervention on the grounds that the authorities may have better knowledge of their own future policy intentions than private market participants. Official intervention may be called for in circumstances where the credibility of the authorities is in question and it is necessary to "buy credibility" by committing the assets of the central bank to the support of its intended future policy. (Mussa 1980: 4)

But intervention can affect exchange rates permanently only by changing the quantity of money:

> [It] is clear from the general principles of the "asset market view" of exchange rates why [nonsterilized] intervention should be of first order importance for the behavior of exchange rates. It is much less clear, from general analytical principles, that [sterilized] intervention, which has no effect on the domestic money supply, should have a significant effect on the behavior of exchange rates, particularly in the long run. In fact, an analysis of the principal channels through which [sterilized] intervention may be presumed to operate suggests that while such intervention may be able to affect the behavior of exchange rates in the short run, it has at best very modest capacity to affect their behavior in the long run. (Ibid.: 25)

Mussa does not provide a formal model containing the channels to which he refers. His model, however, is implicit in his presentation.

Setting aside the effects of intervention on expectations, Mussa goes on to treat spot intervention as a form of monetary policy. A spot purchase of foreign currency by the central bank resembles an ordinary open market purchase of domestic securities in that it increases the money supply and therefore reduces the long-run equilibrium price of the domestic currency. By implication, a spot purchase that is offset (sterilized) by an open market sale of domestic securities cannot affect the long-run equilibrium price of the domestic currency, because it does not affect the money supply.

Mussa's treatment of official intervention is thus based on a simple monetarist model of exchange rate determination in which supplies of assets other than money are unimportant. Transactions in foreign currency are equivalent to transactions in domestic securities, because changes in supplies of domestic securities do not affect the exchange rate. Mussa's conclusions do not reflect the "general principles" of the asset market approach to exchange rate theory but derive from a special case.

I shall examine the effects of official intervention in a more general asset market model of exchange rate determination. It is a streamlined version of the portfolio balance model developed by Allen and Kenen (1980).[1] Our model is useful for the purpose because it contains several channels through which exchange rates influence behavior in goods and asset markets and because the conduct of monetary policy is carefully specified. Furthermore, it can be solved for short-run effects (those taking place before flows of assets have had time to alter the corresponding stocks) and separately for long-run effects (those pertaining to comparisons of stationary states where all flows of assets cease and stocks come to be constant). In consequence, it allows us to pursue the two-way distinction drawn by Mussa between sterilized and nonsterilized intervention on the one hand and between short-run and long-run effects on the other. Finally, the model includes Mussa's monetarist model as a limiting case. When domestic and foreign bonds are perfect substitutes, changes in supplies of domestic bonds do not influence exchange rates.

The model can be used to study shifts in expectations, but I shall not go that far. Instead, I shall assume that expectations are stationary, so as to exclude all expectational effects from my conclusions about intervention and set aside the issues raised in the first quotation from Mussa's paper. I want to concentrate on those raised in the second.

I present the model in the following section and solve it for short-run and long-run effects in section three. I interpret the solutions in section four, with particular reference to Mussa's distinction between sterilized and nonsterilized intervention, and return to his special case in the final section, where I show what happens with perfect substitutability. These are my main conclusions:

- When foreign and domestic bonds are not perfect substitutes, intervention can have permanent effects on the exchange rate even when it is sterilized completely. There is indeed one instance, examined below, in which sterilized intervention is equally effective in the short run and the long run, whereas nonsterilized intervention is effective in the short run but much less effective in the long run.

- When foreign and domestic bonds are perfect substitutes, sterilized intervention is ineffective in the long run. But it is also ineffective in the short run, apart from any influence it may exert on expectations. Official intervention can affect exchange rates only when it is allowed to alter the money supply — when the central bank employs the foreign exchange market to carry out its monetary policy.

1. I use the simplified version of the model presented in Chapter 7 of Allen and Kenen (1980), where there are no nontraded goods, but go further by simplifying the notation and eliminating fiscal policies and goods market disturbances that do not affect asset markets in the short run (because the demand for money is made to depend on wealth but not on income).

THE MODEL

Consider an economy whose households hold three assets – domestic money, domestic (government) bonds, and foreign bonds denominated in foreign currency. Denote their holdings by L^h, B^h, and F^h, and make them depend on interest rates and wealth:

$$L^h = L(r_0, r_1, W^h), \quad L_0 < 0, \; L_1 < 0, \; 0 < L_W < 1 \qquad (4.1)$$

$$B^h = B(r_0, r_1, W^h), \quad B_0 < 0, \; B_1 > 0, \; 0 < B_W < 1 \qquad (4.2)$$

$$\pi F^h = F(r_0, r_1, W^h), \quad F_0 > 0, \; F_1 < 0, \; 0 < F_W < 1 \qquad (4.3)$$

where r_0 is the interest rate on the foreign bond, r_1 is the interest rate on the domestic bond, W^h is household wealth in home currency, and π is the home currency price of the foreign currency (the spot exchange rate), and where

$$W^h = L^h + B^h + \pi F^h \qquad (4.4)$$

By implication, $L_0 + B_0 + F_0 = 0$, $L_1 + B_1 + F_1 = 0$, and $L_W + B_W + F_W = 1$.

Household wealth can be described by the history of saving, S, and the history of capital gains and losses on bond holdings. As bonds are bills in this model, however, there can be no capital gains or losses on account of fluctuations in bond prices (interest rates). Therefore,

$$W^h = \int_0^t S dt + \int_0^t V\left(\frac{\dot{\pi}}{\pi}\right) dt \qquad (4.5)$$

where $V = \pi F^h$.[2] Saving is made to rise with interest rates and income and, following Metzler (1951), to fall with wealth[3]:

$$S = S(r_0, r_1, Y^d, W^h), \quad S_0 > 0, \; S_1 > 0, \; 0 < S_Y < 1, \; S_W < 0 \qquad (4.6)$$

where Y^d is disposable income and is defined by

$$Y^d = Y + r_1 B^h + r_0 \pi F^h - T^h \qquad (4.7)$$

Here, Y is gross domestic product, and T^h is the lump sum tax collected by the government.

---

2. Note that $V > 0$ (because $F > 0$). This economy is a foreign currency creditor. On the importance of this point for the behavior of the model, see Allen and Kenen (1980: 204–205).

3. The wealth effect plays a role in this model analogous to the role of the real balance effect in a monetary model; an increase of wealth raises consumption (absorption) by reducing saving. A negative wealth effect can be justified, of course, only for a stationary economy in which households take a life cycle view of their need to save and there are no legacies.

The supply of money is given by the balance sheet of the central bank:

$$L = B^c + \pi R - W^c \tag{4.8}$$

where L is the stock of money, B^c is the stock of domestic bonds held by the central bank, R is the stock of foreign exchange reserves measured in foreign currency, and W^c is the history of capital gains and losses on the bank's foreign exchange reserves:

$$W^c = \int_0^t \pi R \left(\frac{\dot{\pi}}{\pi} \right) dt \tag{4.9}$$

Changes in B^c represent open market operations in the domestic bond. Changes in R represent interventions in the foreign exchange market. When interventions are not sterilized, R changes by itself, changing the money supply by the same amount. When interventions are completely sterilized, R and B^c change by opposite amounts, leaving the money supply unaffected. (Hereafter, B^c and R are written as $\bar{B}^c$ and $\bar{R}$ because they are policy determined.) The market-clearing equation for domestic money is

$$L^h - L = 0 \tag{4.10}$$

The supply of the domestic (government) bond is given by the history of budget deficits and surpluses. In this chapter, however, the budget is always balanced, so that B is fixed at $\bar{B}$. Furthermore, foreigners do not hold the domestic bond, so that the market-clearing equation is

$$B^h + B^c - \bar{B} = 0 \tag{4.11}$$

The supply of the foreign bond is infinitely elastic at the interest rate r_0 (which is written hereafter as $\bar{r}_0$).

The economy produces a single good, Q, priced at p_1 in domestic currency. Its output is

$$Q = f(p_1) \tag{4.12}$$

In the simplest of classical economies, $f'(p_1) = 0$; in the simplest of Keynesian economies, $f'(p_1) > 0$.[4] Gross domestic product is defined by

$$Y = p_1 Q \tag{4.13}$$

There are three sources of demand for the domestic good—households, foreigners, and the government. Household demand is given by

$$c^h = c^h(p_1, \pi p_0, C), \quad c_1^h < 0, \quad c_0^h > 0, \quad c_C^h > 0 \tag{4.14}$$

---

4. In the simple classical economy, the money wage rate is flexible, and the supply of labor is fixed. In the simple Keynesian economy, the money wage rate is fixed, and the supply of labor is perfectly elastic at that money wage. Combining these assumptions with profit maximization by domestic producers, we obtain the conditions in the text. For details, see Allen and Kenen (1980: ch. 2 and App. A).

where p_0 is the foreign currency price of the foreign good and C is domestic consumption in domestic currency:

$$C = Y^d - S \qquad (4.15)$$

Assume that $c^h(\ldots)$ is homogeneous of zero degree in prices and consumption and that the consumption elasticity is unity. Foreign demand is given by

$$c^f = c^f\left(\frac{p_1}{\pi}, p_0, C^f\right), \quad c_1^f < 0, \quad c_0^f > 0, \quad c_C^f > 0 \qquad (4.16)$$

where C^f is foreign consumption in foreign currency and is fixed at $\overline{C}^f$. Let $c^f(\ldots)$ have properties identical to those of $c^h(\ldots)$. Government demand is fixed at $\overline{G}$ in nominal terms. Therefore, the market-clearing equation for the domestic goods is

$$c^h + c^f + (\overline{G}/p_1) - Q = 0 \qquad (4.17)$$

The economy is not small in the market for its export good. It is small in the market for its import good. The supply of that good is infinitely elastic at its fixed foreign currency price (written hereafter as $\overline{p}_0$).

To close the model, we need the government budget. Outlays are $\overline{G}$ on domestic output, $r_1 B$ on interest, and T^f on transfers to foreigners. Receipts are tax revenues, T^h, and the interest income of the central bank, $r_1 B^c$. As the budget is balanced at all times,

$$\overline{G}_1 + r_1 B^h + T^f - T^h = 0 \qquad (4.18)$$

The lump sum tax, T^h, is manipulated to balance the budget (i.e., to offset variations in $\overline{G}, r_1 B^h$, and T^f). Transfers to foreigners are manipulated to offset interest income earned on the foreign bond[5]:

$$T^f = r_0 \pi F^h \qquad (4.19)$$

These assumptions allow us to rewrite disposable income as

$$Y^d = p_1 f(p_1) - \overline{G} \qquad (4.20)$$

and to show that saving must be equal to the current account balance, which is equal in turn to the trade balance.

The model outlined above can be written compactly, beginning with the three market-clearing equations:

$$L(\overline{r}_0, r_1, W^h) - (\overline{B}^c + \pi\overline{R} - W^c) = 0 \qquad (4.21)$$

---

5. This assumption is, of course, quite arbitrary, but serves to simplify the model substantially. It can be relaxed without impairing the chief conclusions of this paper (see Allen and Kenen 1980:279–85).

$$B(\bar{r}_0, r_1, W^h) + \bar{B}^c - \bar{B} = 0 \tag{4.22}$$

$$c^h(p_1, \pi p_0, Y^d - S) + c^f\left(\frac{p_1}{\pi}, p_0, \bar{C}^f\right) + (\bar{G}/p_1) - f(p_1) = 0 \tag{4.23}$$

But equation (4.20) defines Y^d as a function of p_1 and $\bar{G}$ when the government budget is balanced; equation (4.5) defines W^h as a function of the histories of S and π; equation (4.9) defines W^c as a function of the history of π; and equation (4.6) defines S as a function of $\bar{r}_0, r_1, Y^d$, and W^h. Accordingly, the three market-clearing equations can be solved for changes in π, r_1, and p_1 (or nominal income, Y) resulting from changes in $\bar{B}^c, \bar{R}, \bar{r}_0, \bar{G}, \bar{p}_0, \bar{C}^f$, and other exogenous disturbances.

THE SOLUTIONS

As income does not directly affect the demands for bonds and money, equations (4.21) and (4.22) can be solved separately from equation (4.23) to give the impact (short-run) of various disturbances. Differentiating them (but holding $\bar{r}_0$ and $\bar{B}$ constant),[6]

$$\begin{bmatrix} B_1 & B_W \\ \\ L_1 & L_W \end{bmatrix} \begin{bmatrix} \delta r_1 \\ \\ V\left(\frac{\delta\pi}{\pi}\right) \end{bmatrix} = \begin{bmatrix} -1 & 0 \\ \\ 1 & 1 \end{bmatrix} \begin{bmatrix} \delta\bar{B}^c \\ \\ \pi\delta\bar{R} \end{bmatrix} - \begin{bmatrix} \delta B^a \\ \\ \delta L^a \end{bmatrix} \tag{4.24}$$

where δB^a is an autonomous shift of household demand from the foreign bond to the domestic bond and δL^a is an autonomous shift of demand from the foreign bond to domestic money.

The solutions for the changes in the interest rate are

$$\delta r_1 = -(1/H)[(B_W + L_W)\delta\bar{B}^c + (B_W)\pi\delta\bar{R}^n$$

$$- (L_W)\pi\delta\bar{R}^s + (L_W)\delta B^a - (B_W)\delta L^a] \tag{4.25}$$

where $\pi\delta\bar{R}^n$ denotes a nonsterilized purchase of foreign exchange, $\pi\delta\bar{R}^s$ denotes a sterilized purchase, and $H = B_1 L_W - L_1 B_W > 0$. (The solution for $\pi\delta\bar{R}^n$ is the solution for $\pi\delta\bar{R}$ by itself. The solution for $\pi\delta\bar{R}^s$ is the solution for $\pi\delta\bar{R}$ combined with the solution for $\delta\bar{B}^c = -\pi\delta\bar{R}$, an open market sale of the domestic bond to offset the money supply effect of the foreign exchange purchase.) The signs of these effects are listed in Table 4-1. They are interpreted in the next section.

6. Here and hereafter, the operator δ is used to denote impact (short-run) effects, while d is used to denote steady-state (long-run) effects.

Table 4-1. Short-run Effects of Disturbances and Policies.

Effect on	$\delta \bar{B}^c$	$\pi\delta\bar{R}^n$	$\pi\delta\bar{R}^s$	δB^a	δL^a
r_1	$-$	$-$	$+$	$-$	$+$
π	$+$	$+$	$+$	$-$	$-$
p_1	$+$	$+$	$+^*$	$-^*$	$-$

*Assuming that $S_W L_1 > S_1 L_W$.

The solution for the changes in the exchange rate are

$$\left(\frac{\delta\pi}{\pi}\right) = (1/HV)\,[(-F_1)\,\delta\bar{B}^c + (B_1)\,\pi\delta\bar{R}^n - (L_1)\,\pi\delta\bar{R}^s$$
$$+ (L_1)\,\delta B^a - (B_1)\,\delta L^a] \tag{4.26}$$

The signs of these effects are also listed in Table 4-1. Notice that nonsterilized intervention causes a larger depreciation than an equal amount of sterilized intervention. Defining the effect of nonsterilized intervention as $(\delta\pi/\pi)^n$ and the effect of sterilized intervention as $(\delta\pi/\pi)^s$ and setting $\pi\delta\bar{R}^n = \pi\delta\bar{R}^s$, we have

$$\left(\frac{\delta\pi}{\pi}\right)^n - \left(\frac{\delta\pi}{\pi}\right)^s = (1/HV)(B_1 + L_1)\,\pi\delta\bar{R}^n$$

and $B_1 + L_1 = -F_1 > 0$. The difference is, of course, the same as the effect of an open market purchase shown in equation (4.26).

Differentiating equation (4.23) but holding $\bar{G}$, $\bar{P}_0$, and $\bar{C}^f$ constant, we obtain this expression for the change in the price of the domestic good:

$$\left(\frac{\delta p_1}{p_1}\right) = (1/N)\,[(u_\pi - m_1 S_W V)\left(\frac{\delta\pi}{\pi}\right) - (m_1 S_1)\,\delta r_1] \tag{4.27}$$

where $N = (u_t + \sigma N_Y)$; and $N_Y = S_Y + m_0(1 - S_Y)$, where m_0 and m_1 are the marginal propensities to spend on imported and domestic goods, respectively, and where u_π, u_t, and σ are (positive) combinations of goods market parameters.[7] Substituting the arguments of equations (4.25) and (4.26) for the changes in r_1 and π,

___

7. To be precise, $m_1 = p_1 c_C^h$, and $m_0 = 1 - m_1$, while $u_t = p_1 c^h e_0^h - p_1 c^f e_0^f$, where e_0^h and e_0^f are the (positive) cross-price elasticities of domestic and foreign demands for the domestic good, and $u_\pi = u_t + p_1 c^f$. Finally, $\sigma = Y\,[1 + f'(p_1)(p_1/Q)]$, which measures the effect of a change in p_1 on nominal gross domestic product. Note that N_Y is the simple Keynesian multiplier (the sum of the marginal propensities to save and import defined with respect to disposable income). It can be shown, moreover, that $u_t > 0$ (because $u_t > 0$), which satisfies the Marshall–Lerner–Robinson condition (see Allen and Kenen 1980:54). The exchange rate term, $u_\pi - m_1 S_W V$, in equation (4.27) contains an expenditure-switching (elasticities) effect, u_π, and an expenditure-changing (absorption) effect, $-m_1 S_W V$. The latter has three parts: (a) A depreciation of the domestic currency raises

$$\left(\frac{\delta p_1}{p_1}\right) = (1/NHV)\left\{m_1 V\left[S_1(B_W + L_W) + S_W F_1\right] - F_1 u_\pi\right\}\delta\overline{B}^c \quad (4.28)$$

$$+ (1/NHV)\left[m_1 V(S_1 B_W - S_W B_1) + B_1 u_\pi\right](\pi\delta\overline{R}^n - \delta L^a)$$

$$+ (1/NHV)\left[m_1 V(S_W L_1 - S_1 L_W) - L_1 u_\pi\right](\pi\delta\overline{R}^s - \delta B^a)$$

The effects of an open market purchase and of nonsterilized intervention are unambiguous. The effect of sterilized intervention is not, because $S_W L_1 \gtrless S_1 L_W$. Here and hereafter, however, I shall assume that $S_W L_1 > S_1 L_W$, which is to say that desired saving (absorption) is relatively sensitive to changes in wealth, and the demand for money relatively sensitive to the interest rate. Using language made familiar by recent work on fiscal policy in a closed economy, I assume that "crowding out" does not dominate.[8] The signs listed in Table 4–1 reflect this assumption.

It is not hard to prove that this model is stable—that saving falls monotonically to zero in the course of the response to an exogenous disturbance, causing stocks of wealth and assets to converge to constant levels. Accordingly, the steady-state solutions are meaningful, and they are obtained as follows: The changes in the interest rate and nominal wealth are obtained from equations (4.21) and (4.22). The change in disposable income is obtained from the changes in the interest rate and wealth, using equation (4.6) and the steady-state condition that $S = 0$. The change in p_1 is obtained from the change in disposable income, using equation (4.20). Finally, the change in the exchange rate is obtained from the price and income changes, using equation (4.23). Impact effects on the exchange rate are decided by behavior in the bond and money markets. Long-run effects come from the goods market, given the price and income changes produced by disturbances and domestic policies. This proposition is the analogue of the assertion that "purchasing power parity" obtains only in the long run.

Proceeding in this fashion, one can show that the long-run changes in r_1 are the same as those supplied by equation (4.25). The interest rate is unaffected by the dynamic adaptation that follows a disturbance. The long-run change in nominal wealth is given by

$$dW^h = (1/H)\left[(-F_1)d\overline{B}^c + (B_1)\pi d\overline{R}^n - (L_1)\pi d\overline{R}^s\right. \quad (4.29)$$

$$+ (L_1)dB^a - (B_1)dL^a\right]$$

wealth by $V(\delta\pi/\pi)$, the capital gain on foreign bonds held by domestic households; (b) the increase in wealth reduces desired saving by $S_W V(\delta\pi/\pi)$, raising consumption by the same amount; and (c) the increase of consumption raises the demand for the domestic good by the fraction m_1.

8. See, for example, Blinder and Solow (1973). In Allen and Kenen (1980: esp. ch.5), we show that a number of familiar propositions in international monetary theory, including those pertaining to the influence of capital mobility on the effectiveness of monetary and fiscal policies, depend crucially on this same assumption.

Table 4-2. Long-run Effects of Disturbances and Policies.

Effect on	$d\bar{B}^C$	$\pi d\bar{R}^n$	$\pi d\bar{R}^S$	dB^a	dL^a
r_1	−	−	+	−	+
W^h	+	+	+	−	−
p_1	+	+	+*	−*	−
π	+	+	+*	−*	−

*Assuming that $S_W L_1 > S_1 L_W$.

Moving directly to the change in p_1 obtained from the change in disposable income,

$$\left(\frac{dp_1}{p_1}\right) = -(1/\sigma S_Y)\,[(S_1)\,dr_1 + (S_W)\,dW^h] \tag{4.30}$$

Substituting the arguments of equations (4.25) and (4.29) for the changes in the interest rate and wealth,

$$\left(\frac{dp_1}{p_1}\right) = (1/H\sigma S_Y)\,[S_1\,(B_W + L_W) + S_W F_1]\,d\bar{B}^c \tag{4.31}$$
$$+ (1/H\sigma S_Y)\,(S_1\,B_W - S_W\,B_1)\,(\pi d\bar{R}^n - dL^a)$$
$$+ (1/H\sigma S_Y)\,(S_W\,L_1 - S_1\,L_W)\,(\pi d\bar{R}^s - dB^a)$$

Finally, the change in the exchange rate is given by

$$\left(\frac{d\pi}{\pi}\right) = [(u_t + m_0\,\sigma)/u_\pi]\left(\frac{dp_1}{p_1}\right) \tag{4.32}$$

so that the sign of the change in π is the same as the sign of the change in p_1.[9]
   The signs of the changes in r_1, W^h, p_1, and π are listed in Table 4-2 and are interpreted in the next section.

EFFECTS OF NONSTERILIZED AND
STERILIZED INTERVENTIONS

The comparative static results obtained in the previous section are most readily explained with the aid of a simple asset market diagram. In Figure 4-1, the curve WW traces the sets of combinations of r_1 and W^h that clear the bond mar-

9. In the classical variant of the model, $\sigma = Y$. In the absence of government spending, moreover, $Y = Y^d$, while $Y^d = C$ in the steady state, because there is no saving. Thus, $m_0\,\sigma = m_0\,C$, which measures the value of imports. But trade is balanced in the steady state, so that $m_0\,C = p_1\,c^f$, and this means in turn that $u_t + m_0\,\sigma = u_\pi$. By implication, $(d\pi/\pi) = (dp_1/p_1)$ in the classical variant; "purchasing power parity" holds in the long run when there are no goods market disturbances. For a more general proof, comprising the case in

Figure 4-1. Effects of Nonsterilized Intervention.

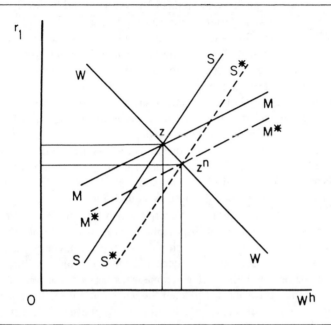

ket; it is downward sloping because an increase in wealth raises the demand for bonds $(B_W > 0)$ and must therefore be offset by a reduction in the interest rate $(B_1 > 0)$. The curve MM traces the sets of combinations that clear the money market; it is upward sloping because an increase in wealth raises the demand for money $(L_W > 0)$ and must therefore be offset by an increase in the interest rate $(L_1 < 0)$. Finally, the curve SS traces the sets of combinations at which saving is zero, given the steady-state level of disposable income; it is upward sloping because an increase in wealth reduces saving $(S_W < 0)$ and must therefore be offset by an increase in the interest rate $(S_1 > 0)$. When "crowding out" does not dominate, SS is steeper than MM.[10]

which government spending is not zero but is fixed in real terms rather than nominal terms, see Allen and Kenen (1980: App. C).

   10. These are the equations for the three asset market curves:
   - Bond market equilibrium (WW):
   $$dr_1 = - (B_W/B_1) dw^h - (1/B_1)(d\overline{B}^c + dB^a)$$
   - Money market equilibrium (MM):
   $$dr_1 = - (L_W/L_1) dw^h + (1/L_1) [(\pi d\overline{R} + dB^c) - dL^a]$$
   - Zero saving (SS):
   $$dr_1 = - (S_W/S_1) dw^h - (S_Y/S_1) dY^d$$

   When SS is steeper than MM, $(S_W/S_1) < (L_W/L_1)$, so that $S_W L_1 > S_1 L_W$.

As asset markets clear instantaneously in this model, short-run equilibria in the bond and money markets are defined by intersections of WW and MM. As saving is zero in the steady state, long-run equilibria are defined by intersections of WW, MM, and SS. When short-run equilibrium is displaced from some such point as z in Figure 4-1, where the three curves intersect, to a point above the SS curve, households will start to save at the initial level of disposable income, and absorption (consumption) will fall; when it is displaced to a point below the SS curve, households will start to dissave, and absorption will rise.

Income and the exchange rate do not appear explicitly in Figure 4-1, but it tells us much about the way that they behave.

What does it say about the behavior of income? As income rises with absorption, a disturbance that displaces asset market equilibrium to a point below the original SS curve raises nominal income above its initial level. Furthermore, a new SS curve must pass through the new equilibrium point, and this tells us what must happen to income in the long run. When the new SS curve lies below the old, the steady-state level of disposable income must be higher than it was before. The interest rate is lower at each point on the new SS curve, and disposable income is thus higher, because saving must be zero on any SS curve. But nominal income rises with disposable income when, as here, there are no changes in taxes other than those needed to keep the budget balanced. Summing up, the location of the new asset market equilibrium point, above or below the original SS curve, tells us how income responds in the short run and where it must wind up in the long run if asset market curves do not shift again.

What does it say about the behavior of the exchange rate? In the short run, before flows can influence stocks, there is only one way to alter nominal wealth—by changing the home currency value of the foreign bonds held in household portfolios. This is, in fact, the short-run function of an exchange rate change, which means that the sign of the short-run change in wealth gives us the sign of the short-run change in the exchange rate. The stock of wealth cannot rise instantaneously unless there is a depreciation of the domestic currency (an increase in π, the price of the foreign currency). With the passage of time, of course, wealth will respond to saving as well as the exchange rate. But the sign of the permanent change in the exchange rate can be inferred from the shift in the SS curve, because the long-run equilibrium level of the exchange rate depends on the long-run level of p_1 and, therefore, the long-run level of nominal income. When the new SS curve lies below the old, for example, so that there must be a permanent increase in nominal income and, therefore, a permanent increase in p_1, there must be a permanent depreciation of the domestic currency.[11]

---

11. This inference, like the one above concerning the long-run change in income, depends on the assumption that $\bar{G}$ is constant. A change in $\bar{G}$ would alter the relationship between Y^d and Y, changing the relationship between Y^d and p_1. The relationship between p_1 and π, moreover, would be altered by a goods market disturbance.

Starting at point z in Figure 4-1, where the three curves intersect, let us examine the effects of nonsterilized intervention. A purchase of foreign currency ($\pi d\bar{R} > 0$) adds to the assets of the central bank and raises the money supply. The MM curve shifts downward to M*M*, raising wealth and reducing the interest rate. The increase in wealth testifies, of course, to a depreciation of the domestic currency—which is what one would expect in the foreign exchange market, where the central bank has bought foreign currency and thus sold domestic currency. The decrease in the interest rate is what one would expect in the domestic bond market; the increase in wealth resulting from the depreciation of the domestic currency raises the demand for the domestic bond, and there has been no change in the supply, so that the interest rate must fall to clear the market.

As the new short-run equilibrium point, z^n, lies below the original SS curve, households start to dissave, raising absorption and nominal income, the result recorded in Table 4-1. With the passage of time, of course, wealth must be affected by dissaving, but asset market equilibrium remains at z^n, because WW and M*M* stay in place. The stock of wealth and the interest rate do not change. The SS curve, however, is displaced to S*S*, which says that there must be a permanent increase in disposable income, a permanent increase in p_1, and a permanent depreciation of the domestic currency. The permanent depreciation, moreover, must be larger than the initial depreciation; the price of foreign currency must rise through time to raise the home currency value of foreign bonds held in households' portfolios and thus to stabilize the stock of wealth in the face of the dissaving that takes place on the way to the new steady state (for more on these dynamics, see Allen and Kenen 1980: ch. 6).

To sum up, a nonsterilized purchase of foreign exchange has short-run and long-run effects on the economy. The interest rate falls, nominal income rises, and the domestic currency depreciates, immediately and permanently.

What happens with sterilized intervention? The answer is given by Figure 4-2. There is no change in the position of the MM curve, because there is no change in the money supply. But the WW curve shifts upward to W*W*, because the central bank must make an open market sale of domestic bonds if it is to make room for its purchase of foreign currency without affecting the money supply. Asset market equilibrium is displaced to z^s. There is an instantaneous increase in wealth, just as there was in Figure 4-1, which says that the domestic currency depreciates. But the interest rate rises instead of falling, because of the increase in the supply of the domestic bond. When SS is steeper than MM, as in Figure 4-2, the point z^s lies below the old SS curve, and households begin to dissave, raising absorption and nominal income. Furthermore, the SS curve gives way to S*S*, which means that disposable income must be higher in the new steady state, that p_1 must be higher too, and that there will be a permanent depreciation of the domestic currency. When "crowding out" does not dominate, then, sterilized intervention raises the interest rate rather than reducing it, but it raises

Figure 4-2. Effects of Sterilized Intervention.

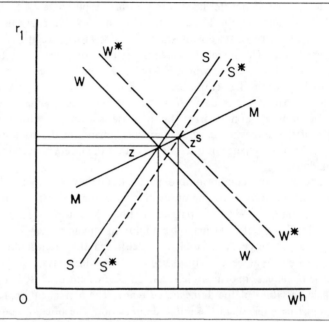

nominal income nonetheless and causes the domestic currency to depreciate, on impact and permanently.[12] There is no clear-cut qualitative distinction of the type that Mussa (1980) draws between the short-run effects of sterilized intervention and its long-run effects.

Consider, next, the consequences of official intervention designed to stabilize the exchange rate in the face of a shift of household demand from the foreign bond to the domestic bond. Setting $(\delta \pi/\pi) = 0$, I solve equation (4.26) for the requisite amounts of intervention: $\pi \delta \bar{R}^n = -(L_1/B_1) \delta B^a$, and $\pi \delta \bar{R}^s = \delta B^a$. In both instances, the central bank must buy foreign currency to keep the domestic currency from appreciating. If it engages in sterilization, the requisite purchase will be larger,[13] and the side effects will be quite different. With non-sterilized intervention, equations (4.25) and (4.27) give

12. As in the case of nonsterilized intervention, the permanent depreciation will be larger than the initial depreciation, because wealth must be kept constant in the face of dis-saving. When SS is flatter than MM, by contrast, the point z^s will lie above the SS curve, so that households will begin to save. Furthermore, the SS curve will shift upward, which says that disposable income must fall, reducing p_1 and causing the domestic currency to appreciate. The long-run change in the exchange rate will be opposite in sign to the short-run change.

13. This is because $-(L_1/B_1) = [L_1/(L_1 + F_1)] < 1$.

$$\delta r_1 = -(1/B_1)\,\delta B^a < 0$$

and

$$\left(\frac{\delta p_1}{p_1}\right) = -(m_1 S_1/N)\,\delta r_1 > 0$$

The interest rate falls, raising nominal income and the price of the domestic good. With sterilized intervention, $\delta r_1 = (\delta p_1/p_1) = 0$. There are no side effects. Furthermore, the long-run effects are different, including the effects on the exchange rate itself. With nonsterilized intervention, equations (4.25) and (4.29) give $dr_1 = \delta r_1 < 0$ (the long-run and short-run effects are the same), and $dW^h = 0$. In consequence, equations (4.30) and (4.32) give

$$\left(\frac{dp_1}{p_1}\right) = -(S_1/\sigma S_Y)\,dr_1 > 0$$

and

$$\left(\frac{d\pi}{\pi}\right) = [(u_t + m_0 \sigma)/u_\pi]\left(\frac{dp_1}{p_1}\right) > 0$$

An act of intervention that prevents appreciation in the short run leads to depreciation in the long run! With sterilized intervention, by contrast, $dr_1 = dW^h = 0$, so that $(dp_1/p_1) = (d\pi/\pi) = 0$. An act of intervention that prevents appreciation in the short run stabilizes the exchange rate in the long run too.

The differences between the two types of intervention are shown in Figure 4-3. The shift of demand between bonds is represented by the movement of the bond market curve from WW to W^aW^a. In the absence of any intervention, asset market equilibrium would be displaced from z to z^a. The domestic currency would appreciate. The effects of nonsterilized interventions are described by the movement of the money market curve from MM to M^nM^n, a movement large enough to keep wealth constant in the fact of the shift in demand and thus to keep the exchange rate constant in the short run. At the new equilibrium point, z^n, the interest rate is lower, and z^n lies below the SS curve, so that absorption rises in the short run, raising nominal income. The SS curve must shift downward, which means that disposable income must be higher in the new steady state, along with nominal income, and that the domestic currency must depreciate eventually.

The effects of sterilized intervention are even easier to show. As it does not affect the money market curve but acts instead on the bond market curve, intervention to stabilize the exchange rate serves merely to shift the bond market curve back from W^aW^a to WW. Asset market equilibrium returns to point z, and there are no side effects at all, in the short run or the long run.

Consider, finally, the effects of intervention designed to stabilize the exchange rate in the face of a shift of household demand from the foreign bond

Figure 4-3.   Effects of a Shift of Demand Between Bonds
with Nonsterilized and Sterilized Intervention.

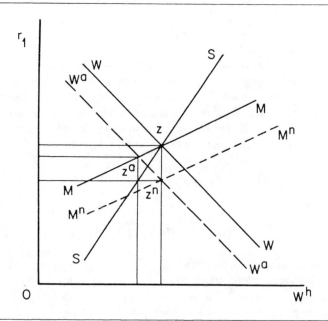

to domestic money. Here, equation (4.26) gives $\pi\delta\bar{R}^n = \delta L^a$, and $\pi\delta\bar{R}^s = -(B_1/L_1)\delta L^a$. Once again, the central bank must buy foreign currency to keep the domestic currency from appreciating, and when it engages in sterilization, the amount of intervention must be larger. In this instance, however, involving an increase in the demand for money, nonsterilized intervention is preferable, because it raises the supply of money. With nonsterilized intervention, there are no effects on the interest rate or nominal income in the short run or the long run and no change in the long-run level of the exchange rate. With sterilized intervention, by contrast, the interest rate rises in the short run and the long run, depressing nominal income and the price of the domestic good, so that the domestic currency must appreciate eventually.

These examples lead to a general conclusion. Nonsterilized intervention is the optimal response to a disturbance that impinges directly on the domestic money market. It can stabilize the exchange rate in the short run and the long run without affecting wealth or income. Sterilized intervention is the optimal response to a disturbance that impinges directly on other asset markets but not on the money market.[14]

14. A shift of household demand from the domestic bond to domestic money ($\delta L^a = -\delta B^a$) would cause the domestic currency to appreciate. From equation (4.26), $(\delta\pi/\pi) = -[(L_1 + B_1)/HV]\,\delta L^a = (F_1/HV)\delta L^a < 0$ (because $F_1 < 0$). But exchange market inter-

SUBSTITUTABILITY AND STERILIZATION

Is there any case in which Mussa would be right about the effects of sterilized intervention? There is one in which he is half right but has therefore to be half wrong. When domestic and foreign bonds are perfect substitutes in households' portfolios, sterilized intervention cannot have any permanent effect on the exchange rate, which is why Mussa is half right. But it cannot have any impact effect either, which is why Mussa is half wrong.

When domestic and foreign bonds are perfect substitutes, $-F_1 \to \infty$, so that $B_1 \to \infty$ (I assume that L_1 is unaffected). Therefore, $H \to \infty$ in equation (4.25), so that $\delta r_1 \to 0$. The domestic interest rate cannot change unless there is a change in the foreign interest rate. Furthermore, equation (4.26) becomes

$$\left(\frac{\delta \pi}{\pi}\right) = (1/L_W V)(\delta \bar{B}^c + \pi \delta \bar{R}^n - \delta L^a) \qquad (4.33)$$

Sterilized intervention has no effect on the exchange rate, even in the short run. (Note that δB^a has also vanished from the exchange rate equation, because it has no economic meaning in this special case. When the two bonds in the model are perfect substitutes, there can be no shift of demand between them.) Turning to the short-run change in p_1, equation (4.28) becomes

$$\left(\frac{\delta p_1}{p_1}\right) = [(u_\pi - m_1 S_W V)/NL_W V](\delta \bar{B}^c + \pi \delta \bar{R}^n - \delta L^a) \qquad (4.34)$$

When sterilized intervention has no effect on any asset market variable, it can have no effect on saving (absorption), the price of the domestic good, or nominal income. And when it does not influence saving or income, it cannot affect the path of the economy. The steady-state values are unchanged.

Look more closely at equations (4.33) and (4.34). Nonsterilized intervention and an open market operation have the same effects on the exchange rate, the price of the domestic good, and thus the level of nominal income. This is because they operate in the same fashion—by altering the money supply. Open market operations in the domestic bond do not affect the interest rate on that bond. In other words, perfect substitutability between the two bonds converts our asset market model from a portfolio balance model into a simple monetarist model of the type implicit in Mussa's analysis.

---

vention is not the optimal response, because this disturbance does not impinge directly on the foreign exchange market. The optimal response is an open market purchase of domestic securities, as it would raise the supply of money to meet the increase in demand, reduce the supply of bonds to meet the decrease in demand, and stabilize the exchange rate in the process. Conclusions similar to those drawn in the text are found in Kouri (1980).

REFERENCES

Allen, Polly R., and Peter B. Kenen. 1980. *Asset Markets, Exchange Rates, and Economic Integration.* London and New York: Cambridge University Press.

Blinder, Alan S., and Robert M. Solow. 1973. "Does Fiscal Policy Matter?" *Journal of Public Economics* 2:319–37.

Kouri, Pentti J.K. 1980. "Monetary Policy, the Balance of Payments, and the Exchange Rate." In David Bigman and Teizo Taya, eds., *The Functioning of Floating Exchange Rates.* Cambridge, Massachusetts: Ballinger Publishing Company.

Metzler, Lloyd A. 1951. "Wealth, Saving and the Rate of Interest." *Journal of Political Economy* 59 (April):930–46.

Mussa, Michael. 1980. "The Role of Official Intervention." Paper prepared for the Group of Thirty, New York.

Triffin, Robert. 1960. *Gold and the Dollar Crisis.* New Haven: Yale University Press.

[3]

Chapter 13

MACROECONOMIC THEORY AND POLICY: HOW THE CLOSED ECONOMY WAS OPENED

PETER B. KENEN

Princeton University

Contents

Handbook of International Economics, vol. II, edited by R.W. Jones and P.B. Kenen
© *Elsevier Science Publishers B.V., 1985*

1. Introduction

This chapter is designed as background to those that follow. It shows how international transactions and relationships were introduced into macroeconomic models and policy in the twenty-five years following the Second World War. It does not trace each step in that complicated process or give credit to each contributor. It uses a simple model to show how issues were defined, how they were analyzed, and how well or badly the dominant approach reflected the realities of economic life.[1]

This chapter does not bring us up to date. That task has been left to Frenkel and Mussa, whose survey of recent developments in Chapter 14 starts shortly before this one ends, and to the authors of the specialized chapters that complete this volume. Nevertheless, there are three ways in which this introduction can cast light on current work and controversy.

First, it introduces tools of analysis that are (or ought to be) employed in current work. Modern models of exchange-rate determination focus sharply on money and bond markets. They cannot describe the path of the exchange rate, however, without showing what happens to the current-account balance, and the evolution of that balance is governed in part by the price elasticities and income propensities that were the main ingredients of older models. The Marshall–Lerner–Robinson condition, discussed later in this chapter, was developed to show how a change in the exchange rate affects the current-account balance. It is found in recent models too, but tucked away in stability conditions and equations dealing with the path of the economy. The Keynesian multiplier, adapted to the open economy by Metzler (1942a), Machlup (1943), and Meade (1951), was used to show how changes in domestic activity affect the balance of payments and to trace the propagation of business fluctuations. It is found in recent models too, but lurking alongside the elasticities conditions.

Second, the period on which this chapter concentrates was one in which there was widespread agreement about the aims and instruments of economic policy. Great weight was given to full employment and to fiscal policy. Less weight was given to price stability and to monetary policy. There were vigorous disagreements about the choice between fixed and flexible exchange rates, the contribution of "money illusion" to the success of fiscal and exchange-rate policies, and the conduct of monetary policy. These were the precursors of debates that rage

---

[1] The approach followed in this chapter owes much to the ideas and work of Ronald McKinnon; see especially McKinnon (1981). He and I had planned to write this chapter jointly and conferred extensively at an early stage. Unfortunately, he had to withdraw from the project in order to honor prior commitments. I am grateful to him for suggestions and advice, but I must bear all blame for defects in the chapter.

today. Yet there was less dissonance than we endure today. Debates were conducted by appealing to beliefs that were firmly held by most of the participants. They did not develop from deep disagreements about the way in which economies behave. No one had told us that "rational expectations" keep policies from having permanent effects on output or employment. No one had told us that currency markets are inhabited by hosts of risk-neutral speculators capable of gobbling up the central banks' reserves.

Arguments about fixed and flexible exchange rates dealt mainly with the best technique for altering rates promptly. Here is how I put the issue when I was younger and the world was simpler:

> The issue, in the end, is horribly subjective. Will it be easier to persuade the central banks that speculators are not gnomes and that they can be trusted to manage the exchange rates, or instead to convince them that their own self-esteem does not depend upon the preservation of a fixed parity, but rather on their skill in choosing a new rate? [Kenen (1969a, p. 364)].

Not much was said about the ways in which exchange-rate changes can influence wages and prices, nominal rates of return on financial instruments, or the demand for real balances.

Arguments about the use of monetary policy dealt mainly with the size and stability of lags in the influence of money on aggregate demand. The case for a "predictable" monetary policy was based on the belief that lags are long and changeable, so that "fine tuning" of the money supply or close concentration on the management of interest rates can amplify economic fluctuations. Little was said about the possibility emphasized so often now that nominal interest rates and money stocks can rise and fall together, rather than moving in opposite directions, because expectations about inflation are sensitive to monetary policy. The distinction between anticipated and unanticipated changes in the money supply had not made its appearance.

Finally, we need to be reminded frequently that models which appear to be very general are rooted shallowly in recent experience. The actors within any economic model base their own decisions on experience. The ways in which households, firms, and governments respond to information are conditioned by earlier successes and mistakes. They may be maximizing something or other, but their strategies are almost always based on imperfect information and imperfect methods for collecting and assessing it. The institutional framework within which they operate is itself a product of experience. Economic institutions and arrangements can change rapidly, and arrangements designed de novo by governments, because others have malfunctioned or broken down, reflect all too faithfully the dominant diagnosis of their predecessors' defects. Finally, economists design their own models to fit certain sets of facts, frequently subsets of "stylized facts" distilled from recollection and observation by methods that we do not articulate clearly, and the need to be "relevant" leads us to build models that fit the recent facts most closely. Theory is inspired by history, but good theorists do not always have long memories.

2. Stylized facts and economic analysis

In the period on which this chapter concentrates, two sets of stylized facts had enormous influence on theory and policy. International monetary relations were governed by the Bretton Woods Agreement of 1944, which reflected the dominant interpretation of international monetary history before the Second World War — of errors made in monetary reconstruction during the twenties and in monetary management during the thirties. The analysis and conduct of domestic policy were dominated by the stylized facts from which Keynes constructed *The General Theory* (1936).

2.1. The stylized facts of Bretton Woods

The architects of the Bretton Woods Agreement are often criticized for having insufficient faith in markets and excessive faith in governments. The criticism is half right.

Those who met at Bretton Woods did not believe that markets can regulate exchange rates in a satisfactory way. The dominant interpretation of experience was given by Nurkse in *International Currency Experience* (1944):

> The twenty years between the wars have furnished ample evidence concerning the question of fluctuating *versus* stable exchanges. A system of completely free and flexible exchange rates is conceivable and may have certain attractions in theory; and it might seem that in practice nothing would be easier than to leave international payments and receipts to adjust themselves through uncontrolled exchange variations in response to the play of demand and supply. Yet nothing would be more at variance with the lessons of the past.
>
> Freely fluctuating exchanges involve three serious disadvantages. In the first place, they create an element of risk which tends to discourage international trade. The risk may be covered by "hedging" operations where a forward exchange market exists; but such insurance, if obtainable at all, is obtainable only at a price and therefore generally adds to the cost of trading. ...
>
> Secondly, as a means of adjusting the balance of payments, exchange fluctuations involve constant shifts of labour and other resources between production for the home market and production for export. Such shifts may be costly and disturbing; they tend to create frictional unemployment, and are

obviously wasteful if the exchange-market conditions that call for them are temporary. ...

Thirdly, experience has shown that fluctuating exchanges cannot always be relied upon to promote adjustment. Any considerable or continuous movement of the exchange rate is liable to generate anticipations of a further movement in the same direction, thus giving rise to speculative capital transfers of a disequilibrating kind. ... Self-aggravating movements of this kind, instead of promoting adjustment in the balance of payments, are apt to intensify any initial disequilibrium and to produce what may be called "explosive" conditions of instability. We have observed such forces at work in several cases of freely variable exchange rates; we may recall in particular the example of the French franc during the years 1924–26 [Nurkse (1944, pp. 210–211)].

The architects of Bretton Woods, however, did not trust governments either. The dominant interpretation of experience gave three reasons for concern.

Governments had made serious mistakes in choosing new exchange rates after the First World War:

An exchange rate by definition concerns more currencies than one. Yet exchange stabilization was carried out as an act of national sovereignty in one country after another with little or no regard for the resulting interrelationship of currency values in comparison with cost and price levels. This was so even where help was received from financial centers abroad. Stabilization of a currency was conceived in terms of gold rather than of other currencies. ... From the very start, therefore, the system was subject to stresses and strains. The two most familiar but by no means the only sources of disequilibrium arose from the successive stabilization of the pound sterling and the French franc early in 1925 and late in 1926 respectively, the one at too high and the other at too low a level in relation to domestic costs and prices [Nurkse (1944, pp. 116–117)].

It was therefore decided at Bretton Woods that countries joining the International Monetary Fund would have to choose their parities in consultation with the Fund. (Unfortunately, this decision led to another problem. Countries had to choose their parities too soon, before they could assess, let alone correct, the economic damage done by the war.)

National sovereignty in exchange-rate policy is open to abuse. Exchange rates can be manipulated for "beggar-my-neighbor" purposes. This was the conventional interpretation of the devaluations that took place in the thirties:

In contemporary discussion much stress was laid on the competitive aspects of currency devaluation. In many quarters devaluation was regarded primarily as a means of improving a country's foreign trade balance and hence its volume of domestic employment — an effective means but one that operated necessarily at the expense of other countries and invited retaliation [Nurkse (1944, p. 129)].

Therefore, the Bretton Woods Agreement called on governments to notify the Fund before changing their exchange rates and prohibited them from making large exchange-rate changes without its consent. The only justification for an exchange-rate change, moreover, was a "fundamental disequilibrium." A country with a temporary deficit in its balance of payments was expected to finance it by drawing down reserves and drawing on the Fund.

Finally, governments could not be expected to deflate their economies in order to balance their external accounts. They had not followed the "rules of the game" during the 1920s and 1930s, and they should not be expected to do so in the future.[2] The theory of balance-of-payments adjustment under fixed exchange rates emphasized price changes. But these require changes in output and·employment that may not be acceptable:

> Experience has shown that stability of exchange rates can no longer be achieved by domestic income adjustments if these involve depression and unemployment. Nor can it be achieved if such income adjustments involve a general inflation of prices which the country concerned is not prepared to endure. It is therefore only as a consequence of internal stability, above all in the major countries, that there can be any hope of securing a satisfactory degree of exchange stability as well [Nurkse (1944, p. 229)].

We come thus to a second set of stylized facts, having to do with internal stability.

2.2. The stylized facts of Keynesian macroeconomics

Keynes led the British delegation to Bretton Woods, and though the plan adopted there came mainly from American proposals, it owed much to his influence. And this was not his first appearance in the international monetary arena. The book that made him famous, *The Economic Consequences of the Peace* (1919), attacked the economic and financial clauses of the Versailles Treaty. Furthermore, the foreign-exchange markets held center stage in his first major book on monetary theory, *A Tract on Monetary Reform* (1923).

---

[2] The "rules" required contraction of the money supply when reserves were falling and expansion when they were rising. In most cases examined by Nurkse, however, the central banks' foreign and domestic assets moved in opposite directions, reducing or preventing money-supply changes. In some instances, "sterilization" took place automatically because of the ways in which central banks and governments financed their intervention in the foreign-exchange markets. In other cases, it was undertaken deliberately [Nurkse, (1944, pp. 68–88)]. Bloomfield (1963) found evidence of sterilization even before the First World War.

In *The General Theory* (1936), however, we find no discussion of exchange rates, international aspects of income determination, or the need for international cooperation to achieve national stability. "Keynesian macro theory focused on the national economy, and the national government was, explicitly or implicitly, asserted to be the natural form of organization for achieving macroeconomic stability" [Lindbeck (1979, p. 1)].

Keynes probably made the right tactical choice in focusing on the national economy. The concepts introduced in *The General Theory* were not easy to grasp. The policy implications were unorthodox. It was therefore sensible to concentrate on monetary and fiscal policies for a closed economy, not to deal at the same time with foreign repercussions, exchange rates, reserves, and the problem of protection — matters that Keynes had tackled before and would take up again. His choice had important consequences, however, for the way in which other economists would analyze international issues. They opened the Keynesian model of the national economy by adding international transactions, instead of revising the model systematically to allow for the effects of foreign trade and payments on the basic behavioral relationships.

This incremental approach was not harmful for a while. In the years right after the Second World War, foreign trade and payments were indeed additional. They had only marginal effects on domestic markets and behavior. As trade and payments grew, however, the approach became less helpful. Furthermore, some features of *The General Theory* were based on British experience in the 1920s and 1930s, which made it less than general.

In earlier debates about economy policy, Keynes had argued that wage rigidity was the main cause of Britain's economic plight. Money wage rates had fallen sharply in 1921–22, along with prices, but did not continue to fall thereafter, even though unemployment was very high. Keynes went farther. Money wage rates were not likely to rise sharply, he believed, in response to an increase in aggregate demand, a devaluation of the pound, or the use of import tariffs.[3] In *The General Theory*, he converted wage rigidity from a defect to a virtue, although he was careful to point out that he was describing a closed economy:

> ...I am now of the opinion that the maintenance of a stable general level of money-wages is, on a balance of considerations, the most advisable policy for a closed system; whilst the same conclusion will hold good for an open system, provided that equilibrium with the rest of the world can be secured by means of fluctuating exchanges. There are advantages in some degree of flexibility in the wages of particular industries so as to expedite transfers from those which are relatively declining to those which are relatively expanding. But the money-wage level as a whole should be maintained as stable as possible, at any rate in the short period [Keynes (1936, p. 270)].

[3] Keynes' views and the policy debate itself are summarized in Eichengreen (1981).

This opinion was based largely on another — that prices are determined by demand and supply conditions in domestic markets — so that stable wages can lead to stable prices:

> This policy will result in a fair degree of stability in the price-level. ... Apart from "administered" or monopoly prices, the price-level will only change in the short period in response to the extent that changes in the volume of employment affect marginal prime costs; whilst in the long period they will only change in response to changes in the cost of production due to new technique and new or increased equipment [Keynes (1936, pp. 270–271)].

These views animated the Keynesian approach to wages, prices and exchange rates. As domestic prices depend chiefly on domestic wages, and money wages tend to be rigid, a change in the exchange rate can alter real wages and the level of employment without undermining domestic price stability. It will change the home-currency prices of foreign goods and the foreign-currency prices of domestic goods. But it will not necessarily change the home-currency prices of domestic goods.

Here is how Meade put the matter in *The Balance of Payments* (1951), the most ambitious adaptation of Keynesian analysis to international economic problems:

> There is... no absolute criterion by which it can be decided whether there is sufficient wage flexibility to operate the gold-standard mechanism successfully. It depends upon the degree of wage rate adjustment which it is expected that the adoption of this mechanism will demand. ... If it were judged that there were insufficient flexibility of *money* wage rates to meet the demands which are likely to be put upon a gold-standard system, then some other method of adjustment (such as variable exchange rates) would have to be chosen in its place.
>
> But it would be useless to turn to the mechanism of variable exchange rates unless there were sufficient flexibility of *real* wage rates, because any spontaneous disturbance which, if a new equilibrium is to be found, requires a change in the real terms of trade between A and B is likely to require some change in real wage rates in A and B. For example, a shift of demand away from B's products on to A's products will... require a movement in the terms of trade against B to shift demand back again... and, therefore, in so far as imported products are consumed by wage earners it involves a fall in the real wage in B.
>
> Under the gold standard the necessary reduction in the real wage of labour will be brought about partly by the reduced demand for labour in B causing a reduction in the money wage rate in B, and partly by the increased demand for A's products leading to a rise in the money prices of A's products. ... With variable exchange rates the decline in the real wage rate in B will be brought about by the depreciation of B's currency which will make A's products more

expensive in terms of B's money. Money wage rates in B and the money prices of B's products will remain unchanged, but imports from A will be higher in price.

We may conclude, therefore, that for the gold-standard mechanism to work effectively there must be "sufficient" flexibility of money wage rates; and for the variable-exchange-rate mechanism to work effectively there must be "sufficient" divorce between movements in the cost of living and movements in money wage rates.... [Meade (1951, pp. 201–203)].

Many economists disagreed with Keynes about the rigidity of the money wage. Few were prepared to claim, however, that it is flexible enough to make the gold standard work effectively. It was for this very reason, indeed, that economists started to criticize the Bretton Woods system in the 1960s. The rules of the system, the attitudes of governments, and the freeing of capital movements, permitting speculative attacks on currencies whose rates might be expected to change, had combined to make exchange rates very rigid. The world had thus wandered into a "disequilibrium system" in which there was no way to change the terms of trade. Money wage rates were too rigid. So were exchange rates.[4]

To be consistent, of course, critics of the system had to hold strong views about the cost of living or the real wage. On the one hand, they could hold with Keynes that the prices which figure importantly in the cost of living are determined mainly in domestic markets, so that the cost of living is not affected substantially by a change in the exchange rate. This is the view implicit in the model that Keynesians developed from *The General Theory*. On the other hand, they could hold (or hope) with Meade that "money illusion" permeates the labor market, divorcing the money wage from the cost of living and imparting flexibility to the real wage.

Keynes himself was quite consistent in another way. Even as the prices of domestic goods are determined in his model by domestic markets, so too are the prices of domestic assets and, therefore, the interest rate. In *The General Theory*, the interest rate depends on its own future — on forecasts about interest rates conditioned by experience. (It should also depend on income and wealth, as Keynes' own followers were quick to note, but that is not the issue here.) In an open economy, however, the domestic interest rate depends in part on foreign interest rates and on expectations about exchange rates. Keynes was not unaware of this important point; he came close to making it explicitly in *A Tract on Monetary Reform* (1923), where he worked out the interest-parity condition for the forward exchange rate. But he chose to neglect it a decade later. Finally, the

---

[4] The phase "disequilibrium system" was used by Mundell (1961a), who had in mind one additional feature of the system — the tendency of governments to sterilize changes in reserves — which meant that there could be no changes in price levels even if wage rates were flexible.

money supply is determined domestically in Keynes' model by open-market operations in domestic bonds. There are no operations in foreign exchange.

This approach was not an auspicious starting point for those who sought to study international problems. Consciously or carelessly, they were too faithful to Keynes' model. They neglected the links between domestic and foreign interest rates, as well as the influence of exchange-rate expectations. They neglected the crucial problem of managing the money supply itself. In most Keynesian models of the open economy, including Meade's model, the domestic interest rate is the chief instrument of monetary policy. The central bank holds a stock of foreign currency large enough to peg the exchange rate and a stock of domestic securities large enough to sterilize changes in reserves. It controls the money supply, and it can use the money supply to control the interest rate.

2.3. The insular economy

The Keynesian model of the closed economy was too simple, and so was the open version. Nevertheless, the open version represented quite faithfully many characteristics of the national economies that emerged from the Second World War. McKinnon (1981) has described those economies as *insular*. Their international transactions did not impinge dramatically on their domestic markets, because those markets were not integrated closely with foreign markets. Opportunities for arbitrage in goods and assets were severely limited by the trade, capital, and currency countries put in place in the 1920s and 1930s and the additional barriers erected during the war.

Many new trade barriers were thrown up in the 1920s and 1930s. They were not dismantled until the sixties. The United States adopted the Smoot–Hawley Tariff, the highest in its history, in 1930. The United Kingdom opted for protection two years later. Some countries started to use quotas and other direct controls, and these were reinforced by strict exchange controls after the outbreak of the Second World War. Liberalization got under way soon after the war in the

Table 2.1
Average trade-to-income ratios

Period	U.K.	U.S.
1915–24	41.5	12.4
1925–34	35.4	7.7
1935–44	23.1	6.8
1945–54	32.3	7.4
1955–64	31.5	7.1
1965–74	35.2	10.2

Source: Grassman (1980).

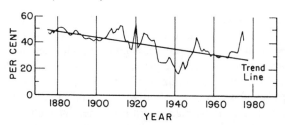

Figure 2.1. Sum of exports and imports as a percentage of gross national product, United Kingdom, 1875–1975. *Source*: Grassman (1980).

framework of the General Agreement of Tariffs and Trade (GATT) and in the Organization for European Economic Cooperation (OEEC), but progress was slow.

The effects of protection and other restrictions show up clearly in conventional measures of economic openness. Grassman (1980) has computed ten-year averages of trade-to-income ratios (sums of exports and imports as percentages of gross national product) for the United Kingdom and the United States (Table 2.1). The ratios drop steadily at first, recover in the first postwar decade, but fall back slightly in the next, even though trade liberalization had begun. Grassman traces the same process relative to trend, and his results for Britain are reproduced in Figure 2.1. The second quarter of this century shows up as the main aberration.[5]

Openness is an "average" concept. It cannot measure faithfully the extent to which foreign transactions impinge on domestic markets. But the change in openness that has taken place, most notably in the case of the United States, does serve to remind us of the difference between the world of the 1940s and 1950s and the world that we know today. American exports were but 5 percent of gross national product in 1950; they rose to 10 percent in 1980. Restrictions on capital flows were widespread and intensive thirty years ago; most of them have been dismantled, and those that remain are made much less effective by opportunities to lend and borrow in Eurocurrency markets. National economies were much more insular in the decades following the Second World War than they are today, and this fact was reflected by the typical model of the open economy. It was insular in three respects.

[5] These numbers tend to understate the recent increase in openness, because the rates of growth of GNP reflect in part rapid rates of growth of public-sector spending (i.e. spending on nontradables). The same point is made by Grassman (1980). The change in the situation of the United States is signaled by the numbers but is not described vividly enough. It would be hard to find an American industry that is not acutely sensitive today to foreign competition, whether it be competition in the domestic market or in export markets.

(1) The share of foreign trade in gross national product was relatively small and, more important, substantial trade barriers restricted the role of commodity arbitrage. In consequence, exchange rates could be changed without significant effects on domestic prices. Domestic prices were determined by domestic wages, and wages were determined by conditions in domestic labor markets. The Phillips curve was firmly anchored even before it was discovered.

(2) The international capital market did not function freely. Therefore, private capital movements could not automatically finance deficits and surpluses on current account. By implication, those deficits and surpluses could not raise or reduce asset stocks or wealth by enough to induce large changes in aggregate demand. (The private flows that did occur could also continue for long periods, because they were small in relation to the corresponding stocks.)

(3) The national monetary systems was insulated. On the one hand, official interventions in foreign-exchange markets were sterilized; they did not affect the monetary base. On the other hand, short-term interest rates could be controlled by monetary policy; they were not influenced by foreign interest rates or exchange-rate expectations.

In the review of theory undertaken below, I stress the roles of these assumptions. In the survey of subsequent developments at the end of this chapter, I show how they were challenged.

3. Incomes, prices, and the current account

Capital movements did not figure importantly in the models of the fifties. When comparing balance-of-payments adjustment under fixed and flexible exchange rates, Meade (1951, ch. 15) was careful to include them, but they could be deleted without altering his argument. (It is indeed better to remove them, because they appear asymmetrically in Meade's comparison. With fixed exchange rates, they occur on account of endogenous changes in interest rates, resulting from endogenous changes in money supplies. There is no sterilization. With flexible exchange rates, they occur on account of exogenous changes in interest rates, because monetary policies are adjusted to maintain internal balance.) Capital movements played more important roles in the models of the 1960s. In Metzler (1960), they reflected changes in saving and investment, which were in turn reflected in the current-account balance. In Fleming (1962) and Mundell (1962, 1963), they reflected changes in monetary policy similar to those in Meade's analysis, but these took place with fixed as well as flexible exchange rates.

The models of the fifties concentrated on the current-account balance and even more narrowly on the trade balance. (When capital movements are neglected, interest-income payments can be neglected too.) Most of the models, moreover, were ultra-Keynesian, in that they fixed the prices of domestic goods rather than the money wage.[6] Two types of models were popular: (1) those in which each country produces a single traded good and (2) those in which each country produces a nontraded good as well as a traded good. In models of the first type, exchange-rate changes induce substitution in consumption by altering the terms of trade (and the "real" exchange rate is thus measured by the terms of trade). In models of the second type, exchange-rate changes induce substitution in production and consumption by altering the relative price of the nontraded good (and the "real" exchange rate is measured by that relative price).[7] I use the first type of model in the rest of this chapter.

3.1. The basic model

There are two goods: x_1 is produced at home, and its home-currency price is p_1, while x_2 is produced abroad, and its foreign-currency price is p_2^*. The nominal exchange rate is π and is measured in units of home currency per unit of foreign currency.

As x_1 is the only good produced at home and x_2 the only one produced abroad, nominal incomes (gross national products) are given by

$$Y = p_1 x_1 \quad \text{and} \quad Y^* = p_2^* x_2. \tag{3.1}$$

As both goods are consumed in each country and nominal consumption is equal to disposable income *less* saving,

$$C = p_1 c_1 + \pi p_2^* c_2 = (Y - T) - S$$

and

$$C^* = \frac{p_1}{\pi} c_1^* + p_2^* c_2^* = (Y^* - T^*) - S^*, \tag{3.2}$$

---

[6] Fixed prices can be squared with fixed wages by imposing a Ricardian assumption (fixed labor requirements per unit of output). As many models of the fifties adopted another Ricardian assumption (complete specialization), they should perhaps be called Ricardian–Keynesian. Various labor-market specifications can be handled simultaneously with a device adopted by Allen and Kenen (1980). Changes in income are measured first in nominal terms. They become output changes when prices are fixed (the case considered in the text); they become price changes when employment is fixed (the classical case considered in most monetary models); they become combinations of output and price changes when the money wage is fixed (the typical Keynesian case). Labor-market specifications are examined thoroughly in Chapter 16 of this Handbook.

[7] This is the only form of substitution in most such models, because the country is deemed to be small in all foreign markets (its terms of trade are fixed). A few models, however, allow both sorts of substitution by making the country large in one foreign market. Meade (1951) deals with both sorts of substitution in his *Mathematical Supplement* but drops the nontraded good from the model used in most of his book, making it into the first type of model. Salter (1959) develops the small-country version of the second type. For more on goods-market specifications, see Chapter 16 of this Handbook.

where c_i ($i = 1, 2$) is the quantity of good i consumed at home, and c_i^* is the quantity consumed abroad, while T and T^* are lump-sum taxes, and S and S^* are private-sector savings.

The home government buys a fixed quantity, g_1, of the domestic good; the foreign government buys a fixed quantity, g_2^*, of the foreign good. Therefore, the budget deficits are

$$D = p_1 g_1 - T \quad \text{and} \quad D^* = p_2^* g_2^* - T^*. \tag{3.3}$$

As g_1 and g_2^* are fixed and their prices are fixed too, changes in T and T^* are reflected fully by D and D^*, and the latter are used as fiscal-policy variables throughout this section. Budget deficits are financed by issuing bonds.[8]

In some applications of the model, it will be important for the interest rate to influence aggregate demand. It could do so by affecting investment, but investment is omitted to keep the model simple. Accordingly, saving is made to depend on disposable income and on the local interest rate:

$$S = s(r, Y - T) \quad \text{and} \quad S^* = s^*(r^*, Y^* - T^*), \tag{3.4}$$

where $0 < s_Y < 1$, $0 < s_Y^* < 1$, and $s_r, s_r^* > 0$.

These are the market-clearing equations for the domestic and foreign goods:

$$c_1 + c_1^* + g_1 - x_1 = 0 \quad \text{and} \quad c_2 + c_2^* + g_2^* - x_2 = 0. \tag{3.5}$$

In the simplest Keynesian model, where prices are fixed, goods markets are cleared by output changes. In the simplest classical model, where outputs are fixed, goods markets are cleared by price changes.

The current-account balance can be obtained from either of the two market-clearing equations. Multiplying the equation for x_1 by p_1, using eqs. (3.1) and (3.2) to replace $p_1 c_1$ with $p_1 x_1 - \pi p_2^* c_2 - T - S$, and using eq. (3.3) to replace $p_1 g_1 - T$ with D,

$$p_1 c_1^* - \pi p_2^* c_2 = S - D. \tag{3.6}$$

As $p_1 c_1^*$ is the level of domestic exports expressed in domestic currency and $\pi p_2^* c_2$ is the level of domestic imports, the left-hand side of (3.6) is the trade balance and is equal in this model to the current-account balance. The right-hand side says that the current-account balance must be matched by the difference

---

[8] The inclusion of government bonds, however, introduces two complications. First, disposable income must be redefined. It becomes gross nation product *plus* interest income on the government bonds held by the public *less* the lump-sum tax. Second, the budget deficit must be redefined. It becomes expenditure *plus* interest payments to the public *less* the lump-sum tax. Both complications can be removed by dividing the lump-sum tax into two parts. The first part is determined exogenously. The second part is set equal at all times to the flow of interest payments and thus changes endogenously whenever there are changes in the interest rate or quantity of debt held by the public. It cancels interest income from the definition of the budget deficit. The first part is the one denoted by T (and T^*) in the text.

between saving and the budget deficit. (In a more general model, it would be matched by the difference between saving *less* investment and the budget deficit.)

Equation (3.6) can be used to explain the asset-market implications of budget deficits financed by issuing bonds. If the demand for money depends on the interest rate and income but not on wealth, saving does not raise it. Therefore, saving must show up as a flow demand for bonds, and bonds are the only other assets available. Under a flexible exchange rate, moreover, the current-account balance must always be zero, because there are no capital movements here. Therefore eq. (3.6) says that $D = S$. The flow supply of bonds produced by a budget deficit is equal to the flow demand for bonds produced by private saving. Under a fixed exchange rate, the current-account balance can differ from zero, but it is financed by reserve flows, and these are sterilized. Therefore, eq. (3.6) says that $D + \dot{R} = S$, where $\dot{R}$ is the rate of increase of reserves measured in domestic currency and it is matched by central-bank bond sales. The flow supply of bonds produced by a budget deficit is augmented or reduced by sterilizing reserve flows, and the adjusted flow supply forthcoming from this process is equal to the flow demand produced by private saving. The bond market remains in flow equilibrium at a constant interest rate whether the exchange rate is fixed or flexible.[9]

Goods are gross substitutes in private consumption, and the demand functions are homogeneous of degree zero in prices and consumption:

$$c_i = f_i\left(p_1, \pi p_2^*, C\right) \quad \text{and} \quad c_i^* = f_i^*\left(\frac{p_1}{\pi}, p_2, C^*\right), \tag{3.7}$$

where $f_{ii}, f_{ii}^* < 0$, and $f_{ij}, f_{ij}^* > 0$ for $i = 1, 2$. Furthermore, $m_1 + m_2 = 1$, and $m_1^* + m_2^* = 1$, where $m_i = p_i f_{ic}$, and $m_i^* = p_i^* f_{ic}^*$. Let demands be homothetic, so that $m_i C = p_i c_i$ and $m_i^* = p_i^* c_i^*$.[10]

As prices are constant here and hereafter, they can be set at unity, and the market-clearing equations can be rewritten:

$$f_1(1, \pi, C) + f_1^*\left(\frac{1}{\pi}, 1, C^*\right) + g_1 - Y = 0,$$

$$f_2(1, \pi, C) + f_2^*\left(\frac{1}{\pi}, 1, C^*\right) + g_2^* - Y^* = 0,$$

[9]An increase in income raises the demand for money and lowers the demand for bonds, but the central bank can satisfy these changes in demand by open-market purchases. It can maintain equilibrium in the money and bond markets at a constant interest rate. This is the assumption implicit in models that treat the interest rate as a policy instrument.

[10]When demand functions are homogeneous of degree zero in prices and nominal consumption and demands are homothetic, $e_{ij} = e_{ii} - 1$, where e_{ij} is the cross-price elasticity, $(p_j/c_i)f_{ij}$, and e_{ii} is the own-price elasticity, $-(p_i/c_i)f_{ii}$. With gross substitutability, $e_{ij} > 0$, so that $e_{ii} > 1$. Analogous properties attach to the foreign elasticities. These relationships are invoked below to show that the Marshall–Lerner–Robinson condition is satisfied automatically when goods are gross substitutes, demand functions are homogenous of degree zero, and demands are homothetic.

where

$$C = Y - T - s(r, Y - T) \quad \text{and} \quad C^* = Y^* - T^* - s^*(r^*, Y^* - T^*).$$

The left-hand side of the current-account equation can be rewritten as

$$B = f_1^*\left(\frac{1}{\pi}, 1, C^*\right) - \pi f_2(1, \pi, C),$$

where B is the current-account balance measured in home currency, and it is set equal to zero initially. I describe these hereafter as the basic equations of the model.

3.2. Income, imports, and the multiplier

The most Keynesian contribution to balance-of-payments analysis was the foreign-trade multiplier — the adaptation to an open economy of the basic Keynesian approach to income determination. It was used to show how economic fluctuations spread from country to country, how they affect the current-account balance, and how they should be countered by economic policies.[11]

The multiplier can be derived from the basic equations given above. Differentiate those equations totally (but hold g_1, g_2^*, and π constant); set $\pi = 1$, for simplicity, and solve for the income changes:

$$dY = \left(\frac{1}{K}\right)\left\{\left[m_1 s_Y^* + m_1^*(1 - s_Y^*)\right]\left[dA - (1 - s_Y)dT - s_r dr\right]\right.$$
$$\left. + m_1^*\left[dA^* - (1 - s_Y^*)dT^* - s_r^* dr^*\right] + s_Y^* dB^a\right\},$$

$$dY^* = \left(\frac{1}{K}\right)\left\{\left[m_2^* s_Y + m_2(1 - s_Y)\right]\left[dA^* - (1 - s_Y^*)dT^* - s_r^* dr^*\right]\right.$$
$$\left. + m_2\left[dA - (1 - s_Y)dT - s_r dr\right] - s_Y dB^a\right\},$$

where

$$K = m_1^*(1 - s_Y^*)s_Y + m_2(1 - s_Y)s_Y^* + s_Y s_Y^*,$$

where dA is a spontaneous increase in domestic consumption (absorption), dA^* is a spontaneous increase in foreign consumption, and dB^a is a spontaneous shift in domestic or foreign demand from the foreign to the home good.[12] In the

---

[11] It was also used to analyze the transfer problem debated by Keynes (1929) and Ohlin (1929). See Metzler (1942b), Samuelson (1952, 1971), and Johnson (1956).

[12] The shifts dA and dA^* correspond to parametric shifts in the savings functions. The shift dB^a corresponds to a parametric shift in the demand functions such that $dB^a = p_1(dc_1^a + dc_1^{*a})$, where $p_1 dc_1^a = -\pi p_2^* dc_2^a$, and $p_1 dc_1^{*a} = -\pi p_2^* dc_2^{*a}$. The term K looks unusually complicated but is actually identical to the most common formulation. Define $m = m_2(1 - s_Y)$ and $m^* = m_1^*(1 - s_Y^*)$, so that m and m^* are the marginal propensities to import. Then $K = ms_Y^* + m^* s_Y + s_Y s_Y^*$, which is the most common formulation.

language used by Johnson (1961), dA and dA^* are shifts in expenditure, and dB^a is a switch in expenditure. The change in the current-account balance follows directly:

$$dB = \left(\frac{1}{K}\right)\left\{ m_1^* s_Y \left[dA^* - \left(1 - s_Y^*\right) dT^* - s_r^* dr^* \right] \right.$$
$$\left. - m_2 s_T^* \left[dA - \left(1 - s_Y\right) dT - s_r dr \right] + s_Y s_Y^* dB^a \right\}.$$

The shift in domestic expenditure, the effect of a change in domestic fiscal policy, and the effect of a change in domestic monetary policy appear jointly in all three equations. So do their foreign counterparts. In the absence of capital movements, changes in fiscal and monetary policies are equivalent to spontaneous shifts in expenditure and are thus interchangeable, because they affect Y, Y^*, and B only by changing expenditure. The spontaneous switch in expenditure, by contrast, appears by itself in all three equations (and with opposite signs in the Y and Y^* equations). We have not yet come to its policy counterpart.

An increase in domestic expenditure, whether spontaneous or the result of a policy change, raises incomes in both countries and drives the home country's current account into deficit.[13] An increase in foreign expenditure raises income in both countries too but drives the current account into surplus. Finally, a spontaneous switch in expenditure from foreign to home goods raises domestic income, reduces foreign income, and drives the current account into surplus.

It is easy to show that income changes are equilibrating in their effects on the current-account balance. If an increase in domestic expenditure did not raise foreign income, the current-account deficit would be larger than the one above. By raising foreign income, it raises the foreign demand for imports and reduces the current-account deficit. If a switch in expenditure from foreign to home goods did not raise domestic income and reduce foreign income, the current-account surplus would equal the switch in expenditure and would likewise be larger than the one above. The increase in domestic income raises the domestic demand for imports, the decrease in foreign income reduces the foreign demand for imports, and the two together cut the current-account surplus.

But equilibration is incomplete. A permanent shift or switch in expenditure leads to a permanent surplus or deficit. This was the feature of the multiplier

---

[13] Without imposing additional restrictions on the model, we cannot know whether it raises Y by more than it raises Y^*. When demand conditions are *identical* (i.e. $s_Y = s_Y^*$ and $m_i = m_i^*$), then $(dY/dA) = (dY/dA^*)$, and $(dY^*/dA^*) = (dY^*/dA)$, but $(dY/dA) \gtrless (dY^*/dA^*)$ as $m_1 \gtrless m_2$. When demand conditions are *symmetrical* and each country's marginal propensity to consume its own good exceeds its marginal propensity to consume the other's good (i.e. $s_Y = s_Y^*$, as before, but $m_1 = m_2^*$ and $m_1 > m_2$), then $(dY/dA) = (dY^*/dA^*)$, and $(dY/dA^*) = (dY^*/dA)$, but $(dY/dA) > (dY^*/dA^*)$, and $(dY^*/dA^*) > (dY^*/dA)$. All "own" effects exceed the corresponding "cross" effects. (In this same case, the sum of the marginal propensities to import is necessarily smaller than unity, a condition that plays an important role in several applications of the model, including analyses of the transfer problem.)

model that drew most criticism. Imbalances cannot last forever. The deficit country's central bank must run out of reserves eventually. At some point, then, governments or central banks must act to eradicate imbalances or allow their countries' money stocks to change in response to those imbalances. This point was made early on. [See Meade (1951, ch. 15) and Tsiang (1961).] It did not come to the fore, however, until money itself came to the fore — until the emphasis in balance-of-payments analysis shifted from goods markets to money and bond markets, and therefore from flows to stocks.

Moving on from positive to normative conclusions, let us see what the multiplier model had to say about the theory of economic policy. Suppose that the domestic and foreign economies begin in "internal balance" (i.e. at levels of Y and Y^* that correspond to full employment and price stability) and in "external balance" (i.e. with $B = 0$). How can their governments defend these states against spontaneous disturbances?

Clearly, a spontaneous increase in domestic expenditure can be offset completely by an increase in domestic taxes, an increase in the domestic interest rate, or some combination of the two. Therefore, these are "optimal" responses. If they are not adopted, the foreign government faces a dilemma. It would have to raise its taxes or interest rate to maintain internal balance, but would then move farther from external balance. It would have to reduce its taxes or interest rate to maintain external balance, but would then drive its own economy farther from internal balance. Faced with these unsatisfactory options, the foreign government is sure to complain — much as surplus countries usually complain that it is the obligation of deficit countries to deal with these problems — and it would be justified in this instance.

The problem is more complicated, however, when there is a spontaneous switch in expenditure from foreign to home goods. No combination of fiscal and monetary policies can defend internal balance in both countries and defend external balance simultaneously. If both countries followed policies for internal balance, the external imbalance would get larger. If they followed policies for external balance, both would be driven farther from internal balance. This is the true "conflict" or "dilemma" case, and it calls for the use of policies to switch expenditure rather than shift it. A change in the exchange rate is one such policy.

3.3. Exchange rates and elasticities

The methods used to study exchange-rate determination and the effects of changes in exchange rates were at first Marshallian rather than Keynesian. The exchange rate was treated as the price that clears the foreign-exchange market, and that market was treated like any other — as a flow market for foreign or domestic currency with well-defined demand and supply curves. The partial-equilibrium models in Machlup (1939) and Haberler (1949) are good examples. Furthermore, one can trace back to Marshall (1923) the sufficient condition for devaluation to improve the current-account balance, although it was discovered independently by Lerner (1944) and Robinson (1947). But the treatment was Keynesian in one important way. The typical analysis did not distinguish clearly between a change in the nominal exchange rate and a change in the real rate (the terms of trade in the model used here). As the prices of domestic goods are determined internally in an insular economy, a change in the nominal exchange rate was expected to produce an identical change in the real rate.

The Marshall–Lerner–Robinson condition can be derived directly from the basic equations set out above. Differentiating the equation for the current-account balance with respect to the nominal exchange rate, π, while holding Y, Y^*, T, T^*, g_1, g_2^*, r, and r^* constant,

$$dB = dB^a + m_1^* dA^* - m_2 dA + e_\pi \left(\frac{d\pi}{\pi} \right),$$

where

$$e_\pi = \left(c_1^* \right) e_{11}^* + \left(\pi c_2 \right) e_{22} - \left(\pi c_2 \right).$$

Here, e_{11}^* is the own-price elasticity of foreign demand for the domestic good, and e_{22} is the own-price elasticity of domestic demand for the foreign good. When $B = 0$ initially, $c_1^* = \pi c_2$, so that $e_\pi = c_1^*(e_{11}^* + e_{22} - 1)$. A devaluation of the domestic currency ($d\pi > 0$) improves the current-account balance when the sum of the two demand elasticities is larger than unity.[14]

---

[14] The definition of e_π in the text describes the effect of a change in π on the home-currency value of the current-account balance. The effect on the foreign-currency value is given by

$$e_\pi^* = \left(\frac{c_1^*}{\pi} \right) e_{11}^* + \left(c_2 \right) e_{22} - \left(\frac{c_1^*}{\pi} \right) = \left(\frac{c_1^*}{\pi} \right) \left[e_{11}^* + \left(\frac{\pi c_2}{c_1^*} \right) e_{22} - 1 \right].$$

As Robinson (1947) and Hirschman (1949) pointed out, this condition is less stringent when $B < 0$ than when $B > 0$. When $B < 0$ initially, $\pi c_2 > c_1^*$, so that the weight attached to e_{22} increases. When domestic prices are not constant, the condition is more complicated. With upward sloping supply curves (and $B = 0$ initially), it is

$$e_\pi' = c_1^* \left[\frac{e_{11}^* (n_1 + 1)}{e_{11}^* + n_1} + \frac{e_{22} (n_2^* + 1)}{e_{22} + n_2^*} - 1 \right] > 0,$$

where n_1 is the own-price elasticity of the domestic supply curve and n_2^* is the own-price elasticity of the foreign supply curve. Clearly, $e_\pi > 0$ is sufficient (but not necessary) for $e_\pi' > 0$. Note that $e_\pi > 0$ in the basic equations of the model, because demand functions are homogeneous of degree zero in prices and consumption, demands are homothetic, and goods are gross substitutes in consumption. Using the relationships given in footnote 10, we can write $e_\pi = c_1^* + (c_1^*)e_{12}^* + (\pi c_2)e_{21}$, where e_{12}^* is the cross-price elasticity of foreign demand for the domestic good and e_{21} is the cross-price elasticity of domestic demand for the foreign good. As e_{12}^*, $e_{21} > 0$ with gross substitutability, $e_\pi > 0$. On this and related points, see Hahn (1959), Jones (1961), and Negishi (1968). Finally, $e_\pi > 0$ is a sufficient condition for local stability in the flow foreign-exchange market when trade flows are the only sources of demand and supply in that market. See Haberler (1949) and Sohmen (1969, ch. 1).

The role of the Marshall–Lerner–Robinson condition is illustrated in Figure 3.1, adapted from Haberler (1949). The upper panels show demand and supply curves for exports and imports plotted against prices in domestic currency. The lower panels show them plotted against prices in foreign currency. (The prices p_1 and p_2^* are constant and were set at unity in the basic equations. They are shown explicitly in Figure 3.1 to clarify the presentation.)

Look first at the lower-left-hand panel. The foreign-currency price of the export goods begins at Oa, and the quantity demanded is Oc. Export receipts in foreign

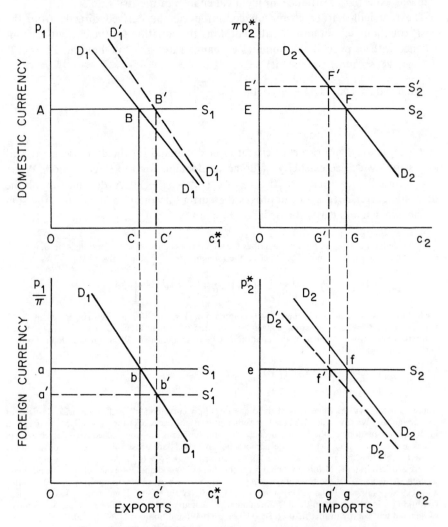

Figure 3.1. The elasticities approach to the analysis of devaluation.

currency are *Oabc*. A devaluation of the domestic currency has no effect on p_1 in an insular economy but reduces the foreign-currency price. Let it fall to *Oa'* and thus raise export volume to *Oc'*. Export receipts in foreign currency go to *Oa'b'c'*. This outcome is translated into domestic currency in the upper-left-hand panel. The export price remains at *OA* in domestic currency, but export volume rises to *OC'*. Seen from the standpoint of domestic firms, the outcome is a shift in the demand curve to $D_1'D_1'$ and an increase in export receipts to *OAB'C'*.

Look next at the upper-right-hand panel. The home-currency price of the import good begins at *OE*, and the quantity demanded is *OG*. Import payments in domestic currency are *OEFG*. A devaluation of the domestic currency has no effect on p_2^* but raises the domestic-currency price to *OE'* [i.e. $(E'E/OE) \approx (a'a/Oa)$]. Import volume falls to *OG'*, and import payments in domestic currency go to *OE'F'G'*. This outcome is translated into foreign currency in the lower-right-hand panel. The import price remains at *Oe* in foreign currency, but import volume falls to *Og'*. Seen from the standpoint of foreign firms, the outcome is a shift in the demand curve to $D_2'D_2'$ and a decrease in import payments to *Oef'g'*.

Let the trade balance be zero initially, so that *OABC* = *OEFG* and *Oabc* = *Oefg*. Suppose that e_{11}^* (the elasticity of $D_1 D_1$) is unity in the neighborhood of *b*. Then *Oa'b'c'* = *Oabc* and export receipts are unchanged in foreign currency. Suppose that e_{22} (the elasticity of $D_2 D_2$) is greater than zero. Then *Oef'g'* < *Oefg*, and import payments fall in foreign currency. The values chosen for e_{11}^* and e_{22} satisfy the Marshall–Lerner–Robinson condition, and the devaluation improves the trade balance in foreign currency. When export proceeds are unchanged in foreign currency, their value in domestic currency must rise in proportion to the devaluation. When import payments fall in foreign currency, their value in domestic currency can rise or fall, but it cannot rise in proportion to the devaluation. Accordingly, $(OAB'C'/OABC) = (OE'/OE)$, but $(OE'F'G'/OEFG) < (OE'/OE)$, so that $OAB'C' > OE'F'G'$ and the trade balance improves in domestic currency.

This diagram can be used to work through other cases (the one, for instance, in which $e_{22} = 1$ and $e_{11}^* > 0$). I leave that to the reader, however, and turn instead to the main defect of the elasticities analysis illustrated in Figure 3.1.

We began by assuming that *Y*, *Y**, *T*, *T**, *r*, and *R** are constant. These assumptions hold *C* and *C** constant too, absent spontaneous shifts in consumption. When *C* and *C** are constant, however, *Y* and *Y** cannot be constant. If the Marshall–Lerner–Robinson condition is satisfied, the expenditure-switching effects of a devaluation must raise *Y* and lower *Y**.

Look first at the situation in the market for the home good. When domestic consumption is constant in domestic currency, a change in domestic spending on the imported good must be matched by an equal but opposite change in domestic spending on the home good. Therefore, domestic spending on the home good rises when $e_{22} > 1$ and falls when $e_{22} < 1$. Even when it falls, however, the decrease is smaller than the increase in foreign spending on the home good. An improvement in the current-account balance must raise aggregate demand for the home good.

Look next at the situation in the market for the foreign good. As foreign spending on the domestic good remains constant in foreign currency when $e_{11}^* = 1$, foreign spending on the foreign good remains constant too. Whenever $e_{22} > 0$, however, domestic spending on the foreign good falls in foreign currency. An improvement in the current-account balance must raise aggregate demand for the foreign good.

To get the story right, one must rework the elasticities analysis in a broader framework.

3.4. *Exchange rates and absorption*

The defect in the elasticities analysis illustrated in Figure 3.1 was known to its earliest exponents. In fact, the expenditure-switching effects of a devaluation were emphasized by Robinson (1947), because she was concerned to show how exchange-rate changes affect employment. The effects were modeled formally by several authors, including Harberger (1950), and can be replicated by differentiating the basic equations above with respect to π as well as other variables (i.e. by holding only g_1 and g_2^* constant).[15] Solving for the income changes,

$$dY = \left(\frac{1}{K}\right)\left\{\left[m_1 s_Y^* + m_1^*(1 - s_Y^*)\right](dA + dE) + m_1^*(dA^* + dE^*)\right.$$
$$\left. + s_Y^*\left[dB^a + (e_\pi)\left(\frac{d\pi}{\pi}\right)\right]\right\},$$

$$dY^* = \left(\frac{1}{K}\right)\left\{\left[m_2^* s_Y + m_2(1 - s_Y)\right](dA^* - dE^*) + m_2(dA - dE)\right.$$
$$\left. - s_Y\left[dB^a + (e_\pi)\left(\frac{d\pi}{\pi}\right)\right]\right\},$$

where $dE = -[(1 - s_Y)dT + s_r dr]$ and $dE^* = -[(1 - s_Y^*)dT^* + s_r^* dr^*]$, thus representing the expenditure-changing effects of monetary and fiscal policies. The change in the current-account balance is

$$dB = \left(\frac{1}{K}\right)\left\{m_1^* s_Y(dA^* + dE^*) - m_2 s_Y^*(dA + dE)\right.$$
$$\left. + s_Y s_Y^*\left[dB^a + (e_\pi)\left(\frac{d\pi}{\pi}\right)\right]\right\}.$$

[15]When the market-clearing equation for the domestic good is differentiated with respect to the exchange rate, the exchange-rate term appears as $(c_1 e_{12} + c_1^* e_{11}^*)(d\pi/\pi)$. But one can show that $c_1 e_{12} = \pi c_2 e_{21}$ [see Allen and Kenen, (1980, p. 36)], and I have shown in footnote 10 that $e_{21} = e_{11} - 1$. Thus, $(c_1 e_{12} + c_1^* e_{11}^*) = e_\pi$. Analogous substitutions are employed when differentiating the other market-clearing equation (along with the assumption that $B = 0$ initially). The appearance of e_π in the derivatives of the market-clearing equations recalls a statement made at the beginning of this chapter,

Note that the exchange-rate change is paired in each equation with the spontaneous switch in expenditure. It is therefore the expenditure-switching policy that was missing earlier.

Four propositions follow from these equations.

(1) A devaluation of the domestic currency raises domestic output but reduces foreign output.

(2) Because of its effects on Y and Y^* and their effects on trade flows, a devaluation improves the current-account balance by an amount smaller than the switch in expenditure defined by the Marshall–Lerner–Robinson condition.

(3) A change in the exchange rate is an optimal policy response to a spontaneous switch in expenditure, and it is also an optimal response for a country that faces a shift in foreign expenditure.

(4) If countries are at full employment, however, a change in the exchange rate by itself cannot be expected to improve the current-account balance.

The first proposition is the one anticipated in work with Figure 3.1. A devaluation of the domestic currency raises the demand for the domestic good, and domestic output must increase to clear the market for the domestic good. The devaluation reduces the demand for the foreign good, and foreign output must decrease to clear the market for the foreign good. By implication, devaluation is a "beggar-my-neighbor" remedy for unemployment.[16]

The second proposition follows from the first. An increase in domestic output raises domestic imports, and a decrease in foreign output reduces domestic exports. Therefore, the improvement in the current-account balance is smaller than the initial switch in expenditure. Nevertheless, the improvement is permanent, because equilibration is incomplete in the multiplier model and reserve flows are sterilized. In monetary models of the balance of payments, by contrast, a devaluation leads to a temporary surplus because there is no sterilization; reserve flows cause changes in money supplies that lead in turn to shifts in levels of expenditure. [See, for example, Dornbusch (1973)].

---

that the Marshall–Lerner–Robinson condition shows up in recent models as a condition for goods-market stability.

[16]Two qualifications are in order. Although a devaluation raises real output and thus raises real income measured in terms of the domestic good, it may not increase economic welfare. Using the term applied by Bhagwati (1958) to the welfare effects of economic growth, a devaluation can be "immiserizing" if it causes a large deterioration in the terms of trade. (This qualification also applies to the point made below, that an exchange-rate change can offset the output effects of a spontaneous switch in expenditure or shift in foreign expenditure.) Furthermore, one can build models in which a devaluation reduces domestic output. See, for example, Salop (1974), where the supply of labor depends on the real wage defined in terms of a price index containing the foreign good. By reducing the real wage, devaluation reduces the supply of labor and, therefore, domestic output. Alternatively, consider an economy that has debt-service payments denominated in foreign currency. A devaluation increases the amount of domestic currency that must be used to make those payments, and this can reduce domestic consumption. Possibilities of this sort led Cooper (1971) to warn against relying heavily on models that concentrate exclusively on trade flows and especially against assuming, as here, that trade is balanced initially.

The third proposition follows from an observation made above. The effects of a change in the exchange rate are paired with those of spontaneous switches in expenditure. Therefore, a change in the exchange rate is an optimal response to a spontaneous switch. It can maintain internal balance in both countries while maintaining external balance between them. Furthermore, a change in the exchange rate is the best response for a country that confronts the policy dilemma posed by a shift in foreign expenditure. (Return to a case considered earlier. An increase in domestic expenditure, whether due to a spontaneous increase in consumption or a change in domestic policy, raises income in the foreign country and saddles it with a current-account surplus. That country cannot deal with this situation by changing its fiscal or monetary policy. But it can solve its problem by revaluing its currency. This response will drive the domestic economy farther from internal balance, but that is the result of its own failure to stabilize expenditure by changing its fiscal or monetary policy.)

The fourth proposition takes us outside the basic equations of the model by introducing price changes, but I will pursue it briefly because of its importance for the theory of policy.

If the domestic economy begins at full employment, a devaluation of its currency cannot improve its current-account balance unless the devaluation is accompanied by a reduction in demand for the domestic good. It cannot increase domestic output to accommodate the increase in demand brought about by expenditure switching. If demand for the domestic good is not reduced, the market for that good will be cleared by a price increase — one that keeps the real exchange rate from changing and therefore precludes any switch in expenditure. This will happen even in an insular economy, where prices are determined internally. It will happen even under the assumption adopted by Keynes (1936) that prices depend mainly on the money wage. If labor is fully employed initially, excess demand for the domestic good will show up as excess demand for labor, raising the money wage.

The importance of this fourth proposition was widely recognized and became the basic postulate of the "absorption" approach to the analysis of devaluation. When resources are fully employed, a devaluation cannot improve the current-account balance unless domestic absorption (expenditure) is reduced to accommodate the expenditure-switching effect of the devaluation. But the postulate generated two lines of analysis. It led one group of economists, including Alexander (1952, 1959), to look for ways in which a devaluation could affect absorption endogenously. It led another group, including Meade (1951), to build it into the theory of economic policy.

Those who hunted for endogenous links between the nominal exchange rate and the level of absorption worked with the basic national-income identity

$$B = Y - A = (S - I) - D,$$

where A is total absorption (the sum of consumption, investment, and government spending). They sought ways in which a devaluation could affect saving, investment, or both.[17]

Alexander (1952) and Machlup (1956), among others, stressed effects on the demand for real cash balances. By raising the domestic price of the imported good, a devaluation raises the price level, increasing the demand for real cash balances. This raises saving (hoarding) and reduces absorption. Their argument was revived by Dornbusch (1973) in the context of a simple monetary model; he showed that a devaluation would improve the current-account balance even if it had no influence whatsoever on the real exchange rate (i.e. no expenditure-switching effect).

Laursen and Metzler (1950) stressed effects on saving that do not derive from the demand for real cash balances. In the absence of money illusion, nominal consumption is homogeneous of first degree in nominal income. But real consumption is not necessarily homogeneous of first degree in real income. In Keynes (1936), for example, the marginal propensity to consume is smaller than the average propensity, and this means that an increase in the price level reduces real consumption. By implication, the price-raising effect of a devaluation will cut back absorption endogenously and will thus improve the current-account balance.[18]

3.5. Exchange rates and optimal policy

To show how the basic postulate of the absorption approach was built into the theory of economic policy, let us examine a single small economy using the famous diagram introduced by Swan (1963).[19] The vertical axis of Figure 3.2

[17]Early advocates of the absorption approach went too far in this direction, arguing that one should concentrate on these effects to the exclusion of expenditure-switching (elasticity) effects. They were not wrong analytically in attempting to show that a devaluation can improve the current-account balance by raising saving or reducing investment (i.e. cutting back absorption), even when it does not switch expenditure. The same point was made by Dornbusch (1973), Johnson (1977), and other advocates of the monetary approach. If domestic prices are not flexible, however, a devaluation that does not switch expenditure can improve the current-account balance only by reducing domestic output and driving the economy away from internal balance. It is a roundabout way of shifting expenditure and not an optimal response to a spontaneous switch in expenditure. This was not always realized, even by those who tried to synthesize the absorption and elasticity approaches.

[18]For a simple proof, see Sohmen (1969, pp. 133–135). The Laursen–Metzler effect vanishes when the marginal and average propensities are equal (and operates perversely when the marginal propensity is larger than the average). Recent criticisms of the Laursen–Metzler argument, including those that come from models in which current consumption depends on wealth or on intertemporal utility maximization, can be treated as criticisms of the assumption that the marginal propensity is smaller than the average.

[19]To represent a small economy by the basic equations, it is convenient to assume that $m_2[(1 - s_Y)\,dY + (dA + dE)] \approx 0$ in the total derivative of the Y^* equation (i.e. that the effects of changes in domestic consumption are too small to disturb equilibrium in the market for the foreign good). On

shows expenditure policy, E, which can be either monetary or fiscal policy, as they are interchangeable at this stage. An upward movement, then, denotes a tax cut or reduction in the interest rate. The horizontal axis shows the nominal and real exchange rates. They must move together, because goods prices do not change when the economy stays in internal balance (and it will not be allowed to stray far from internal balance). A rightward movement denotes a devaluation or depreciation of the domestic currency.

The DD curve shows how the exchange rate can be combined with expenditure policy to maintain internal balance. It is downward sloping because a devaluation or depreciation of the domestic currency switches domestic and foreign demands to the domestic good and requires a more restrictive expenditure policy to maintain internal balance. (At points above the DD curve, there is inflationary pressure; at points below, there is unemployment.) The FF curve shows how the exchange rate can be combined with expenditure policy to maintain external balance. It is upward sloping because a devaluation or depreciation improves the current-account balance and requires a less restrictive expenditure policy to maintain external balance. (At points above the FF curve, the current account is in deficit; at points below, it is in surplus.) The intersection of DD and FF at P

---

this assumption,

$$dY = \left(\frac{1}{k}\right)\left[\left(\frac{s^*}{k^*}\right)e_\pi\left(\frac{d\pi}{\pi}\right) + m_1(dA + dE) + dQ\right],$$

$$dB = \left(\frac{1}{k}\right)\left[s_Y\left(\frac{s_Y^*}{k^*}\right)e_\pi\left(\frac{d\pi}{\pi}\right) - m_2(dA + dE) + s_Y dQ\right],$$

where $k = s_Y + m_2(1 - s_Y)$, $k^* = s_Y^* + m_1^*(1 - s_Y^*)$, and $dQ = (s_Y^*/k^*)dB^a + (m_1^*/k^*)(dA^* + dE^*)$. Note that a switch in expenditure and a shift in foreign expenditure look alike to the small economy and thus call for identical policy responses. (This point was anticipated in the text, where an exchange-rate change was shown to insulate an economy from a switch in expenditure *and* from a shift in foreign expenditure.) Denote by Y^t and B^t the target levels of Y and B, so that $Y = Y^t$ in internal balance and $B = B^t$ in external balance. The DD curve in Figure 3.2 can then be obtained from the income equation:

$$dE = -\left(\frac{1}{m_1}\right)\left[\left(\frac{s_Y^*}{k^*}\right)e_\pi\left(\frac{d\pi}{\pi}\right) + dQ - k\,dY^t\right] - dA.$$

It is negatively sloped. The FF curve can be obtained from the current-account equation:

$$dE = \left(\frac{s_Y}{m_2}\right)\left[\left(\frac{s_Y^*}{k^*}\right)e_\pi\left(\frac{d\pi}{\pi}\right) + dQ - \left(\frac{k}{s_Y}\right)dB^t\right] - dA.$$

It is positively sloped. Statements made in the text about shifts in the curves derive from these equations. Note that the FF curve is steeper absolutely than the DD curve when $(s_Y/m_2) > (1/m_1)$ or $s_Y[(1 - s_Y)/(1 + s_Y)] > m_2(1 - s_Y)$. This condition cannot hold unless s_Y, the marginal propensity to save, exceeds $m_2(1 - s_Y)$, the marginal propensity to import. It is the more likely to hold, the larger the marginal propensity to save and the smaller the marginal propensity to import (i.e. the less open the domestic economy).

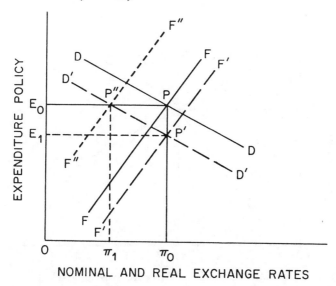

Figure 3.2. Policies for internal and external balance with a spontaneous increase in domestic expenditure and a spontaneous switch in expenditure.

defines an optimal policy combination — one that confers internal and external balance.

A spontaneous increase in domestic expenditure shifts *DD* downward, because a more restrictive expenditure policy is needed to maintain internal balance. It shifts *FF* downward too, because a more restrictive expenditure policy is needed to maintain external balance. In fact, the curves shift downward together, to $D'D'$ and $F'F'$, displacing P to P'. A change in expenditure policy from E_0 to E_1 can maintain internal and external balance without a change in the exchange rate.

A spontaneous switch in expenditure to the domestic good (or an increase in the level of foreign expenditure) shifts *DD* downward, because a more restrictive expenditure policy is needed to maintain internal balance. Let it shift to $D'D'$, just as it did in the previous example. This disturbance, however, shifts *FF* upward, because a less restrictive expenditure policy is needed to maintain external balance. It goes to $F''F''$, displacing P to P''. A change in the exchange rate from π_0 to π_1 (a revaluation or appreciation of the domestic currency) can maintain internal and external balance without a change in expenditure policy.

Both exercises illustrated in Figure 3.2 appear to violate a fundamental proposition in the theory of economic policy — that the number of policy instruments must be at least as large as the number of policy targets [Tinbergen (1952, ch. iv)]. Two policy targets were represented in Figure 3.2, internal and external balance. In each exercise, however, it was sufficient to change just one policy instrument — expenditure policy in the first and the exchange rate in the

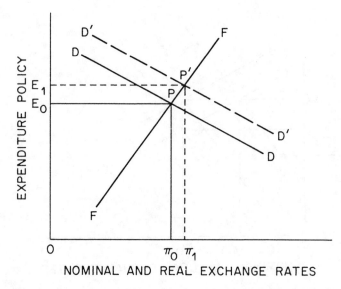

Figure 3.3. Policies for internal and external balance with an increase in the labor force.

second. But these were special cases. The economy began at an optimal policy point, and the disturbances that drove it from that point had properties that paired them with the policy instruments. The first was an increase in expenditure and could thus be offset by an expenditure-changing policy. The second was a switch in expenditure and could thus be offset by an expenditure-switching policy. When the disturbances do not have these properties, both policy instruments have to be adjusted. An illustration is supplied in Figure 3.3.

Suppose that the domestic labor force increases. Output must be raised to maintain full employment. The DD curve shifts upward to $D'D'$, because a less restrictive expenditure policy is needed for internal balance. The FF curve stays in place, however, so that the optimal policy combination is displaced from P to P'. Expenditure policy must be adjusted from E_0 to E_1, and the domestic currency must be devalued (or depreciate) from π_0 to π_1.

When working with Figure 3.2, we were able to pair disturbances with policies. When working with Figure 3.3, we are tempted to pair targets with instruments. With an increase in the labor force, for example, it seems natural to say that expenditure policy should be used to increase output and exchange-rate policy should be used to prevent a deterioration in the current-account balance. But the pairing of targets with instruments is a tricky business. It is the "assignment problem" and was studied by Mundell (1960) using what he called the "principle of effective market classification". Each instrument should be assigned to the policy target on which it has the greatest relative effect.

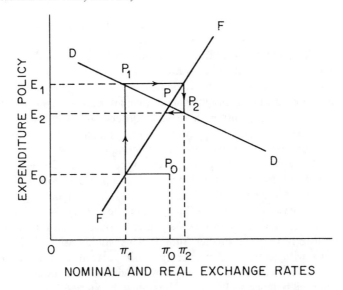

Figure 3.4. A stable assignment of instruments to targets.

The solution to the assignment problem is illustrated in Figure 3.4. Suppose that the domestic economy begins at P_0, with unemployment and a balance-of-payments surplus. Assign exchange-rate policy to external balance, assign expenditure policy to internal balance, and suppose that the managers of exchange-rate policy are the first to act. They will revalue the domestic currency from π_0 to π_1, taking the economy to the FF curve and achieving external balance. As there is still unemployment (more than there was to start), the managers of expenditure policy will adjust it from E_0 to E_1, taking the economy to the DD curve and achieving internal balance. At the new policy point P_1, however, there is a current-account deficit, because it lies above the FF curve. Accordingly, the domestic currency will be devalued from π_1 to π_2, which will trigger an additional adjustment of expenditure policy from E_1 to E_2. The next policy point is P_2. The policy path is described by the cobweb P_0, P_1, P_2, etc. and converges on the intersection of the DD and FF curves.[20]

This indirect decentralized procedure seems wasteful. The exchange rate goes up and down. So does expenditure policy. To move directly to the optimal point

---

[20]In this particular example, the managers of the policy instruments act sequentially and each instrument is adjusted by the full amount required to hit its policy target. In more general analyses of the assignment problem, instruments are altered simultaneously, and the size of each adjustment is a fraction of the one required to hit the policy target (i.e. a fraction of the gap between the current and desired values of the target variable). See, for example, Cooper (1969) and Patrick (1973).

P, however, policy makers must possess all of the information needed to construct the *DD* and *FF* curves and must know where those curves lie at all times. (Economists make assumptions of this sort when ascribing "rational expectations" to households and firms. But we all know that governments are dumber than private decision-makers!) The authorities, however, can recognize a balance-of-payments deficit or surplus, incipient unemployment, and incipient inflation. By pairing their policy instruments with these disorders, they can wend their way through the cobweb in Figure 3.4 without knowing much about the structure of the economy or the exogenous disturbances affecting it.

It is essential, however, to get the assignment right. In Figure 3.4, exchange-rate policy was assigned to external balance and expenditure policy to internal balance. This is the "conventional" assignment, but it is the right assignment only because the *FF* curve is steeper absolutely than the *DD* curve. If the sizes of slopes were reversed, the conventional assignment would be unstable; the policy point would move farther and farther from P. This would happen in a very open economy — one with a marginal propensity to import larger than its marginal propensity to save.[21] In such an economy, exchange-rate policy should be assigned to internal balance and expenditure policy to external balance.

3.6. The behavior of a flexible exchange rate

In the story told by Figure 3.4, the exchange rate was adjusted periodically, in the manner prescribed by the Bretton Woods Agreement. The same apparatus can be used to describe the behavior of a flexible exchange rate. In the underlying model, the exchange rate is the price that clears the foreign-exchange market, and the only flows that cross the market come from the current account and from exogenous capital flows of a sort introduced below. Furthermore, expectations are stationary, which means that traders will not lead or lag their foreign-exchange purchases in order to profit from exchange-rate fluctuations. Accordingly, the *FF* curve can be regarded as the market-clearing curve for the foreign-exchange market, and therefore the source of information about the behavior of a flexible exchange rate.[22]

The argument is illustrated in Figure 3.5. The economy begins at P_0, as in Figure 3.4, but P_0 has to lie on the initial *FF* curve. The economy cannot leave

[21]Strictly speaking, one in which $m_2(1 - s_Y) > s_Y[(1 - s_Y)/(1 + s_Y)]$; see footnote 19 above.
[22]Solving the current-account equation in footnote 19 for the change in π,

$$\left(\frac{\mathrm{d}\pi}{\pi}\right) = \left(\frac{1}{e_\pi}\right)\left(\frac{k^*}{s_Y^*}\right)\left[\left(\frac{m_2}{s_Y}\right)(\mathrm{d}A + \mathrm{d}E) - \mathrm{d}Q + \left(\frac{k}{s_Y}\right)\mathrm{d}B^t\right],$$

where $B^t > 0$ can be taken to reflect the effect of an exogenous capital outflow requiring (and causing) a depreciation of the domestic currency. Note that $e_\pi > 0$ has become a condition for stability of the foreign-exchange market, a point made by Haberler (1949) and Sohmen (1969).

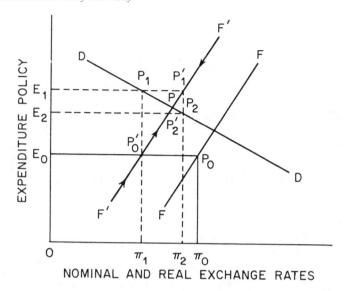

Figure 3.5. The behavior of a flexible exchange rate.

that curve, even momentarily, when the exchange rate is flexible. A spontaneous capital inflow begins and shifts FF to $F'F'$ because it requires an appreciation of the domestic currency to clear the foreign-exchange market. The exchange rate moves at once from π_0 to π_1. The foreign-exchange market does the job assigned heretofore to a policy-maker. But there is unemployment in the new situation, as P_0' lies below DD, and expenditure policy must be adjusted from E_0 to E_1 in order to achieve internal balance. The economy moves along $F'F'$ to P_1', because the domestic currency depreciates at once from π_1 to π_2. Unemployment is replaced by inflationary pressure, as P_1' lies above the DD curve, and expenditure policy must be adjusted from E_1 to E_2. The policy path is P_0, P_0', P_1', P_2', etc. rather than a cobweb. Nevertheless, the policy point converges on P, just as it did in Figure 3.4.

In Figure 3.5 the slopes of DD and FF show how the economy reacts to the way that expenditure policy is managed. If DD is flatter absolutely than FF, the economy will converge to P, even when expenditure policy is altered by large amounts (i.e. to achieve internal balance at the current exchange rate). The exchange rate will oscillate but not explosively. If DD is steeper than FF, the economy will not converge to P when expenditure policy is managed in this way. The exchange rate will oscillate explosively. But policy-makers are not as dumb as those who inhabit Figure 3.5. They can alter expenditure policy by smaller amounts and take explicit account of the exchange-rate changes produced by their decisions. (Matters become more difficult, however, when exchange-rate changes have lagged effects on trade flows and incomes.)

3.7. The choice between fixed and flexible exchange rates

The consensus favoring pegged exchange rates represented in the passages quoted from Nurkse (1944) began to break down rather quickly. Although Meade did not advocate flexible exchange rates in *The Balance of Payments* (1951), he did stress the need for adjustable exchange rates when the money wage is rigid, in order to deal with "conflict" situations. In 1953, however, Friedman published his celebrated case for flexible rates, and Meade came over two years later.[23] Many others crossed the aisle in the 1960s.

The growth of support for flexible exchange rates derived in part from disenchantment with the Bretton Woods regime. What some now remember nostalgically as exchange-rate stability was viewed at the time as exchange-rate rigidity. Furthermore, many economists had started to voice doubts about the compatibility of an adjustable peg with free capital movements. The issue had been raised by Meade some years earlier:

> ... an adjustable-peg mechanism can be successfully operated only if there is some direct control over speculative capital movements between the currencies concerned. And ... this involves the maintenance of the apparatus of exchange control over all transactions and raises difficult problems in the decision as to what are, and what are not, speculative capital movements. This is undoubtedly a grave disadvantage of this mechanism of adjustment [Meade (1951, pp. 228–229)].

There was a more fundamental change in view, however, concerning the effect of private speculation on a flexible exchange rate. Nurkse (1944) said that it had been destabilizing. Meade (1951) said that it might be destabilizing.[24] But Friedman (1953) said that it should be stabilizing:

> People who argue that speculation is generally destabilizing seldom realize that this is largely equivalent to saying that speculators lose money, since speculation can be destabilizing in general only if speculators on the average sell when the currency is low in price and buy when it is high [Friedman (1953, p. 175)].

---

[23] See Friedman (1953) and Meade (1955).

[24] Central banks, he said, might have to intervene to counter "perverse" or "grossly excessive" speculation: "By such means, the monetary authorities can attempt to make the market for foreign exchange approximate toward what it would have been if there had been free competitive speculation with correct foresight of future movements. In this case all that the authorities have to do is to anticipate more correctly than private speculators the future course of exchange rates. And in so far as they do so they will make a profit at the expense of the private speculator" [Meade (1951, p. 224)]. Note that Meade anticipated the point made by Friedman (1953) concerning stability and profitability, and he also posed the issue about which we are still arguing — who can forecast exchange rates more accurately?

Friedman's assertion provoked a debate that has not yet ended.[25] But a growing number of economists, including Meade (1955), took positions closer to Friedman than to Nurkse. Private speculation would be forthcoming in directions and amounts sufficient to smooth exchange-rate fluctuations.[26] By implication, the advocates of flexible exchange rates rejected the elasticity pessimism that was another feature of earlier opinion — the fear that the Marshall–Lerner–Robinson condition would not be satisfied or would be barely satisfied.[27] Once private speculation had driven the nominal exchange rate to its "correct" level, the current-account balance would adjust rapidly, as producers and consumers responded to the new real exchange rate.

Friedman, Meade, and those who joined them disagreed among themselves on many major issues. Yet monetarists and Keynesians came to a common view concerning the exchange rate because they agreed tacitly on three propositions — that the typical economy is insular, that flexible exchange rates can therefore provide significant national autonomy in matters of macroeconomic policy, and that governments require that sort of autonomy because of differences in national objectives.

Recall the long passage from Meade (1951) in which he said that exchange-rate changes alter the domestic prices of imported goods but not those of domestic goods — an argument that drew on Keynesian assumptions about wage and price determination. Friedman made the same sort of statement:

A rise in the exchange rate produced by a tendency toward a surplus makes foreign goods cheaper in terms of domestic currency, even though their prices are unchanged in terms of their own currency, and domestic goods more expensive in terms of foreign currency, even though their prices are unchanged in terms of domestic currency [Friedman (1953, p. 162)].

Exceptions were recognized. Panama is too small and open to be an "optimum currency area" and should therefore maintain a fixed exchange rate with the U.S. dollar.[28] Belgium should maintain a fixed exchange rate with the deutsche mark. For larger and more insular economies, however, flexible rates seemed to make much sense.

---

[25]See the survey in Sohmen (1969, ch. III), where Friedman wins hands down. The debate has started up again, however, in the context of a larger debate about the usefulness of official intervention.

[26]The issue of sufficiency has come into question; see, for example, McKinnon (1979, ch. 7).

[27]On reasons for and answers to this earlier pessimism, see Orcutt (1950).

[28]The notion of an "optimum currency area" was introduced by Mundell (1961b), but he defined it differently than those who adopted it. In his paper, countries (regions) are exposed to real disturbances of the sort illustrated in our model by a spontaneous switch in expenditure. If factors of production moved freely between countries, endogenous factor flows could restore external balance, and there would be no need for changes in the terms of trade (the real exchange rate). Countries could afford to maintain fixed exchange rates. They would comprise an optimum currency area. As factors do not move freely enough and rigid money wages make for sticky prices, exchange-rate changes are required

We have already seen why a flexible exchange rate was thought to protect an economy from switches in demand and from fluctuations in foreign demand. In Figure 3.2, a spontaneous switch in expenditure displaced the internal-balance curve from DD to $D'D'$ and the external-balance curve from FF to $F''F''$. If the exchange rate is pegged at π_0, the authorities confront a policy conflict. There are inflationary pressures and a current-account surplus at the initial policy point (P is above $D'D'$ and below $F''F''$). Internal balance can be achieved by an expenditure policy that takes the economy to $D'D'$ at P', but this will make the current-account surplus bigger. External balance can be achieved by an expenditure policy that takes the economy to $F''F''$ at a point vertically above P, but this will exacerbate inflationary pressures. With a flexible exchange rate, however, the domestic currency will appreciate immediately from π_0 to π_1, taking the economy to P''. Internal balance will be maintained without any change in expenditure policy.

But belief in the need for national autonomy and its feasibility was perhaps the leading theme in the 1950s and 1960s. Johnson (1972a) put the point this way:

> The fundamental argument for flexible exchange rates is that they would allow countries autonomy with respect to their use of monetary, fiscal and other policy instruments, consistent with the maintenance of whatever degree of freedom in international transactions they choose to allow their citizens, by automatically ensuring the preservation of external equilibrium [Johnson (1972a, p. 199)].

With flexible exchange rates, for example, countries can choose different points on their Phillips curves:

> On the one hand, a great rift exists between nations like the United Kingdom and the United States, which are anxious to maintain high levels of employment and are prepared to pay a price for it in terms of domestic inflation, and other nations, notably the West German Federal Republic, which are strongly averse to inflation. Under the present fixed exchange-rate system, these nations are pitched against each other in a battle over the rate of inflation that is to prevail in the world economy, since the fixed rate system diffuses that rate to all the countries involved in it. Flexible exchange rates would allow each country to pursue the mixture of unemployment and price trend objectives it prefers, consistent with international equilibrium, equilibrium being secured by appreci-

---

to alter the terms of trade and restore external balance. Mundell's economies are insular in wage and price determination, but some are more open than others to capital and labor movements. In other papers on the subject, it is the insularity of wage and price determination that varies across countries. Fixed exchange rates were recommended for those that are not insular — whose money wages depend importantly on import prices — because changes in exchange rates can then lead to changes in domestic prices that undermine the quality of the domestic currency. See McKinnon (1963) and the surveys by Kenen (1969b) and Tower and Willett (1976).

ation of the currencies of "price-stability" countries relative to the currencies of "full-employment" countries [Johnson (1972a, p. 210)].

Although Friedman (1968) had already warned that the not-so-long-run Phillips curve is vertically sloped — that countries cannot choose between unemployment and inflation — Johnson's views were widely shared. Whitman (1972), for example, suggested that members of an optimum currency area ought to have similar policy preferences and similar "possibility surfaces" linking unemployment rates, inflation rates, and growth rates, and Corden (1972) cited differences in preferences and Phillips curves as the major obstacles to European monetary integration.

4. Interest rates and the capital account

Although the case for flexible exchange rates put forth in the 1950s was endorsed by many economists in the 1960s, it did not make much headway in official circles. Early debates on reform of the monetary system focused mainly on liquidity, not adjustment, and when they did turn to adjustment, they paid very little attention to exchange rates.[29] Even after the breakdown of the pegged-rate system, the negotiations on long-run reform sought to restore a system of "stable but adjustable" exchange rates. Floating was not sinful but was not to be permanent. It was a way for governments to ask for help from market forces when searching for new parities.

The breakdown of the pegged-rate system, however, was important in the history of exchange-rate theory. Even as it led to the adoption of flexible exchange rates by the major industrial countries, it demonstrated clearly the obsolescence of the macroeconomic model on which the case for flexibility was commonly based. The suggestion by Friedman (1968) that the Phillips curve is vertical had already challenged implicit assumptions about wage–price dynamics and raised doubts about the usefulness of national autonomy. The breakdown of pegged exchange rates reflected the increase of capital mobility, challenged explicit assumptions about insularity, and called into question the feasibility of national autonomy.

More realistic models of exchange-rate behavior began to appear soon after the advent of flexible exchange rates. Innovation took place very quickly, because of work done in the 1960s. The models of the 1970s are reviewed in Chapter 14 of this Handbook. I conclude this chapter by surveying briefly the innovations of the 1960s that made way for those models — the introduction of capital mobility into the flow models of the 1950s and the introduction of stock equilibrium, especially money-market equilibrium.

---

[29] The official debates and documents are reviewed in Solomon (1977, chs. iv, x, and xiv).

4.1. Capital flows and optimal policy

Capital movements appeared frequently in the models of the 1950s. They embellished the description of the adjustment process given by Meade in *The Balance of Payments* (1951). They played a more important role in the story told by Metzler (1960). I concentrate here, however, on their role in the theory of economic policy developed by Fleming (1962) and Mundell (1962, 1963).

Capital mobility was added to the model I have used thus far in the same way that trade had been added to the Keynesian model of a closed economy. Two new equations were tacked on without changing old ones:

$$\dot{F} = F(r, r^*), \qquad F_r > 0, \quad F_{r^*} < 0, \tag{4.1}$$

$$\dot{R} = B + \dot{F}, \tag{4.2}$$

where $\dot{F}$ is an inflow of capital, $\dot{R}$ is an inflow of reserves, and both are measured in domestic currency. When $\dot{F} > 0$, foreigners are buying domestic government debt, because government bonds are the only securities available in our basic model. When $\dot{R} > 0$, the domestic economy has a balance-of-payment surplus, so that the definition of external balance is $\dot{R} = 0$ rather than $B = 0$. The small-country version of the model is one where r^* does not change. The limiting case of "perfect" capital mobility is one where $F_r \to \infty$ and $r = r^*$ (the central bank has no control over the domestic interest rate). One should, of course, make an additional change in the model; an interest-income term should be added to the current account. This amendment was usually neglected, however, because it requires another amendment — the definition and inclusion of the integral of $\dot{F}$.[30]

In the absence of capital mobility, monetary and fiscal policies were interchangeable in their effects on the balance of payments, and they could be lumped together as expenditure policies. With the introduction of capital mobility, monetary policy acquires an additional influence on the balance of payments, by way of its effect on the capital account, and we must distinguish carefully between the two policies. The main implications come out clearly in the small-country case.[31]

---

[30] This point was noted early on and one implication emphasized. An increase in r can worsen the balance of payments. By raising interest payments to foreigners, it can weaken the current account by more than it strengthens the capital account. The net effect of capital mobility on the balance of payments is $\dot{F} - rF$, where $F = \int \dot{F}$, and its partial derivative with respect to r is $F_r - F$. Therefore, the balance of payments improves if and only if $F_r > F$. See, for example, Gray (1964). When $F_r < F$, incidentally, the model can become unstable.

[31] The equations in footnote 19 must be rewritten as

$$dY = \left(\frac{1}{k}\right)\left\{\left(\frac{s_Y^*}{k^*}\right)e_\pi\left(\frac{d\pi}{\pi}\right) + m_1[dA - (1 - s_Y)dT - s_r dr] + dQ\right\},$$

$$d\dot{R} = \left(\frac{1}{k}\right)\left\{s_Y\left(\frac{s_Y^*}{k^*}\right)e_\pi\left(\frac{d\pi}{\pi}\right) - m_2[dA - (1 - s_Y)dT - s_r dr] + s_Y dQ + kF_r dr\right\}.$$

In Figure 3.3 above, it was not possible to maintain internal and external balance without changing the exchange rate. In Figure 4.1, they can be maintained by exploiting the difference between the balance-of-payments effects of monetary and fiscal policies. Monetary policy (the interest rate) is shown on the vertical axis, and fiscal policy (the tax rate) is shown on the horizontal axis. Upward movements on the vertical axis and rightward movements on the horizontal axis denote increasingly restrictive policies (indications opposite to those employed in Figures 3.1 through 3.5).

The *II* curve shows how monetary and fiscal policies can be combined to maintain internal balance. It is downward sloping because an increase in *T* reduces domestic expenditure and requires a decrease in *r* to offset it. (At points above the *II* curve, there is unemployment; at points below it, there is inflationary pressure.) The *XX* curve shows how the two policies can be combined to maintain external balance. It is also downward sloping because an increase in *T* improves the balance of payments by reducing imports and requires a decrease in *r* to offset it. (At points above the *XX* curve, $\dot{R} > 0$; at points below it, $\dot{R} < 0$.) The *XX* curve is flatter than the *II* curve. The decrease in the interest rate required to maintain external balance is smaller than the one required to maintain internal balance. Its effect on the balance of payments includes an effect on the capital account (a decrease in inflows or increase in outflows), as well as an expenditure-increasing effect on imports.[32]

Suppose that the economy starts at *P*. Let its labor force grow, raising the income level required for internal balance. The internal-balance curve shifts from *II* to *I'I'*. Less restrictive policies are needed to maintain internal balance, and the policy point is displaced from *P* to *P'*. The tax rate must be reduced from T_0 to T_1 in order to raise income to the levels needed for internal balance, and the interest rate must be raised from r_0 to r_1 in order to produce the improvement in the capital account needed for external balance (the one needed to offset the increase in imports induced by the increase in income).

The assignment of instruments to targets implicit in the language of the previous paragraph is the right assignment. Tell the finance ministry to use the tax

---

[32] The income equation in the previous footnote gives the *II* curve:

$$dr = -\left(\frac{1}{s_r}\right)(1 - s_Y)\,dT + \left(\frac{1}{m_1 s_r}\right)\left[\left(\frac{s_Y^*}{k^*}\right)e_\pi\left(\frac{d\pi}{\pi}\right) + m_1\,dA + dQ - k\,dY^t\right].$$

The balance-of-payments equation gives the *XX* curve:

$$dr = -\left(\frac{1}{u_r}\right)(1 - s_Y)\,dT - \left(\frac{1}{m_2 u_r}\right)\left[s_Y\left(\frac{s_Y^*}{k^*}\right)e_\pi\left(\frac{d\pi}{\pi}\right) - m_2\,dA + s_Y\,dQ - k\,d\dot{R}^t\right],$$

where $u_r = s_r + (k/m_2)F_r$, so that $u_r > s_r$ and $u_r \to \infty$ as $F_r \to \infty$. $\dot{R}^t$ is the target value of the balance of payments. The slopes of the *II* and *XX* curves do not depend on the size of the marginal propensity to import. The condition encountered earlier, that $s_Y[(1 - s_Y)/(1 + s_Y)] > m_2(1 - s_Y)$, does not determine the assignment of instruments to targets in the present case. (It is important, however, for the sizes of shifts in the *II* and *XX* curves.)

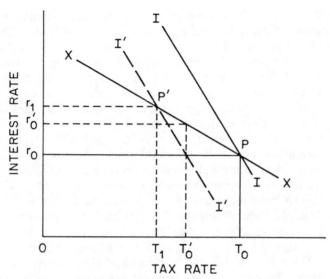

Figure 4.1. Monetary and fiscal policies for internal and external balance under a fixed exchange rate.

rate for internal balance. Tell the central bank to use the interest rate for external balance. The finance ministry will cut the tax rate from T_0 to T_0' in order to achieve internal balance, and this will cause a balance-of-payments deficit by putting the policy point below the XX curve. The central bank will raise the interest rate from r_0 to r_0' in order to achieve external balance, and this will cause unemployment by putting the policy point above the $I'I'$ curve. The finance ministry will cut the tax rate again, the central bank will raise the interest rate again, and the policy point will move gradually to P'. (Note that T and r move monotonically, instead of oscillating as they did in Figure 3.4.)

4.2. Capital mobility and policy autonomy under fixed exchange rates

Heretofore, the interest rate has been used as the instrument of monetary policy. With perfect capital mobility, however, the XX curve becomes horizontal, and the central bank loses control of the interest rate. Therefore, we must look more closely at the mechanics of monetary policy, and we must reexamine the relationship between monetary policy and fiscal policy.

Suppose that there is no capital mobility (so that $\dot{R} = B = S - D$, as before). When the finance ministry cuts taxes to stimulate demand, S and D rise, but S rises by less than D. The current account deteriorates, and there is an outflow of

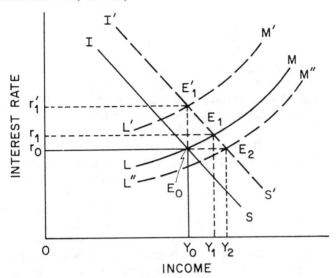

Figure 4.2. Fiscal policy and capital mobility under fixed exchange rates.

reserves. In earlier examples, the central bank sterilized that outflow. In this one, it will not. The short-run and long-run results are shown in Figure 4.2, using *IS* and *LM* curves.[33] A tax cut shifts the *IS* curve rightward to *I'S'*, displacing the equilibrium point from E_0 to E_1, raising the interest rate from r_0 to r_1, and raising income from Y_0 to Y_1. This is the permanent result for a closed economy, but it is the short-run result for an open economy with a fixed exchange rate. The outflow of reserves resulting from the current-account deficit reduces the money supply and shifts the *LM* curve. That curve must move leftward until $S = D$ so that $\dot{R} = 0$ and the money stock is stabilized. Therefore, it must move to *L'M'*, displacing the equilibrium point to E_1', raising the interest rate to r_1', and bringing income back to Y_0, its initial level. The money-supply effects of the current-account deficit "crowd out" enough consumption to offset completely the stimulus to spending afforded by the tax cut.[34]

Suppose that there is some capital mobility (so that $\dot{R} = B + \dot{F} = S - D + \dot{F}$). The tax cut raises S by less than it raises D, producing a current-account deficit,

[33] The *IS* curve is the goods–market relationship between income and the interest rate. It is downward sloping because an increase in the interest rate reduces income by raising saving and thus reducing consumption. Its position depends on the level of taxation and on the exchange rate. The *LM* curve is the money-market relationship between income and the interest rate. It is upward sloping because an increase in the interest rate is needed to clear the money market when an increase in income raises the demand for money. Its position depends on the size of the money stock.

[34] Return to the equations in footnote 31. When $\dot{R} = 0$ (and $F_r = 0$), then $(1 - s_Y)\,dT + s_r\,dr = 0$, and this means that $dY = 0$.

but it does not necessarily cause an outflow of reserves. Let the interest rate rise to r_1, as before, but let it induce a capital inflow just large enough to take up the excess flow supply of bonds (i.e. let $\dot{F} = D - S$). Income rises to Y_1 and stays there indefinitely, because there is no shift in the *LM* curve. There may indeed be sufficient capital mobility to generate an inflow of reserves and drive the *LM* curve to the right. This is what happens with perfect capital mobility. The interest rate remains at r_0, the *LM* curve moves to $L''M''$, and income rises to Y_2. There is a larger current-account deficit here, but it serves to offset the capital inflow and therefore to terminate the increase in the money stock.

Consider, next, the use of monetary policy to influence aggregate demand. If there is no capital mobility, an open-market purchase of government bonds increases the money stock and decreases the interest rate. The short-run and long-run results are shown in Figure 4.3. The *LM* curve shifts to $L'M'$, displacing equilibrium from E_0 to E_1, reducing the interest rate from r_0 to r_1, and raising income from Y_0 to Y_1. This is the permanent result in a closed economy, but is again the short-run result in an open economy with a fixed exchange rate. The increase in income produces a current-account deficit and an outflow of reserves. If the central bank can sterilize that outflow, it can keep the economy at E_1. Otherwise, the money stock begins to fall, and it must go on falling until it has dropped back to its initial level. The *LM* curve drifts back to its starting point, the interest rate rises to r_0, and income returns to Y_0.

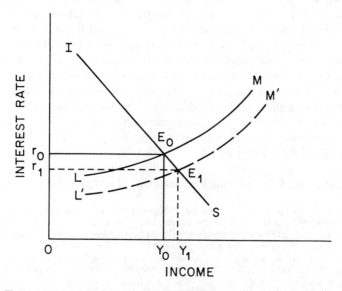

Figure 4.3. Monetary policy and capital mobility under fixed exchange rates.

The introduction of capital mobility makes matters worse. A reduction in the interest rates from r_0 to r_1 causes a capital outflow ($\dot{F} < 0$), adding to the outflow of reserves and reversing more rapidly the increase in income. There is, indeed, no increase whatsoever with perfect capital mobility. An open-market purchase of government bonds causes a capital outflow that is exactly equal to the open-market purchase, and there is no observable movement in the diagram — no shift in the *LM* curve, even temporarily, no change in the interest rate, and no change in income. The central bank has no control over the domestic interest rate. More important, it has no control over the money stock. The only effect of an open-market purchase is a change in the composition of its balance sheet; it loses reserve as rapidly as it buys bonds.

4.3. Capital mobility and policy autonomy under flexible exchange rates

Under a flexible exchange rate, there is no intervention in the foreign-exchange market. Therefore, the central bank can control the money stock, even with perfect capital mobility. This is the basic sense in which a flexible exchange rate furnishes autonomy. But capital mobility has important effects on the behavior of a flexible exchange rate and on the functioning of national policies.

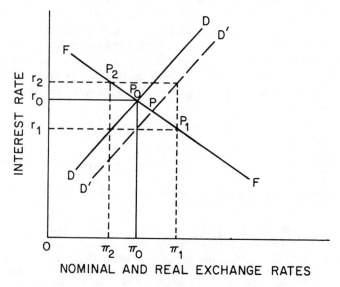

Figure 4.4. The behavior of a flexible exchange rate with high capital mobility.

The behavior of a flexible exchange rate is described in Figure 4.4, which is another version of the Swan (1963) diagram. The interest rate is shown on the vertical axis and is used to represent monetary policy. The nominal and real exchange rates are shown on the horizontal axis. Combinations of the interest rate and exchange rate that confer internal balance are given by the *DD* curve. It is upward sloping here because a depreciation of the domestic currency switches expenditure to the domestic good and must be offset by a more restrictive monetary policy. Combinations that confer external balance are shown by the *FF* curve. It is downward sloping because a depreciation of the domestic currency improves the current account and must be offset by a less restrictive monetary policy. (A less restrictive policy has two effects. It increases imports by raising expenditure, and it reduces the capital inflow or raises the capital outflow.) In earlier versions of this diagram, the *FF* curve was steeper absolutely than the *DD* curve. In Figure 4.4, the *FF* curve is flatter, reflecting the influence of high capital mobility. The higher the degree of capital mobility, the larger the exchange-rate change required to offset an interest-rate change. With perfect capital mobility, the *FF* curve is horizontal.[35]

As the foreign-exchange market determines the exchange rate, it is assigned implicitly to external balance, and monetary policy must be assigned to internal balance. When the *FF* curve is flatter than the *DD* curve, however, the central bank must be careful. If it does not make allowance for the change in the exchange rate resulting from a change in monetary policy, it can introduce explosive oscillations. Let there be growth in the labor force, introducing unemployment. The internal-balance curve shifts from *DD* to *D'D'*, because a lower interest rate is needed to raise output. If the interest rate is cut from r_0 to r_1, the reduction needed for internal balance at the current exchange rate, there will be a capital outflow (or smaller capital inflow), as well as an increase in imports. The policy point will move from P_0 to P_1, and the domestic currency will depreciate from π_0 to π_1. Unemployment will give way to inflation (P_1 lies below *D'D'*), and

---

[35] The equation for the *DD* curve is obtained by rearranging the equation for the *II* curve in footnote 32:

$$dr = \left(\frac{1}{m_1 s_r}\right)\left(\frac{s_Y^*}{k*}\right)e_\pi\left(\frac{d\pi}{\pi}\right) + \left(\frac{1}{m_1 s_r}\right)[m_1\,dA - m_1(1 - s_Y)\,dT + dQ - k\,dY^t].$$

The equation for the *FF* curve is obtained by rearranging the equation for the *XX* curve (and omitting $\dot{R}^t$, the target value for the balance of payments):

$$dr = -\left(\frac{s_Y}{m_2 u_r}\right)\left(\frac{s_Y^*}{k*}\right)e_\pi\left(\frac{d\pi}{\pi}\right) + \left(\frac{1}{m_2 u_r}\right)[m_2\,dA - m_2(1 - s_Y)\,dT - s_Y\,dQ].$$

The *FF* curve is flatter absolutely than the *DD* curve when $(s_Y/m_2 u_r) < (1/m_1 s_r)$, or $m_2(1 - s_Y) > [s_Y - k(F_r/s_r)][(1 - s_Y)/(1 + s_Y)]$, and this condition can obtain for large values of F_r (high capital mobility), even when the marginal propensity to import is much smaller than the marginal propensity to save.

the central bank will have to raise the interest rate. If the rate goes directly to r_2, as required for internal balance, the policy point will move to P_2, and the domestic currency will appreciate to π_2. Inflation will give way again to unemployment, but more than before, and the central bank will have to cut the interest rate. The path of the policy point is P_0, P_1, P_2, etc. and it does not converge on P.

The instability illustrated here does not condemn exchange-rate flexibility. It serves merely to remind us of the point made before, that the central bank cannot afford to ignore its own influence on the exchange rate, especially when capital mobility is high.

There are, of course, other ways to deal with the same problem. It would be possible, for instance, to use fiscal policy rather than monetary policy. When capital mobility is high, however, fiscal policy is not very powerful.

Under a fixed exchange rate, capital mobility enhanced the effectiveness of fiscal policy. Under a flexible exchange rate, capital mobility decreases its effectiveness. Figure 4.5 shows why. A tax cut shifts the *IS* curve rightward to $I'S'$, raising the interest rate from r_0 to r_1, and raising income from Y_0 to Y_1. This is the old outcome for a closed economy. But it is not the outcome for an open economy with a flexible exchange rate, not even in the short run. It does not allow for the change in the exchange rate. When capital mobility is low, the domestic currency depreciates; the increase in income raises imports by more than the

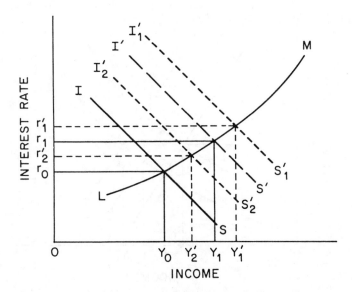

Figure 4.5. Fiscal policy and capital mobility under flexible exchange rates.

increase in the interest rate raises the capital inflow. The expenditure-switching effect of the depreciation shifts the *IS* curve from *I'S'* to some position such as $I_1'S_1'$ and generates a bigger increase in income. It rises all the way to Y_1'. When capital mobility is high, however, the domestic currency appreciates; the increase in the interest rate raises the capital inflow by more than the increase in income raises imports. The expenditure-switching effect shifts the *IS* curve from *I'S'* to some position such as $I_2'S_2'$ and generates a smaller increase in income. It drops only to Y_2'. With perfect capital mobility, the appreciation offsets the whole fiscal stimulus and keeps the *IS* curve from shifting. The interest rate remains at r_0, because it cannot change with perfect capital mobility, and income does not rise at all. Fiscal policy is completely ineffective.

Under a fixed exchange rate, the influence of monetary policy is transitory, and capital mobility reduces its effectiveness, diminishing its temporary influence on income. Under a flexible exchange rate, the influence of monetary policy is permanent, and capital mobility raises its effectiveness. In Figure 4.6, an open-market purchase of government bonds shifts the *LM* curve to *L'M'*, reducing the interest rate from r_0 to r_1 and raising income from Y_0 to Y_1. This is the old outcome for a closed economy. In an open economy with a flexible exchange rate, something more must happen. The domestic currency must depreciate, and the size of the depreciation must increase with capital mobility. Therefore, the *IS*

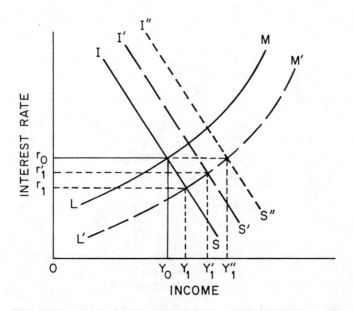

Figure 4.6. Monetary policy and capital mobility under flexible exchange rates.

curve shifts to some position such as $I'S'$, adding to the increase in income. It rises all the way to Y_1'. With perfect capital mobility, the increase in income is even larger. The domestic interest rate must stay at r_0, and this says that the IS curve must shift to $I''S''$, driving income to Y_1''. (This conclusion is related to the point made in the discussion of Figure 4.4, that there is a risk of instability when capital mobility is high. The central bank must make adequate allowance for the large shifts in the IS curve that take place with large changes in the nominal exchange rate.)

4.4. Flows, stocks, and asset-market equilibrium

Most of the analysis just summarized is found in the papers by Fleming (1962) and Mundell (1962, 1963) that introduced capital mobility into the theory of economic policy. Related contributions are surveyed by Whitman (1970). At one important point, however, I drew on papers by McKinnon and Oates (1966) and McKinnon (1969). They were among the first to show that the Fleming–Mundell view of economic policy depended strategically on sterilizing reserve flows. If those flows are allowed to affect the money stock, they erode the influence of monetary policy, even in the absence of capital mobility, and they weaken the influence of fiscal policy unless capital mobility is high.

The link between reserve flows and the money stock, however, is only one of several links between flows and stocks that are missing from the Fleming–Mundell model. Consider the basic accounting relationship used so often earlier, rewritten and amended to include investment:

$$\dot{R} - \dot{F} - B = \dot{R} - \dot{F} + D - S + I = 0.$$

A balance-of-payments surplus (inflow of reserves) raises the money stock. A capital inflow raises stocks of debt to foreigners (or reduces stocks of claims on foreigners). A budget deficit financed by bond issues raises the stock of government securities. Private saving raises the stock of wealth. And investment raises the capital stock. A change in any stock, moreover, has effects on flows.

We have already seen how reserve flows alter the money stock, undermining the influence of monetary policy, and noted that this process can be deferred only for as long as central banks can sterilize reserve flows. The monetary approach to the balance of payments is built on this basic proposition.[36] It views a balance-of-

---

[36] The monetary approach has a long history, going back to David Hume. It was resurrected by Polak (1957) and Hahn (1959) but owes much of its influence to Mundell (1968, 1971) and Johnson (1972b), because they could connect it with monetarist models of the closed economy developed by Friedman (1956) and Patinkin (1956). One can take a monetary view of the balance of payments without using a monetarist model, but most monetary models are monetarist. Real income and the real interest rate are determined on the "real" side of the economy, and they in turn determine the demand for real balances. In a small (price-taking) country with a fixed exchange rate, then,

payments deficit as a manifestation of excess supply in the money market, which will be self-correcting in the long run. A balance-of-payments deficit cannot endure unless the central bank perpetuates the excess supply of money by sterilizing reserve losses. Here is Johnson's formulation:

> The central propositions of the monetary approach are, first, that the balance of payments is a monetary phenomenon and requires analysis with the tools of monetary theory and not barter or "real" trade theory; second, that money is a stock, whereas real theory traditionally deals with flows, so that an adequate balance-of-payments theory must integrate stocks and flows; and third, that the money stock can be changed in two alternative ways, through domestic credit creation or destruction and through international reserve flows, the policy choice being important for balance-of-payments analysis [Johnson (1977, p. 251)].

There are, he said, three implications:

> First, and as a fundamental proposition, balance-of-payments deficits and surpluses... are monetary symptoms of monetary disequilibria that will cure themselves in time without any inherent need for a government balance-of-payments policy. If the natural processes of adjustment cannot be allowed to work themselves out, because of inadequacy of international reserves, the policy indicated to speed the natural adjustment process is deliberate monetary contraction. Devaluation, or alternatively import restrictions and export-promoting policies, is a substitute for monetary contraction, logically having the same effect but achieving it by deflating the real stock of money backed by domestic credit through raising the domestic price level rather than by deflating the nominal stock of money through open market sales, and its effect is a transient one of accelerating the inherent natural process of adjustment to equilibrium. ...
> Second, on a fixed exchange rate system inflation is a world monetary phenomenon, which cannot be prevented by national monetary policy or its ineffective substitute, a national "wage–price policy," and can only be counteracted by any national policy if the currency is first freed to find its own level on the foreign exchange market (or the pegged rate is regularly and systematically altered to national anti-inflationary policy).
> Third, in a regime of floating exchange rates inflation is *not* a world but a national problem. ... Inflation does, however, remain a "world" or "externally-caused" problem to the extent that countries' exchange rate policies aim

---

the money market must be cleared by movements in reserves. See, for example, Dornbusch (1973). The monetary approach is developed more fully in Chapter 14 of this Handbook, and applied to the problem of exchange-rate determination. For earlier and more skeptical assessments, see Whitman (1975) and Hahn (1977).

at maintaining some conventional value or range of values of their currencies...,
or more subtly the policy-makers aim at maintaining a conventional relation
between the domestic and foreign interest rates. ... An important corollary of
this proposition is that, contrary to widespread belief, a floating rate system
yields little if any extra freedom for the independent exercise of national
economic policy, if freedom means freedom from external influences and
changes and is defined implicitly to mean independence exercised without cost
in the form of disturbance [Johnson (1977, pp. 265–266)].

How different is this passage from the one quoted earlier, in which Johnson made
the case for national autonomy and for a flexible exchange rate to achieve it! This
one is an epitaph for insularity.

Another approach to the balance of payments originated in the 1960s. It is the
portfolio-balance approach. Its origins and history, however, are different from
those of the monetary approach. It was not set out all at once, in a group of
formal models, and had no home comparable to the International Trade Workshop
at Chicago, which nurtured the monetary approach. It was developed gradually
by many contributors, who began to understand the importance of the links
between certain flows and stocks and to build them, one by one, into their own
models.[37]

The portfolio-balance approach grew out of the debates of the 1960s about the
way to estimate capital-flow equations. The first efforts of the 1960s were based
on the simple specifications in the Fleming–Mundell model, represented by eq.
(4.1) above, which linked flows of capital with levels of interest rates. Critics
pointed out that one should work with stocks, not flows. Capital movements
should be treated as episodic stock adjustments, following the theory of portfolio
selection developed by Markowitz (1959) and Tobin (1967, 1969). Formally, eq.
(4.1) should be replaced by equations of this sort:

$$F^d = F(r, r^*, W^*), \qquad F_r > 0, \quad F_{r^*} < 0 \quad \text{and} \quad F_W > 0, \tag{4.1a}$$

$$\dot{F} = \gamma(F^d - F), \quad \gamma > 0, \tag{4.1b}$$

where F^d is the foreign (stock) demand for the domestic bond, F is the stock
actually held, W^* is foreign wealth, and γ is the speed of adjustment (the rate at
which foreigners adjust their portfolios).

---

[37]The paper by McKinnon and Oates (1966) did contain a formal model that anticipated in a
number of respects the full-fledged portfolio-balance models of the 1970s. There was only one bond in
that model, however, and thus one interest rate. In this sense, the model was closer to a monetary
model with perfect capital mobility than to the typical portfolio-balance model with imperfect capital
mobility. A number of recent papers have shown that the difference in assumptions about capital
mobility is one of the most important differences between the two groups of models. See the
discussion and citations in Chapter 15 of this Handbook.

Branson (1968) was among the first to put stock-adjustment terms into capital-flow equations, and they added greatly to the quality of his results.[38] He was likewise among the first to emphasize the implications for the Fleming–Mundell model. The policy combination shown in Figure 4.1, where the interest rate was assigned to external balance and the tax rate assigned to internal balance, will work for a while but cannot work permanently in a stationary model. An increase in the interest rate leads to a permanent shift in portfolios but does not produce a permanent improvement in the balance of payments. Foreigners start to buy domestic bonds as soon as the interest rate rises, but the capital inflow falls off as the portfolio shift is completed.[39]

The next major step in the evolution of the portfolio-balance approach was taken when eq. (4.1b) was replaced by instantaneous stock adjustment.[40] The third step was taken when a number of economists introduced *two* links between saving and the stock of wealth. Eq. (3.4) above was replaced by these assertions:

$$S = \dot{W} = s(r, Y - T, W), \tag{3.4a}$$

where $0 < s_Y < 1$, $s_r > 0$, and, most importantly, $s_W < 0$. Saving raises wealth, and an increase in wealth reduces saving.[41]

In a typical portfolio-balance model, portfolio shifts occur instantaneously, but capital flows take place too, whenever there is saving or dissaving. Capital flows are not permanent, however, because saving and dissaving are not permanent; saving goes to zero as it raises wealth, and dissaving goes to zero as it lowers wealth. Therefore, these models have a self-correcting mechanism, but it is different from the one in monetary models, and it focuses attention on the current-account balance. A current-account surplus has its counterpart in saving (in flow demands for bonds and money), but saving raises wealth, and that in turn reduces saving. When saving and the current-account surplus go to zero, more-over, the overall balance of payments must go to zero too. Flow demands for bonds and money vanish completely. Monetary models, by contrast, focus attention directly on the balance of payments. A balance-of-payments surplus has its counterpart in hoarding (a flow demand for money), but hoarding raises the supply of money, and that in turn reduces hoarding.

---

[38]Similar specifications were used by Willett and Forte (1969), Miller and Whitman (1970, 1972), Bryant and Henderschott (1972), Branson and Willett (1972), and Kouri and Porter (1974).

[39]See Branson and Willett (1972); also Whitman (1970) and the papers cited there. Fleming and Mundell (1964) had made the same sort of point in their paper on official intervention in the forward exchange market but did not see its general applicability. See also Kenen (1965), who criticized Tsiang (1959) for failing to distinguish between stock and flow effects of changes in the forward rate.

[40]See, for example, Branson (1975) and Girton and Henderson (1977).

[41]See, for example, Branson (1976), Kenen (1976), and Allen and Kenen (1980); the basic formulation goes back to Metzler (1951).

5. Conclusion

I have carried my story as far as I can without poaching on domains assigned to others. The story is brought up to date later in this Handbook, by Frenkel and Mussa in Chapter 14 and by the discussion of asset-market processes by Branson and Henderson in Chapter 15.

I have tried to show how stylized facts influenced the modeling of open economies in the 1950s and 1960s, paying particular attention to the way in which Keynesian models of the closed economy were opened to trade and capital flows. I have also tried to trace the origins of recent work — the monetary and portfolio approaches — paying particular attention to the ways in which they have introduced stock–flow relationships into models of the open economy. Those approaches made fundamental contributions and paved the way for further work — for introducing expectations into explanations of exchange-rate behavior and studying the problems of policy formation in interdependent national economies.

Those new approaches, however, may have had one detrimental influence. They have drawn our attention in two directions and thus drawn it away from the central issues of economic policy. The Keynesian models with which most economists worked in the 1950s and 1960s were designed to deal with the medium run — with the problems of achieving economic stability over an old-fashioned business cycle. The newer approaches have drawn attention to the very short run — to market processes determining exchange rates from day to day and week to week — and drawn attention to the very long run — to the never-never land of the stationary state where stocks of money, bonds, and wealth have adjusted fully. We may have to come back to the medium run of the typical Keynesian model if we are to deal in a useful way with the hardest problems of the world economy.

References

Alexander, S.S. (1952), "Effects of a devaluation on a trade balance", International Monetary Fund Staff Papers, 2:263–278. Reprinted in: R.E. Caves and H.G. Johnson, eds., Readings in international economics (Irwin, Homewood, 1968) 359–373.

Alexander, S.S. (1959), "Effects of a devaluation: A simplified synthesis of elasticities and absorption approaches", American Economic Review, 49:22–42.

Allen, P.R. and P.B. Kenen (1980), Asset markets, exchange rates, and economic integration (Cambridge University Press, London).

Bhagwati, J.N. (1958), "Immiserizing growth: A geometrical note", Review of Economic Studies, 25:201–205. Reprinted in: R.E. Caves and H.G. Johnson, eds., Readings in international economics (Irwin, Homewood, 1968) 300–305.

Bloomfield, A.I. (1963), Short-term capital movements under the pre-1914 gold standard (International Finance Section, Princeton University, Princeton).

Branson, W.H. (1968), Financial capital flows in the U.S. balance of payments (North-Holland, Amsterdam).

Branson, W.H. (1975), "Stocks and flows in international monetary analysis", in: A. Ando, R. Herring, and R. Marston, eds., International aspects of stabilization policies (Federal Reserve Bank of Boston and International Seminar in Public Economics, Boston) 27–50.

Branson, W.H. (1976), "Portfolio equilibrium and monetary policy with foreign and nontraded assets", in: E. Claassen and P. Salin, eds., Recent issues in international monetary economics (North-Holland, Amsterdam) 241–250.

Branson, W.H. and T.D. Willett (1972), "Policy toward short-term capital movements; some implications of the portfolio approach", in: F. Machlup, W.S. Salant, and L. Tarshis, eds., International mobility and movement of capital (National Bureau of Economic Research, New York) 287–310.

Bryant, R.C. and P.H. Hendershott (1972), "Empirical analysis of capital flows: Some consequences of alternative specifications", in: F. Machlup, W.S. Salant, and L. Tarshis, eds., International mobility and movement of capital (National Bureau of Economic Research, New York) 207–240.

Cooper, R.N. (1969), "Macroeconomic policy adjustment in interdependent economies", Quarterly Journal of Economics, 83:1–24.

Cooper, R.N. (1971), Currency devaluation in developing countries (International Finance Section, Princeton University, Princeton).

Corden, W.M. (1972), Monetary integration (International Finance Section, Princeton University, Princeton).

Dornbusch, R. (1973), "Currency depreciation, hoarding, and relative prices", Journal of Political Economy, 81:893–915.

Eichengreen, B.J. (1981), Sterling and the tariff, 1929–32. (International Finance Section, Princeton University, Princeton).

Fleming, J.M. (1962), "Domestic financial policies under fixed and under floating exchange rates", International Monetary Fund Staff Papers, 9:369–379.

Fleming, J.M. and R.A. Mundell (1964), "Official intervention on the forward exchange market", International Monetary Fund Staff Papers, 11:1–17.

Friedman, M. (1953), "The case for flexible exchange rates", in: M. Friedman, Essays in positive economics (University of Chicago Press, Chicago) 157–203. Reprinted in: R.E. Caves and H.G. Johnson, eds., Readings in international economics (Irwin, Homewood, 1968) 413–437.

Friedman, M. (1956), "The quantity theory of money – a restatement", in: M. Friedman, ed., Studies in the quantity theory of money (University of Chicago Press, Chicago) 3–21.

Friedman, M. (1968), "The role of monetary policy", American Economic Review, 58:1–17.

Girton, L. and D. Henderson (1977), "Central bank operations in foreign and domestic assets under fixed and flexible exchange rates", in: P.B. Clark, D.E. Logue, and R.J. Sweeney, eds., The effects of exchange rate adjustments (U.S. Treasury, Washington) 151–178.

Grassman, S. (1980), "Long-term trends in openness of national economies", Oxford Economic Papers, 32:123–133.

Gray, H.P. (1964), "Marginal cost of hot money", Journal of Political Economy, 72:189–192.

Haberler, G. (1949), "The market for foreign exchange and the stability of the balance of payments: A theoretical analysis", Kyklos, 3:193–218.

Hahn, F.H. (1959), "The balance of payments in a monetary economy", Review of Economic Studies, 26:110–125.

Hahn, F.H. (1977), "The monetary approach to the balance of payments", Journal of International Economics, 7:231–249.

Harberger, A.C. (1950), "Currency depreciation, income and the balance of trade", Journal of Political Economy, 58:47–60. Reprinted in: R.E. Caves and H.G. Johnson, eds., Readings in international economics (Irwin, Homewood, 1968) 341–358.

Hirschman, A.O. (1949), "Devaluation and the trade balance: A note", Review of Economics and Statistics, 31:50–53.

Johnson, H.G. (1956), "The transfer problem and exchange stability", Journal of Political Economy, 64:212–225. Reprinted in: R.E. Caves and H.G. Johnson, eds., Readings in international economics (Irwin, Homewood, 1968) 148–171.

Johnson, H.G. (1961), "Towards a general theory of the balance of payments", in H.G. Johnson, International trade and economic growth (Harvard University Press, Cambridge) 153–168. Reprinted in: R.E. Caves and H.G. Johnson, eds., Reading in international economics (Irwin, Homewood, 1968) 374–388.

Johnson, H.G. (1972a), "The case for flexible exchange rates", in: H.G. Johnson, Further essays in monetary economics (Allen and Unwin, London) 198–222.

Johnson, H.G. (1972b), "The monetary approach to balance-of-payments theory", Journal of Financial and Quantitative Analysis, 7:1555–1572. Reprinted in: J.A. Frenkel and H.G. Johnson, eds., The monetary approach to the balance of payments (University of Toronto Press, Toronto, 1976) 147–167.

Johnson, H.G. (1977), "The monetary approach to the balance of payments: A non-technical guide", Journal of International Economics, 7:251–268.

Jones, R.W. (1961), "Stability conditions in international trade: A general equilibrium analysis", International Economic Review, 2:199–209.

Kenen, P.B. (1965), "Trade, speculation, and the forward exchange rate", in: R.E. Baldwin, et al., Trade, growth and the balance of payments (Rand-McNally, Chicago) 143–169.

Kenen, P.B. (1969a), "The future of gold: A round table", American Economic Review, 59:362–364.

Kenen, P.B. (1969b), "The theory of optimum currency areas: An eclectic view", in: R.A. Mundell and A.K. Swoboda, eds., Monetary problems of the international economy (University of Chicago, Chicago) 41–60.

Kenen, P.B. (1976), Capital mobility and financial integration: A survey (International Finance Section, Princeton University, Princeton).

Keynes, J.M. (1919), The economic consequences of the peace (Macmillan, London).

Keynes, J.M. (1923), A tract on monetary reform (Cambridge University Press, London).

Keynes, J.M. (1929), "The German transfer problem", Economic Journal, 39:1–7.

Keynes, J.M. (1936), The general theory of employment, interest, and money (Macmillan, London).

Kouri, P.J.K. and M.G. Porter (1974), "International capital flows and portfolio equilibrium", Journal of Political Economy, 82:443–467.

Laursen, S. and L.A. Metzler (1950), "Flexible exchange rates and the theory of employment", Review of Economics and Statistics, 32:281–299.

Lerner, A.P. (1944), The economics of control (Macmillan, New York).

Lindbeck, A. (1979), Inflation and open economies (North-Holland, Amsterdam).

Machlup, F. (1939), "The theory of foreign exchanges", Economica, 6:375–397.

Machlup, F. (1943), International trade and the national income multiplier (Blakiston, Philadelphia).

Machlup, F. (1956), "The terms of trade effects of devaluation upon real income and the balance of trade", Kyklos, 9:417–452.

Markowitz, H.M. (1959), Portfolio selection (Wiley, New York).

Marshall, A. (1923), Money, credit, and commerce (Macmillan, London).

McKinnon, R.I. (1963), "Optimum currency areas", American Economic Review, 53:717–725.

McKinnon, R.I. (1969), "Portfolio balance and international payments adjustment", in: R.A. Mundell and A.K. Swoboda, eds., Monetary problems of the international economy (University of Chicago Press, Chicago) 199–234.

McKinnon, R.I. (1979), Money in international exchange: The convertible currency system (Oxford University Press, New York).

McKinnon, R.I. (1981), "The exchange rate and macroeconomic policy: Changing postwar perceptions", Journal of Economic Literature, 19:531–557.

McKinnon, R.I. and W.E. Oates (1966), The implications of international economic integration for monetary, fiscal, and exchange-rate policies (International Finance Section, Princeton University, Princeton).

Meade, J.E. (1951), The balance of payments (Oxford University Press, London).

Meade, J.E. (1955), "The case for variable exchange rates", Three Banks Review, 27:3–28.

Metzler, L.A. (1942a), "Underemployment equilibrium in international trade", Econometrica, 10:97–112.

Metzler, L.A. (1942b), "The transfer problem reconsidered", Journal of Political Economy, 50:397–414. Reprinted in: H.S. Ellis and L.A. Metzler, eds., Readings in the theory of international trade (Blakiston, Philadelphia, 1949) 179–197.

Metzler, L.A. (1951), "Wealth, saving and the rate of interest", Journal of Political Economy, 59:930–946.

Metzler, L.A. (1960), "The process of international adjustment under conditions of full employment: A Keynesian view", published in: R.E. Caves and H.G. Johnson, eds., Readings in international economics (Irwin, Homewood, 1968) 465–486.

Miller, N.C. and M.v.N. Whitman (1970), "A mean-variance analysis of United States long-term portfolio foreign investment", Quarterly Journal of Economics, 84:175–196.

Miller, N.C. and M.v.N. Whitman (1972), "The outflow of short-term funds from the United States: Adjustment of stocks and flows", in F. Machlup, W.A. Salant, and L. Tarshis, eds., International mobility and movement of capital (National Bureau of Economic Research, New York) 253–286.

Mundell, R.A. (1960), "The monetary dynamics of international adjustment under fixed and flexible exchange rates", Quarterly Journal of Economics, 74:227–257.

Mundell, R.A. (1961a), "The international disequilibrium system", Kyklos, 14:154–172.

Mundell, R.A. (1961b), "A theory of optimum currency areas", American Economic Review, 51:657–665.

Mundell, R.A. (1962), "The appropriate use of monetary and fiscal policy for internal and external stability", International Monetary Fund Staff Papers, 9:70–77.

Mundell, R.A. (1963), "Capital mobility and stabilization policy under fixed and flexible exchange rates", Canadian Journal of Economics, 29:475–485. Reprinted in: R.E. Caves and H.G. Johnson, eds., Readings in international economics (Irwin, Homewood, 1968) 487–499.

Mundell, R.A. (1968), "Barter theory and the monetary mechanisms of adjustment", in: R.A. Mundell, International economics (Macmillan, New York) 111–139. Reprinted in: J.A. Frenkel and H.G. Johnson, eds., The monetary approach to the balance of payments (University of Toronto Press, Toronto, 1976) 64–91.

Mundell, R.A. (1971), "The international distribution of money in a growing world economy", in: R.A. Mundell, Monetary theory (Goodyear, Pacific Palisades) 147–169. Reprinted in: J.A. Frenkel and H.G. Johnson, eds., The monetary approach to the balance of payments (University of Toronto Press, Toronto, 1976) 92–108.

Negishi, T. (1968), "Approaches to the analysis of devaluation", International Economic Review, 9:218–227.

Nurkse, R. (1944), International currency experience (League of Nations, Geneva).

Ohlin, B. (1929), "The reparation problem: Transfer difficulties, real and imagined", Economic Journal, 39:172–173.

Orcutt, G.H. (1950), "Measurement of price elasticities in international trade", Review of Economics and Statistics, 32:117–132. Reprinted in: R.E. Caves and H.G. Johnson, eds., Readings in International Economics (Irwin, Homewood, 1968) 528–552.

Patinkin, D. (1956), Money, interest, and prices (Harper & Row, New York).

Patrick, J.D. (1973), "Establishing convergent decentralized policy assignment", Journal of International Economics, 3:37–52.

Polak, J.J. (1957), "Monetary analysis of income formation and payments problems", International Monetary Fund Staff Papers, 6:1–50.

Robinson, J. (1947), Essays in the theory of employment (Blackwell, Oxford).

Salop, J. (1974), "Devaluation and the balance of trade under flexible wages", in: G. Horwich and P.A. Samuelson, eds., Trade, stability, and macroeconomics (Academic Press, New York) 129–151.

Salter, W.E.G. (1959), "International and external balance: The role of price and expenditure effects", Economic Record, 35:226–238.

Samuelson, P.A. (1952), "The transfer problem and transport costs: The terms of trade when impediments are absent", Economic Journal, 62:278–304. Reprinted in: J.E. Stiglitz, ed., The collected scientific papers of Paul A. Samuelson, II (MIT Press, Cambridge, 1966) 985–1011.

Samuelson, P.A. (1971), "On the trail of conventional beliefs about the transfer problem", in: J.N. Bhagwati, et al., eds., Trade, balance of payments and growth (North-Holland, Amsterdam) 327–351. Reprinted in: R.C. Merton, ed., The collected scientific papers of Paul A. Samuelson, III (MIT Press, Cambridge, 1972) 374–398.

Sohmen, E. (1969), Flexible exchange rates (University of Chicago Press, Chicago).

Solomon, R. (1977). The international monetary system, 1945–1976 (Harper & Row, New York).

Swan, T.W. (1963), "Longer-run problems of the balance of payments", in: H.W. Arndt and W.M. Corden, eds., The Australian economy: A volume of readings (Cheshire Press, Melbourne) 384–395. Reprinted in: R.E. Caves and H.G. Johnson, eds., Readings in international economics (Irwin, Homewood, 1968) 455–464.

Ch. 13: Macroeconomic Theory and Policy   677

Tinbergen, J. (1952), On the theory of economic policy (North-Holland, Amsterdam).

Tobin, J. (1967), "Liquidity preference as behavior toward risk", in: D.D. Hester and J. Tobin, eds., Risk aversion and portfolio choice (Wiley, New York) 1–26.

Tobin, J. (1969), "A general equilibrium approach to monetary theory", Journal of Money, Credit and Banking, 1:15–30.

Tower, E. and T.D. Willett (1976), "The theory of optimum currency areas" (International Finance Section, Princeton University, Princeton).

Tsiang, S.C. (1959), "The theory of forward exchange and effects of government intervention on the forward exchange market", International Monetary Fund Staff Papers, 7:75–106.

Tsiang, S.C. (1961), "The role of money in trade-balance stability: Synthesis of the elasticity and absorption approaches", American Economic Review, 51:912–936. Reprinted in: R.E. Caves and H.G. Johnson, eds., Readings in international economics (Irwin, Homewood, 1968) 389–412.

Whitman, M.v.N. (1970), Policies for internal and external balance (International Finance Section, Princeton University, Princeton).

Whitman, M.v.N. (1972), "Place prosperity and people prosperity: The delineation of optimum policy areas", in: M. Perlman and C.J. Levin, eds., Spatial, regional and population economics (Gordon and Breach, New York) 395–393.

Whitman, M.v.N. (1975), "Global monetarism and the monetary approach to the balance of payments", Brookings Papers on Economic Activity, 3:121–166.

Willett, T.D. and F. Forte (1969), "Interest rate policy and external balance", Quarterly Journal of Economics, 83:242–262.

[4]

Forward Rates, Interest Rates, and Expectations Under Alternative Exchange Rate Regimes*

PETER B. KENEN

Princeton University,
Princeton, NJ 08544

A model comprising spot and forward foreign exchange markets and a domestic credit market is used to examine the trade-off between volatility in the nominal exchange rate and domestic interest rate. It also shows how a slowly crawling spot rate can raise interest rate volatility and the amplitude of reserve flows. Finally, the paper extends a finding by Driskill and McCafferty that the exchange rate effects of external shocks are differently affected by the responsiveness of speculation to expected profits; high responsiveness makes the spot exchange rate more sensitive to foreign financial shocks but less sensitive to trade balance shocks.

From September 1974 through November 1976, the Australian dollar was pegged to a trade-weighted index (TWI) of foreign currencies; its value in terms of the US dollar was adjusted daily to stabilize its value in terms of the TWI. After the devaluation on 28 November 1976, Australia moved to a crawling peg. The rate of crawl was not predetermined, but frequent changes were made in the peg between the Australian dollar and TWI, and these were implemented by corresponding changes in the bilateral rate with the US dollar (the rate at which the Reserve Bank bought up the net positions of Australian trading banks at the close of each business day).[1]

These arrangements came under attack in the second half of 1983. They were criticized by the financial press and other observers because Australia appeared to be purchasing short-run stability in the foreign exchange market at the price of instability in domestic financial markets. The nominal exchange rate was less volatile than those of most other advanced countries, whether measured in terms of the TWI or US dollar, but short-term interest rates had become more volatile than those of many other countries. The arrangements were attacked in the foreign exchange market because participants came to believe that a revaluation could be expected, but the authorities refused to validate that expectation by speeding up the crawl. In the third quarter of 1983, private capital inflows averaged more than $635 million per month; in the fourth quarter, more than $1.2 billion per month. Official reserves rose by $2.9 billion in the fourth quarter alone, driving the growth rate of the money supply far above target.

In October 1983, the Reserve Bank made several changes in exchange rate arrangements designed to reduce the capital inflow. These proved to be inadequate. On 9 December 1983, the Australian dollar was allowed to float, and most exchange controls were rescinded.

* This paper was drafted during my visit to the Australian National University, made possible by a Professorial Fellowship awarded by the Reserve Bank of Australia. It has benefited from comments by referees and by participants in seminars at the Reserve Bank, the ANU, and the Universities of Adelaide, Melbourne, and New South Wales.

[1] There was one large change in the peg; on 8 March 1983, the Australian dollar was devalued by 10 per cent in terms of the TWI. For a detailed description of Australia's exchange rate arrangements, see Polasek and Lewis (1985); for an empirical analysis of the crawl, see Gross and Hogan (1982).

This paper was inspired by Australian experience before the float. It uses a simple model of foreign exchange and financial markets to show when and why there will be a trade-off between volatility in the nominal exchange rate and in the domestic interest rate. It also explores the problem of modelling expectations under alternative exchange rate arrangements and shows how a slowly crawling rate can amplify interest rate volatility.

The model has three markets, and they are linked by the activities of domestic firms. In the domestic credit market, supply depends on the reserves of the commercial banks, which depend in turn on the central bank's open market operations and its interventions on the foreign exchange market. Demand is the difference between the total demand for credit by domestic firms and their net foreign borrowing, which depends in turn on the covered interest differential. In the forward foreign exchange market, supply depends on the activities of speculators, who sell foreign currency forward whenever the prevailing forward rate is higher than their forecast of the future spot rate. Demand depends on the volume of foreign borrowing by domestic firms, because they buy foreign currency forward to cover their foreign currency debts. In the spot foreign exchange market, supply depends on the volume of borrowing by domestic firms, because they sell foreign currency spot whenever they borrow it. Demand is identified with the state of the current account balance.

The model is used to examine a number of issues. It is made to replicate the familiar proposition that monetary policy is more effective under a floating rate than under a pegged rate, but new reasons are adduced for that proposition. The model is also made to show how the exchange rate regime affects the transmission of external shocks. Under a pegged exchange rate, for example, foreign financial shocks are transmitted strongly to domestic financial markets; under a floating rate, their influence is weaker. This is the sense in which there is a trade-off between exchange rate stability and interest rate stability.

Later, the model is modified to deal with a wider range of exchange rate arrangements. The central bank is assumed to keep the spot rate from changing by more than a fraction of the change that would take place if the rate was floating freely, and speculators are assumed to base their expectations on that hypothetical floating rate. It is then shown how the interest rate and balance of payments depend on the difference between the speed at which the authorities permit the spot rate to move

and the speed at which it would move if it was free to float. When the central bank leans heavily against the wind, permitting the spot rate to change by only a small fraction of the change that would take place under a free float, changes in the interest rate and balance of payments produced by domestic and foreign disturbances can be even larger than those that occur when the spot exchange rate is rigidly pegged. From this standpoint, then, a slow crawl may be inferior to a rigid peg.

The model does not afford a basis for choosing among alternative exchange rate arrangements; it does not take adequate account of connections between the financial and real sides of the economy. It is likewise too simple to represent the Australian financial system. Nevertheless, it captures certain features of that system, and it is more elaborate than most other models concerned with spot and forward markets, including the classic model in Tsiang (1959), on which it draws heavily, and the model in Driskill and McCafferty (1982), which also focuses on volatility. The model deals with flow equilibria rather than the stock equilibria found in portfolio balance models. It ignores intertemporal connections between spot and forward markets.[2] But it has three markets rather than two, and the domestic interest rate is determined endogenously.

I The Model

The three markets in this model are linked by covered interest arbitrage. An increase in the foreign interest rate shifts borrowing by domestic firms from foreign to domestic lenders. This shift shows up in the market for domestic credit as an increase in demand, and it tends therefore to raise the domestic interest rate. It shows up in the market for forward foreign exchange as a decrease in demand, because firms that borrow less from

---

[2] If speculators sell foreign currency forward today, they will have to buy it back spot tomorrow. This point is modelled formally by McCormick (1977) and was discussed in Kenen (1965). In that paper, incidentally, I criticized Tsiang for separating speculators, arbitrageurs, and hedgers; a firm engaged in international trade will be all three, and factors affecting its involvement in speculation, including its net worth and attitude toward risk, will affect its involvement in arbitrage and hedging. The same criticism applies to the model in this paper (albeit less forcefully, because there is no trade related hedging in the forward market).

foreign lenders have smaller repayments to cover, and it tends therefore to reduce the forward premium on the foreign currency. Finally, it shows up in the market for spot foreign exchange as a decrease in supply, because the capital inflow falls, and it tends therefore to raise the spot price of the foreign currency.

The Market for Bank Credit

The flow supply of credit from domestic banks rises with the growth rate of the banks' reserves and with the domestic interest rate:

$$L^s = L^s(R, \ r), \ L^s_1 > 0, \ L^s_2 > 0 \qquad (1)$$

where R is the increase in the banks' reserves and r is the domestic interest rate. The increase in bank reserves is

$$R = E + B \qquad (2)$$

where E is the increase in domestic assets held by the central bank and B is the increase in its foreign assets (and equals the balance of payments surplus measured in domestic currency).[3]

The flow demand for bank credit is the difference between the total flow demand for credit by domestic firms and net foreign borrowing by those firms:

$$L^d = L^t(r) - L^f(c), \ L^t_1 < 0, \ L^f_1 < 0 \qquad (3)$$

where c is the covered interest differential:

$$c = r^* + p - r. \qquad (4)$$

Here, r^* is the foreign interest rate and p is the forward premium on the foreign currency:

$$p = (x^f - x)/x \qquad (5)$$

where x^f is the forward exchange rate and x is the spot exchange rate, both measured in units of domestic currency per unit of foreign currency. Initially, $r = r^*$, and $x = x^f = 1$, so that $p = c = 0$.[4]

In many models of spot and forward markets, covered interest parity holds at all times ($c = 0$); in other words, $L^f_1 \to -\infty$. This supposition is introduced later as a limiting case, and that is the

[3] Equation (2) ignores the effects of changes in the demand for currency and other factors that impinge on the central bank's balance sheet.

[4] The model can be made more general by writing the total flow demand as $L^t(r, \ r^* + p)$, $L^t_1 < 0$, $L^t_2 < 0$. But the substitution of this formulation for the one in equation (3) does not change the sign of any outcome in this paper unless an increase in r^* or p reduces the total flow demand by more than it reduces net foreign borrowing (i.e., unless $L^t_2 > L^f_1$).

most informative way to treat it. In Eurocurrency markets, c is close to zero, for reasons described by Herring and Marston (1976). Elsewhere, it can differ markedly from zero, because of restrictions on capital movements or risk aversion on the part of arbitrageurs. No exchange rate risk attaches to covered interest arbitrage, but default risk attaches to a forward contract and may also attach to the debt instruments involved.[5]

The market for bank credit clears at all times:

$$L^s - L^d = 0. \qquad (6)$$

The Forward Market

The forward market accommodates arbitrage and speculation. There is no trade related hedging.[6] The flow supply of forward exchange is therefore identified with pure speculation:

$$F^s = (1/x^f)F^s(x^f - x^e), \ F^s_1 > 0 \qquad (7)$$

where x^e is the expected spot exchange rate, and $x^e = x$ initially.[7] The flow demand for forward

[5] For more on this issue, see Eaton and Turnovsky (1983), who model the way that default risk and exchange rate risk affect the influence of monetary policy on the behaviour of a floating exchange rate. (Their conclusions are consistent with those shown in Tables 3 and 4, below, for the effects of changes in E.)

[6] We could add trade related hedging by assuming that a fraction z of the current account deficit, defined in equation (12) below, shows up in the forward market, so that the fraction $1-z$ shows up in the spot market. This amendment complicates the algebra but alters the sign of only one outcome. Under a pegged exchange rate, an autonomous increase in the current account deficit reduces c in the absence of trade related hedging; it can raise or reduce c in the presence of such hedging. (Australian readers will note that the omission of trade related hedging makes the forward market in this paper much like the Australian 'hedge' market and omits the 'official' forward market. Arbitrage and speculation have been accommodated in the hedge market; trade related transactions have been accommodated in the 'official' forward market. On this interpretation, p stands for the hedge-market premium, and the analysis applies to the Australian case without major modification.)

[7] The function $F^s(x^f - x^e)$ is defined in domestic currency and multiplied by $(1/x^f)$ to express the variable F^s in foreign currency. In many recent models of exchange rate behaviour, speculators are risk neutral and free to assume indefinitely large positions, long or short, in the spot or forward market; in other words, $F^s_1 \to \infty$. This supposition is treated later as a limiting case (just like the supposition that $L^f_1 \to -\infty$). Work by McCallum (1977) suggests that the elasticity of speculation is less than infinite, even when estimated in the context of a rational-expectations model.

foreign exchange is identified with covering by firms engaged in net foreign borrowing:

$$F^d = (1/x^f) \, L^f(c). \qquad (8)$$

The forward market clears without official intervention:

$$F^s - F^d = 0. \qquad (9)$$

In one version of this model, exchange rate expectations are exogenous:

$$dx^e = dx^{ea}. \qquad (10a)$$

In a second version, they are endogenous and depend on the behaviour of the currency spot rate:

$$dx^e = bdx, \; 0 \leqslant b \leqslant 1. \qquad (10b)$$

It should be noted that equations (10a) and (10b) are concerned with expectations about the level of the spot rate, not the rate of change. When $b = 0$ in equation (10b), speculators believe that the future spot rate will be what the actual spot rate was initially; in other words, the current change in x is deemed to be temporary. When $b = 1$ speculators believe that the future spot rate will be what the actual spot rate is currently; in other words, the current change in x is deemed to be permanent. In a third version of the model, dealing with a crawling peg or managed float, expectations depend on the spot rate that would be observed if the rate were floating freely, rather than the actual (managed) spot rate. An algebraic representation is given later.

The Spot Market

The flow supply of spot foreign exchange comes from net foreign borrowing (the capital inflow):

$$S^s = (1/x)L^f(c). \qquad (11)$$

The flow demand for spot foreign exchange is identified with the current account deficit:

$$S^d = (1/x)T(x, q), \; T_1 < 0, \; T_2 > 0. \qquad (12)$$

A depreciation of the domestic currency reduces the current account deficit (the Marshall-Lerner-Robinson condition is always satisfied); but the deficit can change for other reasons too — the shifts denoted by changes in q.[*] The balance of payments surplus is

---

[*] The current account deficit is defined in domestic currency, so S^s and S^d are defined in foreign currency. If the current account balance traced out a J curve after a change in x, T_1 would be positive, and this could destabilize the floating rate version of the model.

$$B = x(S^s - S^d) \qquad (13)$$

and $B = 0$ under a floating rate.

II Disturbances to Equilibrium

Differentiating the entire model and using more compact notation, we obtain this system:

$$
\begin{bmatrix}
(e+n) & -e & 0 & k \\
e & -(e+s)-s(1-b) & 0 & \\
e & -e & t & -1
\end{bmatrix}
\begin{bmatrix}
dr \\
dp \\
dx \\
dB
\end{bmatrix}
$$
$$
=
\begin{bmatrix}
1 \\
1 \\
1
\end{bmatrix}
edr^* +
\begin{bmatrix}
-kdE \\
-sdx^{ea} \\
dT^a
\end{bmatrix}
\qquad (14)
$$

where $e = -L_1^f > 0$, $n = L_2^s - L_1^s > 0$, $s = F_1^s > 0$, $k = L_1^s > 0$, $t = -T_1 > 0$, and $dT^a = T_2 dq \gtrless 0$.

The first row in this system relates to the credit market, the second to the forward market, and the third to the spot market. The term e is the arbitrage effect, describing the decrease in foreign borrowing caused by an increase in the covered interest differential. The term n is the credit supply effect, describing the increase in the excess supply of bank credit caused by an increase in the domestic interest rate. The term s is the speculative effect, describing the increase in the speculative supply of forward foreign exchange caused by an increase in the difference between the forward and expected spot rates. The term k is the reserve effect, describing the increase in the supply of bank credit caused by a faster increase in the banks' reserves. The term t is the trade effect, defining the decrease in the demand for spot foreign exchange caused by a depreciation of the domestic currency. Finally, dT^a is an autonomous increase in the demand for spot foreign exchange caused by an autonomous increase in the current account deficit.

The same set of equations is represented in Figure 1, where $r = r^*$ initially, and $x = x^f = x^e$, so that $p = c = 0$. The three curves are obtained by solving equations (14) for the change in r required to clear each market when there is a change in p, given the values of x, r^*, E, and q. (The spot market equation is converted into a market-clearing equation by setting $B = 0$.)

The *SS* curve describes equilibrium in the spot

98 *Exchange Rates and the Monetary System*

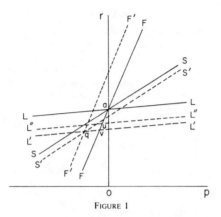

FIGURE 1

market. An increase in p requires an equal increase in r to keep c constant and prevent any change in the capital inflow. Therefore, the SS curve is a 45° line. Above SS, c falls and raises the capital inflow, producing excess supply in the spot market; B rises with a pegged exchange rate, and x falls with a floating rate. An increase in x shifts SS downward. The current account improves, producing excess supply in the spot market, so r must fall at each p in order to raise c and reduce the capital inflow.[9]

The FF curve describes equilibrium in the forward market. It is steeper than the SS curve because an increase in p has two effects on the forward market. First, it raises c, which reduces the arbitrage demand for forward foreign exchange. Second, it raises x^f, given x, which opens a gap between x^f and x^e and raises the speculative supply of forward foreign exchange. The increase in r required to clear the forward market must be large enough to offset both effects and must therefore exceed the increase in p. (In different terms, r must rise by enough to turn c negative, not just return it to zero, because the arbitrage demand must rise to match the increase in the speculative supply.) Above FF, c falls and raises the arbitrage demand, producing excess

[9] An increase in r^* shifts the SS curve upward; by raising c at each r and p, it reduces the capital inflow and produces excess demand in the spot market, so r must rise at each p to bring c back to zero. (As an increase in r^* also shifts the FF and LL curves upward, its effects are hard to illustrate and are not shown below.) An autonomous increase in the current account deficit $(dT^a > 0)$ also produces excess demand in the spot market and shifts SS upward.

demand in the forward market and thus raising x^f. An increase in x shifts FF upward unless $b = 1$. At the initial p, x^f rises by as much as x, but x^e rises by less than x when $b < 1$. Hence, x^f rises by more than x^e, stimulating speculative sales and producing excess supply in the forward market, and r must thus rise at each p to reduce c and raise the arbitrage demand. An autonomous increase in the expected spot rate $(dx^{ea} > 0)$ shifts FF downward. By raising x^e, it opens a (negative) gap between x^f and x^e, depressing speculative sales and producing excess demand in the forward market.

The LL curve describes equilibrium in the credit market. It is flatter than the SS curve because an increase in r has three effects on the credit market. First, it raises the supply of domestic credit. Second, it reduces the total demand for credit by domestic firms. Third, it lowers c, shifting the demand for credit from domestic to foreign lenders. Accordingly, p must rise by more than r to clear the credit market. (It must rise by enough to turn c positive, because foreign borrowing must fall to match the combined effects of the increase in the supply of credit and decrease in the total demand for credit.) Above LL, the same three effects of an increase in r generate excess supply in the credit market, reducing r. A change in x does not affect the position of LL, but an increase in B or E shifts it downward. By increasing the banks' reserves, an increase in B or E creates supply in the credit market, so r must fall to clear that market by reducing supply and raising demand.

Solutions with a Floating Spot Rate

When the spot exchange rate floats freely, B stays at zero, and equations (14) can be solved for the changes in r, p, and x caused by various disturbances. The determinant is $- D$, where

$$D = n[t(e + s) + es(1 - b)] + ets$$

and these are the solutions[10]:

$$dr = (1/D)ets(dx^{ea} + dr^*) - (1/D)es(1 - b)dT^a$$
$$- (1/D)[t(e + s) + es(1 - b)]kdE \qquad (15)$$

$$dp = (1/D)s(e + n)[tdx^{ea} - (1 - b)dT^a]$$
$$- (1/D)e[t + s(1 - b)](ndr^* + kdE) \,(16)$$

[10] Strictly, the solutions for autonomous changes in expectations $(dx^{ea} \neq 0)$ should be presented separately and evaluated at $b = 0$. But the outcomes in Table 1 would not be affected.

$$dx = (1/D)es(dx^{ea} + ndr^* + kdE)$$
$$+ (1/D)s[t(e+n) + en]dx^{ea} \qquad (17)$$

$$dx^f = (1/D)s[t(e+n) + en]dx^{ea}$$
$$+ (1/D)[s(e+n)b + en]dT^a$$
$$- (1/D)e[(t-s) + s(1-b)](ndr^* + kdE) \qquad (18)$$

$$dc = (1/D)st(ndx^{ea} + ndr^* + kdE)$$
$$- (1/D)ns(1-b)dT^a \qquad (19)$$

The signs of these effects are shown in Table 1, and two sets are illustrated in Figures 1 and 2, along with the corresponding pegged rate results.[11]

Figure 1 illustrates the short-run effects of an easier monetary policy: an increase in E, representing faster growth in the banks' reserves and, therefore, an increase in the flow supply of credit. It was shown before that the credit market curve shifts downward in response to an increase in E. It goes from LL to $L'L'$ in Figure 1, and there is excess supply in the credit market at the initial point a, where r was Oa (and equal to r^*), and p and c were zero. The domestic interest rate begins to fall, raising c and reducing the capital inflow, and excess demand develops in the spot market. Therefore, the domestic currency starts to depreciate, shifting the spot market curve downward from SS to $S'S'$ and shifting the forward market curve upward from FF to $F'F'$. Asset markets return to equilibrium at q, where $L'L'$, $S'S'$, and $F'F'$ intersect. The domestic interest rate has fallen, the foreign currency has gone to a discount forward, and c has risen (because r has fallen by more than p). There is a reduction in the capital inflow, matched by an improvement in the current account balance resulting from the depreciation of the domestic currency. (The sign of the change in x^f is ambiguous, however, because x has risen but p has fallen.)

[11] Note that c cannot change in response to changes in E, r^*, or exchange rate expectations when $t = 0$. Changes in c generate capital flows, which call for the current account to change when the exchange rate floats freely. If the current account does not respond immediately to a change in the spot exchange rate, covered interest parity will be maintained in the face of certain disturbances, even though the supply of arbitrage funds is not perfectly elastic. (By contrast, an autonomous shift in the current account balance changes c even when t is zero; the initial shift in the current account accommodates the resulting capital flow.)

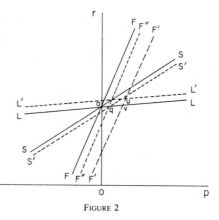

FIGURE 2

TABLE 1

Signs of Effects of Various Disturbances under a Floating Exchange Rate

Effect	Disturbance			
	dE	dx^{ea}	dr^*	dT^a
dr	−	+	+	−
dp	−	+	−	−
dx	+	+	+	+
dx^f	*	+	*	+
dc	+	+	+	−

*Negative if $b = 0$; otherwise ambiguous.

Figure 2 illustrates the effects of an autonomous change in exchange rate expectations. It was shown before that the forward market curve shifts downward in response to an increase in x^e. It goes from FF to $F'F'$ in Figure 2, and there is excess demand in the forward market at the initial equilibrium point. The foreign currency goes to a premium forward, raising c and reducing the capital inflow, as in the previous case, so excess demand develops in the spot market. The domestic currency starts to depreciate, shifting the spot market curve downward from SS to $S'S'$ and the forward market curve upward from $F'F'$ to $F''F''$. Asset markets return to equilibrium at q, where LL, $S'S'$, and $F''F''$ intersect. The domestic interest rate has risen, the foreign currency has gone to a premium forward and c has risen (because r has risen by less than p). There is, again, a reduction in the capital inflow, matched by an improvement in the current account resulting from the depreciation of the domestic currenty.[12] (In this case, however, x^f has risen, because x and p have both risen.)

Solutions with a Pegged Spot Rate

When the spot exchange rate is pegged, B varies but x does not, and equations (14) can be solved for the changes in r, p, and B caused by various disturbances. The determinant is

$$H = n(e + s) + es(1 + k)$$

and these are the solutions[13].

$$d\bar{r} = (1/H)es(1 + k)(dx^{ea} + dr^*) + (1/H)(e + s)kdT^a$$
$$- (1/H)(e + s)kdE \qquad (15')$$

$$d\bar{p} = (1/H)s[n + e(1 + k)]dx^{ea}$$
$$- (1/H)e(ndr^* - kdT^a + kdE) \qquad (16')$$

$$d\bar{B} = - (1/H)se(ndx^{ea} + ndr^* + kdE)$$
$$- (1/H)[n(e + s) + es]dT^a \qquad (17')$$

$$d\bar{x}^f = d\bar{p} \qquad (18')$$

$$d\bar{c} = (1/H)s(ndx^{ea} + ndr^* - kdT^a + kdE) \qquad (19')$$

The signs of these effects are shown in Table 2, and two sets of outcomes are illustrated in Figures 1 and 2.

In Figure 1, which shows the effects of an increase in E, there is again a downward shift in the credit market curve from LL to $L'L'$, and excess supply in the credit market at the initial values of r and p. The domestic interest rate starts to fall, raising c and reducing the capital inflow, and excess demand develops in the spot market. When the exchange rate is pegged, however, the central bank satisfies that excess demand by selling foreign currency from its own reserves. There are no shifts in the SS and FF curves, because the exchange rate does not change. Therefore, asset market equilibrium moves at once from a to v, where $L'L'$ intersects FF. But the supply of bank loans starts to contract, because reserve losses by the central bank reduce growth in the cash reserves held by

[12] With an increase in E, r had to fall to clear the credit market, because the disturbance created excess supply. With an expectation of depreciation, r has to rise to clear that market, because the increase in p induces firms to switch from foreign to domestic borrowing, creating excess demand in the credit market.

[13] Overbars are used to denote the pegged rate solutions.

the commercial banks, and the credit market curve moves upward from $L'L'$ to $L''L''$. Asset market equilibrium moves from v to u, where $L''L''$ intersects FF. The domestic interest rate has fallen, the foreign currency has gone to a discount forward, and c has risen (because r has fallen by more than p). There is a reduction in the capital inflow, due to the increase in c, but no change in the current account balance. Accordingly, the balance of payments remains in deficit at u, an outcome confirmed by the fact that u lies below SS, where there is excess supply in the spot market.[14]

In Figure 2, which shows the effects of an autonomous change in exchange rate expectations, there is again a downward shift in the forward market curve, from FF to $F'F'$, and excess demand in the forward market at the initial values of r and p. The foreign currency goes to a premium forward, raising c and reducing the capital inflow, and excess demand develops in the spot market. As before, however, the central bank satisfies that excess demand by drawing down its reserves, and there are no shifts in the SS and $F'F'$ curves. Asset market equilibrium moves at once to v, where LL intersects $F'F'$. But the flow supply of bank credit falls, and the credit market curve moves upward from LL to $L'L'$, so asset market equilibrium moves from v to u, where $L'L'$ intersects $F'F'$. The domestic interest rate has risen, the foreign currency has gone to a premium forward, and c has risen (because r has risen by less than p). There is a reduction in the capital inflow, due to the

[14] To prove that $L''L''$ must lie between $L'L'$ and LL, not at one of the extremes, we have merely to show that the limiting cases involve contradictions. The curve cannot stay at $L'L'$ because the balance of payments deficit offsets some of the increase in E that shifted the curve from LL to $L'L'$. The curve cannot go all the way to LL (and thus intersect SS at a) because there would be no balance of payments deficit to offset part of the increase in E. (In the new equilibrium at u, commercial bank reserves are rising faster than they were before the increase in E but not as fast as they would in the absence of the balance of payments deficit. The situation at u cannot last indefinitely, however, because the central bank cannot continue to lose reserves; it must rescind the increase in E eventually in order to shift the credit market curve back to LL and eliminate the balance of payments deficit. An analogous caveat applies to the outcome at u in Figure 2. In that case, however, the central bank must reduce E below its initial level, not merely rescind an increase; it must shift the credit market curve upward from $L'L'$ to the intersection of the SS and $F'F'$ curves, raising r and p to even higher levels.)

increase in c, but no change in the current account balance. Accordingly, the balance of payments remains in deficit at u.

TABLE 2
Signs of Effects of Various Disturbances under a Pegged Exchange Rate

	Disturbance			
Effect	dE	dx^{ea}	dr^*	dT^a
dr	−	+	+	+
dp	−	+	−	+
dB	−	−	−	−
dx^f	−	+	−	+
dc	+	+	+	−

III Comparisons of Outcome under Floating and Pegged Rates

The solutions in the previous section lead to several important conclusions regarding the effects of exchange rate arrangements on responses to exogenous disturbances.

The Effectiveness of Monetary Policy

An increase in E may be deemed to represent an attempt by the monetary authorities to stimulate aggregate demand — to encourage borrowing for capital formation — by raising the supply of credit. Viewed from this standpoint, the results obtained in the previous section replicate and reinforce a familiar conclusion. Monetary policy is more effective under floating than pegged rates.[15] In Figure 1, asset market equilibrium moves all the way to q under a floating rate but moves only to u under a pegged rate. The domestic interest rate falls farther under a floating rate, and monetary policy is thus more effective.[16]

In this particular model, however, the difference in effectiveness is not due exclusively to the credit contraction that takes place with a pegged rate — the effect of the loss of reserves on which

---

[15] See Mundell (1968) and the survey of subsequent literature in Kenen (1985).

[16] There is, of course, another way in which monetary policy is made more effective by a floating rate. The domestic currency depreciates, switching domestic and foreign demands from foreign to domestic goods. Furthermore, the depreciation can raise aggregate demand by raising wealth. These exchange rate effects are additional to the larger interest rate effects discussed in the text.

comparisons usually concentrate. It is due in part to the effects of speculation.

The difference between outcomes at q and u, the floating rate and pegged rate equilibria, can be divided into two components, using the point v. The movement from v to u represents the effect of the credit contraction that takes place with a pegged rate. The movement from v to q represents the effect of speculation that takes place with a floating rate. It is brought about by the depreciation of the domestic currency, which raises x^f by more than x^e when $b<1$, causing speculators to sell foreign currency forward. Their sales drive down p, which reduces the increase in c and curtails the shift by domestic firms from foreign to domestic borrowing. Therefore, the interest rate must fall farther to clear the credit market.

Insulation from External Shocks

It used to be said that a floating exchange rate would insulate domestic markets from external shocks. But recent work has shown that this claim must be qualified. Complete insulation occurs in trade balance models, where there are no capital movements and the exchange rate is determined entirely by trade flows. It can occur in other models, but only in the long run, when the economy has reached a stationary state where capital movements have ceased, and only in respect of certain goods market disturbances.

The discussion of exchange rate arrangements in Australia revived this issue in a new form. Under pegged exchange rates, it was said, financial shocks originating in the outside world are transmitted strongly to domestic financial markets by international capital movements. Under floating rates, their effects are weakened. In other words, floating exchange rates can partially insulate financial markets precisely when they cannot insulate goods markets — when exchange rates are affected by capital movements.

Figure 2 illustrates this argument clearly. Under a floating exchange rate, an exogenous change in exchange rate expectations takes the economy to q. Under a pegged rate, it takes the economy to u. Under both arrangements, r and p rise, but they rise by less with a floating rate. (As before, the difference in outcomes is due partly to credit contraction under a pegged rate, which takes asset markets from v to u, and partly to speculation under a floating rate, which takes them from v to q.)

Another comparison supports the argument. An

increase in the foreign interest rate raises r and reduces p under both exchange rate arrangements, and the decrease in p is smaller with a pegged rate, but the increase in r is smaller with a floating rate.[17]

IV The Role of Risk Aversion

Two parameters in this model reflect the effects of attitudes toward risk. An increase in e represents a reduction in risk aversion on the part of borrowers (arbitrageurs); a fall in the covered interest differential induces them to shift more borrowing from domestic to foreign lenders. Risk neutrality obtains when $e \to \infty$. An increase in s represents a reduction in risk aversion on the part of speculators; a rise in the gap between x^f and x^e induces them to sell more foreign currency forward. Risk neutrality obtains when $s \to \infty$.

Reduced Risk Aversion by Borrowers

To ascertain the effects of reduced risk aversion on the part of borrowers, we differentiate the arguments of equations (15) through (19) and (15′) through (19′) with respect to e. Using equation (15), for example,

$$\partial(dr/dE)/\partial e = [(1/D)ts]^2 k > 0$$

which is opposite in sign to (dr/dE) and says that a reduction in risk aversion by borrowers lowers the effect of an increase in E on the domestic interest rate (i.e., diminishes the effectiveness of monetary policy).

Selected effects of reductions in risk aversion are given in Table 3 for floating and pegged exchange rates. Three findings are noteworthy. All changes in c get smaller, and they vanish completely with risk neutrality. (This is, of course, the standard outcome; the larger the elasticity of arbitrage flows with respect to changes in c, the smaller the deviations from covered interest parity.) All changes in x and B get larger, except those resulting from shifts in demand for spot foreign exchange. Changes in r^* and x^e have larger effects on r, but changes in E have smaller effects (the result above that monetary policy becomes less effective), and the effects of shifts in demand for spot foreign exchange get larger with a floating rate but smaller with a pegged rate.

[17] The comparison of changes in r are based on equations (15) and (15′); the comparison of changes in p is based on equations (16) and (16′). The same equations can be used to compare the sizes of the changes in r and p shown in Figures 1 and 2.

Reduced Risk Aversion by Speculators

The effects of reduced risk aversion on the part of speculators are obtained in a similar way — by differentiating with respect to s. Selected effects are given in Table 4. The effects on changes in c and p are opposite to sign in those in Table 3. The effects on changes in r, x, and B are identical. Note, in particular, that monetary policy becomes less effective in this case too, and that the results for x and B replicate and extend a finding by Driskill and McCafferty (1982); changes in r^* and other financial disturbances have larger effects on x and B as speculators become less risk averse, but changes in the demand for spot foreign exchange produced by trade balance changes have smaller effects on x and B.[18]

TABLE 3

Impact of Reduced Risk Aversion by Borrowers

Effect	Disturbance			
	dE	dx^{ea}	dr^*	dT^a
dc	lowers	lowers	lowers	lowers
dx or dB	raises	raises	raises	lowers
dr	lowers	raises	raises	*
dp	raises	lowers	raises	**

*Raises with floating rate; lowers with pegged rate.
**Lowers with floating rate; raises with pegged rate.

TABLE 4

Impact of Reduced Risk Aversion by Speculators

Effect	Disturbance			
	dE	dx^{ea}	dr^*	dT^a
dc	raises	raises	raises	raises
dx or dB	raises	raises	raises	lowers
dr	lowers	raises	raises	*
dp	lowers	raises	lowers	*

*Raises with floating rate; lowers with pegged rate.

[18] One other result is worth noting. When $s \to \infty$, equation (18) becomes

$$dx^f = (1/D')[t(e+n) + en]dx^{ea} + (1/D')b(e+n)dT^a$$
$$+ (1/D')eb(ndr^* + kdE)$$

where $D' = t(e+n) + en(1-b)$. Therefore, the effects of changes in r^* and E are positive, resolving the ambiguity in Table 1. When this equation is evaluated at $b = 0$, moreover, $dx^f = dx^{ea}$, which is a special case of the general result reported in the text below.

Using the Forward Rate to Predict the Spot Rate

Another result emerges from this sort of analysis. From equations (10a) and (10b), $dx^e = dx^{ea} + bdx$. Therefore, equations (17) and (18) give

$$dx^e - dx^f = (1/D)en[t(dx^{ea} + dr^* + dE) - (1 - b)dT^v]$$

which measures the error made in using the forward rate to predict the spot rate when the latter is floating. Clearly, this error rises with reductions in risk aversion on the part of borrowers and falls with reductions in risk aversion on the part of speculators. When $s \to \infty$, moreover, $dx^e - dx^f \to 0$, and the forward rate is an unbiased predictor of the future spot rate. Similar results obtain when the spot rate is pegged. From equations (17') and (18').

$$dx^e - dx^f = (1/H)e[n(dx^{ea} + dr^*) + k(dT^a - dE)]$$

so that the error rises with reductions in e and falls with reductions in s (and when $s \to \infty$, $dx^e - dx^f \to 0$, as before).

V Modelling a Managed Float

Like most comparisons between exchange rate regimes, those in the previous section have two limitations. First, they concentrate on polar cases — freely floating rates and firmly pegged rates. Second, they compare results based on different ways of modelling expectations. Under pegged rates, changes in exchange rate expectations occurred exogenously; under floating rates, they occurred endogenously as well. Comparisons made this way may be valid. As Lucas (1976) has pointed out, expectations are regime dependent. Thus, the pegged rate results in equations (15') through (19') may be deemed to represent outcomes when pegs are credible, and they can be compared in a meaningful way with the floating rate results in equations (15) through (19), where expectations about the future spot rate are influenced by the current spot rate. But when market participants believe that a pegged rate can change, we must represent the manner in which they form their expectations before we can compare exchange rate regimes.

The approach adopted here allows us to model a continuum of exchange rate regimes and to model expectations in a way that facilitates comparisons across regimes. The monetary authorities and market participants are assumed to know how the spot rate would behave currently if it floated

freely — to know the exchange rate effects of disturbances given by equation (17).[19] The authorities use their knowledge to manage the actual spot rate. Market participants use their knowledge to form expectations about the future spot rate.

Managing the Spot Rate

The monetary authorities intervene to keep the actual spot rate from changing by more than a fraction, g, of the change that would take place currently if the rate was floating freely:

$$d\hat{x} = gdx, \quad 0 \leqslant g \leqslant 1 \qquad (20)$$

where $\hat{x}$ is the actual spot rate and x is the floating rate whose behaviour is described by equation (17). (Note that $dx > 0$ for all disturbances considered here.) When $g = 1$, the spot rate floats freely. When $g = 0$, the rate is pegged. And when $0 < g < 1$, the rate can be said to crawl. But the rate of crawl is not fixed, even when g is fixed, because $\hat{x}$ depends on x as well as g. Equation (20) should thus be taken to describe the intensity with which the authorities 'lean against the wind' rather than a true crawling peg.[20]

Forecasting the Spot Rate

In earlier parts of this paper, speculators based their views about the future spot rate on the behaviour of the current spot rate. Here, they base them on the same floating rate solutions that the authorities use to regulate the spot rate:

$$d\hat{x}^e = hdx, \quad 0 \leqslant h \leqslant 1 \qquad (21)$$

where $\hat{x}^e$ is the expected spot rate and x is given

---

[19] In what follows, however, we omit from the set of disturbances the exogenous change in the expected spot rate.

[20] Under a true crawl, equation (20) would give way to $\hat{x} = (1 + z)\hat{x}_{t-1}$, where z is fixed or is made to depend on an 'objective indicator' such as the rate of change or level of official reserves, a moving average of earlier changes in the actual spot rate, or the deviation of $\hat{x}_{t-1}$ from purchasing power parity (*PPP*). For recent contributions to the literature on crawling pegs, see Williamson (1981); on the optimization of z in a welfare theoretic context, see Mathieson (1976); on the use of objective indicators, see Kenen (1975), Branson and de Macedo (1982), and Shelburn (1984); on the use of *PPP*, see Dornbusch (1982).

once again by equation (17).[21] When $h=0$, speculators do not revise their views about the future spot rate even when there are changes in $\hat{x}$ and x. This case is analogous to the earlier one in which $b=0$. Changes in x are deemed to be temporary.[22] When $h=1$, speculators revise their forecast of the future spot rate by the full amount of the (hypothetical) floating rate change, even when it is different from the actual spot rate change. When $h=g$, speculators revise their forecast of the future spot rate by the full amount of the actual spot rate change, even when it is different from the (hypothetical) floating rate change. This case can be described as a credible crawl; the speculators believe that the spot rate change permitted currently by the authorities will suffice to deal permanently with the effects of the particular disturbance that led the authorities to allow it.[23]

When exchange rate behaviour is based on equations (20) and (21), the set of equations (14) gives way to

$$
\begin{bmatrix} (e+n) & -e & k \\ e & -(e+s) & 0 \\ e & -e & -1 \end{bmatrix} \begin{bmatrix} d\hat{r} \\ d\hat{p} \\ d\hat{B} \end{bmatrix} = \begin{bmatrix} 1 \\ 1 \\ 1 \end{bmatrix} edr^* + \begin{bmatrix} -kd\bar{E} \\ 0 \\ dT^a \end{bmatrix}
$$
$$
- \begin{bmatrix} 0 \\ s(h-g) \\ gt \end{bmatrix} dx \qquad (22)
$$

which is identical to the pegged rate version of the system (14) apart from the omission of the autonomous change in expectations and the addition of the exchange rate vector. The

---

[21] In a model with explicit exchange rate dynamics, involving interactions between asset markets and good markets, any disturbance is apt to produce a series of changes in a floating spot rate, x, and well-informed speculators will base their views about x^e on future values of x rather than its current value. But the model in this paper does not generate dynamics, so the current and future values of x are the same when disturbances are permanent. Therefore, the size of h can be taken to reflect speculators' judgements about the permanence of disturbances and the authorities' willingness to allow the future level of $\hat{x}$ to reflect the current (but hypothetical) value of x.

[22] When $h=0$ and $g=0$, the spot rate is pegged, and the changes in r, p, B, x^f, and c are given by equations (15') through (19').

[23] When $h=b$ and $g=1$, the spot rate floats freely and the changes in r, p, x, x^f, and c are given by equations (15) through (19).

determinant is H, as before, and the solutions can be written as amendments to the pegged rate solutions given above.

Starting with the change in the domestic interest rate,

$$
d\hat{r} = d\dot{r} + (1/H)G^r(hg_r - g)dx \qquad (23)
$$

where $G^r = (e+s)tk + es(1+k)$, and $g_r = (1/G^r)es(1+k)$. When $g < hg_r$, an increase in E reduces r by less than in the earlier pegged rate case, and all other disturbances raise r by more than in that case.[24] Hereafter, we will say that the crawl worsens the r outcome when $g < hg_r$, is neutral when $g = hg_r$, and improves the r outcome when $g > hg_r$.[25]

Turning to the change in the forward premium,

$$
d\hat{p} = d\dot{p} + (1/H)G^p(hg_p - g)dx \qquad (24)
$$

where $G^p = s(e+n) + ek(s+t)$, and $g_p = (1/G^p)s[(e+n) + ek]$. When $g < gh_p$, an increase in E or r^* reduces p by less than in the earlier pegged rate case, and an increase in demand for spot foreign exchange raises p by more than in that case. When $g > hg_p$, the outcomes are reversed. (It would not be appropriate, however, to say that these modifications worsen or improve the p outcomes, because those outcomes do not have clear normative interpretations.)

Finally, the change in the balance of payments is given by

$$
d\hat{B} = d\bar{B} - (1/H)G^B(hg_B - g)dx \qquad (25)
$$

where $G^B = es(n+t) + nt(e+s)$, and $g_B = (1/G^B)esn$. When $g < hg_B$, all disturbances examined here lead to larger balance of payments deficits than in the earlier pegged rate case. When $g > hg_B$, the outcomes are reversed. It can therefore be said that

---

[24] An increase in E can even raise r. Suppose that $g=0$, so the spot rate is pegged, but $h=1$, so speculators believe that it will be changed in the future by the full amount of the (hypothetical) floating rate change:

$$
dr = -(1/HD)\{t(e+s)[n(e+s) + es] - (es)^2(1+k)\}kdE
$$

so that r rises when $(es)^2(1+k) > t(e+s)[n(e+s) + es]$. An increase in E can likewise raise p.

[25] An increase in E reduced r by less in the earlier pegged rate case than in the corresponding floating rate case, and an increase in r^* raised r by more than in the floating rate case. In these instances, then, a crawl that worsens the r outcome with reference to the earlier pegged rate outcome (i.e., in the sense used here) worsens it by more with reference to the floating rate outcome. Analogous statements can be made with regard to the effects on p.

the crawl worsens the B outcomes when $g < hg_B$, is neutral when $g = hg_B$, and improves the B outcomes when $g > hg_B$.[26]

The Case for Crawling Rapidly

It is easily shown that $0 < g_B < g_r < g_p < 1$, and two consequences follow.

First, consider a credible crawl, where $g = h$. Speculators do not expect any additional change in the spot rate, because they believe that the change permitted currently by the authorities is large enough to deal permanently with the disturbance that led to the current change. In this case, $g > hg_r > hg_B$, and the crawl improves the interest rate and balance of payments outcomes. The same thing is true, of course, when $g > h$, and the improvements are larger, because speculators expect part of the current change in x to be reversed. It must be noted, moreover, that these results do not depend on the 'rightness' of the authorities' actions, only on the speculators' views about their rightness.

Second, consider cases in which $g < h$. Speculators expect an additional change in the spot rate to take place in the future, because they believe that the change permitted currently is not large enough. The results can be ordered this way:

If $g < hg_B$, the crawl worsens the r and B outcomes. Monetary policy is less effective than with a credible peg, and external shocks such as changes in r^* and the current account balance cause larger changes in domestic interest rates. All disturbances also cause changes in reserves larger than those with a credible peg.

If $g = hg_B$, the crawl worsens the r outcomes but is neutral with respect to the B outcomes.

If $hg_B < g \leqslant hg_r$, the crawl does not worsen the r outcomes and improves the B outcomes.

If $g < hg_r$, the crawl improves the r and B outcomes. Monetary policy is more effective than with a credible peg, and external shocks cause

smaller changes in domestic interest rates. All disturbances cause changes in reserves smaller than those with a credible peg.

Note finally that a crawl fast enough to be neutral with respect to the forward premium $(g = hg_p)$, a criterion that is not intrinsically attractive, serves nevertheless to improve the r and B outcomes.

When governments choose to let the exchange rate crawl or 'lean against the wind' rather than float freely, they may produce results inferior to those obtained with a rigidly pegged rate. The risks of this happening, however, are reduced by allowing the rate to crawl quickly. To keep it from destabilizing the domestic interest rate, however, the crawl must be quicker than the one required to keep it from destabilizing the balance of payments.

REFERENCES

Branson, W. H., and de Macedo, J.B. (1982), 'The Optimum Weighting of Indicators for a Crawling Peg', *Journal of International Money and Finance*, **1**, 165-78.

Dornbusch, R. (1982), 'PPP Exchange-Rate Rules and Macroeconomic Stability', *Journal of Political Economy*, **90**, 158-65.

Driskill, R., and McCafferty, S. (1982), 'Spot and Forward Rates in a Stochastic Model of the Foreign Exchange Market', *Journal of International Economics*, **12**, 313-31.

Eaton, J., and Turnovsky, S. J. (1983), 'Exchange Risk, Political Risk, and Macroeconomic Equilibrium', *American Economic Review*, **73**, 183-9.

Gross, E.M.A., and Hogan, W. P. (1982), 'Short Term Management of the Australian Exchange Rate, 1977-82', Department of Economics Working Paper 66, University of Sydney.

Herring, R. J., and Marston, R. C. (1976), 'The Forward Market and Interest Rates in the Eurocurrency and National Money Markets', in C. H. Stem, *et al.* (eds), *Eurocurrencies and the International Monetary System*, American Enterprise Institute, Washington, 139-63.

Kenen, P. B. (1965), 'Trade, Speculation, and the Forward Exchange Rate', in R. E. Baldwin, *et al.*, *Trade, Growth, and the Balance of Payments*, North-Holland, Amsterdam, 143-69.

—— (1975), 'Floats, Glides, and Indicators', *Journal of International Economics*, **5**, 107-52.

—— (1985), 'Macroeconomic Theory and Policy: How the Closed Economy Was Opened', in R. W. Jones and P. B. Kenen (eds), *Handbook of International Economics*, Vol. II, North-Holland, Amsterdam, 625-77.

Lucas, R. E. (1976), 'Econometric Policy Evaluation: A Critique', in K. Brunner (ed.), *The Phillips Curve and Labor Markets*: Supplement to the *Journal of Monetary Economics*, 19-46.

---

[26] The changes in x^f and c are given by

$$d\hat{x}^f = d\hat{x}^f + (1/H)G^f(hg_f - g)dx, \text{ and } d\hat{c} = d\hat{c} - (1/H)G^f(hg_c - g)dx$$

where $G^f = e(tk - n)$, $g_f = (1/G^f)s[e + n] + ke]$, and $g_e = (1/G^f)en$. If $tk > n$ so that $G^f > 0$, then $g_f > 0$ and $g_c < 0$. The effects on the changes in x^f will depend on the sizes of g and gh_f, but any crawl $(g > 0)$ will cause c to rise by more or fall by less than in the earlier pegged rate case. If $tk < n$ so that $G^f < 0$, then $g_f < 0$ and $g_c > 0$. Any crawl will cause x^f to rise by more or fall by less than in the earlier pegged rate case, but the effects on the change in c will depend on the sizes of g and hg_c.

McCallum, B. T. (1977), 'The Role of Speculation in Canadian Forward Exchange Markets, Some Evidence Assuming Rational Expectations', *Review of Economics and Statistics*, **59**, 145-51.

McCormick, F. (1977), 'A Multiperiod Theory of Forward Exchange', *Journal of International Economics*, **8**, 269-82.

Mathieson, D. J. (1976), 'Is There an Optimal Crawl?' *Journal of International Economics*, **6**, 183-202.

Mundell, R. A. (1968), 'Capital Mobility and Stabilization Policy under Fixed and Flexible Exchange Rates', in *International Economics*, Macmillan, New York, 250-71.

Polasek, M., and Lewis, M. K. (1985), 'Foreign Exchange Markets and Capital Inflow', in M. K. Lewis and R. H. Wallace (eds), *Australia's Financial Institutions and Markets*, Longman Cheshire, Melbourne.

Shelburn, M. R. (1984), 'Rules for Regulating Intervention under a Managed Float', Studies in International Finance 55, International Finance Section, Princeton University.

Tsiang, S. C. (1959), 'The Theory of Forward Exchange and Effects of Government Intervention on the Forward Exchange Market', International Monetary Fund, *Staff Papers*, **7**, 75-163.

Williamson, J. (ed., 1981), *Exchange Rate Rules*, Macmillan, London.

5

2 The Coordination of
Macroeconomic Policies

Peter B. Kenen

2.1 Introduction

For the last three years, beginning with the Plaza Communiqué of September 1985, governments have been hard at work on policy coordination, including the improvement of the process itself. We have seen nothing like it since the mid-1970s and the run-up to the Bonn Economic Summit of 1978. Economists have also been at work, modeling and measuring the gains from policy coordination and devising new approaches. But some have turned against it. The obstacles are large, they say, the potential gains are small, and there is the risk that governments will get it wrong—that macroeconomic coordination will make matters worse.

Some economists were skeptical initially. In 1981, for example, Max Corden argued that coordination is not needed because the international monetary ''non-system'' has a logic of its own:

> The key feature of the present system is that it is a form of international *laissez-faire*. First of all, it allows free play to the private market, not just to trade in goods and non-financial services but, above all, to the private capital market. Secondly, it allows free play to governments and their central banks to operate in the market and—if they wish and where they can—to influence and even fix its prices or its quantities. Thus it is a fairly free market where many governments, acting in their own presumed interests and not necessarily taking much account of the interests of other governments, are participants. (60).

Peter B. Kenen is Walker Professor of Economics and International Finance and Director of the International Finance Section at Princeton University.

This paper is based partly on research conducted while the author was Visiting Fellow at the Royal Institute of International Affairs, supported by a fellowship from the German Marshall Fund. An earlier version appears as the concluding chapter in Kenen (1988a).

Roland Vaubel (1981) went even further, arguing that governments should compete in providing the most attractive economic environment, measured primarily by price stability, and that policy coordination is harmful because it reduces competition among governments. Coordination can also raise the costs of policy mistakes because governments will do the same wrong things collectively rather than make mutually canceling errors.

On Corden's "market" view, each government can and should be free to choose its own monetary and fiscal policies but also to choose its exchange rate arrangements and decide for itself whether to borrow or lend on international capital markets. This sort of policy decentralization would probably be optimal if all economies were very small; each country's decisions regarding its exchange rate would have only trivial effects on other countries' effective exchange rates, and its decisions to borrow or lend would not have much influence on world interest rates.

What happens, however, when economies are large? Each country's policies affect other countries, and structural interdependence gives rise in turn to policy interdependence. The conventional case for coordination starts here.[1] But the strength of the case depends on the extent of the underlying structural interdependence, the governments' policy objectives, and the number of policy instruments at their command.

Stanley Fischer (1988) has surveyed recent research on these issues and has joined the skeptics:

> The notion of international policy coordination is appealing and appears to hold out the promise of major improvements in economic performance. However, estimates of the quantitative impacts of policy decisions in one economy on other economies are quite small. These results, together with explicit calculations of the benefits of coordination, suggest the gains will rarely be significant. Furthermore, theoretical analysis finds many circumstances under which coordination worsens rather than improves economic performance.
>
> The interest in policy coordination in the United States has been strongest when advocates of coordination were hoping to use international policy agreements to bring about changes in domestic policies that they regarded as either undesirable or eventually untenable. It is entirely possible though that formal coordination would sometimes require a country to undertake policy actions of which it disapproved.
>
> So long as exchange rates remain flexible—and they will likely remain flexible among the three major currency areas—macroeconomic policy coordination among the major blocs is unlikely to advance beyond the provision of mutual information and occasional agreements for specific policy trade-offs. Both information exchanges and occasional policy agreements when the circumstances are right are useful and should be encouraged.
>
> But more consistent ongoing policy coordination in which countries, including the United States, significantly modify national policies "in recognition of international policy interdependence" is not on the near hor-

izon. Fortunately, the evidence suggests that the potential gains from coordination are in any event small: the best that each country can do for other countries is to keep its own economy in shape. (38–39).

Martin Feldstein was even blunter in comments written shortly after the stock market crash of October 1987:

> Unfortunately, ever since the 1985 Plaza meeting, the [U.S.] administration and the governments of other industrial nations have emphatically asserted that international economic coordination is crucial to a healthy international economy in general and to continued U.S. growth in particular. Since such assertions are not justified by the actual interdependence of the industrial economies, Americans have been inappropriately worried about whether coordination would continue.
>
> Because foreign governments will inevitably pursue the policies that they believe are in their own best interests, it was inevitable that international coordination would eventually collapse. . . . But what contributed to the market decline was not the collapse of international macroeconomic coordination per se but the false impression created by governments that healthy expansion requires such coordination.
>
> The U.S. should now in a clear but friendly way end the international coordination of macroeconomic policy. We should continue to cooperate with other governments by exchanging information about current and future policy decisions, but we should recognize explicitly that Japan and Germany have the right to pursue the monetary and fiscal policies that they believe are in their own best interests.
>
> It is frightening to the American public and upsetting to our financial markets to believe that the fate of our economy depends on the decisions made in Bonn and Tokyo. Portfolio investors, business managers and the public in general need to be reassured that we are not hostages to foreign economic policies, that the U.S. is the master of its own economic destiny, and that our government can and will do what is needed to maintain healthy economic growth (Feldstein 1987).

When thoughtful economists like Fischer and Feldstein express themselves this forcefully, policymakers should listen. But when they listen carefully, they are likely to conclude that two quite different concepts of coordination are at issue. The critics of coordination are castigating governments for pursuing objectives that bear very little resemblance to the objectives that actually animate the governments' own efforts.

Economists typically adopt what can be described as a policy-optimizing approach to coordination,[2] and their use of game-theoretic methods to represent that process has led them to treat the participating governments as antagonists engaged in what Putnam and Henning (1986) have described as policy barter—the trading of commitments about policy instruments without any trading of analyses or forecasts. In this particular framework, moreover, exchange rate stabilization does not play a central role; it is at most a *method* for optimizing policies and is usually a second-best method at that.

Governments, by contrast, appear to adopt what can be described as a regime-preserving or public goods approach to policy coordination. It has different implications for the ways in which governments interact and for the role of exchange rate stabilization. Mutual persuasion takes the place of adversarial bargaining; exchange rate stabilization becomes a public good rather than a rule for optimizing policies. Furthermore, the regime-preserving approach sheds light on certain puzzling questions: Why does policy coordination move in and out of fashion? Why are disagreements about policy objectives cited so often as "obstacles" to coordination, when they can be expected to raise the gains from policy-optimizing coordination? Why do governments argue about sharing the "burdens" of coordination, when each of them should be expected to benefit from policy optimization?

2.2   Perspectives on Policy Coordination

Governments engage in many forms of economic cooperation. They exchange information about their economies, policies, and forecasts. They provide financial assistance to other governments, bilaterally and multilaterally, ranging from balance of payments support to long-term development aid. They act jointly to supervise or regulate various sorts of economic activity.

Coordination is the most rigorous form of economic cooperation because it involves mutually agreed modifications in the participants' national policies. In the macroeconomic domain, it involves an exchange of explicit, operational commitments about the conduct of monetary and fiscal policies. Commitments of this sort can be framed contingently, with reference to mutually agreed norms or targets; a government can promise to cut taxes, for example, if the growth rate of real GNP or nominal demand is lower than the rate it has promised to deliver. But commitments to targets, by themselves, do not constitute coordination. Commitments about instruments are the distinguishing feature of coordination, setting it apart from other forms of economic cooperation.[3]

2.2.1   Forms of Coordination

Coordination can result from episodic bargaining about specific policy packages or from a once-for-all bargain about policy rules or guidelines.

The Bonn Summit of 1978 is usually cited as the leading instance of episodic bargaining, although the Bonn bargain was not confined to macroeconomic matters. The Federal Republic of Germany and Japan made promises about their fiscal policies, and the United States made promises about its energy policies (Putnam and Bayne 1987, ch. 4). The Bretton Woods Agreement of

1944 is sometimes cited as a once-for-all bargain about rules, although it was too vague to meet my definition of full-fledged coordination. The exchange rate obligations were explicit; the corresponding policy commitments were implicit. The latter became somewhat tighter, however, as the Bretton Woods system evolved. The International Monetary Fund (IMF) began to attach strict policy conditions to the use of its resources, and Working Party 3 of the Organization for Economic Cooperation and Development (OECD) devoted close attention to the macroeconomic side of the exchange rate system.

These arrangements began to resemble rule-based policy coordination, but some would say that they were not symmetrical enough. The obligations of deficit countries were more clearly defined and commonly accepted than those of surplus countries. But symmetry is different from reciprocity or mutuality. The Bretton Woods system was *not* symmetrical—although the most striking asymmetries arose from the special role of the dollar rather than the imbalance between obligations borne by deficit and surplus countries. Nevertheless, the obligations were mutual in the important contingent sense emphasized earlier. They applied in principle to every country when it ran a balance of payments deficit. (Concern to preserve this contingent mutuality explains the reluctance of the IMF to depart from the uniform treatment of its members when attaching conditions to the use of its resources.)

The Louvre Accord of 1987 can be described as a combination of the two techniques for policy coordination. There were rule-based obligations, too loosely defined perhaps, which linked the use of interest rate policies to the maintenance of exchange rate stability. There was an ad hoc bargain about fiscal policies, although it served mainly to codify the goals that governments had already chosen unilaterally.[4]

A number of rule-based systems have been proposed in recent years, including those of McKinnon (1984, 1988), Meade (1984), and Williamson and Miller (1987). McKinnon proposes a gold standard without gold. The major central banks would choose an appropriate growth rate for the global money stock and would then conduct their monetary policies to realize that growth rate. Each of them would also use nonsterilized intervention to peg its exchange rate, causing its national money stock to grow faster than the global stock when its currency was strong and more slowly than the global stock when its currency was weak. The system would work symmetrically, however, so that exchange rate pegging would not affect the growth rate of the global money stock. The Williamson-Miller proposal would not peg exchange rates but is more comprehensive than McKinnon's proposal; it covers fiscal policies as well as interest rate or monetary policies.[5] Because it would involve a rule-based bargain to coordinate national policies, and we will discuss it later, the Williamson-Miller framework is reproduced as figure 2.1.

The distinction between types of policy bargains—between ad hoc agreements on policy packages and long-lasting agreements on policy rules—is helpful in sorting out arguments and issues. But it is far less fundamental than the distinction drawn in the introduction to this paper, which pertains to the rationale for policy coordination.

2.2.2   The Policy-Optimizing Approach

Many economists look upon policy formation as an optimizing process and are thus inclined to treat policy coordination as an extension of that process. Each government is deemed to have a welfare function defined in terms of its policy targets, and it sets its policy instruments to maximize that function. Its actions may affect other governments' decisions, but it disregards that possibility. When all governments behave this way, however, they end up in a suboptimal situation, the noncooperative or Nash equilibrium. They have neglected the policy interdependence resulting from structural interdependence, and they can bargain their way to a better situation, the cooperative or Pareto equilibrium. By changing the settings of their policy instruments in a mutually agreed manner, they can get closer to their policy targets and raise each country's welfare.[6]

The Blueprint

The participating countries [the Group of Seven] agree that they will conduct their macroeconomic policies with a view to pursuing the following two intermediate targets:

(1) A rate of growth of domestic demand in each country calculated according to a formula designed to promote the fastest growth of output consistent with gradual reduction of inflation to an acceptable level and agreed adjustment of the current account of the balance of payments.

(2) A real effective exchange that will not deviate by more than [10] percent from an internationally agreed estimate of the "fundamental equilibrium exchange rate," the rate estimated to be consistent with simultaneous internal and external balance in the medium term.

To that end, the participants agree that they will modify their monetary and fiscal policies according to the following principles:

(A) The *average level* of world (real) short-term interest rates should be revised up (down) if aggregate growth of national income is threatening to exceed (fall short of) the sum of the target growth of nominal demand for the participating countries.

(B) *Differences* in short-term interest rates among countries should be revised when necessary to supplement intervention in the exchange markets to prevent the deviation of currencies from their target ranges.

(C) National *fiscal policies* should be revised with a view to achieving national target rates of growth of domestic demand.

The rules (A) to (C) should be constrained by the medium-term objective of maintaining the real interest rate in its historically normal range and of avoiding an increasing or excessive ratio of public debt to GNP.

Figure 2.1   The Williamson-Miller blueprint for a target zone system
Source: Williamson and Miller (1987, 2); brackets and italics in original.

Viewed from this standpoint, policy coordination serves to internalize the effects of economic interdependence, which no single government can capture on its own by setting its policies unilaterally. To use a different metaphor, policy coordination gives each government partial control over other governments' policy instruments. Therefore, it relieves the shortage of instruments that prevents each government from reaching its own targets (see, e.g., Buiter and Eaton 1985, and Eichengreen 1985).

No one can quarrel with the logic of the policy-optimizing approach. It has given precise operational meaning to the notion of policy interdependence, provided a framework for measuring the costs of neglecting it, and linked this special subject with the much larger literature on macroeconomic theory and policy. But it tends to be more normative than positive. It tells us what governments can hope to achieve by multinational optimization and warns against some of the risks. It is less useful, however, in helping us to understand what governments are actually trying to accomplish, the obstacles they face, and the institutional arrangements they employ.

2.2.3   The Regime-Preserving Approach

Some economists, many political scientists, and most policymakers look at policy coordination from a different standpoint.[7] It is needed to produce certain public goods and defend the international economic system from economic and political shocks, including misbehavior by governments themselves.

Much of this important work was done by the United States in the first two postwar decades. It was the hegemonic power, having the ability and self-interested concern to stabilize the world economy by its actions. Furthermore, it had been largely responsible for writing the rules of the system and designing the institutions. It could thus be expected to defend them whenever they were threatened. Equally important, other governments could not accomplish very much without American cooperation. Matters are different now. It is still difficult to get very far without American cooperation, and little is likely to happen until Washington decides that something must be done. But the United States cannot act alone. The economic and political costs are too high.

It is easy to find examples of regime-preserving cooperation in recent economic history. They include the mobilization of financial support for the dollar and sterling in the 1960s and the joint management of the London gold pool, the "rescue" of the dollar in 1978, the speedy provision of bridge loans to Mexico at the start of the debt crisis in 1982, and the Plaza Communiqué of 1985, which was meant to defend the trade regime rather than alter the exchange rate regime.

The bargain struck at Bonn in 1978 can likewise be described as regime-preserving coordination. It reflected an agreed need for collective action on two fronts: for more vigorous recovery from the global recession of 1974–75, to combat rising unemployment, especially in Europe, and for energy conservation to reduce the industrial countries' dependence on imported oil and limit the ability of OPEC to raise oil prices.

When viewed from this different perspective, policy coordination becomes the logical response to the dispersion of power and influence that ended American hegemony. Public goods must be produced and institutional arrangements defended by common or collective action. When seen this way, moreover, disagreements about the benefits and costs of policy coordination take on a different but familiar aspect. They become debates about burden sharing.

2.3   Two Views of Exchange Rate Management

The two views of policy coordination yield different ways of looking at exchange rate management. Seen from the policy-optimizing viewpoint, it involves the use of a simple policy rule to internalize the effects of economic interdependence. Seen from the regime-preserving viewpoint, it embodies a commitment by governments to improve the global economic environment by pursuing exchange rate stability as a policy objective (strictly speaking, an intermediate objective conducive to the pursuit of stable and liberal trade policies and an efficient allocation of resources nationally and globally).

2.3.1   Exchange Rates in the Policy-Optimizing Framework

The earliest theoretical work on policy-optimizing coordination dealt mainly with the pegged rate case. Recent work has taken the opposite tack, partly because of the change in the actual exchange rate regime and partly because mathematical tractability exerts an unfortunate influence on the economist's research agenda.

Although many economists doubt that exchange rate expectations are truly rational, they tend to disparage any other view. Yet it is hard to solve a theoretical model in which rational expectations are combined with imperfect capital mobility. Accordingly, most such models assume that foreign and domestic assets are perfect substitutes. On this assumption, however, exchange rate pegging precludes any other use of monetary policy, greatly reducing the scope for policy coordination.[8] Therefore, exchange rate pegging is typically viewed as a second-best alternative to fully optimal coordination. It is attractive mainly because a simple, rule-based regime is less vulnerable to cheating or reneging, which many economists have regarded as a major obstacle to fully optimal coordination (see, e.g., Canzoneri and Gray 1985, and McKibbin and Sachs 1986).

When foreign and domestic assets are imperfect substitutes, however, the case for exchange rate pegging becomes much stronger, even in the policy-optimizing framework. Purchases and sales of foreign assets (intervention) can be used to peg the exchange rate; purchases and sales of domestic assets (open market operations) can be used to pursue domestic policy objectives. Using this framework to ask how exchange rate arrangements affect the need for policy-optimizing coordination, I have reached an unorthodox conclusion (Kenen 1987a, 1988c). A simple agreement to peg exchange rates, without any additional coordination, is better from each government's national standpoint than an agreement to let rates float and pursue fully optimal coordination. This is because exchange rate arrangements affect the ways in which exogenous shocks influence outputs and prices.

Working with a standard portfolio-balance model, I have studied the effects of various exogenous shocks, including fiscal policy shocks, under pegged and floating rates and asked how those two exchange rate regimes affect each government's ability to stabilize its output and price level on its own, without attempting to coordinate its monetary policy with those of other countries. In effect, I have used the policy-optimizing framework to look anew at an old question, whether a floating exchange rate can confer policy autonomy on the governments of interdependent economies. It cannot. On the contrary, a pegged exchange rate proves to be superior in three of the five cases studied (a permanent shift in demand between the countries' bonds, a temporary increase in one country's saving reflecting a permanent increase in desired wealth, and a balanced budget increase in one government's spending). The ranking of exchange rate regimes is ambiguous in the other two cases (a permanent switch in demand between the countries' goods and a permanent increase in one country's stock of debt resulting from a temporary tax cut).

My model is summarized in the appendix to this paper. It contains two countries, the U.S. and EC, each with its own good, bond, and currency. The two goods and bonds are traded and are imperfect substitutes; each currency is held only in the issuing country. Asset markets and goods markets clear continuously, but goods prices are sticky. An increase in demand for the U.S. good, for example, does not raise its dollar price immediately. There is instead a temporary increase in U.S. output. But wages and prices start to rise in response to the increase in output, and they go on rising until output returns to its long-run equilibrium level. U.S. bonds are dollar bonds issued by the U.S. government when it runs a budget deficit; EC bonds are ecu bonds issued by the EC government. The two countries' money supplies are managed by their central banks, using open market operations in their own bond markets. When the exchange rate is pegged, however, money supplies are affected by intervention in the foreign-exchange market; intervention can be sterilized when, as here, two countries' bonds are imperfect substitutes, but sterilization is not automatic.

Expectations are static, and the model begins in long-run equilibrium, where there is no saving or investment, budgets and trade flows are balanced, and prices are constant. When this situation is disturbed, moreover, the two economies move gradually to a new long-run equilibrium, driven by changes in wealth induced by transitory saving and, in the floating rate case, by capital gains or losses on holdings of foreign-currency bonds. Governments are well behaved. They do not try to move their economies away from the stationary state but use their monetary policies merely to optimize the adjustment process initiated by an exogenous shock. Furthermore, each government has enough confidence in the other's integrity to give it open-ended access to reserves.

Casting these assumptions in game-theoretic terms, each government may be said to start at the bliss point defined by its own social welfare (loss) function, and their bliss points will be identical initially even if the governments have different preferences. Therefore, the Nash and Pareto equilibria will coincide. When the situation is disturbed, however, each government will seek to minimize the welfare loss resulting from the output and price effects of the shock. But there are two sorts of shocks. Some can be shown to shift both bliss points together, so that the Nash and Pareto equilibria will continue to coincide. In these special cases, each government can use its own monetary policy to neutralize completely the output and price effects of the shock and thus move directly to its new bliss point. There is no welfare loss and no need for policy coordination. Other shocks can be shown to shift the bliss points differently, so that the Nash and Pareto equilibria will no longer coincide, and monetary policies cannot be expected to neutralize the output and price effects of those shocks. Each government must then settle for a second-best solution, involving a departure from its bliss point and a welfare loss, and policy coordination is needed to minimize that loss.[9]

This strategy is illustrated in figures 2.2 and 2.3, which focus on the pegged rate case. The vertical axis in figure 2.2 measures the permanent change in the U.S. price level resulting from an open market operation or exogenous shock, and the horizontal axis measures the temporary change in U.S. output. As the U.S. economy starts in long-run equilibrium and the U.S. government wants to stay there, the origin in figure 2.2 represents the U.S. bliss point in output and price space, and points on the elliptical indifference curve surrounding it are welfare-inferior to it. (There is, of course, one such curve for each value of the U.S. social welfare function.) The line BB and arrows on it show what happens to the U.S. economy when the U.S. central bank makes an open market purchase. Output rises temporarily, and the price level rises permanently. The line FF and arrows on it show what happens when the EC central bank makes an open market purchase. Under a pegged exchange rate, the case considered here, the change in the U.S. price level will be the same when the size of the open market purchase is the same, but the change in U.S. output will be smaller. Therefore, FF is steeper than BB.

The apparatus in figure 2.2. can be used to derive a reaction curve showing how the U.S. central bank responds to the effects of an open market purchase by the EC central bank. An EC open market purchase takes the U.S. economy to a point such as T', and the options open to the U.S. central bank are shown by the line B'B', parallel to BB. The best option is at H', where B'B' is tangent to the indifference curve; the U.S. central bank must make an open market sale

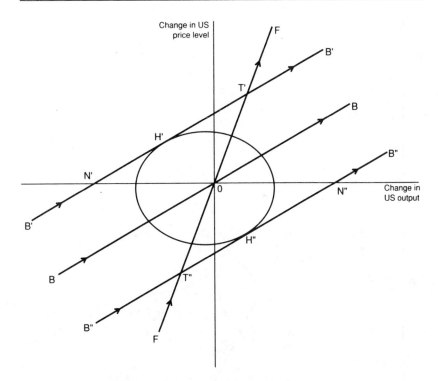

Fig. 2.2   U.S. policy preferences and policy responses

to minimize the welfare loss resulting from the EC open market purchase. But the U.S. price level is higher at H′ than at the origin, which says that the U.S. open market sale is smaller than the EC open market purchase. (The global money supply has risen, raising both countries' prices.)

Turning to figure 2.3, the vertical axis measures holdings of EC bonds by the EC central bank, and the horizontal axis measures holdings of U.S. bonds by the U.S. central bank. The point P is the initial U.S. bliss point and the EC bliss point too, because the EC economy also starts in long-run equilibrium and the EC government wants to stay there. The line I_1 is the U.S. reaction curve, showing how the U.S. central bank responds to an EC open market purchase. It is negatively sloped, because the U.S. central bank will make an open market sale, reducing its holdings of U.S. bonds. It is steeper absolutely than a 45° line, because the U.S. open market sale is smaller than the EC open market purchase. The line I_2 is the EC reaction curve, derived from the EC counterpart of figure 2.2.

Returning to figure 2.2, consider the effects of an exogenous shock that drives the U.S. economy to a point such as N′, depressing U.S. output temporarily but having no permanent effect on the U.S. price level. (That is what actually happens with a permanent switch in demand from the U.S. bond

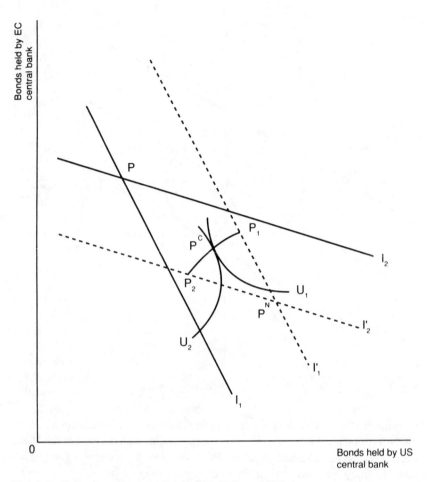

Fig. 2.3   Policy reactions curves for the U.S. and EC

to the EC bond.) The U.S. central bank could go again to H′, accepting a
permanent increase in the U.S. price level in order to reduce the size of the
temporary cut in U.S. output. But there is another possibility. Suppose that
the U.S. central bank makes an open market purchase large enough to take the
U.S. economy from N′ to T′ and the EC central bank makes an open market
sale large enough to take the U.S. economy from T′ to the origin. The output
and price effects of the shock will be neutralized completely. This outcome is
shown in figure 2.3 by shifting the U.S. bliss point to P_1, where the EC central
bank holds fewer bonds and the U.S. central bank holds more bonds, then
shifting the U.S. reaction curve from I_1 to I'_1 making it pass through the new
U.S. bliss point.[10]

Now suppose that the same exogenous shock drives the EC economy to the
EC counterpart of point N″ in figure 2.2, raising EC output temporarily and
having no permanent effect on the EC price level. The effects of the shock can

be neutralized completely if the EC central bank makes an open market sale large enough to take the EC economy from N″ to T″ and the U.S. central bank makes an open market purchase large enough to take the EC economy from T″ to the origin. In figure 2.3, the EC bliss point shifts to P_2, where the EC central bank holds fewer bonds and the U.S. central bank holds more bonds, and the new EC reaction curve must be I'_2.

If each central bank optimizes its policy independently, without taking account of the other's decisions, the two will wind up in Nash equilibrium at P^N. If they coordinate their policies by some sort of bargaining, they will wind up in Pareto equilibrium at a point such as P^C, lying on the so-called contract curve connecting P_1 and P_2, and it is easy to prove that P^C is better than P^N from each country's standpoint. Bliss points such as P_1 and P_2 are surrounded by elliptical indifference curves, and two such curves are drawn in figure 2.3. They are the curves whose tangency defines the point P^C. But U_1, the U.S. indifference curve, cuts I'_1 between P^N and P_1, which says that the U.S. welfare loss is smaller at P^C than at P^N, while U_2, the EC indifference curve, cuts I'_2 between P^N and P_2, which makes an analogous statement about EC welfare. These are the gains from policy-optimizing coordination.

This sort of policy coordination cannot neutralize completely the output effects of the shock; it can only minimize the resulting welfare losses. The effects of a shock are neutralized completely only when a government can reach its new bliss point, and P^C lies between those bliss points. If the bliss points shifted together, however, they would continue to coincide, and the new reaction curves would intersect at the new common bliss point, just as they did initially. That is precisely what happens under a pegged exchange rate. The bliss points shift together in three of the five cases studied, permitting the two central banks to neutralize completely the output and price effects of the shocks without having to coordinate their policies.

2.3.2   Exchange Rates in the Regime-Preserving Framework

In the previous section, the policy-optimizing framework was used to prove that exchange rate pegging can substitute for more ambitious forms of policy coordination. But two strong assumptions were needed. First, the two economies were well behaved. They began in long-run equilibrium and returned to it after every shock. Disturbances were permanent but did not have permanent effects on output. Second, governments were well behaved. They did not defy or try to manipulate the long-run properties of their economies in ways that might have interfered with the viability of a pegged exchange rate. When these assumptions are violated, we step through the looking glass, from a world in which exchange rate pegging reduces the need for policy coordination to one in which coordination is required merely to achieve exchange-rate stability.

When we take that step, moreover, we have to change our frame of reference—to shift from the policy-optimizing framework to the regime-preserving framework. Unless we treat exchange rate stability as an international public good, something that governments want but cannot produce individually, it is hard to explain how exchange-rate stability can become the rationale for policy coordination. The critics of coordination go wrong here, but so do the defenders. They debate the merits of the Louvre Accord for being something different than it was. The G-7 governments were not trying to manage the global economy. They were trying to manage exchange rates. They started rather tentatively, hoping to keep the dollar from "overshooting" and thus allow the adjustment process to work itself out, but became more ambitious as time wore on. They deserve to be graded fairly, however, for what they were trying to accomplish and how they set about it, not by an extraneous standard.

There is enough to debate even when the issues are narrowly defined by the regime-preserving framework. How much importance should governments attach to the production of exchange rate stability? What should they be willing to sacrifice in order to produce it? How much can they achieve by intervention? How closely must they coordinate their monetary and fiscal policies? How frequently should they revise their exchange rate targets? Can they continue to depend on informal understandings of the sort embodied in the Louvre Accord, or must they adopt more formal rules? Should exchange rate bands be hard and narrow, as in the Bretton Woods system and EMS, or soft and wide, as proposed by Williamson (1985 [1983])? Can governments reform exchange rate arrangements without reforming reserve arrangements?

I have explored most of these issues elsewhere (Kenen 1987c, 1988a) and tried to show how they are linked. Thus, judgments about the feasibility of revising exchange rate targets must condition one's judgments about the appropriate size of the exchange rate band, and the width of the band cannot be chosen without knowing whether it should be hard or soft. If a hard band is appropriate, moreover, intervention must play a major role in exchange rate management; a hard band cannot be defended merely by manipulating short-term interest rates. But changes in reserve arrangements may be needed to facilitate and finance large amounts of intervention.

There have been remarkable changes in the importance that governments attach to exchange rate stability and in their self-confidence—what they think they can achieve by altering or challenging the market's expectations.

At the Versailles Summit of 1982, the G-7 governments created a working group to study the role of intervention, and the group's report was predictably critical of using it extensively. Intervention could be helpful in some special circumstances, but mainly for drawing the market's attention to the implications of monetary policies. Intervention could not and should not be used to oppose market forces (Working Group 1983). The same view was expressed in a second, more comprehensive report on the monetary system commissioned by the Williamsburg Summit in 1983. It worried about the volatility of floating exchange rates and warned that "large movements in real exchange rates may lead to patterns of international transactions that are unlikely to be sustainable," but it laid most of the blame for exchange rate instability on "inadequate and inconsistent policies that have led to divergent economic performance" (Deputies 1985, paras. 17, 20). In effect, governments endorsed the view then prevalent among economists that foreign-exchange markets process information efficiently and should not be blamed for the policies on which they are asked to pass judgment. That would be shooting the messenger who brings embarrassing news (Frenkel 1987).

A few months later, however, governments took a different view. On September 22, 1985, in the Plaza Communiqué, they sent the messenger back to the market to say that the market was not doing its job:

> The Ministers and Governors agreed that exchange rates should play a role in adjusting external imbalances. In order to do this, exchange rates should better reflect fundamental economic conditions than has been the case. They believe that agreed policy actions must be implemented and reinforced to improve the fundamentals further, and that in view of the present and prospective changes in fundamentals, some further orderly appreciation of the main non-dollar currencies against the dollar is desirable. They stand ready to cooperate more closely to encourage this when to do so would be helpful.

And they took the next step in the Louvre Accord of February 22, 1987:

> The Ministers and Governors agreed that the substantial exchange-rate changes since the Plaza Agreement will increasingly contribute to reducing external imbalances and have now brought their currencies within ranges broadly consistent with underlying economic fundamentals, given the policy commitments summarized [earlier] in this statement.
>
> Further substantial exchange-rate shifts among their currencies could damage growth and adjustment prospects in their countries.
>
> In current circumstances, therefore, they agreed to cooperate closely to foster stability of exchange rates around current levels.

In the months that followed, the G-7 governments intervened massively to support the dollar. They let it depreciate slightly in the spring but held it to a very narrow range thereafter, until the stock market collapse in October.

The rationale for trying to stabilize exchange rates can be summed up in two statements. Those who produce exchange rates in the foreign-exchange market are differently motivated from those who consume them in the markets for goods, services, and long-term assets. Furthermore, exchange rates are very flexible, like other asset prices, whereas goods prices are sticky, so that nominal and real exchange rates move together.

A growing body of evidence supports the first assertion. Inhabitants of the foreign-exchange market have been shown to behave myopically, even irrationally,[11] and this would be reason enough to challenge the conventional wisdom of the early 1980s, which held that markets are wiser than governments. But the second assertion is more important. If goods prices were perfectly flexible, there would be little cause to worry about exchange rate arrangements. Goods markets would optimize relative prices continuously, including real exchange rates, even if they had to cope with nonsensical messages from the foreign-exchange market. Governments could then stabilize their money stocks and allow the foreign-exchange market to determine nominal exchange rates, or they could peg exchange rates and allow the market to determine national money stocks. It is the stickiness of goods prices that makes the exchange rate regime important. When nominal exchange rates affect real exchange rates, they also affect economic activity—its level, location, and composition.

The strength of the connection between nominal and real exchange rates is shown clearly in figure 2.4, which draws attention to the huge swing in real rates during in the 1980s. This may have been the most expensive round-trip in recent history, save perhaps for the swing in oil prices that began and ended earlier. It would have been expensive even if the effects of the strong dollar had been fully reversed once the exchange rate movement was reversed. According to Branson and Love (1988), the appreciation of the dollar from 1980 to 1985 wiped out more than one million jobs in U.S. industry, affecting more than 5.3 percent of the work force in manufacturing. But the costs of the swing may prove to be even bigger because its effects may not be reversed completely.

Whole industries and regions in the United States may be affected permanently because plants that were shut down when they became uncompetitive will not be reopened. They were not inefficient in 1980, when the

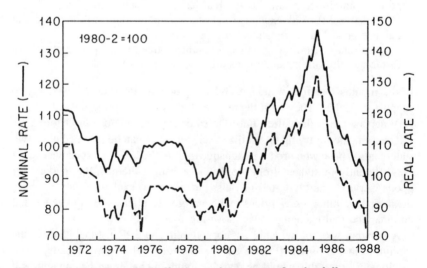

Fig. 2.4   Real and nominal effective exchange rates for the dollar
Source: J. P. Morgan, *World Financial Markets,* various issues; includes currencies of fifteen industrial countries weighted by bilateral trade in manufactures.

exchange rate swing began, but have been rendered obsolete by decisions and events resulting from that swing. Export and domestic markets have been lost to foreign competitors, who invested heavily to capture them and will not give them up, even though they are less profitable than they were initially.[12] This is not a mercantilist dirge. It is a lament for lost resources—for the physical and human capital that has been misallocated, not only in the United States but in other countries too.

These real resource costs have been compounded by permanent damage to the trading system. Although it was deeply opposed to protectionism, the Reagan administration was unable to resist pressures from industries severely hurt by the appreciation of the dollar. It imposed new trade restrictions or tightened old ones on imports of automobiles, steel, textiles, and apparel, and most of them remain in place.

But was this trip unnecessary, or was the foreign-exchange market doing a job that goods markets could not do because goods prices are not flexible enough? That is the key question.

Krugman (1989) dismisses the question curtly, saying that there was no fundamental reason for raising the real value of the dollar in 1984 only to reduce it in 1985. He argues persuasively that this part of the round-trip reflected irrational behavior by the foreign-exchange market. But it is hard to blame the *whole* round-trip on that sort of behavior. The appreciation of the dollar began with the tightening of U.S. monetary policy in 1979. It was driven thereafter by the capital inflow induced by the combination of tight money with a growing budget deficit. In this simple but meaningful sense, the first part of the trip was unavoidable under a floating exchange rate.

Suppose that Louvre Accord had been in force at the start of the 1980s. What would have happened to the dollar? A number of economists have played back this period using different policies or policy rules and a different exchange rate regime (see, e.g., Currie and Wren-Lewis 1988, Williamson and Miller 1987, and Frenkel, Goldstein, and Masson, ch. 1 in this volume). All of them conclude that the world would have been a better place. But most of the improvement can be traced to the modification of U.S. policies, not to the modification of the exchange rate regime. In fact, the exchange rate rules used in most such exercises are too loose to have much influence. The point at issue, moreover, has to do with the behavior of exchange rates under the policies actually followed rather than the modification of those policies. There are two reasons. First, it is hard to believe that the Reagan administration would have forsworn its idiosyncratic fiscal experiment in deference to policy rules or guidelines endorsed by an earlier administration. Second, and more generally, it is wrong to contrast the existing exchange rate regime under imperfect policies with an alternative regime under perfect policies.

If the G-7 governments had been committed to exchange rate management at the start of the 1980s, the new U.S. policy mix would have forced them to intervene heavily to prevent the dollar from appreciating, which would have put strong upward pressure on the U.S. money supply and strong downward pressure on other countries' money supplies.[13] These monetary side effects of exchange rate stabilization would have produced political pressures that might perhaps have forced the U.S. government to act earlier and more decisively on the budgetary front. At the same time, the G-7 governments would have been warned of the need to adjust exchange rates—to revalue the dollar gradually in small steps, but by less than it rose in fact under the influence of market forces.

How, then, should we apportion blame for the whole round-trip? Some blame must be borne by U.S. policies, which would have caused the dollar to appreciate significantly whether exchange rates were floating freely or closely managed. But much blame must be borne by the foreign-exchange market, not just for producing the speculative bubble of 1984–85 but also for taking a myopic view two or three years earlier. If the inhabitants of the market had been endowed with the marvelous attributes displayed by those who populate many economists' models, they would have known that the U.S. budget and trade deficits could not last indefinitely and that the dollar would have to return eventually to something near its 1980 level. When the dollar started to appreciate, then, they would have bet against it, selling dollars rather than buying them and reducing the net capital inflow. In other words, they would have engaged in stabilizing speculation on a scale sufficiently large to keep nominal and real exchange rates from changing substantially.[14]

The basic lesson taught by the experience of 1980–87 has to do with the high cost of imperfect policies under floating exchange rates. The core of the case for exchange rate management is the simple but sad fact that policies and markets are usually imperfect and interact in costly ways under freely floating rates.

2.4   Obstacles to Policy Coordination

Economists have used the policy-optimizing framework to measure the potential gains from policy coordination. An early attempt by Oudiz and Sachs (1984) found that the gains were disappointingly small. In one of their exercises, for example, the coordination of fiscal and monetary policies by Germany, Japan, and the United States had very little influence on the fiscal instruments and rather small effects on economic performance; when measured in units equivalent to percentage point changes in real income, the welfare gains were smaller than 1 percent of GNP. But subsequent studies have produced bigger numbers. Holtham and Hughes Hallett (1987) have reported welfare gains, measured in income-equivalent units, as large as 6 or 7 percent of GNP and not smaller than 3 or 4 percent, depending on the model used. There would thus seem to be large unexploited gains from policy-optimizing coordination.

Why don't governments exploit those gains? Four reasons are commonly given. First, governments are apt to renege on their bargains and cannot trust each other. Second, governments subscribe to different views about economic behavior and the workings of the world economy. Third, governments have different policy targets. Fourth, political and constitutional constraints interfere with the bargaining process.

The first explanation has been demolished. The rest make sense. But they seem more cogent when they are invoked to explain the apparent scarcity of regime-preserving coordination than when they are used to account for a shortage of policy-optimizing coordination.

2.4.1   Reneging and Reliability

The concern about reneging derives in large part from the stylized way in which economists have represented public and private decision-making and the resulting concern with the problem of time consistency. The issue is illustrated neatly by the Barro-Gordon (1983) model, in which wages and prices are set by the private sector in light of its expectations concerning the inflation rate, which depends in turn on its expectations concerning the money supply. If the government promises to raise the money supply by, say, 5 percent and the private sector expects the government to keep its word, wages and prices will rise immediately by 5 percent, in line with the expected growth rate of the money supply. At this point, the government has two options. If it keeps its promise, it will exactly validate the actual inflation rate, and there will be no change in output or employment. If it breaks its promise and raises the money supply by, say, 10 percent, it will stimulate output and employment, because the inflation rate cannot change until wages and prices cån be adjusted. If it breaks its word frequently, however, it will lose credibility. The private sector will cease to pay attention to the government's promises; it will start to base its expectations on the actual growth rate of the money supply, not the rate that the government keeps promising. The inflation rate will rise, and the rapid growth rate of the money supply will serve merely to validate the higher inflation rate. It will no longer stimulate output and employment.[15]

The argument, however, depends on three assumptions: (1) the private sector makes binding decisions about wages and prices; (2) the government can and should make promises about its own behavior to facilitate planning by the private sector; and (3) the "game" played by the government vis-à-vis the private sector is the only game in town.

The assumption about binding private sector decisions is unexceptional. In fact, the resulting stickiness of wages and prices is one basic reason for wanting to stabilize nominal exchange rates. The case for predictable behavior by governments is equally hard to challenge in principle but has to be qualified carefully. Governments may need to keep markets guessing by creating uncertainty about their tactics; they need short-term flexibility, which is not necessarily incompatible with medium-term predictability. Furthermore, governments cannot be rigidly predictable in an uncertain world. If they were the only source of uncertainty facing the private sector, governments could produce economic stability by being perfectly predictable. When governments and the private sector are *both* plagued by uncertainties, the rigid pursuit of predictable policies can cause instability.[16] But the third feature of the Barro-Gordon (1983) model is far too restrictive. Governments play many games simultaneously, including the all-important political game. If a government cheats on any other player, all of them can punish it. In fact, they can choose a new government at the next election. In the international context, moreover, governments can commit themselves rather firmly because the costs of cheating are very high. A government that breaks its promises to other governments cannot make more bargains with them. This consideration is particularly important for the major industrial countries, which have to cooperate not only in macroeconomic matters but in many economic, political, and strategic domains.[17]

Governments try to refrain from making commitments they cannot expect to honor and try to honor those they make:

> If we take seriously the claim that policy-makers in an anarchic world are constantly tempted to cheat, certain features of the [1978] Bonn story—certain things that did *not* happen—seem quite anomalous. We find little evidence that the negotiations were hampered by mutual fear of reneging. For example, even though the Bonn agreement was negotiated with exquisite care, it contained no special provisions about phasing or partial conditionality that might have protected the parties from unexpected defection. Moreover, the Germans and the Japanese both irretrievably enacted their parts of the bargain in September [1978], more than six months before [President Carter's] action on oil price decontrol and nearly two years before decontrol was implemented.
>
> Once the Germans and Japanese had fulfilled their parts of the bargain, the temptation to the President to renege should have been overpowering, if the standard account of international anarchy is to be believed. Moreover, the domestic political pressure on him to renege was clearly very strong. But virtually no one on either side of the final decontrol debate dismissed the Bonn pledge as irrelevant. (Putnam and Henning 1986, 100)

But these results seem natural enough when we treat the Bonn bargain as an exercise in regime-preserving coordination and bear in mind the complex and continuing relationships among the participating governments. Each stood to gain from its own "concessions" as well as those of its partners, and each was concerned to preserve its reputation for reliability. In President Carter's own words, "Each of us has been careful not to promise more than he can deliver" (Putnam and Henning 1986, 100).

2.4.2   Disagreements about Economic Behavior

Governments *do* disagree about economic behavior. German and American governments have disagreed for years about the responsiveness of unemployment to aggregate demand and even about the way that aggregate demand responds to fiscal and monetary policies. For a time, moreover, U.S. officials denied that there was any connection between the American budget and trade deficits, while other governments connected them simplistically, without leaving enough room for the role of the exchange rate.[18] But economists disagree in turn about the way that disagreements among governments affect policy coordination.

Frankel and Rockett (1988) have tried to show that misperceptions about economic behavior can lead to welfare-worsening policy bargains. They use ten large multicountry models to represent U.S. and European views about economic behavior and assume that each party uses its own model to measure the welfare effects of striking a bargain with the other. The governments do not exchange information. Instead, they engage in policy barter, agreeing to coordinate their policies whenever each government's own calculations lead it to believe that coordination will be beneficial, given its own model and objectives.

After they have taken the governments through the bargaining process and know the new settings of the policy instruments, Frankel and Rockett ask what will happen to each country, using the "true" model of the world economy. Because they must measure the effects of every bargain using all ten models, they must analyze 100 potential bargains and 1,000 possible outcomes. They find that the United States gains in 494 cases, loses in 398, and is unaffected in the remaining 108, while Europe gains in 477 cases, loses in 418, and is unaffected in the remaining 105. The parties' "success rates" are about 60 percent.

These are interesting results, but they must be interpreted cautiously. Frankel (1988, 27) himself concludes that "ministers in Group of 7 and Summit meetings might do better to discuss their beliefs directly rather than telling the others how to adjust their policies." But that is what governments have been doing all along, and there is a simple way to represent the outcome.

Suppose as before that each government believes in one model and also knows the other's model. If it is not perfectly confident about the rightness of its views, prudential considerations should lead it to ask how a policy bargain would affect its welfare on the working supposition that the other government is using the right model; it should not strike a bargain unless it can expect to gain under both governments' models. If it wants to persuade its partner to accept its own proposals, an important part of the actual bargaining process, reputational considerations should lead it to make sure that its own proposals would raise its partner's welfare under both governments' models. These concerns, taken together, impose a strong condition on the bargaining process. It should not even start unless both governments can expect to gain under both governments' models.

Holtham and Hughes Hallett (1987) came to this conclusion by a different route and applied the strong condition to the Frankel-Rockett (1988) bargains.

They used six models, not ten, and had thus to analyze thirty-six possible bargains.[19] But they ruled out twenty of those bargains because they violated the strong condition. (Three were ruled out because Europe would be worse off on the U.S. view of the world, eight because the United States would be worse off on the European view, and the other nine because both sides would be worse off on the other's view.) This leads me to my first conclusion: disagreements about economic behavior can be a major obstacle to policy-optimizing coordination. They can keep governments from getting together. But Holtham and Hughes Hallett went on to measure the welfare effects of the other sixteen bargains and found that the success rate was quite high. It was 73 percent for the United States and 83 percent for Europe.[20] This leads to my second conclusion: when prudential and reputational considerations block bargains that should not take place, policy coordination is not very dangerous to the participants' health.

It would be hard to conduct this sort of exercise for an instance of regime-preserving coordination. But one would expect the same sort of result. When governments disagree about the workings of the world economy, they are bound to hold different views about the costs of policy coordination, even when they agree completely about the benefits. Suppose that two governments are considering the use of interest rate policies for exchange rate stabilization. If they hold different views about the way that interest rates affect aggregate demand, they will also disagree about the costs of exchange rate stabilization.

Disagreements about economic behavior may be very potent in blocking this sort of coordination. When governments are willing to contemplate policy-optimizing coordination, it must be because they believe that a suitable policy bargain will allow them to make welfare-improving changes in their own national policies. When they are made to contemplate regime-preserving coordination, they may still believe that their national policies continue to be optimal and will thus want their partners to make the policy changes required for the common good.

2.4.3   Disagreements about Policy Objectives

The same possibility arises when governments have different policy objectives—the third in the list of reasons for the scarcity of coordination. In fact, such differences cannot explain why governments fail to engage in policy-optimizing coordination. On the contrary, they make it more attractive.

An example drawn from Eichengreen (1985) illustrates this point. Indeed, it makes a stronger point. Governments that have incompatible objectives can nevertheless benefit from policy-optimizing coordination.

Consider two identical economies with rigid wage rates and greedy governments. Each government wants to hold three-quarters of the global gold stock. If they pursue their targets independently, raising their interest rates competitively to attract capital inflows and gold, they will wind up with identical gold stocks but high unemployment rates. There are two ways to deal with this outcome. The two governments can agree to reduce their interest rates without even talking about their targets. That is the sort of policy barter that many economists have in mind when they talk about policy-optimizing coordination. Alternatively, the governments can reveal and modify their policy targets. But what if they reveal them and refuse to modify them? That is when conflicts or differences in targets obstruct coordination.

This case is too simple to take seriously—or is it? It does not differ from the case in which governments pursue incompatible current account targets, and they seem to do that frequently. It does not differ from the case in which they attach different weights to different targets, including the common or collective targets that they can achieve only at some cost in terms of their domestic targets. When collective targets are at issue, moreover, debates about objectives are unavoidable. The aims of the exercise have to be identified, and differences in preferences are bound to surface. When governments engage in policy barter, they can agree on means without discussing ends. When they engage in mutual persuasion—which is what normally happens—it is hard to agree on means without agreeing on ends.

2.4.4 Political and Constitutional Constraints

The fourth reason for the shortage of coordination applies to both varieties. Once again, however, it provides a more compelling explanation for the scarcity of regime-preserving coordination. There are political and constitutional obstacles to every sort of international cooperation, but they are hardest to surmount when the costs are clear and close to home and the benefits are not.

The political obstacles to policy coordination have been dramatized by the budgetary problems of the United States. How can the United States engage in international bargaining about fiscal policies when congressional leaders can say that the president's budget is "dead on arrival" on Capitol Hill? In the last days of World War I, the German general staff was said to believe that the situation was serious but not hopeless, while the Austrian general staff thought that it was hopeless but not serious. The Viennese view may be more appropriate here. The budgetary deadlock of the 1980s does not signify permanent paralysis. Nor should we neglect the political problems faced by other major countries in making and adjusting fiscal policies:

> The political system in Japan has traditionally restrained the powers of the Prime Minister to a far greater degree than the U.S. constitution limits the power of the American President. Always conscious of factional politics, the Prime Minister must answer to "policy tribes" which are groups of politicians committed to one-dimensional special interests. The Prime Minister must also placate vast armies of bureaucrats, not always from a position of strength. In Japan, it has often been said, politicians reign, but bureaucrats rule. (Funabashi 1988, 91)

The German situation is similar for different reasons:

> Although the ruling coalition has no difficulty in obtaining sufficient parliamentary support for its taxing and spending priorities, in practice its

control over fiscal policy is undermined by the following two factors. First, since the 1970s . . . the SPD has received control of the Ministry of Finance, while the FDP has staffed the Ministry of Economics, an arrangement that has weakened the federal government's ability to undertake comprehensive or drastic measures. Second, the federal government controls less than 50 percent of public investment, and only about 15 percent of the nation's total public spending and investment, the remainder coming from the *land* and local governments. (Funabashi 1988, 117)

There is, of course, a fundamental difference between these situations and the U.S. situation. Once the German and Japanese governments have decided to make a policy change, they can commit themselves formally, and the U.S. government cannot, because it cannot commit the Congress. But the record is not so very bad. President Carter was careful not to promise more than he could deliver—and he did deliver eventually. In another context, moreover, the White House obtained in advance a promise of rapid congressional action on the trade policy bargain produced by the Tokyo round of GATT negotiations— the "fast track" that Congress would follow in agreeing to accept or reject those parts of the bargain requiring new legislation. The Bush administration should perhaps propose a similar standby arrangement in the fiscal policy package it takes to Capitol Hill to break the budgetary deadlock.

The basic problems are political, not constitutional. No democratic government can make major policy changes without working hard to persuade the public that the new policies will be better than the old, if not indeed the best of all possible policies. When the time comes to coordinate policies, "Each national leader already has made a substantial investment in building a particular coalition at the domestic [game] board, and he or she will be loath to construct a different coalition simply to sustain an alternative policy mix that might be more acceptable internationally" (Putnam and Bayne 1987, 11). In brief, fiscal policies are not very flexible in any democracy, regardless of its constitution.

Policy coordination is made more difficult by jurisdictional divisions within governments. The problem is most serious on the monetary side, especially in Germany and the United States which have independent central banks. Here again, however, constitutional arrangements matter less than political realities, and independent central banks maintain their independence by being extremely astute politically. They cannot permit politicians to precommit them or to take their consent for granted, and they can be expected to make their views known, privately or publicly. Once they have given their consent, however, they are apt to be very reliable partners, because credibility is their most important asset. Furthermore, they rely on each other to protect their independence. On a number of recent occasions, central banks have refused to make interest rate changes until they could be sure that foreign central banks were ready to move with them.[21]

Finally, monetary policies can be altered rapidly and incrementally, without building a new political consensus. That is why a change in monetary policy is usually the first signal of a change in official thinking about the economic outlook. Therefore, monetary policies can be coordinated more deftly than fiscal policies, despite jurisdictional divisions in some countries.

2.5   The Framework for Policy Coordination

Rigidities in making fiscal policies and differences of view about the ways in which they work are probably sufficient to account for the apparent scarcity of policy-optimizing coordination—why governments fail to exploit all of the potential gains. They may even account for a more important failure. Quantitative studies of policy coordination have to start with a benchmark—the counterpart of the noncooperative equilibrium. They must therefore define fully optimal policies for each government acting unilaterally, and this is an instructive exercise. The welfare gains obtained by optimizing policies are often larger than the gains obtained thereafter by moving from noncooperative to cooperative policies. Dealing with policy coordination between the United States and Europe, Hughes Hallett (1987) obtains these welfare measures:

Simulation	United States	Europe
Baseline	466.2	346.2
Noncooperative	103.6	81.3
Cooperative	96.2	55.8

These are loss-function calculations, measuring the welfare costs of the governments' failure to reach their targets, so reductions are good things. But the biggest reductions occur on the way from the actual (baseline) situation to optimal noncooperative policies, not from noncooperative to cooperative (coordinated) policies. Political and institutional rigidities combine with the uncertainties of the real world to interfere with any sort of optimization, let alone optimal coordination.

The same rigidities and disagreements also help to account for the apparent scarcity of regime-preserving coordination, and disagreements about targets are important too. They combine to produce disagreements about burden sharing. But disagreements of this sort are more readily susceptible to resolution than those which arise when one government tries to tell another how to pursue its own self-interest. For this reason, if no other, we can perhaps be optimistic about the prospects for the sorts of policy coordination required to support exchange rate management.

What sorts of coordination are needed? The Williamson-Miller (1987) framework supplies an appropriate starting point. Intervention and interest rate differences would be used to stabilize exchange rates, while the global average of real interest rates and national fiscal policies would be used to regulate nominal expenditure. Conflicts between external and internal balance would be reconciled in the usual way, by periodic adjustments in real exchange rates. This is a far more sensible assignment than the one proposed by McKinnon (1988), who believes that fiscal policies should regulate current account balances because real exchange rates do not affect them, that the global money supply should be used to control the global price level, and that nonsterilized intervention should keep nominal exchange rates in line with purchasing power parity. Fiscal policies cannot control current account balances without imposing unemployment on deficit countries and inflationary pressures on surplus countries. They may be needed to validate changes in real exchange rates but cannot replace them.[22]

Yet the Williamson-Miller (1987) framework fails to address some difficult issues. While monetary policies must be coordinated closely to influence capital flows and offset expectations of exchange rate realignments, they cannot be assigned to that task exclusively, nor can fiscal policies be assigned exclusively to managing nominal demand. On the one hand, fiscal policies affect current account balances and, therefore, the size of the task faced by monetary policies. On the other hand, fiscal policies cannot be adjusted frequently enough to stabilize aggregate demand. Monetary policies must do some of the work that fiscal policies could do if they were more flexible, and exchange rate changes must do the rest.

It is important to distinguish between exchange rate management and the rigid defense of pegged exchange rates within very narrow bands. In my own view, the bands should be hard but wide and should be adjusted frequently to rectify disequilibria, including those that result from rigid fiscal policies. It is also important to distinguish between fiscal differences and fiscal shocks. International differences in fiscal policies do not necessarily destabilize exchange rates. They have not done so in the EMS, even though they continue to be quite large (see Gros and Thygesen 1988, 7). In fact, differences in fiscal policies can compensate for differences in national savings rates that would otherwise produce current account imbalances. The lessons to be learned from the 1980s relate to the effects of large fiscal shocks, which are bad news indeed, and the framework for multilateral surveillance currently being developed by the G-7 governments should focus very sharply on that problem.

Appendix

This appendix presents the model used to derive the results reported in the text. The model contains two countries, the U.S. and EC, but is written entirely in U.S. dollar terms. All nominal variables are dollar denominated except those with primes and those pertaining to the EC bond (F, F^c, etc.) which are denominated in EC ecu. The subscripts 1 and 2 denote U.S. and EC variables respectively; asterisks denote long-run values and exogenous shifts in demands for goods and assets.

The U.S. Economy

U.S. households hold U.S. money, U.S. bonds, and EC bonds. Their wealth is

(1) $$W_1 = L_1 + B_1 + \pi F_1,$$

where W_1 is U.S. wealth, L_1 and B_1 measure U.S. holdings of U.S. money and bonds, F_1 measures U.S. holdings of EC bonds denominated in ecu, and π is the exchange rate in dollars per ecu. (An increase in π is a depreciation of the dollar.) The time path of U.S. wealth is

(2) $$(dW_1/dt) = S_1 + F_1(d\pi/dt),$$

where S_1 is U.S. saving, and the last term measures the capital gain conferred by a depreciation of the dollar.

The U.S. money supply is

(3) $$L_1 = B^c - R,$$

where L_1 is the money supply, B^c is the central bank's holdings of U.S. bonds, and R measures its reserve liabilities to the EC central bank. (An increase in B^c reflects an open market purchase by the U.S. central bank; an increase in R reflects nonsterilized intervention in the foreign-exchange market—a dollar purchase by the U.S. or EC central bank to keep π from rising.)

The supply of dollar bonds can change only gradually as the U.S. government runs a budget deficit or surplus. The market-clearing equation for the U.S. bond is

(4) $$B = B_1 + B_2 + B^c,$$

where B_1 and B_2 are the quantities held by U.S. and EC residents and B^c is the quantity held by the U.S. central bank. The evolution of B is governed by a stylized fiscal policy:

(5) $$(dB/dt) = g(B^* - B), 0 < g < 1.$$

The U.S. government chooses a target level of debt, B^*, and runs a budget deficit or surplus until target and actual debt levels are equal. The government cuts taxes to run a deficit, then rescinds the tax cut gradually to satisfy equation (5). The government's budget is

(6) $\quad g(B^* - B) = G_1 + r_1 B - T_1 - T_{12} - r_1 B^c, \; T_{12} = r_1 B_2 - r_2 \pi F_1,$

where G_1 is the government's spending on U.S. and EC goods, r_1 and r_2 are the interest rates on U.S. and EC bonds, T_1 is the lump sum tax that the government adjusts continuously to run the desired surplus or deficit, and T_{12} is an intergovernmental transfer payment from the EC to the U.S. that removes all interest income terms from the definitions of the current account balance and disposable income.

The demand for money by U.S. households is defined with reference to the value of U.S. output and varies inversely with the U.S. interest rate around $\bar{r}$, its initial level:

(7) $\qquad\qquad L_1 = (1/v)\mathrm{Exp}[-\delta_1(r_1 - \bar{r})]p_1 Q_1, \; \delta_1 > 0,$

where Q_1 is U.S. output and p_1 is its price. The demand for the EC bond by U.S. households is defined with reference to U.S. wealth and varies with the difference between U.S. and EC interest rates:

(8) $\qquad \pi F_1 = \beta_1 \mathrm{Exp}[-\tfrac{1}{2}\phi(r_1 - r_2)]W_1, \; 0 < \beta_1 < 1, \; \phi > 0.$

The demand for the U.S. bond by U.S. households is defined residually by equations (1), (7), and (8).

Saving depends on the difference between desired and actual wealth:

(9) $\qquad\qquad\qquad S_1 = s(W_1^* - W_1), \; 0 < s < 1.$

Desired wealth, in turn, depends on the domestic interest rate and on disposable income:

(10) $\qquad W_1^* = \alpha \mathrm{Exp}[\Theta_1(r_1 - \bar{r})]Y_1^d, \; 0 < s\alpha < 1, \; 0 < \Theta_1 < \phi.$

The term $s\alpha$ is the marginal propensity to save out of disposable income (and must thus lie between zero and unity); the restriction on Θ_1 puts a lower bound on capital mobility. Disposable income is

(11) $\quad Y_1^d = p_1 Q_1 + r_1 B_1 + r_2 \pi F_1 - T_1 = p_1 Q_1 - G_1 + g(B^* - B),$

where equation (6) has been used to replace the lump sum tax T_1.

Households and the government have identical preferences with regard to goods, and a_1 measures the share of the EC good in total U.S. spending. Therefore,

(12) $\quad p_1 c_{11} = (1 - a_1)(Y_1^d - S_1 + G_1), \; p_2 c_{21} = a_1(Y_1^d - S_1 + G_1).$

On these same assumptions, the U.S. consumer price index is

(13) $$q_1 = p_1^{1 - a_1} p_2^{a_1}.$$

Finally, the market-clearing equation for the U.S. good is

(14) $$Q_1 = c_{11} + c_{12},$$

where c_{12} is the quantity of the U.S. good imported by the EC for household and government consumption.

The EC Economy

It is not necessary to write out all of the EC equations, since they resemble their U.S. counterparts. The equations for EC wealth, however, look different because they are written in terms of the dollar (the foreign currency) rather than the ecu:

(1') $$W_2 = \pi(L_2' + F_2) + B_2,$$

(2') $$(dW_2/dt) = S_2 + (L_2' + F_2)(d\pi/dt),$$

where W_2 is EC wealth, L_2' and F_2 measure holdings of EC money and bonds in ecu, B_2 measures holdings of U.S. bonds in dollars, and S_2 is EC saving in dollars. The supplies of the two ecu assets are given by

(3') $$L_2' = F^c + (1/\pi)R,$$

(4') $$F = F_1 + F_2 + F^c,$$

(5') $$(dF/dt) = g(F^* - F),$$

where F, F^c and F^* play the roles that B, B^c, and B^* played in the U.S. equations. The EC budget equation is

(6') $$g(F^* - F) = G_2' + r_2 F - T_2' + (1/\pi)T_{12} - r_2 F^c,$$

where G_2' and T_2' play the roles that G_1 and T_1 played in the U.S. budget equation. The EC demands for money and the U.S. bond are

(7') $$L_2 = (1/v)\text{Exp}[-\delta_2(r_2 - \bar{r})]p_2 Q_2$$

(8') $$B_2 = \beta_2 \text{Exp}[\tfrac{1}{2}\phi(r_1 - r_2)]W_2$$

The EC demand for the EC bond is defined residually. The remaining EC equations, for saving, desired wealth, disposable income, levels of EC spending on the U.S. and EC goods, and the consumer price index, are identical to their U.S. counterparts, equations (9) through (13), apart from subscripts. The market-clearing equation for the EC good is made redundant by Walras's Law.

Strategic Simplifications

Four conditions are imposed on the initial situation. Prices are normalized at unity $(p_1 = p'_2 = \pi = 1$, so that $p_2 = \pi p'_2 = q_1 = q_2 = \pi q'_2 = 1)$. Interest rates are equalized $(r_1 = r_2 = \bar{r})$. Net reserves are zero $(R = 0)$. Both economies start in a stationary state $(S_1 = S_2 = 0, B^* = B,$ and $F^* = F)$, so trade is balanced initially $(p_1 c_{12} = p_2 c_{21})$.

Two restrictions are imposed on economic behavior. Each country's spending is biased toward its own home good, so that $a_1 < \frac{1}{2}$ and $(1 - a_2) < \frac{1}{2}$, where a_1 and a_2 are the shares of the EC good in U.S. and EC spending, espectively. When the U.S. and EC interest rates are equal, as they are to start, the share of the foreign-currency asset in each country's wealth is equal to the share of the imported good in that country's spending, so that $\beta_1 = a_1$ and $\beta_2 = (1 - a_2)$.

Finally, outputs and levels of government spending are the same in the U.S. and EC $(Q_1 = Q_2 = Q,$ and $G_1 = G'_2 = G)$, and all behavioral parameters are the same $(\delta_1 = \delta_2 = \delta,$ and $\Theta_1 = \Theta_2 = \Theta)$. Under these assumptions, moreover, $W_1 = W_2$, and $a_1 = (1 - a_2) = a$, because trade is balanced initially.

The model is solved for the short-run and long-run effects of six disturbances: open market purchases of the domestic bond in the U.S. and EC $(dB^c > 0$ and $dF^c > 0)$, a permanent shift by U.S. or EC households from the EC bond to the U.S. bond $(dB^*_2 > 0)$, a permanent shift in U.S. or EC spending from the U.S. good to the EC good $(dc^*_2 > 0)$, permanent increases in government spending in the U.S. and EC matched by increases in lump sum taxes $(dG_1 > 0$ and $dG'_2 > 0)$, permanent increases in desired wealth causing temporary increases in saving $(dW^*_1 > 0$ and $dW^*_2 > 0)$, and temporary tax cuts in the U.S. and EC causing permanent increase in stocks of debt $(dB^* > 0$ and $dF^* > 0)$. As prices are sticky in both countries, p_1 and p'_2 are held at unity to obtain the short-run solutions, but Q_1 and Q_2 vary. As outputs return eventually to their natural levels, Q_1 and Q_2 are held at their initial levels to obtain the long-run solutions, but p_1 and p'_2 vary.

The Short-Run Solutions

The pegged rate solutions are obtained by holding π at unity and allowing R to vary:

$$(15) \quad dR = (1/H)\{aW\phi[n(vdB^c - vdF^c) - (1 - 2a)(dx_1 - dx_2) + 2dc^*_2]$$
$$- [s(1 - 2a)W\Theta + nQ\delta]dB^*_2\},$$

where

$$H = s(1 - 2a)J + 2a(Q\delta + nvW\phi),$$
$$n = 2a + s\alpha(1 - 2a),$$
$$J = W\Theta + \alpha Q\delta,$$
$$dx_1 = s(\alpha dG_1 - dW_1^*) + (1 - s\alpha)gdB^*,$$
$$dx_2 = s(\alpha dG_2' - dW_2^*) + (1 - s\alpha)gdF^*.$$

An open market purchase of domestic bonds reduces the reserves of the country involved; so do the two forms of fiscal expansion and a permanent fall in desired wealth (a temporary decrease in household saving). A switch in demand to the U.S. bond raises U.S. reserves. A switch in demand to the EC good raises EC reserves.

The changes in outputs are

(16) $dQ_1 = (1/H)(1/J)\{[H_1vdB^c + H_2vdF^c + v(H_1 - H_2)dB_2^*]$
$+ (1/s)(M_1dx_1 + M_2dx_2) - J[(Q\delta + 2avW\phi)dc_2^* - H_f d\bar{\pi}]\},$

(16') $dQ_2 = (1/H)(1/J)\{[H_1vdF^c + H_2vdB^c - v(H_1 - H_2)dB_2^*]$
$+ (1/s)(M_1dx_2 + M_2dx_1) + J[(Q\delta + 2avW\phi)dc_2^* - H_f d\bar{\pi}]\},$

where

$$H_1 = [s(1 - 2a)J + a(Q\delta + nvW\phi)]W\Theta, \quad H_2 = a(Q\delta + nvW\phi)W\Theta,$$
$$M_1 = s(1 - 2a)J(Q\delta + avW\phi) + aQ\delta (Q\delta + nvW\phi),$$
$$M_2 = a[Q\delta(Q\delta + 2avW\phi) - s(1 - 2a)W\Theta(vW\phi)],$$
$$H_f = a[(Q\delta + 2avW\phi)U_f + 2v(1 - a)Ws(1 - 2a)W\Theta],$$
$$U_f = Q + s(1 - 2a)W.$$

These effects are unambiguous, with one exception noted shortly. An open market purchase of the domestic bond raises both countries' outputs but raises domestic output by more than foreign output ($H_1 > H_2$). Both forms of fiscal expansion raise domestic output but can raise or lower foreign output, and a reduction in desired wealth has the same effects. A switch in demand to the U.S. bond raises U.S. output and reduces EC output, and a switch in demand to the EC good has the opposite effects. The final terms in equations (16) and (16') describe the effects of a once-for-all devaluation of the dollar, which raises U.S. output and reduces EC output.

The floating rate solutions are obtained by holding R at zero and allowing π to vary:

(17) $d\pi = (1/a)(A/U)dR,$

where dR is the vector of changes in reserves given in equation (15), and

$$U = 2\{(1 - a)[s(1 - 2a)J + 2aQ\delta] + a\phi U_f\}.$$

These effects are unambiguous, because those in equation (15) were unambiguous. The dollar depreciates under a floating rate whenever U.S. reserves would fall under a pegged rate.

The changes in outputs are

$$
(18) \quad dQ_1 = (1/U)\{(1/J)[U_1 vdB^c - U_2 vdF^c - (1/W)JQ\delta U_f dB_2^*]
$$
$$
+ (1/J)(1/s)Q\delta[V_1 dx_1 + V_2 dx_2] - 2Q\delta(1 - a)dc_2^*,
$$

$$
(18') \quad dQ_2 = (1/U)\{(1/J)[U_1 vdF^c - U_2 vdB^c + (1/W)JQ\delta U_f dB_2^*]
$$
$$
+ (1/J)(1/s)Q\delta[V_1 dx_2 + V_2 dx_1] + 2Q\delta(1 - a)dc_2^*\},
$$

where

$$
U_1 = 2(1 - a)W\Theta[s(1 - 2a)J + aQ\delta] + a(J + W\Theta)\phi U_f,
$$
$$
U_2 = aQ\delta[\alpha\phi U_f - 2(1 - a)W\Theta],
$$
$$
V_1 = 2(1 - a)[s(1 - 2a)J + aQ\delta] + a\phi U_f,
$$
$$
V_2 = a[2(1 - a)Q\delta + \phi U_f].
$$

These terms are unambiguous (even U_2, as $\phi > \Theta$). An open market purchase of the domestic bond raises domestic output but reduces foreign output. Both forms of fiscal expansion raise both outputs, as does a permanent fall in desired wealth. A switch in demand to the U.S. bond reduces U.S. output and raises EC output, and a switch in demand to the EC good has the same effects.

The Long-Run Solutions

These are the long-run solutions for the pegged rate case:

$$
(19) \quad dR = (1/2N)\{[(1 - 2a)W\Theta + 2aW\phi](vdB^c - vdF^c)
$$
$$
- 2(Q\delta)dB_2^* + Q\delta[(1 - 2a)(\alpha dG_1 - dW_1^*)
$$
$$
- (1 - 2a)(\alpha dG_2' - dW_2^*) + (dB^* - dF^*)]
$$
$$
+ [(1 - 2a)J + 2aW\phi](1/a)dc_2^*\},
$$

where

$$
N = v(1 - 2a)W\Theta + 2avW\phi + Q\delta.
$$

There is an important difference between the signs of these effects and those in equation (15), pertaining to the short run. In the short run, both forms of fiscal expansion raise the reserves of the country involved, and a permanent fall in desired wealth has the same effect; in the long run, however, they reduce its reserves. The changes in the two price indexes are

$$(20) \qquad dq_1 = (1/2JQ)[W\Theta(vdB^c + vdF^c) + Q\delta(dB^*$$
$$+ \alpha dG_1 - dW_1^*) + Q\delta(dF^* + \alpha dG_2' - dW_2^*)]$$
$$- (1/2Q)(1 - 2a)(1/a)dc_2^* + (1/2)d\bar\pi,$$

$$(20') \quad dq_2' = (1/2JQ)[\ \ldots\ ] + (1/2Q)(1 - 2a)(1/a)dc_2^* - (1/2)d\bar\pi,$$

where the term [. . .] in equation (20') is identical to the corresponding term in equation (20). A switch in demand to the U.S. bond has no permanent effect on the countries' price levels; it does not appear in equations (20) and (20'). A switch in demand to the EC good drives them apart, raising the EC price level and reducing the U.S. price level, and a devaluation has the opposite effects, but all of the other disturbances raise them by the same amounts.

These are the long-run solutions for the floating rate case:

$$(21) \qquad\qquad d\pi = (2N/QK)dR,$$

where dR is the vector of changes in reserves given in equation (19) and

$$K = (1 - 2a)J + 2aW(\delta + \phi).$$

The changes in the two price indexes are

$$(22) \quad dq_1 = (1/JQK)\{K_1 vdB^c - K_2 vdF^c - Q\delta JdB_2^* + JK_0 dc_2^*$$
$$+ Q\delta[(1 - 2a)J + aW(\delta + \phi)](dB^* + \alpha dG_1 - dW_1^*)$$
$$+ aQ\delta[W(\delta + \phi) - J]dF^* + aQ\delta W(\delta + \phi)(\alpha dG_2' - dW_2^*)\},$$

$$(22') \quad dq_2' = (1/JQK)\{K_1 vdF^c - K_2 vdB^c + Q\delta JdB_2^* - JK_0 dc_2^*$$
$$+ Q\delta[(1 - 2a)J + aW(\delta + \phi)](dF^* + \alpha dG_2' - dW_2^*)$$
$$+ aQ\delta[W(\delta + \phi) - J]dB^*$$
where
$$+ aQ\delta W(\delta + \phi)(\alpha dG_1 - dW_1^*)\},$$

$$K_1 = W\Theta[(1 - 2a)J + aW(\delta + \phi)] + (aW\phi)J,$$
$$K_2 = aW\delta(\alpha Q\phi - W\Theta),$$
$$K_0 = (1 - 2a)\alpha\delta G + aW(\delta + \phi).$$

An open market purchase of the domestic bond raises the domestic price level and reduces the foreign price level (as $\phi > \Theta$). A temporary tax cut causing a permanent increase in debt raises the domestic price level but can raise or lower the foreign price level. A balanced budget increase in government spending raises both price levels, as does a permanent fall in desired wealth. A switch in demand to the U.S. bond reduces the U.S. price level and raises the EC price level, and a switch in demand to the EC good has the opposite effects.

The Bliss-Point Shifts

To obtain the countries' bliss-point shifts, we would set $dQ_1 = dQ_2 = dq_1 = dq_2' = 0$ and solve the appropriate output and price equations for the requisite changes in B^c and F^c. Under a pegged exchange rate, for example, equations (16) and (20) would be solved for the U.S. bliss-point shifts, and equations (16') and (20') would be solved for the EC bliss-point shifts. This is laborious and not really necessary. It is simpler to set $dQ_1 = dQ_2$ and solve the appropriate output equations for the changes in B^c and F^c that stabilize Q_1 and Q_2. These will represent common bliss-point shifts if it can be shown that $dq_1 = d_2' = 0$ when the changes in B^c and F^c are inserted in the price equations.

Here is the simplest illustration. With a switch in demand from the EC bond to the U.S. bond $(dB_2^* > 0)$ and a pegged exchange rate, equations (16) and (16') say that $dB^c = - dF^c = dB_2^*$ will stabilize both countries' outputs. But the switch in demand does not affect price levels, and when $dB^c + dF^c = 0$, equations (20) and (20') say that $dq_1 = dq_2' = 0$. Therefore, the bliss points shift together. But the changes in B^c and F^c that stabilize Q_1 and Q_2 with a floating exchange rate, obtained from equations (18) and (18'), do not stabilize q_1 and q_2' when used in equations (22) and (22').

The same results obtain with balanced budget changes in government spending and changes in desired wealth. They do not obtain in the remaining cases, with temporary tax cuts leading to permanent changes in supplies of debt, and switches in demand between goods. With a U.S. tax cut, for example, outputs are stabilized with a pegged exchange rate when

$$dB^c = - (1/v)(1/W\Theta)(Q\delta + avW\phi)(1/s)(1 - s\alpha)gdB^*,$$

$$dF^c = (1/v)(1/W\Theta)(avW\phi)(1/s)(1 - s\alpha)gdB^*.$$

But these solutions give $dq_1 = dq_2' = - (1/2)\delta(1/s)[(1 - s\alpha)g - s]dB^*$, which goes to zero when $g = s/(1 - s\alpha)$ but not otherwise.

Notes

1. Corden examines these issues in a subsequent paper (Corden 1986), paying particular attention to the interdependence of fiscal policies. He concedes that large countries' budget deficits can have large effects on real exchange rates and interest rates. But he does not depart substantially from his earlier conclusion. Governments should mitigate the adverse effects of their neighbors' policies by making compensatory changes in their own domestic policies rather than rely on agreed rules or procedures to limit or correct fiscal policy differences.

2. In earlier papers (Kenen 1987a, 1987b, 1988b), I used different names for the approaches described in this and the next paragraph, but each attempt to label them ran into difficulties.

3. Similar definitions are used by Bryant (1980, 465), Artis and Ostry (1986, 75) and Frankel (1988, 1). The varieties of cooperation are discussed in Kenen (1987a). Some authors are less emphatic about including commitments about instruments in the definition of coordination. But the concept becomes too elastic without them. At the start of the 1980s, governments firmly agreed to combat inflation but said nothing about the settings of their monetary and fiscal policies, and the outcome was unsatisfactory — huge movements in real exchange rates and in current account balances. No one would want to identify that outcome with policy coordination. In fact, the subsequent revival of full-fledged coordination was partly a reaction to that outcome.

4. Describing the negotiations that led to the Louvre Accord, Funabashi (1988, chs. 5–8) depicts it differently: Japan and the Federal Republic of Germany agreed reluctantly to take new fiscal measures in exchange for a commitment by the United States to help stabilize dollar exchange rates by joint intervention. There were no commitments about monetary policies. This characterization is not wholly accurate. The United States was also pressed to make fiscal policy commitments, and it had agreed to the stabilization of the yen-dollar exchange rate some months before the Louvre Accord (even before Japan agreed to take new fiscal measures). Furthermore, the disagreement about German interest rates that cropped up in October 1987, the "collapse" of coordination to which Feldstein refers, suggests that the Louvre Accord included understandings about interest rate policies, even if there were no formal undertakings.

5. The most recent version of Meade's proposal, developed in Blake, Vines, and Weale (1988), is even more comprehensive than the Williamson-Miller proposal, having a wealth target as well as a GDP target, and it uses a different rule to define the exchange rate target.

6. Following Hamada (1974, 1976), the Nash and Pareto equilibria are usually depicted by reaction curves, as in figure 2.3. These curves appear to say that governments respond directly to changes in other governments' policies. If that were true, however, the Nash equilibrium would degenerate; each government would soon notice that other governments do not stand pat when it alters its own policies. Therefore, reaction curves should be deemed to say that governments respond to the *effects* of their partners' policies. They can then react repeatedly to each others' policies without becoming aware of policy interdependence. For surveys of research on policy-optimizing coordination, see Cooper (1985), Kenen (1987a), and Fischer (1988); on recent theoretical developments, see Oudiz and Sachs (1985).

7. Cooper (1985) and Kindleberger (1986) are prominent among the economists; for the views of political scientists and policymakers, see Putnam and Bayne (1987, ch. 1), and the sources cited there. Paul Krugman has persuaded me that the policy-optimizing framework can be used to represent regime-preserving coordination by including the international public good in the governments' welfare functions. That, indeed, is done in some recent papers; a measure of exchange rate variability is included in the governments' loss functions to represent their collective interest in exchange rate stability. I still believe, however, that the regime-preserving approach is sufficiently different in its implications to justify the sharp distinction drawn in this paper.

8. It is still necessary to decide what should be done with one country's money supply or with the global money supply. In many representations of pegged rate regimes, that decision is left to a single country (the United States in the Bretton Woods system and Germany in the EMS); McKinnon (1984) would handle the problem collectively, as would Williamson and Miller (1987), who would use the global money supply to manage the average short-term interest rate (see fig. 2.1). This is the fundamental issue

facing the designers of a European central bank. The question of substitutability, central to the functioning of policy coordination under pegged exchange rates, is also central to the functioning of official intervention in foreign-exchange markets; see Marston, ch. 6 in this volume.

9. Other economists have suggested or used the same basic approach. Buiter and Eaton (1985) show that Nash and Pareto equilibria are both bliss-point equilibria when policy targets and instruments are equal in number; Giavazzi and Giovannini (1986) anticipate my approach to the ranking of exchange rate regimes but do not carry it out; Turnovsky and d'Orey (1986) adopt the same strategy but deal only with temporary disturbances.

10. The size of the bliss-point shift does not depend on the particular shape of the ellipse in figure 2.2 (on the preferences of the U.S. government); it depends only on the slopes of the BB and FF curves (on the structures of the U.S. and EC economies).

11. See, for example, Dominguez (1986), Frankel and Froot (1986, 1987), and Krugman (1989); recent research on this issue is surveyed by Dornbusch and Frankel (1987).

12. This theme is developed by Krugman (1989), drawing partly on work by Dixit (1989) concerning the effects of uncertainty about the future exchange rate. A firm that has made the investment required to enter a market may decide to remain in that market even when the exchange rate turns against it, even though it cannot cover its variable costs, if the firm is sufficiently uncertain about the permanence of the new exchange rate. Conversely, a firm that has left a market may decide not to make the investment required to reenter it when the exchange rate moves in its favor. For more on the allocational effects of the exchange rate swing, see Marris (1987, 54–60).

13. These tendencies would have developed even under existing institutional arrangements, which automatically sterilize the effects of foreign official intervention on the U.S. money supply (and likewise sterilize the effects of U.S. intervention when conducted by the U.S. Treasury rather than the Federal Reserve); see Kenen (1988a, ch. 5). To prevent the dollar from appreciating, foreign official institutions would have been forced to sell dollars and thus to sell the U.S. government securities in which they invest their dollar reserves. To prevent U.S. interest rates from rising sharply under the influence of those sales and thus enlarging the capital inflow to the United States, the Federal Reserve System would have been compelled to undertake open market purchases of government securities, and these would have raised the U.S. money supply. Furthermore, foreign central banks could not have sterilized the domestic money-supply effects of their own and U.S. intervention without reducing their interest rates and thus enlarging the capital flow. These monetary effects of exchange rate management have also been cited by Frenkel (1987) and Dornbusch (1988) in criticizing McKinnon's rules for exchange rate management and by Williamson and Miller (1987) in defending their own proposals from those, like myself, who favor tighter arrangements.

14. In this case, however, the current account deficit would have been smaller, and interest rates might have risen in the United States, in order to crowd out domestic investment and thus make room for the budget deficit.

15. Taken to its logical conclusion, the Barro-Gordon model restates the basic proposition of the "new" macroeconomics—that monetary policy cannot affect the real economy—but casts it as a long-run tendency. If a government protects its reputation by keeping its promises, it can never alter output or employment. If it risks its reputation by breaking its word, it will vitiate its ability to surprise the private sector. Rogoff (1985) uses the same basic model to show why international policy coordination can be welfare-worsening, but his results have been challenged by Currie, Levine, and Vidalis (1987) and by Carraro and Giavazzi (1988).

16. Bryant (1987) has made the same point and applied it more generally to the problems of time consistency and reneging. He points out that all policy promises are contingent on forecasts about the state of the world, explicitly or implicitly. It is therefore impossible for anyone to know whether a government is reneging on previous promises or adapting to new circumstances.

17. These considerations are finding their way into the formal literature on policy-optimizing coordination; see Canzoneri and Henderson (1987). But the emphasis is still too narrow; it treats policy coordination as a repeated game but neglects the broad context in which the game is played.

18. Some of these disagreements may really testify to disputes about objectives. It may be more convenient for governments to say "That won't work" than to say "We don't like that." If this is true, however, apparent disagreements about behavior should not interfere with policy-optimizing coordination because disagreements about objectives can actually enhance the gains from that sort of coordination. An illustration follows shortly.

19. Holtham and Hughes Hallett used an early version of the Frankel-Rockett paper, which gave complete results for six models. The final version of the paper shows results that differ appreciably from those in the early version but gives complete results for only four models. It is therefore impossible to update the calculations reported in the text. (When they are updated for the four models shown in tables 4 and 5 of the final version, seven of the sixteen bargains violate the strong condition, and the success rates for the remaining nine approach 75 percent, up from 69 percent for all twenty-four bargains.)

20. These numbers cannot be compared directly to the 60 percent success rate reported by Frankel and Rockett, which covered all ten models. The corresponding rate for the six models used by Holtham and Hughes Hallett was 62 percent.

21. See Funabashi (1988, chs. 2 and 7). But his assessment of monetary cooperation is more critical than mine. He seems to regard the central bankers' silence at certain G-5 meetings as reflecting a reluctance to coordinate their policies. It should perhaps be seen as reflecting their reluctance to endorse the rather ambitious commitments made by finance ministers.

22. See Dornbusch (1988) and Krugman (1989). Simulations by Currie and Wren-Lewis (1988) support this view; feedback rules based on the Williamson-Miller framework do better than rules that use fiscal policies to regulate current account balances and monetary policies to regulate aggregate demand.

References

Artis, M., and S. Ostry. 1986. *International economic policy coordination.* London: Royal Institute of International Affairs.

Barro, R. J., and D. Gordon. 1983. Rules, discretion, and reputation in a model of monetary policy. *Journal of Monetary Economics* 12:101–21.

Blake, A., D. Vines, and M. Weale. 1988. Wealth targets, exchange rate targets, and macroeconomic policy. CEPR Discussion Paper no. 247. London: Centre for Economic Policy Research.

Branson, W. H., and J. P. Love. 1988. U.S. manufacturing and the real exchange rate. In R. C. Marston, ed., *Misalignment of exchange rates: Effects on trade and industry.* Chicago: University of Chicago Press.

Bryant, R. C. 1980. *Money and monetary policy in interdependent nations.* Washington, DC: Brookings Institution.

_____. 1987. Intergovernmental coordination of economic policies. In P. B. Kenen, ed., *International monetary cooperation: Essays in honor of Henry C. Wallich.* Essays in International Finance no. 169. Princeton: International Finance Section, Princeton University.

Buiter, W. H., and J. Eaton. 1985. Policy decentralization and exchange rate management in interdependent economies. In J. S. Bhandari, ed., *Exchange rate management under uncertainty.* Cambridge, MA: MIT Press.

Canzoneri, M. B., and J. A. Gray. 1985. Monetary policy games and the consequences of noncooperative behavior. *International Economic Review* 26:547–564.

Canzoneri, M. B. and D. B. Henderson. 1987. Is sovereign policymaking bad? Paper presented at the NBER conference on the European Monetary System. Cambridge, MA: National Bureau of Economic Research.

Carraro, C., and F. Giavazzi. 1988. Can international policy coordination really be counterproductive? CEPR Discussion Paper no. 258. London: Centre for Economic Policy Research.

Cooper, R. N. 1985. Economic interdependence and coordination of economic policies. In R. W. Jones and P. B. Kenen, eds., *Handbook of international economics,* vol. 2. Amsterdam: North Holland.

Corden, W. M. 1981. The logic of the international monetary non-system. In F. Machlup, G. Fels, and H. Muller-Groeling, eds., *Reflections on a troubled world economy: Essays in honor of Herbert Giersch.* London: St. Martins Press.

_____. 1986. Fiscal policies, current accounts, and real exchange rates: In search for a logic of international policy coordination. *Weltwirtschaftliches Archiv* 122 (no.3):423–38.

Currie, D., P. Levine, and N. Vidalis, 1987. International cooperation and reputation in an empirical two-block model. In R. C. Bryant and R. Portes, eds., *Global macroeconomics: Policy conflict and cooperation.* London: Macmillan.

Currie, D., and S. Wren-Lewis, 1988. A comparison of alternative regimes for international macropolicy coordination.

Deputies of the Group of Ten. 1985. *Report on the functioning of the international monetary system.* Reprinted in *IMF Survey: Supplement* (July). Washington, DC: International Monetary Fund.

Dixit, A. 1989. Entry and exit decisions of firms under uncertainty. *Journal of Political Economy* 97:620–38.

Dominguez, K. M. 1986. Are foreign exchange forecasts rational? New evidence from survey data. International Finance Discussion Paper no. 281. Washington, DC: Board of Governors of the Federal Reserve System.

Dornbusch, R. 1988. Doubts about the McKinnon standard. *Journal of Economic Perspectives* 2 (Winter):105–12.

Dornbusch, R., and J. Frankel. 1987. The flexible exchange rate system: Experience and alternatives. NBER Working Paper no. 2464. Cambridge, MA: National Bureau of Economic Research.

Eichengreen, B. 1985. International policy coordination in historical perspective. In W. H. Buiter and R. C. Marston, eds., *International economic policy coordination.* New York: Cambridge University Press.

Feldstein, M. 1987. The end of policy coordination. *The Wall Street Journal,* November 9.

Fischer, S. 1988. Macroeconomic policy. In M. Feldstein, ed., *International economic cooperation.* Chicago: University of Chicago Press.

Frankel, J. A. 1988. *Obstacles to international macroeconomic policy coordination.* Princeton Studies in International Finance no. 64. Princeton: International Finance Section, Princeton University.

Frankel, J. A. and K. A. Froot. 1986. Explaining the demand for dollars: International rates of return and the expectations of chartists and fundamentalists. Department of Economics Working Paper no. 8603. University of California at Berkeley.

———. 1987. Using survey data to test standard propositions regarding exchange rate expectations. *American Economic Review* 77:133–53.

Frankel, J. A. and K. E. Rockett. 1988. International macroeconomic policy coordination when policymakers do not agree on the true model. *American Economic Review* 78:318–40.

Frenkel, J. A. 1987. The international monetary system: Should it be reformed? *American Economic Review* 77 (May):205–10.

Funabashi, Y. 1988. *Managing the dollar: From the Plaza to the Louvre.* Washington, DC: Institute for International Economics.

Giavazzi, F., and A. Giovannini. 1986. Monetary policy interactions under managed exchange rates. CEPR Discussion Paper no. 123. London: Centre for Economic Policy Research.

Gros, D., and N. Thygesen. 1988. The EMS: Achievements, current issues and directions for the future. CEPS Paper no. 35. Brussels: Center for European Policy Studies.

Hamada, K. 1974. Alternative exchange rate systems and the interdependence of monetary policies. In R. Z. Aliber, ed., *National monetary policies and the international financial system.* Chicago: University of Chicago Press.

———. 1976. A strategic analysis of monetary interdependence. *Journal of Political Economy* 84:677–700.

Holtham, G., and A. J. Hughes Hallett. 1987. International policy cooperation and model uncertainty. In R. C. Bryant and R. Portes, eds., *Global macroeconomics: Policy conflict and cooperation.* London: Macmillan.

Hughes Hallett, A. J. 1987. Macroeconomic policy design with incomplete information: A new argument for coordinating economic policies. CEPR Discussion Paper no. 151. London: Centre for Economic Policy Research.

Kenen, P. B. 1987a. Exchange rates and policy coordination. Brookings Discussion Papers in International Economics no. 61. Washington, DC: Brookings Institution.

———. 1987b. What role for IMF surveillance? *World Development* 15:1445–56.

———. 1987c. Exchange rate management: What role for intervention? *American Economic Review* 77 (May):194–99.

———. 1988a. *Managing exchange rates.* London: Royal Institute of International Affairs.

———. 1988b. International money and macroeconomics. In K. A. Elliott and J. Williamson, eds., *World economic problems.* Washington, DC: Institute for International Economics.

———. 1988c. Exchange rates and policy coordination in an asymmetric model. CEPR Discussion Paper no. 240. London: Centre for Economic Policy Research.

Kindleberger, C. P. 1986. International public goods without international government. *American Economic Review* 76:1–13.

Krugman, P. 1989. *Exchange Rate Instability.* Cambridge, MA: MIT Press.

McKibbin, W. J., and J. D. Sachs. 1986. Comparing the global performance of alternative exchange rate arrangements. Brookings Discussion Papers in International Economics no. 49. Washington, DC: Brookings Institution.

McKinnon, R. I. 1984. *An international standard for monetary stabilization.* Policy Analyses in International Economics no. 8. Washington, DC: Institute for International Economics.

———. 1988. Monetary and exchange rate policies for international stability: A proposal. *Journal of Economic Perspectives* 2 (Winter):83–103.

Marris, S. 1987. *Deficits and the dollar: The world economy at risk*. rev. ed. Policy Analyses in International Economics no. 14. Washington, DC: Institute for International Economics.

Meade, J. E. 1984. A new Keynesian Bretton Woods. *Three Banks Review* (June).

Oudiz, G., and J. Sachs. 1984. Macroeconomic policy coordination among the industrial economies. *Brookings Papers on Economic Activity* 1:1–64.

———. 1985. International policy coordination in dynamic macroeconomic models. In W. H. Buiter and R. C. Marston, eds., *International economic policy coordination*. New York: Cambridge University Press.

Putnam, R. D., and N. Bayne. 1987. *Hanging together: The seven-power summits*. 2d ed. London: Sage Publications.

Putnam, R. D. and C. R. Henning. 1986. The Bonn summit of 1978: How does international economic policy coordination actually work? Brookings Discussion Papers in International Economics no. 53 (October). Washington, DC: Brookings Institution.

Rogoff, K. 1985. Can international monetary cooperation be counterproductive? *Journal of International Economics* 18:199–217.

Turnovsky, S. J., and V. d'Orey, 1986. Monetary policies in interdependent economies with stochastic disturbances. *Economic Journal* 96:696–721.

Vaubel, R. 1981. Coordination or competition among national macroeconomic policies? In F. Machlup, G. Fels, and H. Muller-Groeling, eds., *Reflections on a troubled world economy: Essays in honor of Herbert Giersch*. London: St. Martins Press.

Williamson, J. 1985 [1983]. *The Exchange Rate System*. 2d ed. Policy Analyses in International Economics no. 5. Washington, DC: Institute for International Economics.

Williamson, J. and M. H. Miller. 1987. *Targets and indicators: A blueprint for the international coordination of economic policies*. Policy Analyses in International Economics no. 22 (September). Washington, DC: Institute for International Economics.

Working Group on Exchange Market Intervention 1983. *Report*. Washington, DC: U.S. Treasury.

6

4

Exchange Rates and Policy Co-ordination in an Asymmetric Model

P. B. KENEN

---

1 Introduction

Most of the large theoretical literature on optimal exchange rate arrangements adopts a national approach to the problem. It compares the effects of various disturbances on a single small open economy under alternative exchange rate regimes. This approach is unsatisfactory for studying exchange rate arrangements among the large industrial countries. No such country can choose to peg or float its currency without affecting the behaviour of the other countries' currencies. Large countries must choose their regime collectively, and comparisons of alternative regimes must therefore adopt a cosmopolitan approach to the problem.

In earlier papers (Kenen, 1987a, b), I developed one such approach, based on a simple criterion. Using a portfolio balance model containing two countries, the US and the EC, I asked how pegged and floating exchange rates affect each government's ability to achieve its own policy objectives independently without having to co-ordinate its monetary policy with that of the other country.[1] In effect, I used the game-theoretical framework commonly employed in studying interactive policies to look anew at an old question: whether a floating exchange rate can confer policy autonomy on interdependent economies. I found that it cannot. On the contrary, a pegged but adjustable exchange rate proved to be superior to a floating rate in most of the cases studied.

In the face of a permanent switch between the countries' bonds, a pegged rate was fully optimal. Each country's government was able to stabilize its output and price level by a once-and-for-all open-market operation in its own bond market. There was no need for policy co-ordination. A floating rate was not fully optimal, as the governments could not prevent output and price changes and had to co-ordinate their monetary policies to minimize the welfare losses resulting from those changes. In other words, a pegged rate was first best, a floating rate with policy co-ordination was second best and a floating rate without co-ordination was third best.

The same ranking obtained in two other cases, a permanent balanced budget change in one government's spending and a temporary change in private saving reflecting a permanent change in desired wealth. However, the results were different in the remaining cases, a temporary cut in lump sum taxes producing a budget deficit and permanent increase in debt, and a permanent switch in demand between the countries' goods. A pegged rate was not first best in the sense used above, but a floating rate was not first best either, and policy co-ordination was required to minimize the welfare losses produced by the output and price effects of those two disturbances.

However, there were other ways in which a pegged exchange rate was superior to a floating rate. Under a pegged exchange rate, some of the output and price effects of a change in one country's taxes could be offset by an opposite change in the other country's taxes, and the two governments could then offset the rest of the effects by independent open-market operations. This was not possible under a floating exchange rate. Furthermore, a once-and-for-all adjustment in a pegged exchange rate, combined with independent open-market operations, could neutralize the output and price effects of a permanent switch in demand between the countries' goods.

All these conclusions, however, reflect certain strong assumptions imposed on the basic model:

1 The two economies began and ended in stationary states, where outputs and prices were constant and trade flows were balanced; permanent disturbances did not have permanent effects on output or the inflation rate.
2 Price and exchange rate expectations were static.
3 The two governments were well behaved, as they did not try to manipulate their economies but used their monetary policies merely to optimize the adjustment process initiated by an exogenous shock. Furthermore, each government had sufficient confidence in the other's integrity to give it open-ended access to reserves.
4 Each country specialized completely in the production of one good, and the prices of the goods were sticky. Both countries' consumers bought both goods, but each country's consumers displayed a preference for their own home good.
5 The two countries' bonds were imperfect substitutes, so that sterilized intervention could be used to peg the exchange rate, and open-market operations could be used to influence the domestic economy differently from the foreign economy.
6 The two economies were identical in size and perfectly symmetrical in behaviour.

The first four assumptions are retained in this paper, but the last two are relaxed in order to investigate two questions: What can be said about exchange rate arrangements under conditions of perfect capital mobility, when sterilized intervention is ineffective and monetary policies cannot influence the domestic economy differently from the foreign economy? What can be said about the ranking of exchange rate arrangements when two economies differ in size and are not perfectly symmetrical?

The analysis begins with a brief presentation of the basic model used by Kenen (1987b). It reproduces the principal results and adds results concerning fiscal policies. Thereafter, it relaxes the fifth and sixth assumptions, looking first at the effects of assuming that US and EC bonds are perfect substitutes, and then at the effects of assuming that one country is larger than the other and that the two economies are not perfectly symmetrical.

2   The basic model

Consider two countries, the US and the EC, whose currencies are the dollar and the ecu respectively. Each country supplies one good, one bond and one currency. The two goods and bonds are traded and are imperfect substitutes; each currency is held only in the issuing country. Asset markets and goods markets clear continuously, but goods prices are sticky. An increase in demand for the US good, for example, does not raise its price immediately. There is instead a temporary increase in US output that reduces unemployment below its 'natural' level. But wages and prices start to rise in response to the increase in output and go on rising until output and unemployment return to their natural levels. US bonds are dollar bonds issued by the US government when it runs a budget deficit; EC bonds are ecu bonds issued by the EC government. The two countries' money supplies are managed by their central banks using open-market operations in their own bond markets. When the dollar–ecu exchange rate is pegged, however, money supplies can be affected by intervention in the foreign exchange market; intervention can be sterilized, but sterilization is not automatic.

Expectations are static, as was indicated earlier, and the model begins in long-run equilibrium where there is no saving or investment, budgets and trade flows are balanced and unemployment rests at its natural rate so that wages and prices are stationary. When the situation is disturbed, moreover, each economy moves gradually to a new long-run equilibrium, driven by changes in wealth induced by transitory saving and, with a floating exchange rate, by capital gains or losses on holdings of foreign currency bonds.

As governments do not try to drive their economies away from the stationary state, they can be said to begin at the 'bliss points' defined by their own social welfare functions, and those bliss points are the same. In game-theoretical terms, the Nash and co-operative solutions coincide. When the situation is disturbed, however, each government must take steps to minimize the welfare loss resulting from the output and price changes caused by the disturbance. But there are two sorts of disturbances. Some can be shown to shift both bliss points together, so that the Nash and co-operative solutions continue to coincide. By implication, each government can use its own monetary policy to neutralize completely the output and price effects of the disturbance and thus move directly to its bliss point, forestalling any welfare loss and any need for policy co-ordination. Other disturbances can be shown to shift the bliss points differently, so that the Nash and co-operative solutions no longer coincide and monetary policies cannot neutralize completely the output and price effects of the disturbances. Each government must settle for a second-best solution, involving a departure from its bliss point and a welfare loss, and policy co-ordination is needed to minimize the loss.

The model is written in dollar terms. All nominal variables are dollar denominated except those with primes and those that pertain to the EC bond (F, F^c etc.), which are ecu denominated. The subscripts 1 and 2 are used to denote US and EC variables respectively; asterisks denote long-run values and exogenous changes in demands for goods and assets. As the economies are strongly symmetrical, I describe the US economy completely and then describe the EC economy briefly.

2.1   The US economy

US households hold three assets, US money, US bonds and EC bonds, so that their wealth is given by

$$W_1 = L_1 + B_1 + \pi F_1 \tag{4.1}$$

where W_1 is US wealth measured in dollars, L_1 and B_1 measure US holdings of US money and bonds, F_1 measures US holdings of EC bonds and π is the exchange rate in dollars per ecu. (An increase in π is a depreciation of the dollar.) The time path of US wealth is

$$\frac{dW_1}{dt} = S_1 + F_1 \frac{d\pi}{dt} \tag{4.2}$$

where S_1 is US saving and the second term measures the capital gain conferred by a depreciation of the dollar, which raises the dollar value of the EC bonds held by US households.

The next three equations define the supplies of the two dollar assets. The US money supply is

$$L_1 = B^c - R \tag{4.3}$$

where L_1 is the money supply, B^c is the central bank's holdings of US bonds and R is the dollar value of its reserve liabilities to the EC central bank. An increase in B^c represents an open-market purchase by the US central bank. An increase in R represents non-sterilized intervention in the foreign exchange market – a dollar purchase by the US or EC central bank to keep π from rising.[2] It also measures a balance of payments surplus for the EC and deficit for the US. The supply of dollar bonds is fixed at any point in time; it can change only gradually as the US government runs a budget deficit or surplus. The market-clearing equation for the US bond is

$$B = B_1 + B_2 - B^c \qquad (4.4)$$

where B_1 and B_2 are the quantities held by US and EC residents and B^c is the quantity held by the US central bank. The evolution of B is governed by a stylized fiscal policy:

$$\frac{dB}{dt} = g(B^\star - B) \qquad 0 < g < 1 \qquad (4.5)$$

The US government chooses a target level of debt $B^\star$ and runs a budget deficit or surplus until target and actual debt levels are equal. To run a budget deficit, the government cuts taxes and then rescinds the tax cut gradually to satisfy equation (4.5).[3] The government's budget is given by

$$g(B^\star - B) = G_1 + r_1 B - T_1 - T_{12} - r_1 B^c$$

$$T_{12} = r_1 B_2 - r_2 \pi F_1 \qquad (4.6)$$

where G_1 is the dollar value of US government spending on US and EC goods, r_1 and r_2 are the interest rates on US and EC bonds, T_1 is the lump sum tax that the government adjusts continuously to run the desired surplus or deficit and T_{12} is an intergovernmental transfer payment from the EC to the US that removes all interest income terms from the definitions of the current account balance and disposable income.[4] A change in G_1 should be regarded as a balanced budget change in government spending; once $B^\star$ has been chosen, determining the budget surplus or deficit, any change in G_1 must be offset by a change in T_1 to keep it from affecting the surplus or deficit.

The demand for money by US households varies directly with the value of US output and varies inversely with the US interest rate around its initial level:

$$L_1 = \frac{1}{v} \exp\left[-\delta_1(r_1 - \bar{r})\right] p_1 Q_1 \qquad \delta_1 > 0 \qquad (4.7)$$

where Q_1 is the volume of US output, p_1 is its dollar price and r is the initial interest rate.[5] The demand for the EC bond by US households depends on US wealth and on the difference between the US and EC interest rates:

$$\pi F_1 = \beta_1 \exp\left[-\tfrac{1}{2}\phi(r_1 - r_2)\right] W_1 \qquad 0 < \beta_1 < 1 \qquad \phi > 0 \qquad (4.8)$$

The demand for the US bond by US households is defined residually by equations (4.1), (4.7) and (4.8).

The level of saving is made to depend on the difference between desired and actual wealth:

$$S_1 = s(W_1^\star - W_1) \qquad 0 < s < 1 \qquad (4.9)$$

Desired wealth, in turn, depends on the domestic interest rate and on disposable income:

$$W_1^* = \alpha \exp\left[\theta_1 (r_1 - \bar{r})\right] Y_1^d \qquad 0 < s\alpha < 1 \qquad 0 < \theta_1 < \phi \qquad (4.10)$$

The term $s\alpha$ is the marginal propensity to save out of disposable income, which is why it must lie between zero and unity. The restriction on θ_1 puts a lower bound on capital mobility. Disposable income is

$$Y_1^d = p_1 Q_1 + r_1 B_1 + r_2 \pi F_1 - T_1 = p_1 Q_1 - G_1 + g(B^* - B) \qquad (4.11)$$

where equation (4.6) has been used to replace the lump sum tax T_1.

Households and the government have the same preferences with regard to goods, and a_1 measures the share of the EC good in total spending by US households and the US government. Therefore

$$p_1 c_{11} = (1 - a_1)(Y_1^d - S_1 + G_1) \qquad p_2 c_{21} = a_1 (Y_1^d - S_1 + G_1) \qquad (4.12)$$

On these same assumptions, the US consumer price index is

$$q_1 = p_1^{1-a_1} p_2^{a_1} \qquad (4.13)$$

Finally, the market-clearing equation for the US good is

$$Q_1 = c_{11} + c_{12} \qquad (4.14)$$

where c_{12} is the quantity of the US good imported by the EC for household and government consumption.

2.2   The EC economy

It is not necessary to write out all the EC equations, since they resemble their US counterparts. The equations for EC wealth look different, however, because they are written in terms of the foreign currency (i.e., in dollars rather than ecu):

$$W_2 = \pi (L_2' + F_2) + B_2 \qquad (4.1')$$

$$\frac{dW_2}{dt} = S_2 + (L_2' + F_2)\frac{d\pi}{dt} \qquad (4.2')$$

where W_2 is EC wealth measured in dollars, L_2' and F_2 measure holdings of EC money and bonds in ecu, B_2 measures EC holdings of US bonds in dollars and S_2 is EC saving measured in dollars. The supplies of the two ecu assets are

$$L_2' = F^c + \frac{1}{\pi} R \qquad (4.3')$$

$$F = F_1 + F_2 + F^c \qquad (4.4')$$

Exchange rates and policy co-ordination 89

$$\frac{\mathrm{d}F}{\mathrm{d}t} = g(F^\star - F) \qquad (4.5')$$

where F, F^c and $F^\star$ play the same roles that B, B^c and $B^\star$ played in the US equations. The EC budget equation is

$$g(F^\star - F) = G_2' + r_2 F - T_2' + \frac{1}{\pi} T_{12} - r_2 F^c \qquad (4.6')$$

where G_2' and T_2' play the same roles that G_1 and T_1 played in the US budget equation. The EC demands for money and for the US bond are

$$L_2 = \frac{1}{v} \exp\left[-\delta_2(r_2 - \bar{r})\right] p_2 Q_2 \qquad (4.7')$$

$$B_2 = \beta_2 \exp\left[\tfrac{1}{2}\phi(r_1 - r_2)\right] W_2 \qquad (4.8')$$

The EC demand for the EC bond is defined residually. The remaining EC equations, defining saving, desired wealth, disposable income, the levels of EC spending on the two goods and the consumer price index, are identical with their US counterparts (equations (4.9) – (4.13)) apart from subscripts. The market-clearing equation for the EC good is omitted because it is made redundant by Walras' law.

2.3 Strategic simplifications

Four conditions are imposed on the initial situation. Prices are normalized at unity ($p_1 = p_2' = \pi = 1$, so that $p_2 = \pi p_2' = q_1 = q_2 = \pi q_2' = 1$). Interest rates are equalized ($r_1 = r_2 = \bar{r}$). Net reserves are set at zero ($R = 0$). The two economies begin in a stationary state ($S_1 = S_2 = 0$, $B^\star = B$ and $F^\star = F$), which means that trade is balanced initially ($p_1 c_{12} = p_2 c_{21}$).

Two additional restrictions are imposed on economic behaviour.

1 Each country's consumption is biased toward its own home good, so that $a_1 < \tfrac{1}{2}$ and $1 - a_2 < \tfrac{1}{2}$, where a_1 and a_2 are the shares of the EC good in US and EC consumption respectively.
2 When the US and EC interest rates are equal, as they are to start, the share of the foreign currency asset in each country's wealth is equal to the share of the imported good in its consumption, so that $\beta_1 = a_1$ and $\beta_2 = 1 - a_2$.[6]

Finally, in this first version of the model, outputs and levels of government spending are the same in the two countries ($Q_1 = Q_2 = Q$ and $G_1 = G_2' = G$), and all behavioural parameters are the same ($\delta_1 = \delta_2 = \delta$ and $\theta_1 = \theta_2 = \theta$). Under these assumptions, moreover, $W_1 = W_2$, and because trade is balanced initially, $a_1 = 1 - a_2 = a < \tfrac{1}{2}$.

The model is solved for the short-run and long-run effects of six disturbances:

an open-market purchase of the domestic bond in the US or EC ($dB^c > 0$ and $dF^c > 0$), a permanent shift by US or EC households from the EC bond to the US bond ($dB_2^* > 0$), a permanent shift in US or EC expenditure from the US good to the EC good ($dc_2^* > 0$), a permanent balanced budget increase of government spending in the US or EC ($dG_1 > 0$ and $dG_2' > 0$), a permanent increase in desired wealth causing a temporary increase in saving ($dW_1^* > 0$ and $dW_2^* > 0$) and a temporary tax cut in the US or EC causing a permanent increase in the stock of debt ($dB^* > 0$ and $dF^* > 0$). As prices are sticky in both countries, p_1 and p_2' are held at unity to obtain the short-run solutions, but Q_1 and Q_2 are allowed to vary. As outputs return to their natural levels eventually, Q_1 and Q_2 are held at their initial levels to obtain the long-run solutions, but p_1 and p_2' are allowed to vary.

2.4   *The short-run solutions*

Results for the pegged rate case are obtained by holding π at unity and allowing R to vary:

$$dR = \frac{1}{H} \{ aW\phi [n(vdB^c - vdF^c) - (1 - 2a)(dx_1 - dx_2) + 2dc_2^*]$$

$$- [s(1 - 2a)W\theta + nQ\delta]dB_2^* \} \qquad (4.15)$$

where

$$H = s(1 - 2a)\mathcal{J} + 2a(Q\delta + nvW\phi)$$

$$n = 2a + s\alpha(1 - 2a)$$

$$\mathcal{J} = W\theta + \alpha Q\delta$$

$$dx_1 = s(\alpha dG_1 - dW_1^*) + (1 - s\alpha)gdB^*$$

$$dx_2 = s(\alpha dG_2' - dW_2^*) + (1 - s\alpha)gdF^{*7}$$

The signs of these effects are unambiguous. An open-market purchase of domestic bonds reduces the reserves of the country involved, as do the two forms of fiscal expansion and a permanent fall in desired wealth (a temporary decrease in household saving). A switch in demand to the US bond raises US reserves, and a switch in demand to the EC good raises EC reserves.

The changes in outputs are:

$$dQ_1 = \frac{1}{H} \frac{1}{\mathcal{J}} \left\{ [H_1 vdB^c + H_2 vdF^c + v(H_1 - H_2)dB_2^*] \right.$$

$$\left. + \frac{1}{s}(M_1 dx_1 + M_2 dx_2) - \mathcal{J}[(Q\delta + 2avW\phi)dc_2^* + H_f d\bar{\pi}] \right\} \qquad (4.16)$$

$$dQ_2 = \frac{1}{H}\frac{1}{\jmath}\left\{\left[H_1 vdF^c + H_2 vdB^c - v(H_1 - H_2)dB_2^*\right]\right.$$

$$\left. + \frac{1}{s}(M_1 dx_2 + M_2 dx_1) + \jmath\left[(Q\delta + 2avW\phi)dc_2^* - H_f d\bar{\pi}\right]\right\} \quad (4.16')$$

where

$$H_1 = \left[s(1 - 2a)\jmath + a(Q\delta + nvW\phi)\right]W\theta$$

$$H_2 = a(Q\delta + nvW\phi)W\theta$$

$$M_1 = s(1 - 2a)\jmath(Q\delta + avW\phi) + aQ\delta(Q\delta + nvW\phi)$$

$$M_2 = a\left[Q\delta(Q\delta + 2avW\phi) - s(1 - 2a)W\theta(vW\phi)\right]$$

$$H_f = a\left[(Q\delta + 2avW\phi)U_f + 2v(1 - a)Ws(1 - 2a)W\theta\right]$$

$$U_f = Q + s(1 - 2a)W$$

An open-market purchase of the domestic bond raises both countries' outputs but raises domestic output by more than foreign output ($H_1 > H_2$). The two forms of fiscal expansion raise domestic output but can raise or reduce foreign output ($M_2 \gtreqless 0$), and a fall in desired wealth has the same effects. A switch in demand to the US bond raises US output and reduces EC output, and a switch in demand to the EC good has the opposite effects. The final terms in equations (4.16) and (4.16′) describe the effects of a once-and-for-all devaluation of the dollar, which raises US output and reduces EC output.

The results for the floating rate case are obtained by holding R at zero and allowing π to vary:

$$d\pi = \frac{1}{a}\frac{A}{U}dR \quad (4.17)$$

where dR is the vector of changes in reserves given by equation (4.15) and

$$U = 2\{(1 - a)\left[s(1 - 2a)\jmath + 2aQ\delta\right] + a\phi U_f\}$$

The signs of these effects are unambiguous, because those in equation (4.15) were unambiguous. The dollar depreciates under a floating rate whenever US reserves would fall under a pegged rate.

The corresponding changes in outputs are given by

$$dQ_1 = \frac{1}{U}\left[\frac{1}{\jmath}\left(U_1 vdB^c - U_2 vdF^c - \frac{1}{W}\jmath Q\delta U_f dB_2^*\right)\right.$$

$$\left. + \frac{1}{\jmath}\frac{1}{s}Q\delta(V_1 dx_1 + V_2 dx_2) - 2Q\delta(1 - a)dc_2^*\right] \quad (4.18)$$

$$dQ_2 = \frac{1}{U}\left[\frac{1}{\mathcal{J}}\left(U_1\,vdF^c - U_2\,vdB^c + \frac{1}{W}\mathcal{J}Q\delta U_f\,dB_2^\star\right)\right.$$
$$\left. + \frac{1}{\mathcal{J}}\frac{1}{s}Q\delta\left(V_1\,dx_2 + V_2\,dx_1\right) + 2Q\delta\left(1 - a\right)dc_2^\star\right] \qquad (14.8')$$

where

$$U_1 = 2\left(1 - a\right)W\theta\left[s\left(1 - 2a\right)\mathcal{J} + aQ\delta\right] + a\left(\mathcal{J} + W\theta\right)\phi U_f$$

$$U_2 = aQ\delta\left[\alpha\phi U_f - 2\left(1 - a\right)W\theta\right]$$

$$V_1 = 2\left(1 - a\right)\left[s\left(1 - 2a\right)\mathcal{J} + aQ\delta\right] + a\phi U_f$$

$$V_2 = a\left[2\left(1 - a\right)Q\delta + \phi U_f\right]$$

These signs are likewise unambiguous (even that of U_2, as $\phi > \theta$). An open-market purchase of the domestic bond raises domestic output but reduces foreign output. The two forms of fiscal expansion raise both outputs, as does a permanent fall in desired wealth. A switch in demand to the US bond reduces US output and raises EC output, and a switch in demand to the EC good has the same effects.[8]

2.5   The long-run solutions

The long-run solutions for the pegged rate case are as follows:

$$dR = \frac{1}{2N}\left\{\left[\left(1 - 2a\right)W\theta + 2aW\phi\right]\left(vdB^c - vdF^c\right) - 2\left(Q\delta\right)dB_2^\star\right.$$
$$+ Q\delta\left(1 - 2a\right)\left[\left(\alpha dG_1 - dW_1^\star\right) - \left(\alpha dG_2' - dW_2^\star\right)\right]$$
$$\left. + Q\delta\left(dB^\star - dF^\star\right) + \left[\left(1 - 2a\right)\mathcal{J} + 2aW\phi\right]\frac{1}{a}dc_2^\star\right\} \qquad (4.19)$$

where

$$N = v\left(1 - 2a\right)W\theta + 2avW\phi + Q\delta$$

There is an important difference between the signs of these effects and those in equation (4.15) pertaining to the short-run changes in reserves. In the short run, both types of fiscal expansion raise the reserves of the country involved, and a permanent fall in desired wealth has the same effect; in the long run, however, they reduce its reserves.

The changes in the two price indexes are given by

$$dq_1 = \frac{1}{2\mathcal{J}Q}\left[W\theta\left(vdB^c + vdF^c\right) + Q\delta\left(dB^\star + dF^\star - dW_1^\star - dW_2^\star\right)\right]$$

Exchange rates and policy co-ordination 93

$$+ \alpha Q \delta (dG_1 + dG_2')] - \frac{1}{2Q}(1 - 2a)\frac{1}{a}dc_2^{\star} + \frac{1}{2}d\bar{\pi} \qquad (4.20)$$

$$dq_2' = \frac{1}{2\mathcal{J}Q}[\ldots] + \frac{1}{2Q}(1 - 2a)\frac{1}{a}dc_2^{\star} - \frac{1}{2}d\bar{\pi} \qquad (4.20')$$

where the term $[\ldots]$ in equation (4.20′) is identical to the corresponding term in equation (4.20). A switch in demand to the US good has no permanent effect on the countries' price levels; it does not appear in equations (4.20) and (4.20′). A switch in demand to the EC good drives them apart, raising the EC price level and reducing the US price level, and a devaluation of the dollar has the opposite effects. All other disturbances raise them by the same amounts.

The long-run solutions for the floating rate case are as follows:

$$d\pi = \frac{2N}{QK}dR \qquad (4.21)$$

where dR is the vector of changes in reserves given in equation (4.19) and

$$K = (1 - 2a)\mathcal{J} + 2aW(\delta + \phi)$$

The changes in the two price indexes are given by

$$dq_1 = \frac{1}{\mathcal{J}QK}\{K_1 vdB^c - K_2 vdF^c - Q\delta\mathcal{J}dB_2^{\star} + \mathcal{J}K_0 dc_2^{\star}$$

$$+ Q\delta[(1 - 2a)\mathcal{J} + aW(\delta + \phi)](dB^{\star} + \alpha dG_1 - dW_1^{\star})$$

$$+ aQ\delta[W(\delta + \phi) - \mathcal{J}]dF^{\star} + aQ\delta W(\delta + \phi)(\alpha dG_2' - dW_2^{\star})\} \quad (4.22)$$

$$dq_2' = \frac{1}{\mathcal{J}QK}\{K_1 vdF^c - K_2 vdB^c + Q\delta\mathcal{J}dB_2^{\star} - \mathcal{J}K_0 dc_2^{\star}$$

$$+ Q\delta[(1 - 2a)\mathcal{J} + aW(\delta + \phi)](dF^{\star} + \alpha dG_2' - dW_2^{\star})$$

$$+ aQ\delta[W(\delta + \phi) - \mathcal{J}]dB^{\star} + aQ\delta W(\delta + \phi)(\alpha dG_1 - dW_1^{\star})\} \quad (4.22')$$

where

$$K_1 = W\theta[(1 - 2a)\mathcal{J} + aW(\delta + \phi)] + (aW\phi)\mathcal{J}$$

$$K_2 = aW\delta(\delta Q\phi - W\theta)$$

$$K_0 = (1 - 2a)\alpha\delta G + aW(\delta + \phi)$$

An open-market purchase of the domestic bond raises the domestic price level and reduces the foreign price level (as $\phi > \theta$). The permanent increase in debt resulting from a temporary tax cut raises the domestic price level but can raise or reduce the foreign price level. A balanced budget increase in government spending raises both price levels, as does a permanent fall in desired wealth. A switch in demand to the US bond reduces the US price level and raises the EC price level, and a switch in demand to the EC good has the opposite effects.

2.6   The bliss point shifts

In Kenen (1987b), the short-run changes in Q_1 and Q_2 and the long-run changes in q_1 and q_2' are used to derive reaction curves for the US and EC governments, depicting the way in which each government adjusts to an open-market purchase by the other, and to show how the two curves shift in response to the disturbances analysed above. I will not repeat the analysis here but will show how the bliss points shift, to show when they stay together, permitting first-best policy responses without policy co-ordination, and when they are driven apart, requiring second-best policy responses and calling for co-ordination.

To obtain the countries' bliss point shifts, we set $dQ_1 = dQ_2 = dq_1 = dq_2' = 0$ and solve the appropriate output and price equations for the requisite changes in B^c and F^c. Under a pegged exchange rate, for example, equations (4.16) and (4.20) must be solved for the US bliss point shifts, and equations (4.16') and (4.20') must be solved for the EC bliss point shifts. This is laborious and not really necessary. It is simpler to set $dQ_1 = dQ_2$ and solve the appropriate output equations for the changes in B^c and F^c that stabilize Q_1 and Q_2. These will represent common bliss point shifts if it can be shown that $dq_1 = dq_2' = 0$ when the changes in B^c and F^c are substituted into the relevant price equations.

The simplest illustration is as follows. With a switch in demand from the EC bond to the US bond ($dB_2^\star > 0$) and a pegged exchange rate, equations (4.16) and (4.16') say that $dB^c = -dF^c = dB_2^\star$ will stabilize both countries' outputs. But the switch in demand does not affect the two countries' price levels, and when $dB^c + dF^c = 0$, equations (4.20) and (4.20') say that $dq_1 = dq_2' = 0$. Therefore the two countries' bliss points shift together.[9] But the changes in B^c and F^c that stabilize Q_1 and Q_2 under a floating exchange rate, obtained from equations (4.18) and (4.18'), do not stabilize q_1 and q_2' when used in equations (4.22) and (4.22').

The same results obtain with balanced budget changes in government spending and changes in desired wealth. But they do not obtain in the two remaining cases: temporary tax cuts leading to permanent changes in stocks of debt, and a switch in demand to the EC good. With a US tax cut, for example, outputs are stabilized with a pegged exchange rate when

$$dB^c = -\frac{1}{v}\frac{1}{W\theta}\left(Q\delta + avW\phi\right)\frac{1}{s}\left(1 - s\alpha\right)gdB^\star$$

$$dF^c = \frac{1}{v}\frac{1}{W\theta}\left(avW\phi\right)\frac{1}{s}\left(1 - s\alpha\right)gdB^\star$$

But these solutions give

$$\mathrm{d}q_1 = \mathrm{d}q_2' = -\frac{1}{2}\delta\frac{1}{s}\left[(1 - s\alpha)g - s\right]\mathrm{d}B^{\star}$$

which goes to zero when $g = s/(1 - s\alpha)$ but not otherwise.[10]

2.7 Additional results

More results can be obtained from the basic model. One pertains to the effects of a switch in demand between goods. The rest pertain to fiscal policies.

A devaluation of the dollar can offset the price effects of a switch in demand to the EC good. From equations (4.20) and (4.20') $\mathrm{d}q_1 = \mathrm{d}q_2' = 0$ when

$$\mathrm{d}\bar{\pi} = \frac{1}{Q}(1 - 2a)\frac{1}{a}\mathrm{d}c_2^{\star}$$

On substituting this change in exchange rate into equations (4.16) and (4.16'), it can be shown that $\mathrm{d}Q_1 = \mathrm{d}Q_2 = 0$ when

$$\mathrm{d}B^c = -\mathrm{d}F^c = \left[\frac{1}{v}(H_1 - H_2)\right]\left[\frac{1}{Q}(1 - 2a)\frac{1}{a}H_\mathrm{f}\right.$$
$$\left. - (Q\delta + 2avW\phi)\right]\mathrm{d}c_2^{\star}$$

which says that the bliss points shift together. Therefore a devaluation of the dollar is the first-best response to the switch in demand to the EC good. A change in the pegged exchange rate can stabilize q_1 and q_2', and independent open-market operations can then stabilize Q_1 and Q_2, taking account of the switch in demand and the change in exchange rate.[11]

Suppose that the US raises the stock of dollar debt by cutting taxes temporarily but the EC raises taxes temporarily to reduce the stock of ecu debt by the same amount, so that $\mathrm{d}F^{\star} = -\mathrm{d}B^{\star}$. From equations (4.16) and (4.16'), outputs will be stabilized when

$$\mathrm{d}B^c = -\mathrm{d}F^c = -\frac{1}{v}W\theta(Q\delta + 2avW\phi)\frac{1}{s}(1 - s\alpha)g\mathrm{d}B^{\star}$$

There must be monetary contraction in the US, because Q_1 would rise without it, and an equal amount of monetary expansion in the EC, because Q_2 would fall without it. When $\mathrm{d}B^c + \mathrm{d}F^c = \mathrm{d}B^{\star} + \mathrm{d}F^{\star} = 0$, however, equations (4.20) and (4.20') say that $\mathrm{d}q_1 = \mathrm{d}q_2' = 0$. If one country offsets the other country's tax cut, the two bliss points shift together with a pegged exchange rate. But this cannot happen with a floating rate, because the bliss points do not shift together unless $g = s/(1 - s\alpha)$.

It would, of course, be difficult for any government to offset promptly and precisely the tax policy pursued by another government. Therefore it is worth asking what would happen if one country cut its taxes and the other one did nothing and to compare the effects under pegged and floating rates. More generally, how large are the output and price effects of various disturbances under the two exchange rate regimes?

Equations (4.16) and (4.18) can be used to compare the effects on Q_1 (the effects on Q_2 are symmetrical). Subtracting the floating rate effects from the pegged rate effects, we obtain

$$
dQ_1^p - dQ_1^f = \frac{1}{\mathcal{J}HU}\Bigg\{ (UH_1 - HU_1)\,vdB^c + (UH_2 + HU_2)\,vdF^c
$$
$$
+ \left[Uv(H_1 - H_2) + H\frac{1}{W}\mathcal{J}Q\delta U_f \right] dB_2^\star
$$
$$
- \mathcal{J}\big[U(Q\delta + 2avW\phi) - H2Q\delta(1 - a) \big] dc_2^\star
$$
$$
+ \frac{1}{s}\big[(UM_1 - HQ\delta V_1)\,dx_1 + (UM_2 - HQ\delta V_2)\,dx_2 \big] \Bigg\}
$$

As $UH_1 < HU_1$, an open-market purchase of the US bond produces a larger increase in Q_1 under a floating rate. This result replicates the familiar assertion that a floating exchange rate 'bottles up' the domestic effects of an increase in the money supply because the whole increase stays at home; it is not diminished by a loss of reserves. But an open-market purchase of the EC bond produces a larger increase in Q_1 under a pegged rate (it reduces Q_1 under a floating rate), and the same result obtains with a switch in demand to the US bond.[12]

A switch in demand to the EC good produces a larger decrease in Q_1 under a pegged rate; the loss of reserves with a pegged rate reduces the US money supply, which tends to depress US output further, while the depreciation of the dollar under a floating rate shifts demand to the US good, which partially reverses the fall in US output. Finally, $UHM_1 > HQ\delta V_1$ but $UHM_2 < HQ\delta V_2$, so that fiscal expansion by the US has a larger effect on US output under a pegged rate, but fiscal expansion by the EC has a larger effect on US output under a floating rate.[13]

Equations (4.20) and (4.22) can be used to compare the effects on q_1 (the effects on q_2' are symmetrical). An open-market purchase of the US bond produces a larger price increase under a floating rate; this matches the ordering of output effects and reflects the depreciation of the dollar, which raises the dollar price of the EC good. But an open-market purchase of the EC bond produces a larger price increase under a pegged rate, because it reduces q_1 under a floating rate. A switch in demand to the US bond does not affect q_1 under a pegged rate but raises it under a floating rate, while a switch in demand to the EC good reduces q_1 under a pegged rate but raises it under a floating rate.

A temporary tax cut in the US raises q_1 by more with a floating rate, because the dollar depreciates over the long run, raising the dollar price of the EC good; the same thing happens with a balanced budget increase in US government spending. A temporary tax cut in the EC raises q_1 by less with a floating rate because the dollar appreciates, and the same thing happens with a balanced budget increase in EC spending. Thus a domestic fiscal expansion, regardless of type, has a larger effect on domestic output under a pegged rate but a smaller effect on the price level, while a foreign fiscal expansion has a smaller effect on domestic output under a pegged rate but a larger effect on the price level. If a government is very averse to inflation and fears that its partners will run large budget deficits, it will want a floating rate. If it is very averse to output changes, it will want a pegged rate.

Heretofore, fiscal policies have been treated as part of the stabilization problem, and not part of the solution. What role might they play as part of the solution?

One point emerges from cursory inspection of the output and price equations. Under both pegged and floating exchange rates, a balanced budget change in government spending can neutralize completely the domestic and foreign effects of a change in desired wealth. But a change in B^* can do this only with a pegged rate and only when $g = s/(1 - s\alpha)$.[14]

Under a pegged exchange rate, moreover, changes in G_1 and G_2 or B^* and F^* can neutralize the output and price effects of a switch in demand to the US bond, taking the place of open-market operations. They can also substitute for open-market operations in stabilizing outputs when the dollar is devalued to neutralize the price effects of a switch in demand to the EC good. In all other instances, however, changes in fiscal policies are less than fully optimal, and so policy co-ordination would be required to minimize the welfare costs of output and price changes.

3 The limiting case of perfect capital mobility

When dollar and ecu are perfect substitutes, $\phi \to \infty$ and the switch in demand between bonds drops out of the model completely.

The short-run solutions for the pegged-rate case are[15]

$$dR = \frac{1}{2}(dB^c - dF^c) - \frac{1}{2nv}(1 - 2a)(dx_1 - dx_2) + \frac{1}{nv}dc_2^* \quad (4.23)$$

$$dQ_1 = \frac{1}{2\mathfrak{J}}\{W\theta(vdB^c + vdF^c) + \frac{1}{n}[nQ\delta + s(1 - 2a)\mathfrak{J}]\frac{1}{s}dx_1$$

$$+ \frac{1}{n}[2aQ\delta - s(1 - 2a)W\theta]\frac{1}{a}dx_2\} + \frac{1}{n}(aU_f d\tilde{\pi} - dc_2^*) \quad (4.24)$$

$$dQ_2 = \frac{1}{2\mathfrak{J}}\{W\theta(vdB^c + vdF^c) + \frac{1}{n}[nQ\delta + s(1 - 2a)\mathfrak{J}]\frac{1}{s}dx_2$$

$$+ \frac{1}{n}[2aQ\delta - s(1 - 2a)W\theta]\frac{1}{s}dx_1\} - \frac{1}{n}(aU_f d\tilde{\pi} - dc_2^*) \quad (4.24')$$

The signs of these effects are identical to those obtained with imperfect substitutability, but there is an important difference in size. An open-market purchase of one country's bond has the same effect on both outputs; it does not affect domestic output more strongly than foreign output.

The short-run solutions for the floating rate case are

$$d\pi = \frac{nv}{aU_f} dR \qquad (4.25)$$

where the dR are given by equation (4.23), and

$$dQ_1 = \frac{1}{2\mathcal{J}}\left[(\mathcal{J} + W\theta)\,v dB^c - (\alpha Q\delta)\,v dF^c + Q\delta\frac{1}{s}(dx_1 + dx_2)\right] \qquad (4.26)$$

$$dQ_2 = \frac{1}{2\mathcal{J}}\left[(\mathcal{J} + W\theta)\,v dF^c - (\alpha Q\delta)\,v dB^c + Q\delta\frac{1}{s}(dx_1 + dx_2)\right] \qquad (4.26')$$

Here, open-market purchases have different effects on domestic and foreign outputs. In this limiting case, moreover, the switch in demand between goods has no output effects whatsoever; the change in the floating exchange rate is just large enough to reverse the switch in demand.

The long-run solutions for the pegged rate case are

$$dR = \frac{1}{2}\left[(dB^c - dF^c) + \frac{1}{av}dc_2^\star\right] \qquad (4.27)$$

$$dq_1 = \frac{1}{2\mathcal{J}Q}\left[W\theta\,(v dB^c + v dF^c) + Q\delta\,(dB^\star + \alpha dG_1)\right.$$

$$\left. + Q\delta\,(dF^\star + \alpha dG_2')\right] - \frac{1}{2}\left[Q(1 - 2a)\frac{1}{a}dc_2^\star - d\tilde\pi\right] \qquad (4.28)$$

$$dq_2' = \frac{1}{2\mathcal{J}Q}[\ldots] + \frac{1}{2}\left[Q(1 - 2a)\frac{1}{a}dc_2^\star - d\tilde\pi\right] \qquad (4.28')$$

The price equations are the same as equations (4.20) and (4.20') for the case of imperfect substitutability.

The long-run solutions for the floating rate case are

$$d\pi = \frac{1}{2Q}v dR \qquad (4.29)$$

$$dq_1 = \frac{1}{2Q\mathcal{J}}\left[(W\theta + \mathcal{J})\,v dB^c - (\alpha Q\delta)\,v dF^c + Q\delta\,(dB^\star + \alpha dG_1)\right.$$

$$\left. + Q\delta\,(dF^\star + \alpha dG_2')\right] + (1/Q)\,dc_2^\star \qquad (4.30)$$

$$dq_2' = \frac{1}{2Q\mathcal{J}}\left[(W\theta + \mathcal{J})\,v dF^c - (\alpha Q\delta)\,v dB^c + Q\delta\,(dB^\star + \alpha dG_1)\right.$$

$$+ Q\delta \left(dF^{\star} + \alpha dG_2'\right)\Big] - \frac{1}{Q} dc_2^{\star} \qquad (4.30')$$

The effects of open-market purchases and fiscal policies are identical to those in the corresponding output equations, but the switch in demand to the EC good reappears because the change in exchange rate raises the dollar price of the EC good and reduces the ecu price of the US good.

Under a pegged exchange rate, open-market operations cannot be used independently because they have the same effects on both countries' outputs and prices. This means that monetary policies can no longer be used to offset a balanced budget change in government spending. Nor can one country offset the other country's tax cut, as it could with imperfect capital mobility, because monetary policies cannot neutralize the remaining output changes. In some cases, however, open-market operations can be replaced by fiscal policies, and they can be used jointly with fiscal policies in another case.

As before, a change in G_1 can offset completely the domestic and foreign effects of a change in $W_1^{\star}$ (this can be done with a floating rate as well). Furthermore, fiscal policies can still stabilize Q_1 and Q_2 completely when the dollar is devalued by just enough to neutralize the price effects of a switch in demand to the EC good. They can replace monetary policies. With perfect capital mobility, moreover, changes in $B^{\star}$ and $F^{\star}$ can be combined with a joint change in monetary policies to neutralize the output and price effects of a balanced budget change in government spending or change in desired wealth. In the case of a change in $W_1^{\star}$, for example, equations (4.24), (4.25) and (4.28) or (4.28') can be solved simultaneously for the requisite changes in $B^{\star}$ and $F^{\star}$ and the change in the sum of B^c and F^c.

$$dB^{\star} = -dF^{\star} = \frac{s}{2(1 - s\alpha)g} dW_1^{\star}$$

$$dB^c + dF^c = \frac{1}{v} \frac{Q\delta}{W\theta} dW_1^{\star}$$

With an increase in $W_1^{\star}$, the US must raise taxes, the EC must reduce them, and the two governments must agree to conduct open-market purchases that raise the sum of their money supplies.

Under a floating exchange rate, fiscal policies have the same effects on both outputs and both prices, and so they cannot be used independently. Nevertheless, one country can offset completely a tax cut by the other, which could not be done with imperfect capital mobility, even with the aid of open-market operations. But monetary policies have different effects on domestic and foreign outputs, and their price effects resemble their output effects. Therefore they can be used independently to neutralize certain disturbances, even when this was not possible with imperfect capital mobility. With an increase in $W_1^{\star}$, for example, outputs and prices can be stabilized by setting $dB^c = dF^c = (Q\delta/W\theta)dW_1^{\star}$, without any change in $B^\star$, or $F^\star$, which is simpler than the pegged rate solution, where changes in $B^\star$ and $F^\star$ had to be combined with a change in the sum of B^c and F^c. With a switch in demand to the EC good, however, the changes in B^c and F^c that stabilize q_1 and dq_2' work to destabilize Q_1 and Q_2, and fiscal policies cannot help; because they have the same effects on both countries' outputs and prices, they cannot cause them to converge. A floating exchange rate is never the optimal response to the switch in demand between goods, because the change in exchange rate drives q_1 and q_2 in opposite directions.

4   An asymmetrical model

The US and EC economies can be made less alike by removing two restrictions imposed on the basic model. First, let $\theta_1 \neq \theta_2$ and $\delta_1 \neq \delta_2$. Second, let $Q_2 = \sigma Q_1$ and $G_2 = \sigma G_1$, so that $W_2 = \sigma W_1$ initially, and $a_1 = \sigma(1 - a_2)$ because trade is balanced initially.[16]

This version of the model can be written compactly, in a way that resembles earlier versions, by working with averages of US and EC variables. To this end, define $Q = (Q_1 + Q_2)/2$, etc., so that $Q_1 = uQ$ and $Q_2 = \sigma uQ$, where $u = 2/(1 + \sigma)$.[17] In what follows, moreover, we seek to determine whether exchange rate pegging continues to display attractive properties when the US and EC economies are not symmetrical – whether it allows complete domestic stabilization with a switch in demand between bonds, a balanced budget change in government spending and a change in desired wealth, and facilitates stabilization with a temporary tax cut and a switch in demand between goods. Therefore we need not solve the model for a floating exchange rate, but only for a pegged rate.

The short-run changes in reserves are

$$
\begin{aligned}
dR = \frac{1}{A} \Big\{ &\sigma u a\, W\phi \big[ua\left(W\theta_1 + \sigma W\theta_2\right) + 2a\alpha Q\delta_2 + s\alpha\left(1 - 2a\right)\mathcal{J}_2 \big] v dB^c \\
&- ua\, W\phi \big[ua\left(W\theta_1 + \sigma W\theta_2\right) + 2a\alpha Q\delta_1 + s\alpha\left(1 - 2a\right)\mathcal{J}_1 \big] v dF^c \\
&- \big[uaQ\left(\delta_2\mathcal{J}_1 + \sigma\delta_1\mathcal{J}_2\right) + s\left(1 - 2a\right)\mathcal{J}_1\mathcal{J}_2 \big] dB_2^\star \\
&- \sigma u a\, W\phi \big[s\left(1 - 2a\right)\mathcal{J}_2 + uaQ\left(\delta_2 - \delta_1\right) \big] \frac{1}{s} dx_1 \\
&+ ua\, W\phi \big[s\left(1 - 2a\right)\mathcal{J}_1 - \sigma uaQ\left(\delta_2 - \delta_1\right) \big] \frac{1}{s} dx_2 \\
&+ ua\, W\phi \left(\mathcal{J}_1 + \sigma\mathcal{J}_2\right) dc_2^\star \Big\}
\end{aligned}
\tag{4.31}
$$

where

$$A = uaQ\left(\delta_2\mathcal{J}_1 + \sigma\delta_1\mathcal{J}_2\right) + s\left(1 - 2a\right)\mathcal{J}_1\mathcal{J}_2 + uanv\, W\phi\left(\mathcal{J}_1 + \sigma\mathcal{J}_2\right)$$

$$\mathcal{J}_1 = W\theta_1 + \alpha Q\delta_1$$

$$\mathcal{J}_2 = W\theta_2 + \alpha Q\delta_2$$

The changes in reserves have the same signs as those in equation (4.15) for the symmetrical model, apart from two ambiguities. Fiscal expansion by the US ($dx_1 > 0$) can raise EC reserves if $\delta_2 < \delta_1$, and fiscal expansion by the EC ($dx_2 > 0$) can reduce EC reserves if $\delta_2 > \delta_1$.

The short-run changes in outputs are

$$dQ_1 = \frac{1}{A}\left\{ H_{11}vdB^c + H_{12}vdF^c + vH_{10}dB_2^\star + \frac{1}{s}\left(M_{11}dx_1 + M_{12}dx_2\right) \right.$$

$$\left. - M_{10}dc_2^\star + \left[2\left(1 - a\right)WvH_{10} + M_{10}U_f\right]\left(a\sigma u^2\right)d\tilde{\pi}\right\} \qquad (4.32)$$

$$dQ_2 = \frac{1}{A}\left\{ H_{22}vdF^c + H_{21}vdB^c - vH_{20}dB_2^\star + \frac{1}{s}\left(M_{22}dx_2 + M_{21}dx_1\right) \right.$$

$$\left. + M_{20}dc_2^\star - \left[2\left(1 - a\right)WvH_{20} + M_{20}U_f\right]\left(a\sigma u^2\right)d\tilde{\pi}\right\} \qquad (4.32')$$

where

$$H_{11} = W\theta_1\left[uaQ\delta_2 + s\left(1 - 2a\right)\mathcal{J}_2\right] + uavW\phi\left[ua\left(W\theta_1 \right.\right.$$
$$\left.\left. + \sigma W\theta_2\right) + s\alpha\left(1 - 2a\right)W\theta_1\right]$$

$$H_{12} = H_{11} - H_{10}$$

$$H_{10} = s\left(1 - 2a\right)W\theta_1\mathcal{J}_2 + ua\Omega$$

$$\Omega = Q\left(W\theta_1\delta_2 - W\theta_2\delta_1\right)$$

$$H_{22} = W\theta_2\left[\sigma uaQ\delta_1 + s\left(1 - 2a\right)\mathcal{J}_1\right] + \sigma uavW\phi\left[ua\left(W\theta_1 \right.\right.$$
$$\left.\left. + \sigma W\theta_2\right) + s\alpha\left(1 - 2a\right)W\theta_2\right]$$

$$H_{21} = H_{22} - H_{20}$$

$$H_{20} = s\left(1 - 2a\right)W\theta_2\mathcal{J}_1 - \sigma ua\Omega$$

$$M_{11} = Q\delta_1\left[uaQ\delta_2 + s\left(1 - 2a\right)\mathcal{J}_2\right]$$
$$+ uavW\phi\left\{\left[ua + s\alpha\left(1 - 2a\right)\right]Q\left(\delta_1 + \sigma\delta_2\right) + s\left(1 - 2a\right)\sigma W\theta_2\right\}$$

$$M_{12} = M_{11} - s\left(1 - 2a\right)M_{10}$$

$$M_{10} = Q\delta_1\mathcal{J}_2 + uavW\phi\left(\mathcal{J}_1 + \sigma\mathcal{J}_2\right)$$

$$M_{22} = Q\delta_2\left[\sigma uaQ\delta_1 + s\left(1 - 2a\right)\mathcal{J}_1\right]$$
$$+ uavW\phi\left\{\left[\sigma ua + s\alpha\left(1 - 2a\right)\right]Q\left(\delta_1 + \sigma\delta_2\right) + s\left(1 - 2a\right)W\theta_1\right\}$$

$$M_{21} = M_{22} - s\left(1 - 2a\right)M_{20}$$

$$M_{20} = Q\delta_2\mathcal{J}_1 + uavW\phi\left(\mathcal{J}_1 + \sigma\mathcal{J}_2\right)$$

The domestic and foreign effects of monetary policies are unambiguously positive (as H_{11}, H_{22}, H_{12} and H_{21} are positive), and the domestic effects of fiscal policies are also positive (as M_{11} and M_{22} are positive). But the foreign effects of fiscal policies are ambiguous (as M_{12} and M_{21} are ambiguous). Thus far, then, the output effects have the same signs as those in equations (4.16) and (4.16′) for the fully symmetrical version. But H_{10} and H_{20} are ambiguous, because Ω can be positive or negative, and this was not true in equations (4.16) and (4.16′), where their counterparts were positive. In consequence, the domestic effects of open-market operations are not necessarily larger than their foreign effects, and a switch between bonds has ambiguous output effects. Finally, M_{10} and M_{20} are positive, and so we know the effects of a switch in demand to the EC good ($dc_2^\star > 0$), but the output effects of a change in exchange rate contain an ambiguity (as they depend in part on H_{10} and H_{20}).

The long-run changes in reserves are

$$
\begin{aligned}
dR = \frac{1}{E} \Big(& \big\{ \big[(1 - 2a)\, W\theta_1 \mathcal{J}_2 + \sigma W\phi \big[ua\,(W\theta_1 + \sigma W\theta_2) + 2a\alpha Q\delta_2 \big] \big\} v dB^c \\
& - \big\{ (1 - 2a)\, W\theta_2 \mathcal{J}_1 + W\phi \big[ua\,(W\theta_1 + \sigma W\theta_2) + 2a\alpha Q\delta_1 \big] \big\} v dF^c \\
& - Q\big(\delta_2 \mathcal{J}_1 + \sigma\delta_1 \mathcal{J}_2 \big) dB_2^\star \\
& + \sigma Q\big[(1 - 2a)\,\delta_1 \mathcal{J}_2 - ua\, W\phi\, (\delta_2 - \delta_1) \big]\big(\alpha dG_1 - dW_1^\star\big) \\
& - Q\big[(1 - 2a)\,\delta_2 \mathcal{J}_1 - \sigma ua\, W\phi\, (\delta_2 - \delta_1) \big]\big(\alpha dG_2' - dW_2^\star\big) \\
& + \sigma\big[Q\delta_1 \mathcal{J}_2 + ua\Omega - ua\, W\phi Q\, (\delta_2 - \delta_1) \big] dB^\star \\
& - \big[Q\delta_2 \mathcal{J}_1 - \sigma ua\Omega + \sigma ua\, W\phi Q\, (\delta_2 - \delta_1) \big] dF^\star \\
& + \frac{1}{ua}\big[(1 - 2a)\, \mathcal{J}_1 \mathcal{J}_2 + ua\, W\phi\, (\mathcal{J}_1 + \sigma \mathcal{J}_2) \big] dc_2^\star \Big)
\end{aligned}
$$

(4.33)

where

$$
E = \sigma M_{10} + M_{20} + v(1 - 2a)\big(W\theta_2 \mathcal{J}_1 + \sigma W\theta_1 \mathcal{J}_2 \big)
$$

Changes in fiscal policies and desired wealth have ambiguous effects on reserves, just as they did in equation (4.31). Otherwise, the long-run changes in reserves bear the same basic relationships to the short-run changes that were shown to prevail in the symmetrical model. The fiscal-policy and wealth terms have opposite signs in equations (4.31) and (4.33), whereas the effects of open-market operations and switches in demand have the same signs in both equations.

The long-run changes in price levels are

$$
\begin{aligned}
dq_1 = \frac{1}{uQE} \Big(& \big\{ E_1 v dB^c + E_2 v dF^c + v\big(E_1 - E_2 \big) dB_2^\star \\
& + \big[E_0 + v(1 - 2a)\, QW\theta_2 \delta_1 \big]\big(\alpha dG_1 - dW_1^\star \big)
\end{aligned}
$$

Exchange rates and policy co-ordination 103

$$+ \left[E_0 + v(1 - 2a) QW\theta_1\delta_2 \right] (\alpha dG_2' - dW_2^\star)$$

$$+ \left[E_0 + v(1 - 2a) QW\theta_1\delta_2 - v(1 - ua)\Omega \right] dB^\star$$

$$+ \left[E_0 + v(1 - 2a) QW\theta_1\delta_2 + vua\Omega \right] dF^\star \}$$

$$+ \frac{1}{ua} \left[QM_{10} + v(1 - 2a) QW\theta_1\mathcal{J}_2 + uavW\Omega \right] (a\sigma u^2) d\bar{\pi}$$

$$- \frac{1}{ua} \left[M_{10} + v(1 - 2a) W\theta_1\mathcal{J}_2 - uaE \right] dc_2^\star \Big) \tag{4.34}$$

$$dq_2' = \frac{1}{uQE} \Big(\{\dots\}$$

$$- \frac{1}{\sigma ua} \left[QM_{20} + v(1 - 2a) QW\theta_2\mathcal{J}_1 - \sigma uavW\Omega \right] (a\sigma u^2) d\bar{\pi}$$

$$+ \frac{1}{\sigma ua} \left[M_{20} + v(1 - 2a) W\theta_2\mathcal{J}_1 - uaE \right] dc_2^\star \Big) \tag{4.34'}$$

where the term $\{\dots\}$ in equation (4.34') is identical with the corresponding term in equation (4.34) and

$$E_0 = Q\delta_1 Q\delta_2 + uavW\phi Q(\delta_1 + \sigma\delta_2)$$

$$E_1 = QW\theta_1\delta_2 + v\left[(1 - 2a) W\theta_1 W\theta_2 + uaW\phi(W\theta_1 + \sigma W\theta_2) \right]$$

$$E_2 = E_1 - \Omega$$

The effects of open-market operations, balanced budget changes in government spending and changes in desired wealth have the same signs as those in equations (4.20) and (4.20') pertaining to the symmetrical model. All other effects become ambigious, because they depend on Ω. Note, in particular, that a switch in demand between bonds can raise or reduce price levels, depending on the sign of Ω, although it did not affect price levels in the symmetrical model.

In the symmetrical model, a pegged exchange rate was fully optimal for dealing with the output and price effects of a switch in demand between bonds, a balanced budget change in government spending and a change in desired wealth. It was not fully optimal for dealing with the effects of temporary tax cuts or a switch in demand between goods. However, it facilitated stabilization in those two cases. Do these results continue to hold?

With a switch in demand between bonds, outputs and prices are stabilized when $dB^c = -dF^c = -dB_2^\star$, the same result that obtained before. With a balanced budget change in government spending or change in desired wealth, the changes in B^c and F^c that stabilize Q_1 and Q_2 come from equations (4.32) and (4.32'). With an increase in US government spending, for example.

$$dB^c = -\frac{1}{D}\frac{1}{v}(M_{11}H_{22} - M_{21}H_{12})\alpha dG_1$$

$$dF^c = -\frac{1}{D}\frac{1}{v}(M_{21}H_{11} - M_{11}H_{21})\alpha dG_1$$

where

$$D = H_{11}H_{22} - H_{12}H_{21} = [s(1 - 2a) W\theta_1 W\theta_2]A$$

Substituting these solutions into equations (4.34) and (4.34′) gives

$$dq_1 = dq_2' = \frac{1}{uQE}\frac{1}{D}\{[E_0 + v(1 - 2a) QW\theta_2\delta_1]D$$
$$- [E_1(M_{11}H_{20} + M_{21}H_{10}) - \Omega(M_{21}H_{11} - M_{11}H_{21})]\alpha dG_1$$

and laborious algebra shows that $dq_1 = dq_2' = 0$. Therefore a pegged exchange rate is still optimal in this case also.

In the symmetrical model, the output and price effects of a temporary tax cut in one country could be offset by raising taxes in the other country and using open-market operations independently. Can that be done here? Setting $dF^* = -dB^*$ and using equations (4.32) and (4.32′) to obtain the output-stabilizing monetary policies,

$$dB^c = -\frac{1}{D}\frac{1}{v}(1 - 2a)(M_{10}H_{22} + M_{20}H_{12})(1 - s\alpha)g dB^*$$

$$dF^c = \frac{1}{D}\frac{1}{v}(1 - 2a)(M_{10}H_{21} + M_{20}H_{11})(1 - s\alpha)g dB^*$$

so that

$$dq_1 = dq_2' = \frac{1}{uQE}\frac{1}{D}\{(1 - 2a)(1 - s\alpha)g[E_1(M_{20}H_{10} - M_{10}H_{20})$$
$$- \Omega(M_{20}H_{11} + M_{10}H_{21})] - v\Omega D\} dB^*$$

But

$$[E_1(\ldots) - \Omega(\ldots)] = \frac{1}{s}v\Omega D$$

so that

$$dq_1 = dq_2' = \Omega\frac{1}{uQE}\frac{1}{s}v[(1 - 2a)(1 - s\alpha)g - s] dB^*$$

and this does not go to zero, even when $g = s/(1 - s\alpha)$, the condition that cropped up frequently in earlier parts of this paper.

Finally, consider the use of a change in exchange rate to offset the price effects of a switch in demand to the EC good. It is easy to show that this cannot be done when the US and EC economies are not perfectly symmetrical. To begin, use equations (4.34) and (4.34′) to show how a switch in demand combined with a devaluation of the dollar affects the average price level:

$$\frac{1}{2}(dq_1 + dq_2') = \frac{1}{2}\frac{1}{uQ}\frac{1}{\sigma ua}\left[Q(a\sigma u^2)\,d\tilde{\pi} - (1 - 2a)\,dc_2^\star\right]$$

Clearly, this is not zero unless

$$d\tilde{\pi} = \frac{1}{Q}(1 - 2a)\frac{1}{a\sigma u^2}\,dc_2^\star$$

which is equivalent to the result obtained for the symmetrical model (where $\sigma = u = 1$). But a devaluation of this size does not stabilize q_1 and q_2', taken individually. Substituting into equations (4.34) and (4.34′) gives

$$dq_1 = -dq_2' = -\Omega\frac{1}{uQE}\frac{1}{Q}\alpha[Q + v(1 - 2a)\,G]\,dc_2^\star$$

which is not zero unless Ω is zero. Note further that open-market operations cannot offset the remaining changes in price levels because q_1 and q_2' move together in response to a change in B^c or F^c. (If $\Omega > 0$, for example, so that $dq_1 < 0$ and $dq_2' > 0$, changes in B^c and F^c that stabilize q_1 will amplify the change in q_2'.)

In brief, the particular asymmetries studied in this paper do not affect the extent to which a pegged exchange is fully optimal and thus dominates a floating rate. Nevertheless, they prevent it from facilitating stabilization in cases where it is not fully optimal but has attractive attributes in a world of perfectly symmetrical economies.

Notes

1 Other economists have suggested or used the same approach. Buiter and Eaton (1985) show that Nash and Pareto equilibria are both bliss point equilibria when policy targets and instruments are equal in number; Giavazzi and Giovannini (1986) anticipate my approach to the ranking of regimes but do not carry it out; Turnovsky and d'Orey (1986) adopt the same strategy but deal only with temporary disturbances. Some of my findings have been anticipated by Laskar (1986), who shows that a floating exchange rate can exacerbate the target instrument problem by changing the prices of imported goods and thus making it harder for monetary policy to stabilize the price level.

2 When intervention is conducted by the EC central bank, an increase in R comes about directly. When it is conducted by the US central bank, the increase comes about because the US central bank borrows ecu from the EC central bank and thus incurs a reserve liability.

3 Note that the coefficient g has no subscript, which implies that it is the same in the

US and EC, even when the two economies are not perfectly symmetrical. This is also true of certain coefficients in equations (4.7) – (4.10).

4 The same device is used by Allen and Kenen (1980, ch. 2). The final term in equation (4.6) is the central bank's interest income on its holdings of the US bond, which it pays over to the government.

5 The US demand for money should be made to depend on the EC interest rate as well as on the US interest rate because US residents hold EC bonds, but this link is omitted for simplicity. The same objection can be raised against equation (4.10), defining desired wealth.

6 In the language of portfolio balance modelling, households choose the minimum variance portfolio when there is no difference between expected returns on foreign and domestic assets (and that happens here whenever interest rates are equal because expectations are stationary). See, for example, Branson and Henderson (1985).

7 Unless otherwise indicated, expressions such as H, $\mathcal{J}$ and n are uniformly positive. Equations for the changes in interest rates and other variables can be found in Kenen (1987b).

8 The differences between the pegged rate and floating rate effects of the shift in demand to the US bond reflect the exchange rate effects of that shock. Under a pegged exchange rate, it raises the US money supply, raising US output; under a floating rate, it causes the dollar to appreciate, reducing US output.

9 In this particular case, moreover $dR = -B_2^*$, from equation (4.15), which says that sterilized intervention is the first-best policy response to a switch in demand between bonds. The same point is made by Kenen (1982) and Henderson (1984).

10 It should be noted, however, that governments can meet this condition. They have the power to choose g, as well as the long-run changes in debt.

11 As $dB^c + dF^c = 0$, the open-market operations do not affect the size of the change in exchange rate required to stabilize q_1 and q_2'. The US and EC government must agree on the size of the change in exchange rate but do not even have to consult about the monetary policies that they will pursue individually to offset the remaining output effects.

12 I have not compared the absolute sizes of the increases in Q_1 under a pegged rate with the absolute sizes of the decreases under a floating rate.

13 This last result is not surprising, because fiscal expansion by the EC has ambiguous effects on Q_1 under a pegged rate.

14 Under a floating rate, a change in B^* will neutralize the domestic effects when $g = s/(1 - s\alpha)$, but it will not neutralize the foreign price effects, because changes in B^* and W_1^* take different coefficients in equation (4.22').

15 Changes in W_1^* and W_2^* are omitted from this and subsequent equations because they have the same effects as balanced budget changes in government spending.

16 This last relationship reduces the openness of the larger economy and thus vitiates much of the effect of introducing a difference in size, but that cannot be helped when, as here, demand functions are Cobb–Douglas and trade must be balanced initially. It is also worth noting that the larger country's holdings of its own bond exceed those of the smaller country by more than the difference in scale. As $W_2 = \sigma W_1$ and $L_2 = \sigma L_1$ in the initial situation, $B_2 + \pi F_2 = \sigma(B_1 + \pi F_1)$. But $\pi F_1 = B_2$, because $\pi F_1 = \beta_1 W_1 = a_1 W_1$ and $B_2 = \beta_2 W_2 = (1 - a_2) W_2$. In consequence, $\sigma B_1 = \pi F_2 + (1 - \sigma)\pi F_1$, and $B_1 > (1/\sigma)\,\pi F_2$ if $\sigma < 1$; when the US is the larger economy,

US holdings of the US bond are disproportionately larger than EC holdings of the EC bond.

17 Correspondingly, $a_1 = \beta_1 = ua$, and $(1 - a_2) = \beta_2 = \sigma ua$, as before.

References

Allen, P. R. and Kenen, P. B. (1980) *Asset Markets, Exchange Rates, and Economic Integration*. Cambridge: Cambridge University Press.

Branson, W. H and Henderson, D. W. (1985) The specification and influence of asset markets. In R. W. Jones and P. B. Kenen (eds), *Handbook of International Economics*, vol. 2. Amsterdam: North-Holland.

Buiter, W. H. and Eaton, J. (1985) Policy decentralization and exchange rate managment in interdependent economies. In J. S. Bhandari (ed.), *Exchange Rate Management under Uncertainty*. Cambridge, MA: MIT Press.

Giavazzi, F. and Giovannini, A. (1986) Monetary policy interactions under managed exchange rates. CEPR Discussion Paper 123, Centre for Economic Policy Research, London.

Henderson, D. W. (1984) Exchange market intervention operations: Their role in financial policy and their effects. In J. F. O. Bilson and R. C. Marston (eds), *Exchange Rate Theory and Practice*. Chicago, IL: University of Chicago Press.

Kenen, P. B. (1982) Effects of intervention and sterilization in the short run and the long run. In R. N. Cooper, P. B. Kenen, J. B. de Macedo and J. van Ypersele (eds), *The International Monetary System under Flexible Exchange Rates*. Cambridge, MA: Ballinger.

—— (1987a) Global policy optimization and the exchange rate regime, *Journal of Policy Modeling* 9, Spring.

—— (1987b) Exchange rates and policy coordination, *Brookings Discussion Papers in International Economics* 52, The Brookings Institution, Washington.

Laskar, D. (1986) International cooperation and exchange rate stabilization, *Journal of International Economics* 21, August.

Turnovsky, S. J. and d'Orey, V. (1986) Monetary policies in interdependent economies with stochastic disturbances: A strategic approach, *Economic Journal* 96, September.

7

INTERNATIONAL ECONOMIC JOURNAL
Volume 5, Number 1, Spring 1991

1

DEBT BUYBACKS AND FORGIVENESS
IN A MODEL WITH VOLUNTARY REPUDIATION

PETER B. KENEN*

Princeton University

Debt reduction is usually analyzed in models where default is involuntary and the gains from debt reduction derive from various disincentives linked to a large debt overhang. This paper uses a model in which default is voluntary and shows that debt reduction can be beneficial even in the absence of those disincentives, by inducing debtors to renounce or postpone repudiation. This is likely to happen when debts are large compared to the penalties incurred by debtors if they repudiate. Furthermore, debtors can gain from debt buybacks even after allowing fully for the opportunity costs of using reserves for that purpose. [430]

1. INTRODUCTION

At the 1988 economic summit in Toronto, the seven major industrial countries agreed to reduce the debts or debt-service payments of low-income debtors, mainly in Africa. In March 1989, Nicholas Brady, Secretary of the Treasury of the United States, urged the commercial banks to accept debt-reducing arrangements with the middle-income debtors, mainly in Latin America, and called on the International Monetary Fund and the World Bank to earmark some of their policy-based lending for the debt-reducing process; some of it could be used to promote debt-for-bond swaps at significant discounts and to replenish the debtors' reserves following cash buybacks, and some of it could be used to underwrite the interest payments on new or modified debt contracts.

Events moved rapidly thereafter. The Fund and World Bank adopted guidelines for the implementation of the Brady Plan, and extended new credits to several countries in accordance with those guidelines. Two of those countries (Mexico and the Philippines) have reached debt-reducing agreements with their commercial-bank creditors, and others are negotiating with their creditors. Several other countries have begun discussions with the Fund and Bank, with their creditors, or both, and three countries (Bolivia, Chile, and Uruguay) have

*Research on this paper was financed by the International Finance Section at Princeton University. I thank Avinash Dixit, Mark Gersovitz, Giuseppe Bertola, Leonardo Bartolini, and other participants in seminars at Princeton University, the University of Maryland, and the Korea Development Institute for comments on earlier versions of the paper.

2   PETER B. KENEN

reached agreements with their creditors without seeking help from the Fund and Bank. Questions have been raised, however, about the size and distribution of the gains from debt reduction, producing a large body of analytical work.

Recent papers by Krugman (1989), Bulow and Rogoff (1988, 1989a), Froot (1989), and Williamson (1989) have examined the benefits of debt forgiveness and debt buybacks under various assumptions about the penalties that creditors impose when debtors default and the disincentive effects of a large debt overhang.[1] In most of that literature, however, defaults occur involuntarily, when a stochastic shock produces a "bad state" in which debtors cannot meet their obligations. In this paper, by contrast, debtors behave as in Eaton and Gersovitz (1981). They decide to repudiate their debts when the benefits exceed the costs, including the costs of the penalties imposed by their creditors.[2]

When debt forgiveness and debt buybacks are analyzed in this context, the results are different from those obtained in previous studies. Even when debt impairs economic efficiency in the debtor country or interferes with the functioning of the debtor's policies, debt reduction will not be mutually beneficial to the debtor and its creditors unless it induces the debtor to postpone or renounce the repudiation of its remaining debt. when debt reduction does have that effect, however, and the stock of debt is large, debt forgiveness can benefit both parties, and a buyback at the price prevailing in the secondary market can be beneficial too, even when the assets used for the buyback yield a rate of return to the debtor higher than the cost of servicing its debt.

The paper starts by modeling the debtor's behavior, turns next to the creditors' situation, and then studies conditions in which debt forgiveness and debt buybacks will be mutually beneficial.

2. OPTIMAL BEHAVIOR BY THE DEBTOR

Throughout this paper, decisions are made and announced at the start of the

---

[1]See also Corden (1988), Dooley (1988a, 1988b), and Helpman (1989).

[2]Rotemberg (1988) combines the Eaton-Gersovitz framework with a game-theoretic model to show that a debt buyback can benefit creditors and debtors by obviating the need for creditors to spend real resources on bargaining. To "act tough," he argues, and thus prevent repudiation, "one must spend real resources harassing the borrower." His result, however, depends crucially on the assumption that the cost of harrassment rises with the stock of debt. By contrast with the case studied here, moreover, outright debt forgiveness cannot be mutually beneficial in Rotenberg's model. Ghosh (1989) uses the Eaton-Gersovitz framework to study debt forgiveness in a model where there is new lending; he shows that it can raise investment and growth in the debtor country by reducing the debtor's incentive to repudiate and thus relaxing the credit constraint on new lending. He does not study buybacks, however, and confines attention to the impact on the debtor.

DEBT BUYBACKS AND FORGIVENESS   3

year, affecting transactions due to occur at the end of the year. All agents have perfect foresight and access to the same information. The debtor's obligations are inherited, reflecting previous borrowing, and creditors are not prepared to roll them over or make new loans.

The debtor has undertaken to service its debt by paying Y dollars per year for n years.[3] If it honors its obligations fully, their present value will be

$$D = \sum_{t=1}^{n} Y \delta^t = (1/r)Y(1 - \delta^n),$$ (1)

where $\delta = 1/(1 + r)$, and r is the interest rate as well as the subjective discount rate for debtors and creditors. If the debtor plans to repudiate its remaining obligations at the start of year k $(1 \leqslant k \leqslant n)$, their present value will fall to

$$D_k = \sum_{t=1}^{k-1} Y \delta^t = (1 - \phi)D, \quad \phi = \delta^{k-1}(1 - \delta^m)/(1 - \delta^n),$$ (1')

where m is the number of debt-service payments that will not be made when the debtor repudiates in year k (i.e., $m = n + 1 - k$). Hence, $\phi = 1$ and $D_k = 0$ when the debtor repudiates immediately, making $k = 1$ and $m = n$.

The debtor holds financial assets (reserves) with face value A, which yield an interest rate no higher than r but furnish other benefits to the debtor, such as the capacity for import smoothing and exchange-rate stabilization. They are thus deemed to yield a total return equal to $r + u$. If the debtor holds those assets permanently, their present value will be

$$B = \sum_{t=1}^{\infty}(r + u) A \delta^t = (1/r)(r + u)A.$$ (2)

If the debtor repudiates at the start of year k, however, its creditors may seize a fraction of its assets $(0 \leqslant \alpha \leqslant 1)$, reducing their present value to

$$B_k = \sum_{t=1}^{k-1}(r + u)A \delta^t + \sum_{t=k}^{\infty}(r + u)A(1 - \alpha)\delta^t$$

$$= (1/r)(r + u)A(1 - \alpha \delta^{k-1}).$$ (2')

Assume that the stock of reserves is smaller than the present value of the debtor's contractual obligations $(A < D)$.

Repudiation exposes the debtor to additional penalties. Exports must be dis-

---

[3]In earlier versions of this paper, the debtor paid interest for n years and repaid the whole principal at the end of the nth year. But this produced algebraic complications and a discontinuity in behavior; the debtor's incentive to repudiate was small until the start of the nth year but became very large at that point.

4   PETER B. KENEN

guised to prevent creditors from seizing them, and imports must be bought with cash when trade-credit lines are cut. In effect, the debtor can expect to experience a deterioration in its terms of trade. This terms-of-trade effect is permanent, but its size is deemed to fall as repudiation is postponed, because creditors are less likely to punish debtors that have met their obligations for many years, and the creditors' own cohesion is apt to decline with time, reducing their ability to impose effective sanctions. The annual cost of repudiation, in and after year k, is therefore denoted by $L\tau^m$, $\tau > 1$, and the present value of that cost will be

$$L_k = \sum_{t-k}(L\tau^m)\delta^t = (1/r)L(\tau^m)\delta^{k-1}. \tag{3}$$

Finally, debt is deemed to have income-reducing fiscal effects. Large debt-service payments require high tax rates that discourage capital formation and the repatriation of flight capital (Krugman, 1989). Furthermore, large debt-service payments in foreign currency can prevent a devaluation from improving the trade balance, because a devaluation widens the budget deficit, which speeds up the growth of the money supply and thus raises the inflation rate (Sachs, 1987, Dornbusch, 1988, and Reisen, 1989). Therefore, the debtor must rely on less efficient policy measures to produce the trade surplus it needs to service its debt. These fiscal effects are treated here as being proportional to the annual debt-service payment and to last until it ceases. Their present value is thus given by

$$G = \sum_{t-1}^{n}gY\delta^t = (1/r)gY(1 - \delta^n), \quad g > 0. \tag{4}$$

With repudiation in year k, however, their present value falls to

$$G_k = \sum_{t-1}^{k-1}gY\delta^t = (1/r)gY(1 - \delta^{k-1}). \tag{4'}$$

The full cost of servicing debt completely is thus given by

$$C = D + G - B = (1/r)[(1 + g)Y(1 - \delta^n) - A(r + u)]. \tag{5}$$

The full cost of servicing debt for $k - 1$ years and repudiating at the start of year k is given by

$$C_k = D_k + G_k - B_k + L_k = C - \delta^{k-1}(1/r)R_k, \tag{5'}$$

where

$$R_k = (1 + g)Y(1 - \delta^m) - [L\tau^m + \alpha A(r + u)]. \tag{6}$$

When $R_k = 0$, then $C_k = C$, and the debtor is indifferent between meeting the rest of its obligations and repudiating those obligations at the start of year k (and

DEBT BUYBACKS AND FORGIVENESS 5

I assume that it does not repudiate). When $R_k > 0$, however, then $C_k < C$, and repudiation is unambiguously advantageous.

Before turning to the creditors' calculations, consider three questions:

(1) How is the debtor's incentive to repudiate affected by its circumstances? Choosing an arbitrary year, $k \leqslant n$, and differentiating eq. (6) with respect to D, L, α, and A:

$$(dR_k/dY) = (1 + g)(1 - \delta^m) > 0,$$

$$(dR_k/dL) = -\tau^m < 0,$$

$$(dR_k/d\alpha) = -(r + u)A < 0,$$

$$(dR_k/dA) = -\alpha(r + u) \leqslant 0.$$

These results accord with intuition. The incentive to repudiate rises with an increase in the annual debt-service payment (which means, of course, that it rises with an increase in the interest rate). It falls with an increase in the strength of the sanctions to which the debtor is exposed (with increases in L and α). And it falls with an increase in the debtor's assets if some of them can be seized when the debtor repudiates (if $\alpha > 0$).

(2) What would the debtor do if it was willing to meet its obligations fully but was given the opportunity to buy back some of its debt at par? The answer is obtained by differentiating eq. (5) with respect to Y and A, then setting $dA = dD = (1/r)(1 - \delta^n)dY$, so that

$$(dC/dD) = -(1/r)v, \quad v = u - rg.$$

When $v < 0$, the debtor can reduce its debt burden, C, by buying back some of its debt at par (it should indeed be willing to buy it at a premium). I rule out this possibility by assuming that $v \geqslant 0$. When $v > 0$, by contrast, larger reserves confer benefits in use bigger than the cost of a larger debt overhang, so the debtor will want to borrow in order to raise its reserves. This is impossible, however, because I have assumed that creditors will not lend.[4]

(3) If the debtor does not repudiate today, will it do so later? If not, the model degenerates and is not very interesting. Hence, R_k must be made to rise through time, and this can be done by assuming that

$$\sigma_k = R_k - R_{k-1} = (\tau - 1)L\tau^m - (1 - \delta)(1 + g)Y\delta^m > 0. \tag{7}$$

---

[4] The case in which $v > 0$ resembles the one studied by Bulow and Rogoff (1988, 1989a), where a buyback cannot benefit the debtor, because it will want to engage in capital formation rather than repurchase debt, even when debt reduction has output-increasing effects ($g > 0$). In this paper, by contrast, a buyback can be beneficial to the debtor when the debtor plans to repudiate its debt and the terms of the buyback induce it to postpone repudiation.

6   PETER B. KENEN

This is the rationale for making $\tau > 1$. If $\tau \leqslant 1$, R_k would fall through time, and a debtor unwilling to repudiate today would not repudiate later. The assumption embodied in eq. (7) plays a vital role in the rest of the analysis.[5]

3. OPTIMAL BEHAVIOR BY THE CREDITORS

The creditors' assets consist of claims on the debtor and other safe assets having face value Q and the same interest rate, r, as claims on the debtor.[6] If creditors know that the debtor does not expect to repudiate, they will value their assets at

$$V = D + Q = (1/r)Y(1 - \delta^n) + Q. \tag{8}$$

If creditors know that the debtor plans to repudiate in year k, and it is not costly for them to impose the sanctions described in the previous section, they will value their assets at

$$V_k = D_k + Q + \sum_{t=k}^{\infty} \alpha r A \delta^t = V - \phi D + \alpha A \delta^{k-1}. \tag{8'}$$

By implication, individual creditors will be willing to swap debt with each other at a discount no larger than

$$w^s = \phi - \alpha (A/D) \delta^{k-1}, \tag{9}$$

---

[5]It should be noted that R_k and σ_k depend on m, the interval between the year in which the debtor will repudiate and the year in which it will pay off its debt completely if it does not repudiate. This makes the debtor's behavior time consistent. If the debtor decides at $t = 1$ to repudiate at $t = k$, fixing the value of m, it will not change its plans at $t = 2$, etc. (I thank Giuseppe Bertola for drawing this matter to my attention.) The results obtained by making $\tau > 1$ could also be obtained by assuming that the fiscal costs of a debt overhang rise with time, but that would make the model depend too heavily on the presence and size of those costs. The stochastic approach often adopted to analyze debt problems could be added to this model by making appropriate assumptions about expectations concerning future values of L. The "good state" would be one in which R_k was negative for all $k < n$ because L was thought to be large; the "bad state" would be one in which R_k was positive because L was thought to be small. The rest of the analysis would follow without significant modifications. Assumption about future values of L could also be used to replicate the framework suggested by Williamson (1989); pessimistic creditors would assign lower values to L than would optimistic creditors and would thus expect earlier repudiation.

[6]The safe asset Q might be expected to bear an interest rate lower than r, because D is exposed to repudiation. That would be the case, however, only if the possibility of repudiation had been anticipated when the debt was contracted initially, and bankers' statements at that time suggest that it was not. The terms of loans to developing countries protected commercial banks from interest-rate risk and exchange-rate risk but not from sovereign risk.

DEBT BUYBACKS AND FORGIVENESS   7

and this will be the discount in the secondary market. It is less than ϕ when creditors can expect to seize some of the debtor's assets, because each buyer of the debt obtains a *pro rata* share of the creditors' contingent claim to the debtor's assets.[7]

But creditors may quote a different discount to the debtor when it wants to buy back debt. On the one hand, a buyback reduces the debtor's reserves and, therefore, the assets that creditors can seize when the rest of the debt is repudiated. On the other hand, a buyback by the debtor can affect the date on which the debtor will repudiate and, therefore, the present value of the remaining debt. To analyze these possibilities separately, I distinguish between "small" and "large" reductions in the contractual value of the debtor's obligations. A small reduction is, by definition, too small to affect the debtor's plans. A large reduction is, by definition, big enough to change those plans by causing the debtor to renounce or postpone repudiation.

4. EFFECTS OF A SMALL BUYBACK

Suppose that $R_k > 0$ for some $k > 1$, so that the debtor plans to repudiate, and that the debtor can use reserves to buy back debt at a discount w, so that $dA = (1 - w)dD$. The effect of the buyback on the debtor is obtained by differentiating eq. (5′) with respect to D:

$$(dC_k/dD) = (1 + g)[(1 - \delta^{k-1})/(1 - \delta^n)]$$
$$- (1 - w)(1/r)(r + u)(1 - \alpha \delta^{k-1}).$$

The debtor will voluntarily buy back debt whenever $(dC_k/dD) > 0$ (so that the buyback reduces C_k). Accordingly, the debtor will want to buy back debt

---

[7]Nevertheless, we must assume that $D(1 - \delta^m) > \alpha A(1 - \delta^n)$. Unless this condition is satisfied, $w^s < 0$ and $V < V_k$, which say that creditors will *want* the debtor to repudiate. This condition is not automatically satisfied by assuming that $D > A$, because $(1 - \delta^m) < (1 - \delta^n)$ for $k > 1$. Note that eqs. (8′) and (9) assume implicitly that creditors cannot collude along the lines described by Bulow and Rogoff (1989b). If they could collude, they would refuse to buy back debt before year k, the year in which the debtor is expected to repudiate. They would continue to collect interest and amortization until the end of year $k - 1$, then offer to buy back debt at a discount that would leave the debtor indifferent between repudiation in year k and the creditors' offer. The gains from that sort of buyback would go to the creditors, as they would be partially compensated for the debt-service payments they were due to receive after year $k - 1$. Collusion would not be difficult in a world like the one modeled in this paper; because it assumes perfect foresight, it rules out any reason for creditors to disagree and any incentive for cheating. But collusion is difficult in an uncertain world, where creditors are apt to disagree concerning the debtor's intentions, opening the way for a buyback in advance — the sort analyzed later in this paper.

whenever the discount w is larger than

$$w^d = [1/(1 - \alpha \delta^{k-1})] \{[\phi - \alpha \delta^{k-1}]$$
$$+ [v/(r + u)] [(1 - \delta^{k-1})/(1 - \delta^n)]\}. \tag{10}$$

When $v > 0$ and $\alpha = 0$, then w^d is larger than w^s. The debtor will not buy back debt at the market price. when $\alpha > 0$, of course, w^d can be larger or smaller than w^s, but that will not be the relevant comparison, as the creditors' decision to deal with the debtor will not depend on w^s. When a single creditor sells debt to another, the debtor's reserves do not change, so α A does not change. When a group of creditors sell debt to the debtor, the debtor's assets fall, reducing α A, and the creditors will want compensation for the fall in the value of their remaining claims.[8] The discount that will govern their behavior is obtained by differentiating eq. (8′) with respect to D and A, then setting dA $= -$dQ $= (1 -$ w)dD:

$$(dV_k/dD) = (1 - \phi) - (1 - w)(1 - \alpha \delta^{k-1}).$$

Creditors will voluntarily sell debt to the debtor whenever (dV_k/dD) is negative (so that the debt sale raises V_k). Accordingly, creditors will sell debt to the debtor whenever the discount is smaller than

$$w^c = [1/(1 - \alpha \delta^{k-1})](\phi - \alpha \delta^{k-1}). \tag{11}$$

When $\alpha = 0$, of course, $w^c = w^s$, which means that $w^d > w^c$ whenever v is positive. This result resembles the one obtained by Bulow and Rogoff (1989a). A small buyback cannot be mutually beneficial when the assets used in the buyback yield a rate of return to the debtor higher than the cost of servicing its debt. And this result obtains even when $g > 0$, the case in which a buyback has output-increasing effects.[9] The same result obtains, moreover, when $\alpha > 0$, because

$$w^d - w^c = [v/(r + u)] [1/(1 - \alpha \delta^{k-1})] [(1 - \delta^{k-1})/(1 - \delta^n)],$$

and this is strictly positive whenever $v > 0$.

---

[8]A single creditor selling all of its claims to the debtor would not be affected by the fall in the debtor's assets and would deal with the debtor at the market price. But the "sharing clause" prevents a single creditor from dealing with a debtor in a manner harmful to the other creditors. When they deal jointly with the debtor, moreover, creditors can be expected to take account of the fall in the value of their claims that occurs when the debtor draws down assets to buy back debt.

[9]The derivation is different here, however, because it comes from the assumption that the debtor would not swap reserves for debt if it was willing to meet its obligations fully (i.e., that v $= u - rg > 0$).

5. DEBT FORGIVENESS AND THE TIMING OF REPUDIATION

Before examining the consequences of a large debt buyback, let us look at outright debt forgiveness. In the model used by Krugman (1989), debt forgiveness is mutually beneficial when the debtor finds itself on the downward-sloping portion of the Debt Relief Laffer Curve, and the debtor is bound to be there when its debt gets very large. In this model, by contrast, debt forgiveness cannot be mutually beneficial unless the amount of forgiveness is large enough to change the date on which the debtor plans to repudiate the rest of its obligations. A smaller amount of forgiveness has output-increasing effects when $g > 0$, but the debtor appropriates the whole gain.

To see how debt forgiveness works in the model, suppose that $R_{k-1} = 0$ for some $k \leqslant n$, so that the debtor is indifferent between honoring and repudiating its obligations at the start of year $k - 1$. In that case, eq. (7) says that $R_k = \sigma_k > 0$, so that $C_k = C - \delta^{k-1}(1/r)\sigma_k$, and the debtor will repudiate at the start of year k.

Now reduce the annual debt-service payment from Y to Y', defined below by eq. (12), and use eq. (5) to define

$$C' = (1/r)[(1 + g)Y'(1 - \delta^n) - A(r + u)].$$

Then set $C' = C_k$, so that the debtor will be indifferent between repudiating its original obligations at the start of year k and making the smaller debt-service payment Y' for n years. The amount of forgiveness required for this purpose is

$$Y - Y' = [\delta^{k-1}/(1 - \delta^n)][\sigma_k/(1 + g)] > 0. \tag{12}$$

After its debt is reduced, however, the debtor must decide whether to pay Y' per year for n years or to renege on the new bargain. It has thus to calculate

$$\begin{aligned}
R_k' &= (1 + g)Y'(1 - \delta^m) - [L\tau^m + \alpha A(r + u)] \\
&= [(1 - \delta^{k-1})/(1 - \delta^n)]\sigma_k,
\end{aligned}$$

and this is positive (because σ_k is positive), giving the debtor an incentive to repudiate. Therefore, this first approach yields a time-inconsistent solution and is unsatisfactory. We need instead to calculate the amount of debt forgiveness that will induce the debtor to meet its obligations fully after they have been reduced.

The debt-service payment required for that purpose is denoted by Y'' and is obtained by defining

$$\begin{aligned}
R_n'' &= (1 + g)Y''(1 - \delta^m) - [L\tau^m + \alpha A(r + u)] \\
&= (1 + g)Y''(1 - \delta) - [L\tau + \alpha A(r + u)],
\end{aligned}$$

because $m = 1$ when $k = n$. When $R_n'' = 0$, the debtor will be prepared to pay

Y'' for n $-$ 1 years and will be indifferent between paying and repudiating in year n. But we started by assuming that $R_{k-1} = 0$. Hence, we can obtain the amount of debt forgiveness that rules out repudiation by setting $R_n'' = R_{k-1} = 0$, and this procedure yields

$$Y - Y'' = [R_n/(1 + g)(1 - \delta)] > 0, \tag{13}$$

because $R_n > 0$ when $R_{k-1} = 0$ for $k \leqslant n$.

The debtor has to gain from debt forgiveness of this sort; otherwise, it would not renounce repudiation.[10] It is not hard to show, moreover, that the creditors can also gain when the initial debt is large. This will happen when $V'' > V_k$, where V'' is defined by substituting Y'' for Y in eq. (8) and V_k is defined as usual by eq. (8′). But $V'' > V_k$ whenever

$$\lambda_m(1 + g)Y > (1 - \delta)r(1 + g)\alpha A \delta^{k-1} + (1 - \delta^n)(\tau^m - 1)L\tau,$$

where $\lambda_m = (1 - \delta^m)[(1 - \delta)\delta^{k-1} + \delta(1 - \delta^n)] > 0$. Both sides of this inequality are positive when $\tau > 1$. But the size of the expression on the left increases with Y, the debt-service payment without debt forgiveness, while the size of the expression on the right increases with L and with αA, the penalties for repudiation. The whole statement says that the Debt Relief Laffer Curve found in Krugman (1989) is alive and well and living in this model too. Creditors can gain from outright debt forgiveness when the debt is large enough. In Krugman (1989), however, the Debt Relief Laffer Curve came into being because debt forgiveness raised the debtor's real income and thus raised the size of the partial payment that the debtor was able to make in the "bad state" when it could not meet all of its obligations. In this model, by contrast, it comes into being because debt forgiveness induces the debtor to renounce repudiation. The output-raising effects of debt forgiveness appear in the condition shown above, and it is more likely to be satisfied when those effects are large. But they could be omitted completely (by setting $g = 0$) without changing the basic story told by that condition.

Smaller amounts of debt forgiveness can likewise benefit both parties. They can induce the debtor to postpone repudiation rather than renounce it. When $R_{k-1} = 0$, as before, so that $R_k = \sigma_k$, the debtor will postpone repudiation by one year when the debt-service payment is reduced from Y to Y^i so as to satisfy

[10]Having set $R_n'' = 0$, we know that $R_k'' < 0$ for $k < n$. Therefore, we know that $C'' \leqslant C_k''$ for all k^n, where C'' and C_k'' are defined by replacing Y with Y'' in eqs. (5) and (5′). Furthermore, $C'' < C$ because of debt forgiveness, whereas $C_k > C$ for some $k \leqslant n$ as the debtor was planning to repudiate in the absence of forgiveness. Hence, $C'' < C_k$, and the debtor is better off than it was initially.

DEBT BUYBACKS AND FORGIVENESS   11

$$R^i_k = (1 + g)Y^i(1 - \delta^m) - [L\tau^m + \alpha A(r + u)] = 0,$$

and this condition gives

$$Y - Y^i = [\sigma_k/(1 + g)(1 - \delta^m)] > 0. \tag{14}$$

The debtor will repudiate the reduced debt at the start of year $k + 1$ but will be better off than it was without forgiveness, because it is cheaper to pay Y^i for k years than to pay Y for $k - 1$ years.[11] As in the previous case, however, the effect on the creditors depends on the size of the initial debt. They will gain when $V^i_{k+1} > V_k$, where V^i_{k+1} is defined by substituting Y^i for Y in eq. (8) and V_k is defined as before. Hence, they will gain whenever

$$\lambda_n(1 + g)Y > (1 - \delta)r(1 + g)\alpha A\delta^{k-1}(1 - \delta^m)$$
$$+ (1 - \delta^k)(\tau - 1)L\tau^m,$$

where $\lambda_n = (1 - \delta)[(1 - \delta^k)\delta^m + \delta^{k-1}(1 - \delta^m)] > 0$. This condition resembles the one obtained in the previous case. Debt forgiveness will be mutually beneficial when the debt is large compared to the penalties for repudiation.

6. EFFECTS OF A LARGE BUYBACK

When a small amount of debt was bought back at a discount larger than w^d, the debtor gained and creditors lost. How does a large buyback work? Suppose, as before, that $R_{k-1} = 0$ (so that $R_k = \sigma_k$), making the debtor plan to repudiate at the start of year k, and focus on the case in which creditors cannot seize the debtor's assets ($\alpha = 0$), so that $R_k = (1 + g)Y(1 - \delta^m) - L\tau^m$. The debtor will postpone repudiation for one year if

$$R^i_k = (1 + g)Y^i(1 - \delta^m) - L\tau^m = 0,$$

so that eq. (14) defines the size of the buyback.

When it buys back this amount of debt, however, the debtor's reserves are reduced to

$$A^i = A - (1 - w^i)(1/r)(1 - \delta^n)(Y - Y^i), \tag{15}$$

where w^i is the discount at which the transaction takes place, and the effect on the debtor will depend on that discount. The debtor will not gain unless

[11]Before the cut in the debt-service payment, the debtor's burden was $C_k = (1/r)[(1 + g)Y(1 - \delta^n) - A(r + u)] - \delta^{k-1}(1/r)\sigma_k$. After the cut from Y to Y^i, postponing repudiation from t $= k$ to $t = k + 1$, it is $C^i_{k+1} = (1/r)[(1 + g)Y^i(1 - \delta^n) - A(r + u)] - \delta^k(1/r)\sigma^i_{k+1}$, where $\sigma^i_{k+1} = \sigma_{k+1} + (1 - \delta)(1 + g)(Y - Y^i)\delta^{m-1}$. But $C_k > C^i_{k+1}$ when $[(1 - \delta^{k-1}) + (1 - \delta)\delta^n]\sigma_k + \delta^k(1 - \delta^m)\sigma_{k+1} > 0$, and this is always true.

$$r(1 + g)[\delta^n(1 - \delta)\sigma_k + \phi\delta(1 - \delta^n)\sigma_{k+1}] >$$
$$[(r + u)(1 - \delta^n)(\phi - w^i) + v(1 - \delta^{k-1})]\sigma_k.^{12}$$

In the present case, where $\alpha = 0$, this condition has two interpretations.

First, eq. (10) says that $(r + u)(1 - \delta^n)\phi + v(1 - \delta^{k-1}) = (r + u)(1 - \delta^n)w^d$, so that the condition becomes

$$r(1 + g)[\delta^n(1 - \delta)\sigma_k + \phi\delta(1 - \delta^n)\sigma_{k+1}] >$$
$$(r + u)(1 - \delta^n)(w^d - w^i)\sigma_k,$$

which says that the debtor can gain from a large buyback even when the discount is too small for the debtor to gain from a small buyback (i.e., when $w^d > w^i$).

Second, eq. (9) says that $\phi = w^s$, the discount in the secondary market. When $w^i = w^s$, moreover, the condition becomes

$$r(1 + g)[\delta^n(1 - \delta)\sigma_k + \phi\delta(1 - \delta^n)\sigma_{k+1}] > v(1 - \delta^{k-1})\sigma_k,$$

which says that the debtor can gain from making a large buyback even when it has to pay the market price. When $v > 0$, of course, the cost of using reserves to buy back debt exceeds the output-increasing effect of reducing the debt; that is why a small buyback at the market price was harmful to the debtor. By postponing repudiation, however, a large buyback reduces the penalty that the debtor faces, and this additional benefit can more than offset the high cost of using reserves (as well as the cost of servicing debt for an additional year).

As creditors can gain from outright debt forgiveness when it postpones repudiation, they are even more likely to gain from a large debt buyback. They will be better off whenever $V^i_{k+1} > V_k$, where

$$V^i_{k+1} = (1/r)(1 - \delta^k)Y^i + Q + (A - A^i).$$

and this will be true whenever

$$\delta^{k-1}(1 - \delta)L\tau^m > (1 - \delta^n)(w^i - \phi)\sigma_k.$$

We have already seen, however, that $\phi = w^s$ when $\alpha = 0$, so that this condition will be met whenever $w^i \leqslant w^s$. Accordingly, a buyback at the market price can be mutually beneficial when it induces the debtor to postpone repudiation.

---

[12]As in the previous note, the debtor will gain when $C_k > C^i_{k+1}$, but C^i_{k+1} must be redefined to allow for the reduction in the debtor's reserves: $C^i_{k+1} = (1/r)[(1 + g)Y^i(1 - \delta^n) - A^i(r + u)] - \delta^k(1/r)\sigma^i_{k+1}$, which can be combined with eq. (15) to produce the statement in the text.

DEBT BUYBACKS AND FORGIVENESS 13

REFERENCES

Bulow, Jeremy, and Rogoff, Kenneth, "The Buyback Boondoggle," *Brookings Papers on Economic Activity*, 2, 1988.

——————, "Sovereign Debt Repurchases: No Cure for Overhang," Working Paper 2850, National Bureau of Economic Research, Cambridge, 1989 (a).

——————, "A Constant Recontracting Model of Sovereign Debt," *Journal of Political Economy*, February 1989 (b).

Corden, W. Max, "Debt Relief and Adjustment Incentives," *International Monetary Fund Staff Papers*, December 1988.

Dooley, Michael P., "Buy-Backs and Market Valuation of External Debt," *International Monetary Fund Staff Papers*, June 1988 (a).

——————, "Self-Financed Buy-Backs and Asset Exchanges," *International Monetary Fund Staff Papers*, December 1988 (b).

Dornbusch, Rudiger, "Our LDC Debts," in M. Feldstein, ed., *The United States in the World Economy*, Chicago: University of Chicago Press, 1988.

Eaton, Jonathan, and Gersovitz, Mark, "Debt with Potential Repudiation," *Review of Economic Studies*, March 1981.

Froot, Kenneth A., "Buybacks, Exit Bonds, and the Optimality of Debt and Liquidity Relief," *International Economic Review*, Feruary 1989.

Ghosh, Atish R., "Debt Forgiveness and Economic Growth," Unpublished Manuscript, 1989.

Helpman, Elhanan, "Voluntary Debt Reduction: Incentives and Welfare," *International Monetary Fund Staff Papers*, September 1989.

Krugman, Paul R., "Market-Based Debt-Reduction Schemes," in J. A. Frenkel, M. P. Dooley, and P. Wickham, eds., *Analytical Issues in Debt*, Washington, D.C.: International Monetary Fund, 1989.

Reisen, Helmut, "Public Debt, External Competitiveness, and Fiscal Discipline in Developing Countries," *Princeton Studies in International Finance*, 66, International Finance Section, Princeton University, Princeton, 1989.

Rotemberg, Julio J., "Sovereign Debt Buybacks Can Lower Bargaining Costs," Working Paper 2767, National Bureau of Economic Research, Cambridge, 1988.

Sachs, Jeffrey, "Trade and Exchange Rate Policies in Growth-Oriented Adjustment Programs," in V. Corbo, M. Goldstein, and M. Khan, eds., *Growth-Oriented Adjustment Programs*, International Monetary Fund and World Bank, Washington, D.C., 1987.

Williamson, John, *Voluntary Approaches to Debt Relief*, Revised Edition, Policy Analyses in International Economics, 25, Institute for International Economics, Washington, 1989.

Mailing Address : Professor Peter B. Kenen, International Finance Section, Department of Economics, Princeton University, 300 Fisher Hall, Princeton, NJ 08544-1021, U.S.A.

13

Exchange Rate Arrangements, Seigniorage, and the Provision of Public Goods

Peter B. Kenen

I. Introduction

The Delors Committee Report on European monetary union[1] revived an old debate about fiscal policies in a monetary union. Believing that "divergent national budgetary policies would undermine monetary stability" and noting "that the centrally managed Community budget is likely to remain a very small part of total public sector spending and that much of this budget will not be available for cyclical adjustments," the Report concluded correctly that "the task of setting a Community-wide fiscal policy stance will have to be performed through the coordination of national budgetary policies" (Delors (1989), pp. 24–25). This conclusion, however, was followed by another that may be inconsistent with it and is controversial on its own (Delors (1989), p. 24):

I have benefited greatly from discussions with Alessandra Casella, from suggestions by Avinash Dixit, and from comments by participants in seminars at the Bank of Canada and Princeton University, but they bear no responsibility for the contents of the paper. Work on the paper was supported by the International Finance Section at Princeton University.

[1]Committee for the Study of Economic and Monetary Union, *Report on Economic and Monetary Union in the European Community* (Luxembourg, 1989); the Committee was chaired by Jacques Delors, President of the Commission of the European Communities. The report is cited hereafter as Delors (1989).

In the budgetary field, binding rules are required that would: firstly, impose effective upper limits on budget deficits of individual member countries of the Community, although in setting these limits the situation of each member country might have to be taken into consideration; secondly, exclude access to direct central bank credit and other forms of monetary financing while, however, permitting open market operations in government securities; thirdly, limit recourse to external borrowing in non-Community currencies.

These recommendations raise many questions, which can be grouped beneath three headings: stabilization, credibility, and seigniorage.

Stabilization

Having relinquished the use of monetary policy, does a member of a monetary union need to lean more heavily on fiscal policy to stabilize its own economy? The answer must be "yes" in principle, unless you believe that fiscal policy is completely ineffective or that the members of a monetary union should not expect to experience country-specific shocks to output and employment. In the United States, however, the world's largest monetary union, few state governments appear to follow contracyclical policies, and many are bound by balanced-budget rules, which have procyclical effects. Yet students of U.S. experience have also pointed out that the contra-cyclical behavior of the federal budget substitutes partially for local autonomy, and they have warned that a monetary union will not work well in Europe unless the budget of the European Community (EC) is made more flexible or supplemented by large-scale transfers to countries or regions that suffer adverse real shocks.[2]

Credibility

The debate about the Delors Committee Report has gradually revealed the main concern that caused its authors to recommend strict limits on national budget deficits. They were determined to protect the independence and credibility of the new European central bank, and its credibility will be impaired if it is expected to rescue member governments whenever they borrow their way into a debt crisis. It can be argued, however, that strict limits on new borrowing may not be necessary or sufficient for this purpose. They may not be necessary if capital markets can discipline national

---

[2] These issues and the relevant literature are reviewed in Eichengreen (1990).

governments by charging them more when they borrow more.[3] They may not be sufficient if national governments have large debts initially, because a debt overhang can lead to a debt crisis even when the debtor is not borrowing more.

Seigniorage

Some European governments have counted heavily on money creation to finance their budget deficits,[4] and they cannot expect to do that in a monetary union. This has led economists such as van der Ploeg (1990) to warn that a monetary union could produce a shortage of public goods. But Casella (1990) has come to the opposite conclusion. She has shown that a monetary union can help to prevent the excessive production of public goods that occurs when fiscal policies are not coordinated, and her analysis is the starting point for this paper.

Building on earlier work with Feinstein (Casella and Feinstein (1989)), Casella uses a two-country model to show how monetary arrangements can affect the supply of public goods. Each country has a private sector that produces and exports many varieties of a differentiated consumer good and a government that produces a single public good. An increase in output of the public good raises household welfare directly but reduces it indirectly by shrinking the number of varieties of the consumer good, and this indirect loss is shared by the two countries' households, which buy both countries' goods. Therefore, decentralized decision making leads each country to produce too much of the public good, and fiscal policies have to be coordinated to achieve the first-best allocation of resources. In Casella's model, however, the first-best allocation can be achieved by monetary coordination, because governments rely entirely on newly printed money to pay for the production of the public goods.

A monetary union is one form of monetary coordination, but it poses special problems in Casella's model, because country size and the strength of the demand for the public good affect the optimal distribution of new money. The particular characteristics of her model lead Casella to conclude that the smaller member of a two-country union will usually require and obtain more than proportional power in managing the union. Otherwise, it cannot count on

---

[3] A variant of this argument appears in Corden (1983).
[4] See, for example, Drazen (1989).

obtaining enough of the newly created money and will not join the union.[5]

Combining Inflation and Taxation

Casella assumes that governments are indifferent between two ways to pay their bills, issuing new money and collecting lump-sum taxes, and some of her results depend directly on this strong assumption. I will show what happens when it is relaxed—when governments are not indifferent between using the inflation tax and using lump-sum taxes and they differ in their policy preferences. The introduction of these preferences complicates the model greatly, forcing me to simplify it in some other ways. Accordingly, I have suppressed most of the cross-country differences featured in Casella's model and will not be able to say very much about the issue on which she concentrates—the effects of differences in country size on the appropriate constitution for a monetary union. But I will be able to analyze several other issues—the influence of various exchange rate arrangements on resource allocation, inflation rates, and tax rates, and the degree to which monetary coordination can substitute for fiscal coordination.

The first part of the paper outlines the basic model. It is an abbreviated version of Casella's presentation but makes some minor modifications and adds the national governments' policy preference functions.[6]

The second part solves the model for the national currency case, in which each country's households hold that country's currency (there is no currency substitution). It deals extensively with two policy regimes: a floating exchange rate with policy autonomy and a floating rate with comprehensive coordination. It asks what happens

---

[5] It should be noted that Casella's model and the adaptation here violate the injunction of the Delors Report that governments should not have direct access to central bank credit. A weak version of that injunction is introduced below, however, when the central bank of a monetary union is forbidden to discriminate in distributing new money.

[6] Casella's own model draws on the Dixit-Stiglitz (1977) representation of monopolistic competition and the trade-theoretic adaptation in Krugman (1981). Her basic conclusions, however, and those in this paper do not depend strongly on the use of that model; they can be obtained from old-fashioned trade models, where an increase in one country's spending on its public good will affect the welfare of the other country's households by affecting the terms of trade rather than the number of varieties of the consumer good.

in each instance when the two countries differ in size and in their policy preferences (DSP), when they are identical in size (IS) but differ in their preferences, and when they are identical in size and in their policy preferences (ISP).

The third part of the paper extends the analysis of the national currency case by looking at three more regimes: a floating exchange rate with partial policy coordination (monetary but not fiscal), a pegged rate with comprehensive coordination, and a pegged rate with partial coordination.[7]

The fourth part of the paper solves the same model for the common currency case, in which each country's households hold both countries' currencies (there is perfect currency substitution) or hold a single currency issued jointly by those countries. It examines three policy regimes: policy autonomy, comprehensive coordination, and partial coordination. The last two regimes are equivalent to monetary unions with and without fiscal coordination, and they will be analyzed under two arrangements—one in which the union's central bank can discriminate freely when issuing new money to its members, and one in which it is constrained to treat them identically. To limit the length of the paper and emphasize the influence of policy preferences, analysis of these common currency regimes is confined to the IS and ISP cases.

I will show that a floating exchange rate with comprehensive coordination is the first-best regime; it can accommodate differences in policy preferences but can still achieve the optimal allocation of real resources between each country's private and public sectors. A floating rate with partial coordination is a second-best regime; it cannot fully accommodate different policy preferences and thus leads to a less efficient resource allocation. Pegged exchange rates likewise interfere with the accommodation of policy preferences, distorting resource allocation, even when national policies are fully coordinated.

A common currency has interesting properties. When govern-

---

[7] It would be possible, of course, to have a pegged exchange rate without any policy coordination, but this regime cannot be modeled without adding another asymmetry; one central bank must lead and the other must follow. The analysis would be interesting, because the European Monetary System (EMS) has been described this way, which makes it the most appropriate benchmark for measuring the welfare effects of a European monetary union. But it is a difficult case to model, as we will see when we come to a similar case, where both countries issue a common currency but do not coordinate their monetary policies.

ments issue it independently, without any coordination, there is no equilibrium in Casella's model, yet that is not true here. But governments produce more public goods than in any other case, because they try to tax their partner's households by issuing larger amounts of money. A monetary union solves this problem, but it cannot accommodate differences in policy preferences. Hence, it tends to replicate the inefficiencies associated with pegged-rate regimes.

II. The Model

The model comprises two countries ($j = 1$, 2) having σ_j identical households and n_j identical firms. Each household supplies labor, earns wage income, pays lump-sum taxes, buys goods from the private sector, and partakes of the public good produced by its government. There is a one-period lag, however, between the time at which it receives its wage income and the time at which it pays taxes and buys goods from the private sector, and it holds a cash balance in the interim, since money is the only store of value.[8] Each firm produces its own variety of the differentiated consumer good under decreasing-cost conditions. Each household consumes all n varieties ($n = n_1 + n_2$).

The utility of the typical household in the jth country is represented by

$$u_j = (1 - g)\ln\left[\left(\sum_{i=1}^{n} c_{ij}^{\theta}\right)^{\frac{1}{\theta}}\right] + g \ln\left(z_j \sigma_j^{1-\mu}\right),$$

$$0 < g < 1, \quad 0 < \theta < 1, \tag{1}$$

where c_{ij} is the household's consumption of the ith variety of the consumer good and $\sigma_j z_j$ is total output of the jth country's public good.[9] The parameter μ is used to distinguish between two types of public good. When $\mu = 0$, the utility provided by the public good is independent of the number of households partaking of it. That is

---

[8] There are no other lags in the model, and I omit time subscripts whenever possible.

[9] Note that u_j is not affected by the output of the other country's public good. If that were true, an increase in one country's spending on its public good could be beneficial to the other country's households rather than being harmful, as it is in this paper.

Casella's specification. When $\mu = 1$, by contrast, households crowd each other out, and the utility provided by the public good varies inversely with the number of households. This distinction proves to be crucial for the effect of country size on household welfare.[10] Note that the parameters g, θ, and μ do not have country subscripts. Take this to mean that they do not vary from country to country. The elasticity of substitution between any two varieties of the consumer good is given by $1/(1 - \theta)$.

Labor is the only input in the model, and the quantity required by the ith firm to produce its own variety of the consumer good is

$$L_{ij} = \alpha + \beta X_{ij}, \tag{2}$$

where X_{ij} is total output of the ith variety, so that

$$X_{ij} = \sum_{j=1}^{2} \sigma_j c_{ij}. \tag{3}$$

Because the n_j varieties have the same labor requirements and figure identically in the utility function, they must have the same price, p_j, and profits must be zero with free entry:

$$p_j X_{ij} = w_j L_{ij}, \tag{4}$$

where w_j is the wage rate. Using equation (2) to replace L_{ij} and differentiating with respect to X_{ij}, we equate marginal cost to marginal revenue and can thus obtain

$$p_j = \left(\frac{\beta}{\theta} \right) w_j. \tag{5}$$

Hence, the output of each variety is

$$X_{ij} = X = \frac{\alpha \phi}{\beta}, \qquad \phi = \frac{\theta}{1 - \theta}. \tag{6}$$

Each firm chooses the same level of output, given by the tangency between its average-cost curve and demand curve. By implication, each country's private sector adjusts to policy changes and shocks by changing the number of varieties, not the output of each variety.

---

[10] A public broadcasting system exemplifies the first type of public good; a system of schools or hospitals exemplifies the second. But many public goods fall between these polar cases.

Changes in the number of varieties are achieved by the entry or exit of firms.

The two countries' goods prices are linked by the exchange rate, expressed in units of the first country's currency:

$$p_1 = ep_2. \tag{7}$$

Clearly, the exchange rate cannot be constant unless the two countries have the same inflation rates.

Under the assumptions imbedded in the utility function, the same fraction of each household's disposable income is spent on each variety of the consumer good. Accordingly,

$$c_{ij} = c_j = \left(\frac{1}{n}\right)\left(\frac{w_{jt-1} - w_{jt}\tau_j}{p_{jt}}\right) = \left(\frac{1}{n}\right)\left(\frac{\theta}{\beta}\right)\left[\left(\frac{1}{1 + \pi_j}\right) - \tau_j\right], \tag{8}$$

where π_j is the jth country's inflation rate and $w_{jt}\tau_j$ is the nominal lump-sum tax paid in period t, so that τ_j is the real lump-sum tax.[11]

The public good is produced under constant-cost conditions, and a suitable choice of units allows us to define the quantity of labor needed by

$$L_{jz} = \sigma_j z_j. \tag{9}$$

Production of the public good must be financed by taxation or money creation, which means that the jth government's budget constraint can be written as

$$z_j = \tau_j + m_j, \quad m_j = \left(\frac{1}{\sigma_j}\right)\left(\frac{M_{jt} - M_{jt-1}}{w_{jt}}\right), \tag{10}$$

where M_{jt} is the nominal money stock at the end of period t, so that m_j is the real increase in the money stock per household.

As labor is fully employed,

$$\sigma_j = n_j(\alpha + \beta X) + \sigma_j z_j = n_j\left(\frac{\alpha}{1 - \theta}\right) + \sigma_j z_j, \tag{11}$$

---

[11] Because the supply of labor is inelastic in this model, τ_j is equivalent in form and effect to a proportional tax on the current nominal wage, w_{jt}.

so that

$$n = \sigma\left(\frac{1-\theta}{\alpha}\right)\Gamma, \quad \sigma = \sigma_1 + \sigma_2, \quad \Gamma = \sum_{j=1}^{2} s_j(1 - z_j), \quad \text{and} \quad s_j = \frac{\sigma_j}{\sigma}.$$

$$(12)$$

Therefore, equation (1) can be rewritten as

$$u_j = A + (1-g)\phi\ln\Gamma + (1-g)\ln\left[\left(\frac{1}{1+\pi_j}\right) - \tau_j\right]$$

$$+ g\left[\ln z_j + (1 - \mu)\ln s_j\right],$$

$$(13)$$

where

$$A = (1-g)\left[\phi\ln\left(\frac{1-\theta}{\alpha}\right) + \ln\left(\frac{\theta}{\beta}\right)\right] + \left[(1-g)\phi + g(1-\mu)\right]\ln\sigma.$$

Note that the term Γ contains the two z_j, which says that each country's decision concerning its z_j affects the utility of the other country's households. This is the basic externality in the model and the rationale for policy coordination.

This concludes the presentation of Casella's model and brings us to the governments' policy preferences.

Each government is deemed to maximize a welfare function containing the utility of the typical household and its own policy preference function:

$$W_j = u_j - \lambda Q_j,$$

$$(14)$$

The jth government's policy preference function is

$$Q_j = \frac{1}{2}\left[v_j\left(\frac{\tau_j}{z_j}\right)^2 + (1 - v_j)\left(\frac{m_j}{z_j}\right)^2\right], \quad 0 < v_j < 1.$$

$$(15)$$

The cost of using a policy instrument, τ_j or m_j, rises quadratically as the government relies more heavily on it to finance production of the public good.

It might be more appropriate to write the policy preference function in terms of the inflation rate, π_j, rather than the cause of the inflation rate, m_j. We will soon see, however, that the two formulations are formally equivalent in the national currency case but that the use of π_j would complicate the common currency case, where the common inflation rate depends on both of the m_j. In other words, the use of π_j would introduce an additional externality. It might likewise be argued that the policy preference functions do not really belong in the model, as the costs of money creation and taxation are already reflected in the households' utility functions. But perfect internal consistency is not the ultimate virtue in a model too simple to be realistic.

As they are used repeatedly hereafter, it is worth writing out the partial derivatives of the policy preference functions:

$$\frac{\partial Q_j}{\partial \tau_j} = \left(\frac{1}{m_j}\right)^3 m_j q_j, \quad \frac{\partial Q_j}{\partial m_j} = -\left(\frac{1}{z_j}\right)^3 \tau_j q_j,$$

$$q_j = v_j \tau_j - \left(1 - v_j\right)m_j = v_j z_j - m_j.$$

This completes the model.

III. The National Currency Case

When households hold only their own country's currency, the demand for the currency must equal total wage payments, because households have to carry them forward from the period in which they earn them to the period in which they spend them. Therefore, money market equilibrium obtains when

$$M_{jt} = \sigma_j w_{jt}, \tag{16}$$

so that

$$m_j = \frac{\pi_j}{1 + \pi_j}. \tag{17}$$

Equation (17) says that countries can have identical inflation rates if and only if $m_1 = m_2$. It also supports the assertion made earlier that it does not much matter whether the policy preference function is written in terms of m_j or π_j in the national currency case.

Using equation (17) to solve for π_j and replacing it in equation (13),

$$u_j = A + (1 - g)[\phi \ln \Gamma + \ln(1 - z_j)] + g[\ln z_j + (1 - \mu)\ln s_j]. \tag{18}$$

Note that τ_j and m_j do not appear separately in equation (18). Hence, a government that wants merely to maximize u_j has simply to choose the appropriate z_j. That is what governments do in Casella's model. Putting the same point formally,

$$\frac{\partial u_j}{\partial \tau_j} = \frac{\partial u_j}{\partial m_j} = \frac{\partial u_j}{\partial z_j} = -(1-g)\left[\phi s_j\left(\frac{1}{\Gamma}\right) + \left(\frac{1}{1-z_j}\right)\right] + g\left(\frac{1}{z_j}\right).$$

Note further that

$$\frac{\partial u_1}{\partial z_2} = -(1-g)\phi s_2\left(\frac{1}{\Gamma}\right), \quad \frac{\partial u_2}{\partial z_1} = -(1-g)\phi s_1\left(\frac{1}{\Gamma}\right).$$

A Floating Exchange Rate with Policy Autonomy

With a floating exchange rate between the two countries' currencies and no international coordination of monetary or fiscal policies, the jth country's fiscal and monetary authorities will maximize W_j with respect to τ_j and m_j, and they will obtain these first-order conditions:[12]

$$\frac{\partial W_j}{\partial \tau_j} = \frac{\partial u_j}{\partial z_j} - \lambda\left(\frac{1}{z_j}\right)^3 m_j q_j = 0, \quad \frac{\partial W_j}{\partial m_j} = \frac{\partial u_j}{\partial z_j} + \lambda\left(\frac{1}{z_j}\right)^3 \tau_j q_j = 0. \quad (19)$$

Subtracting one from the other,

$$\lambda\left(\frac{1}{z_j}\right)^2 q_j = 0. \tag{20}$$

This condition cannot be satisfied, however, unless, $q_j = 0$, which gives us the optimal values of m_j and τ_j:

$$m_j = v_j z_j, \quad \tau_j = (1 - v_j) z_j. \tag{21}$$

The marginal (and average) yield from each revenue-raising instrument is equated to the marginal cost of using it.

---

[12] The second-order conditions for this and other exercises are shown in Annex I.

When $q_j = 0$, moreover, equations (19) say that

$$(1-g)\left[\phi k_j\left(\frac{1}{\Gamma}\right) + \left(\frac{1}{1-z_j}\right)\right] - g\left(\frac{1}{z_j}\right) = 0, \qquad (22)$$

where $k_j = s_j$.

As τ_j and m_j do not appear individually in equation (22), a government's policy preferences do not impinge on its decisions about z_j, the output of the public good, and it can partition its policy problem. It can use equation (22) to choose the appropriate z_j, then use equations (21) to choose the τ_j and m_j that minimize the cost of providing the public good.[13] For this same reason, moreover, a floating rate regime without coordination can accommodate different policy preferences. The governments' decisions about the z_j are interdependent, because both of the z_j appear in Γ, but their decisions about the τ_j and m_j can be taken independently. The latter are reconciled by the floating exchange rate, which offsets the gap between the inflation rates that arises when governments create different amounts of money per household.

Note finally that equation (22) puts strict limits on the z_j. It is, of course, impossible for them to be negative or larger than unity, but equation (22) narrows the limits. Feasible z_j must be positive and smaller than unity.

Before we carry the analysis further, let us look at the governments' problem with comprehensive policy coordination.

A Floating Exchange Rate with Comprehensive Coordination

With a floating exchange rate and comprehensive policy coordination, the two countries' monetary and fiscal authorities can be deemed to maximize a weighted sum of their welfare functions, with the weights based on the countries' populations:

$$W_T = s_1 W_1 + s_2 W_2. \qquad (23)$$

---

[13] The policy problem in this particular case does not differ greatly from the one in Casella's paper, where the government chooses the optimal z_j and finances its spending by issuing money, levying a lump-sum tax, or using the two together. Whenever, $q_j = 0$, in fact, the results in this paper regarding the z_j match those in Casella's paper. (To replicate her results, we have merely to drop the policy preference function from the optimization problem by setting $\lambda = 0$.)

The first-order conditions for the jth country's instruments are

$$\frac{\partial W_T}{\partial \tau_j} = s_1\left(\frac{\partial u_1}{\partial z_j}\right) + s_2\left(\frac{\partial u_2}{\partial z_j}\right) - \lambda s_j\left(\frac{1}{z_j}\right)^3 m_j q_j = 0, \tag{24a}$$

$$\frac{\partial W_T}{\partial m_j} = s_1\left(\frac{\partial u_1}{\partial z_j}\right) + s_2\left(\frac{\partial u_2}{\partial z_j}\right) + \lambda s_j\left(\frac{1}{z_j}\right)^3 \tau_j q_j = 0. \tag{24b}$$

Subtracting one from the other, we obtain equation (20) once again and, therefore, equations (21) and (22), but with $k = 1$ instead of $k = s_j$.

Although the two governments engage in comprehensive coordination, each of them is still free to choose the τ_j and m_j that satisfy its preferences; the floating exchange rate continues to offset the gap between the π_j that arises when the governments have different preferences. Looking at this outcome from another standpoint, the governments seem to be coordinating their decisions about the τ_j and m_j but are really coordinating their decisions about the z_j. And that is what they should do in this model, where the externality involves the z_j.

Because the two regimes examined above yield very similar equations for the z_j (they differ only in the values of the k_j), the rest of the analysis can deal with them jointly.

Optimal Supplies of the Public Goods

To show how policy coordination affects household welfare, we must show how it affects the z_j. We begin by rewriting equation (22):

$$k_j(1 - g)\phi(1 - z_j)z_j - \Gamma(g - z_j) = 0. \tag{25}$$

There are two such equations, of course, one for each country, and they must be solved simultaneously, because Γ appears in both. In the IS case, however, where the $s_j = \frac{1}{2}$, the two equations are the same and have only one feasible solution, $z_1 = z_2 = z$.[14] As $\Gamma = 1 - z$ in this case, the equations are easy to solve:

$$z = \frac{g}{H}, \qquad H = 1 + k(1 - g)\phi, \tag{26}$$

---

[14] See Annex II.

where $k = \frac{1}{2}$ with policy autonomy and $k = 1$ with comprehensive coordination. It will be useful, moreover, to define and evaluate total output of the public good, $z_T = z_1 + z_2$, to facilitate comparisons with other regimes. With policy autonomy,

$$z_T = \frac{2g}{1 + \frac{1}{2}(1-g)\phi}, \tag{27a}$$

and with comprehensive coordination,

$$z_T' = \frac{2g}{1 + (1-g)\phi}. \tag{27b}$$

Comprehensive coordination reduces total output of the public good $(z_T' < z_T)$.

Policy Coordination and Welfare

Policy coordination raises household welfare too, and this is easy to prove in the IS case. Using equation (26) to replace z_j in equation (13) and differentiating with respect to k,

$$\frac{\partial u_j}{\partial k} = \frac{g(1-g)\phi^2(1-k)}{(1+k\phi)H}.$$

An increase in k raises utility when $k < 1$, and utility is maximized when $k = 1$. It would thus appear that a floating exchange rate combined with comprehensive coordination yields the first-best allocation of resources between the public and private sectors. The floating exchange rate accommodates the difference between the governments' policy preferences, and comprehensive coordination optimizes the number of varieties of the consumer good by reducing total output of the public good and releasing resources to the private sector.

Some Comparative Statics

Before examining other regimes, let us see how the optimal z_j are affected by the weight of the public good in the utility function and relative country size, how welfare is affected by relative size, and how it is affected by the size of the whole two-country world.

The first two questions can be answered by differentiating equations (25) with respect to the z_j, s_j, and g (remembering that $k_j = s_j$ with policy autonomy and $k_j = 1$ with comprehensive coordination), then evaluating the results for the IS case (in which $z_j = z$ initially):

$$
\begin{bmatrix} (1-g)D + \frac{1}{2}(g-z) & \frac{1}{2}(g-z) \\ \frac{1}{2}(g-z) & (1-g)D + \frac{1}{2}(g-z) \end{bmatrix} \begin{bmatrix} dz_1 \\ dz_2 \end{bmatrix}
$$

$$
= (1-z) \begin{bmatrix} (1+kz\phi)dg - (1-g)z\phi dk_1 \\ (1+kz\phi)dg - (1-g)z\phi dk_2 \end{bmatrix},
$$

where $D = 1 + k(1-z)\phi$, while $dk_j = ds_j$ with policy autonomy but $dk_j = 0$ with comprehensive coordination. With policy autonomy, then,

$$
dz_1 = \left(\frac{1 + \frac{1}{2}z\phi}{H} \right) dg - (1-z) \left(\frac{z\phi}{D} \right) ds_1,
$$

$$
dz_2 = \left(\frac{1 + \frac{1}{2}z\phi}{H} \right) dg + (1-z) \left(\frac{z\phi}{D} \right) ds_1,
$$

but with comprehensive coordination,

$$
dz_j = \left(\frac{1 + z\phi}{H} \right) dg.
$$

As one would expect, an increase in the weight of the public good raises output of the public good, with and without coordination. The effects of a change in the s_j, however, are felt only in the absence of coordination. An increase in the relative size of one country reduces its optimal z_j and has the opposite effect in the other country. This result is due to the basic externality that was built into the model and to the difference between the technologies used by the private and public sectors. If countries begin to differ in size, do not coordinate their policies, and did not adjust their z_j in response to the difference in size, both countries' households would experience a welfare-reducing reduction in the number of varieties of the consumer good. But governments will respond to the difference in size and will do so differently. The (newly) larger country has more influence on the number of varieties of the consumer good, so it will try to compensate its citizens by cutting output per household of the public good, releasing resources to the private sector, and raising the number of varieties of the consumer good. The (newly) smaller country has less influence on the number of varieties, so it will try to compensate its citizens by raising output per household of the public good, even though this will reduce the number of varieties of the consumer good.

The responses of the z_j to a change in the s_j do not depend on the nature of the public good (represented by the parameter μ). The nature of that good, however, is crucial for the ultimate effect on household welfare. Continuing to work with the IS case, consider the effect of increasing the size of the first country on the welfare of that country's households. From equation (13),[15]

$$\frac{du_1}{ds_1} = \frac{1}{z}\left(\frac{g-z}{1-z}\right)\frac{dz_1}{ds_1} + 2g(1-\mu).$$

We have therefore to deal with two pairs of possibilities:

(1) When the utility provided by the public good varies inversely with the number of households ($\mu = 1$), the last term of the expression drops out entirely. With comprehensive coordination, moreover, $(dz_1/ds_1) = 0$, so an increase in the relative size of a country does not affect its households' welfare. With policy autonomy, however, $(dz_1/ds_1) < 0$, so an increase in relative size reduces the households' welfare.

(2) When the utility provided by the public good is independent of the number of households ($\mu = 0$), an increase in the relative size of a country raises its households' welfare, with and without coordination. With comprehensive coordination, the first term of the expression goes to zero, as before, but the second term is positive. With policy autonomy, the first term is negative, the second term is positive, but the difference between them is positive.[16]

Finally, consider an increase in the size of the whole two-country world, measured by σ, the number of households, without changing the relative sizes of the countries. Using equation (13) again,

$$\frac{du_j}{d\sigma} = \frac{dA_j}{d\sigma} = \frac{1}{\sigma}\left[(1-g)\phi + g(1-\mu)\right],$$

[15] This formulation reflects the fact that $d\Gamma/ds_1 = 0$ in the IS case.
[16] Replacing (dz_1/ds_1) and simplifying, $(du_1/ds_1) = (1/D)[2g + (1-g)\phi z]$.

which is always positive, even when $\mu = 0$, because of the increase in the number of varieties provided by the increase in the number of households.

IV. Three More Policy Regimes

The two regimes examined in the previous section are similar in one vital way. They both rely on a floating exchange rate to offset the difference between national inflation rates arising from different policy preferences; inflation rates will differ when the m_j differ, and this will happen, even in the IS case, whenever the v_j differ. But the two regimes have different implications for resource allocation. As governments can use inflation and taxation to finance production of the public good, comprehensive coordination, covering monetary and tax policies, suffices to coordinate the governments' decisions about production of the public good. It prevents the excessive fall in the number of varieties of the consumer good that occurs when governments choose their z_j individually.

Nevertheless, a floating exchange rate cannot fully offset a difference in policy preferences when governments coordinate their monetary policies but do not coordinate their tax policies. Furthermore, comprehensive coordination cannot fully optimize the number of varieties of the consumer good when the exchange rate does not float. These are some of the results obtained in this section, which examines three more policy regimes: a floating exchange rate with partial coordination, a pegged rate with comprehensive coordination, and a pegged rate with partial coordination. (It is impossible to have a pegged rate without any coordination, because the exchange rate cannot be pegged in this particular model unless the two economies have the same inflation rates.)

For brevity and tractability, I confine the analysis to the IS case, where $s_j = \frac{1}{2}$. At times, in fact, I will have to go on to the ISP case, where the v_j are equal, too. This case was not considered before because the results for a floating exchange rate are not very interesting. As the m_j are equal in the ISP case, a floating rate cannot change. Put differently, pegging is redundant. That will be true here too, of course, but the ISP case will be the only one in which we can obtain solutions for the optimal z_j. (When comparing the z_j with those obtained before, however, we must keep in mind the special nature of the cases under study. The exchange rate cannot change. The importance of this point will be seen most clearly at the end of the section, when we look at the results for a pegged exchange rate with partial coordination; they will be the same as those for the corresponding floating rate case.)

A Floating Exchange Rate with Partial Coordination

With a floating exchange rate and monetary but not fiscal coordination, the monetary authorities will maximize W_T and the fiscal authorities will maximize the W_j. These are the first-order conditions for the jth country's instruments:

$$\frac{\partial W_j}{\partial \tau_j} = \frac{\partial u_j}{\partial z_j} - \lambda \left(\frac{1}{z_j} \right)^3 m_j q_j = 0, \tag{28a}$$

$$\frac{\partial W_T}{\partial m_j} = \frac{1}{2} \left[\frac{\partial u_1}{\partial z_j} + \frac{\partial u_2}{\partial z_j} + \lambda \left(\frac{1}{z_j} \right)^3 \tau_j q_j \right] = 0. \tag{28b}$$

Subtracting one from the other,

$$q_j = \frac{1}{2}(1 - g)\phi \left(\frac{1}{\lambda \Gamma} \right) z_j^2. \tag{29}$$

Therefore, the optimal τ_j and m_j are

$$m_j = \left[v_j - \frac{1}{2}(1 - g)\phi \left(\frac{1}{\lambda \Gamma} \right) z_j \right] z_j,$$

$$\tau_j = \left[(1 - v_j) + \frac{1}{2}(1 - g)\phi \left(\frac{1}{\lambda \Gamma} \right) z_j \right] z_j. \tag{30}$$

When the governments coordinate their monetary policies but not their fiscal policies, they cannot partition their policy problem; the ratio of τ_j to m_j is not independent of z_j, as it was before, but rises with z_j, and there is less reliance on m_j relative to τ_j for each and every z_j. It is, indeed, impossible to rule out solutions in which the m_j are negative.[17]

What happens to the z_j under this regime? Substituting the solutions for the τ_j and m_j into equation (28a),

$$\frac{1}{2}(1 - g)\phi(2z_j - \tau_j)(1 - z_j) - \Gamma(g - z_j) = 0,$$

---

[17] For more on this point, see Annex I, which examines the second-order conditions that correspond to equations (28a) and (28b).

or

$$\tfrac{1}{2}(1-g)\phi\left[(1+v_j)-\tfrac{1}{2}(1-g)\phi\left(\frac{1}{\lambda\Gamma}\right)z_j\right]z_j(1-z_j)-\Gamma(g-z_j)=0.$$

$$(31)$$

There are, again, two such equations, one for each country, but they are cubic, even in the IS case. Therefore, we impose two simplifications. (1) We move on to the ISP case, where $v_j = v$, so that the two equations are identical. (2) We assume that the z_j are equal when the equations are the same.[18] Even after we impose these restrictions, the common equation is not easy to solve, but it can be used to define

$$z_T'' = \frac{2g+(1-g)\phi\tau}{1+(1-g)\phi},$$

$$(32)$$

because the τ_j are the same when the v_j and z_j are the same. Using equations (27a) and (27b), it is then possible to show that

$$z_T'' - z_T' = \frac{(1-g)\phi\tau}{1+(1-g)\phi} > 0,$$

$$z_T'' - z_T = -\frac{(1-g)\phi m}{1+\tfrac{1}{2}(1-g)\phi} < 0 \quad \text{iff} \quad m > 0.$$

The cut in total output of the public good is smaller with partial coordination than with comprehensive coordination. When $m < 0$, indeed, the sum of the z_j is larger than it was with policy autonomy.[19] In brief, partial coordination cannot take us all the way to the first-best outcome and may indeed take us in the opposite direction.

A Pegged Exchange Rate with Comprehensive Coordination

To peg the exchange rate in this model, the two countries' central banks must equalize their m_j, but there are two ways to do that. One central bank can lead and the other can follow, as in many

---

[18] In the previous section, we relied on a *proof* that the z_j were equal before moving to the IS case. Here, we rely on a weaker proposition—the demonstration in Annex II that the assumption in the text does not produce a contradiction. (It does produce a contradiction under the first common currency regime studied in the next section.)

[19] Remember, however, that these results hold only for the ISP case, because equation (32) holds only for that case.

models of the EMS and of the earlier Bretton Woods system. Alternatively, they can coordinate their policies, by maximizing W_T with respect to a common value for the two m_j. I do not examine the first possibility, although it may be the best benchmark for appraising the welfare effects of European monetary union, being the closest approximation to the previous regime. I focus entirely on the second possibility, but distinguish, as before, between comprehensive and partial coordination.

With comprehensive coordination, the two countries' monetary and fiscal authorities can be deemed to maximize W_T by choosing optimal values for the τ_j and for the (common) $m_{i'}$, denoted hereafter by $\tilde{m}$, and these are the first-order conditions:[20]

$$\frac{\partial W_T}{\partial \tau_j} = s_1\left(\frac{\partial u_1}{\partial z_j}\right) + s_2\left(\frac{\partial u_2}{\partial z_j}\right) - s_j\lambda\left(\frac{1}{z_j}\right)^3 \tilde{m}q_j = 0, \tag{33a}$$

$$\frac{\partial W_T}{\partial \tilde{m}} = s_1\left(\frac{\partial u_1}{\partial z_1} + \frac{\partial u_1}{\partial z_2}\right) + s_2\left(\frac{\partial u_2}{\partial z_1} + \frac{\partial u_2}{\partial z_2}\right)$$

$$+ s_1\lambda\left(\frac{1}{z_1}\right)^3 \tau_1 q_1 + s_2\lambda\left(\frac{1}{z_2}\right)^3 \tau_2 q_2 = 0. \tag{33b}$$

Subtracting equations (33a) from equation (33b),

$$s_1\left(\frac{1}{z_1}\right)^2 q_1 + s_2\left(\frac{1}{z_2}\right)^2 q_2 = 0. \tag{34}$$

Therefore,

$$\tilde{m} = \frac{s_1 v_1\left(\dfrac{1}{z_1}\right) + s_2 v_2\left(\dfrac{1}{z_2}\right)}{s_1\left(\dfrac{1}{z_1}\right)^2 + s_2\left(\dfrac{1}{z_2}\right)^2}. \tag{35}$$

In this instance, moreover, $\tau_j = z_j - \tilde{m}$. Accordingly, the τ_j will differ whenever the z_j differ, and that will happen whenever the v_j differ, even in the IS case, where the s_j are equal. Rewriting equations

---

[20] Although the analysis that follows deals only with the IS case, these first-order conditions are written for the general (DSP) case, so that they can be compared with their floating rate counterparts, equations (19) and (24).

(33a) for that case,

$$(1-g)\left[\phi\left(\frac{1}{\Gamma}\right) + \left(\frac{1}{1-z_j}\right)\right] - g\left(\frac{1}{z_j}\right) + \lambda\left(\frac{1}{z_j}\right)^3 \tilde{m}(v_j z_j - \tilde{m}) = 0,$$

which does not produce identical solutions for the two z_j unless we go to the ISP case, where the v_j are equal. In that case, however, exchange rate pegging is redundant, because comprehensive coordination will stabilize a floating rate.[21]

It is hard to solve for the z_j in the IS case, but we can say something about the solutions. It is clear, for example, that $\tilde{m}$ will be positive but that one of the τ_j can be negative:

$$\tau_1 = \psi + \frac{z_1 - z_2}{z_2^2\left[\left(\frac{1}{z_1}\right)^2 + \left(\frac{1}{z_2}\right)^2\right]}, \qquad \tau_2 = \psi - \frac{z_1 - z_2}{z_1^2\left[\left(\frac{1}{z_1}\right)^2 + \left(\frac{1}{z_2}\right)^2\right]},$$

where

$$\psi = \frac{(1-v_1)\left(\frac{1}{z_1}\right) + (1-v_2)\left(\frac{1}{z_2}\right)}{\left(\frac{1}{z_1}\right)^2 + \left(\frac{1}{z_2}\right)^2} > 0.$$

But both τ_j cannot be negative because the sum of them cannot be negative:

$$\tau_1 + \tau_2 = 2\psi + \frac{(z_1 + z_2)(z_1 - z_2)^2}{z_1^2 + z_2^2}.$$

Furthermore, the sum of the two equations (33a) is

$$(1-g)\left[\phi\left(\frac{1}{\Gamma}\right)(z_1 + z_2) + \left(\frac{z_1}{1-z_1}\right) + \left(\frac{z_2}{1-z_2}\right)\right]$$

$$- 2g + \lambda\tilde{m}\left[\left(\frac{1}{z_1}\right)^2 q_1 + \left(\frac{1}{z_2}\right)^2 q_2\right] = 0.$$

---

[21] To confirm this assertion, assume provisionally that the z_j are equal when the v_j are equal and rewrite the previous equation for common values of the v_j and z_j. It becomes identical to the IS version of the corresponding equation for comprehensive coordination under a floating rate (in which case, of course, the z_j are equal because the solution is unique).

But the last term on the left side is zero, from equation (34), so that we can write

$$(1-g)\phi\left(\frac{1}{\Gamma}\right)\tilde{z}_T' - 2g = -(1-g)\left[\frac{z_1(1-z_2)+z_2(1-z_1)}{(1-z_1)(1-z_2)}\right],$$

where $\tilde{z}_T' = z_1 + z_2$. And using equation (27b), we obtain

$$\tilde{z}_T' - z_T' = -\frac{1}{2}\left[\frac{1-g}{1+(1-g)\phi}\right]\left[\frac{(z_1-z_2)^2}{(1-z_1)(1-z_2)}\right] < 0.$$

When governments engage in comprehensive policy coordination, total output of the public good is smaller with a pegged exchange rate than with a floating rate. The combination of comprehensive coordination and exchange rate pegging tends to *overcompensate* for the externality produced by policy autonomy and a floating rate. This result comes up again in the corresponding common currency case and thus echoes the result obtained by van der Ploeg (1990) that monetary union can cause a shortage of public goods. (He obtains his result from a different model, however, and ascribes it to monetary unification rather than exchange rate pegging.)

A Pegged Exchange Rate with Partial Coordination

When the governments peg the exchange rate by choosing $\tilde{m}$ jointly but do not coordinate their fiscal policies, the first-order conditions are given by equation (28a), for the maximization of the W_j with respect to the τ_j, and by equation (33b), for the maximization of W_T with respect to $\tilde{m}$. Subtracting the former from the latter,

$$2s_1 s_2(1-g)\phi\left(\frac{1}{\Gamma}\right) - \lambda\left[s_1\left(\frac{1}{z_1}\right)^2 q_1 + s_2\left(\frac{1}{z_2}\right)^2 q_2\right] = 0, \qquad (36)$$

so that

$$\tilde{m} = \frac{s_1 v_1\left(\frac{1}{z_1}\right) + s_2 v_2\left(\frac{1}{z_2}\right) - 2s_1 s_2(1-g)\phi\left(\frac{1}{\lambda\Gamma}\right)}{s_1\left(\frac{1}{z_1}\right)^2 + s_2\left(\frac{1}{z_2}\right)^2}. \qquad (37)$$

This equation replicates the basic result obtained for a partially coordinated float. There is comparatively less reliance on money creation than with comprehensive coordination, and we cannot rule out solutions in which $\tilde{m} < 0$. In the IS case, moreover,

$$\tilde{m} = \frac{v_1\left(\dfrac{1}{z_1}\right) + v_2\left(\dfrac{1}{z_2}\right) - (1-g)\phi\left(\dfrac{1}{\lambda\Gamma}\right)}{\left(\dfrac{1}{z_1}\right)^2 + \left(\dfrac{1}{z_2}\right)^2}.$$

This is the same result obtained for a floating rate with partial coordination and for a pegged rate with comprehensive coordination. The z_j are equal when the v_j are equal. When the v_j are equal, however, pegging is redundant, and the expression for $\tilde{m}$ becomes the same as the one for the (common) m_j obtained with a floating exchange rate and partial coordination. We need not carry the analysis further.

V. The Common Currency Case

When the two currencies are perfect substitutes or there is just one common currency, prices and wages cannot differ across countries, and the demand for money by the two countries' households must equal the sum of the money stocks supplied by the two central banks, whether they issue them separately or jointly. Therefore, equations (16) and (17) must be replaced by

$$M_{1t} + M_{2t} = \sigma w_t, \tag{38}$$

$$s_1 m_1 + s_2 m_2 = \frac{\pi}{1 + \pi}. \tag{39}$$

The m_j should now to be interpreted as (1) the real increase per jth country household in the stock of the jth currency or in the stock of the common currency issued by the jth country's central bank, or (2) the real increase per jth country household in the stock of the common currency issued to the jth government by the central bank of a monetary union. They are formally equivalent.

Using equation (39) to solve for the common inflation rate, π, replacing π in equation (13), and setting $s_j = \frac{1}{2}$ to move to the IS case (which will be used through this section), we obtain the common currency version of the utility function:

$$u_j = A' + (1-g)(\phi \ln \Gamma + \ln G_j) + g \ln z_j, \tag{40}$$

where

$$A' = A + g(1 - \mu)\ln\tfrac{1}{2}, \quad \text{and} \quad G_j = 1 - \tfrac{1}{2}(m_1 + m_2) - \tau_j,$$

so that $G_1 = \Gamma + \tfrac{1}{2}(\tau_2 - \tau_1)$ and $G_2 = \Gamma + \tfrac{1}{2}(\tau_1 - \tau_2)$. Thus, the shift to a common currency introduces a second externality. The utility of the typical household depends on both z_j, which appear in Γ, and on both m_j, which appear in the G_j.[22] Therefore, the partial derivatives of the u_j with respect to the τ_j and m_j are no longer equal to their partial derivatives with respect to the z_j. Instead,

$$\frac{\partial u_j}{\partial \tau_j} = -\tfrac{1}{2}(1 - g)\left[\phi\left(\frac{1}{\Gamma}\right) + 2\left(\frac{1}{G_j}\right)\right] + g\left(\frac{1}{z_j}\right),$$

$$\frac{\partial u_j}{\partial m_j} = -\tfrac{1}{2}(1 - g)\left[\phi\left(\frac{1}{\Gamma}\right) + \left(\frac{1}{G_j}\right)\right] + g\left(\frac{1}{z_j}\right),$$

$$\frac{\partial u_1}{\partial \tau_2} = \frac{\partial u_2}{\partial \tau_1} = -\tfrac{1}{2}(1 - g)\phi\left(\frac{1}{\Gamma}\right),$$

$$\frac{\partial u_1}{\partial m_2} = -\tfrac{1}{2}(1 - g)\left[\phi\left(\frac{1}{\Gamma}\right) + \left(\frac{1}{G_1}\right)\right],$$

$$\frac{\partial u_2}{\partial m_1} = -\tfrac{1}{2}(1 - g)\left[\phi\left(\frac{1}{\Gamma}\right) + \left(\frac{1}{G_2}\right)\right].$$

We will consider three policy regimes—national autonomy, comprehensive coordination, and partial coordination, and will interpret

---

[22] We noted earlier, moreover, that there would be a third externality if the Q_j were defined in terms of the inflation rate, because it depends on both m_j, and this can be demonstrated easily using equations (15) and (39). When the policy preference function is written in terms of the common inflation rate, π, rather than the increase in the money stock, m_j, it becomes:

$$Q_j = \left(\tfrac{1}{2}\right)\left(\frac{1}{z_j}\right)^2 \left(v_j \tau_j^2 + (1 - v_j)[\tfrac{1}{2}(m_1 + m_2)]^2\right),$$

and each country's Q_j depends on both countries' m_j. But this interdependence vanishes in a monetary union if the central bank cannot discriminate freely when distributing new money. If the m_j are equal, we return to the result obtained in the national currency case, where it did not matter whether the policy preference function was written in terms of the π_j or the m_j.

the last two as monetary unions with and without fiscal coordination.

A Common Currency with Policy Autonomy

When the two countries can issue a common currency independently, each government has an incentive to subsidize its households—to replace lump-sum taxes ($\tau_j > 0$) with lump-sum subsidies ($\tau_j < 0$) and to finance the subsidies, as well as production of the public good, by issuing additional money. There is no limit to this process in Casella's model and, therefore, no well-defined Nash equilibrium.[23] But the policy preference functions limit the process in this model by making it increasingly expensive for governments to reduce the τ_j and raise the m_j.

The relevant first-order conditions resemble those pertaining to policy autonomy under a floating exchange rate between the two national currencies, but they cannot be written as they were before, because the partial derivatives of the u_j with respect to the τ_j and m_j do not equal their partial derivatives with respect to the z_j. They are

$$\frac{\partial W_j}{\partial \tau_j} = \frac{\partial u_j}{\partial \tau_j} - \lambda \left(\frac{1}{z_j}\right)^3 m_j q_j = 0, \quad \frac{\partial W_j}{\partial m_j} = \frac{\partial u_j}{\partial m_j} + \lambda \left(\frac{1}{z_j}\right)^3 \tau_j q_j = 0. \quad (41)$$

Therefore,

$$q_j = -\tfrac{1}{2}(1-g)\left(\frac{1}{\lambda G_j}\right) z_j^2. \quad (42)$$

When we use this expression to replace the q_j in equations (41), however, we obtain four quadratic equations in the τ_j and m_j (or, equivalently, the z_j and m_j). The problem is intractable even in the ISP case, because the strategy used before produces a contradiction here. Let the $v_j = v$ and assume provisionally that the z_j and m_j are equal in the ISP case.[24] Under these assumptions, equation (42) yields

$$\tfrac{1}{2}(1-g)z^2 + \lambda(1-z)(vz - m) = 0,$$

---

[23] To see that this is so, set $\lambda = 0$ in equations (41) below. There is no solution that can satisfy both of them.

[24] Under these conditions, the τ_j must be equal, and $G_j = \Gamma = 1 - z$.

and these are the optimal setting of the instruments:

$$m = vz + \tfrac{1}{2}(1-g)\left(\tfrac{1}{\lambda}\right)\left(\frac{z^2}{1-z}\right),$$

$$\tau = (1-v)z - \tfrac{1}{2}(1-g)\left(\frac{1}{\lambda}\right)\left(\frac{z^2}{1-z}\right). \tag{43}$$

There is comparatively more reliance on money creation than in the corresponding national currency case, and the lump-sum tax can give way to a lump-sum subsidy ($\tau < 0$). But when we use equation (43) to replace m in equations (41), we obtain

$$[(1-g)\phi z - 2(g-z) - (1-g)vz](1-z) - \tfrac{1}{2}(1-g)^2\left(\frac{1}{\lambda}\right)z^2 = 0, \tag{44}$$

and there can be *two* feasible solutions for z, which means that the z_j may not be equal.[25]

Consider a special symmetrical case, however, in which $g = \tfrac{1}{4}(1-g)^2(1/\lambda)$ and $\lambda[(1+\phi) + (1-v)] = (1-g)$.[26] The only solution for the output of the public good is $z = \tfrac{1}{2}$, so that

$$m = \tfrac{1}{2}\left[v + 2\left(\frac{g}{1-g}\right)\right], \quad \tau = \tfrac{1}{2}\left[(1-v) - 2\left(\frac{g}{1-g}\right)\right],$$

$$\text{and} \quad q = -\left(\frac{g}{1-g}\right).$$

In this same special case, moreover, $\tau < 0$ satisfies the second-order conditions corresponding to equations (41).[27] In other words, we obtain a well-behaved version of Casella's result. The lump-sum tax gives way to a lump-sum subsidy.

Finally, we can show that total output of the public good may be larger with a common currency and policy autonomy than in the corresponding national currency case. If the z_j are equal when the v_j are equal, even when there are two such solutions, equations (27a)

---

[25] See Annex II.

[26] The rationale for choosing this case is provided in Annex II.

[27] See Annex I for details.

and (44) can be used to obtain

$$\hat{z}_T - z_T = \left[\frac{2}{1 + \frac{1}{2}(1-g)\phi}\right]\left[(1-g)v(1-\hat{z})\hat{z} + \frac{1}{2}(1-g)^2\left(\frac{1}{\lambda}\right)\hat{z}^2\right] > 0,$$

where the $\hat{z}$ are the common currency values and $\hat{z}_T$ is the sum of those values.

Note that this last result pertains to the ISP case, where the exchange rate between the two national currencies did not change when the governments pursued independent policies. Hence, the result does not reflect any difference in exchange rate behavior between the common currency and national currency cases. It reflects instead the change in the governments' behavior produced by the externality introduced by a common currency. As part of each country's inflation tax is borne by the other country's households, both governments have an incentive to produce very large quantities of the public good.

A Common Currency with Comprehensive Coordination

When the two countries issue a common currency jointly or create a single central bank to issue it for them, they may be deemed to maximize W_T with respect to the m_j. When they coordinate their fiscal policies too, they may be deemed to maximize W_T with respect to the τ_j. The relevant first-order conditions resemble those obtained for comprehensive coordination under a floating exchange rate between the two national currencies, but they have to be rewritten:

$$\frac{\partial W_T}{\partial \tau_j} = \frac{1}{2}\left[\frac{\partial u_1}{\partial \tau_j} + \frac{\partial u_2}{\partial \tau_j} - \lambda\left(\frac{1}{z_j}\right)^3 m_j q_j\right] = 0, \tag{45a}$$

$$\frac{\partial W_T}{\partial m_j} = \frac{1}{2}\left[\frac{\partial u_1}{\partial m_j} + \frac{\partial u_2}{\partial m_j} + \lambda\left(\frac{1}{z_j}\right)^3 \tau_j q_j\right] = 0. \tag{45b}$$

Therefore,

$$\left(\frac{1}{z_1}\right)^2 q_1 = -\left(\frac{1}{z_2}\right)^2 q_2 = \frac{1}{2}(1-g)(\tau_2 - \tau_1)\left(\frac{1}{\lambda}\right)\left(\frac{1}{G_1 G_2}\right), \tag{46}$$

which says that the q_j cannot be equal unless they are zero, and they cannot be zero unless the τ_j are equal.

In Casella's model, comprehensive coordination has powerful effects when the s_j are equal. It offsets the externality arising from the use of a common currency, and it also offsets the tendency for governments to produce too much of the public good. In fact, the z_j given by this common currency regime are the same as the z_j given by the first-best national currency regime—the one with comprehensive coordination and a floating exchange rate.[28] Accordingly, Casella concludes that a currency union cannot be Pareto-superior to a floating rate regime but is not inferior to it in the IS case. (Her own paper, however, is chiefly concerned with the differences between a currency union and a floating rate regime when the s_j are not equal.)

In the model used here, by contrast, the common currency values of z_j differ from country to country and are thus different from their floating rate values (which are equal across countries). That is because the q_j cannot be equal in this model unless the τ_j are equal, and that will not normally happen unless the v_j are equal. When policy preferences differ, then, a currency union cannot precisely neutralize the tendency for governments to provide too much of the public good, even with comprehensive coordination.

There are two ways to illustrate this basic point without solving for the z_j explicitly. First, we can show that total output of the public good is smaller with comprehensive coordination and a common currency than with comprehensive coordination and a floating exchange rate. Using equations (27a), (45b), and (46),

$$\hat{z}'_T - z'_T = -\tfrac{1}{2}\left[\frac{1-g}{1+(1-g)\phi}\right]\left(\frac{1}{G_1 G_2}\right)(\tau_1 - \tau_2)^2,$$

where $\hat{z}'_T$ is the sum of the z_j with comprehensive coordination and a common currency. This difference is negative whenever the τ_j differ.

Second, we can use equation (46) to write

$$m_1\left(\frac{1}{z_1}\right)^2 + m_2\left(\frac{1}{z_2}\right)^2 = v_1\left(\frac{1}{z_1}\right) + v_2\left(\frac{1}{z_2}\right), \tag{47}$$

and this equation will allow us to show that comprehensive coordination in a currency union can yield results identical to those provided by a pegged exchange rate, not those provided by a floating rate, as in Casella's model.

---

[28] Once again, we can replicate Casella's result by setting $\lambda = 0$ in equation (45a) or (45b). The resulting equations are the same across countries and have only one feasible solution. Hence, $z_1 = z_2 = z$, and z is given by equation (26) with $k_j = 1$.

Suppose that the central bank of the monetary union cannot discriminate when issuing new money. It must issue identical amounts per household to both countries' governments.[29] Then equation (47) yields

$$m_j = m = \frac{v_1\left(\dfrac{1}{z_1}\right) + v_2\left(\dfrac{1}{z_2}\right)}{\left(\dfrac{1}{z_1}\right)^2 + \left(\dfrac{1}{z_2}\right)^2}.$$

This is identical to the result obtained with comprehensive coordination and a pegged exchange rate; it can be derived from equation (35) by setting $s_j = \frac{1}{2}$ to generate the IS case. It is possible to show, in fact, that a monetary union with $m_j = m$ combined with fiscal coordination is identical to a pegged rate regime with comprehensive coordination. The coordination or unification of monetary policies offsets the externality created by the use of a common currency. But precisely because it emulates a pegged rate regime, a monetary union tends to overcompensate for the externality affecting production of the public good. The effects of that externality always emerge when the v_j differ (except, of course, in the floating rate cases examined early in this paper).

A Common Currency with Partial Coordination

When the central bank of a monetary union cannot discriminate when issuing new money, but must issue the same amounts per household to both governments, and the governments do not coordinate their fiscal policies, the relevant first-order conditions are given by equations (28a) and (33b), as in the corresponding pegged rate case. Accordingly, the outcomes for a monetary union without discrimination or fiscal coordination are the same as the outcomes for a pegged rate regime with partial coordination. There is comparatively less reliance on money creation than with comprehensive coordination, and the amount of money creation, $\tilde{m}$, can be negative. In the IS case, moreover, the solution for $\tilde{m}$ is the same as the one obtained for a floating exchange rate and partial coordination.

---

[29] As was indicated earlier, this is a "weak form" of the recommendation in the Delors Report (1989) that the central bank of a European monetary union should not lend directly to national governments.

VI. Summary and Concluding Note

The main results of this analysis can be summarized succinctly by reviewing the principal effects of floating exchange rates, a monetary union, and fiscal coordination on total output of the public good and by comparing the results with those in Casella's paper.

Because it can insulate each economy from its partner's inflation rate, a floating exchange rate is the only regime that can prevent differences in policy preferences from affecting the allocation of resources between the public and private sectors. Accordingly, it sets the stage for policy coordination to optimize that allocation. By implication, the results in this paper strengthen the case for floating exchange rates implicit in Casella's paper.

When the members of a monetary union do not differ in size, the governments have the same policy preferences, and the governments coordinate their fiscal policies, the union does not distort resource allocation. Total output of the public good is the same as it would be with a floating exchange rate between the members' currencies and comprehensive coordination. When the governments have different preferences, however, a monetary union resembles a pegged rate regime, and total output of the public good is smaller than it would be with a floating rate. In other words, the monetary union *overcompensates* for the externality distorting resource allocation. Therefore, the results in this paper qualify those in Casella's paper.

When governments coordinate their monetary policies but do not coordinate their fiscal policies, there is comparatively less reliance on money creation than with comprehensive coordination or national autonomy. This result holds for floating and pegged rates and for a common currency. But total output of the public good tends to be larger than with comprehensive coordination and can sometimes be larger than with national autonomy. In brief, partial coordination does not always lead part way from the allocation under national autonomy to the first-best allocation under comprehensive coordination. These results have no counterpart in Casella's paper, because her model does not allow her to examine partial coordination.

A general cost-benefit analysis of the case for monetary union, in Europe or anywhere else, should take account of the issues studied in this paper. But others may be more important. How does exchange rate uncertainty affect capital formation? How high are the transactions costs imposed by using and holding many national currencies? How large are the costs of adjusting to country-specific shocks when nominal exchange rates are fixed or fused by a monetary union, when labor mobility is low, and when there are no endogenous fiscal transfers from one country to another? This list of questions is incomplete. The Commission of the European Communities (1990) has raised many more. The list is long enough, however, to warn that the model used in this paper deals with one corner of a complicated puzzle.

ANNEX I

The Second-Order Conditions

National Currency Regimes

In the national currency case, the second derivatives of the utility function are

$$\frac{\partial^2 u_j}{\partial \tau_j \partial \tau_j} = \frac{\partial^2 u_j}{\partial m_j \partial m_j} = \frac{\partial^2 u_j}{\partial z_j \partial z_j} = -(1-g)\phi\left[s_j\left(\frac{1}{\Gamma}\right)\right]^2$$

$$-(1-g)\left(\frac{1}{1-z_j}\right)^2 - g\left(\frac{1}{z_j}\right)^2 < 0,$$

$$\frac{\partial^2 u_1}{\partial z_2 \partial z_2} = -(1-g)\phi\left[s_2\left(\frac{1}{\Gamma}\right)\right]^2 < 0, \quad \frac{\partial^2 u_2}{\partial z_1 \partial z_1} = -(1-g)\phi\left[s_1\left(\frac{1}{\Gamma}\right)\right]^2 < 0.$$

The second derivatives of the policy preference functions are

$$\frac{\partial^2 Q_j}{\partial \tau_j \partial \tau_j} = \left(\frac{1}{z_j}\right)^4 m_j(m_j - 2q_j), \quad \frac{\partial^2 Q_j}{\partial m_j \partial m_j} = \left(\frac{1}{z_j}\right)^4 \tau_j(\tau_j + 2q_j),$$

$$\frac{\partial^2 Q_j}{\partial \tau_j \partial m_j} = \left(\frac{1}{z_j}\right)^4 [(\tau_j - m_j)q_j - \tau_j m_j],$$

which can be positive or negative (because q_j can be positive or negative).

A Floating Exchange Rate with Policy Autonomy

The jth government maximizes W_j, the first-order conditions are given by equations (19) in the text, and the corresponding second-order conditions are

$$\frac{\partial^2 W_j}{\partial \tau_j \partial \tau_j} < 0, \quad \begin{vmatrix} \dfrac{\partial^2 W_j}{\partial \tau_j \partial \tau_j} & \dfrac{\partial^2 W_j}{\partial \tau_j \partial m_j} \\[3mm] \dfrac{\partial^2 W_j}{\partial \tau_j \partial m_j} & \dfrac{\partial^2 W_j}{\partial m_j \partial m_j} \end{vmatrix} > 0.$$

But $q_j = 0$ when the first-order conditions are met, so that

$$\frac{\partial^2 W_j}{\partial \tau_j \partial \tau_j} = \frac{\partial^2 u_j}{\partial z_j \partial z_j} - \lambda v_j^2 \left(\frac{1}{z_j}\right)^2,$$

$$\frac{\partial^2 W_j}{\partial m_j \partial m_j} = \frac{\partial^2 u_j}{\partial z_j \partial z_j} - \lambda (1 - v_j)^2 \left(\frac{1}{z_j}\right)^2,$$

and

$$\frac{\partial^2 W_j}{\partial \tau_j \partial m_j} = \frac{\partial^2 u_j}{\partial z_j \partial z_j} + \lambda v_j (1 - v_j) \left(\frac{1}{z_j}\right)^2,$$

which satisfy the second-order conditions.

A Floating Exchange Rate with Comprehensive Coordination

The two governments maximize W_T, the first-order conditions are given by equations (24a) and (24b), and the second-order conditions are

$$\frac{\partial^2 W_T}{\partial \tau_1 \partial \tau_1} < 0, \quad \begin{vmatrix} \dfrac{\partial^2 W_T}{\partial \tau_1 \partial \tau_1} & \dfrac{\partial^2 W_T}{\partial \tau_1 \partial m_1} \\[3mm] \dfrac{\partial^2 W_T}{\partial \tau_1 \partial m_1} & \dfrac{\partial^2 W_T}{\partial m_1 \partial m_1} \end{vmatrix} > 0,$$

$$\begin{vmatrix} \dfrac{\partial^2 W_T}{\partial \tau_1 \partial \tau_1} & \dfrac{\partial^2 W_T}{\partial \tau_1 \partial m_1} & \dfrac{\partial^2 W_T}{\partial \tau_1 \partial \tau_2} \\[3mm] \dfrac{\partial^2 W_T}{\partial \tau_1 \partial m_1} & \dfrac{\partial^2 W_T}{\partial m_1 \partial m_1} & \dfrac{\partial^2 W_T}{\partial m_1 \partial \tau_2} \\[3mm] \dfrac{\partial^2 W_T}{\partial \tau_1 \partial \tau_2} & \dfrac{\partial^2 W_T}{\partial m_1 \partial \tau_2} & \dfrac{\partial^2 W_T}{\partial \tau_2 \partial \tau_2} \end{vmatrix} < 0,$$

and so on. Once again, however, $q_j = 0$, when the first-order conditions are met, so that

$$\frac{\partial^2 W_T}{\partial \tau_j \partial \tau_j} = s_j \left[\frac{\partial^2 u_T}{\partial z_j \partial z_j} - \lambda v_j^2 \left(\frac{1}{z_j} \right)^2 \right],$$

$$\frac{\partial^2 W_T}{\partial m_j \partial m_j} = s_j \left[\frac{\partial^2 u_T}{\partial z_j \partial z_j} - \lambda (1 - v_j)^2 \left(\frac{1}{z_j} \right)^2 \right],$$

$$\frac{\partial^2 W_T}{\partial \tau_j \partial m_j} = s_j \left[\frac{\partial^2 u_T}{\partial z_j \partial z_j} + \lambda v_j (1 - v_j) \left(\frac{1}{z_j} \right)^2 \right],$$

where

$$\frac{\partial^2 u_T}{\partial z_j \partial z_j} = - \left[(1 - g) \phi s_j \left(\frac{1}{\Gamma} \right)^2 + (1 - g) \left(\frac{1}{1 - z_j} \right)^2 + g \left(\frac{1}{z_j} \right)^2 \right] < 0,$$

while

$$\frac{\partial^2 W_T}{\partial \tau_1 \partial \tau_2} = \frac{\partial^2 W_T}{\partial \tau_1 \partial m_2} = \frac{\partial^2 W_T}{\partial m_1 \partial \tau_2} = \frac{\partial^2 W_T}{\partial m_1 \partial m_2} = - s_1 s_2 (1 - g) \phi \left(\frac{1}{\Gamma} \right)^2 < 0,$$

and it can then be shown, albeit laboriously, that the second-order conditions are satisfied.

A Floating Exchange Rate with Partial Coordination

The fiscal authorities maximize the W_j while the monetary authorities maximize W_T, the first-order conditions are given by equations (28a) and (28b), and the second-order conditions are

$$\frac{\partial^2 W_j}{\partial \tau_j \partial \tau_j} < 0, \qquad \frac{\partial^2 W_T}{\partial m_1 \partial m_1} < 0, \qquad \begin{vmatrix} \dfrac{\partial^2 W_T}{\partial m_1 \partial m_1} & \dfrac{\partial^2 W_T}{\partial m_1 \partial m_2} \\[2mm] \dfrac{\partial^2 W_T}{\partial m_1 \partial m_2} & \dfrac{\partial^2 W_T}{\partial m_2 \partial m_2} \end{vmatrix} > 0,$$

which must be evaluated at

$$q_j = v_j z_j - m_j = \tfrac{1}{2} (1 - g) \phi \left(\frac{1}{\lambda \Gamma} \right) z_j^2 > 0,$$

so that

$$\frac{\partial^2 W_j}{\partial \tau_j \partial \tau_j} = \frac{\partial^2 u_j}{\partial z_j \partial z_j} - \lambda \left(\frac{1}{z_j}\right)^4 m_j (m_j - 2q_j),$$

$$\frac{\partial^2 W_T}{\partial m_j \partial m_j} = \frac{\partial^2 u_T}{\partial z_j \partial z_j} - \lambda \left(\frac{1}{z_j}\right)^4 \tau_j (\tau_j + 2q_j),$$

and the cross-partial derivative has the same value as before. Clearly, the first second-order condition is satisfied when $m_j <$ or when $m_j > 2q_j$ (which confirms the statement in the text that we cannot exclude outcomes in which $m_j < 0$), and it is easy to show that other conditions are satisfied.

The pegged rate regimes are not examined here, because they resemble their floating rate counterparts in the ISP case, the only case in which they are tractable.

Common Currency Regimes

In the common currency case, the second derivatives of the household utility function are

$$\frac{\partial^2 u_j}{\partial \tau_j \partial \tau_j} = -\left[\frac{1}{4}(1-g)\phi\left(\frac{1}{\Gamma}\right)^2 + (1-g)\left(\frac{1}{G_j}\right)^2 + g\left(\frac{1}{z_j}\right)^2\right],$$

$$\frac{\partial^2 u_j}{\partial m_j \partial m_j} = -\left[\frac{1}{4}(1-g)\phi\left(\frac{1}{\Gamma}\right)^2 + \frac{1}{4}(1-g)\left(\frac{1}{G_j}\right)^2 + g\left(\frac{1}{z_j}\right)^2\right],$$

$$\frac{\partial^2 u_j}{\partial \tau_j \partial m_j} = -\left[\frac{1}{4}(1-g)\phi\left(\frac{1}{\Gamma}\right)^2 + \frac{1}{2}(1-g)\left(\frac{1}{G_j}\right)^2 + g\left(\frac{1}{z_j}\right)^2\right].$$

The other cross-partial derivatives are not needed here.

A Common Currency with Policy Autonomy

The jth government maximizes W_j, the first-order conditions are given by equations (41) in the text, and the corresponding second-order conditions are the same as those shown above for the corresponding floating rate case. Evaluating the relevant expressions for the special case where $g = \frac{1}{4}(1-g)^2(1/\lambda)$ and $z = \frac{1}{2}$,

$$\frac{\partial^2 W_j}{\partial \tau_j \partial \tau_j} = -\left[(1-g)(1+\phi) + 4g\right]$$

$$-4(1-g) - 4\left[\frac{(1-g)^2}{g}\right]m\left[m + 2\left(\frac{g}{1-g}\right)\right],$$

$$\frac{\partial^2 W_j}{\partial m_j \partial m_j} = -\left[(1-g)(1+\phi) + 4g\right] - 4\left[\frac{(1-g)^2}{g}\right]\tau\left[\tau - 2\left(\frac{g}{1-g}\right)\right],$$

$$\frac{\partial^2 W_j}{\partial \tau_j \partial m_j} = -\left[(1-g)(1+\phi) + 4g\right] - 2(1-g)$$

$$-4\left[\frac{(1-g)^2}{g}\right]\left[m\tau + \left(\frac{g}{1-g}\right)(\tau - m)\right].$$

The first condition is always met (because $m > 0$), and the second condition can be written as

$$4\left[\frac{(1-g)^2}{g}\right]\left(\left[(m-\tau) + 4\left(\frac{g}{1-g}\right)\right]\left[(1-g)(1+\phi) + 4g - 4(1-g)\tau\right]\right) > 0,$$

so that $\tau < 0$ is sufficient to meet it.

The other common currency regimes are not examined here, because they resemble their pegged rate counterparts in the IS case and their floating rate counterparts in the ISP case.

ANNEX II

Mapping Solutions for Optimal Output of the Public Good

A Floating Exchange Rate with Policy Autonomy or Comprehensive Coordination

Rewriting equation (25) of the text, using the version for the first country:

$$\left[s_1 + k_1(1-g)\phi\right](1-z_1)z_1 + \left[gs_1 + s_2(1-z_2)\right]z_1 - g\left[s_1 + s_2(1-z_2)\right] = y_1.$$

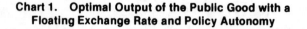

**Chart 1.   Optimal Output of the Public Good with a
Floating Exchange Rate and Policy Autonomy**

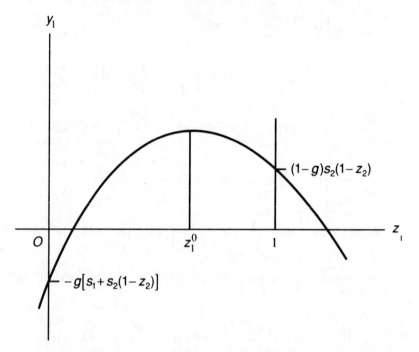

For feasible values of z_2, then, $y_1 < 0$ when $z_1 = 0$, and $y_1 > 0$ when $z_1 = 1$. Furthermore,

$$\frac{\partial y_1}{\partial x_1} = [s_1 + k_1(1-g)\phi](1-2z_1) + [gs_1 + s_2(1-z_2)],$$

and

$$\frac{\partial^2 y_1}{\partial z_1 \partial z_1} = -2[s_1 + k_1(1-g)\phi] < 0.$$

Therefore, y_1 reaches a maximum when

$$z_1^0 = \tfrac{1}{2}\left[1 + \frac{gs_1 + s_2(1-z_2)}{s_1 + k_1(1-g)\phi}\right],$$

so that $\tfrac{1}{2} < z_1^0 < 1$. These results are reproduced in Chart 1. When $0 < z_2 < 1$, there is only one feasible solution for z_1. But this proposition holds both ways, which means that there is only one such solution for the two z_j.

A Floating Exchange Rate with Partial Coordination

Rewriting equation (31) of the text,

$$\tfrac{1}{2}(1-g)\phi\left[(1+v)(1-z)-\tfrac{1}{2}(1-g)\phi\left(\frac{1}{\lambda}\right)z\right]z-(g-z)(1-z)=y,$$

so that

$$\frac{\partial y}{\partial z}=\tfrac{1}{2}(1-g)\phi\left[(1+v)(1-2z)-(1-g)\phi\left(\frac{1}{\lambda}\right)z\right]+\left[(1+g)-2z\right],$$

and

$$\frac{\partial^2 y}{\partial z\partial z}=-\left[2+(1-g)\phi(1+v)+\tfrac{1}{2}(1-g)^2\phi^2\left(\frac{1}{\lambda}\right)\right]<0.$$

Setting the first derivative equal to zero and solving,

$$z^0=\frac{(1+g)+\tfrac{1}{2}(1-g)\phi(1+v)}{2+(1-g)\phi(1+v)+\tfrac{1}{2}(1-g)^2\phi^2\left(\frac{1}{\lambda}\right)},$$

so that $0<z^0<1$ (because $g<1$). Therefore, the mapping of the equation for common value of z resembles the mapping of the one for the individual z_i in the previous section, with only one feasible solution for z.

A Common Currency with Policy Autonomy

Rewriting equation (44) of the text,

$$\left[(1-g)\phi z-2(g-z)-(1-g)vz\right](1-z)-\tfrac{1}{2}(1-g)^2\left(\frac{1}{\lambda}\right)z^2=y,$$

so that $y=-2g$ when $z=0$, and $y=-\tfrac{1}{2}(1-g)^2(1/\lambda)$ when $z=1$. Furthermore,

$$\frac{\partial y}{\partial z}=\left[1+(1-g)\phi+(1-v)+vg\right](1-2z)+2\left[g-\tfrac{1}{2}(1-g)^2\left(\frac{1}{\lambda}\right)z\right],$$

and

$$\frac{\partial^2 y}{\partial z\partial z}=-2\left[1+(1-g)\phi+(1-v)+vg+\tfrac{1}{2}(1-g)^2\left(\frac{1}{\lambda}\right)\right]<0.$$

**Chart 2.   Optimal Output of the Public Good with a
Common Currency and Policy Autonomy**

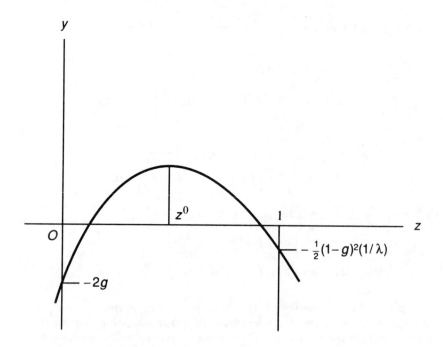

Therefore, y reaches a maximum when

$$z^0 = \left(\tfrac{1}{2}\right)\left(\frac{[1+(1-g)\phi+(1-v)+vg]+2g}{[1+(1-g)\phi+(1-v)+vg]+\tfrac{1}{2}(1-g)^2\left(\dfrac{1}{\lambda}\right)}\right) < 1.$$

These results are reproduced in Chart 2. There are two feasible solutions
for z if $y > 0$ when $z = z^0$, one such solution if $y = 0$, and no solution if
$y < 0$. When $g = \tfrac{1}{4}(1-g)^2(1/\lambda)$, however, $z^0 = \tfrac{1}{2}$, and the corresponding value of y is

$$y^0 = \tfrac{1}{4}(1-g)\left[(1+\phi)+(1-v)-(1-g)\left(\dfrac{1}{\lambda}\right)\right],$$

so that $y^0 = 0$ when $\lambda[(1+\phi)+(1-v)] = (1-g)$. The only solution for
the output of the public good is $z = z^0 = \tfrac{1}{2}$, which is the special symmetrical case examined in the text.

REFERENCES

Casella, Alessandra, "Participation in a Currency Union," NBER Working Paper No. 3220 (Cambridge, Massachusetts: National Bureau of Economic Research, 1990).

——, and Jonathan Feinstein, "Management of a Common Currency," in *A European Central Bank? Perspectives on Monetary Unification After Ten Years of the EMS,* ed. by Marcello de Cecco and Alberto Giovannini (Cambridge, England: Cambridge University Press, 1989).

Commission of the European Communities, "One Market, One Money: An Evaluation of the Potential Benefits and Costs of Forming an Economic and Monetary Union," *European Economy* (Luxembourg), No. 44 (October 1990).

Committee for the Study of Economic and Monetary Union (Delors Committee), *Report on Economic and Monetary Union in the European Community* (Luxembourg, 1989).

Corden, W.M., "The Logic of the International Monetary Non-System," in *Reflections on a Troubled World Economy: Essays in Honor of Herbert Giersch,* ed. by Fritz Machlup and others (New York: St. Martins, 1983).

Dixit, Avinash K., and Joseph E. Stiglitz, "Monopolistic Competition and Optimum Product Diversity" *American Economic Review* (Nashville, Tennessee), Vol. 67 (June 1977), pp. 297–308.

Drazen, Allan, "Monetary Policy, Capital Controls and Seigniorage in an Open Economy," in *A European Central Bank? Perspectives on Monetary Unification After Ten Years of the EMS,* ed. by Marcello de Cecco and Alberto Giovannini (Cambridge, England: Cambridge University Press, 1989).

Eichengreen, Barry, "One Money for Europe? Lessons from the U.S. Currency Union," *Economic Policy* (Cambridge, England), No. 10 (April 1990), pp. 117–87.

Krugman, Paul R., "Intraindustry Specialization and the Gains from Trade," *Journal of Political Economy* (Chicago), Vol. 89 (October 1981), pp. 959–73.

Ploeg, F. van der, "Does Economic and Monetary Union Lead to a Too Small Public Sector in Europe?," paper presented to the Conference on Fiscal Aspects of European Economic Integration (New Haven, March 1990).

PART II

MEASUREMENT

[9]

THE DEMAND FOR INTERNATIONAL RESERVES*
Peter B. Kenen and Elinor B. Yudin

IF economists could measure the need for reserves, they might be able to agree on the right way to reform the international monetary system. Most of the economists who propose drastic reform do so because they anticipate a shortage of reserves; some even believe that the shortage is upon us. Those who advocate more gradual change believe that reserves are adequate now and for the next several years; some even believe that reserves are excessive.

Unfortunately, there is no way to measure the adequacy of reserves — not even to make historical comparisons. Scitovsky's comments illustrate several of the problems involved in appraising the global stock of reserves:

If the world supply of reserves were adequate, the drawing down of some countries' reserves to unduly low levels would be matched by some other countries' excessive accumulation of reserves, and the desire to eliminate balance-of-payments deficits in the former would be matched by the desire to eliminate the surpluses in the latter.[1]

On this definition, global reserves would not be adequate unless countries behaved symmetrically toward payments surpluses and payments deficits. Hence, Scitovsky's criterion assumes that every government or central bank has a precise demand for reserves; if it acts to restrict aggregate expenditure when its reserves fall below a certain level, it will also act to stimulate expenditure when reserves exceed that same level. Behavior, however, may not be this simple. A government willing to tolerate losses of reserves without taking restrictive action may still prefer to accumulate more reserves than to expand demand and court inflation. Even if each country had a unique demand for reserves, moreover, a fixed global total

of reserves could be more or less "adequate" depending on its distribution. Finally, Scitovsky's criterion, like most others, involves important normative judgments, implicitly endorsing global price stability as a policy objective and assuming that a symmetrical response to deficits and surpluses will accomplish payments adjustments with appropriate speed.[2]

It is even difficult to measure the stock of reserves, as the several reserve assets and reserve credits now in use are not perfect substitutes for one another; equal amounts of gold, currency, and credit may make unequal contributions to a nation's external liquidity. Liquidity is a state of mind. Most of the economists concerned with these problems take account of central-bank gold and foreign currency, IMF gold tranches, and automatic drawing rights under bilateral credit arrangements. Others count all assets susceptible to mobilization at moments of crisis — all IMF drawing rights, the long-term foreign assets of official institutions, and "potential" bilateral credits. Some prefer to deal with gross assets and gross drawing rights, others make allowance for "liquid" liabilities.

Yet quantitative methods may answer important factual questions pertaining to liquidity. We may ask, for example, if national holdings of reserves, defined consistently if not perfectly, exhibit any marked regularity or rational pattern. If they do, we may be able to describe the national demand for reserves of a "typical" country, then to appraise the distribution of global reserves.

The Measurement of Payments Disturbances

Measurement always requires a yardstick. A dollar total of reserves, gross or net, is meaningless. But the yardstick generally used to measure liquidity — the ratio of reserves to imports — does not tell us very much. This

* The authors are Professor of Economics and research assistant in the International Economics Workshop, Columbia University. They are indebted to fellow members of the Workshop and to the Seminar in International Economics, Harvard University, for criticism and suggestions. Professor Jon Cunnyngham provided valuable guidance in the design of computations. Research on the project was financed by a Ford Foundation grant to the International Economics Workshop, Columbia University.
[1] Tibor Scitovsky in [8], 208.

[2] Several recent studies stress these important normative issues — the links between the question of adequacy and the problem of adjustment. See Caves [1]; Machlup, et al., [4], 53–54; and the Report of the Group of Ten [5], 4–5.

familiar ratio merely shows how long a country could finance its imports if it were suddenly deprived of all its foreign-exchange earnings. A better yardstick would direct our attention to the more likely contingency. It would compare the level of reserves to the variations in payments and receipts that countries actually expect to experience.

Governments have many reasons for holding reserve assets, including the requirements of domestic monetary legislation or long-standing custom. But the paramount reason for holding reserves is the commitment to maintain stable exchange rates in the face of payments disturbances. Trade and private service flows, government transactions and capital movements are subject to several disturbances — secular, cyclical, seasonal, and random. Under a system of flexible exchange rates, the net current impact of all these disturbances would be manifest as changes in the exchange rates. If exchange rates were perfectly rigid, by contrast, the net current impact of these disturbances would be manifest as changes in official reserves and official liabilities — the counterparts of central-bank intervention supporting the exchange rates. Under the arrangements that actually prevail, small changes in exchange rates occur automatically, absorbing some disturbances.[3] Changes in policy, moreover, especially in exchange controls, have suppressed or offset significant disturbances. However, most of the countries surveyed in this study have been compelled to intervene in the foreign-exchange market and the larger disturbances afflicting trade and payments are usually reflected in their reserves.

The adequacy of official reserves and credit facilities must be appraised in relation to expected future disturbances, not in relation to those of the past. But the size and duration of future disturbances may perhaps be gauged by examining past disturbances, manifest as changes in official reserves. In Triffin's words:

The order of magnitude of deficits calling for reserve financing might first be gauged quantitatively on the

basis of past experience. This first approximation should then be revised, upward or downward, in the light of other pertinent evidence about the probable course of external and internal developments.[4]

Recorded changes in reserves do not measure past disturbances with any great accuracy — even with respect to countries that have abjured exchange control and have not altered their exchange rates. Changes in domestic policy, especially in monetary policy, can offset substantial disturbances, and the endogenous responses of the private sector have also been important in many instances. Finally, reserves may sometimes change autonomously, as central banks may intervene in the foreign-exchange market when there has been no apparent disturbance, selling gold and foreign currency when the exchange rate is above its "lower support point," and buying when the rate is below its "upper support point." They also engage in forward foreign-exchange operations and intergovernmental credit transactions that distort statistics on reserves and thereby distort any measure of disturbances derived from those statistics. Yet changes in reserves remain the best available measure of disturbances. In their very nature, moreover, they are certain to reflect the disturbances sufficient in size or duration to compel official intervention —disturbances requiring the use or acquisition of official reserves.

Inspection of the major countries' published reserve statistics suggested that the monthly changes in each nation's reserves can be described stochastically — that the changes may even be normally distributed.[5] If this were so,

---

[4] Robert Triffin [7], 35.

[5] The reserve statistics used in this study span the five-year period 1958–1962. They include official holdings of gold and convertible foreign exchange, the net IMF position (whether positive or negative), and, prior to 1959, the net EPU position of member countries. All data were drawn from *International Financial Statistics*. It might have been better to include credits available through EPU, rather than credits drawn or granted, and to have included the IMF gold tranche which cannot turn negative, rather than the net IMF position which does turn negative when countries draw on their credit tranches. But these substitutions would not have altered many of the month-to-month changes. The monthly changes in reserves were computed directly from the gross reserve figures, but adjusted to exclude the discontinuities introduced by the termination of EPU (January 1959). One might also have adjusted the published statistics for drawings on bilateral credit facilities, for the creation of and drawings on IMF "standby"

---

[3] In one important case studied here (Canada), the exchange rate was allowed to fluctuate extensively. More important, the rate was deliberately altered. In two other cases (Germany and the Netherlands), there were smaller but significant changes in exchange rates, interrupting the continuity of the data.

a country's balance of payments could be described as a simple random walk. But the monthly changes in reserves also displayed a significant serial correlation; successive observations were not independent. If, then, a country's balance of payments is to be described stochastically, one must use a Markov process rather than a random walk. We consequently sought to describe each country's balance of payments by a simple autoregressive scheme:

$$\triangle R_t = \rho \triangle R_{t-1} + \epsilon_t, \quad 0 < \rho < 1 \quad (1)$$

where ϵ_t has $N(\bar{\epsilon}, \sigma_\epsilon^2)$. In other words, the monthly "surplus" or "deficit" in the balance of payments, as measured by the change in gross reserves, $\triangle R_t$, was treated as reflecting a current disturbance, ϵ_t, drawn from a normal population with mean $\bar{\epsilon}$ and variance σ_ϵ^2, and the "carry-forward" of all past disturbances embodied in $\rho \triangle R_{t-1}$. The past disturbances will be subject to cumulative decay when $0 < \rho < 1.$[6] This compound hypothesis, if valid, would be quite convenient, allowing the complete description of a country's payments experience in terms of three parameters: $\bar{\epsilon}$, mean of the net disturbance; σ_ϵ^2, its variance; and ρ, its carry-forward or duration.[7] To test

this hypothesis, we have computed simple least-squares estimates of:

$$\triangle R_t = \bar{e} + p \triangle R_{t-1}, \quad (1a)$$

where $\bar{e}$ approximates $\bar{\epsilon}$, p is an estimate of ρ, and σ_e (the standard error of estimate) is an estimate of σ_ϵ.[8] We then ran separate statistical tests on the several parts of our composite hypothesis — that $0 < \rho < 1$, that ϵ_t is normally distributed, and that a simple Markov scheme suffices to describe the monthly balance of payments.

Estimates of $\bar{e}$, p, and σ_e for 14 countries are arrayed in table 1.[9] Eight countries' data displayed significant positive values for p; one more series (Germany) displayed a positive value just short of statistical significance.[10] Five other national series gave negative values for p, but only one of these (Finland) was significantly different from zero. In the majority of cases, then, our results were consistent with the supposition that $0 < \rho < 1$. An even larger majority of countries conformed to the next supposition; ten sets of residuals e_t satis-

---

credits, for changes in "liquid" liabilities, or for "special" intergovernment capital transactions such as debt prepayments. These adjustments would have had significant effects on the British statistics and, at the end of the period under study, on the statistics of several continental European countries.

[6] The supposition that ϵ_t is normally distributed obtains support from theory, not just casual observation. If the balance of payments can be viewed as a sum of separate transactions, each of them subject to a stochastic disturbance, the change in reserves will itself display a disturbance equal to the sum of the component disturbances. Although the components of the sum may not be normally distributed, the Central Limit Theorem suggests that the sum will have a normal distribution. The supposition that $0 < \rho < 1$ also obtains support from theory. Some of the constituent disturbances are likely to vanish soon after they appear. Others are likely to endure for several months or years unless they are offset by endogenous responses or by public policy. These offsets, however, will only take hold with the passage of time, eroding the disturbance gradually. A disturbance ϵ_0, therefore, may be deemed to have a net effect $\rho^k \epsilon_0$, k months later. These points are discussed at much greater length in a paper by the junior author, Elinor B. Yudin, *The Demand for Reserves* (International Economics Workshop, Columbia University, 1964, mimeo.). That paper also contains a detailed description of the computations presented below.

[7] The values of the parameters, $\bar{\epsilon}$, σ_ϵ^2, and ρ, obtained below, will, of course, reflect the choice of time interval (the use of monthly data). But the relative national values

of each parameter should not be much affected by this arbitrary choice. Although quarterly estimates of the three parameters would probably differ from the monthly estimates studied here, they are apt to differ in similar degree from one country to the next. It is the relationship among national values, moreover, that matters for the cross-sectional analysis in the next section.

[8] If the residuals e_t are normally distributed, implying that the ϵ_t are normally distributed, a simple least-squares estimate of $\bar{\epsilon}$ and p will approach the desirable large sample properties of asymptotic consistency and efficiency.

[9] Additional estimates were made for the changes in reserves reported by 13 other countries (Brazil, Chile, Colombia, El Salvador, Greece, India, Iran, Iraq, Lebanon, Mexico, Pakistan, Peru, and the Philippines) usually classified as "less-developed" countries. Nine of these countries' reserves gave values for p that were not significantly different from zero; two (Greece and Pakistan) gave significant positive values, two more (Iran and Iraq) gave significant negative values. The latter pair also showed significant (negative) second-order autocorrelation. Four countries' residuals (Brazil, El Salvador, Iraq, and Lebanon) failed the Chi-square test for normality at the 0.05 level, but only one (Lebanon) failed the Bartlett test for homoscedasticity. One would expect — and one finds — that the changes in reserves for these countries are more nearly random than those for the countries in table 1. Most of the underdeveloped countries still use strict exchange controls and have small reserves. Any enduring payments disturbance is usually met by changes in direct controls, so that the monthly changes in reserves should be regarded as the consequence of imperfect synchronization in exchange control, rather than the measure of the payments disturbances.

[10] When the most recent past quarterly change in reserves was substituted for $\triangle R_{t-1}$, the German data gave a significant positive p.

DEMAND FOR INTERNATIONAL RESERVES

TABLE 1. — AUTOREGRESSIVE EQUATIONS: MONTHLY CHANGES IN RESERVES, 1958–1962

Country	Parameters (and standard errors)		Standard Error of Estimate (σ_e) (millions of dollars)	e_t Normally Distributed [b]
	$\bar{e}$ (millions of dollars)	p		
Austria	5.40 (2.66)[a]	0.4664 (0.1198)[a]	18.9958	yes
Belgium	7.65 (4.47)	0.4216 (0.1165)[a]	32.4678	yes
Canada	2.99 (8.64)	0.4914 (0.1149)[a]	66.3340	no
Denmark	2.70 (2.14)	−0.2176 (0.1306)	16.4670	yes
Finland	1.32 (1.12)	−0.3785 (0.1280)[a]	8.3367	yes
Germany	10.12 (33.14)	0.2022 (0.1284)	256.4864	no
Italy	22.32 (9.05)	0.4661 (0.1139)[a]	61.5243	yes
Japan	9.16 (5.02)	0.6457 (0.1001)[a]	33.2173	yes
Netherlands	20.17 (6.87)[a]	−0.0853 (0.1294)	49.3806	no
New Zealand	0.22 (1.97)	0.4331 (0.1177)[a]	15.2923	yes
Norway	1.91 (1.34)	−0.1796 (0.1303)	10.2767	yes
Sweden	3.36 (2.21)	0.3307 (0.1237)[a]	16.4466	yes
Switzerland	17.08 (8.78)	−0.0631 (0.1494)	66.6481	yes
United Kingdom	14.69 (16.77)	0.3302 (0.1244)[a]	127.4753	no[c]

[a] Significantly different from zero at the 0.05 level.
[b] Distributions listed as "yes" are those that satisfied the Chi-square test for normality at the 0.05 level of significance.
[c] Would satisfy the Chi-square test for normality at the 0.01 level of significance.

fied a Chi-square test for normal fit at the 0.05 level of significance.

There is no satisfactory test for the sufficiency of the simple Markov scheme, but two imperfect tests give consistent results. The first test was performed by inserting an additional term into equation (1a):

$$\triangle R_t = \bar{e} + p_1 \triangle R_{t-1} + p_2 \triangle R_{t-2}. \quad (1b)$$

Not one computed p_2 was significantly different from zero, suggesting that the simple scheme set forth by equation (1) provides a sufficient stochastic description of the payments disturbances.[11] The second test applied the Durbin-

[11] This test is imperfect because $\triangle R_{t-1}$ and $\triangle R_{t-2}$ will be intercorrelated when $p_1 > 0$.

Watson ratio to the residuals, e_t, generated from equation (1a). There was no evidence of autocorrelation, positive or negative.[12]

Our hypothesis, however, involves one additional supposition — that σ_e^2 is constant through time. To test this assumption of homoscedasticity, we split each country's residuals, e_t, into two equal groups at the mid-point of the monthly series (June 1960), made separate estimates of σ_e^2 for the two subperiods, and applied the Bartlett test. Our results, arrayed in table 2, were less satisfactory than expected.

TABLE 2. — TESTS FOR STABILITY OF THE STANDARD ERRORS (σ_e)

Country	Bartlett Test (χ^2)	Linear Trend Coefficients and Standard Errors	
		λ	σ_λ
Austria	7.908[b]	14.3987[a]	4.4660
Belgium	0.017	1.5601	13.0310
Canada	30.603[b]	305.0469[a]	86.5924
Denmark	0.290	1.9199	3.0062
Finland	2.228	− 0.9648	0.7330
Germany	0.835	−370.1011	1141.2093
Italy	4.275[a]	87.3123	53.7158
Japan	6.231[a]	27.6118[a]	13.1164
Netherlands	1.405	− 82.6399	58.6199
New Zealand	0.008	− 1.1795	1.9708
Norway	2.116	1.4701	1.1071
Sweden	5.070[a]	− 2.2450	4.7838
Switzerland	5.544[a]	172.4060[a]	69.6477
United Kingdom	0.971	161.9592	186.5336

[a] Significantly different from zero at the 0.05 and 0.01 levels.
[b] Significantly different from zero at the 0.05 level, but not at the 0.01 level.

Six of the 14 sets of residuals showed a change in variance during the five-year period 1958–1962.

Viewed from a different standpoint, however, these same results inspire more pleasure than chagrin, supporting the contention that reserves must grow through time. The Brookings group endorses this important hypothesis:

While the range of potential swings in the balance of payments will probably continue to be a moderate percentage of the total volume of international transactions, these swings have widened greatly in recent years, and the trend of recent developments suggests that they are likely to widen further in the future.[13]

[12] This test is also imperfect, as the Durbin-Watson test should not be applied to data generated from an autoregressive transform. See J. Durbin and G. S. Watson [2], 410.
[13] See W. Salant, *et al.* [6], 136; also the Report of the Group of Ten [5], 8. Triffin [7], ch. 3 made the same

We have obtained additional support for the Brookings view by running a set of simple trend estimates, displayed in table 2. Treating every e_t^2 as a point-estimate of σ_e^2, we have made regression estimates of linear trend:

$$e_t^2 = e_0^2 + \lambda T. \qquad (2)$$

Four of the λ's were statistically significant, and nine of the 14 λ's were positive, suggesting gradual growth in the amplitude of payments disturbances.

Our composite hypothesis ($0 < \rho < 1$, ϵ_t normal, and σ_e^2 constant) is rarely satisfied by any one country's data. Belgium and New Zealand are the only ones whose data pass all tests at the 0.05 level of significance. The Italian, Japanese, Swedish, and British statistics could do so too, but only if the tests for normality and homoscedasticity were substantially relaxed (by accepting the hypotheses of normality and homoscedasticity unless they are contradicted at the 0.01 level of significance rather than the 0.05 level). A majority of national estimates, however, passed each of our tests taken one at a time — even the test for homoscedasticity. Hence, we were content to use our computed parameters, $\bar{e}$, p, and σ_e^2, as yardsticks with which to appraise the need for reserves — as the input to a series of cross-sectional relationships seeking to measure the demand for reserves.

The Demand for Reserves

If countries hold reserves to cope with disturbances — to maintain stable exchange rates — the demand for reserves should depend on expectations as to the size and duration of those disturbances. Each country's demand for reserves should therefore depend on the central bank's expectations concerning the anticipated mean disturbance, $\bar{e}$, the variance of disturbances, σ_e^2, and the "carry-forward," ρ.[14] Yet

any attempt to measure the "typical" demand for reserves by a cross-sectional analysis of information on national payments disturbances must make two heroic assumptions:

First, we are obliged to assume that each central bank or government holds the reserves it desires. This assumption can never be fulfilled with precision, if only because the stock of reserves circulates continuously.[15] Nor can it be fulfilled for all countries together unless the total of reserves is sufficiently large.[16]

Second, we are obliged to assume that the distribution of future disturbances, as forecast by the central banks, resembles the distribution of past disturbances. The values of $\bar{e}$, p and σ_e must be regarded as satisfactory proxies for $\bar{e}$, ρ, and σ_e, and these, in turn, must be thought to resemble the parameters that the authorities contemplate when they appraise the sufficiency of their reserves. This assumption cannot be exactly fulfilled because recorded changes in reserves will always reflect the influence of policies initiated to control the nation's balance of payments and regulate its stock of reserves. A country that deems itself short of reserves may act directly to reduce payments disturbances — or will willingly accommodate a "structural" surplus — thereby compressing σ_e, reducing p, and enlarging $\bar{e}$. We shall assume that the values of σ_e and p shown in table 1 are not materially affected by national policies — that they are satisfactory proxies for σ_e and ρ, the "true" parameters. We shall also assume that these "true" parameters do not greatly differ from those that central banks project for the future. But we do not

---

point much earlier, but did not explicitly relate his argument for growth in reserves to the evolution of payments disturbances.

[14] Alternatively, the demand for reserves might be deemed to depend on the distribution of a single number, jointly generated by these three parameters — on the distribution of anticipated *cumulative* surpluses and deficits. One could derive such a distribution from the three parameters studied in the text, but this would be extremely laborious and should not be necessary. The three parameters,

$\bar{e}$, σ_e^2 and ρ, specify that distribution completely and sufficiently. One might also try to link the level of reserves to the *total* variance, rather than the variance around $\bar{e}$. This procedure would avoid the necessity for separate consideration of $\bar{e}$ and ρ in the equations that follow. But it would also misrepresent the stochastic character of the balance of payments adduced in the previous section.

[15] One might, perhaps, surmount this first objection by seeking to explain *average* national reserves over a period of years. But experiments along these lines gave similar results to those reported in the text (the experiments on single-year reserves).

[16] This second *caveat* does not much impair the validity of our approach because we do not study all the major countries simultaneously. We have deliberately excluded the United States — the main supplier of reserves over the past few years. We have also excluded France because its reserve data were not sufficiently continuous.

have similar confidence in our estimates of $\bar{e}$, as any deliberate attempt to adjust reserve holdings is certain to affect the mean monthly change and, therefore, our values for $\bar{e}$. A country that anticipates a "structural" deficit ($\bar{e} < 0$) and lacks sufficient reserves to finance such a deficit is obliged to defend its position. In consequence, its $\bar{e}$ may differ substantially from its anticipated mean disturbances, $\bar{e}$.[17]

We now suppose that the demand for reserves depends on $\bar{e}$, σ_e, and ρ. As a linear approximation:

$$R_{it} = \beta_0 - \beta_1 \bar{e}_1 + \beta_2 \rho_i + \beta_3 \sigma_{ei}, \qquad (3)$$

where R_{it} measures the ith country's gross reserves at the start of the tth month. To compute a cross-sectional least-squares estimate of this relationship, we employed the parameters arrayed in table 1, but made a systematic adjustment in those statistics. When p was not significant (or significant but negative), it was arbitrarily fixed at zero. The corresponding estimate of $\bar{e}$ was replaced by the mean change in reserves, and the corresponding estimate of σ_e was replaced by the simple standard deviation of the monthly change in reserves.[18] Our first least-squares estimates sought to "explain" the distribution of gross reserves at December 31, 1957 ("initial" reserves). Our second estimate sought to "explain" gross reserves at December 31, 1962 ("terminal" reserves): [19]

[17] In the period under study, of course, the several national values of $\bar{e}$ jointly reflected the massive United States deficits of 1958–1962. These deficits may be viewed as "structural" disturbances afflicting other countries — as an overwhelming increase in the "supply" of reserves, posing an intractable identification problem. We think it equally correct, however, to view them as reflecting European policies deliberately designed to acquire reserves, and, therefore, overlaying or distorting the "true" $\bar{e}$. One can hardly accuse the European countries of excessive zeal in accomplishing a restoration of payments equilibrium. On the contrary, the major European countries were quite content to acquire reserves by way of the United States deficit.

[18] Computations using the "unadjusted" values of $\bar{e}$, p, and σ_e suggested that this adjustment did not have much effect on our final results. As expected, it did increase the standard error of β_2 (pertaining to ρ), but not by enough to alter our conclusions. Estimates were also made using σ_e^2, "adjusted" and "unadjusted," and the results of these computations were slightly different from those described below. In general, the coefficient of multiple correlation ($\bar{R}^2$) was lower, and the influence of ρ was sometimes less pronounced.

[19] The standard errors of the regression coefficients appear in parentheses beneath the coefficients. Asterisks denote statistical significance at the 0.05 level.

$$R_{57} = \begin{matrix} 68.11 + & 5.77\ \bar{e} + & 77.17\ p \\ (177.81) & (15.96) & (378.12) \end{matrix}$$
$$\begin{matrix} + 19.34\ \sigma_e, & \bar{R}^2 = .95, \\ (2.16)* \end{matrix} \qquad (3a)$$

$$R_{62} = \begin{matrix} -159.80 + & 95.89\ \bar{e} + & 1136.62\ p \\ (206.91) & (18.57)* & (440.00)* \end{matrix}$$
$$\begin{matrix} + 16.69\ \sigma_e, & \bar{R}^2 = .96 \\ (2.51)* \end{matrix} \qquad (3b)$$

These equations offer strong support for our hypothesis that the demand for reserves depends on the size and duration of disturbances. They attribute great explanatory power to σ_e (represented by the "adjusted" values of σ_e). They also apply the anticipated sign to β_2, the coefficient attached to ρ, and β_2 is significant with respect to "terminal" reserves. In both equations, however, β_1 takes the "wrong" (positive) sign, and the influence of $\bar{e}$ attains striking significance in the second equation. These results support our *caveat* concerning the computed mean of the disturbances, $\bar{e}$. The $\bar{e}$ may reflect intended reserve accumulation, not the projected mean disturbance determining demand. We therefore delete this variable from subsequent equations.[20]

When $\bar{e}$ is deleted from our first two equations, we obtain these results:

$$R_{57} = \begin{matrix} 89.80 + & 70.23\ p + & 19.95\ \sigma_e \\ (160.61) & (362.40) & (1.26)* \end{matrix}$$
$$\bar{R}^2 = .95, \qquad (3a')$$

$$R_{62} = \begin{matrix} 200.96 + & 1021.19\ p + & 26.98\ \sigma_e \\ (355.51) & (802.14) & (2.78)* \end{matrix}$$
$$\bar{R}^2 = .88. \qquad (3b')$$

The equations still "explain" the distribution of reserves quite well, but β_2 (pertaining to ρ) is no longer significant in the "terminal" equation. Furthermore, the coefficient of multiple correlation, $\bar{R}^2$, declines abruptly with respect to "terminal" reserves, falling below the $\bar{R}^2$ for "initial" reserves. As the "terminal" $\bar{R}^2$ was consistently lower than the "initial" $\bar{R}^2$ in other experiments, we may perhaps infer that the very large increase in reserves generated by the United States payments deficit was not well distributed among other countries.

One would expect the demand for reserves to reflect additional circumstances and considerations, not just expectations concerning disturb-

[20] Note, in passing, that $\bar{e}$ and σ_e are highly intercorrelated.

ances. We have sought to take account of two such considerations — the opportunity cost of holding reserves and the level of "liquid" liabilities that governments regard as claims on their reserves — but have not been successful.

We did not try to devise a direct measure of opportunity cost. Instead, we supposed that reserve accumulation is usually accomplished at the expense of capital formation — public or private, domestic or foreign — and that the "social marginal product" of capital varies inversely with per capita income. On this supposition, per capita income should correlate directly with total reserves. A country with a high per capita income should hold more reserves than a country with a low per capita income.[21]

We had equal difficulty measuring "liquid" liabilities, as the published figures are notoriously poor. There are no statistics for Switzerland, a major banking center, and the British data are organized quite differently from other countries' figures. In the end, we added the gross liabilities of central banks and governments to the net liabilities of "deposit money banks," both as reported in *International Financial Statistics*.[22] Once again, we employed a linear approximation:

$$R_{it} = \beta_0 + \beta_2 p_i + \beta_3 \sigma_{ei} + \beta_4 (Y/P)_i + \beta_5 L_{it},$$
(4)

where $(Y/P)_i$ represents per capita income in the ith country and L_{it} represents that country's liabilities. The addition of per capita income and of liabilities did not much improve the overall fit:

$$R_{57} = -371.78 + 305.95\,p + 20.63\,\sigma_e$$
$$(275.32)\quad(336.44)\quad(1.19)*$$
$$+\ 0.39(Y/P) -\ 0.02\,L_{57},$$
$$(0.21)\quad\quad(0.01)$$
$$\bar{R}^2 = .96,$$
(4a)

[21] The statistics for per capita income were obtained from income data in *International Financial Statistics*. They pertain to 1960.

[22] For the United Kingdom, we used the "old" series on sterling balances, excluding British indebtedness to the IMF. For the Canadian banks, we used foreign currency deposits *less* banks' claims on their foreign branches. When "explaining" initial reserves, we used liabilities at December 31, 1957; when "explaining" terminal reserves, we used liabilities at December 31, 1962. We ran several computations using other constructs (central bank liabilities taken alone, then official and bank liabilities without allowance for bank assets), but we did not find significant departures from the pattern described in the text.

$$R_{62} = 715.40 + 977.98\,p + 28.06\,\sigma_e$$
$$(681.78)\quad(836.39)\quad(2.96)*$$
$$-\ 0.51(Y/P) -\ 0.03\,L_{62},$$
$$(0.52)\quad\quad(0.02)$$
$$\bar{R}^2 = .88.$$
(4b)

Indeed, liabilities took on the "wrong" (negative) sign in both equations, while per capita income took on the "wrong" (negative) sign in the 1962 equation.

In a final experiment, we replaced liabilities with the domestic money supply, M_{it}, to allow for the impact of domestic legislation on the demand for reserves and for the contention that "excessive" domestic liquidity represents a potential claim on reserves.[23] This permutation was not informative. Our results were much as with liabilities:

$$R_{57} = -320.31 + 351.11\,p + 20.92\,\sigma_e$$
$$(290.16)\quad(383.28)\quad(1.55)*$$
$$+\ 0.35(Y/P) -\ 0.02\,M_{57},$$
$$(0.22)\quad\quad(0.02)$$
$$\bar{R}^2 = .96,$$
(4c)

$$R_{62} = 757.13 + 576.12\,p + 25.44\,\sigma_e$$
$$(720.22)\quad(980.99)\quad(4.25)*$$
$$+\ 0.47(Y/P) +\ 0.02\,M_{62},$$
$$(0.57)\quad\quad(0.04)$$
$$\bar{R}^2 = .87.$$
(4d)

Although central banks insist that "liquid" liabilities and the domestic money supply are relevant to any appraisal of their reserves, we could not establish any connection between either item and actual reserves. The prospective volatility of the balance of payments, measured by σ_e, accounted for the bulk of the total variation in the several central banks' holdings of reserves.

The strong partial correlation between R_{it} and σ_e, however, could conceivably reflect the influence of country size. Large countries, one might argue, hold large reserves and likewise experience large disturbances, as measured by the changes in their reserves. To exclude this possibility, we recomputed each of our cross-sectional equations with the addition of national income as a proxy for size. As national income did not display explanatory power and did not alter our other results, we doubt that those results are spurious or accidental.

[23] See Holtrop [3]. We did not employ liabilities and the money stock in the same equation as they are closely correlated.

DEMAND FOR INTERNATIONAL RESERVES   249

TABLE 3. — EXCESS (+) AND SHORTFALL (−) OF GROSS RESERVES COMPUTED FROM "BEST" EQUATIONS

	1957			1962			
Country	Actual Reserves	Computed Reserves	Excess (+) or Short-fall (−)	Actual Reserves	Computed Reserves	Excess (+) or Short-fall (−)	*ē*
Austria	523.00	491.33	31.67	1081.00	1041.72	39.28	5.3991
Belgium	1148.00	770.89	377.11	1753.00	1406.53	346.47	7.8446
Canada	1926.00	1432.61	493.39	2547.00	2270.03	276.97	2.9886
Denmark	172.00	445.99	−273.99	261.00	982.56	−721.56	1.4833
Finland	180.00	279.37	− 99.37	317.00	765.13	−448.13	1.3186
Germany	5197.00	5277.10	− 80.10	6964.00	7286.80	−322.80	29.4500
Italy	1354.00	1336.97	17.03	3644.00	2145.22	1498.78	22.3195
Japan	524.00	774.07	−250.07	2022.00	1410.68	611.32	9.1578
Netherlands	1009.00	1090.82	− 81.82	1946.00	1824.01	121.99	15.6167
New Zealand	152.00	417.76	−265.76	171.00	945.71	−774.71	.2228
Norway	197.00	319.53	−122.53	304.00	817.54	−513.54	1.7833
Sweden	501.00	440.62	60.38	801.00	975.55	−174.55	3.3577
Switzerland	1898.00	1429.63	468.37	2872.00	2266.14	605.86	16.2333
United Kingdom	2374.00	2648.29	−274.29	3311.00	3856.40	−545.40	14.6865

The Distribution of Reserves

Our cross-sectional equations cannot be used to detect an absolute "excess" or "deficiency" of gross reserves. But they can be used cautiously to appraise the distribution of reserves — to estimate the gross reserves each nation would hold if it conformed to "average" behavior and the relative "excess" or "shortfall" in national holdings compared to "average" behavior. Table 3 presents two sets of calculations based on the "best" regression equations we were able to develop. The first three columns of that table list actual and computed reserves for 1957, along with the relative "excess" (+) or "shortfall" (−), the discrepancy between computed and actual holdings. The next three columns list the corresponding figures for 1962, and the final column lists the computed mean disturbance (*ē* adjusted for nil or negative *p*). Computed reserves are derived from the simple regression relationship between R_{it} and σ_e (the only consistently significant relationship we have identified):

$$R_{57} = \begin{array}{c} 113.74 \\ (98.47) \end{array} + \begin{array}{c} 19.88\,\sigma_e, \\ (1.15)* \end{array} \quad \bar{R}^2 = .96, \quad (5a)$$

$$R_{62} = \begin{array}{c} 548.99 \\ (233.07) \end{array} + \begin{array}{c} 25.95\,\sigma_e, \\ (2.73)* \end{array} \quad \bar{R}^2 = .87. \quad (5b)$$

We do not attach great significance to these computations, but have been impressed by certain regularities:

First, we detect a considerable change in the distribution of reserves between 1957 and

1962. The correlation between the successive relative national positions (between columns 3 and 6 of table 3) is a mere 0.49.

Second, we find support for our contention that "new" reserves were not well distributed over this period. Countries displaying large relative deficiencies in 1957 should, perhaps, have made the largest gains in reserves by 1962. In this case, their data would have displayed the largest mean changes, i.e., the largest values for *ē*. Had this been so, in turn, there should have been a negative correlation between the third and seventh columns of table 3. In actual fact, there was no such correlation.[24]

Finally, our computations conform to *a priori* expectations in several strategic respects: They reveal a persistent and substantial relative deficiency in British reserves, sharp gains across the period in the relative positions of Japan and Italy, a deterioration in the relative position of Canada resulting from its payments crisis in 1962, and, surprisingly, a very slight relative deficiency for Germany.[25]

[24] As one would expect, the sixth and seventh columns of table 3 were positively correlated, but not very strongly.

[25] It should be noted in this connection that the level and variation in German reserves caused that country to appear as the extreme observation in the cross-sectional analysis, but that the exclusion of Germany from the entire analysis did not change the pattern or significance of our overall findings. Furthermore, alternative estimates of relative "excesses" and "shortfalls" based on equations including per capita income, liabilities, and *p* (similar to equations 4a and 4b in the text) did not give very different results in respect of distribution. The relative "excess"

REFERENCES

[1] R. E. Caves, "International Liquidity: Toward a Home Repair Manual," *Review of Economics and Statistics*, XLVI (May 1964).

[2] J. Durbin and G. S. Watson, "Testing for Serial Correlation in Least Squares Regression. I," *Biometrica* (1950).

[3] M. W. Holtrop, "Method of Monetary Analysis Used by De Nederlandsche Bank," International Monetary Fund *Staff Papers* (Feb. 1957).

[4] F. Machlup, et al., *International Monetary Arrangements: The Problem of Choice* (Princeton, 1964).

[5] *Ministerial Statement of the Group of Ten and Annex Prepared by Deputies* (Aug. 1964).

[6] W. Salant, et al., *The United States Balance of Payments in 1968* (Washington: The Brookings Institution, 1963).

[7] R. Triffin, *Gold and the Dollar Crisis* (New Haven, 1961).

[8] United States Congress, Subcommittee on International Economic Committee, *Hearings: International Payments Imbalances and Need for Strengthening International Financial Arrangements* (Washington, 1961).

of Canadian reserves increased on this computation, while the position and pattern of change for several small countries, especially Austria, Belgium, and Sweden, was rather different.

[10]

EXPORT INSTABILITY AND ECONOMIC GROWTH*

PETER B. KENEN AND CONSTANTINE S. VOIVODAS

For many years, economists seemed to agree that export instability damages the growth of the less-developed countries. Because of its effects on producers' incomes and, more generally, on foreign-exchange earnings, it was alleged to discourage investment. But faith in this doctrine has been undermined by MACBEAN (1966) and others[1]. MACBEAN's cross-sectional results, relating export fluctuations to the growth of real income and the level of investment, are summarized in *Table 1*. Coupled to his separate country studies, they cause him to assert that there is no systematic relationship between instability and economic growth, although individual countries have, at times, suffered adverse consequences.

MACBEAN's work, however, has itself been criticized from several points of view. MAIZELS (1968), for example, has argued that MACBEAN's cross-sectional technique implies the existence of a 'single, unique relationship between a given degree of fluctuation in exports and the resultant change in the growth rates of GNP'. ERB and SCHIAVO-CAMPO (1969) analyze time-series data, country by country, to adduce significant statistical connections between instability and economic growth.

There are, in addition, major questions to be raised about MACBEAN's findings, even when one accepts his analytical framework:

(1) Has he measured the relevant variables in an appropriate way?
(2) Were special factors at work in the period he chose to study

* This study was sponsored by the International Economics Workshop at Columbia University and was supported by a grant from the University's School of International Affairs. Additional assistance was received from the Center for Advanced Study in the Behavioral Sciences, Stanford, California, during the senior author's Fellowship in 1971–72. The authors are grateful to RONALD FINDLAY, DONALD KEESING, ROGER LAWRENCE and NORMAN MINTZ for critical comments and advice. A complete account of this project is contained in KENEN and VOIVODAS (1972).

1. See especially MASSELL (1964, 1970).

PETER B. KENEN AND CONSTANTINE S. VOIVODAS

Table 1

A Summary of MacBean's Cross-Sectional Results

Equation	R^2
$Y_g = 3.6 + 0.4278\ X_g - 0.0082\ S_x$ $\quad *(0.1267)\quad\ \ (0.2811)$	0.43
$Y_g = 4.1 + 0.3021\ X_g - 0.0089\ S_x + 0.0002\ T + 0.1028\ DR$ $\quad\ (0.1580)\quad\ \ (0.2833)\quad\ (0.0186)\quad (0.0828)$	0.48
$\qquad\qquad\qquad\cdots\cdots\cdots$	
$I_g = -5.6 + 1.09\ X_g + 1.21\ S_x - 0.14\ X_3$ $\qquad\ \ *(0.39)\quad\ (0.70)\quad\ (0.16)$	0.30
$I_g = -4.6 + 0.71\ X_g + 0.95\ S_x + 0.10\ X_3 + 0.19\ X_4 + 0.16\ X_5$ $\qquad\ \ *(0.24)\ \ *(0.39)\quad\ (0.10)\quad *(0.04)\quad *(0.03)$	0.81
$\qquad\qquad\qquad\cdots\cdots\cdots\cdots\cdots$	
$Q = 12.4 + 0.03\ X_g + 0.04\ S_x + 0.05\ X_4 + 0.05\ X_5$ $\qquad\ \ (0.04)\quad\ (0.08)\quad\ (0.07)\quad\ (0.05)$	0.11

Source: MACBEAN (1966), pp. 108–27.
* Statistically significant at the 0.05 level.
The numbers in parentheses are standard errors; the number of observations is 22 for the first two equations and 25 for the next three; the values of the variables are calculated for the period 1950/1 to 1957/8 (for most countries). The variables are:
Y_g rate of growth of real income
I_g rate of growth of real investment
X_g rate of growth of import capacity
S_x index of instability in the importing power of exports
Q average ratio of investment to income
X_3 rate of growth of foreign-exchange reserves
X_4 percentage change in the ratio of capital-goods imports to domestic investment
X_5 percentage change in the ratio of capital-goods imports to total imports
T ratio of foreign trade to income in 1957
DR change in gold and foreign-exchange reserves

Detailed definitions are given by MACBEAN (1966), p. 119. Regression equations dealing with the composition of investment are not reproduced here.

(1950–58), so that different results could be obtained by examining a longer interval?

(3) Was his sample of countries too small or unrepresentative?

This paper examines these three possibilities. It presents a broader statistical analysis, using a different measure of instability, two decades of data, and a larger group of countries. By and large, our results do not contradict MACBEAN's conclusions, but we do produce new results bearing on the general question of export instability and the special questions posed above.

EXPORT INSTABILITY AND ECONOMIC GROWTH

I

A number of statistics have been employed to measure instability[2]. The simplest and best known index is, perhaps, the coefficient of variation. Because it corrects for country size, it is particularly useful in cross-country comparisons of the type attempted here. Unfortunately, it does not distinguish between long-term variations and short-term instability. It will be inappropriately large for countries whose exports have displayed strong trends during the interval to which it is applied.

Trend removal, however, gives rise to other problems; each method of measuring trend generates a different set of residuals and, therefore, a different measure of instability. Some studies use a moving average, then compute percentage differences between actual and trend-value exports[3]. Others employ regression analysis to calculate trend, then use as an index of instability the standard error of estimate of the trend equation divided by the mean of exports —a trend-corrected analogue to the coefficient of variation[4].

The moving-average method suffers from competing flaws. If the time span of the average is made too short, the moving average will include too many short-term movements in exports, and the corresponding index of residuals will understate instability. If, instead, the average is made too long, it will take up too little of the secular movement, and the residuals will overstate instability. The regression method avoids this particular dilemma, but it is apt to furnish a very rigid description of the long-term drift in the export series; most investigators have employed linear or log-linear relationships, settling for the simplest description of the underlying pattern.

The measure of instability used in this study employs a regression equation to correct for trend, but one which may conform more flexibly to the underlying structure of the export data. It relies upon the supposition that total export proceeds, E_t, can be described by a first-order autoregressive scheme, or modified random walk[5]. Let:

2. For more on this problem, see SUNDRUM (1967); also KENEN and VOIVODAS (1972).

3. See, *e.g.*, FLEMING *et al.* (1963), and MacBEAN (1966).

4. See, *e.g.*, United Nations (1961), and MASSELL (1964).

5. This model was used by KENEN and YUDIN (1965) to study instability in the balance of payments.

793

PETER B. KENEN AND CONSTANTINE S. VOIVODAS

$$E_t = \alpha E_{t-1} + U_t \tag{1}$$

where:

$$U_t = \bar{u} + \beta \, \text{Time} + u_t \tag{2}$$

with u_t distributed independently and normally (with a zero mean and constant variance σ_u^2).

The principal measure of export instability to be furnished by this scheme is the standard error of the linear regression equation obtained by substituting (2) into (1):

$$E_t = a_0 + a_1 \, \text{Time} + a_2 E_{t-1} + e_t \tag{3}$$

where a_0 approximates $\bar{u}$; a_1 approximates β; a_2 approximates α; and e_t approximates u_t. The standard error of the regression equation (*i.e.*, σ_e) will serve as a proxy for σ_u, and when multiplied by $(100/\bar{E})$, will be denoted by S. The coefficient a_2 will also be used in the analysis of instability; it is related to the duration of the disturbances, U_t, affecting total export proceeds.

But estimates of S and of a_2 made directly from (3) may be badly biased. As E_{t-1} is the lagged value of the dependent variable, it will not be distributed independently of the error term, e_t. In consequence, a_1 may be biased upward. If, further, the model is misspecified, especially if longer-lagged values of E_t should appear in (1), there will be serial correlation in the error terms themselves. In consequence, σ_e and S will be biased downward (and t-tests applied to a_1 and a_2 will overstate the statistical significance of those coefficients). When these problems occur simultaneously, most authorities recommend a modification of the least-squares approach[6]. We have selected the simplest—first differencing the basic regression equation:

$$\Delta E_t = a_1' + a_2' \Delta E_{t-1} + w_t \tag{4}$$

where $w_t = e_t - e_{t-1}$. This transformation will be the more effective, the higher the simple correlation between E_t and e_t, and the higher the serial correlation in the error terms. The counterpart of S furnished by this transformation will be denoted by S'.

6. See, *e.g.*, ORCUTT and WINOKUR (1969), and GRILICHES (1967).

EXPORT INSTABILITY AND ECONOMIC GROWTH

II

Equations (3) and (4) were fitted to the export data for each of 52 less-developed countries. For each of 30 countries, we produced three pairs of equations spanning different intervals—the years 1950–58 (studied by MACBEAN), 1950–66, and 1956–67. For 22 additional countries, we produced one pair of equations spanning 1956–67[7].

Each such computation gave us three statistics for each country:

An index of instability, S or S' (the standard error of estimate of the regression equation divided by the mean of export proceeds).

A trend term, A or A' (the coefficient a_1 or a'_1 of the regression equation divided by the mean of export proceeds).

An autoregressive term, R or R' (the coefficient a_2 or a'_2 of the regressive equation, without additional modification).

Our results are summarized in *Table 2*.

If we were concerned primarily to defend our random-walk hypothesis, these summary statistics would be disappointing. The autoregressive terms have significant means in all four samples, supporting our supposition, but fewer than half of the national coefficients are significant individually. Furthermore, the mean of R' is always negative[8]. Our principal aim, however, is descriptive—to generate a measure of export instability that is not forced to reflect any preconceived notion concerning the long-term trend or cycle in export proceeds. If exports do not show a trend or autoregressive pattern,

7. The first thirty countries were Argentina, Bolivia, Brazil, Burma, Ceylon, Chile, Colombia, Costa Rica, Dominican Republic, Ecuador, Finland, Ghana, Greece, Guatemala, Honduras, Iceland, India, Iraq, Israel, Mexico, Morocco, Nicaragua, Peru, Philippines, Portugal, Rhodesia-Nyassaland, South Africa, Thailand, Turkey and Venezuela. The second twenty-two were Australia, Cyprus, El Salvador, Ethiopia, Guyana, Iran, Ireland, Jamaica, South Korea, Malaysia, New Zealand, Nigeria, Pakistan, Panama, Paraguay, Spain, Sudan, Syria, Tanzania, Trinidad, Tunisia, and Uruguay. For the individual regression results and notes on the data used, see KENEN and VOIVODAS (1972).

8. This may indicate that the residuals from (3) are themselves random (*i.e.*, that this equation fully describes the autoregressive properties of the export series). If this were so and a_2 were small, as it seems to be, the w_t would display an inverse autocorrelation, and the a'_2 would be biased downward. Unhappily, one cannot test directly for this possibility. The *computed* w_t will not display fully that inverse autocorrelation; it will be 'transferred' to the coefficients a'_2.

PETER B. KENEN AND CONSTANTINE S. VOIVODAS

Table 2

Time-Series Regression Results, Export Proceeds

Characteristic	Equation (3)			
	1950–58	1950–66	1956–67	1956–67
Number of equations (countries) . . .	30	30	30	52
With significant trend terms	6	8	11	20
With significant autoregressive terms .	2	14	11	20
With both	1	2	4	7
Mean values:				
Index of instability	12.14	11.43	9.25	9.23[1]
Deflated trend term	3.83	1.96	3.06	4.70[1]
Autoregressive term	0.16	0.58	0.47	0.40[1]
Standard deviations:				
Index of instability	3.45	3.27	4.57	4.21[1]
Deflated trend term	4.49	1.30	2.00	6.69[1]
Autoregressive term	0.24	0.29	0.34	0.39[1]

Characteristic	Equation (4)			
	1950–58	1950–66	1956–67	1956–67
Number of equations (countries) . . .	30	30	30	52
With significant trend terms	2	12	3	9
With significant autoregressive terms .	1	1	2	3
With both	1	1	0	0
Mean values:				
Index of instability	15.55	12.65	11.06	11.20[1]
Deflated trend term	5.19	5.56	4.89	5.60[1]
Autoregressive term	0.17	−0.07	−0.06	−0.07[1]
Standard deviations:				
Index of instability	5.12	3.53	4.77	4.52[1]
Deflated trend term	5.18	2.75	3.84	4.11[1]
Autoregressive term	0.24	0.26	0.33	0.40[1]

Statistical significance appraised at the 0.05 level, using a two-tailed test.
1. Using 50 countries, not 52 (India and Rhodesia-Nyassaland omitted for statistical reasons).

the method used here will not extract one forcibly. If exports do evince a trend or autoregressive pattern, the method used here will capture it accurately. More generally, the model underlying equations (3) and (4) serves flexibly to isolate any systematic vari-

EXPORT INSTABILITY AND ECONOMIC GROWTH

ation in the data, then to measure directly the remaining random fluctuations.

The statistics in *Table 2*, moreover, display several interesting characteristics: (i) The indexes of instability, S and S', are lower in the later (and longer) intervals, suggesting some decline in export instability. (ii) The autoregressive terms pertaining to equation (3) increase in the later (and longer) intervals, suggesting a change in the character of instability; the sharp short-term fluctuations which followed the Korean War have been replaced by gentler but more persistent disturbances. (iii) The standard deviations of S and S', and A and A' are smallest in the longest interval, suggesting that the histories of the countries in our sample become more nearly comparable over long periods.

III

Now to our principal concern. Using the index of export instability developed above, time intervals longer than were studied by MacBean, and a larger sample of countries, we shall apply cross-section regression methods in an effort to connect export instability with the rates of growth of the less-developed countries. Following MacBean, we shall look first for effects on the rate of growth of gross domestic product, Y_g, then for effects on the growth rate of investment, I_g, and lastly for effects on the ratio of investment to gross domestic product, Q. (The ratio Q is also used to 'explain' Y_g.)

In each instance, we shall test for an inverse relationship—the one that would prevail if instability did deter development. In each, moreover, we shall start with a simple statistical relationship, then make allowance for the role of inflation, measured by the rate of change in the cost of living, P_g, and for the role of trend in foreign exchange earnings, measured by A'. In each instance, finally, we shall begin with the interval used by MacBean and our thirty-country sample, then report the consequence of lengthening the interval and adding to the sample[9].

Beginning with effects on the rate of growth of output, we replicate MacBean's principal results. For 1950–58, the period he studied,

9. For additional regression results, see Kenen and Voivodas (1972).

PETER B. KENEN AND CONSTANTINE S. VOIVODAS

export instability, measured by S', is not a discernible deterrent to development. As a matter of fact, its coefficient is 'wrong signed' (see *Table 3*). We also find that inflation, measured by P_g, has a significant inverse relationship to the rate of growth of output in the same first period.

In the longer and later intervals, however, the influence of P_g is very much reduced[10], while the ratio of investment to gross domestic product, Q, and the trend in exports, A', come to have strong effects. The investment-output ratio has a significant weight in two of the remaining six equations (and is close to significance in a third)[11], and the trend in export proceeds is significant whenever it appears. Yet S' is not significant in any equation, and is wrong-signed in several.

We do adduce one new result concerning instability, but cannot assign it any simple interpretation. The duration of export disturbances, measured by the autoregressive terms of the national time-series equations (4), have positive weights in every cross-sectional regression equation, and reach significance in two of them. This may say that persistent or enduring disturbances do not much impede medium-term planning for the use of export proceeds—or can be built into planning itself. Alternatively, it may say that the disturbances themselves tend to be smaller. (There are significant negative correlations between the autoregressive term, R', and the index of instability, S', in the thirty- and fifty-country samples for 1956–67.)

The link between development measured by Y_g and export instability is necessarily indirect; instability can affect the growth rate of output only by affecting capital formation, and this is only one source of economic growth. If, then, there is an important connection

10. The link with inflation in 1950–58 may be spurious. Five of the thirty countries in this sample had rates of inflation higher than 10 per cent, and five had growth rates lower than 2.5 per cent. Three countries in South America (Argentina, Bolivia and Brazil) belong to both groups. In 1956–57, two of these same countries continued to display high rates of inflation, but their growth rates were no longer low. Notice, moreover, that the same price index was used to deflate gross domestic product and to define P_g.

11. Our expectation concerning the value of Q derives from the simplest HARROD-DOMAR assumptions. Let $K = \sigma Y$, where K is the capital stock, Y is national output, and σ is the (constant) capital-output ratio. Then $I = \Delta K = \sigma \Delta Y$, so that $Q = \sigma Y_g$. Q and Y_g should be directly related. Notice, however, that the coefficient of Q is not significant in any of the fifty-country equations.

EXPORT INSTABILITY AND ECONOMIC GROWTH

Table 3

Cross-Sectional Regression Equations with Growth of Output as the Dependent Variable

Interval[1]	Coun-tries	Equation	$\bar{R}^2$
1950–58	30	$Y_g = 6.11 + 0.052 \, S' + 3.452 \, R' - 0.105 \, P_g + 0.002 \, Q$ (0.527) (1.762) *(3.056) (0.018)	0.340
1950–58	30	$Y_g = 4.72 + 0.082 \, S' + 4.149 \, R' - 0.096 \, P_g - 0.007 \, Q + 0.184 \, A'$ (0.865) *(2.198) *(2.297) (0.092) (1.972)	0.432
1950–66	30	$Y_g = 3.80 - 0.081 \, S' + 1.854 \, R' - 0.061 \, P_g + 0.158 \, Q$ (1.002) (1.621) (1.671) *(2.548)	0.416
1950–66	30	$Y_g = 2.82 - 0.061 \, S' + 1.673 \, R' - 0.052 \, P_g + 0.123 \, Q + 0.223 \, A'$ (0.795) (1.566) (1.500) (1.982) *(2.188)	0.513
1956–67	30	$Y_g = 1.36 + 0.108 \, S' + 0.734 \, R' - 0.006 \, P_g + 0.148 \, Q$ (1.706) (0.777) (0.188) *(2.166)	0.239
1956–67	30	$Y_g = 2.18 + 0.017 \, S' + 0.895 \, R' - 0.001 \, P_g + 0.082 \, Q + 0.233 \, A'$ (0.288) (1.132) (0.015) (0.015) *(3.430)	0.489
1956–67	50[2]	$Y_g = 3.46 + 0.054 \, S' + 0.670 \, R' - 0.023 \, P_g + 0.057 \, Q$ (1.021) (1.159) (0.805) (1.130)	0.071
1956–67	50[2]	$Y_g = 3.33 - 0.003 \, S' + 1.595 \, R' - 0.006 \, P_g + 0.012 \, Q + 0.271 \, A'$ (0.080) *(3.421) (0.268) (0.308) *(5.848)	0.477

* Denotes statistical significance at the 0.05 level.
The numbers in parentheses are t coefficients; Y_g is the rate of growth of gross domestic product; S' is the standard error of equation (4) divided by the mean of export proceeds; R' is the autoregressive coefficient of equation (4); P_g is the rate of change of the price level; Q is the investment-output ratio; A' is the constant (trend) term of equation (4) divided by the mean of export proceeds.
1. Data span used to measure the variables entering the cross-sectional equation.
2. India and Rhodesia-Nyassaland omitted because of deficiencies in basic data.

between development and instability, one should be able to detect it most clearly by examining the growth or level of investment.

MacBean did not find any plausible relationship between the growth rate of investment and the instability of export proceeds. Some of his regression coefficients were significant, but they were positive rather than negative. We had the same experience. In both of our equations for 1950–58, S' has a significant positive weight, and in three of the remaining six equations it is again 'wrong-signed' (see *Table 4*). In that same first period, moreover, inflation seems to have a powerful negative effect on growth, but it does not play the same

PETER B. KENEN AND CONSTANTINE S. VOIVODAS

Table 4

Cross-Sectional Regression Equations with Growth of Investment
as the Dependent Variable

Interval[1]	Coun- tries	Equation	$\bar{R}^2$
1950–58	30	$I_g = -0.75 + 0.710\,S' + 3.817\,R' - 0.280\,P_g$ $*(3.006) \quad (0.859) \quad *(2.866)$	0.089
1950–58	30	$I_g = -0.96 + 0.713\,S' + 3.902\,R' - 0.276\,P_g + 0.025\,A'$ $*(2.930) \quad (0.847) \quad *(2.566) \quad (0.104)$	0.310
1950–66	30	$I_g = 6.39 - 0.025\,S' + 1.587\,R' - 0.061\,P_g$ $(0.123) \quad (0.586) \quad (0.666)$	0.033
1950–66	30	$I_g = 4.14 + 0.006\,S' + 1.068\,R' - 0.047\,P_g + 0.314\,A'$ $(0.030) \quad (0.393) \quad (0.519) \quad (1.207)$	0.087
1956–67	30	$I_g = 5.09 + 0.017\,S' + 2.922\,R' - 0.005\,P_g$ $(0.173) \quad *(2.507) \quad (0.087)$	0.059
1956–67	30	$I_g = 4.58 - 0.154\,S' + 2.823\,R' + 0.013\,P_g + 0.465\,A'$ $(0.876) \quad (1.221) \quad (0.166) \quad *(2.363)$	0.231
1956–67	50[2]	$I_g = 5.59 + 0.060\,S' + 2.799\,R' - 0.054\,P_g$ $(0.549) \quad *(2.232) \quad (0.860)$	0.106
1956–67	50[2]	$I_g = 3.39 - 0.004\,S' + 4.222\,R' - 0.023\,P_g + 0.405\,A'$ $(0.044) \quad *(3.522) \quad (0.405) \quad *(3.465)$	0.295

* Denotes statistical significance at the 0.05 level.
The numbers in parentheses are t coefficients; I_g is the rate of growth of gross domestic product. For other symbols, see the notes to *Table 3*.
1. Data span used to measure the variables entering the cross-sectional equation.
2. India and Rhodesia-Nyassaland omitted because of deficiencies in basic data.

role in other intervals. Here, finally, the A' and R' are significant
only in 1956–67, and the regression equations, as a whole, are somewhat less powerful than those in *Table 3*[12]. In brief, we cannot find
any systematic inverse relationship between instability and the
growth rate of investment.

MACBEAN did not pay much attention to the level of investment.
His efforts to connect it with export instability were less complete—
and no more successful—that his work with the growth rates of out-

12. The investment-output ratio, Q, is not employed in these equations because
there is no simple theoretical justification for predicting its relationship to the
growth rate of investment.

EXPORT INSTABILITY AND ECONOMIC GROWTH

put and investment. Yet the level of investment is the argument most likely to reflect any adverse impact of export instability. A country that suffers from substantial instability may be able to maintain rapid growth in investment, provided the average level of investment is not high relative to average export earnings. If imports of capital goods do not normally absorb a major share of total export earnings, a short-fall of foreign-exchange receipts need not curtail investment significantly. If they do not use a large fraction of total export earnings, a short-fall can have a prompt, serious effect. If, further, instability in export earnings inhibits expansion of the export industries, this effect will also be reflected in the level of total capital formation, not its rate of growth. Here, moreover, we have found occasional statistical connections.

In 1950–58, MACBEAN could not find a single significant relationship between the ratio of investment to income and the instability of foreign-exchange receipts. We are not much more successful at this stage:

$$Q = 14.75 + 0.233 \ S'; \ + 8.418 \ R' - 0.094 \ P_g \quad R^2 = 0.150$$
$$ (1.026) \quad (1.965) \quad (1.000)$$

The coefficient of S' is wrong-signed again. In this instance, moreover, the addition of trend has no effect whatsoever. But in 1950–66 and 1956–67, S' obtains the expected negative sign in every regression equation, and it is significant in the fifty-country sample. Thus:

$$Q = 20.94 - 0.312 \ S'; \ - 0.605 \ R' - 0.070 \ P_g \quad R^2 = 0.106$$
$$ *(2.122) \quad (0.360) \quad (0.833)$$

or:

$$Q = 20.02 - 0.233 \ A' - 0.349 \ S' + 0.213 \ R' - 0.060 \ P_g \quad R^2 = 0.141$$
$$ (1.355) \quad *(2.358) \quad (0.120) \quad (0.619)$$

Export instability does appear to reduce the level of investment.

The results of this analysis can best be summarized as answers to the questions posed at the beginning:

(1) The method of measuring export instability does not seem to matter much. Using the same time period as MACBEAN and a very similar sample of countries, we have managed to replicate most of his results. Many of the partial regression coefficients pertaining to

PETER B. KENEN AND CONSTANTINE S. VOIVODAS

instability have the wrong signs, and some of these attain statistical significance in the investment equation.

(2) The choice of time period matters somewhat more. Thus, the regression coefficients of S' are negative in most of the equations pertaining to our intervals 1950–56 and 1956–67, especially in those that also contain export trends. Our one new result, moreover, crops up only in recent years; the inverse relationship between S' and Q is strongest in the interval 1956–67[13].

(3) Our work does not reveal any major deficiency in the sample of countries chosen by MacBean. To be sure, the negative relationship between S' and Q did not attain significance in any thirty-country sample. But there are few other differences between our two sets of results for 1956–67. The only discernible difference worth noting is the greater statistical significance attaching to A' and R' in the fifty-country sample[14].

In general, our findings do not contradict MacBean. We do not show any pervasive connection between the rate of economic development and the degree of export instability. We do show, however, that some of the perverse results encountered by MacBean—his wrong-signed coefficients for instability—are peculiar to the 1950's, and that there is a strong, plausible connection between instability and the level of investment in the 1960's.

This one new result cannot settle a very complex question. It can, perhaps, be said to reopen the question.

Princeton University   Peter B. Kenen
UNCTAD   Constantine S. Voivodas

13. The effects of using a longer time period, as distinguished from a different time period, are hard to disentangle. The data and equations for 1950–66 may be treated as averages of experience in the two shorter intervals under study here. But the average is something distinct from its parts, because the method employed to measure instability is more reliable over long periods. At the same time, however, our basic data are least perfectly comparable over a long period. (As a practical matter, the best equations for Y_g were obtained in the interval 1956–66, but not those for I_g or for Q.)

14. Note, in this connection, that the simple correlation between A' and R' is much stronger in the fifty-country sample (-0.39 compared with -0.19).

EXPORT INSTABILITY AND ECONOMIC GROWTH

REFERENCES

ERB, G., and SCHIAVO-CAMPO, S.: 'Instability of Exports, of "Developmental Imports", and of National Income in Less-Developed Countries' (unpublished manuscript), 1969.

FLEMING, M., RHOMBERG, R., and BOISSONEAULT, L.: 'Export Norms and Their Role in Compensatory Finance', *International Monetary Fund Staff Papers*, 1963.

GRILICHES, Z.: 'Distributed Lags: A Survey', *Econometrica*, 1967.

KENEN, P.B., and VOIVODAS, C.S.: *Export Instability and Economic Growth*, Working Papers in International Economics, G-72-01, International Finance Section, Princeton University, 1972.

KENEN, P.B., and YUDIN, E.B.: 'The Demand for International Reserves', *Review of Economics and Statistics*, 1965.

MACBEAN, A.: *Export Instability and Economic Development*, Harvard University Press, 1966.

MAIZELS, A.: *Exports and Economic Growth of Developing Countries*, Cambridge University Press, 1968.

MASSELL, B.: 'Export Concentration and Fluctuations in Export Earnings', *American Economic Review*, 1964.

MASSELL, B.: 'Export Instability and Economic Structure', *American Economic Review*, 1970.

ORCUTT, G.H., and WINOKUR, H.S., Jr.: 'First Order Autoregression: Inference, Estimation and Prediction', *Econometrica*, 1969.

SUNDRUM, R.: 'The Measurement of Export Instability' (unpublished manuscript), 1967.

United Nations: *International Compensation for Fluctuations in Commodity Trade*, 1961.

SUMMARY

Does export instability interfere with economic development? Work by McBEAN answers in the negative. He finds no systematic relationship between instability and economic growth. This paper asks three questions about McBEAN's work: (1) Has he measured the relevant variables appropriately? (2) Were special factors at work in the period he studied (1950–58)? (3) Was his sample of countries representative? It presents a broader statistical analysis, using a different index of instability, two decades of data, and more countries. In general, the findings do not contradict McBEAN. But calculations using different time periods (1950–66 and 1956–67) do produce some evidence of interference. Furthermore, the paper finds one new relationship—a strong inverse connection between instability and the *level* of investment in developing countries.

[11]

Reprinted from THE JOURNAL OF FINANCE, Vol. XXIX, No. 2, May, 1974

THE BALANCE OF PAYMENTS AND POLICY MIX: SIMULATIONS BASED ON A U.S. MODEL

PETER B. KENEN*

THIS IS A progress report. It introduces a new medium-sized model of the U.S. balance of payments and, to go with it, a macroeconomic model of the domestic economy. It goes on to illustrate uses of the model, including a simple demonstration of the case for making careful, correct assignments of policy instruments to policy targets.[1]

THE MODEL

The model itself includes 53 stochastic equations and a dozen identities. The stochastic relationships were obtained with quarterly data spanning 1952-1969,[2] using simple single-equation least-squares estimation. Specification was governed by three objectives: (1) to feature explicitly the principal instruments of fiscal and monetary policies—government expenditure, tax rates, and bank reserves; (2) to trace the important connections between domestic economic activity and the balance of payments, and to feed effects of changes in the balance of payments back into the domestic economy,[3] (3) to facilitate simple, sequential programming.

The foreign sector of the model is fairly large. It seeks to forecast separately each major component of the U.S. balance of payments.[4] Furthermore, it offers and tests a number of hypotheses that have not found their way into other models. I argue, for example, that short-term variations in U.S. direct investment depend in chief on changes in monetary conditions affecting the locus and method of financing capital formation abroad, not on changes in the conditions affecting the long-term decision to undertake foreign investment. Finally, the model exploits my own earlier work on the determinants of short-term capital flows in the U.S. balance of payments.[5]

* The author is professor of Economics and International Finance at Princeton University.

This study was begun under the auspices of the International Economics Workshop at Columbia University, and the initial stages were financed by the National Science Foundation under grant GS 2024. Additional assistance was received from the Center for Advanced Study in the Behavioral Sciences, Stanford California, during the author's Fellowship in 1971-72, and from the International Finance Section, Princeton University. I am especially grateful to Carol Gerstl, Constantine Voivodas, Stephen Altheim, Donald Jackson and Nancy Happe for gathering data and processing the regression estimates, to Mary Pori of the CASBS for designing the program used to simulate the model, and to Dennis Warner and Peter Dungan for extending and improving the program.

1. The work reported briefly here is described more fully in Kenen [3].

2. In cases when early data were not available, 1955-1969.

3. There is, however, only one such link in the present version of the model. The computed balance on current account is fed back into the identity defining gross national product.

4. It is larger than the model by Prachowny [7], even though he deals in detail with several components of merchandise trade. It is similar to the model developed by Kwack and Schink [4], but does not require as much exogenous information.

5. Kenen [2].

The domestic sector is constructed with less attention to the lessons taught by formal theory. It is not designed to test competing hypotheses concerning the behavior of consumption, investment, and other components of gross national product.[6] Instead, the requirements of the foreign sector and the desire for simplicity in structure govern to a large extent the selection of dependent and independent variables.

The domestic sector is summarized by Table 1. It is a neo-Keynesian construct aimed at explaining four components of gross national product—personal consumption, fixed capital formation, net investment in inventories, and residential construction—using a handful of exogenous variables. But it also forecasts the unemployment rate, the price level, and certain monetary arguments such as the free reserves of commercial banks. The major exogenous variables are government expenditure (FGO), the owned (unborrowed) reserves of commercial banks (SUR), and the discount rate (RDR).[7]

The foreign sector is summarized by Table 2. It is concerned to forecast the official-settlements measure of the surplus or deficit in the U.S. balance of payments and, using that measure, net U.S. reserves at the end of each quarter (official reserve assets *less* liabilities to foreign official monetary institutions). The equations employ several arguments generated by the domestic sector, including gross national product, corporate savings, the price level, free reserves, and long- and short-term interest rates. In addition, they employ an index of foreign industrial production, an index of foreign (U.S. import) prices, foreign interest rates and foreign stock-price indexes.[8] Finally, they employ a number of dummy variables standing for controls on capital outflows from the United States.

Time does not allow me to describe in detail the implications of individual equations. Three points, however, need to be made: (1) Equations relating to merchandise trade show rapid sensitivity to changes in prices, including implicitly changes in exchange rates. This is because the prices used are indexes of average values, not explicit price quotations; they are the prices at which goods were purchased whenever in the past the purchases occurred. In consequence, the trade equations cannot be used to study the short-term effects of changes in exchange rates. (2) Several capital-account equations invoke the implications of portfolio theory. New acquisitions of foreign assets, including direct-investment claims, are inversely related to stocks of assets acquired in the past. As a result, changes in domestic and foreign interest rates will produce combined effects (once-for-all stock adjustments and continuing flows).

---

6. The decision to build a special domestic sector, rather than use an existing macroeconomic model, may well be questioned. Models superior to this one in specification and power are readily available. Unhappily, those which are small enough to be used easily in experiments like the ones reported here are too small to generate the domestic information needed by the foreign sector, while those which are large enough to supply that information are too large to handle easily.

7. In addition, the Regulation Q ceiling on time-deposit rates, and dummy variables denoting important changes in tax rates. In some simulations not reported here, I treat as additional exogenous variables parameters of the personal and corporate tax equations.

8. All of these variables are deemed to be exogenous, with two exceptions: The Canadian interest rate is treated as a function of its own past value and the U.S. rate, and the Canadian stock-price index is treated as a function of a similar U.S. index generated by the domestic sector. In general, then, the model ignores the effects of the U.S. economy on activity and prices abroad.

TABLE 1
THE DOMESTIC SECTOR OF THE MODEL

Dependent Variable	Independent Variables	Form of Equation	$\bar{R}^2$	DW
Gross national product (FYG)	Personal consumption, fixed capital formation, inventory investment, residential construction, government expenditure, foreign balance	Identity	—	—
Personal consumption (FCO)	Personal income, personal taxes, real money stock, real thrift deposits	Linear autoregressive	0.998	0.91
Fixed capital formation (FFC)	Corporate saving, long-term interest rate, unemployment rate	Log autoregressive	0.992	1.40
Inventory investment (FIN)	Ratio of inventories to gross national product, change in final demand, inflation rate, short-term interest rate	Linear autoregressive	0.667	2.09
Residential construction (FRC)	Housing starts, trend	Linear difference	0.743	2.60
Housing starts (DHS)	Long-term interest rate, change in thrift deposits	Linear autoregressive	0.774	1.47
Unemployment rate (RUN)	Gross national product, growth rate of gross national product, trend	Log	0.890	0.40
Corporate saving (FCS)[a]	Corporate income, dividends, corporate taxes	Identity	—	—
Corporate income (FYC)[a]	Gross national product, growth rate of gross national product	Log autoregressive	0.998	2.32
Corporate dividends (FDV)	Corporate income, long-term interest rate	Linear autoregressive	0.991	2.03
Corporate taxes (FTC)[a]	Corporate income, dummies denoting tax surcharges during Korean and Vietnam wars	Linear	0.997	0.58
Personal income (FYP)[b]	Gross national product, corporate income, dividends, transfers to households, government interest payments	Identity	—	—
Personal taxes (FTP)[b]	Personal income, dummies denoting tax surcharges during Korean and Vietnam wars, dummy denoting effects of tax reforms (1964)	Log	0.995	0.85

Continued overleaf

TABLE 1 (*Continued*)

Dependent Variable	Independent Variables	Form of Equation	$\bar{R}^2$	DW
Transfers to households (FYT)	Unemployment rate, trend	Log	0.989	0.41
Government interest payments (FIG)	Short-term interest rate	Linear autoregressive	0.996	1.58
Wage-rate index (DWE)	Unemployment, price index, trend	Log	0.998	0.53
Price index (DPY)	Wage-rate index, capacity utilization, trend	Log autoregressive	0.999	1.23
Price index for goods output (DPG)	Wage-rate index, capacity utilization, trend	Log autoregressive	0.998	1.24
Price index for exports (DPX)	Price index for goods, capacity utilization, trend	Log	0.970	1.03
Short-term interest rate (RST)	Discount rate, free reserves, growth rate of gross national product	Linear	0.956	1.00
Long-term interest rate (RLT)	Short-term interest rate, change in free reserves	Linear autoregressive	0.979	1.88
Free reserves (SFR)	Change in owned reserves, change in money stock, short-term interest rate, discount rate	Linear autoregressive	0.902	2.18
Money stock (SMO)	Owned reserves, short-term interest rate, discount rate, fixed capital formation	Linear autoregressive	0.996	0.89
Thrift deposits (SSL)	Regulation Q ceiling, short-term interest rate, trend	Linear	0.999	0.84
Stock-price index (DSP)	Short-term interest rate, trend	Linear	0.961	0.47

a Corporate income is defined to include corporate profits and inventory valuation adjustment *plus* indirect business tax and nontax liability *plus* capital consumption allowance *plus* contributions for social insurance (except personal contributions). Corporate taxes are defined symmetrically to include indirect business tax and nontax liability and contributions for social insurance (except personal contributions); corporate saving includes the capital consumption allowance.

b Personal income is defined to include personal contributions to social insurance. Personal taxes are defined symmetrically to include those contributions.

With few exceptions, flows are defined in billions of constant (1958) dollars at seasonally adjusted annual rates; stocks are defined in billions of current dollars at the end of the relevant quarter; index numbers are based on 1958 and seasonally adjusted. For details, see Kenen [3].

TABLE 2
THE FOREIGN SECTOR OF THE MODEL

Dependent Variable	Independent Variables	Form of Equation	$\bar{R}^2$	DW
Export volume (FXG)	Export prices, foreign prices, foreign industrial production, gross foreign aid, dummies denoting dock strikes	Linear	0.950	0.59
Export value (EXG)	Export volume *times* export price index	Identity	—	—
Import volume (FMG)	Export prices, foreign prices, gross national product, dummies denoting dock strikes, trend	Linear	0.968	0.32
Import value (EMG)	Import volume *times* foreign price index	Identity	—	—
Military sales (EXM)	Military payments, trend	Linear	0.848	1.32
Military payments (EMM)	Dummy variable denoting Vietnam war	Linear auto-regressive	0.909	2.18
Service exports (EXS)	Merchandise exports, foreign industrial production, export prices	Linear auto-regressive	0.996	1.99
Service imports (EMS)	Disposable income, foreign prices, dummy denoting dock strike, trend	Linear	0.992	1.04
Income from direct investments (EXYD)	Foreign capacity utilization, trend, dummies denoting U.S. controls on capital outflows (ZDIV, ZDIM)	Linear	0.954	1.54
Income from other investments (EXYO)	Long-term interest rate, trend, dummies denoting U.S. controls on capital outflows (ZDIV, ZDIM)	Linear	0.958	0.74
Investment income paid to foreigners (EMY)	Foreign short-term claims on the United States, short-term interest rate, trend	Log	0.993	1.08
Transfer payments to foreigners (EMT)	Trend	Log	0.924	0.77
Balance on current account (EBGST)[a]	[EXG + EXM + EXS + EXYD + EXYO] *less* [EMG + EMM + EMS + EMY + EMT]	Identity	—	—
Nonmilitary aid *less* repayments (EGC, ERG)	Trends	Linear & Log	0.849 / 0.389	1.61 / 2.15

Continued overleaf

TABLE 2 (*Continued*)

Dependent Variable	Independent Variables	Form of Equation	$\bar{R}^2$	DW
U.S. direct investment abroad (EDI)	Stock of direct investments, corporate saving, long-term interest rates (U.S., Canadian, other foreign), dummies denoting U.S. controls on capital outflows (ZDIV, ZDIM)	Log	0.750	1.62
Stock of U.S. direct investments (EDI)	Direct investment, unrepatriated earnings, prior stock	Identity	—	—
Unrepatriated U.S. earnings (EXYDR)	Direct investment, income from direct investments, dummies denoting U.S. controls on capital outflows (ZDIV, ZDIM)	Linear annual	0.946	2.74
U.S. purchases of new Canadian securities (ENIC)	Change in U.S. dollar price of Canadian dollar; trend	Linear	0.431	1.91
U.S. purchases of other securities (EPIS *less* ENIC)	Long-term interest rates (U.S., Canadian), dummy denoting Interest Equalization Tax (ZIET)	Linear	0.295	1.92
Other U.S. long-term investment (EPIO)	Export value, dummy denoting U.S. controls on capital outflows (ZVCR)	Linear auto-regressive	0.266	2.37
U.S. short-term claims on foreigners reported by banks (STC)	Export value, short-term interest rate, trend, dummy denoting U.S. controls on capital outflows (ZVCR), seasonal dummies	Log auto-regressive	0.997	2.01
Other U.S. short-term investment (ESCO)	Export value, short-term interest rate	Linear auto-regressive	0.195	1.97
Foreign direct investment in U.S. (EDF)	Stock of direct investments, capacity utilization, long-term interest rate	Linear	0.331	2.12
Stock of foreign direct investments (SDF)	Direct investment, unrepatriated earnings, prior stock	Identity	—	—
Unrepatriated foreign earnings (EMYDR)	Stock of foreign direct investments	Linear annual	0.810	1.23
Foreign purchases of U.S. long-term securities (EPFS)[b]	Long-term interest rate, change in stock price indexes (U.S., Canadian)	Linear auto-regressive	0.652	1.96
Foreign short-term claims on U.S. (STL)	Free reserves, trend, seasonal dummies	Log auto-regressive	0.994	1.89

TABLE 2 *(Continued)*

Dependent Variable	Independent Variables	Form of Equation	$\bar{R}^2$	DW
Other foreign investment in U.S. (EPFO)	Long-term interest rate, capacity utilization	Linear	0.578	1.83
Balance on capital account (EBGPC)[a,b]	$[(EGC - ERG) + EDI + EPIS + EPIO + (STC - STC_{-1}) + ESCO]$ *less* $[EDF + EPFS + (STL - STL_{-1}) + EPFO]$	Identity	—	—
Errors and omissions (EOC)[b]	Changes in export value, import value, U.S. short-term claims on foreigners, foreign short-term claims on the United States; dummy denoting apparent discontinuity	Linear	0.570	2.03
Balance of payments (EBP)[c]	$EBGST - EBGPC + EOC$	Identity	—	—
Net reserves (SNR)[c]	$SNR_{-1} + EBP$	Identity	—	—

[a] As U.S. government grants are included in government capital outflows (EGC) rather than transfers (EMT), EBGST and EBGPC are biased. The biases cancel when the two series are used to define the overall balance of payments (EBP). But the bias in EBGST affects the computation of gross national product, because the constant-dollar equivalent of EBGST is used to represent the foreign balance in the first equation of the domestic sector. This and other statistical imperfections in the data are offset crudely by correcting arithmetically the definition of gross national product.

[b] Except foreign purchases of U.S. government bonds and notes. This omission biases the balance on capital account (EBGPC), but the bias is offset crudely by correcting implicitly errors and omissions (EOC).

[c] Because there are no data for the 1950's on foreign official purchases of U.S. government bonds and notes, there are no data on EPB and SNR before 1960. Actual EBP is our own approximation. Actual SNR is obtained by constructing a benchmark and feeding actual EBP into the identity given in this table. The initial value used in our simulations, $20 billion for 1955 IV, is the rounded result of that computation.

With few exceptions, these series are defined in billions of current dollars per quarter, seasonally adjusted. For details, see Kenen [3].

(3) The model forges several connections between the current and capital accounts. Exports, for example, depend upon gross foreign aid; short-term bank claims depend upon the level of merchandise exports.

The power of the model is described by the first three columns of Table 3,

TABLE 3
DYNAMIC FORECASTS, 1956 I THROUGH 1969 IV

Variable	Balance of Payments Forecast from Exact Domestic Data			Best Forecast Using Entire Model with Discount Rate Rule		
	Mean Values	Standard Deviations	Root Mean Squared Errors	Mean Values	Standard Deviations	Root Mean Squared Errors
FXG	5.563	1.269	0.265	5.570	1.128	0.262
FMG	4.842	1.669	0.320	4.850	1.628	0.406
EXG	5.916	1.688	0.277	5.934	1.665	0.269
EMG	4.926	1.821	0.328	4.930	1.769	0.415
EBGST	0.898	0.354	0.527	0.890	0.345	0.571
EDI	0.573	0.223	0.178	0.566	0.229	0.198
EPIS	0.216	0.078	0.135	0.220	0.072	0.130
CSTC	0.144	0.207	0.228	0.147	0.217	0.247
CSTL	0.387	0.425	0.612	0.395	0.329	0.688
EBGPC	1.116	0.576	0.715	1.071	0.453	0.932
EBP	−0.317	0.456	0.634	−0.287	0.403	0.700
SNR	9.635	6.181	2.231	11.699	5.260	2.541
FYG	—	—	—	561.6	91.7	11.30
RUN	—	—	—	4.78	0.71	0.68
DPY	—	—	—	107.9	11.3	2.21
RGY[a]	—	—	—	0.829	0.673	1.07
RPY[b]	—	—	—	0.663	0.219	0.25
RDR	—	—	—	3.67	0.99	0.15
RST	—	—	—	3.66	1.20	0.46

[a] Rate of change of gross national product.
[b] Rate of change of price index.

which show a fourteen-year dynamic forecast of the U.S. balance of payments using exact domestic data.[9] The forecasts of trade flows are very accurate (see the charts in Figure 1A). The forecasts of capital transactions are, as usual, less satisfactory, and the forecast of the overall balance suffers accordingly. Nevertheless, the latter traces quite well general tendencies and major fluctuations (see Figure 1B). It fails badly only in 1956-57, when the export equation misses a surge, and in 1968-69, when the capital-account equations

---

9. Because so many major equations are autoregressive, the root mean squared errors of these long-term forecasts are larger than the errors of quarterly forecasts. Consider the corresponding values of RMSE for the 56 one-quarter forecasts contained within the same 14-year period.

FXG	0.270
FMG	0.319
EBGST	0.495
EBGPC	0.641
EBP	0.530

The difference in errors is largest for the capital account (EBGPC) because it includes a number of autoregressive equations (and forecasts of flows made from forecasts of stocks).

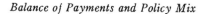

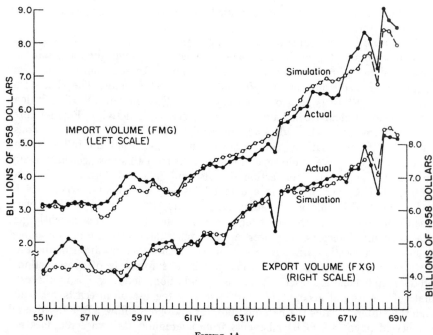

FIGURE 1A

Trade Volume Forecast from Exact Domestic Data

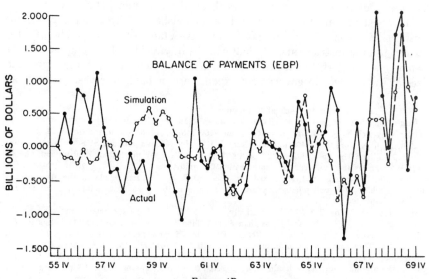

FIGURE 1B

Balance of Payments Forecast from Exact Domestic Data

understate short-term movements related to the Eurocurrency borrowings of U.S. commercial banks.

The second half of Table 3 is more important. It shows what happens when the two sectors of the model are made to generate a single dynamic forecast for the balance of payments and domestic economy. In addition, it reflects an attempt to remedy one major defect of the domestic sector. The short-term interest rate (RST) is pegged too closely to the discount rate (RDR); it does not respond to changes in bank reserves or economic activity. Furthermore, the long-term rate (RLT) depends on RST, so that capital formation, housing starts, and international capital movements do not show the full effects of monetary policies. We made several efforts to correct this flaw, settling finally on a simple policy rule connecting the discount rate with changes in owned reserves (SUR) and reflecting a detailed inspection of actual experience in 1956-1969.[10] This rule gives satisfactory results; the error in RDR is very small, and the error in the short-term interest rate (RST) is not much larger. The payments forecasts, moreover, are not much inferior to the ones obtained from exact domestic data. There is some substantial deterioration in the estimate of import volume (FMG), because it uses forecasts of gross national product and domestic prices. There is, in addition, deterioration in the estimate of the capital account (EBGPC) due to the use of forecasts for trade and U.S. interest rates in the equations for short-term flows. But the overall balance of payments (EBP) benefits from averaging; its own error does not rise appreciably from one forecast to the next.

POLICY SIMULATIONS

To illustrate the uses and limitations of this model, consider the effects of regulating policies by rules like the ones employed in mathematical work on the theory of policy, especially in work on the optimum policy mix.[11]

The construction of policy rules is accomplished in three steps. First, one must make statements about policy targets—statements which identify the need to use the instruments. (I shall call them *criteria*.) Next, one must make statements about the instruments—statements which describe the signs and sizes of the changes in government expenditure or bank reserves. (I shall call

10. The rule is different for each of three subperiods:

From 1955 IV through 1960 IV, inclusively, raise RDR by 25 basis points at the start of any quarter in which SUR will *fall* by more than $100 million (and by an additional 25 points if SUR will fall by more than $400 million). Reduce RDR by 25 basis points if SUR will *rise* by more than $200 million (by an additional 25 points if SUR will rise by more than $250 million, and by another 25 points if it will rise by more than $500 million).

From 1961 I through 1963 II, inclusively, raise RDR by 25 basis points at the start of any quarter in which SUR will *fall* by any amount. Reduce RDR by 25 basis points if SUR will *rise* by more than $400 million.

From 1963 III through 1969 IV, inclusively, raise RDR by 25 basis points at the start of any quarter in which SUR will *rise* by less than $200 million (and by an additional 25 points if SUR will *fall* by more than $100 million). Reduce RDR by 25 basis points if SUR will *rise* by more than $400 million (and by an additional 25 points if SUR will *rise* by more than $800 million).

But never raise the discount rate if it has fallen in the previous quarter (nor cut if it has risen). At no point, moreover, should RDR exceed 7.0 per cent, nor be below 1.5 per cent.

11. On their use in theoretical work, see, e.g., Mundell [5], Cooper [1], Whitman [8], and Patrick [6].

them *instructions*.) Finally, one must link the two sets of statements. Here, I do so by way of a policy index, Q, causing it to rise when a criterion calls for expansion (an increase of expenditure or owned reserves), and causing it to fall when a criterion calls for contraction (a decrease of expenditure or owned reserves).

Consider, first, instructions for the use of the two instruments. The instruction to alter government expenditure (FGO) is the simplest:

$$FGO = FGOA[(1 + 0.01r_g)^Q]$$

where FGOA is actual government expenditure during the quarter in question, and r_g is a percentage chosen in advance for each simulation.[12]

The instruction to alter monetary policy attaches the index Q to the current *change* in owned reserves. Like the instruction to alter government spending, it relates directly to actual history:

$$SUR = SUR_{-1} + (SURA - SURA_{-1}) + [Q(0.001r_s)]$$

where SUR_{-1} is the simulated stock at the end of the previous quarter, SURA and $SURA_{-1}$ are actual stocks at the end of the current and previous quarters, and r_s is a number fixed at the start of each simulation.[13]

The policy criteria are very simple. The economy is inspected at the end of every quarter, and a change in policy can be made after each inspection. The criteria, moreover, contain only two terms—a target value for the target variable and the most recent simulated value of that variable—and the policy index is made to depend on the size of the gap between them. The four criteria used below are:[14]

$$Q = k_u[RUN_{-1} - T(RUN)]$$
$$Q = k_p[T(RPY) - RPY_{-1}]$$
$$Q = k_b[EBP_{-1} - T(EBP)]$$
$$Q = k_r[SNR_{-1} - T(SNR)]$$

where T(RUN) is the target value for the unemployment rate, T(RPY) is the target value for the inflation rate, T(EBP) is the target value for the balance of payments, T(SNR) is the target value for net reserves, and the k's are constants.[15] Hence, the index Q will be positive whenever RUN, EBP, or SNR exceeds its target; it will be negative when RPY exceeds its target.

In every simulation reported here, T(RUN) is set at 4.50 per cent, smaller than the mean of the forecast shown in Table 3 (called hereafter the control

---

12. In all simulations reported below, r_g is set at 3.05 per cent. This number has its origin in other simulations, described in Kenen [3].

13. In all simulations reported below, r_s is set at $60 million per quarter.

14. For other formulations, see Kenen [3].

15. The constants used here are fixed to standardize the values of the policy index: k_u is set so that Q will be unity when RUN_{-1} is 0.25 percentage points above T(RUN); k_p is set so that Q will be unity when RPY_{-1} is 0.125 percentage points *below* target; k_b is set so that Q will be unity when EBP_{-1} is $200 million above target; and k_r is set so that Q will be unity when SNR_{-1} is $2.5 billion above target. These same numbers serve also to define the "limits" used in Table 6 to score the simulations.

run). In consequence, the use of the policy rule aimed at unemployment will impart a small stimulus to the economy whenever the criterion is used successfully. Similarly, T(RPY) is set at 0.500 per cent quarterly (a 2.0 per cent annual inflation rate). As the mean of RPY is 0.663 in the control run, the use of this rule will impart deflationary bias to the simulations. The target values for the balance of payments and net reserves, T(EBP) and T(SNR), are related. During most of 1956-69, the United States ran deficits in its balance of payments. (In the control run, net reserves fall from $20.0 billion at 1955 IV to $3.9 billion at 1969 IV; the quarterly deficit averages $287 million.) The choice of T(EBP), however, is governed by a different consideration: I have set the target value for reserves arbitrarily at $17.5 billion, a full $2.5 billion below the initial level. I thereby suggest that U.S. policy makers would have been willing to lose at least $2.5 billion over the fourteen years 1956-69—that they would not have taken restrictive measures if faced with continuing deficits averaging some $200 million per year.[16] Hence, I set T(EBP) at −$50 million per quarter. This choice imposes deflationary pressures on the domestic economy for much of the fourteen-year period. So does the target value for reserves.

Simulations using these instructions and criteria are summarized by Tables 4 through 6. (See also Figure 2, which traces the behavior of the unemploy-

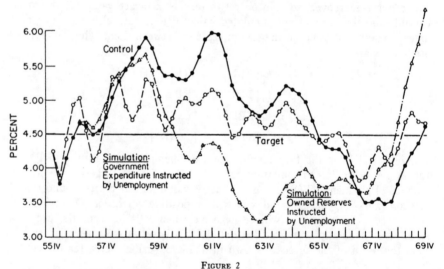

FIGURE 2
Fiscal and Monetary Policies Instructed by Unemployment

ment rate when the criterion aimed at RUN is connected to instructions for FGO and SUR.) Table 4 shows mean values for the target variables and for certain other important series; Table 5 shows standard deviations; Table 6

---

16. This supposition, however, is not consistent with another one implicit in all simulations and the control run. The several dummy variables standing for U.S. controls over capital outflows are allowed to go "on" whatever the behavior of the balance of payments.

TABLE 4

SUMMARY OF POLICY SIMULATIONS, 1956 I THROUGH 1969 IV: MEAN VALUES OF SELECTED VARIABLES

Policy Instrument & Target in Criterion	Mean Value of							
	RUN	RPY	EBP	SNR	FYG	DPY	FGO	SUR
Control^a	4.78	0.663	−0.287	11.699	561.6	107.9	111.8	20.9
Target Value	4.50	0.500	−0.050	17.500	—	—	—	—
Government Expenditure (FGO) Instructed by:								
Unemployment Rate	4.64*	0.691	−0.380	8.097	562.7	109.0	113.2	—
Inflation Rate	5.06	0.632*	−0.121	13.163	555.1	107.6	107.9	—
Balance of Payments	5.00	0.621	−0.162*	14.972	559.4	106.9	109.9	—
Net Reserves	5.13	0.617	−0.078	14.633*	555.0	107.2	107.8	—
High Unemployment	4.55*	0.707	−0.449	7.267	564.9	109.3	114.5	—
Joint Internal Target	4.80*	0.672*	−0.283	9.539	559.4	108.7	111.1	—
Stock of Owned Reserves (SUR) Instructed by:								
Unemployment Rate	4.35*	0.757	−0.726	−5.713	569.0	110.4	—	20.9
Inflation Rate	4.64	0.699*	−0.384	3.654	563.0	109.0	—	19.7
Balance of Payments	4.98	0.633	−0.193*	14.227	558.1	107.3	—	19.2
Net Reserves	5.45	0.593	0.352	18.579*	548.0	107.5	—	20.9

^a Mean values from Table 3; data for government expenditure (FGO) and owned reserves (SUR) are actual values for 1956 I-1969 IV.
* Target variable.

TABLE 5

SUMMARY OF POLICY SIMULATIONS, 1956 I THROUGH 1969 IV: STANDARD DEVIATIONS OF SELECTED VARIABLES

Policy Instrument & Target in Criterion	Standard Deviation of							
	RUN	RPY	EBP	SNR	FYG	DPY	FGO	SUR
Control^a	0.71	0.219	0.403	5.260	91.7	11.3	20.8	3.3
Government Expenditure (FGO) Instructed by:								
Unemployment Rate	0.37*	0.203	0.456	8.013	86.2	12.2	18.8	—
Inflation Rate	0.58	0.183*	0.501	3.925	83.5	10.8	15.9	—
Balance of Payments	1.04	0.247	0.431*	2.908	95.0	10.4	23.1	—
Net Reserves	0.79	0.186	0.459	2.405*	87.7	10.2	18.8	—
High Unemployment	0.45*	0.215	0.430	8.637	88.6	12.4	20.1	—
Joint Internal Target	0.40*	0.191*	0.486	6.596	83.6	11.8	17.2	—
Stock of Owned Reserves (SUR) Instructed by:								
Unemployment Rate	0.72*	0.242	1.060	18.906	86.4	13.9	—	2.2
Inflation Rate	0.58	0.217*	0.817	11.102	86.8	12.3	—	2.1
Balance of Payments	0.75	0.206	0.540*	3.492	90.9	10.6	—	2.6
Net Reserves	0.75	0.112	1.119	11.259*	75.6	10.1	—	3.0

^a Standard deviations from Table 3; data for government expenditure (FGO) and owned reserves (SUR) are actual values for 1956 I-1969 IV.
* Target variable.

TABLE 6

NUMERICAL ANALYSES OF POLICY SIMULATIONS, 1956 I THROUGH 1969 IV

| Policy Instrument & Target in Criterion | Simulation Inside Limits with | | With Control Inside | Simulation Outside Limits | | | Score* |
| | Control Inside | Control Outside | | With Control Outside and | | | |
				On Opposite Side	Simulation No Further	Simulation Further	
Government Expenditure (FGO) Instructed by:							
Unemployment Rate[a]	8	17	4	1	24	2	49
Inflation Rate[b]	23	4	4	0	21	4	48
Balance of Payments[c]	3	15	10	3	13	12	31
Net Reserves[d]	22	2	0	0	32	0	56
High Unemployment[e]	24	12	1	—	19	0	55
Joint Internal Target:							
Unemployment[e]	19	6	6	—	20	5	45
Inflation[f]	23	2	5	—	12	14	37
Stock of Owned Reserves (SUR) Instructed by:							
Unemployment Rate[a]	5	7	7	17	14	6	26
Inflation Rate[b]	25	1	2	0	7	21	33
Balance of Payments[c]	5	6	8	3	10	24	21
Net Reserves[d]	11	2	11	16	4	12	17

* Instances in which simulation and control are inside limits, simulation is inside with control outside, and both are outside but simulation is not further from limits.

a Limits are 4.25 and 4.75 per cent.

b Limits are 0.375 and 0.625 per cent per quarter.

c Limits are −0.250 and 0.150 billion per quarter.

d Limits are 15.0 and 20.0 billion.

e Limit is 4.75 per cent; simulation and control cannot be on opposite sides because there is no second side.

f Limit is 0.625 per cent per quarter; simulation and control cannot be on opposite sides because there is no second side.

scores each simulation according to the frequency with which the rule under study (instruction-*cum*-criterion) puts the target variable inside certain limits[17] or, if outside them, closer than it was in the control run.

Consider a few of the principal results: (1) All four simulations pertaining to the fiscal instrument (FGO) bring the mean value of the target variable closer to its target value. Three of them reduce the standard deviation. All four simulations, moreover, yield plausible trade-offs between target variables. The one aimed at unemployment raises substantially the mean change in prices. The ones aimed at prices, the balance of payments, and the reserve position raise the mean level of unemployment. (2) The simulations pertaining to the monetary instrument are not as successful. The one aimed at unemployment pushes the mean value across the target value; the one aimed at inflation has a perverse effect, raising the mean of RPY rather than reducing it. These results reflect a tendency for SUR to lag behind events due partly to the fact that the rules which govern it deal with the change, not directly with the level. (3) The patterns displayed by the means and standard deviations are confirmed impressively by the scores in Table 6. The ones for fiscal policy are uniformly higher. (4) One reason for using SNR as a policy target is the fact, mentioned earlier, that changes in domestic policies can lead to once-for-all adjustments in domestic holdings of foreign assets. If this phenomenon is important and captured properly by the model, one would expect to see its implications reflected most clearly in the final monetary simulation. Monetary policy is itself concerned to regulate a stock of assets, and it is the only policy examined here that has large effects on interest rates. This particular simulation, however, is unsatisfactory. The mean of SNR is too large; it has crossed its target value. The standard deviation is enormous. The mean of RUN, the cost of the policy, is larger than the others shown in Table 4.[18]

THE OPTIMUM POLICY MIX

I come now to an entertaining exercise—the use of the model and policy rules to study the optimum policy mix. This game has three parts. First, one must select quantitative representations of "external" and "internal" balance, the two aims of macroeconomic policy, choosing among (or amending) the *criteria* stated and tested above. Second, one must connect each criterion to an *instruction* so as to make appropriate changes in the fiscal and monetary instruments. Finally, one must build the new policy rules into the model and study the resulting simulations for 1956-69.

It is not difficult to choose a proxy for external balance. Although my experiments with EBP were not too satisfactory, they were much superior to the experiments with SNR. In this instance, moreover, it is quite appropriate to use a symmetrical policy criterion like the one tested before. Symmetry, indeed, has come to be a cardinal virtue of proposals for reform of the international monetary system—even though it may mean different things to different countries. In consequence, I shall employ:

---

17. For the limits used in Table 6, see note 15, above.

18. The next largest is the one pertaining to the use of FGO for this same policy aim.

Balance of Payments and Policy Mix

$$QX = k_b[EBP_{-1} - T(EBP)]$$

where QX is the policy index used to govern the policy instrument assigned to eternal balance, and k_b is chosen so that QX will be unity when the difference between EBP_{-1} and $T(EBP)$ is \$200 million.

The choice of a proxy for internal balance is somewhat harder. Two domestic criteria are available. Furthermore, symmetry is not virtuous in this context. Low levels of unemployment and inflation are not bad *per se;* they cause concern mainly because they may not be compatible with each other or with other aims of economic policy. Hence, I shall modify the criteria before connecting them to policy instruments.

The first and simpler modification takes a one-sided view of unemployment:

$$QI(1) = k_u[RUN_{-1} - T(RUN)], \text{ when } RUN_{-1} \geqslant T(RUN);$$

otherwise,

$$QI(1) = QI(1)_{-1}.$$

Here, $QI(1)$ is an index used to govern the policy instruments assigned to internal balance, and k_u is a constant chosen so that $QI(1)$ will be unity when the difference between RUN_{-1} and $T(RUN)$ is 0.25 percentage points. A simple simulation using this criterion to regulate government expenditure is summarized in Tables 4 through 6.

The second modification takes a one-sided view of unemployment, but tacks on a one-sided view of inflation:

$$QI(2) = k_p[T(RPY) - RPY_{-1}], \text{ for } RPY_{-1} \geqslant T(RPY);$$

otherwise,

$$QI(2) = QI(2)_{-1}$$

Here, $QI(2)$ is a second index used to govern the policy instrument assigned to internal balance, and k_p is a constant chosen so that $QI(2)$ will be unity when the difference between RPY_{-1} and $T(RPY)$ is 0.125 per cent per quarter.

To use these two criteria together, one must fashion an overall policy index for internal balance, QI. Therefore, when $RUN_{-1} \lesssim T(RUN)$ and $RPY_{-1} \lesssim T(RPY)$ so that $QI(1) = QI(2) = 0$, set $QI = 0$. There is no need to signal expansion or contraction. When, instead, $RUN_{-1} > T(RUN)$ but $RPY_{-1} \lesssim T(RPY)$, set $QI = QI(1)$; similarly, when $RUN_{-1} \lesssim T(RUN)$ but $RPY_{-1} > T(RPY)$, set $QI = QI(2)$. The criterion signaling trouble is given priority. When, however, both of them are signaling at the same time, take an unweighted average:

$$QI = QI(1) + QI(2).$$

A simple simulation using this joint internal criterion is also summarized in Tables 4 through 6.[19]

The results obtained with these new criteria are not at all surprising. The simulation using the one-sided criterion for unemployment cuts the mean of RUN almost to its target value; it is more effective on this score than the

---

19. Simulations using weighted averages are discussed in Kenen [3].

symmetrical criterion. Furthermore, this simulation generates more inflation and a larger deficit in EBP. The simulation using the joint criterion is not as effective *vis-à-vis* unemployment, but does have the expected impact on price changes.

Consider, now, two variants of the optimum policy mix. The first, described by Figures 3 and 4, connects the one-sided criterion aimed at RUN to fiscal policy (FGO), and connects the balance-of-payments criterion to monetary policy (SUR). The second, described by Figures 3A and 4A, substitutes the joint internal criterion for the one-sided RUN criterion.

The results of the first simulation are summarized by the left-hand side of Table 7. They conform to expectation. The mean of RUN is higher than target, at 4.75 per cent (and higher than it was when FGO was used to combat unemployment and nothing was done about the balance of payments). Compare this mean, however, to the one obtained when SUR was aimed at EBP and nothing was done about internal balance (the penultimate simulation in Table 4). That mean was 4.98 per cent, higher than the one in Table 7 (and higher also than the mean of the control run). In brief, this policy assignment is successful in respect of unemployment. Turning to the other half of the assignment, the mean of EBP is larger (absolutely) than the target value. It is much smaller, however, than the mean obtained when FGO was aimed at RUN and nothing was done about external balance (the first and

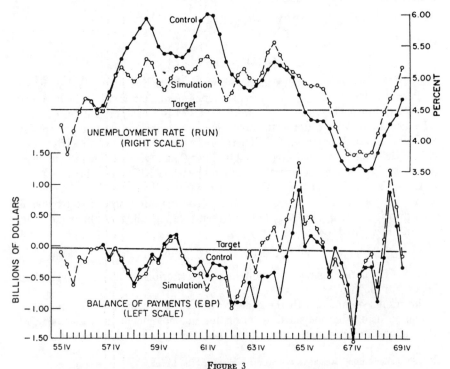

FIGURE 3

The Optimum Policy Mix—Government Expenditure Instructed by Unemployment: Paths of Target Variables

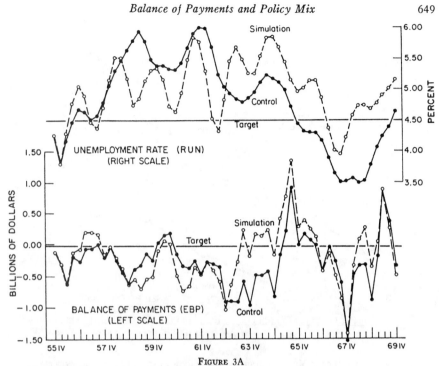

FIGURE 3A

The Optimum Policy Mix—Government Expenditure Instructed by Joint Internal Target:
Paths of Target Variables

fifth simulations in Table 4).[20] The assignment seems successful in respect
of the balance of payments. The more startling test of this assignment, however, occurs when we contrast it with its mirror image. Link the one-sided
criterion aimed at RUN to instructions regulating monetary policy (SUR);
link the criterion aimed at EBP to instructions regulating fiscal policy (FGO).
The results in Figures 5 through 7 speak for themselves: Gross national product oscillates strongly; RUN and EBP are further from target more often
than they were in the control run; the capital account displays gigantic outflows; and the policy instruments move further and further from their control
values. A handful of figures will make the same point:

	FGO to RUN SUR to EBP	SUR to RUN FGO to EBP
Mean Values:		
RUN	4.75	4.85
EBP	−0.18	−1.20
FGO	116.9	89.1
SUR	19.1	26.1
Standard Deviations:		
RUN	0.47	1.07
EBP	0.49	0.70
FGO	20.9	30.7
SUR	2.5	6.5

20. It is also smaller than the mean obtained when SUR was aimed at the balance of payments
and nothing was done about internal balance.

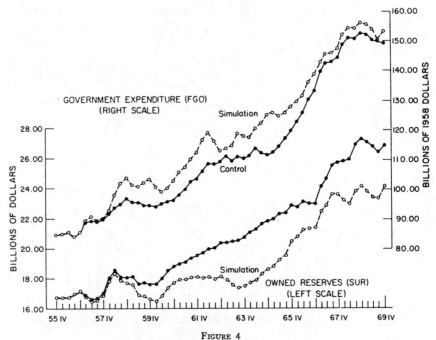

FIGURE 4
The Optimum Policy Mix—Government Expenditure Instructed by Unemployment:
Paths of Policy Instruments

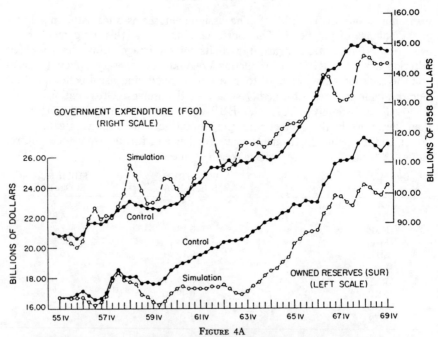

FIGURE 4A
The Optimum Policy Mix—Government Expenditure Instructed by Joint Internal
Target: Paths of Policy Instruments

TABLE 7

DYNAMIC SIMULATIONS, 1956 I THROUGH 1969 IV: THE OPTIMUM POLICY MIX

Variable	Government Expenditure Assigned to Unemployment. Owned Reserves Assigned to the Balance of Payments			Government Expenditure Assigned to the Joint Internal Target. Owned Reserves Assigned to the Balance of Payments		
	Mean Value	Final Value	Standard Deviation	Mean Value	Final Value	Standard Deviation
FXG	5.524	8.107	1.111	5.566	8.236	1.148
FMG	4.861	7.208	1.513	4.735	7.116	1.416
EXG	5.925	9.975	1.666	5.930	9.960	1.666
EMG	4.937	8.073	1.645	4.808	7.970	1.542
EBGST	0.862	1.846	0.362	1.007	2.003	0.414
EDI	0.561	1.013	0.218	0.547	1.060	0.212
EPIS	0.237	0.364	0.072	0.226	0.319	0.062
CSTC	0.144	0.796	0.191	0.165	0.916	0.216
CSTL	0.420	0.568	0.338	0.375	0.453	0.280
EBGPC	0.928	1.767	0.422	1.086	2.425	0.414
EBP	−0.183	−0.166	0.491	−0.175	−0.497	0.480
SNR	13.128	9.766	3.565	13.538	10.205	3.533
FYG	560.7	698.7	86.26	556.5	698.5	83.25
RUN	4.75	5.11	0.47	4.97	5.14	0.49
DPY	108.7	133.7	11.71	108.1	131.3	11.13
RGY	0.806	0.110	0.726	0.809	0.194	1.099
RPY	0.677	1.050	0.196	0.645	0.983	0.184
FGO	116.9	150.5	20.9	113.1	142.4	17.9
SUR	19.1	24.1	2.5	18.9	24.1	2.6
RDR	3.91	6.25	1.00	3.64	5.25	0.81
RST	3.97	6.70	1.20	3.64	5.48	0.99

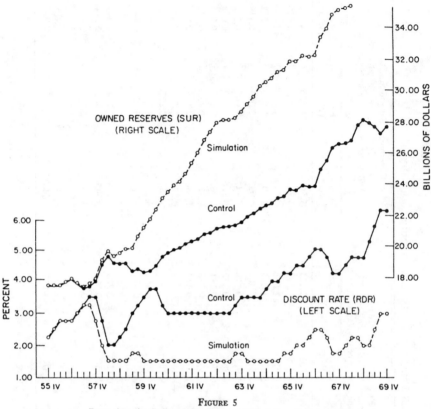

FIGURE 5
Reversing the Policy Mix: Paths of Monetary Instruments

The "conventional" policy assignment is quite stable. Its mirror image is dramatically unstable.

Finally, consider briefly the other simulation summarized by Table 7, the one in which FGO is geared to the joint internal target. Because this experiment represents internal balance by a combination of competing objectives, it is much harder to appraise. Drawing together the relevant mean values from Tables 4 and 7:

	RUN	RPY	EBP
FGO to joint target; SUR to EBP	4.97	0.645	−0.175
FGO to joint target; no other policy	4.80	0.672	−0.283
FGO to one-sided RUN; SUR to EBP	4.75	0.677	−0.183
FGO to one-sided RUN; no other policy	4.55	0.707	−0.449
SUR to EBP; no other policy	4.98	0.633	−0.193
Control run	4.78	0.663	−0.287

Unemployment is higher in this experiment than in any other simulation using RUN as a domestic target. In fact, it is higher than it was in the control run. The assignment fails from this standpoint. By other tests, however, it is quite

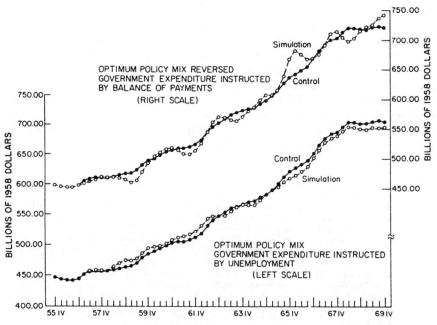

FIGURE 6
Reversing the Policy Mix: Effects on Gross National Product (FYG)

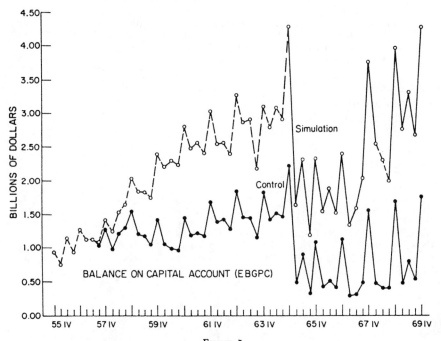

FIGURE 7
Reversing the Policy Mix: Effects on Capital Outflow

successful—mainly because each of the instruments is geared indirectly to the other's target. When fiscal policy is geared to RPY, it helps to stabilize EBP; when monetary policy is geared to EBP, it helps to stabilize RPY. In consequence, the mean of RPY is smaller in this experiment than in any other fiscal simulation, while EBP is smaller (absolutely) than in any other run. And when, once again, the assignments are switched, the balance of payments displays a huge deficit, the policy instruments wander away, and the economy is very unstable.[21] The "conventional" assignment is not especially efficient in this instance. There are more aims than instruments. Nevertheless, it is more efficient than its mirror image.

REFERENCES

1. R. N. Cooper. "Macroeconomic Policy Adjustment in Interdependent Economies," *Quarterly Journal of Economics*, lxxxiii (February 1969).
2. P. B. Kenen. *Portfolio Capital and Monetary Policy*, Working Papers in International Economics, G-73-01. Princeton: International Finance Section, 1973.
3. —————. *The Balance of Payments and Policy Mix: Tradeoffs and Stability*, Working Papers in International Economics, P-73-03. Princeton: International Finance Section. 1973.
4. S. Y. Kwack and G. R. Schink. "A Disaggregated Quarterly Model of United States Trade and Capital Flows: Simulations and Tests of Policy Effectiveness," Paper prepared for the Brookings Conference on Econometric Model Building and Development, 1972 (mimeograph).
5. R. A. Mundell. *International Economics*. New York: Macmillan, 1968.
6. J. D. Patrick. "Establishing Convergent Decentralized Policy Assignment," *Journal of International Economics*, 3(February 1973).
7. M. F. J. Prachowny. *A Structural Model of the U.S. Balance of Payments*. Amsterdam: North-Holland, 1969.
8. M. vN. Whitman. *Policies for Internal and External Balance*, Special Papers in International Economics, No. 9. Princeton: International Finance Section, 1970.

21. The means of RUN and RPY do not change dramatically (the former, however, declines to 4.83 per cent). But the standard deviations are greatly inflated (to 1.07 for RUN, 0.275 for RPY, 0.643 for EBP, 18.4 for FGO, and 5.0 for SUR).

[12]

Exchange Rates, Domestic Prices, and the Adjustment Process

Peter B. Kenen

Clare Pack

Introduction

At the first meeting of the Group of Thirty, many members expressed doubts about the role of the exchange rate in the international adjustment process. Some suggested that exchange-rate changes have their main effects on domestic prices, not on trade balances, and work to widen the dispersion of national inflation rates. Some suggested that exchange-rate changes are not influential in the adjustment process because trade balances are not sufficiently sensitive to changes in relative prices. At the close of the discussion, we were asked to bring to the next meeting a survey of the evidence on these important issues.

This paper is a revised version of that survey. It is based in part on published work and in part on current research at the International Monetary Fund and the Organisation for Economic Cooperation and Development. We are grateful to J. J. Polak of the IMF and to Stephen Marris of the OECD and to their colleagues at those institutions, who made available much new material and gave freely of their time in advising us on the preparation of this survey. We are also grateful to members of the Group of Thirty and its Academic Panel, who gave us comments on an earlier draft. (We take full responsibility, however, for the contents of this survey and the interpretation of the evidence.)

One of the comments we received should be transmitted to our readers. Much of the research we survey and some of our own work as well has an unsatisfactory aspect. In the first part of this paper, we examine the effects of changes in nominal exchange rates on national price levels and those of changes in price levels on nominal exchange rates. In the second part of the paper, we examine the effects of changes in real exchange rates on current-account balances. Under floating exchange rates, however, all of these variables are interdependent, even when the float is heavily managed. Nominal exchange rates, national price levels, and current-account balances respond *jointly* to national economic policies and other disturbances.

1

A country such as the United Kingdom or Mexico, that starts to exploit its own oil reserves, is apt to experience an appreciation of its nominal exchange rate (or a less rapid depreciation relative to its inflation rate), an appreciation of its real exchange rate, and an improvement in its current-account balance—rather than the worsening of the current-account balance that one might expect, watching the appreciation of the real exchange rate. A country with rapid growth in productivity is likely to have the same experience. A country that expands its money supply at a faster than average rate, by contrast, will probably experience an acceleration of domestic inflation and a depreciation of its nominal exchange rate, but there may be very little long-term change in its real exchange rate or current-account balance.

As we revised this paper for publication, we became increasingly aware of the extent to which recent quantitative research relies on or implies one-way causality, rather than emphasizing simultaneity. Our own mode of exposition does so too. For certain purposes, however, one-way causality is a useful framework, especially for purposes of short-term analysis. The calculations we have made, summarized in an appendix, make this point quite clearly. We find that exchange-rate changes have prompt and strong effects on national price levels, yet price changes do not have prompt or strong effects on nominal exchange rates. Accordingly, we continue to employ the notion of one-way causality as an organizing principle, for reporting the results of recent research, but ask that readers bear in mind its serious limitations. In this branch of economics, as in most others, everything depends on everything else.

2

CHAPTER I

Exchange Rates and
Domestic Prices

The Issues

A change in the nominal exchange is bound to affect domestic prices, even in a large rather closed economy like that of the United States. Part of the acceleration of U.S. inflation in 1977-78 reflected the depreciation of the dollar. Conversely, changes in domestic prices affect the exchange rate. If inflation is more rapid in one country than in others, that country's currency is apt to depreciate.

The strength and speed with which these two phenomena occur are matters that economists continue to investigate. It is hard to determine the direction of causation, let alone the size and speed of the response, when exchange rates and price levels are both in motion. The two effects together, however, have one clear implication. They diminish the flexibility of the "real" exchange rate, calling into question the contribution of exchange-rate changes to the adjustment process:

> The strength of domestic effects . . . has led some to wonder whether it is possible to alter "real" exchange rates—the prices of one country relative to those of others expressed in a single currency—thereby to correct international imbalances. [Kenen (1978)]

If differences between inflation rates match—or are matched by—movements in nominal exchange rates, real exchange rates become completely rigid. Exchange-rate changes serve merely to maintain "purchasing-power parity" between pairs of currencies; they cannot influence current-account balances. If a ten per cent inflation in one country results at once in a ten per cent depreciation of the country's

3

currency, the country's competitive position is unchanged. If a ten per cent depreciation results at once in a ten per cent increase of domestic prices, there is again no change in the competitive position.

Few economists contend that the linkage is this tight—that changes in exchange rates and domestic prices are completely synchronized. But a number suggest that the links have tightened in the last few years—that it is increasingly difficult to alter real exchange rates and that the alterations are not likely to last long. The Governor of the Bank of England, Gordon Richardson, took this view in his recent Thornton Lecture:

> Changes in costs arising from exchange rate movements appear nowadays to feed through into an economy more quickly and more completely than used to be the case.
>
> Adjustments in nominal exchange rates can no longer be relied upon to yield, for more than a relatively short period, as large an adjustment of real exchange rates as could once have been anticipated. [Richardson (1979)]

He does not argue that we should return to pegged exchange rates, but others say that this is the appropriate inference.

The problems posed above can be put in different terms. If changes in exchange rates and price levels are tightly linked and the links are more or less symmetrical, floating rates will cause "vicious" and "virtuous" circles. Countries having high inflation rates will watch their currencies depreciate; countries having low inflation rates will watch their currencies appreciate. The exchange-rate changes, in turn, will amplify the differences between inflation rates and generate new rounds of exchange-rate changes. These processes need not be explosive, but they may be very costly to contain. Accordingly, the links between exchange rates and price levels can impair the domestic policy autonomy that floating exchange rates are meant to confer, as well as interfering with the adjustment process.

We have therefore to survey the evidence on exchange-rate and price changes before we can examine the role of the exchange rate in the adjustment process. There is, of course, much literature on this subject, but most of it pertains to experience with large changes in pegged rates, such as the U.K. devaluation of 1967 and the U.S. devaluation of 1971, and we do not deal with that experience here. We look mainly at work done with recent data, because we seek to assess the role of floating rates in the adjustment process and the strength of the self-aggravating tendencies known as vicious and virtuous circles.

4

The Organization of the Survey

To marshall the evidence systematically, we carve our problem into five components:

(1) The direct goods-market effects of exchange-rate changes on domestic prices—the domain of commodity arbitrage and the law of one price.

(2) The indirect goods-market effects—those produced by changes in aggregate demand reflecting the responses of the current-account balance.

(3) The indirect factor-market effects, especially those that take place in labor markets, and the implications of indexation.

(4) The feedbacks from price changes to exchange-rate changes, including the effects of speculation in foreign-exchange markets, that determine whether there will be vicious and virtuous circles.

(5) The influence of macroeconomic policies, particularly monetary policies, on the four sets of effects listed above.

The evidence surveyed here can shed light on a number of additional issues. Are the links between exchange rates and domestic prices stronger in small open economies than in large closed economies like that of the United States? An answer to this question is important for judging the "optimality" of national and regional exchange-rate arrangements, including the European Monetary System. Are the links between exchange rates and domestic prices stronger in one direction than the other? Significant asymmetries would, of course, cause vicious circles larger than the corresponding virtuous circles and might therefore explain some of the recent increase in the average of inflation rates. Can the price effects of exchange-rate changes explain the widening of differences among inflation rates that has accompanied the increase in the average rate? If we could adjust for the effects of exchange-rate changes, we would know more about the "underlying" differences, and they are the ones that have to be eliminated in order to achieve exchange-rate stability.

Before starting to survey the evidence, we make two points about methodology:

First, we plan to stress the influence of the exchange rate on the price level, rather than the influence of the price level on the exchange rate. The latter appears only as the feedback at (4) in our outline. We

5

have two reasons for adopting this approach. The first reason is theoretical: if exchange rates are determined in asset markets, the view that we take today, one would not anticipate a strong causal chain running from price changes to exchange-rate changes. Exchange-rate determination is dominated in the short run by expectations about rates of return on various assets. In consequence, price changes can influence exchange rates only when they lead to forecasts of exchange-rate changes (and only when those forecasts overwhelm all other information on which markets base their expectations about rates of return). The second reason is factual, but not necessarily independent of the first:we have already noted that there is a strong statistical relationship running from exchange rates to prices but no such relationship running from prices to exchange rates. In the appendix to this paper, we show that recent changes in exchange rates can be used to forecast current differences between national inflation rates, but recent differences between inflation rates cannot be used to forecast current changes in exchange rates. See also Goldstein (1979), who points out that the bulk of research on purchasing-power parity says that it holds fairly well in the long run but not in the short run; differences between national inflation rates do not produce offsetting changes in exchange rates.

Second, the evidence surveyed below is rather hard to integrate, because studies of exchange rates and price levels use a variety of exchange-rate and price data. They use different weighting schemes to generate their indexes of effective exchange rates—bilateral weights, global weights, and multilateral (MERM) weights. They use different data on domestic prices—wholesale price indexes, consumer price indexes, and deflators for components of gross national product. These choices have important consequences. Consider, for example, the results obtained by Hooper and Lowrey (1979). Using global trade weights to measure the effective exchange rate for the U.S. dollar, they find that it depreciated by some 14 per cent from the third quarter of 1976 through the third quarter of 1978. Inserting this estimate into an import-price equation, they show that the depreciation led to an 8.0 per cent increase in (non-oil) import prices; by implication, the pass-through discussed below was less than complete. Using bilateral trade weights, however, they find that the dollar depreciated by about 9 per cent, and inserting this estimate into the appropriate import price equation, they show that the depreciation led to a 7.9 per cent increase in import prices; by implication, the pass-through was virtually complete. They point out, moreover, that identical changes in two price indexes can have very different economic meanings. Wholesale price indexes,

6

for instance, may be best for calculating countries' competitive positions (i.e., real exchange rates), but consumer price indexes may be best for calculating real wages or real incomes. For more discussion of these issues, see Kenen and Pack (1979).

The Evidence

We now turn to the evidence linking prices to exchange rates, starting with direct goods-market links.

Direct Effects in Goods Markets

If changes in exchange rates are to influence domestic prices, they have first to influence import prices. A depreciation of the domestic currency must raise import prices expressed in that currency. The size of this effect is the so-called pass-through, mentioned above.

The strength of the pass-through necessarily depends on price elasticities—the elasticity of foreign supply and the elasticity of domestic demand. If the supply of imports is perfectly elastic, the pass-through will be complete, sooner or later, regardless of the elasticity of demand for imports. The increase in import prices will match the depreciation. If the supply is not perfectly elastic, the pass-through will be incomplete, and its size will vary inversely with the elasticity of demand. (The higher the elasticity of demand, the smaller the increase in import prices relative to the depreciation, given the elasticity of supply.) A small country is apt to face a highly elastic supply of imports and may also have a low demand elasticity, because it cannot substitute domestic for foreign goods. Therefore, one would expect it to experience a large pass-through, compared to a bigger country.

Very little research has been done on supply elasticities, but much work has been done on demand elasticities. We survey it thoroughly in the next part of this paper but summarize it briefly here, drawing on an excellent review by Bond (1979) based in turn on recent work by Stern, Francis, and Schumacher (1976) and by Deppler and Ripley (1978). Median estimates of demand elasticities compiled by Stern et al. furnish only weak support for the supposition that small countries have low elasticities. They are quite low for the Netherlands, low also for Belgium and Sweden, higher for France and Italy, and very high for the United States. But there are exceptions to this regularity. The United Kingdom has a low elasticity (due perhaps to its dependence on imported raw materials). Germany and Japan have lower elasticities than France and Italy. Conversely, one small country, Denmark, has an elasticity about

7

as high as those for France and Italy, and Canada is in the same class as the United States (due perhaps to high substitutability between Canadian and U.S. goods). Bond draws attention to additional complications:

> First, the evidence on short-run and long-run elasticities given for food, beverages and tobacco, and for manufactured goods indicates that long-run adjustment to relative prices is greater than short-run adjustment for many countries. Second, the evidence from Deppler and Ripley suggests that these adjustment lags are slow, some taking three to four years to work through. Third, median elasticities for fuels are low for many countries. Indeed for most countries elasticities for foodstuffs, raw materials and fuels tend to be lower than those for manufacturing, confirming that pass-through for countries with a large proportion of these products to total imports is likely to be more complete than for a country with less reliance on imported raw materials, fuels, and foodstuffs.

It is therefore quite difficult to derive estimates of pass-through from estimates of short-run demand elasticities, especially from those for total imports.

Direct estimates of pass-through are available too, and some of them bear out our supposition concerning the effects of country size.[1] Kreinin (1977) finds that pass-through is complete for small and middesized countries but incomplete for large ones. His estimate for the United States is 50 per cent; for Germany, 60 per cent; and for Japan, 80 per cent. But Kreinin's work refers to 1970-72, before the beginning of the current float, and more recent estimates tell a different story. Using data for 1973-78, Spitäller (1979) puts the pass-through at 100 per cent for all countries except Germany (for which he puts it at 75 per cent). In recent studies, moreover, pass-through takes place rapidly and appears to be symmetrical. Most of the change in import prices occurs within two or three quarters of the change in the exchange rate, and no one has reported any systematic difference between the size of the response to a depreciation and of the response to an appreciation.

The next link is the most important. How large is the change in the domestic price level resulting from a change in import prices? Here, of course, one must be careful to identify the price level under study. Traded goods bulk large in indexes of wholesale prices, and one would

---

[1]Direct estimates are made by treating the current change in import prices as a function of current and lagged changes in the exchange rate. They are, in effect, reduced-form estimates; the coefficients of the regression equations are combinations of the relevant price elasticities. These estimates may be biased, because they do not impound the relationship that runs from price changes back to exchange-rate changes, but that relationship may not be strong enough to matter.

8

thus expect those indexes to respond more strongly than, say, indexes of consumer prices.[1] In what follows, however, we concentrate on consumer prices, as they are the ones that have been studied most extensively.

The size of the response of consumer prices will depend importantly on three characteristics of the economy involved: (1) the extent to which imports of final goods enter directly into domestic consumption; (2) the extent to which domestic goods are made from imported inputs; and (3) the degree of substitutability between domestic and imported goods, in both consumption and production. We look first at some evidence that bears upon the third point, then at some that bears upon the overall response.

Adherents of purchasing-power parity frequently explain it in terms of the law of one price—the assertion that the price of a particular product can differ from market to market only insofar as trade barriers and transport costs get in the way of arbitrage between the markets. If this law held perfectly for all products, one would expect the prices of domestic goods to rise by as much as those of imported goods when the latter rise because the currency depreciates. And one would expect the law of one price to hold quite firmly for standardized commodities—for staples such as wheat and cotton, for processed raw materials such as chemicals and metals, and for most types of capital equipment. (One would not expect it to hold as firmly for consumer goods, as they are made to differ in performance or appearance.) The evidence, however, says that the law does not hold well, not even at fine levels of disaggregation or for homogeneous product groups; see, e.g., Isard (1977) and Kravis and Lipsey (1978). By implication, domestic and imported goods are not close substitutes in consumption or production, and one might thus expect the prices of domestic goods to rise by less than those of their imported counterparts.

Confirmation is afforded by recent studies that look at the overall response—the change in consumer prices brought about by a change in import prices. Those studies, moreover, tend to confirm the inference that one would draw from (1) and (2), above. Domestic prices are more sensitive to import prices in small open economies that depend heavily on imported goods. We list on the next page results obtained by Dornbusch and Krugman (1976) and by Spitäller (1978):[2]

---

[1]When GNP deflators are employed instead of consumer prices, the size of the response falls further, and it is more uniform across countries. This is because imports are subtracted from expenditure to calculate gross national product, reducing the effects of openness (and differences in openness) on the response of the price level. See Artus and McGuirk (1978).

[2]This table is adapted from Goldstein (1979). The measure of openness expresses foreign trade in goods and services as a percentage of gross national product; it comes from Salant (1977) and refers to 1972.

9

Country (with measure of openness to trade)	Percentage Change in Index of Consumer Prices Resulting from a One Per Cent Change in Import Prices	
	Dornbusch & Krugman	Spitäller
United States (0.07)	0.14	0.16
Japan (0.10)	0.24	na
France (0.17)	0.16	0.32
Germany (0.21)	0.03	0.08
Italy (0.22)	0.28	0.36
United Kingdom (0.23)	0.19	0.20
Canada (0.24)	0.20	0.24

All of these responses are quite low. So are those obtained by other investigators. And though these responses refer only to first-year effects, most studies find that they reflect no less than half of the entire price increase induced by an increase in import prices.

There are, however, several anomalies here. The Japanese response is fairly high for an economy that is not very open. The German response is extraordinarily low. Two reasons come to mind.

First, the estimates may not relate exclusively to the direct goods-market effects that we are examining here. Some studies make no effort to control for the change in aggregate demand that stems from the shift in the current-account balance induced by a change in the exchange rate. Some make no attempt to control for the change in the wage rate brought about by a change in the cost of living. In other words, some estimates may include indirect effects reviewed later in this section, and these effects may differ from country to country.

Second, significant asymmetries may be at work at this stage in the process. If prices of manufactured goods rise more readily than they decline, and this is the common view, one would expect an increase in import prices to influence consumer prices by more (or more rapidly) than a decrease in import prices. Goldstein (1977) found weak evidence to this effect in his work on Italy, Japan, and the United States. But he did not find it in his work on Germany or the United Kingdom (and not in work on pooled data for all five countries). In his most recent paper, moreover, Goldstein (1979) cites research suggesting that domestic prices may not be as "sticky" as we commonly believe, and if prices are not sticky, they should respond symmetrically to increases and decreases in import prices.

10

Yet the German case cries out for explanation. Why are German prices so much less responsive than those of the United States, when Germany is more open to foreign trade? Is it pure coincidence that Germany, with falling import prices due to the appreciation of the Deutschemark, shows less influence of import prices on consumer prices? The reason may reside in the success of German policies. It may be due, however, to an undetected asymmetry in the effects of import prices on domestic prices or, more plausibly, in the effects of import and domestic prices on money wage rates. We return to this last possibility later in our survey.

If one could impound all indirect effects on prices and make adequate allowance for asymmetries, the numbers in our table might be made to change. But the changes would not be sufficiently large to undermine the chief conclusion. Consumer prices do not rise by as much as import prices. As evidence, we cite research by Hooper and Lowrey (1979), who examined a number of econometric models for the United States in order to produce a consensus estimate of the price response. Having looked at partial equilibrium models, in which the exchange-rate change is exogenous, and at general-equilibrium models, in which it is endogenous, they come to this conclusion: if oil prices are not influenced by the change in the exchange rate and domestic policies are used to stabilize real gross national product, a one per cent depreciation of the real exchange rate for the dollar will cause consumer prices to increase by 0.15 per cent, a number not too different from those listed in our table. If oil prices are affected, rising by the full amount of the depreciation, consumer prices will increase by 0.175 per cent. Once again, the estimates pertain to the first year, but the total effect is not much more than twice as large as the first-year effect.[1]

Indirect Effects in Goods and Factor Markets

Later in this paper, when we summarize our findings, we will argue that a change in the nominal exchange rate does produce a change in the real exchange rate. The latter will be smaller than the former and may be very small for small open economies, but it need not be trivial or transitory. The evidence we summarized above, moreover, says that trade flow are moderately sensitive to a change in the real exchange

---

[1] It should be noted that Hooper and Lowrey move directly from the change in the exchange rate to the change in the price level; they combine the pass-through with the influence of import prices. Furthermore, they work with the change in the *real* exchange rate—a strategy that puzzles us—and their real rate is based on global trade weights (which tend, we saw, to give a lower estimate of pass-through than bilateral trade weights).

11

rate; price elasticities are not negligible. Taken together, these conclu-sions say that a depreciation of one country's currency will increase its exports and reduce its imports, though long lags may be involved. Put differently, a depreciation will shift foreign and domestic demands from foreign to domestic goods.

If domestic prices were absolutely rigid and there were adequate supplies of labor and of other factors of production, this shift in demand would raise real output. Doing so, of course, it would raise the demand for imports, but not by enough to overtake the improvement in the trade balance brought about by the depreciation.[1] Yet prices are far from rigid, which means that some part of the increase in demand for domestic goods will show up as an increase in domestic prices unless it is neutralized by monetary and fiscal policies. How large is this effect and how widely does it differ from one country to the next?

Research on this problem has been conducted by many economists, and several have made international comparisons; these include Lucas (1973), Hamburger and Reisch (1976), Fratianni and Korteweg (1976), Gordon (1977), and Santomero and Seater (1978). Their conclusions differ in detail, and each one tends, of course, to em-phasize the differences, but their findings are consistent with these three assertions:

1. The trade-off between the rate of increase in wages and the level of unemployment—the slope of the so-called Phillips curve—has worsened perceptibly in recent years. There may indeed be no such trade-off in the long run; any increase in aggregate demand will show up eventually as an increase of wages (and prices), not in a reduction of unemployment. The latter will return to its "natural" rate. None of the empirical research that takes account of recent data has been able to refute this dismal hypothesis. See, in particular, the survey by Santomero and Seater (1978).

2. There has been an acceleration of the speed at which an increase of demand, whatever its origin, turns into an increase of domestic prices. Two studies of the British case, by Bergstrom and Wymer (1976) and by Knight and Wymer (1978), show this very clearly, and Spitäller (1978) draws the same conclusion with regard to *all* industrial countries. Comparing the speed of response of prices in 1973-76 with the average for 1958-76, he finds that prices rose three

---

[1]This can be shown by using the Keynesian "foreign-trade multiplier" to analyze the consequences of the shift in the trade balance. The income-adjusted change in the trade balance will be smaller than the shift produced by the exchange-rate change, but it will have the same sign.

12

times as fast in response to changes in underlying forces—in money stocks, output gaps, and import prices. Robinson (1979) makes the same point with respect to import prices, and he suggests that some part of the increase in the speed of response is due to the advent of floating exchange rates, because they have helped to concentrate attention on the real values of national currencies. But most of it should probably be ascribed to the acceleration of inflation itself, and we would not blame floating rates for more than a small part of that acceleration.

3. The trade-off that remains in the short run is far from uniform across countries. In the United States, for example, the increase in aggregate demand brought about by a depreciation and its effects on the trade balance generates more output (less inflation) than in the United Kingdom. In Germany, the decrease in aggregate demand brought about by an appreciation appears to fall more heavily on prices than on output. (The contrast between the United States and the United Kingdom is, of course, consistent with the numbers in our table, insofar as they include the price response to an increase in demand. The findings for Germany, by contrast, are hard to reconcile with the table.)

Price changes that result from variations in the level of aggregate demand can be controlled by stabilizing aggregate demand—by the use of monetary and fiscal policies to reduce domestic spending so as to make room for the trade balance to improve. This is the lesson learned from the "absorption approach" to the theory of the balance of payments, and the lesson holds with equal force under pegged and floating rates. The task is made difficult, however, when wage rates are affected by an increase in demand or respond directly to an increase in the cost of living—when "real wage resistance" is built into the economy by the power of trade unions or by indexation. What do we know about the strength of this phenomenon?

Most observers agree that trade unions are quite strong in the United Kingdom and have much influence, partly political, in Italy and France. They are relatively weak in Japan and Germany. These conclusions are borne out by quantitative work. In a study of real wage resistance, Sachs (1979) calculates an "equilibrium" wage rate for each country (a measure of the marginal product of labor) and compares it with the actual wage rate. Looking at the differences between the two in 1975-76, he finds real wage resistance in the United Kingdom and Italy. The actual wage was above the equilibrium wage. Sachs blames real wage resistance on wage indexation coupled with accommodating monetary policies. In the United Kingdom, Stage III of the incomes policy, starting in October 1973, guaranteed an increase in the real wage. In Italy, 100 per cent indexation was adopted in January 1975,

13

covering a large part of the Italian labor force. In both countries, moreover, economic policies were aimed mainly at reducing unemployment in the wake of the 1974-75 recession, whereas policies in Germany and Japan were aimed primarily at reducing inflation and did not "ratify" real wage resistance. (Furthermore, productivity grew faster in Germany and Japan than in Italy and the United Kingdom, which means that real wages could be raised without raising prices too—that the "equilibrium" wage rate was increasing.)

In another study, Bond (1979) has found large differences from country to country in the strength of the short-run relationship between wage-rate changes and unemployment. In Italy and the United Kingdom, the relationship is rather weak; an increase of unemployment does not slow down wage rates much. In Sweden and the United States, the relationship is even weaker. See also Okun (1978), who has surveyed short-run Phillips curves for the United States and finds that the inflation rate is not very sensitive to the unemployment rate. An increase in unemployment by one percentage point, maintained for a year, reduces the inflation rate eventually, but by no more than half of one percentage point. Turning this result around and putting it in terms of lost output, a ten per cent reduction in gross national product, maintained for a year, is required to cut the inflation rate by one percentage point. Reviewing this and other work on the United States, Goldstein (1979) concludes:

> If these estimates are representative of those for other industrial countries with high current inflation rates (France, Italy, the United Kingdom), it is not surprising that policy makers are wary of anything that requires a large reduction in the inflation rate.

Monetary accommodation may not be so blameworthy. It may be the only course that the authorities can follow after real wage resistance has taken hold. Antipathy to exchange-rate changes is likewise understandable. If a depreciation of the domestic currency will set off a wage-price spiral that can be halted only at great cost, the authorities are bound to place a high premium on exchange-rate stability.

Expectations, Speculation, and Feedback Effects

To round out the analysis, we turn now to the ways in which price changes can affect exchange rates, and we start by repeating what we said before. Exchange rates are determined in the short run by asset-holders' forecasts of what they would earn by having claims and debts in various currencies. Accordingly, there are two main causes of short-run changes in exchange rates:

14

(1) Changes in supplies of claims and debts that cannot be absorbed without adjustments in rates of return.

(2) Changes in expectations resulting from the advent of new information relevant to judgments about rates of return.

On this view, price changes can produce exchange-rate changes only by affecting asset-holders' expectations about future exchange rates.

An increase in one country's prices, however, is quite likely to require a depreciation of that country's currency, and it will also set in motion processes that bring about the requisite depreciation— processes involving the current-account balance, saving, and demands for assets.[1] We need not describe those processes here and need not assume that asset-holders understand them. It is sufficient to assume that experience has taught them to anticipate the long-run result. If one country's prices rise relative to those of other countries, and the increase is deemed to be permanent, asset-holders will come to expect a depreciation of the country's currency and will start to sell it, causing the depreciation to begin at once.

The strength of this short-run effect, however, will depend on the dynamics of exchange-rate speculation. If expectations are formed "rationally," in that asset-holders are able to forecast the path of the exchange rate in the wake of a disturbance, speculation is likely to stabilize the rate—to keep it on the path to long-run equilibrium. But there are other ways in which expectations can be formed. They can be regressive, adaptive, or extrapolative.

If expectations are regressive, a change in the exchange rate is taken to be temporary; the rate is expected to return to its "normal" level, unless and until there is overwhelming evidence that the "normal" level has itself been altered. Asset-holders will be slow to take account of new information, including information contained in price changes. If expectations are adaptive, forecasts are revised in the light of past mistakes; the exchange rate forecast for tomorrow will be based on the one forecast for today adjusted for the errors made in earlier forecasts. Asset-holders may revise their views more quickly than when they hold regressive expectations but still fail to take prompt account of new information.

---

[1]See, e.g., Allen and Kenen (1980), especially Chapter 6.

15

If expectations are extrapolative, however, the change in the exchange rate forecast for tomorrow will have the same sign as the change that took place yesterday, and this sort of forecast can be self-fulfilling. Movements in exchange rates can be made much larger than the movements justified by new information. In other words, extrapolative expectations can produce "band wagon" effects that draw in the most rational of economic actors—those who may believe that rate movements are excessive in the light of available information but act to protect themselves from the behavior of less rational actors. On the one hand, then, extrapolative expectations can cause price changes to induce large exchange-rate changes—large enough to generate vicious and virtuous circles. On the other hand, foreign-exchange markets nervous enough to succumb to this sort of behavior may ignore or misinterpret the new information contained in price changes, and there may then be no firm relationship running from price changes to exchange-rate changes.

This last possibility seems to fit the facts, but speculation may not be the main reason. Although foreign-exchange markets are very volatile, they have been shown to respond in a rational fashion to some types of information. One of us has shown that they respond quite promptly to trade deficits and surpluses.[1] They can, in fact, respond too strongly, failing to take adequate account of the so-called J-curve (the tendency for the trade balance to move in the "wrong" direction immediately after an exchange-rate change). Others have shown that they respond quite promptly to changes in rates of growth of monetary aggregates, especially to unanticipated changes.[2]

Macroeconomic Policies and Price Responses

We have alluded frequently to the importance of national economic policies for the strength of the connection between prices and exchange rates. Let us draw together the strands of the argument.

---

[1] See Kenen (forthcoming), where the size of the U.S. trade balance proves to be more powerful than any other single variable in forecasting the short-term behavior of exchange rates between the dollar and major European currencies, and the size of the Japanese trade balance plays the same role in forecasting the behavior of the rate between the dollar and the yen.

[2] Black (1977) argues that these changes can produce "bandwagon" effects, particularly in the case of currencies whose countries have large money markets and few capital controls (Canada, the United Kingdom, and the United States), but he draws no distinction between anticipated and unanticipated changes. See also Artus (1976), who "explains" a large part of the behavior of the DM-dollar rate in terms of changes in monetary variables but finds evidence of lagged responses that he ascribes to a bandwagon effect. On the role of unanticipated changes in monetary aggregates, see Dornbusch (1977) and Bomhoff and Korteweg (1979).

16

Monetary and fiscal policies do not play an important role at the first stage of the process surveyed above. There is no reason to believe that they influence the pass-through—the change in import prices resulting from a change in the exchange rate. And they may not be important at the second stage. The direct goods-market effects on the general price level depend on the openness of the economy—the extent of its reliance on imported goods in consumption and production—and on the degree of substitutability between imports and domestic output. One would not even want domestic policies to interfere with these direct effects. If consumers and producers were shielded from a change in import prices, an exchange-rate change could not affect the demand for imports and would have no influence on the trade balance.

Monetary and fiscal policies come into play when we reach the indirect and feedback effects. A depreciation of the domestic currency will increase the demand for domestic goods by improving the trade balance and will thus raise domestic prices unless the supply of domestic goods is perfectly elastic. Furthermore, an increase in the demand for domestic goods will add to the demand for labor and thus raise the money wage rate, bringing forth a larger increase in domestic prices. Macroeconomic policies are important at this stage because they can be used to stabilize aggregate demand—to make room for the improvement in the trade balance. The requisite policies, moreover, need not be very painful, as they need not reduce employment. They have merely to prevent an increase in demands for goods and labor.

But a depreciation has another consequence. By raising import prices, it imposes a reduction in the real wage rate, and workers are apt to demand an increase in the money wage rate. If this demand is granted in new union contracts or by indexation, cost-push pressures will present a hard choice for policy—the choice between resistance and accommodation. The choice is hard because resistance will be painful, given the unfavorable short-run trade-off between inflation and unemployment. But it may be more painful if it is deferred—if cost-push pressures are permitted to take hold or are built in by indexation and a wage-price spiral gets under way.

The stance of the authorities in the face of a wage-price spiral can be crucial for the size of the feedback from price changes to exchange-rate changes. Although foreign-exchange markets do not seem to take much notice of price changes by themselves, they are attentive to national policies. Countries that adopt accommodating policies are likely to experience depreciations induced by expectations of additional inflation. By implication, vicious and virtuous circles are not due to

17

exchange-rate flexibility per se and are not foreordained. They stem from the policies adopted in response to the price effects of exchange-rate changes.

This point has been made by many observers, and some of them go further. Thus Gordon (1977) argues that[1]

> Today's dichotomy between healthy nations . . . and sick nations . . . shows up in differences in behavior before the advent of flexible exchange rates in 1973. Growth cycles in the money supply in Germany and Japan appear to have followed a counter-cyclical reaction, whereas accommodation was the rule in Italy and the United Kingdom.

The same argument was spelled out in detail by the BIS in its *Annual Report* for 1977:

> The first striking fact . . . is that both the United Kingdom and Italy got into the vicious circle because of domestic developments. . . . One need not be an orthodox monetarist to regard the 30 per cent rise in the money supply (M3) as the main factor behind the sharp decline in the value of sterling during the same year. . . . In Italy the money supply (M2) was already expanding at an excessive rate in 1973 (and more so early in 1974) but the wage explosion during the same year also played an important role in weakening the lira on the foreign exchanges.

The point can be put in more general terms. Throughout this part of our survey, we have talked about the consequences of exchange-rate changes. One has always to remember, however, that a floating exchange rate does not change by itself:

> Once the exchange rate itself is viewed as endogenous, it becomes less meaningful to talk about exchange rate depreciation *causing* domestic inflation even when the data indicate that exchange rate depreciations lead to upsurges in the domestic inflation rate. Rather, one then has to ask what led the exchange rate to depreciate in the first place. The answer that currently receives the most support from the empirical literature . . . is that the exchange rate will depreciate, ceteris paribus, when [a] country expands its supply of money (relative to the demand for it) faster than . . . other countries. When one couples this with the assumption that exchange rates respond more rapidly to money supply changes than do domestic prices, the 'optical illusion' can be created that exchange rate depreciation is causing domestic inflation à la the vicious circle. . . In reality, it will be the excessive rate of domestic monetary expansion that is the true initiating factor. [Goldstein (1979)]

---

[1]This quotation and the next are reproduced from Goldstein (1979).

18

This is not to imply that monetary changes are the only causes of exchange-rate changes. Nor do we accept the normative inference often drawn from this sort of analysis—that monetary policies should be used primarily to stabilize exchange rates. But it does help to explain—and should help to dissipate—some of the current doubts about exchange-rate flexibility.

Extending the Analysis

At the start of this section we posed several questions about the strength of the connections between prices and exchange rates. We have just answered one of them, concerning the strength of the self-aggravating tendencies known as vicious and virtuous circles. These tendencies are intrinsic to the way in which exchange-rate changes function, but they need not feed upon themselves. Their strength depends on institutional arrangements, especially on the extent of indexation, and on the conduct of domestic policies. Here are our answers to some of the other questions.

Can changes in nominal exchange rates lead to long-lasting changes in real exchange rates? We think that they can and offer an additional piece of evidence. Our own calculations, set out in the appendix and summarized in the first column of Table 1, say that a depreciation of one country's currency will raise that country's prices relative to those of others but that the increase will be smaller than the change in the exchange rate. In the case of the United States, for example, a one per cent depreciation in the effective exchange rate for the dollar will cause the real exchange rate to depreciate by about six-tenths of one per cent. In the case of Japan, a one per cent depreciation in the effective rate for the yen will cause the real rate to depreciate by about four-fifths of one per cent.[1]

Do the links between price changes and exchange-rate changes vary systematically with country size? The table overleaf does not tell us very much. Some other findings, however, shed light on this question. They pertain to the changes in export prices that follow changes in exchange rates. Export price statistics are quite unreliable, and one has to be skeptical about this body of research. Yet one regularity stands out in most studies. The export prices of small countries change by more than

---

[1]These estimates are obtained by subtracting the change in relative prices from the one per cent change in the effective exchange rate. (In the case of the United States, we have $1.00 - 0.39 = 0.61$.) They are first-year estimates, but our month-by-month results suggest that most of the change in relative prices takes place in the first year.

those of large ones and may offset the whole change in the nominal exchange rate; see, e.g., Spitaller (1979) and Robinson, Webb, and Townsend (1979).[1]

What about asymmetries in price responses? There is, we said, no evidence that the pass-through of a depreciation differs from the pass through of an appreciation, and there is very little evidence that consumer prices respond more strongly to an increase than a decrease in import prices. Earlier, however, we called attention to the case of Germany, where price changes have been very small compared to exchange-rate changes, and suggested that German experience may

TABLE I

Exchange-Rate Changes, Price Responses, and Wage Indexation

Country	First-Year Price Response	Depreciation (+) of Effective Exchange Rate	Prevalence of Indexation
Switzerland	0.08	− 44.7	widespread
Germany	0.02	− 33.3	low
Japan	0.10	− 28.7	moderate
France	0.23	2.8	low
Sweden	0.25	3.1	moderate
Canada	0.27	7.3	moderate
United States	0.39	15.3	moderate
United Kingdom	0.25	54.3	widespread
Italy	0.65	76.0	widespread

First-year price response is the percentage change in the ratio of domestic to foreign wholesale prices resulting from a one per cent change in the effective exchange rate. It is the twelve-month sum of distributed-lag (Almon) weights obtained by estimating a second-degree polynominal. For details, see the appendix.

Depreciation of the effective exchange rate is the percentage change in the MERM-weighted index from July 1970 to December 1977. Data from International Monetary Fund, *International Financial Statistics.*

Prevalence of indexation from Braun (1976).

---

[1] Spitäller's work relates to 1973-78, the period of floating rates, and is therefore more relevant than most other studies. For Italy and Canada, he finds that the first-year response is close to unity; the change in export prices offsets almost all of the exchange-rate change. For France, Japan, and the United Kingdom, it is in the neighborhood of 0.6 per cent; but for Germany and the United States, it is only half as large.

20

testify to an important asymmetry in price responses. Real wage resistance, including formal indexation, may work more strongly on one side than the other; an increase in consumer prices is almost certain to raise nominal wage rates, but a decrease in consumer prices is less certain to reduce them. Thus, Switzerland, Germany, and Japan, shown to have had appreciating currencies in Table 1, have had the smallest price responses to exchange-rate changes, although wage indexation is "widespread" in Switzerland and "moderate" in Japan. At the opposite extreme, Italy, the United Kingdom, and the United States have had depreciating currencies and some of the largest price responses. And the response in the United States has been larger than the ones in Sweden and Canada, where wage indexation is about as prevalent as in the United States. Floating rates, combined with monetary accommodation, may have helped to increase the average of inflation rates or, at least, may have prolonged the increase that took place before the start of floating.[1]

Finally, what can we say about the effects of exchange-rate flexibility on the dispersion of national inflation rates? Insofar as prices have responded to exchange-rate changes—and there is no doubt of this— the exchange-rate regime has accounted for some for the increase in dispersion. But the quantitative studies surveyed in this paper are not precise enough to measure the amount. They cannot tell us, for example, what domestic policies would have been pursued if exchange rates had been pegged. If forced to make a guess, however, we would say that the dispersion could not have been less than half as large if exchange rates had been pegged. In other words, there has been a large increase in differences between "underlying" price trends—an increase that began before the start of floating and is, of course, one reason why it would be impractical to return to pegged exchange rates under present circumstances.

---

[1]There is, of course, one other way in which flexible exchange rates can add to inflation rates—by relaxing the constraints on monetary policies that would be imposed by reserve losses under pegged exchange rates. This view has been challenged, however, by those who point out that a large depreciation of the domestic currency may be no less effective in imposing "discipline" and marshalling support for disinflationary policies. See, e.g., Crockett and Goldstein (1976).

21

Chapter II

Exchange-Rate Changes and the Current-Account Balance

The Issues

The contribution of exchange-rate changes to the process of balance-of-payments adjustment depends mainly on these two reactions:

(1) The size and speed of the response of domestic prices to a change in the exchange rate, which determine the response of the real exchange rate to the change in the nominal exchange rate.

(2) The size and speed of the reaction of the current-account balance to the change in the real exchange rate.[1]

Evidence concerning the first reaction was reviewed above. It led us to conclude that price changes do not fully offset changes in nominal exchange rates, so that there can be changes in real exchange rates. But questions have been raised about the second reaction. Some say that it has been getting slower, if not weaker, so that it is harder to correct surpluses and deficits in current-account balances:

> It is by now agreed . . . that trade flows respond slowly to changes in exchange rates, so that exchange-rate changes can produce perverse effects . . . for more than a year or two and can thereby generate destabilizing expectations.

---

[1] As certain service flows, especially tourism, respond to exchange-rate changes, estimates pertaining to the size and speed of this reaction should look to the behavior of the current-account balance, not the merchandise trade balance. Hereafter, however, we confine ourselves to the trade balance, as it is the largest part of the current-account balance and the part on which the bulk of recent research has been concentrated.

22

The slow response of trade flows may be getting slower, because economies are growing more slowly, excess capacity is endemic, and profit margins are low. . . . Labor is becoming a fixed factor of production. . . . In the words of one observer, exchange-rate changes may do little to correct imbalances when commodity and factor markets clear quite slowly and asset markets clear quite fast, and the contrast between market processes may be growing larger. [Kenen (1978)]

The recent behavior of current-account balances has strengthened this new pessimism. The current-account surpluses of Germany, Japan, and Switzerland grew from some $8 billion in 1972 to some $31 billion in 1978, despite the appreciations of their real exchange rates before and after the beginning of the floating-rate regime. The United States, by contrast, ran large current-account deficits in 1977-78, despite the depreciation of its real exchange rate. We have therefore to survey some of the recent evidence on the response of the trade balance to the real exchange rate.

This subject has produced large amounts of research, going back to studies of the interwar period, when interest in the subject was aroused by the first formulations of the "elasticities approach" to balance-of-payments theory. It is therefore quite difficult to summarize the literature, and our problem is compounded because many methods have been used. In early studies of price elasticities, for instance, estimates were based on simple demand functions that did not allow for lags; the econometric methods were primitive by present-day stand-ards; and the data were deficient in a number of respects. For a survey of these problems, see, e.g., Magee (1975). Recent studies are free from some of these defects but are still hard to compare. They use a number of econometric methods, different ways to estimate the rele-vant lags, and different measures of the change in the real exchange rate.[1] For a comprehensive survey of research methods and results,

---

[1] The problem of measurement is discussed in Kenen and Pack (1979), where we point out that price data of the highest quality may be still be inadequate to the purpose at hand:

> When we make [price] comparisons, even when we use them in econometric models, we seek to determine the influence of changes in price levels and exchange rates on trade flows or trade shares. We are interested, moreover, in the sustainabil-ity of the competitive situation. If price changes are modulated, however, in the face of competition, by changing profit margins, they may not reflect fully the underlying situation. When profit margins are "abnormal" on the low side or the high side, the competitive position may not be sustainable. We have already mentioned this possibility in connection with the use of export unit values, but the problem may be much more general. In small open economies, for example, wholesale prices and the GDP deflator are bound to be affected by competitive conditions.
> Putting the point in somewhat different terms, estimates of price elasticities like those surveyed in this section can be badly biased if the price and exchange-rate data used to make them do not measure accurately the long-term changes in relative profitability that are the underlying causes of changes in trade patterns.

23

together with a synthesis of findings, see Stern, Francis, and Schumacher (1976).[1]

Our own survey focusses on these questions:

(1) How large are the relevant price elasticities?

(2) How long are the lags in the response of the trade balance following a change in the real exchange rate?

(3) Have elasticities or lags been affected by the introduction of flexible exchange rates or by some of the other institutional changes that have taken place in recent years?

Our answers to these questions are, of course, tentative but are fairly optimistic.

Price Elasticities

The "elasticities approach" has by now been integrated into more comprehensive balance-of-payments theories that emphasize the influence of aggregate demand (absorption) and the roles of asset markets, especially of money markets. Nevertheless, price elasticities of demand for imports and exports continue to receive attention. They are crucial for the impact of the real exchange rate on the current-account balance. If price elasticities are too low, that balance can move in the "wrong" direction.

Consider the effects of a depreciation and look first at the import side. The increase of import prices measured in home currency will reduce the volume of imports. But when the demand for imports is inelastic, the increase in import prices will be larger than the corresponding decrease in volume, and the total import bill will get bigger, measured in home currency. Look next at the export side. The decrease in export prices measured in foreign currency will raise the volume of exports. But when the demand for exports is inelastic, the decrease in the export prices will be larger than the increase in volume, and total export earnings will get smaller, measured in foreign currency. In each instance, then, a depreciation can enlarge a trade deficit, rather than reducing it.[2]

---

[1]Goldstein (1979) brings the story up to date, and we draw heavily on his paper, as we did in the previous section.

[2]In the simplest two-country model, with infinite price elasticities of supply, fixed levels of activity in each country, and no trade deficit or surplus at the outset, a depreciation or devaluation of the first country's currency gives that country a trade surplus if the price elasticities of demand sum up to a number larger than unity. This is the so-called Marshall-Lerner-Robinson condition. If the elasticities of supply are less than infinite or trade is not balanced at the outset, the critical condition is more complicated (but, by and large, less restrictive). In multi-country models, the relevant condition must take into account all of the bilateral price elasticities, including supply elasticities. In general, however, the larger the various demand elasticities, the larger the improvement in the trade balance attending a depreciaton of one country's exchange rate, given the initial trade pattern, the supply elasticities, and the level of activity in each country. One has to allow for lags, however, and they are discussed later in this paper.

Putting the point in somewhat different terms, estimates of price elasticities like those surveyed in this section can be badly biased if the price and exchange-rate data used to make them do not measure accurately the long-term changes in relative profitability that are the underlying causes of changes in trade patterns.

24

Eight sets of estimates of price elasticities are shown in Table 2, four of them for countries' imports and four more for countries' exports. Those in columns (1) through (3) and columns (5) through (7) come from individual econometric studies; those in columns (4) and (8) are syntheses by Stern et al. (1976), based on their survey and assessment of about 130 separate studies.

The range of results is rather wide; look at the elasticities of import demand for the United States, which run from − 0.45 to − 1.03 in the three recent studies, and the elasticities of export demand, which run from − 1.07 to − 2.32.[1] The differences, we said, are due partly to differences in methodology and data but partly to differences in the time allowed for price changes to affect the relevant trade flows. (Some estimates pertain to the short run, others to the medium or long run.) The estimates by Stern et al., however, refer to the long run, and they lead their authors to this general conclusion: Typical long-run elasticities of the demand for imports vary between − 0.50 and − 1.50 for developed countries, whereas those for exports vary between − 0.50 and − 2.00. But most of the research from which they draw this inference was based on experience in the pegged-rate period (as are the six sets of estimates listed separately in Table 2). And though there has not been much work on the flexible-rate period, by itself, because it has not lasted long enough for well-designed time-series estimation, a handful of new estimates extend into that period; see, e.g., Deppler and Ripley (1978) and Hooper (1978). Taking these new estimates into account, Goldstein (1979) reaches this conclusion: The price elasticities of demand for imports vary between − 0.75 and − 1.25, whereas those for exports vary between − 1.25 and − 2.50. His estimates for imports are higher at the low end and lower at the high end than the estimates by Stern et al., and his estimates for exports are higher at both ends.[2]

Goldstein goes on to point out that price elasticities of demand tend to be larger, the bigger the share of manufactures in the relevant trade flows. They tend also to be larger when trade data are disaggregated by

---

[1] Here and elsewhere in this paper, minus signs denote "right-signed" results for demand elasticities, as quantities should fall when prices rise. Plus signs denote "right-signed" results for supply elasticities, as quantities should rise when prices rise. Some of the estimates in Table 2 are, therefore, "wrong-signed" but may not be cause for alarm (because they fall short of statistical significance).

[2] Note that most estimates of demand elasticities are higher for exports than for imports. The reason is quite simple. When import prices rise, consumers and producers can shift from imported to domestic goods. When export prices rise, consumers and producers in foreign countries have wider options; they can shift from imported to domestic goods but can also shift from the exports of the country with the higher export prices to the exports of third countries.

25

Table 2
Price Elasticities of Demand for Imports and Exports

Country	Imports				Exports			
	(1) Goldstein & Khan	(2) Khan & Ross	(3) Houthakker & Magee	(4) Stern et al	(5) Goldstein & Khan	(6) Hickman & Lau	(7) Houthakker & Magee	(8) Stern et al
United States	-0.45	-1.00	-1.03	-1.66	-2.32	-1.07	-1.51	-1.41
Germany	-0.70	-0.53	ns	-0.88	-0.83	-0.76	-1.25	-1.11
Japan	0.01	0.15	-0.72	-0.78	2.47	-0.46	-0.80	-1.11
France	-1.09	-0.30	ns	-1.08	-1.33	-0.96	-2.27	-1.31
Italy	-0.16	-1.67	ns	-1.03	-3.29	-0.71	-1.12	-0.93
United Kingdom	0.17	0.39	ns	-0.65	-1.32	-1.05	-1.24	-0.48
Canada	—	-2.13	-1.46	-1.30	—	-0.56	-0.59	-0.79
Belgium	-0.62	-0.22	-1.02	-0.83	-1.57	-0.67	ns	-1.02
Netherlands	0.33	0.37	ns	-0.68	-2.73	-0.72	-0.82	-0.95
Austria	—	-0.59	—	-1.32	—	-0.76	-1.30	-0.93

Note. Estimates differ in periods covered, the price indexes employed, the methods of estimation, and the specifications of the demand functions to which the price elasticities pertain, especially in the extent and method of allowing for lags:

(1) Goldstein and Khan (1976): quarterly data for 1955-73 and estimation by ordinary least squares.

(2) Khan and Ross (1975): semiannual data for 1960-72 and estimation by ordinary least squares.

(3) Houthakker and Magee (1969): annual data for 1951-66 and estimation by ordinary least squares (with correction in some cases for serial correlation). The notation ns indicates that the elasticity was not statistically significant and was therefore omitted from the final demand function.

(4) Stern, Francis, and Schumacher (1976) based on a survey of several studies (see Table 2.2.).

(5) Goldstein and Khan (1978): quarterly data for 1955-70 and estimation by full information maximum-likelihood method.

(6) Hickman and Lau (1973): annual data for 1961-69 and estimation by ordinary least squares (with correction for serial correlation).

(7) Same source, coverage, and method as (3).

(8) Same source, coverage, and method as (4).

type of commodity, when demand elasticities are calculated simultaneously with the corresponding supply elasticities, and when the price index for domestic goods is one that does not give much weight to nontraded goods.[1] These last observations on methodology suggest that more work must be done before we have reliable price elasticities. There is, in particular, a shortage of information on supply elasticities. Goldstein and Khan (1978) have done the only recent work with which we are familiar, obtaining significant supply elasticities for seven of eight countries covered (and a cross-country average of 2.76 for the long-run elasticity of export supply).

What we know now, however, leads us to believe that price elasticities are high enough, especially for large industrial countries, to give the exchange rate an important role in coping with current-account deficits and surpluses.

Lagged Responses to Price Changes

Why then has it been so difficult to detect the effects of exchange-rate changes on trade balances? Five reasons come to mind:

First, changes in nominal exchange rates can bring about large changes in domestic prices, offsetting the exchange-rates changes. There may be little change in real exchange rates.

Second, cyclical and secular income changes, at home and abroad, can mask the trade-balance changes induced by exchange-rate changes. This may be one reason for the slow improvement of the U.S. trade balance in 1978-79, following the large depreciation of the real exchange rate in 1977-1978.[2]

Third, trade barriers may be imposed to protect domestic industries from the import competition brought about by an appreciation of the real rate. There has been some such tendency in certain surplus countries at times when the exchange rate was appreciating rapidly.

---

[1] On the effects of simultaneous estimation, see Goldstein and Khan (1978); on the choice of the domestic price index, see Goldstein, Khan, and Officer (1979), where it is shown that price elasticities are higher when wholesale prices are substituted for consumer prices or the GNP deflator.

[2] This point was emphasized by the IMF in its *Annual Report* for 1978:

... the results indicate that an increase of 1 per cent in manufacturing output maintained for three years has a strong negative effect on the trade balance in all [industrial] countries, ranging from 1½ to 3½ per cent of 1977 trade flows. By way of comparison, rather sizeable exchange rate changes, in most cases on the order of 5 to 15 per cent, would be necessary to produce the same trade balance effects. [Cited in Goldstein (1979)]

27

Fourth, producers who must serve foreign and home markets may give high priority to domestic customers, and order books for exports may grow very long. Price differentials may not be decisive when foreign customers must wait for goods that they want now.[1]

Fifth, there are long lags between a change in the exchange rate and the resulting changes in trade volume. It takes time to locate the appropriate supplier or customer, to come to terms with new customers, and to manufacture the goods that they require. In other words, short-run price elasticities may be much smaller than long-run elasticities.

The first of these five reasons was discussed in the first part of this paper. The next three need attention, but we cannot deal with them here. We turn directly to the fifth—lags in the responses to exchange-rate changes.

Even when price elasticities are high, two or three years may elapse before an exchange-rate change has its full effects on the trade balance—effects that correspond to those elasticities.[2] In fact, the first effects can be perverse, as trade flows may not change rapidly enough to offset the price changes caused by the exchange-rate changes. The path of the trade balance will then be described by a J-shaped curve, worsening before beginning to improve.

Interest in this problem started with the devaluation of the pound in 1967 and was stimulated by the subsequent devaluation of the dollar in 1971. In each instance, the trade balance worsened in the months right after the devaluation. Artus (1975) found that the devaluation of the pound had adverse effects on the trade balance through the first half of 1968—for three full quarters following the devaluation. Clark (1974) found that the devaluation of the dollar had adverse effects for a full year. More recent studies by Spitäller (1979) and by Goldstein and Young (1979), concentrating on the flexible-rate period, suggest that these perverse effects are likely to endure for four or five quarters.[3]

---

[1]See, e.g., Greene (1975) and the sources cited there.

[2]See, e.g., Junz and Rhomberg (1973). In the World Trade Model used by the IMF, the lags are somewhat shorter on the import side, where most of the effect of an exchange-rate change takes place within six quarters; Germany is the chief exception among the major industrial countries. On the export side, by contrast, the lags are very long; much of the effect of a price change takes place in the third and fourth years following the exchange-rate change. See Deppler and Ripley (1978), Tables 11 and 12.

[3]In the case of Italy, by contrast, the adverse effects wear off more speedily; see Chiesa, Gomel, Sitzia, Valcamonici, and Vona (1978).

28

Although many efforts have been made to estimate the path of the trade balance after an exchange-rate change—the shape of the J-curve—we have doubts about the productivity of this research. The numerical results are bound to depend in part on the speeds with which import prices, export prices, and internal prices respond to exchange-rate changes, and these speeds will not be the same from episode to episode, even for one country. They will be affected by the state of the economy and, therefore, by monetary and fiscal policies.[1] Furthermore, price changes will differ from country to country, and even if this were not so, the lengths of the lags will differ; the size of an economy and composition of its trade are likely to affect the rate at which exchange-rate changes influence the trade balance.

To make matters worse, the lag structures that emerge from econometric work depend heavily upon the methodology employed. In some studies, for example, Koyck-type estimates are used, and these force the trade-balance lags to fall off exponentially; the bulk of the effect of an exchange-rate change is made to take place quickly. In other studies, Almon estimates are used, and these are made by calculating complicated functions; in consequence, the lags depend on the function that one chooses. The choice of function should, of course, be based on good theory and on careful inspection of the evidence, but an arbitrary element frequently remains.

To illustrate this last point, we compare results obtained by using one such function with the consensus estimate mentioned above, that perverse effects may last for more than a year. In Table 3, we show trade-balance equations for the United States and Japan. In both equations, we rule out any change in the trade balance during the first quarter (the one with the exchange-rate change) and any further change after the sixth quarter. In the case of the United States, the trade balance worsens for one quarter, and the size of the perverse response is not significant statistically. In the case of Japan, the first three changes are perverse (and the first two are significant). In the U.S. equation, moreover, the subsequent improvement in the trade balance is large enough to offset the perverse effect. In the Japanese equation, it is not.[2]

---

[1] We dealt with this issue in the first part of our paper. For detailed work on the United States, see Ahluwalia and Hernandez-Cata (1975) and Hooper (1976).

[2] If we had worked with longer lags, running back for three full years, the improvement might have been much larger—large enough to offset the perverse effect that shows up in the first three quarters—but we are far from sure that this would be the case.

Finally, we must stress one more source of difficulty. The response of the trade balance to a change in the exchange rate will be influenced by views about the *permanence* of the exchange-rate change. If it is viewed as temporary when it first occurs, consumers and producers may be reluctant to incur the costs of shifting between foreign and domestic goods. If they alter their views later, they will start to respond. Thus, the lags in the responses to exchange-rate changes have always to reflect exchange-rate expectations and may therefore be slower in some instances than others. Exchange-rate expectations, however,

---

Table 3
Quarterly Trade-Balance Equations for the United States and Japan 1973 IVQ Through 1978 IIIQ

United States

$$[B^a_t - B^a_{t-1}] = -693.243 - 578.821 \; \dot{Q}^a_t + 652.773 \; \dot{Q}^{af}_t - 43.631 \; \dot{C}_{t-1}$$
$$\quad\quad\quad\quad (1.79) \quad\quad\quad (3.68) \quad\quad\quad\quad (2.14) \quad\quad\quad\quad (3.10)$$

$$+ \sum_k b_k \, [\dot{\pi}^a_{t-k} - \dot{p}^a_{t-k} + \dot{p}^{af}_{t-k}]$$

k	weight	t-statistic
1	− 44.61	0.64
2	31.06	0.74
3	79.44	1.92
4	100.50	2.13
5	94.31	2.12
6	60.80	2.09

Sum of b_k = 321.51,   SE for Sum = 191.04
R^2 = 0.673,   SE = 1597.06,   DW = 2.01,   RHO = − 0.466

B^a_t U.S. trade balance, quarterly, in millions of U.S. dollars.

$\dot{Q}^a_t$ Change in U.S. industrial production (per cent per quarter).

$\dot{Q}^{af}_t$ Change in foreign economic activity (per cent per quarter). For developed and some less developed countries, change in industrial production; for OPEC countries and some other less developed countries, change in import volume. Changes weighted by U.S. exports to individual countries (and to major OPEC countries as a group) in 1976.

$\dot{C}_t$ Change in U.S. dollar price of oil (per cent per quarter).

$\dot{\pi}^a_t$ Change in effective exchange rate for U.S. dollar (per cent per quarter). Changes in dollar prices of 12 major currencies weighted by the corresponding countries' global exports in 1976.

$\dot{p}^a_t$ Change in index of U.S. wholesale prices (per cent per quarter).

$\dot{p}^{af}_t$ Change in index of foreign wholesale prices (per cent per quarter). Constructed in the same way as effective exchange rate.

may depend in turn on the path of the trade balance. If that balance moves perversely in the short run, tracing out a J-curve, asset-holders may come to expect additional exchange-rate changes, and their expectations may be self-fulfilling. Accordingly, the lags do not depend entirely on the time it takes to shift between competing sources of supply, to penetrate new markets, and to fill new orders, and one would not expect them to be stable from one year to the next or one country to another.

Japan

$$[B_t^j - B_{t-1}^j] = 143.869 - 424.298\ \dot{Q}_{t-1}^j + 205.925\ \dot{Q}_{t-1}^{jf} - 18.824\ \dot{C}_{t-1}$$
$$\qquad (0.67) \qquad (3.26) \qquad\quad (2.51) \qquad\quad (2.77)$$

$$+ \sum_k b_k\,[\,\dot{\pi}_{t-k}^j - \dot{p}_{t-k}^j + \dot{p}_{t-k}^{jf}\,]$$

k	weight	t-statistic
1	− 249.40	2.92
2	− 105.00	2.97
3	− 1.74	0.08
4	60.40	1.71
5	81.40	2.09
6	61.27	2.23

Sum of b_k = − 153.12,   SE for Sum = 96.28

R^2 = 0.481,   SE = 1107.86,   DW = 2.17,   RHO = − 0.714

B_t^j Japanese trade balance, quarterly, in millions of U.S. dollars.

$\dot{Q}_t^j$ Change in Japanese industrial production (per cent per quarter).

$\dot{Q}_t^{jf}$ Change in foreign economic activity (per cent per quarter). Constructed in the same way as the corresponding index for the United States (but using Japanese export weights).

$\dot{C}_t$ See above.

$\dot{\pi}_t^j$ Change in effective exchange rate for Japanese yen (per cent per quarter). Changes in yen prices of 12 major currencies weighted by the corresponding countries' trade with Japan (exports *plus* imports) in 1976.

$\dot{p}_t^j$ Change in index of Japanese wholesale prices (per cent per quarter).

$\dot{p}_t^{jf}$ Change in index of foreign wholesale prices (per cent per quarter). Constructed in the same way as effective exchange rate.

Cochrane-Orcutt transformation used to eliminate serial correlation. Distributed lags from second-degree polynomial with first and final weights constrained to zero (i.e., b_k = 0 for k = 0 and k = 7). Numbers in parentheses beneath coefficients are t-statistics, not standard errors. All data except trade weights from IMF, *International Financial Statistics*; trade weights from IMF, *Direction of Trade*.

Note: Global trade weights for π_t^a and p_t^{af} gave results superior to bilateral trade weights, but bilateral trade weights for π_t^j and p_t^{jf} gave results superior to global trade weights.

31

We have therefore to offer an imprecise conclusion. Changes in trade balances are apt to be long-lagged and to be perverse in the short run, but may be substantial in the medium or long run.

Changes in Price Elasticities and Lags

Many reasons are advanced in favor of the view that elasticities have fallen and lags have lengthened in the last few years. Some were cited in a passage quoted at the start of this discussion. Internal adjustments have become more difficult, with slow growth, low profit margins, and high costs of altering patterns of employment. Some refer specifically to flexible exchange rates. McKinnon (1978), for example, suggests that exchange-rate fluctuations make it difficult to judge the permanence of any single change in an exchange rate and thus weaken the incentives of consumers and producers to take full advantage of cost and price differences. By implication, elasticities are likely to be lower and lags likely to be longer. Furthermore, uncertainties associated with exchange-rate fluctuations can cause firms to postpone investments, slowing or reducing the changes in the output mix that must take place to generate changes in trade balances.

But it is hard to marshall a large body of evidence in support of these assertions. We have already given reasons for distrusting any inference that one might draw from calculations about lengths of lags; unless two studies use identical techniques and comparable data, one cannot compare the lag structures they obtain. Similarly, studies of price elasticities cannot be compared unless they use the same sets of price and exchange-rate data (and the same ways of weighting them to measure real exchange rates). Too few studies do so.

There *are* bits of evidence that lend themselves to pessimism. In another paper, one of us has shown that exchange-rate fluctuations may bear some blame for the slow revival of real capital formation after the recession of 1974-75,[1] and this finding is consistent with McKinnon's supposition. Furthermore, the long-run price elasticities computed from the World Trade Model, based on data that extend into the floating-rate period, are slightly lower than the averages of earlier estimates given by Stern et al. (1976) and Goldstein (1979).[2] But these

---

[1] See Kenen (1979), where cross-sectional regressions show that investment grew most slowly in countries whose exchange rates were most volatile.

[2] The estimates for total imports range from -0.50 to -1.00 (whereas those by Stern et al. run to -1.50 and those by Goldstein run from -0.75 to -1.25). The estimates for total exports range from -0.50 to -1.50 (whereas those by Stern et al. run to -2.00 and those by Goldstein run from -1.25 to -2.50).

32

bits of evidence are not strong or numerous enough to justify a major change in our chief conclusion. If countries can combat real wage resistance, compressing the vicious and virtuous circles touched off by exchange-rate changes, they can still employ exchange-rate changes to influence current-account balances substantially and, therefore, to aid in the adjustment process.

References

I. J. Ahluwalia and E. Hernandez-Cata, "An Econometric Model of U.S. Merchandise Imports under Fixed and Fluctuating Exchange Rates, 1953-1973," International Monetary Fund, *Staff Papers*, November 1975.

P. R. Allen and P. B. Kenen, *Asset Markets, Exchange Rates, and Economic Integration*, London and New York, Cambridge University Press (1980).

J. R. Artus, "The 1967 Devaluation of the Pound Sterling," International Monetary Fund, *Staff Papers*, November 1975.

J. R. Artus, "Exchange Rate Stability and Managed Floating: The Experience of the Federal Republic of Germany," International Monetary Fund, *Staff Papers*, July 1976.

J. R. Artus and A. McGuirk, "A Revised Multilateral Exchange Rate Model," International Monetary Fund, unpublished research memorandum, May 1978.

A. R. Bergstrom and C. R. Wymer, "A Model of Disequilibrium Neoclassical Growth and Its Applications to the United Kingdom," in R. Abram, ed., *Statistical Inference in Continuous Time Economic Models*, Amsterdam, Bergstom, 1976.

S. W. Black, *Floating Exchange Rates and National Economic Policy*, New Haven, Yale University Press, 1977.

E. J. Bomhoff and P. Korteweg, "Exchange Rate Variability and Monetary Policy under Flexible Exchange Rates: Some Euro-American Experience, 1973-1978," unpublished paper, July 1979.

M. E. Bond, "Exchange Rates, Inflation and the Vicious Circle," International Monetary Fund, unpublished research memorandum, May 1979.

A. R. Braun, "Indexation of Wages and Salaries in Developed Countries," International Monetary Fund, *Staff Papers*, March 1976.

C. Chiesa, G. Gomel, B. Sitzia, R. Valcomonici, and S. Vona, "Un Modello di Analisi e Previsione del Settore Bilancia die Pagmenti Correnti," Banca D'Italia, March 1978.

34

P. B. Clark, "The Effects of Recent Exchange Rate Changes on the U.S. Trade Balance," in *The Effects of Exchange Rate Adjustments*, Washington, U.S. Treasury, 1974.

A. Crockett and M. Goldstein, "Inflation under Fixed and Flexible Exchange Rates," International Monetary Fund, *Staff Papers*, November 1976.

M. Deppler and D. Ripley, "The World Trade Model: Merchandise Trade," International Monetary Fund, *Staff Papers*, March 1978.

R. Dornbusch, "What Have We Learned from the Float?" unpublished paper, February 1977.

R. Dornbusch and P. Krugman, "Flexible Exchange Rates in the Short Run," *Brookings Papers on Economic Activity*, 1976(3).

M. Fratianni and P. Korteweg, "Inflation—Alternative Explanations and Policies—A Comment on the Hamburger and Reisch Paper," in K. Brunner and A. Meltzer, eds., *Institutions, Policies and Economic Performance*, Amsterdam, North-Holland, 1976.

M. Goldstein, "Downward Price Inflexibility, Ratchet Effects and the Inflationary Impact of Import Price Changes: Some Empirical Evidence," International Monetary Fund, *Staff Papers*, November 1977.

M. Goldstein, "Have Flexible Exchange Rates Made Macroeconomic Policy More Difficult: A Survey of the Issues and the Evidence," unpublished paper, August 1979.

M. Goldstein and M. S. Khan, "Large versus Small Price Changes and the Demand for Imports," International Monetary Fund, *Staff Papers*, March 1976.

M. Goldstein and M. S. Khan, "The Supply and Demand for Exports: A Simultaneous Approach," *Review of Economics and Statistics*, May 1978.

M. Goldstein, M. S. Khan, and L. Officer, "Prices of Tradable and Nontradable Goods in the Demand for Total Imports," *Review of Economics and Statistics*, November 1979.

M. Goldstein and J. Young, "Exchange Rate Policy: Some Current Issues," *Finance and Development*, March 1979.

R. J. Gordon, "World Inflation and Monetary Accommodation in Eight Countries," *Brookings Papers on Economic Activity*, 1977(2).

M. L. Greene, *Waiting Time: A Factor in Export Demand for Manufactures*, Princeton, International Finance Section, Princeton University, 1975.

35

M. J. Hamberger and R. D. Reisch, "Inflation, Unemployment and Macroeconomic Policy in Open Economies: An Empirical Analysis," in K. Brunner and A. Meltzer, eds., *Institutions, Policies and Economic Performance*, Amsterdam, North-Holland, 1976.

B. Hickman and L. Lau, "Elasticities of Substitution and Export Demand in a World Trade Model," *European Economic Review*, December 1973.

P. Hooper, "Forecasting U.S. Export and Import Prices and Volumes in a Changing World Economy," Board of Governors of the Federal Reserve System, International Finance Discussion Paper (mimeograph), December 1976.

P. Hooper, "The Stability of Income and Price Elasticities in U.S. Trade, 1957-77," Board of Governors of the Federal Reserve System, International Finance Discussion Paper (mimeograph), July 1978.

P. Hooper and B. Lowrey, "Impact of the Dollar Depreciation on the U.S. Price Level: An Analytical Survey of Empirical Evidence," Board of Governors of the Federal Reserve System, International Finance Discussion Paper (mimeograph), April 1979.

H. S. Houthakker and S. P. Magee, "Income and Price Elasticities in World Trade," *Review of Economics and Statistics*, August 1975.

P. Isard, "How Far Can We Push the 'Law of One Price'?" *American Economic Review*, December 1977.

H. Junz and R. Rhomberg, "Price Competitiveness in Export Trade Among Industrial Countries," *American Economic Review*, May 1973.

P. B. Kenen, "The Exchange-Rate Regime: An Annotated Agenda for Discussion by the Consultative Group on International Economic and Monetary Affairs," (mimeograph), 1978.

P. B. Kenen, "Exchange-Rate Variability: Measurement and Implications," International Finance Section, Princeton University, Research Memorandum (mimeograph), June 1979.

P. B. Kenen, "Exchange Rates and Domestic Prices: A Multicountry Model," International Finance Section, Princeton University, Research Memorandum (forthcoming).

P. B. Kenen and C. Pack, "The Measurement of Effective Exchange Rates: A Survey," International Finance Section, Princeton University, Research Memorandum (mimeograph), August 1979.

M. S. Khan and K. Z. Ross, "Cyclical and Secular Income Elasticities of the Demand for Imports," *Review of Economics and Statistics*, August 1975.

M. D. Knight and C. R. Wymer, "A Macroeconomic Model of the United Kingdom," International Monetary Fund, *Staff Papers*, December 1975.

36

I. Kravis and R. Lipsey, "Price Behavior in the Light of Balance of Payments Theories," *Journal of International Economics*, May 1978.

H. Kreinin, "The Effects of Exchange Rate Changes on the Prices and Volume of Foreign Trade," International Monetary Fund, *Staff Papers*, July 1977.

R. E. Lucas, "Some International Evidence on Output-Inflation Tradeoffs," *American Economic Review*, June 1973.

S. P. Magee, "Prices, Incomes, and Foreign Trade," in P. B. Kenen, ed., *International Trade and Finance: Frontiers for Research*, London and New York, Cambridge University Press, 1975.

R. I. McKinnon, "Exchange-Rate Instability, Trade Balances, and Monetary Policy in Japan and the United States," unpublished manuscript, 1978.

A. Okun, "Efficient Disinflationary Policies," *American Economic Review*, May 1978.

G. Richardson, "The Prospects for an International Monetary System," City University, London, The Henry Thornton Lecture (mimeograph), June 1979.

P. Robinson, T. Webb, and M. Townsend, "The Influence of Exchange Rate Changes on Prices: A Study of 18 Industrial Countries," *Economica*, February 1979.

J. Sachs, "Wage Indexation, Flexible Exchange Rates and Macroeconomic Policy," Board of Governors of the Federal Reserve System, International Finance Discussion Paper (mimeograph), April 1979.

W. Salant, "International Transmission of Inflation," in L. Krause and W. Salant, eds., *Worldwide Inflation*, Washington, The Brookings Institution, 1977.

A. M. Santomero and J. J. Seater, "The Inflation-Unemployment Trade-Off: A Critique of the Literature," *Journal of Economic Literature*, June 1978.

E. Spitäller, "A Model of Inflation and its Performance in the Seven Main Industrial Countries, 1958-76," International Monetary Fund, *Staff Papers*, June 1978.

E. Spitäller, "Short-Run Effects of Exchange Rate Changes on the Terms of Trade," International Monetary Fund, unpublished research memorandum, March 1979.

R. M. Stern, J. Francis, and B. Schumacher, *Price Elasticities in International Trade*, London, Macmillan, 1976.

37

APPENDIX

Statistical Tests of Interdependence Between Exchange Rates and Relative Domestic Prices

The tables in this appendix summarize a series of statistical exercises in which we seek to measure the strength of relationships between exchange-rate changes and price-level changes. In the first set of exercises, we try to "explain" monthly changes in each country's exchange rate by prior changes in that country's prices relative to those of other countries. In the second set of exercises, we try to "explain" monthly changes in each country's prices relative to those of other countries by prior changes in that country's exchange rate.

The exchange-rate changes used in this analysis are trade-weighted averages (effective rates); the weights are the global exports of the other countries in 1976. (Additional calculations based on bilateral trade weights are summarized in Table II.) The price changes refer to wholesale price indexes (and those of the other countries in each pairwise comparison are likewise weighted by the global exports of those countries). The exchange-rate changes, however, are based on end-of-month quotations, whereas the price changes can refer to any date within the corresponding month.

The statistical technique employed in this analysis is the estimation of a polynomial distributed lag covering a twelve-month period. Thus, the change in the exchange rate is made to depend on a weighted average of changes in relative prices during the previous twelve months. The detailed results in Tables 1 through 9 come from the estimation of a second-degree polynomial (unconstrained at either end); summary statistics for the corresponding Cochrane-Orcutt transformations and for a third-degree polynomial are listed in Tables 10 and 11.

The study uses data for fifteen countries (the United States, United Kingdom, Canada, Japan, Austria, Belgium, Denmark, Finland, France, Germany, Italy, the Netherlands, Norway, Sweden, and

38

Switzerland); the figures come from *International Financial Statistics*. Results are reported, however, for nine countries, not for the fifteen used to calculate the changes in exchange rates and price levels. The computations cover 58 months, starting with March 1974. Earlier data could not be employed, as we would then be using lagged changes in exchange rates that took place before the move to floating rates.

In interpreting the tables, it should be remembered that the exchange rate has been defined as the domestic price of the foreign currency, so that a depreciation raises it. Similarly, the price series are changes in the home price indexes *less* weighted averages of changes in the foreign indexes. Thus, theory would predict a positive relationship between the two sets of changes in both types of exercise. When home prices rise relative to foreign prices, one would anticipate a depreciation of the home currency. When the home currency depreciates, moreover, one would anticipate an increase in home prices relative to foreign prices.

In Tables 1 through 9, however, we find no support for the first hypothesis. Like other tests of the same type, cited in the body of this paper, our tests show no strong positive relationship between exchange-rate changes and earlier price changes. In some instances, indeed, the sums of weights attached to the price changes are negative, not positive. (The explanation we would give for the failure of this test is one mentioned in the text. Exchange rates are determined in the short run by asset-market processes, and though the expectations that dominate those processes may be affected by national price changes, other factors may be much more influential.)

We do find some support, by contrast, for the second hypothesis. Differences between national price changes *are* affected by earlier exchange-rate changes. In several cases, moreover, the relationship is significant statistically (in that the sums of weights are more than twice as large as their standard errors). The United States is one such case, with a sum of weights in the neighborhood of 0.40, indicating that a one per cent depreciation of the dollar will increase by four-tenths of one per cent the gap between the U.S. inflation rate and the weighted average of foreign inflation rates. Italy, Sweden, and Canada are other examples, with the sum of weights being about 0.60 in the case of Italy. (The results for the United Kingdom and Japan come close to significance and reach it in some of the additional experiments summarized by Tables 10 and 11.) We find no strong relationship, however, for France, Germany, or Switzerland.

Table 1
United States

Exchange Rate as a Function of Relative Prices			Relative Prices as a Function of Exchange Rate		
Lag (months)	Weight	t-Statistic	Lag (months)	Weight	t-Statistic
1	− 0.1094	0.383	1	0.0024	0.090
2	− 0.0309	0.171	2	0.0257	1.318
3	0.0277	0.250	3	0.0438	2.809
4	0.0666	0.746	4	0.0564	3.905
5	0.0857	0.836	5	0.0637	4.258
6	0.0851	0.730	6	0.0657	4.160
7	0.0647	0.549	7	0.0622	3.824
8	0.0246	0.232	8	0.0534	3.324
9	− 0.0353	0.391	9	0.0393	2.490
10	− 0.1150	1.123	10	0.0198	1.220
11	− 0.2144	1.306	11	− 0.0051	0.274
12	− 0.3336	1.267	12	− 0.0353	1.493

$R^2 = 0.0342$, DW = 2.49

Sum of weights: − 0.4841

Standard error: 0.8889

$R^2 = 0.2563$, DW = 1.52

Sum of weights: 0.3920

Standard error: 0.1278

Table 2
United Kingdom

Exchange Rate as a Function of Relative Prices			Relative Prices as a Function of Exchange Rate		
Lag (months)	Weight	t-Statistic	Lag (months)	Weight	t-Statistic
1	0.2283	0.958	1	0.0023	0.073
2	0.1283	0.859	2	0.0135	0.595
3	0.0486	0.518	3	0.0223	1.271
4	− 0.0109	0.130	4	0.0288	1.736
5	− 0.0500	0.508	5	0.0330	1.871
6	− 0.0688	0.620	6	0.0349	1.875
7	− 0.0673	0.606	7	0.0345	1.852
8	− 0.0456	0.467	8	0.0317	1.799
9	− 0.0348	0.045	9	0.0267	1.611
10	0.0589	0.750	10	0.0193	1.108
11	0.1416	1.099	11	0.0097	0.431
12	0.2445	1.137	12	− 0.0023	0.072

$R^2 = 0.0289$, DW = 1.52

Sum of weights: 0.6041

Standard error: 0.6388

$R^2 = 0.0700$, DW = 1.14

Sum of weights: 0.2543

Standard error: 0.1422

40

Table 3
France

Lag (months)	Weight	t-Statistic	Lag (months)	Weight	t-Statistic
	Exchange Rate as a Function of Relative Prices			**Relative Prices as a Function of Exchange Rate**	
1	0.1294	0.971	1	0.1534	2.580
2	0.1010	1.250	2	0.1216	3.071
3	0.0742	1.618	3	0.0921	3.411
4	0.0489	1.288	4	0.0648	2.802
5	0.0251	0.525	5	0.0397	1.593
6	0.0029	0.051	6	0.0168	0.617
7	−0.0178	0.318	7	−0.0038	0.139
8	−0.0370	0.764	8	−0.0223	0.862
9	−0.0547	1.438	9	−0.0385	1.632
10	−0.0709	1.631	10	−0.0525	2.071
11	−0.0855	1.117	11	−0.0643	1.816
12	−0.0986	0.771	12	−0.0739	1.387

$R^2 = 0.0935$, DW = 2.13
Sum of weights: 0.0168
Standard error: 0.3765

$R^2 = 0.2282$, DW = 1.28
Sum of weights: 0.2328
Standard error: 0.2198

Table 4
Germany

Lag (months)	Weight	t-Statistic	Lag (months)	Weight	t-Statistic
	Exchange Rate as a Function of Relative Prices			**Relative Prices as a Function of Exchange Rate**	
1	−0.0363	0.066	1	−0.0271	1.869
2	0.0534	0.142	2	−0.0159	1.363
3	0.1205	0.473	3	−0.0065	0.625
4	0.1651	0.813	4	0.0011	0.106
5	0.1872	0.914	5	0.0070	0.650
6	0.1866	0.854	6	0.0111	1.004
7	0.1636	0.745	7	0.0134	1.219
8	0.1180	0.584	8	0.0140	1.322
9	0.0498	0.280	9	0.0128	1.294
10	−0.0410	0.217	10	0.0098	1.056
11	−0.1542	0.562	11	0.0051	0.535
12	−0.2901	0.679	12	−0.0013	0.115

$R^2 = 0.0159$, DW = 2.02
Sum of weights: 0.5225
Standard error: 1.6160

$R^2 = 0.0881$, DW = 1.62
Sum of weights: 0.0234
Standard error: 0.0955

41

Table 5
Italy

Exchange Rate as a Function of Relative Prices			Relative Prices as a Function of Exchange Rate		
Lag (months)	Weight	t-Statistic	Lag (months)	Weight	t-Statistic
1	0.0500	0.305	1	0.1775	6.371
2	0.0256	0.244	2	0.1414	6.866
3	0.0038	0.055	3	0.1095	6.558
4	−0.0153	0.252	4	0.0816	5.168
5	−0.0318	0.456	5	0.0577	3.524
6	−0.0456	0.588	6	0.0380	2.227
7	−0.0568	0.728	7	0.0223	1.303
8	−0.0653	0.922	8	0.0107	0.646
9	−0.0711	1.145	9	0.0031	0.197
10	−0.0743	1.083	10	−0.0004	0.022
11	−0.0748	0.723	11	0.0002	0.011
12	−0.0727	0.450	12	0.0049	0.183

$R^2 = 0.0251$, DW = 1.85
Sum of weights: −0.4284
Standard error: 0.5625

$R^2 = 0.4692$, DW = 1.30
Sum of weights: 0.6465
Standard error: 0.1517

Table 6
Sweden

Exchange Rate as a Function of Relative Prices			Relative Prices as a Function of Exchange Rate		
Lag (months)	Weight	t-Statistic	Lag (months)	Weight	t-Statistic
1	−0.1496	0.538	1	0.0901	3.523
2	−0.0803	0.394	2	0.0665	3.792
3	−0.0312	0.190	3	0.0462	3.597
4	−0.0023	0.015	4	0.0293	2.495
5	0.0064	0.040	5	0.0156	1.244
6	−0.0050	0.030	6	0.0052	0.392
7	−0.0366	0.219	7	−0.0018	0.133
8	−0.0883	0.547	8	−0.0055	0.437
9	−0.1602	1.023	9	−0.0060	0.507
10	−0.2523	1.508	10	−0.0031	0.246
11	−0.3645	1.751	11	0.0031	0.182
12	−0.4969	1.758	12	0.0125	0.509

$R^2 = 0.0553$, DW = 2.00
Sum of weights: −1.6610
Standard error: 1.5264

$R^2 = 0.2124$, DW = 2.42
Sum of weights: 0.2521
Standard error: 0.1067

Table 7
Switzerland

Exchange Rate as a Function of Relative Prices			Relative Prices as a Function of Exchange Rate		
Lag (months)	Weight	t-Statistic	Lag (months)	Weight	t-Statistic
1	−0.3709	0.720	1	−0.0180	0.848
2	−0.4047	1.053	2	−0.0079	0.523
3	−0.4202	1.315	3	0.0005	0.041
4	−0.4175	1.341	4	0.0072	0.630
5	−0.3966	1.205	5	0.0123	1.015
6	−0.3574	1.033	6	0.0157	1.242
7	−0.3000	0.861	7	0.0174	1.395
8	−0.2244	0.671	8	0.0174	1.487
9	−0.1305	0.420	9	0.0158	1.418
10	−0.0183	0.062	10	0.0125	1.020
11	0.1120	0.342	11	0.0075	0.461
12	0.2606	0.613	12	0.0009	0.038

$R^2 = 0.0369$, DW = 1.69
Sum of weights: −2.6679
Standard error: 2.8879

$R^2 = 0.0441$, DW = 1.84
Sum of weights: 0.0812
Standard error: 0.1079

Table 8
Canada

Exchange Rate as a Function of Relative Prices			Relative Prices as a Function of Exchange Rate		
Lag (months)	Weight	t-Statistic	Lag (months)	Weight	t-Statistic
1	−0.0977	0.431	1	0.0480	1.441
2	0.0064	0.039	2	0.0501	2.218
3	0.0879	0.666	3	0.0502	3.130
4	0.1467	1.199	4	0.0483	3.392
5	0.1829	1.451	5	0.0445	2.896
6	0.1964	1.501	6	0.0386	2.310
7	0.1873	1.435	7	0.0307	1.796
8	0.1556	1.256	8	0.0208	1.268
9	0.1012	0.884	9	0.0089	0.576
10	0.0241	0.213	10	−0.0049	0.300
11	−0.0756	0.561	11	−0.0208	0.971
12	−0.1979	1.067	12	−0.0387	1.261

$R^2 = 0.0515$, DW = 2.09
Sum of weights: 0.7174
Standard error: 1.1455

$R^2 = 0.1786$, DW = 1.99
Sum of weights: 0.2757
Standard error: 0.1186

43

Table 9
Japan

Exchange Rate as a Function of Relative Prices			Relative Prices as a Function of Exchange Rate		
Lag (months)	Weight	t-Statistic	Lag (months)	Weight	t-Statistic
1	−0.2720	1.023	1	0.0442	2.437
2	−0.1891	1.001	2	0.0256	2.022
3	−0.1121	0.822	3	0.0106	1.085
4	−0.0412	0.378	4	−0.0007	0.808
5	0.0237	0.240	5	−0.0085	0.840
6	0.0827	0.870	6	−0.0126	1.178
7	0.1357	1.534	7	−0.0131	1.234
8	0.1827	2.145	8	−0.0099	1.016
9	0.2237	2.231	9	−0.0032	0.367
10	0.2587	1.779	10	0.0072	0.829
11	0.2878	1.318	11	0.0212	1.874
12	0.3108	0.990	12	0.0388	2.319

$R^2 = 0.0944$, DW = 1.76	$R^2 = 0.1907$, DW = 1.54
Sum of weights: 0.8915	Sum of weights: 0.0994
Standard error: 0.7324	Standard error: 0.0599

44

Table 10
Summary Statistics for Various Estimators: Multilateral Weights

Estimator and Country	Exchange Rate as a Function of Relative Prices		Relative Prices as a Function of Exchange Rate	
	Sum of Weights	Standard Error	Sum of Weights	Standard Error
Second Degree Polynomial				
United States	-0.4841	0.8889	0.3920	0.1278*
United Kingdom	0.6041	0.6388	0.2543	0.1422
France	0.0168	0.3765	0.2328	0.2198
Germany	0.5225	1.6160	0.0234	0.0955
Italy	-0.4284	0.5625	0.6465	0.1517*
Sweden	-1.6610	1.5264	0.2521	0.1067*
Switzerland	-2.6679	2.8879	0.0812	0.1079
Canada	0.7174	1.1455	0.2757	0.1186*
Japan	0.8915	0.7324	0.0994	0.0599
Cochrane-Orcutt Transform of Second Degree Polynomial				
United States	-0.2733	0.6616	0.3607	0.1441*
United Kingdom	0.5918	0.8808	0.2722	0.2184
France	-0.0413	0.3497	-0.0956	0.3657
Germany	-0.1226	1.6487	-0.0060	0.1120
Italy	-0.3202	0.6154	0.5528	0.1853*
Sweden	-1.3975	1.5197	0.2183	0.0853*
Switzerland	-2.9848	3.3807	0.0012	0.0675
Canada	0.5761	1.0717	0.2796	0.1207*
Japan	0.9516	1.0729	0.1275	0.0667
Third Degree Polynomial				
United States	-0.6697	0.8554	0.4010	0.1256*
United Kingdom	0.6699	0.6531	0.2536	0.1431
France	0.0251	0.3797	0.2264	0.2202
Germany	0.2301	1.6026	0.0151	0.0960
Italy	-0.4223	0.5673	0.6505	0.1411*
Sweden	-1.6662	1.5367	0.2525	0.1063*
Switzerland	-2.6633	2.9159	0.0811	0.1090
Canada	0.7781	1.1655	0.2741	0.1197*
Japan	0.5471	0.7148	0.1597	0.0660*

*Sum of weights has the expected sign and is more than twice the size of its standard error.

45

Table 11

Summary Statistics for Various Estimators: Bilateral Weights

Estimator and Country	Exchange Rate as a Function of Relative Prices		Relative Prices as a Function of Exchange Rate	
	Sum of Weights	Standard Error	Sum of Weights	Standard Error
Second Degree Polynomial				
United States	-0.2098	0.6764	0.3908	0.2097
United Kingdom	0.4206	0.6900	0.3353	0.1313*
France	0.4154	0.3923	0.0560	0.2277
Germany	-0.4546	1.0403	0.2381	0.1326
Italy	-0.4046	0.6389	0.5176	0.1743*
Sweden	-0.7738	0.9288	0.3817	0.1186*
Switzerland	-2.3258	1.8604	0.1023	0.1126
Canada	0.1007	0.6945	0.3518	0.1875
Japan	0.9806	0.7971	0.1731	0.0696*
Cochrane-Orcutt Transform of Second Degree Polynomial				
United States	-0.0130	0.5212	0.3650	0.2408
United Kingdom	0.4201	0.9235	0.3501	0.1950
France	0.2219	0.4409	-0.2119	0.3850
Germany	-0.9550	1.1174	0.1568	0.1497
Italy	-0.3117	0.6785	0.3760	0.2319
Sweden	-0.4698	0.9691	0.3530	0.0983*
Switzerland	-2.2548	2.2935	0.0298	0.0854
Canada	0.1241	0.6888	0.3984	0.1941*
Japan	1.4490	0.8629	0.1864	0.0970
Third Degree Polynomial				
United States	-0.2012	0.6525	0.3903	0.2079
United Kingdom	0.5325	0.7019	0.3339	0.1319*
France	0.4224	0.3955	0.0615	0.2289
Germany	-0.5223	1.0469	0.2279	0.1326
Italy	-0.3988	0.6447	0.5211	0.1635*
Sweden	-0.7698	0.9376	0.3814	0.1194*
Switzerland	-2.3067	1.8777	0.1002	0.1139
Canada	0.1805	0.7129	0.3518	0.1894
Japan	0.2322	0.6852	0.1783	0.0820*

*Sum of weights has the expected sign and is more than twice as large as its standard error.

46

[13]

The Role of the Dollar
as an
International Currency

Peter B. Kenen

There has been much talk in recent years about the decline of the dollar as an international currency. Some say that it was the inevitable consequence of the decline in the international role of the United States — the end to American hegemony. Some say it was due to avoidable mistakes in US monetary policy — that the inflation of the 1970s undermined international confidence in the dollar. Those who have tried to explain it, however, outnumber those who have tried to measure it, and this paper fills the gap. It collates available information on the uses of the dollar in international trade, in foreign-exchange markets and in international financial markets.

This is an exercise in measurement without theory, but it does come to conclusions. There was some decline in the use of the dollar in international trade shortly after the shift to more flexible exchange rates a decade ago, and I ascribe the decline to that shift, not to the weakness of the dollar in the foreign-exchange markets. There has been some significant decline in the use of the dollar as a reserve asset and thus some movement toward a multiple reserve-currency system. But the dollar is still the dominant currency in the international financial system, even in the reserve system narrowly defined. Paraphrasing Mark Twain's remark on hearing that a newspaper had published his obituary, reports of the death of the dollar are greatly exaggerated.

To organize the evidence surveyed in this paper, I adopt the typology used by Cohen (1971) and Whitman (1974), cross-classifying the uses of

3

the dollar by function and by sector.[1] It is shown in Figure 1 (page 16). Data are collated on three of these six uses — in the invoicing of trade, the denomination of deposits, loans and bonds, and the definition of parities. Before presenting them, however, I shall comment briefly on the other three.

1. The Dollar as Means of Payment in Foreign-Exchange Markets

If you were in London and wanted to buy Deutschemark with Swiss franc, you would have first to buy sterling with your francs, then buy marks with the sterling. In most major countries, the domestic currency is used as the vehicle for retail trading in foreign currencies, but the dollar is used as the vehicle for wholesale trading. If a British bank wants to buy marks with francs, it has first to buy dollars with its francs and then buy marks with its dollars. In 1979, some 90 to 99 percent of all wholesale trading took place through the dollar in the London, Zurich and Frankfurt markets.[2] Before starting new work on this subject to see if there has been a change, I discussed the situation with central bankers and foreign-exchange dealers. They said that the percentages are similar today. The dollar is still dominant in foreign-exchange trading.

As most foreign-exchange trading goes through the dollar, one should not be surprised to find that the dollar is the principal intervention currency for central banks and governments. This was true a few years ago, and those with whom I raised the subject recently said that it is true today.[3] There is only one large exception, along with a handful of small ones. The large one arises in connection with the exchange-rate arrangements of the European Monetary System.* When an EMS currency reaches the edge of the band set by those arrangements, the participating countries must intervene directly in EMS currencies. They may still use the dollar, however, for discretionary intra-marginal interventions, which they seem to do frequently. The small exceptions arise in less-developed countries. As there are no wholesale markets in many of those countries, the commercial banks that make the retail market can adjust their working balances only by dealing directly with the central bank, which must stand ready to buy and sell all of the major currencies in order to accomodate the commercial banks. These exceptions are not new, however, not in the EMS nor in the less-developed countries. They do not represent a significant change in the use of the dollar for official intervention.

In brief, informal questioning has led me to conclude that there have been no major changes in the role of the dollar as chief vehicle and

---

* All currencies of the European Economic Community except Great Britain and Greece.

intervention currency in the foreign-exchange markets, and I have not carried the matter farther.

2. The Dollar as Store of Value in the Reserve System

The use of the dollar for official intervention forges a strong link between its role in foreign-exchange markets and its role as an official reserve asset. When a government or central bank intervenes in the foreign-exchange market to keep its country's currency from appreciating, it adds to its foreign-currency reserves, and its new reserves will be dollar balances. Before August, 1971, governments and central banks could sell dollar balances for gold; the US Treasury stood ready (in principle) to sell gold at $35 per ounce. Today, they can buy gold only on the open market (and some of them bought it at the Treasury's gold auctions, held intermittently in 1975-79). But they do not have to keep the dollars they acquire when they intervene in the foreign-exchange markets; they can sell those dollars for other foreign currencies. This is what some of them started to do after the closing of the gold window.

Developing countries were the first to embark on diversification. According to IMF statistics, summarized in Table 1, the share of the dollar in their currency reserves rose from 1973 through 1976, with the "liquidation" of sterling as a reserve currency. (Its share in the currency reserves of developing countries fell from 13 percent early in 1973 to 3 percent at the end of 1976.) Thereafter, however, the share of the dollar fell quite sharply, going from almost 78 percent of currency reserves at the end of 1976 to a low of 58 percent at the end of 1980. There was a small increase in 1981, but the calculations in Table 2 suggest that it was due to the appreciation of the dollar, which reduced the dollar values of other currencies and thus raised the dollar's share in total currency reserves. (I will come back to this matter in another context.)

The developed countries started a bit later and have not gone as far. The share of the dollar in their currency reserves did not begin to fall until 1978, and the fall was not dramatic. The share peaked at 89 percent at the end of 1977 and stood at almost 79 percent four years later.[4] Some developed countries cannot diversify easily — Germany cannot hold Deutschemark, and Japan cannot hold yen. Furthermore, the EMS countries are not supposed to hold significant amounts of their partners' currencies. But the developed countries have probably gone farther than my numbers indicate. For reasons made clear by examples provided below diversification by developing countries can mask the extent of diversification by developed countries.

5

Let us look at the matter from the other side — at the shares of the new reserve currencies (the Deutschemark, Swiss franc, and yen) — in total currency reserves. Their share in the reserves of developing countries was 12 percent at the end of 1975 and rose to 23 percent at the end of 1981. Their share in the reserves of developed countries remained in the neighborhood of 5 percent through the end of 1977 but rose to 16 percent at the end of 1981.

There have thus been large differences from country to country in the timing and extent of diversification, reflecting differences in attitudes and circumstances. Quoting from the most recent annual report of the International Monetary Fund (IMF, 1982, pp. 65-66):

> Differences in the currency composition of foreign exchange reserves among country groups arise from a number of factors. Historical ties account for the higher shares of the French franc and the pound sterling in the holdings of some developing countries, and regional financial and trade agreements explain the much higher shares of "unspecified" currencies in the portfolios of these countries. For industrial countries, the elements that appear to bear on their reserve asset preferences are the nature of their exchange arrangements and policy objectives (particularly regarding the extent of foreign exchange market intervention), the distribution of their trade flows among the several key currency countries, the currency composition of government borrowing on foreign capital markets, and to some extent, profit and risk considerations. The authorities of many developing countries may be able to give more weight . . . to the ordinary portfolio selection criteria of profit maximization and risk minimization than is possible for the larger industrial countries, whose foreign exchange holdings are so large that the attempt to diversify holdings would tend to upset exchange markets. The currency composition of external payments is, of course, also an important factor affecting the denomination of foreign exchange holdings of these countries. More generally, it can be said that countries — industrial or developing — intervening in US dollars tend to hold, on average, a relatively high proportion of their reserves in that currency in order to reduce transactions costs, even if they peg their currency to a currency basket like the SDR.

A similar list of motives and concerns was given by central banks in answers to a questionnaire produced by the Group of Thirty (*How Central Banks Manage Their Reserves*, 1982, p. 10):

> Nearly all agree that the dollar's almost continuous decline and large exchange rate fluctuations from 1971 onward gave the original impetus to reserve diversification and more active reserve management.
> The replies suggest that, once started, the main factor contributing to diversification and more active reserve asset management was the desire of many countries to maintain the real value of their resources at a time of steeply rising liquidity or at least to increase the return on their assets. That became additionally important for commodity producers whose reserves increased substantially after the 1972/73 raw materials' boom and for oil exporters whose reserves rose sharply after the large increases in world oil prices. . . .

The desire to match foreign exchange liabilities and assets acquired growing importance on changing patterns of trade and even more so because of heavy balance of payments borrowing by many countries after 1973. Several banks also stated that foreign currency matching became important in guiding the direction and extent of diversification rather than originally motivating diversification.

Commercial bankers interviewed in connection with this study stressed the central banks' concerns with returns and risk but said that some of their clients have made mistakes. One respondent spoke of "wild and ill-informed trading" by some of his official clients, saying that they have lost money (*How Central Banks Manage Their Reserves*, 1982, p. 6).

There has been debate about the long-run implications of official diversification — the movement toward a multiple reserve-currency system. Some say that such a system is "inherently" unstable; others say that it will improve the adjustment process by imposing "discipline" on a large number of governments.[5] But it is hard to measure accurately the extent of diversification, let alone to forecast its long-run implications. I am increasingly skeptical about the quality of the published data summarized in Table 1 (page 17) and about the quantity of information they convey. They have serious defects, and they are hard to interpret.

There are two defects in the data. First, some central banks do not report their currency holdings to the IMF (the main source of published data). Second, some governments hold foreign currencies that are not included in their reserves. (Some of these holdings show up in the BIS data on official balances in the Eurocurrency markets. When BIS data on DM holdings in those markets are combined with Bundesbank data on DM holdings in Germany, total official holdings of DM turn out to be much larger than those published by the Fund.)

The problems of interpretation are even more worrisome. I can illustrate them by three examples involving two countries, Germany and Korea, that use the dollar when they intervene in foreign-exchange markets.

1. Both countries start out holding dollars. Germany holds $7 billion. Korea holds $2 billion. Korea decides to diversify and sell $1 billion for DM. Germany buys the dollars to keep its currency from appreciating. Korea winds up with 50 percent of its reserves in dollars, which was its intention, but the share of the dollar in global reserves falls by only 10 percentage points. German reserves rise to $8 billion, and so do German dollar holdings. Korean reserves stay at $2 billion, but Korean dollar holdings fall to $1 billion. Therefore, the share of the dollar in global reserves drops from 100 to 90 percent.[6]

2. The two countries start with the same quantities of dollars and DM that they held at the end of the first example, and the share of the dollar in global reserves is 90 percent. Let Germany run a $4 billion balance-of-

payments deficit (i.e., use $4 billion of dollar reserves to keep the DM from depreciating); let Korea run a $4 billion surplus (i.e., acquire $4 billion of dollar reserves to keep the won from appreciating). Suppose that Korea wants to hold half of its reserves in DM. It must sell $2 billion for DM, and Germany must buy them, as in the first example. German reserves and dollar holdings fall first from $8 to $4 billion, then rise to $6 billion. Korean reserves rise from $2 to $6 billion, and Korean dollar holdings rise in the end to $3 billion. The share of the dollar in global reserves falls from 90 to 75 percent.

3. The two countries start with the same quantities of dollars and DM that they held at the end of the second example. Both hold $6 billion of reserves, but Germany holds only dollars and Korea holds half of its reserves in DM. Let the DM appreciate in terms of the dollar by 50 percent, in response to market forces. If Korea does not sell DM for dollars, the share of the dollar falls. Nothing happens to German reserves, but the dollar value of Korean reserves increases to $7.5 billion on account of the 50 percent increase in the dollar value of its DM holdings. This reduces the share of the dollar in global reserves from 75 to 66⅔ percent.

The term "diversification" has been used to cover all of these events. In the first example, however, there is a clear shift away from the dollar and downward pressure on the dollar in the foreign-exchange market. The amount of diversification, moreover, is larger than the resulting reduction in the share of the dollar, because German reserves grow when Korea diversifies, and Germany cannot diversify its own reserves in this two-currency case. In the second example, there is no shift in asset preferences. The decline in the share of the dollar is due to a redistribution of reserves from a country having a high dollar share to one having a low dollar share. In the third example, there is again a shift away from the dollar, as Korea does not buy them to avoid a change in the composition of its currency reserves, but it does not involve official dollar sales in the foreign-exchange market.

We can be sure that there has been outright diversification of the sort illustrated by the first example — sales of dollars for other currencies. We cannot know how much there has been, however, without access to data on currency holdings by individual countries. We can likewise be sure that some of the changes in currency shares were due to changes in exchange rates; in 1981, for instance, total dollar holdings fell, but the appreciation of the dollar raised its share in total currency reserves (see Table 2, pages 18 and 19).

In their answers to the survey by the Group of Thirty, quoted earlier, central bankers said that diversification started when the dollar weakened on the foreign-exchange markets, but it was perpetuated by other motives, including the increase of uncertainty that they traced to the advent of floating exchange rates.[7] The work I have done on other uses of the dollar underscores the need to draw this distinction. Changes in the use of the dollar in international trade and in international financial markets are more readily explained by the increase of uncertainty resulting from the change in the exchange-rate regime than by fluctuations in actual exchange rates.

3. The Dollar as Unit of Account in International Trade

Research on the use of the dollar in international trade was begun by Grassman (1976).[8] He showed that the Swedish kronor is the currency most often used to invoice Swedish exports; the dollar came in second but was very far behind, and sterling was less important than the mark. His study, however, dealt with the just one year. It did not trace changes in the use of the dollar. Studies for other industrial countries must be used instead. They are summarized in Tables 3 and 4 (pages 20 and 21).

In all instances, the data confirm Grassman's finding. The exporter's own currency is more important than the dollar. In most instances, moreover, the exporter's currency became more important between 1972 and 1976, and the importance of the dollar fell. The story on the import side is striking, too. One would not expect the importer's currency to dominate the data; it should not be more important than the exporters' currencies in invoicing imports from the industrial countries, given the large roles of the exporters' currencies shown by the export data. Nevertheless, the importer's currency dominates the data in three of the six cases in Table 3, and the dollar dominates the importer's currency in only one such case.[9]

The decline in the role of the dollar that took place on the export side is frequently ascribed to the depreciation of the dollar that started in 1971. The data do not support this explanation. In all six cases covered by Table 3, the share of the dollar fell after the dollar began to depreciate. But look at the annual data in Table 4. In most cases shown there, the share of the dollar was slow to recover when the dollar appreciated, and the recovery was incomplete (the share of the dollar was lower in 1976 than in 1971 or 1972). More telling, there is just one case (Belgium) in which the share of the dollar dropped significantly in or after 1977, when the dollar started to depreciate again. In the German case, the share of the dollar rose after 1976, and the increase took place at the expense of the mark. The Danish, French and Dutch cases are similar.[10] It would therefore appear that the decline in the use of the dollar in international trade reflected the increase of uncertainty attending the change in the exchange-rate regime.

What can be said about the use of the dollar in invoicing trade with the United States and with third countries? In bilateral trade between Germany and the United States, Scharrer (1980) finds that the exporter's currency

9

dominates. Yet the share of the dollar in German exports to the United States is higher than its share in German exports to other countries (and much higher than in German exports to other industrial countries); see Table 5 (page 22). I have pieced data together from several sources to calculate the share of the dollar in several countries' exports. My calculations are displayed in Table 6 (page 23) and can be summarized this way:

Share of Dollar	Exports to	
in Exports of	United States	Other Countries
Belgium...	57	10
France..	45	8
Germany..	34	3
Italy..	46	27
Japan...	89	75
Netherlands	68	11
United Kingdom	52	12

The share of the dollar is fairly large in the invoicing of exports to the United States. With one exception (Japan), it is fairly small in the invoicing of exports to third countries.[11]

The dollar is still used extensively in the invoicing of exports by the less-developed countries. Figures for German imports from those countries are shown in Table 5. The share of the dollar in imports from Latin America is above 75 percent; its share in imports from Africa and Asia is above 50 percent; and its share in imports from Arab oil-exporting countries is about 95 percent, reflecting the use of the dollar in the oil market.[12] Page (1981) has tried to estimate the share of the dollar in the invoicing of world trade. She finds that it is used to invoice 55 percent, with 32 percentage points provided by third-country trade. Some two-thirds of third-country use is, in turn, contributed by exports from the less-developed countries, with oil trade accounting for a large part of that contribution.

4. The Dollar as Store of Value in International Financial Markets

I turn next to the role of the dollar as store of value in the Eurocurrency and Eurobond markets. I am not concerned here with the share of the dollar in optimal or actual portfolios. Eurocurrency statistics cannot say much about those shares, because big pieces are omitted from each data set.[13] They cannot say much about the banks' portfolios and can say even less about their customers' portfolios. There are additional problems, including two illustrated earlier in this paper. Many banks participate in the Euromarkets; and it would be foolish to suppose that they are identical in needs or preferences. Therefore, the share of the dollar in bank claims can be affected by the distribution of those claims — by the relative size and number of participants having a strong preference for dollar claims. It is also affected by exchange rates. My work has focused on that issue.

The basic Eurocurrency statistics are displayed in Tables 7 and 8. (Pages 24 and 25.) They appear to show a significant decline in the importance of the dollar.[14] Its share in total Eurocurrency claims fell from 77 percent in 1970 to a low of 67 percent in 1978 and stood at 71 percent at the end of 1981. Its share in claims on nonbanks traced a similar path.[15] These figures, however, measure nondollar claims in dollar equivalents and are therefore affected by the large exchange-rate change that took place in the 1970s.

There are several ways to deal with this problem, including the one illustrated in Table 2, which is concerned with foreign-currency reserves. I have used two methods here. Both start by converting nondollar data back into national currency units. The first method reconverts them into dollar equivalents using constant exchange rates and computes percentages analogous to those in Table 8. The second method keeps them in national currency units and calculates the rate of growth in the use of each currency. Both methods were used to study the use of the dollar in the Eurocurrency market; the results are shown in Tables 9 and 10. (Pages 26 and 27.) The second method was used to study the use of the dollar in the Eurobond market; the results are shown in Tables 11 and 12.[16] (Pages 28 and 29.)

Shares of the dollar in Eurocurrency claims appear again in Table 9. The numbers in the first column of this table resemble those in the first column of Table 8; they show the share of the dollar measured at current exchange rates. (They differ from the numbers in Table 8 because they omit nondollar claims in currencies other than the Deutschemark, Swiss franc, pound sterling and French franc, for want of adequate information about those claims.) The numbers in the second column of Table 9 are the shares of the dollar calculated at constant (1975) exchange rates. As nondollar currencies were worth more at 1975 rates than they were at 1970 rates, the share of the dollar begins at a lower level in the second column. Furthermore, it falls in 1971, after the first devaluation of the dollar. It rises in 1972, however, is higher in 1973 than it was to start, and it continues to rise thereafter. On this calculation, the dollar became increasingly important.

The second method gives a similar result. Here are the average rates of growth in Eurocurrency claims measured in national currency units:

US dollar 23.1
Deutschemark... 20.0

11

Swiss franc	15.6
Pound sterling	39.7
French franc	21.6

There has been no significant decline in the use of the dollar to denominate bank claims. The rate of growth in the quantity of dollar claims was larger than the rates of growth in Deutschemark, Swiss franc and French franc claims. Furthermore, the growth rate of dollar claims was much more stable; its variance was smaller than those of other growth rates. In brief, the apparent decline in the use of the dollar shown by Table 8 was due to valuation changes, not a shift to the use of other currencies.[17]

Turning to new issues in the Eurobond market, the shares of dollar issues in total issues measured at current and constant exchange rates are shown in Table 12. Let us look at the series that exclude bonds issued by US borrowers but include those issued by international institutions.

When measured at current exchange rates, the share of dollar issues was lower in the last three years before the sharp recovery of the dollar (1977-79), than it was in the first three years of dollar weakness (1971-73); it averaged 60.3 percent in the former period and 66.8 percent in the latter. When measured at constant exchange rates, the share is lower at the start of the period, falls in years when the dollar weakened sharply (1971, 1977, and 1978), but was higher in 1977-79 than it was in 1971-73, averaging 64.7 percent and 61.4 percent respectively. The use of the dollar is sensitive to exchange-rate fluctuations, but it has not diminished over time.

Standing back from the details, it would seem right to draw these general conclusions:

1. The role of the dollar in international financial markets has not fallen sharply in recent years. There is thus no urgent need to defend it, even if that role is deemed to be important to the interests of the United States. There has been some significant movement toward a multiple-currency monetary system and, more narrowly, a multiple-currency reserve system, but that tendency has not cut deeply into the use of the dollar as a store of value in international financial markets.

2. It is clear, nonetheless, that periods in which the dollar was weak saw temporary cutbacks in its use, especially in the Eurobond market. These in turn probably intensified its weakness, as well as interfered with the smooth functioning of the markets themselves. Greater exchange-rate stability could therefore contribute to the long-term usefulness of the dollar as an international currency.

5. The Dollar as Unit of Account in Setting Parities

Finally, I have studied the use of the dollar as a unit of account in the official sector of the monetary system — its use in setting parities for national currencies — by examining the exchange-rate regimes of less-developed countries. The results are summarized in Table 13. (Page 30.)

There has been a sharp decline in the use of the dollar as the unit of account for pegging exchange rates. In 1974, 61 of 98 countries covered by my survey pegged their currencies to the dollar, and their imports accounted for 72 percent of the total imports of the 98 countries. During the next seven years, 33 comparatively large countries "defected" from this group. Nine countries joined the group, but they were comparatively small. By 1981, then, only 37 countries pegged their currencies to the dollar, with their imports accounting for just 20 percent of the total imports of the 115 countries covered by my survey.

It should be noted, however, that none of the "defectors" adopted another national currency for pegging (and that there were defectors from other currencies, too). Most of the defectors adopted basket pegs, indicators and other exchange-rate regimes (including some that let their currencies float). The change in the role of the dollar as a unit of account was a by-product of the move to more flexible exchange rates on the part of less-developed countries — a move mirroring the one by developed countries.

The decline in this use of the dollar looks to be larger than the decline in any other use. But it is not especially important for the functioning of the system or for the role of the dollar in the system. The interesting issue comes up tangentially. The exchange-rate practices of less-developed countries are more important than their exchange-rate regimes in determining effective exchange rates for them and for their trading partners. It would therefore be useful to examine their policies, especially those of the NICs, from this standpoint. The effective exchange rate for the dollar may be influenced more heavily by countries that peg to the dollar but change their pegs frequently than by those that peg to baskets but give large weights to the dollar or by those that do not peg at all but manage their currencies in ways that keep their dollar rates quite stable.

NOTES

[1] Different typologies are used by Krugman (1980) and Magee and Rao (1980) in their work on "vehicle currencies" in international trade. Their papers, however, blur the important distinction between the use of a currency in foreign-exchange trading and its use in the conduct of merchandise trade. Economies of scale can be achieved by using a single currency as vehicle for foreign-exchange trading. The number of price quotations can be minimized; the frequency of trading can be maximized; and risk management is simplified. Therefore, as noted below, the dollar continues to serve as the main vehicle currency in foreign-exchange markets. But the same economies are not necessarily realized by using a single currency in merchandise trade — not as a unit of account nor as a means of payment.

[2] The figure for Paris was 60 percent, down from 70 percent in 1970. These data come from

central banks and were published in, *Foreign Exchange Markets Under Floating Rates*, Group of Thirty (1980), p. 15.

[3] See also, *How Central Banks Manage Their Reserves*, Group of Thirty (1982), which summarizes central-bank replies to a questionnaire and says that the dollar is the "only intervention currency for all practical purposes " (p. 4).

[4] These figures and the ones in Table 1 minimize the apparent decline in the share of the dollar because they include, in dollar holdings and in total currency reserves, the dollar equivalents of the European Currency Units (ECU) issued against dollars in the EMS. When one goes to the opposite extreme, treating *all* ECU as currency reserves, even those issued against gold, the share of the dollar declines more dramatically; it goes from 89 percent of currency reserves at the end of 1977 (when there were no ECU) to a low of 54 percent at the end of 1980, then rises to 56 percent at the end of 1981. (These and additional figures are given in the notes to Table 1.)

[5] For more on these arguments, see Kenen (1981a).

[6] By adding another country to this example, one can illustrate a point made in the text, that diversification by developing countries can mask the extent of diversification by developed countries. Start as before, with German reserves at $7 billion, Korean reserves at $2 billion, and all reserves in dollars. Suppose that Sweden starts with $5 billion of reserves, which are also invested in dollars. Let Sweden switch $2 billion into DM (with Germany buying the dollars). If this were the only instance of diversification, the share of the dollar in global reserves would fall to 7/8 or 87.5 percent, and its share in the reserves of developed countries (Germany plus Sweden) would fall to 6/7 or 85.7 percent. Now let Korea diversify too, switching $1 billion into DM (with Germany buying the dollars again). The share of the dollar in global reserves would fall to 14/17 or 82.4 percent, but its share in the reserves of developed countries would go back up to 13/15 or 86.7 percent.

[7] One central banker pointed out that periods of dollar strength could induce additional diversification, instead of discouraging it, because central banks could move out of the dollar "with more ease and less embarrassment to the United States" (*How Central Banks Manage Their Reserves*, Group of Thirty, 1982, p. 11).

[8] Page (1981) cites earlier work at the IMF and gives a good survey of the literature; see also Page (1977).

[9] In one of the remaining cases (Denmark), the importer's currency was a bit more important in 1976; in the other (the Netherlands), the dollar overtook the importer's currency in 1979. Note that the share of the dollar rises on the import side from 1972 to 1976 (and goes on rising in two cases). This is probably due to the influence of the increase in the price of oil, as oil is typically traded against dollars.

[10] The Japanese data tell a different story. The share of the dollar in Japanese exports fell sharply in 1975-1980, but it was unusually high initially; see Kenen (1981b), Table 4.

[11] My figures for exports to the United States come from a study by Makin cited in Magee and Rao (1980). The one for Germany is higher than Scharrer's figure shown in Table 5, and those for Belgium and France are lower than the ones in Page (1981). My figures for exports to third countries are deduced from other numbers but may not be far off. Here are the shares of the dollar in Belgian and French exports reported in Page (1981):

Destination	Belgium	France
Denmark	4	7
Germany	2	3
Italy	6	4
Japan	49	14
Netherlands	3	6
Norway	3	5
Sweden	5	12
United Kingdom	22	6

Most of these numbers are smaller than my own, but they pertain to trade with industrial countries. The share of the dollar is higher in exports to the less-developed countries. Data for Germany are shown in Table 5, and Page (1981) gives these numbers for Britain:

    Exports to non-oil countries 11

    Exports to oil-exporting countries 4

[12] Page (1981) reports these figures for British imports:

    Imports from non-oil countries 37

    Imports from oil-exporting countries 86

[13] The claims of the Eurobanks, for example, omit foreign-currency claims on residents and all claims denominated in domestic currency. Furthermore, they omit the claims of home and branch offices domiciled outside the BIS reporting area. Thus, they include the dollar claims of US banks in London but omit their sterling claims, and they exclude the claims of the banks' head offices in the United States. For additional examples, see Kenen (1982a).

[14] I concentrate here on the banks' claims; their liabilities tell the same sort of story. See Kenen (1982a), Table 2.

[15] The share of the dollar tends to be higher in claims on banks than on nonbanks, and it is especially high in claims reported by British banks (see Kenen, 1982a, Table 7). I was thus led to look at the interbank market for an explanation of both phenomena. I was wrong. The dollar *is* used heavily in the interbank market, accounting for some 75 percent of total interbank liabilities at the end of 1980. But much of the interbank market, strictly defined, is excluded from the BIS data used in this paper; claims of banks on other banks in London are treated as claims on residents, not on foreigners.

[16] The first procedure cannot be used too well in work on the Eurobond market because year-to-year fluctuations in issues are very large.

[17] There is, of course, a danger in using quantities to measure changes in currency use. Suppose that governments issue huge quantities of dollar debt. (The US government can do so to finance a budget deficit. Other governments can do so, too. In fact, Eurocurrency claims on nonbanks include large quantities of dollar debt issued by the governments of less-developed countries.) The role of the dollar measured by the quantity of dollar debt has to rise somewhere in the system — someone has to hold it. But the dollar may depreciate in the process. On this view, the use of the dollar reflects the quantity of dollar debt issued and should not be measured at constant exchange rates. I cannot rule out this interpretation, but I have doubts about its relevance. It would hold strictly in respect of "outside" debt. Eurocurrency claims should probably be treated as "inside" debt, even though much of it is issued by governments. The decision to denominate that debt in dollars is not taken independently by the debtor; it is taken jointly by debtor and creditor. (We know very little about the process, however, and someone should probably look at it carefully.)

15

Figure 1.
The Uses of the Dollar as an International Currency

Function	Sector Private	Official
Unit of Account	Currency used in invoicing merchandise trade	Currency used in defining parities
Means of Payment	Vehicle currency in foreign-exchange markets	Intervention currency in foreign-exchange markets
Store of Value	Currency in which deposits, loans, and bonds are denominated	Currency in which reserves are held

16

Table 1

Shares of National Currencies in Identified Official Holdings of
Foreign Exchange

(Ends of Years 1975 through 1981)

Country Group and Currency	1975	1976	1977	1978	1979 [a]	1980 [a]	1981[a]
All Countries							
US dollar	79.4	79.6	79.4	76.9	73.8	68.3	70.6
Pound sterling	3.9	2.0	1.6	1.5	1.9	2.9	2.3
Deutschemark	6.3	7.0	8.3	9.9	11.5	13.9	12.5
Swiss franc	1.6	1.4	2.0	1.4	2.3	3.1	2.8
Japanese yen	0.5	0.7	1.2	2.5	2.9	3.8	4.1
Other currencies[1]	1.8	1.4	1.4	1.4	1.7	2.2	2.1
Unspecified	6.5	7.9	6.2	6.3	5.9	5.8	5.6
Industrial Countries							
US dollar	87.3	86.9	89.0	86.2	83.5	77.9	78.9
Pound sterling	1.1	0.7	0.5	0.5	0.6	0.6	0.6
Deutschemark	4.0	3.8	4.0	6.6	7.5	12.4	11.3
Swiss franc	0.9	0.9	0.7	0.4	1.3	1.5	1.5
Japanese yen	0.2	0.4	0.3	1.6	2.0	2.8	3.1
Other currencies[1]	0.4	0.5	0.2	0.3	0.4	0.5	0.7
Unspecified	6.2	7.0	5.1	4.4	4.5	4.2	3.9
Developing Countries							
US dollar	70.8	72.7	68.6	62.6	62.6	58.1	61.7
Pound sterling	6.8	3.2	2.8	3.0	3.4	5.3	4.1
Deutschemark	8.8	10.1	12.9	15.0	16.1	15.4	13.8
Swiss franc	2.3	1.9	3.4	2.9	3.3	4.8	4.3
Japanese yen	0.9	1.1	2.2	4.0	4.0	4.9	5.2
Other currencies[1]	3.3	2.4	2.7	3.1	3.0	3.9	3.6
Unspecified	7.1	8.6	7.4	9.3	7.5	7.6	7.3

Source: IMF (1982), Table 18.
[1] French franc and Dutch guilder.
[a] The dollar and total currency reserves of all countries include the dollar equivalents of the European Currency Units (ECU) issues against dollars; the ECU issued against gold are excluded entirely. When *all* ECU are treated as currency reserves, the figures for the industrial countries look this way:

Asset	1979	1980	1981
US dollar	62.2	54.3	55.9
ECU	24.0	29.0	26.9
All other and unspecified	13.8	16.7	17.1

Table 2

Quantity and Price Changes Affecting the Share of the Dollar in Total Official Holdings of Foreign Exchange, 1977-1981

(in Billions of SDR)

Item	1977	1978	1979	1980	1981
Total of Identified Currency Reserves					
Value at end of previous year	139.5	177.7	197.5	222.7	266.3
Increase in quantity	42.6	28.2	21.0	23.6	– 10.5
Value at end of current year					
before price change	182.1	205.9	218.5	246.4	255.8
Effect of price change	– 4.4	– 8.4	4.2[a]	20.0[a]	9.8[a]
Value at end of current year	177.7	197.5	222.7	266.3	265.6
US dollar					
Value at end of previous year	120.6	150.4	162.1	147.0	156.2
Increase in quantity	36.3	22.3	– 13.7[b]	4.2	– 8.7
Value at end of current year					
before price change	156.9	172.7	148.4	151.2	147.4
Effect of price change	– 6.5	– 10.6	– 1.4	5.0	15.0
Value at end of current year	150.4	162.1	147.0	156.2	162.4

Table 3

Quantity and Price Changes Affecting the Share of the Dollar in Total Official Holdings of Foreign Exchange, 1977-1981

(in Billions of SDR)

Share of US Dollar in Total of Identified Currency Reserves					
End of previous year	86.4	84.6	82.1	66.0	58.6
End of current year					
Before effect of price change	86.1	83.9	67.9	59.7	57.6
After effect of price change	84.6	82.1	66.0	58.6	61.1
Memorandum: Share of US dollar in all currency reserves at end of current year	79.4	76.9	62.4	55.9	58.4

Source: IMF (1982), Table 17, and own calculations. Data are not comparable to those in Table 1, because they include all ECU as currency reserves and exclude reserves in "unspecified" currencies; the share of the dollar in all currency reserves, including all ECU and reserves in "unspecified" currencies, are shown in the memorandum. The Fund calculates quantity changes quarterly; the quarterly change in each currency component is multiplied by the average of the SDR prices of the currency at the beginning and end of each quarter. As the annual changes are the sums of the quarterly changes, they are not free of price effects; they include the effects of changes from quarter to quarter in the averages of SDR prices used to obtain the quarterly changes in quantity. Nevertheless the crude division between quantity and price effects shows that there was some diversification away from the dollar in 1977-80 (that the decrease in the share of the dollar was not due totally to price effects) and that the process did not end in 1980 (that the increase in the share of the dollar in 1981 *was* due totally to price effects).

[a] Includes effect of change in SDR equivalent of gold price used in EMS to value the ECU issued against gold.

[b] Mainly due to transfer of dollars from national reserves to the European Monetary Cooperation Fund in connection with the issue of ECU.

Table 3

Currency Distributions of Exports and Imports, *Selected Years*

Country and Year	Exports			Imports		
	Exporter's Currency	US Dollar	All Other	Importer's Currency	US Dollar	All Other
Belgium:						
1972	47.3	11.9	40.8	29.9	18.3	51.8
1976	47.8	12.0	40.2	26.5	25.1	48.4
1979	44.2	12.5	43.3	28.4	23.4	48.2
Denmark:						
1972	46.0	16.0	37.0	21.0	21.0	58.0
1976	54.0	14.0	32.0	25.0	23.0	52.0
1979	51.0	16.0	33.0	27.0	27.0	46.0
France:						
1972	59.4	10.3	30.3	31.5	15.6	52.9
1976	68.3	9.4	22.3	31.5	29.1	39.4
1979	62.4	11.6	26.0	35.8	28.7	35.5
Germany:						
1972	84.1	6.5	9.4	49.9[a]	18.6[a]	31.5[a]
1976	86.9	5.0	8.1	42.0[a]	31.3[a]	26.7[a]
1979	82.6	7.2	10.2	43.7[a]	30.5[a]	25.8[a]
Italy:						
1972	50.7[a,b]	28.3[a,b]	21.0[a,b]	22.5[a,b]	32.1[a]	45.4[a]
1976	39.1[a]	27.9[a]	33.0[a]	16.0[a]	42.5[a]	41.5[a]
1979	na	na	na	na	na	na
Netherlands:						
1972	44.2	13.2	42.6	24.3	17.7	58.0
1976	50.2	13.0	36.8	31.4	22.7	45.9
1979	42.9	19.0	38.1	29.1	31.5	39.4

Sources: Data for all countries except Italy from Page (1981) and additional tables supplied by Ms. Page. Data for Italy from Scharrer (1980).

[a] Based on payments data.

[b] 1971.

Table 4
Currency Distributions of Exports, 1971-1980

Country and Currency	1971	1972	1973	1974	1975	1976	1977	1978	1979	1980[a]
Belgium:										
Exporter's currency	46.2	47.3	49.9	53.0	50.9	47.8	45.8	44.4	44.2	40.4
US dollar	14.5	11.9	9.7	8.2	10.0	12.0	14.6	12.6	12.5	13.8
Other currencies	39.3	40.8	40.4	39.7	39.1	30.2	39.6	43.0	43.3	45.8
Denmark:										
Exporter's currency	41.0	47.0	52.0	54.0	54.0	54.0	53.0	53.0	51.0	47.0
US dollar	22.0	16.0	15.0	14.0	13.0	14.0	16.0	16.0	16.0	14.0
Other currencies	37.0	37.0	33.0	32.0	33.0	32.0	31.0	31.0	33.0	39.0
France:										
Exporter's currency	na	59.4	66.4	68.3	69.1	68.3	65.4	64.1	62.4	na
US dollar	na	10.3	8.7	8.8	8.2	9.4	10.9	11.2	11.6	na
Other currencies	na	30.3	24.9	22.9	22.7	22.3	23.7	24.7	26.0	na
Germany:										
Exporter's currency	na	84.1	85.5	88.3	89.2	86.9	86.0	83.6	82.6	82.3
US dollar	na	6.5	5.3	3.8	4.4	5.0	6.2	7.4	7.2	7.2
Other curriencies	na	9.4	9.2	7.9	6.4	8.1	7.8	9.0	10.2	10.5
Netherlands:										
Exporter's currency	44.4	44.2	45.3	46.3	50.0	50.2	48.6	49.4	42.9	43.5
US dollar	16.7	13.2	10.1	13.2	15.0	13.0	15.8	11.9	19.0	16.5
Other currencies	38.9	42.6	44.6	40.5	35.0	36.8	35.6	38.7	38.1	40.0

Source: See Table 3.

[a] For Germany, first three calendar quarters; for other countries, first half year.

21

Table 5

Distributions of German Trade by Currency and Partner, 1979

Partner	Deutschemark	US dollar	All Other
German Exports:			
EC countries	81.0	2.4	16.6
Other Western Europe	86.4	3.6	10.0
Eastern Europe	82.4	16.4	1.2
United States	75.6	24.3	0.1
Canada	42.9	4.9	52.2
Japan	80.7	2.8	16.5
Australia, etc.	89.7	7.0	3.3
Africa	93.8	5.2	1.0
Latin America	83.8	16.2	—
Asia	87.9	9.3	2.8
Memorandum:			
Arab oil producers	92.3	6.0	1.7
German Imports:			
EC countries	53.5	13.8	32.7
Other Western Europe	54.0	23.4	22.6
Eastern Europe	90.4	8.7	0.9
United States	11.3	73.9	14.8
Canada	9.4	63.8	26.8
Japan	45.3	13.4	41.3
Australia, etc.	33.5	43.7	22.8
Africa	26.6	55.7	17.7
Latin America	18.4	77.9	3.7
Asia	29.4	51.5	19.1
Memorandum:			
Arab oil producers	3.9	95.6	0.5

Source: Scharrer (1980); data for first half of calendar year.

22

Table 6
The Role of the Dollar in the Export Trade of Major Industrial Countries, 1976

Item	Belgium	France	Germany	Italy	Japan	Netherlands	United Kingdom
1. Percentage of total exports invoiced in dollars	12.0	9.4	5.0	27.9[a]	78.5[b]	13.0	15.5[c]
2. Percentage of exports to United States invoiced in dollars	57.0	45.0	34.0	46.0	89.0	68.0	52.0
3. Exports to United States as percentage of total exports	3.6	4.6	5.6	6.5	23.6	2.9	9.4
4. Exports to other countries as percentage of total exports	96.4	95.4	94.4	93.5	76.4	97.1	90.6
5. Computed percentages of total exports invoiced in dollars							
a. Exports to United States	2.1	2.1	1.9	3.0	21.0	2.0	4.9
b. Exporters to other countries	9.9	7.3	3.1	24.9	57.5	11.0	10. 6
6. Computed percentage of exports to other countries invoiced in dollars	10.3	7.6	3.3	26.6	75.3	11.3	11.7

Sources: Data on line (1) from sources for Table 3 and from Kenen (1981b), Table 4. Data on line (2) from unpublished study by Makin reproduced in Magee and Rao (1980); pertain to 1975. Data on line (3) from Scharrer (1980). Data on line (4) are the complements to the entries on line (3). Data on line (5a) are the products of the entries on lines (2) and (3). Data on line (5b) are the differences between the entries on lines (1) and (5a). Data on line (6) are the entries on line (5b) divided by the entries on line (4).

[a] Based on payments data.
[b] Based on letters of credit; data for 1975.
[c] Unweighted average of data for first and second halves of 1976.

Table 7

Foreign Currency Claims on Nonresidents Reported by European Banks

(Billions of US dollars at End of Year)

Year	Total			On Nonbanks		
	Total	Dollars	Other	Total	Dollars	Other
1970	78.3	60.4	17.9	16.6	11.9	4.7
1971	100.1	71.5	28.6	21.2	14.4	6.8
1972	131.8	98.0	33.8	26.3	18.3	8.0
1973	187.6	132.1	55.5	38.7	24.7	14.0
1974	215.2	156.2	58.9	53.1	35.0	18.1
1975	258.2	190.2	68.0	61.4	40.9	20.5
1976	305.3	224.0	81.3	73.5	50.8	22.7
1977	384.8	268.4	116.4	97.2	65.6	31.7
1978	502.0	339.5	162.5	127.2	84.3	43.0
1979	639.8	428.0	211.8	156.5	104.3	52.1
1980	751.2	518.7	232.5	193.5	131.6	61.9
1981	839.0	592.5	246.5	230.9	159.7	71.2

Source: BIS (various years). When two figures are given for a single year, the later (revised) one is used here. When calculating changes, however, the earlier (initial) figure is used to obtain the change from the previous year, and the later (revised) figure is used to obtain the next change. Significant changes in coverage occur in 1973, 1974, and 1977.

Detail may not add to total because of rounding.

Table 8

Foreign Currency Claims on Nonresidents Reported by
European Banks

(Dollar Claims as Percentages of Totals at End of Year)

Year	Total	On Nonbanks
1970	77.1	71.7
1971	71.4	67.9
1972	74.3	69.6
1973	70.4	63.8
1974	72.6	65.9
1975	73.7	66.6
1976	73.4	69.1
1977	69.7	67.5
1978	67.6	66.3
1979	66.9	66.6
1980	69.0	68.0
1981	70.6	69.2

Source: Table 7.

Table 9

Foreign Currency Claims on Nonresidents Reported by European Banks
*(Dollar Claims as Percentages of Totals at End of Year Measured at
Current and Constant Exchange Rates)*

Year	Current Exchange Rate	Constant Exchange Rate
1970	75.3	67.4
1971	69.8	63.4
1972	72.4	67.0
1973	72.0	69.4
1974	74.7	75.0
1975	75.5	74.6
1976	75.8	76.2
1977	72.3	75.2
1978	71.1	76.7
1979	70.2	76.7
1980	72.5	76.8
1981	75.4	78.0

Source: The data on which this table is based come from the same source as those in Table 7. The dollar shares at current exchange rates are similar to those in Table 8 but omit from nondollar claims those in currencies other than the Deutschemark, Swiss franc, pound sterling, and French franc. The dollar shares at constant exchange rates are obtained by converting the dollar equivalents of nondollar claims into their own units, using end-of-year exchange rates from *International Financial Statistics*, then converting back into dollar equivalents at the average-in-year exchange rate for 1975. Data relate to total claims, not to those on nonbanks alone (for which there are no published data for currencies other than the dollar).

Table 10

Foreign Currency Claims on Nonresidents Reported by European Banks

(Percentage Rates of Change in Selected Assets Measured in National Currency Units)

Year	US dollars	Deutsche- mark	Swiss francs	Pounds sterling	French francs
1971	18.4	43.7	46.1	149.0	15.9
1972	37.1	23.2	−8.3	46.3	40.1
1973	36.5	30.0	61.1	46.0	−77.0
1974	17.1	−1.7	−25.2	−34.5	−20.6
1975	21.7	29.6	10.4	13.8	75.2
1976	17.8	5.4	8.7	29.0	10.8
1977	17.1	23.6	2.7	83.9	20.5
1978	26.5	20.3	−4.4	28.8	51.9
1979	26.0	21.0	35.2	39.4	32.9
1980	21.2	11.8	43.0	8.6	65.9
1981	14.4	12.6	23.4	26.4	na
Average[a]	23.1	20.0	17.4	39.7	21.6
Average[b]	23.1	19.9	15.6	34.9	9.0

Source: The data on which this table is based come from the same source as those in Table 7, but the figures for currencies other than the dollar have been converted from dollar equivalents into their own units. Thus, the percentage changes in Deutschemark claims shown in the second column are the changes in the *number* of Deutschemark represented by those claims, not in the dollar equivalents. Conversions were made using end-of-year exchange rates in *International Financial Statistics*. Data relate to total claims, not to those on nonbanks alone (for which there are no published data for currencies other than the dollar).

[a] Simple average of annual changes.

[b] Compound rates of change (inclusive of changes due to changes in coverage of BIS data).

27

Table 11

Eurobond Issues

(Billions of US Dollars)

Issuer and Currency	1970	1971	1972	1973	1974	1975	1976	1977	1978	1979	1980	1981
All Issuers:												
US dollars	1.96	2.24	4.31	2.89	3.08	4.92	10.00	12.34	7.69	10.21	13.30	21.25
Deutschemark	0.60	0.86	1.23	1.00	0.64	2.89	2.82	5.22	6.53	4.77	3.46	1.38
Other	0.43	0.66	1.39	0.71	0.80	2.50	2.55	1.92	1.72	2.37	3.29	3.86
US Issuers:												
US dollars	0.63	1.00	1.77	0.71	0.10	0.22	0.40	1.19	0.97	2.78	3.96	5.70
Deutschemark	0.05	0.09	0.09	0.05	—	—	—	0.01	0.23	0.06	0.12	0.03
Other[a]	0.09	0.02	0.17	0.06	0.01	0.09	—	0.10	0.09	0.03	0.31	0.12
International Institutions:												
US dollars	0.06	0.07	0.68	0.65	1.83	1.06	2.25	1.98	1.81	0.70	1.36	1.70
Deutschemark	—	—	0.01	0.02	0.16	0.34	0.67	0.24	0.82	1.09	—	0.04
Other[a]	0.08	0.06	0.20	0.22	0.08	0.08	0.17	0.26	0.24	0.25	0.35	0.75
Dollar Issues as Percentages of Total Issues												
All Issuers	65.5	59.6	62.2	62.8	68.1	47.2	65.1	63.3	48.2	58.8	66.3	80.2
All Except US	59.9	46.8	51.8	57.7	67.6	46.4	64.1	61.3	45.9	51.3	59.6	80.7
All Except US & International	61.3	46.4	46.4	52.9	49.1	42.0	61.9	58.4	41.7	54.1	57.2	76.3

Source: BIS (various issues).

[a] Calculated as residual.

Table 12

Eurobond Issues in Dollars and Deutschemark at Current and Constant Exchange Rates

(Billions of US Dollars)

Issuer and Currency	1970	1971	1972	1973	1974	1975	1976	1977	1978	1979	1980	1981
All Issuers Except US												
US dollars	1.34	1.24	2.54	2.18	2.98	4.61	9.60	11.15	6.72	7.43	9.34	15.55
Deutschemark	0.55	0.77	1.14	0.95	0.64	2.89	2.82	5.21	6.30	4.71	3.34	1.35
Deutschemark at constant exchange rate	0.81	1.09	1.48	1.03	0.67	2.89	2.89	4.92	5.14	3.51	2.47	1.24
All Issuers Except US & International												
US dollars	1.28	1.17	1.86	1.53	1.15	3.53	7.35	9.17	4.91	6.73	7.98	13.85
Deutschemark	0.55	0.77	1.13	0.93	0.48	2.55	2.15	4.97	5.48	3.62	3.34	1.31
Deutschemark at constant exchange rate	0.81	1.09	1.46	1.01	0.51	2.55	2.20	4.69	4.47	2.70	2.47	1.20
Dollar Shares												
All Except US												
Current rates	71.1	61.7	69.0	69.6	82.3	61.5	77.3	68.1	51.6	61.2	73.7	92.0
Constant rates	62.3	53.2	63.2	67.9	81.4	61.5	76.9	69.4	56.7	67.9	79.1	92.6
All Except US & International												
Current rates	70.0	60.3	62.2	63.0	70.5	58.1	77.4	64.8	47.3	65.0	68.9	91.4
Constant rates	61.2	51.8	56.0	60.2	69.3	58.1	77.0	66.2	52.3	71.4	74.6	92.0

Source: Basic data from Table 11; Deutschemark issues at constant exchange rate are dollar equivalents converted into Deutschemark at average exchange rates for the then-current years and converted back into dollars at the average exchange rate for 1975; exchange rates from *International Financial Statistics*.

Table 13

Exchange-Rate Regimes of Developing Countries, Distributions in
1974 and 1981

(percentages of total)

Exchange-Rate Regime	1974	1981
By Number of Countries:		
Dollar peggers	62.2	32.2
Sterling peggers	9.2	0.9
French franc peggers	13.3	12.2
Other currency peggers	1.0	2.6
SDR peggers	—	12.1
Own basket peggers	—	15.6
Using indicators	—	2.6
Having other exchange-rate regimes	14.3	21.7
By Value of 1978 Imports:		
Dollar peggers	72.3	20.0
Sterling peggers	5.4	*
French franc peggers	2.6	2.5
Other currency peggers	*	*
SDR peggers	—	7.8
Own basket peggers	—	20.4
Using indicators	—	7.5
Having other exchange-rate regimes	19.6	41.7

Source: Kenen (1982b), Table 3.

Detail may not add to total because of rounding.

* Less than 0.1 percent.

30

REFERENCES

Bank for International Settlements, *Annual Report*, Basle, various issues.

Cohen, Benjamin J., *The Future of Sterling as an International Currency*, New York: St. Martin's 1971.

Grassman, Sven, "Currency Distribution and Forward Cover in Foreign Trade," *Journal of International Economics*, May 1976, 6, 215-221.

Group of Thirty, *Foreign Exchange Markets under Floating Rates*, New York, 1980.

Group of Thirty, *How Central Banks Manage Their Reserves*, New York, 1982.

International Monetary Fund, *Annual Report 1982*, Washington, 1982.

Kenen, Peter B., (1981a) "The Analytics of a Substitution Account," Banca Nazionale del Lavoro, *Quarterly Review*, December 1981, 139, 403-426.

Kenen, Peter B., (1981b) "The Role of the US Dollar as Unit of Account and Means of Payment in International Trade," International Finance Section Research Memorandum, Princeton University, 1981.

Kenen, Peter B., (1982a) "The Role of the US Dollar as Store of Value in International Financial Markets," International Finance Section Research Memorandum, Princeton University, 1982.

Kenen, Peter B., (1982b) "The Use of the US Dollar in Pegging Exchange Rates," International Finance Section Research Memorandum, Princeton University, 1982.

Krugman, Paul, "Vehicle Currencies and the Structure of International Exchange," *Journal of Money, Credit, and Banking*, August 1980, 13, 513-526.

Magee, Stephen P., and Ramesh K.S. Rao, "Vehicle and Nonvehicle Currencies in International Trade," *American Economic Review*, May 1980, 70, 368-373.

Page, S.A.B., "Currency Invoicing in Merchandise Trade," *National Institute Economic Review*, August 1977, 77-81.

Page, S.A.B., "The Choice of Invoicing Currency in Merchandise Trade," *National Institute Economic Review*, November 1981, 60-72.

Scharrer, Hans-Eckart, "Currencies and Currency Hedging in German Foreign Trade," *Studies on Economic and Monetary Problems and on Banking History*, 18, Deutsche Bank, 1980.

Whitman, Marina v.N., "The Current and Future Role of the Dollar: How Much Symmetry?," *Brookings Papers on Economic Activity*, 1974, 555-570.

[14]

NOTES

MEASURING AND ANALYZING THE EFFECTS OF SHORT-TERM VOLATILITY IN REAL EXCHANGE RATES

Peter B. Kenen and Dani Rodrik*

Abstract—This paper examines short-term volatility in the real effective exchange rates of industrial countries and its impact on their imports. It yields three conclusions. First, volatility has not diminished as markets have gained experience with floating exchange rates; the trend appears to be in the opposite direction for some countries. Second, exposure to short-term volatility has differed among countries; Japan and Sweden have experienced much more than most other industrial countries. Third, volatility appears to depress the volume of international trade. This third finding is consistent with results reported by Cushman and by Akhtar and Hilton and challenges earlier findings by Hooper and Kohlhagen.

Introduction

This paper presents new data on short-term volatility in real exchange rates and examines its effects on the volume of international trade. The project summarized here deals with eleven developed countries and with data for the floating-rate period. The present paper is an updated version of Kenen and Rodrik (1984), which details our methodology and data sources.

Methodology

The effective exchange rates used in this study are based on the bilateral rates between each country's currency and those of the other ten countries covered by the study. Each bilateral rate is weighted by the other country's share in the ten-country total of exports or imports of the country under study. Thus, countries are treated symmetrically because their effective rates are made to depend on a common set of bilateral rates, rather than being determined in part by links with omitted countries. The bilateral rates are deflated by consumer-price indexes to obtain *real* effective exchange rates.

Concern about the impact of exchange-rate volatility derives from the belief that unexpected changes in real exchange rates influence behavior by risk-averse decisionmakers (Artus, 1983, and Brodsky, 1984). Risk

aversion is usually modeled by assuming that decisionmakers maximize objective functions in which unexpected events show up as squared deviations from expected values. Accordingly, quadratic measures of exchange-rate volatility promise conceptual consistency with the maintained hypothesis of risk-averse behavior. We use three such measures, each based implicitly on a different view about the formation of expectations. There are, in turn, two versions of each measure; one uses data for the 24-month period preceding the quarter for which a measure is reported (described henceforth as the current quarter), and the other uses data for the 12-month period.[1]

The first measure is the standard deviation of the monthly (percentage) change in the real exchange rate. It assumes implicitly that the change in the real rate expected in any month of the period is the average change for the whole period. The 24-month version of this measure is denoted by $I1A$, and the 12-month version by $I1B$.

The second measure is the standard deviation (error) of the real exchange rate obtained from a log-linear trend equation. It assumes implicitly that the level of the real rate expected in any month is its trend value for that month. The two versions of the measure are denoted by $I2A$ and $I2B$.

The third measure is the standard deviation (error) of the real exchange rate obtained from a first-order autoregressive equation. It assumes implicitly that the level of the real rate expected in any month is the one predicted by the autoregressive equation.[2] The two versions of the measure are denoted by $I3A$ and $I3B$.

Trends and Cross-Country Differences in Short-Term Volatility

Previous studies of exchange-rate volatility have concentrated on differences between the floating-rate and pegged-rate periods. They show that there has been more short-term volatility under floating rates (see, e.g.,

Received for publication July 19, 1984. Revision accepted for publication May 13, 1985.

* Princeton University and Harvard University, respectively.

An early version of this study was prepared for the Group of Thirty. The research described in the paper was supported in part by the International Finance Section at Princeton University. Helpful comments from Jeffrey Carmichael and from referees are gratefully acknowledged.

[1] Therefore, comparable measures of volatility cannot be reported for quarters earlier than 1975I, although we use exchange-rate data from the start of the floating-rate period in the construction of our measures. Precise descriptions of the volatility measures are given in Kenen and Rodrik (1984).

[2] The trend and autoregressive equations were re-estimated for each 24-month and 12-month period.

IMF, 1979; Kenen, 1979; and Brodsky, Helleiner, and Sampson, 1981). If volatility is costly, however, one would also like to know whether it has risen or fallen *during* the floating-rate period and whether some countries have experienced more than others.

There was widespread surprise in the early years of floating at the size of the short-term fluctuations in exchange rates, but these were expected to diminish as markets learned to cope with rapid changes in market conditions. Volatility was deemed to represent a transitory sort of market inefficiency. But volatility has not diminished. Figure 1 plots the indexes ΠA for the five SDR countries. Those for the United States, Japan, and the United Kingdom were at least as high in 1984 as they were in 1975. Of the eleven countries covered by this study, only two (Germany and Italy) can be said to have experienced appreciable declines in exchange-rate volatility, whereas two others (Canada and Sweden) experienced increases.[3]

Although our measures of short-term volatility are based on a common set of bilateral exchange rates, trends in volatility are not strongly correlated. Volatility in the U.S. real rate is positively correlated with volatility in the Japanese rate but negatively with volatility in the Canadian and Italian rates; volatility in the German real rate is positively correlated with volatility in the French, Italian, and Dutch rates but negatively with volatility in the Canadian and U.K. rates (see Kenen and Rodrik, 1984, table 2). Although the German and Swiss real rates moved together closely through much of the floating-rate period, their indexes of short-term volatility show no correlation whatsoever.

Average levels of exchange-rate volatility differ greatly across countries. The differences show up in table 1, which also shows large cross-country differences in the variability of exchange-rate volatility. Regardless of the index used to measure volatility, Japan and Sweden

[3] The Swedish series, however, reflect the effects of discrete devaluations (which must likewise be borne in mind when interpreting table 1).

TABLE 1.— MEANS AND STANDARD DEVIATIONS OF 24-MONTH PERCENTAGE-CHANGE INDEXES OF EXCHANGE-RATE VOLATILITY (ΠA_i^m), QUARTERLY OBSERVATIONS FROM 1975I THROUGH 1984III

Country	Mean		Standard Deviation	
United States	1.4385	(5)	0.4338	(5)
Canada	1.0894	(8)	0.2743	(10)
Japan	2.4841	(2)	0.7401	(2)
Belgium	0.8003	(11)	0.3324	(7)
France	1.2243	(7)	0.3086	(9)
Germany	1.0561	(9)	0.3254	(8)
Italy	1.3041	(6)	0.6669	(3)
Netherlands	0.9277	(10)	0.2071	(11)
Sweden	2.7117	(1)	1.1389	(1)
Switzerland	1.6891	(4)	0.4513	(4)
United Kingdom	2.0012	(3)	0.3472	(6)

Note: All numbers in this table have been multiplied by 100 (i.e., the mean value of the index for the United States is actually 0.014385). Numbers in parentheses are ranks.

stand out as having experienced more than other developed countries. In this instance and with other measures too, the mean values of the Japanese and Swedish indexes are almost twice as high as the average of mean values for all other countries. Furthermore, Japan has experienced the largest variation in short-term volatility. The United Kingdom and Switzerland follow in average volatility; Italy and Switzerland follow in variability of volatility. At the opposite extreme, the Netherlands and Belgium have experienced the lowest levels of volatility (and also show small variations in volatility), an outcome that presumably reflects their participation in European exchange-rate arrangements combined with the importance of other European currencies in their exchange-rate indexes.

Exchange-Rate Volatility and Trade

Several studies have tried to detect a systematic relationship between exchange-rate volatility and the volume of international trade.[4] Gupta (1980) estimated export supply equations for five developing countries and found a statistically significant relationship for two; export supply was negatively related to short-term volatility in the nominal exchange rate. Coes (1981) studied Brazilian experience and found that the reduction of real exchange-rate uncertainty following the adoption of a crawling peg in 1968 had large positive effects on ex-

[4] For an extensive survey see IMF (1984); also Cushman (1985), which extends Cushman's earlier bilateral analysis to include third-country effects explicitly, and De Grauwe and de Bellefroid (1986), which uses cross-sectional regressions to show that exchange-rate volatility helps to explain differences in rates of growth of bilateral trade flows (and that volatility in real rates has more explanatory power than volatility in nominal rates).

FIGURE 1.— INDEXES OF EXCHANGE-RATE VOLATILITY FOR FIVE COUNTRIES; 24-MONTH PERCENTAGE-CHANGE MEASURES (ΠA_i^m)

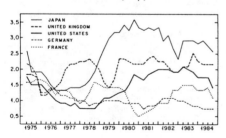

ports. Rana (1981) examined the imports of ASEAN countries and found that volatility had negative effects on volume in the cases of South Korea, Taiwan, and the Philippines. Three papers have focused on industrial countries like those covered by our study, and we summarize their findings in somewhat more detail.

Hooper and Kohlhagen (1978) examined the effects of exchange-rate volatility on trade flows and export prices in 1965–75. Their regression analysis covered the bilateral trade of Germany and the United States with other industrial countries, and they used mean weekly absolute differences between current spot exchange rates and past forward rates to represent nominal exchange risk. They could find no significant impact on the *volume* of trade, although import and export *prices* appeared to be affected. This finding has been widely cited and was not challenged until recently.

Akhtar and Hilton (1983) estimated volume and price equations for German and U.S. multilateral trade in the floating period. They represented exchange risk by measures of nominal and real exchange-rate variability (the standard deviations of daily effective exchange rates within each quarter). They found that nominal exchange-rate variability had statistically significant effects on both countries' manufactured exports and on German manufactured imports. Their results for real variability were mixed but broadly consistent with those for nominal variability.

Cushman (1983) followed the methodology adopted by Hooper and Kohlhagen but studied the effects of volatility in real exchange rates. He measured volatility by standard deviations of quarterly changes in real rates. Examining 14 bilateral trade flows in 1965–77, he found that volatility had significant negative effects on six flows (U.S. exports to Canada, France, and Japan, U.S. imports from Canada and Japan, and German exports to the United Kingdom). In three of these cases, however, other variables had wrong-signed coefficients in his regression equations. In two other cases, moreover, exchange-rate volatility showed significant positive trade effects.

Like Cushman, we work with volatility in the real exchange rate. Our approach has three distinguishing features: (1) We use several measures of volatility, based on 12 or 24 monthly observations. (2) Our equations focus exclusively on the floating-rate period, going from 1975I part way through 1984 (depending on the availability of data). The exclusion of the pegged-rate period precludes the possibility of specification bias stemming from the change in the exchange-rate regime. (3) We estimate equations for global rather than bilateral trade flows (and use effective exchange rates rather than bilateral rates). Once again, we are trying to minimize specification problems, most notably those arising from the fact that bilateral trade flows depend not only on the prices of the exporting and importing countries but also on those of other exporting countries.

Our basic regression equation is simpler than those used by Cushman and by Hooper and Kohlhagen:

$$\log V_t = \beta_0 + \beta_1 \log R_{t-1}^m + \beta_2 \log Y_t \\ + \beta_3 T + \beta_4 \Pi A_t^m \qquad (1)$$

where V_t is the index of the volume of manufactured imports during quarter t, R_{t-1}^m is the import-weighted real exchange rate of the importing country during the previous quarter, Y_t is an index of activity (industrial production) in the importing country, T is a trend term, and ΠA_t^m is the index of volatility defined above. We estimated this equation, with and without trend term, for all six measures of exchange-rate volatility used in this paper. When we did not obtain a satisfactory price term, β_1, we shifted to an Almon lag:

$$\log V_t = \alpha_0 + \sum_k a_k \log R_{t-k}^m + \alpha_2 \log Y_t \\ + \alpha_3 T + \alpha_4 \Pi A_t^m \qquad (1a)$$

and estimated this equation, with and without trend term, for all six measures of volatility.[5] These specifications assume that the importing country is small, but they are consistent with the large body of empirical work on price and income effects in international trade; the small-country assumption appears to work well on the import side, even for the United States.[6]

Our results are summarized in table 2, which lists equations chosen for the quality of their price and activity terms, rather than the sign or significance of their volatility terms, and for overall goodness of fit. The relative price term has the expected (negative) sign in every case and is statistically significant in all but three (Belgium, Germany, and Sweden). The activity term is uniformly positive and statistically significant in all but five (Belgium, France, Netherlands, Sweden, and Switzerland).[7]

Turning to the volatility term, the 24-month indexes usually give better results than their 12-month counterparts; they account for all of the statistically significant outcomes. More important, seven of the eleven volatility terms have the expected negative sign, and four of these are statistically significant (those for the United States, Canada, Germany, and the United Kingdom). Furthermore, no positive term is statistically significant. These

---

[5] The Almon lags were generated from a third-degree polynomial with no constraint on the value of the current term and a zero constraint on the longest-lagged term ($k = 8$).

[6] For a recent survey see Goldstein and Khan (1985); for evidence on the U.S. case see Richardson (1976).

[7] Data for Sweden were not available for the latter part of the period, and the regressions cover only 20 observations; this may explain the poor fit for that country. For more discussion and other regressions, including regressions relating to export volume, see Kenen and Rodrik (1984).

TABLE 2.—EFFECTS OF EXCHANGE-RATE VOLATILITY ON IMPORT VOLUME: SUMMARY OF REGRESSION RESULTS

Country	Constant	Real Exchange Rate		Domestic Activity	Trend	Exchange-Rate Variability	Volatility Index	R^2	D.W.[b]
		Simple Lag	Almon Lag[a]						
United States	−4.78	−0.81	—	1.19	0.01	−14.90	I1A	0.97	1.90
	(2.41)	(4.39)		(4.71)	(4.96)	(4.38)			
Canada	−9.82	−0.89	—	2.09	—	−5.15	I2A	0.77	—
	(6.26)	(4.14)		(9.39)		(2.18)			
Japan	−1.80	−0.23	—	1.14	0.01	3.04	I1A	0.96	1.51
	(0.74)	(2.29)		(3.57)	(1.84)	(1.79)			
Belgium[c]	0.86	−0.50	—	0.70	0.01	1.46	I1B	0.63	2.38
	(0.28)	(1.71)		(1.77)	(2.94)	(0.51)			
France[d]	1.52	−1.39	—	0.55	0.02	−3.65	I1B	0.94	—
	(0.70)	(4.92)		(1.14)	(17.50)	(1.58)			
Germany	−0.09	−0.01	—	1.08	0.01	−8.47	I1A	0.98	—
	(0.11)	(0.05)		(5.56)	(14.27)	(2.54)			
Italy[e]	3.47	−2.55	—	2.41	—	2.39	I3B	0.72	2.44
	(1.09)	(4.68)		(8.22)		(0.70)			
Netherlands	0.61	−1.64	—	0.59	0.01	−5.94	I2B	0.37	2.26
	(0.26)	(2.87)		(1.07)	(2.48)	(1.31)			
Sweden[f]	−1.77	−0.04	—	1.36	—	−3.78	I1A	0.31	2.39
	(0.30)	(0.10)		(1.21)		(0.56)			
Switzerland	3.34	—	−0.97	0.02	0.02	2.92	I2B	0.91	—
	(6.22)		(2.04)	(1.02)	(8.22)	(1.37)			
United Kingdom	−12.75	−0.59	—	2.36	0.01	−8.84	I1A	0.93	1.46
	(5.11)	(3.66)		(7.11)	(5.59)	(2.29)			

Note: Numbers in parentheses are *t*-statistics; unless otherwise indicated, equations span the period 1975I to 1984II or 1984III.
[a] Sum of Almon lag coefficients a_k and *t*-statistic for that sum.
[b] Statistic not shown when equation has been corrected for first-order serial correlation.
[c] Data span 1975I to 1984I.
[d] Data span 1976III to 1984II.
[e] Data span 1975I to 1983IV.
[f] Data span 1975I to 1979IV.

findings were fairly robust across alternative specifications and volatility indexes, and they are thus strongly suggestive. The short-term volatility of real exchange rates does appear to have a depressing effect on the volume of international trade.

Concluding Remarks

This paper yields three conclusions. First, the volatility of real exchange rates has not diminished as markets have gained experience with floating exchange rates. Second, experience with volatility has differed greatly across countries. Japan and Sweden in particular have experienced more short-term volatility than European countries maintaining cooperative exchange-rate arrangements. Finally, and most important, the volatility of real exchange rates appears to depress the volume of international trade.

REFERENCES

Akhtar, M. A., and R. Spence Hilton, "Exchange Rate Uncertainty and International Trade: Some Conceptual Issues and New Estimates for Germany and the United States," Federal Reserve Bank of New York, Dec. 1983.

Artus, Jacques R., "Toward a More Orderly Exchange Rate System," *Finance and Development* 20 (Mar. 1983), 10–13.

Brodsky, David A., "Fixed versus Flexible Exchange Rates and the Measurement of Exchange Rate Instability," *Journal of International Economics* 16 (May 1984), 295–306.

Brodsky, David A., Gerald K. Helleiner, and Gary P. Sampson, "The Impact of the Current Exchange Rate System on Developing Countries," *Trade and Development* (3) (1981), 31–52.

Coes, Donald V., "The Crawling Peg and Exchange Rate Uncertainty," in John Williamson (ed.), *Exchange Rate Rules* (New York: St. Martins, 1981).

Cushman, David O., "The Effects of Real Exchange Rate Risk on International Trade," *Journal of International Economics* 15 (Aug. 1983), 45–63.

——, "Has Exchange Risk Depressed International Trade? The Impact of Third Country Exchange Risk," mimeograph, 1985.

De Grauwe, Paul, and Bernard de Bellefroid, "Long-Run Exchange Rate Variability and International Trade," mimeograph, 1986.

Goldstein, Morris, and Mohsin S. Khan, "Income and Price Effects in Foreign Trade," in P. B. Kenen and R. W. Jones (eds.), *Handbook of International Economics*, Vol. II (Amsterdam: North-Holland, 1985).

Gupta, Shashikant, "Exchange Risk in International Trade Under Alternative Exchange Systems: The Developing

Countries' Experience," unpublished Ph.D. dissertation, Michigan State University, 1980.

Hooper, Peter, and Steven W. Kohlhagen, "The Effect of Exchange Rate Uncertainty on the Prices and Volume of International Trade," *Journal of International Economics* 8 (Nov. 1978), 483–511.

International Monetary Fund (IMF), *Annual Report* 1979, Washington, D.C., 1979.

_____, *Exchange Rate Volatility and World Trade*, Occasional Paper no. 28, Washington, D.C., July 1984.

Kenen, Peter B., "Exchange Rate Instability: Measurement and Implications," International Finance Section Research Memorandum, Princeton University, June 1979.

Kenen, Peter B., and Dani Rodrik, "Measuring and Analyzing the Effects of Short-term Volatility in Real Exchange Rates," Working Paper in International Economics (G-84-01), International Finance Section, Department of Economics, Princeton University, Mar. 1984.

Rana, Radumna B., *ASEAN Exchange Rates: Policies and Trade Effects* (Singapore: ASEAN Economic Research Unit, Institute of Southeast Asian Studies, 1981).

Richardson, J. David, "Some Issues in the Structural Determination of International Price Responsiveness," in Herbert Glejser (ed.), *Quantitative Studies of International Economic Relations* (Amsterdam: North-Holland, 1976).

[15]

European Economic Review 36 (1992) 1523–1532. North-Holland

Intramarginal intervention in the EMS and the target-zone model of exchange-rate behavior*

Kathryn M. Dominguez

Harvard University, Cambridge MA, USA and NBER, Cambridge MA, USA

Peter B. Kenen

Princeton University, Princeton NJ, USA

Received May 1991, final version received October 1991

Exchange-rate data produced by the European Monetary System (EMS) contradict important predictions made by the standard target-zone model. We show that the contradictions reflect a misinterpretation of policies pursued by the EMS countries. They intervened intramarginally, to keep exchange rates well within their bands, not at the edges of the bands, to keep rates from crossing them. In the Basle–Nyborg Agreement of 1987, however, they agreed to make fuller use of the band, and exchange rates behave differently thereafter. The effect appears clearly in the behavior of the French franc and less decisively in the behavior of the Italian lira. We conclude by examining and rejecting other explanations for the observed difference in exchange-rate behavior.

1. Introduction

Governments adhering to the exchange-rate rules of the European Monetary System (EMS) must keep the spot exchange rates for their currencies inside narrow bands. During the period 1979–1989, the band for the French franc had a width of 4.5% (2.25% on each side of its central rate), and the band for the Italian lira had a width of 12%. Yet the actual rate for the franc remained in a narrower range during most of the period, and the lira was always within a narrower range.

Correspondence to: Professor K.M. Dominguez, NBER, 1050 Massachussetts Avenue, Cambridge, MA 01238-5398, USA.

*The research reported in this paper was supported by the International Finance Section at Princeton University. We are grateful to Pierre Perron and James Stock for statistical advice and to Giuseppe Bertola, William Branson, and Paul Söderlind for helpful comments on earlier drafts. A fuller treatment of the issues covered in this paper will be found in Dominguez and Kenen (1991).

1524   *K.M. Dominguez and P.B. Kenen, Intramarginal intervention in the EMS*

We argue that the behavior of those exchange rates reflected a deliberate effort by the governments concerned to keep them well within the bands. The strategy was implemented by official intervention in the foreign-exchange market and, at times, by interest-rate policies. The rationale for the strategy was stated succinctly by the Bank of France in a paper quoted by Edison and Kaminsky (1990, p. 7):

> Within the framework of the European exchange rate mechanism, full use of the 2.25% fluctuation margin may, if the intervention points are reached, lead market participants to think that a realignment is imminent. It is therefore not surprising that most interventions are intramarginal. Action of this kind does not entail any exchange rate objective, within a fluctuation margin which is in any case narrow. In certain circumstances, however, it may be desirable not to go beyond, at least temporarily, the exchange rate considered by the market to be a psychological threshold. On other occasions, and particularly at times of acute crisis, it may, on the other hand, be useful to move swiftly to the exchange rate level at which the speculation in the market on a realignment would no longer be profitable.

When central banks intervened intramarginally they were not permitted to draw on the credit facilities of the EMS. In so doing they had frequently to act unilaterally, because the Bundesbank did not engage in intramarginal intervention to support the franc or lira against the DM.[1]

In 1987, however, agreement was reached on the limited use of EMS credit facilities for intramarginal intervention and, as a *quid pro quo*, fuller use of the exchange-rate band. Under the Basle–Nyborg Agreement of September 12, 1987, EMS members undertook 'to lay emphasis on the use of interest rate differentials to defend the stability of the EMS parity grid, to use the permitted fluctuation margins flexibly in order to deter speculation and to avoid prolonged bouts of intramarginal intervention' [Communiqué quoted in Ungerer et al. (1990, p. 88)].

This paper offers evidence that the Basle–Nyborg Agreement was taken seriously. Actual exchange-rate behavior was significantly different after the agreement than it was before, particularly in the case of the franc. This finding has two implications. First, governments may mean what they say – a possibility often discounted by economists. Second, intramarginal intervention may explain why EMS exchange rates have not conformed to the principal predictions of the target-zone model.

We begin by reviewing the main features and predictions of the target-zone

---

[1]This may help to explain why the French authorities abandoned their narrow-band policy at times when the franc was weak. By allowing the exchange rate to move to the edge of the band, they forced the Bundesbank to intervene (and could also use EMS credit facilities to finance their own interventions).

model and relevant empirical work. We go on to examine the behavior of EMS exchange rates to test for a regime change after the Basle–Nyborg Agreement. Finally, we defend our interpretation of the shift in exchange-rate behavior against a different interpretation – that markets, not governments, were responsible for it.

2. The main features and implications of the target-zone model

The target-zone model of exchange-rate behavior was developed by Krugman (1987) and refined by Froot and Obstfeld (1991), Flood and Garber (1991), and Krugman (1991). It is based on a simple equation linking the log of the exchange rate, e_t, with a univariate representation of the fundamentals determining the rate, f_t, and with the expected change in e_t:

$$e_t = f_t + \alpha \frac{1}{dt} E_t \, de_t,$$

where f_t is assumed to follow Brownian motion. Whenever e_t reaches the upper or lower edge of the band defining the target zone, the monetary authorities intervene to halt it, and this is done by changing f_t itself (not by acting directly on e_t, *given* f_t).

Under the assumptions of the target-zone model, a credible commitment to intervene at both edges of the band produces an S-shaped curve linking the exchange rate to the fundamentals. If the unconditional distribution of the f_t is uniform within the band, then the unconditional distribution of the e_t will be bi-modal, with a high frequency of observations at each edge of the band.[2]

Several empirical studies have used EMS exchange-rate data to test the target-zone model, because EMS rules appear to resemble the main features of the model. Although there have been several realignments since 1979, the year the EMS was inaugurated, the exchange-rate bands are narrow and have been defended firmly between realignments.[3] But exchange-rate behavior in the EMS fails to conform to the principal predictions of the

---

[2]The S-shaped relationship also implies that the variance of e_t will fall as the exchange rate approaches the edge of the band; the flatter the relationship between e_t and f_t, the smaller the response of e_t to a given change in f_t.

[3]Exchange rates for the franc and lira have crossed the edges of their bands on a few occasions. Some of these instances reflect the fact that our data come from the New York market, and EMS central banks are not required to intervene outside Europe. In at least one instance, however, the Bank of France allowed the franc to float on the eve of a realignment [see, e.g., Ungerer et al. (1990, p. 51)]. Furthermore, it has not always intervened on the scale required to force the franc into its new band right after a realignment. (By forcing the franc into the new band, it would have increased the profits of those who had sold francs before the realignment.)

target-zone model. The franc–DM and lira–DM exchange rates have tended to cluster in the middle of the band. Furthermore, econometric tests have failed to establish that the S-shaped relationship between e_t and f_t is in fact nonlinear. [See e.g., Bertola and Caballero (1992), Bodnar and Leahy (1990), and Flood et al. (1991).]

In his initial formulation of the target-zone model, Krugman (1987, 1991) allowed official intervention only at the edges of the band. This was sufficient for his purpose – to show that a credible commitment to the band could keep the exchange rate inside it without any actual intervention (i.e., that stabilizing speculation would substitute for intervention). But EMS central banks have intervened within the band, and anyone using EMS data to verify the forecasts of the target-zone model must allow for the influence of that intervention. The work described below suggests that intramarginal intervention may be a major reason for differences between the behavior of EMS exchange rates and the predictions of the model.

3. Another look at EMS experience

The franc was allowed to reach the lower limit of its band for many weeks in 1980 and in early 1981 and was at or near the upper limit for many weeks in 1981 and 1982. Thereafter, however, it remained well within the limits until the fourth quarter of 1987, apart from brief periods just before the realignments of March 1983, April 1986, and January 1987, and in the weeks following the first two of those realignments. After the Basle–Nyborg Agreement, however, the franc began to fluctuate more freely and approached the upper limit of the band several times in 1988 and 1989. The lira has been allowed to touch both limits of its band, but not very often. Fewer than 0.4% of the daily exchange-rate quotations were closer than 2 percentage points to the upper limit, and fewer than 5.1% were that close to the lower limit.[4] In 1988 and 1989, however, the lira appears to have spent far more time in the upper portion of its band.

Are these apparent changes in exchange-rate behavior sufficiently large and significant to represent a regime change? Did the Basle–Nyborg Agreement make a difference? To answer these questions, we look first at exchange-rate behavior in subperiods marked off by successive realignments, then at behavior before and after the Basle–Nyborg Agreement.

There were five realignments of the franc–DM rate in the 1980s and seven realignments of the lira–DM rate. Table 1 shows distributions of daily

---

[4]Both countries' monetary authorities appear to have been more tolerant of large strong-currency deviations than large weak-currency deviations. In the case of the franc, some 9.1% of the daily quotations were closer than 0.75 percentage points to the upper, weak-currency limit, but 15.1% were that close to the lower, strong-currency limit.

K.M. Dominguez and P.B. Kenen, *Intramarginal intervention in the EMS* 1527

Table 1

Percentage distributions of deviations from central rates for periods bounded by realignments: French franc.

Size of deviation	Period					
	I	II	III	IV	V	VI
Beyond −2.25	0.91	0.00	0.00	0.13	0.00	0.00
−2.25 to −1.50	29.22	15.53	22.95	15.67	33.52	0.00
−1.50 to −0.75	22.83	29.81	4.92	6.91	6.04	7.13
−0.75 to 0.00	14.61	17.39	45.90	44.75	9.34	19.52
0.00 to 0.75	13.70	2.48	24.59	32.54	45.60	16.82
0.75 to 1.50	9.13	7.45	0.00	0.00	3.30	40.78
1.50 to 2.25	7.99	27.33	1.09	0.00	2.20	15.75
Beyond 2.25	1.60	0.00	0.55	0.00	0.00	0.00
Number	438	161	183	753	182	743

quotations for the franc in the six subperiods set off by the realignments.[5] The data exclude quotations for the weeks adjacent to the realignments, because the Bank of France reports that it shifted temporarily to a different strategy right before a realignment and seems to have pursued another strategy right after a realignment.[6]

There are visible differences among the distributions in table 1 and in their counterparts for the lira, but are they significant? First, we ask if they have different means. Second, we apply the Kolmogorov–Smirnov criterion for maximum differences, which furnishes a test for differences between distributions when those distributions cannot be parameterized. Suppose we have samples from two independently distributed populations of a variable x and use $H(x)$ and $J(x)$ to denote the (unspecified) cumulative density functions for those populations. We can estimate the functions H and J from the empirical distribution functions $H_m(x)$ and $J_n(x)$, where m and n are the numbers of observations in the samples. If the null hypothesis, $H = J$, is true, there

---

[5]Tables pertaining to the lira have been omitted for brevity. They can be obtained from the authors and are presented in Dominguez and Kenen (1991). Realignments affecting the franc–DM rate took effect on October 5, 1981, June 14, 1982, March 21, 1983, April 7, 1986, and January 12, 1987, and these were the starting dates for periods II–VI in table 1. Realignments affecting the lira–DM rate took effect on those same dates and on March 23, 1981 and July 22, 1985 (which were the starting dates for periods II–VIII used in corresponding work on the behavior of the lira). The first period for each currency begins on January 2, 1980, although the previous realignment affecting the franc and lira took effect on September 24, 1979. The final period for each currency ends on December 29, 1989.

[6]See the Bank of France quotation in the text above (and comment in note 3, explaining why the franc was allowed to remain below the lower, strong-currency limit of its band right after certain realignments). In the case of the franc, the omitted quotations account for 7.4% of all quotations closer than 0.75 percentage points to the upper limit of the band and for 5% of all quotations closer than 0.75 percentage points to the lower limit. In the case of the lira, they account for 67% of quotations closer than 2 percentage points to the upper limit but for less than 4% of quotations closer than 2 percentage points to the lower limit.

should be close agreement between $H_m(x)$ and $J_n(x)$ for all x. The Kolmogorov–Smirnov two-sample test asks whether the maximum difference between $H_m(x)$ and $J_n(x)$ is large enough to reject the null hypothesis.[7] The test statistic is

$$D_{mn} = \max_x \left| (H_n(x) - J_m(x)) \right|,$$

and the critical value for the 0.01 level significance is approximated by

$$1.63 \sqrt{\frac{n+m}{nm}}.$$

Exchange rates are known to be serially correlated, and the sample distributions of the franc and lira deviations from their central rates violate the Kolmogorov–Smirnov assumption of independence. But Boldin (1982) and Pierce (1985) show that test statistics computed from autoregressive residuals have the same limiting null distributions as statistics computed from independent observations. Hence, we applied the Kolmogorov–Smirnov test to residuals from an ARMA(1,1) regression of the franc and lira deviations from their central rates.[8]

Table 2 shows the two sets of test results for the franc–DM rate. There are many significant differences between pairs of means, and some of the Kolmogorov–Smirnov statistics exceed their critical values. But the third, fourth and fifth distributions differ less among themselves than from the first, second and sixth distributions. (In the case of the lira–DM rate, all but two differences between pairs of means are statistically significant, as are several of the Kolmogorov–Smirnov statistics. But the fourth, fifth, sixth and seventh distributions tend to differ less among themselves than from the eighth distribution, measured by the sizes of the test statistics.)

We are therefore encouraged to perform another set of tests. We put aside the first two subperiods for the franc and the first three for the lira (those ending with the realignment of June 1982). The distributions for those subperiods differ appreciably from most of the others, and may represent a learning period, early in the history of the EMS. Next, we regroup the rest of the exchange-rate quotations into the distributions shown in table 3, for the periods before and after the Basle–Nyborg Agreement of September 1987. Since the French and Italian authorities appear to have been less tolerant of

---

[7]Tests based on the Kolmogorov–Smirnov statistic are sensitive to all types of departures from the null hypothesis $H = J$ and are therefore not sensitive to the particular type of difference between H and J. For a full account, see Pratt and Gibbons (1981, ch. 17).

[8]The ARMA(1,1) models of the franc and lira deviations were estimated using non-linear least squares. The AR coefficient were 0.98 and 0.99, and the MA coefficient were 0.13 and 0.11, for the franc and lira, respectively. The four coefficients were statistically significant at the 0.01 level.

Table 2

Significance tests for differences between distributions of deviations from central rates for periods bounded by realignments: French franc.

Period	Period				
	I	II	III	IV	V
Differences between means (z statistics)					
II	3.68[a]				
III	0.24	3.50[a]			
IV	1.30	3.32[a]	0.96		
V	0.83	3.69[a]	0.63	0.06	
VI	18.60[a]	6.89[a]	18.00[a]	28.40[a]	12.00[a]
Differences between distributions (Kolmogorov–Smirnov statistics)[b]					
II	0.10				
III	0.10	0.13			
IV	0.12[a]	0.20[a]	0.07		
V	0.11	0.12	0.04	0.08	
VI	0.13[a]	0.16[a]	0.14[a]	0.10[a]	0.14[a]

[a]Statistically significant at the 0.01 level.
[b]The formula for the critical value of the Kolmogorov–Smirnov statistic is given in the text; it depends on the sizes of the sample distributions, shown in table 1.

Table 3

Percentage distributions of deviations from central rates before and after the Basle–Nyborg Agreement.

French franc			Italian lira		
Deviation	Before	After	Deviation	Before	After
Positive and negative deviations					
Beyond −2.25	0.08	0.00	Beyond −6.0	0.08	0.00
−2.25 to −1.50	17.21	0.00	−6.0 to −4.0	9.65	0.00
−1.50 to −0.75	9.58	0.35	−4.0 to −2.0	16.25	0.00
−0.75 to 0.00	43.07	5.20	−2.0 to 0.0	53.22	6.93
0.00 to 0.75	29.05	21.66	0.0 to 2.0	18.45	37.09
0.75 to 1.50	0.47	52.51	2.0 to 4.0	2.35	55.63
1.50 to 2.25	0.47	20.28	4.0 to 6.0	0.00	0.35
Beyond 2.25	0.08	0.00	Beyond 6.0	0.00	0.00
Number	1,284	577	Number	1,274	577
Positive deviations only					
0.00 to 0.75	96.63	22.94	0.0 to 2.0	88.68	39.85
0.75 to 1.50	1.55	55.60	2.0 to 4.0	11.32	59.78
1.50 to 2.25	1.55	21.47	4.0 to 6.0	0.00	0.37
Beyond 2.25	0.26	0.00	Beyond 6.0	0.00	0.00
Number	386	545	Number	265	537

positive than negative deviations, we also show distributions of the positive (weak-currency) deviations before and after the agreement.

The results of significance tests for these distributions are shown in table 4.

Table 4

Significance tests for differences between distributions of deviations from central rates before and after the Basle–Nyborg Agreement.

Currency	Differences between means (z statistics)	Differences between distributions (Kolmogorov–Smirnov statistics)[a]
Distributions of positive and negative deviations		
French franc	47.41[b]	0.13[b]
Italian lira	48.75[b]	0.11[b]
Distributions of positive deviations		
French franc	35.2[b]	0.10[c]
Italian lira	19.1[b]	0.09[c]

[a]The formula for the critical value of the Kolmogorov–Smirnov statistic is given in the text. It depends on the sizes of the sample distributions, shown in table 3.
[b]Statistically significant at the 0.01 level.
[c]Statistically significant at the 0.05 level.

The difference between the means are highly significant, and the z-statistics are much larger than those in table 2 for the differences between the final and previous subperiods. The differences between the means of the positive (weak-currency) deviations are likewise very large. Furthermore, the Kolmogorov–Smirnov criterion rejects decisively the null hypothesis that there was no significant change in exchange-rate behavior after the Basle–Nyborg Agreement.

4. Concluding comments

We close by examining two potential difficulties with our interpretation of the evidence. The first has to do with the effectiveness of intervention. If intervention is ineffective, especially when sterilized, the differences between the distributions of exchange rates cannot possibly represent a change in the strategy governing intervention. The second difficulty is more general. The wider fluctuations of EMS exchange rates after the Basle–Nyborg Agreement may reflect the influence of market forces rather than a change in intervention strategy.

The target-zone model is based on the monetary model of exchange-rate determination. Intervention is represented by a change in f_t, which drives the whole model. But intervention in the EMS has not always taken this simple form. Some of it has been sterilized [see, e.g., Mastropasqua et al. (1988)]. Recent empirical work, however, leads us to believe that sterilized intervention can affect exchange rates. First, it can influence some fundamentals relevant to models of exchange-rate behavior as long as foreign and domestic bonds are not perfect substitutes. Second, it can influence expectations, including, but not exclusively, expectations about the fundamentals. For evidence concerning both possibilities, see Dominguez (1990), Dominguez and Frankel (1990), and earlier work surveyed in Kenen (1987).

The second difficulty is subtler. The large and frequent weak-currency deviations shown by the French franc in the two years after the Basle–Nyborg Agreement may be due to market forces rather than a change in intervention policy. On that supposition, however, one would expect *less* evidence of large-scale intervention in the years before the Basle–Nyborg Agreement than in the years following.

What do we know about the amounts of intervention before and after the agreement? Unfortunately EMS intervention data are not publicly available. However, Edison and Kaminsky (1990) present data on the *frequency* of French intervention during the subperiods between realignments.[9] These data do not say anything about the volume of intervention (and do not segregate instances of intervention related to conditions in the EMS from instances related to other objectives, such as the aims of the Plaza and Louvre Agreements). Nevertheless, they are suggestive. Intervention was far *more* frequent in Periods III–V than it was in Period VI (which includes but does not coincide exactly with the period after the Basle–Nyborg Agreement).[10] Thus, the data are consistent with compliance with both aims of the Basle–Nyborg Agreement – avoiding 'prolonged bouts of intervention' as well as making fuller use of the band. The franc was allowed to display more weakness than it had before.

[9]Data on reserve changes are publicly available. However, as Mastropasqua et al. (1988) show, changes in reserves are poor proxies for amounts of intervention. They show that changes in reserves differ both in sign and size from actual intervention figures for France, Germany and Italy in 1983–1985.

[10]The data presented in Edison and Kaminsky (1990) do not include instances of intervention in currencies other than the U.S. dollar. Therefore, they may understate the relative frequency of intervention in recent years, insofar as there has been more use of EMS currencies.

References

Bertola, G. and R.J. Caballero, 1992, Target zones and realignments, American Economic Review 82, June.

Bodnar, G. and J. Leahy, 1990, Are target zone models relevant? Unpublished manuscript.

Boldin, M.V., 1982, Estimation of the distribution of noise in an autoregression scheme, Theory of Probability and its Applications 27, no. 4.

Dominguez, K.M., 1990, Market responses to coordinated central bank intervention, Carnegie Rochester Series on Public Policy 32, Spring.

Dominguez, K.M. and J. Frankel, 1990, Does foreign exchange intervention matter? Disentangling the portfolio and expectations effects for the mark, Working paper 3299 (National Bureau of Economic Research, Cambridge, MA).

Dominguez, K.M. and P.B. Kenen, 1991, On the need to allow for the possibility that governments mean what they say: Interpreting the target-zone model of exchange-rate behavior in the light of EMS experience, Working paper 3670 (National Bureau of Economic Research, Cambridge, MA).

Edison, H.J. and G.L. Kaminsky, 1990, Target zones, intervention, and exchange rate volatility: France, 1979–1990, Unpublished manuscript.

Flood, R.P. and P.M. Garber, 1991, The linkage between speculative attack and targe zone models of exchange rates, Quarterly Journal of Economics 106, Nov.

Flood, R.P., A.K. Rose and D.J. Mathieson, 1991, An empirical exploration of exchange rate target zones, Working paper WP/91/15 (IMF, Washington, DC).

Froot, K.A. and M. Obstfeld, 1991, Exchange-rate dynamics under stochastic regime shifts: A unified approach, Journal of International Economics 31, Nov.

Kenen, P.B., 1987, Exchange rate management: What role for intervention? American Economic Review 77, May.

Krugman, P., 1987, Trigger strategies and price dynamics in equity and foreign exchange markets, Working paper 2459 (National Bureau of Economic Research, Cambridge, MA).

Krugman, P., 1991, Target zones and exchange rates dynamics, Quarterly Journal of Economics 106, Aug.

Krugman, P. and J. Rotemberg, 1990, Target zones with limited reserves, Working paper 3418 (National Bureau of Economic Research, Cambridge, MA).

Mastropasqua, C., S. Micossi and R. Rinaldi, 1988, Interventions, sterilisation and monetary policy in European Monetary System countries, 1979–87, in: F. Giavazzi, S. Micossi and M. Miller, eds., The European Monetary System (Cambridge University Press, Cambridge).

Pierce, D.A., 1985, Testing normality in autoregressive models, Biometrika 72.

Pratt, J. and J. Gibbons, 1981, Concepts of nonparametric theory (Springer-Verlag, New York).

Ungerer, H., J.J. Hauvonen, A. Lopez-Claros and T. Mayer, 1990, The European Monetary System: Developments and perspectives, Occasional paper 73 (International Monetary Fund, Washington, DC).

PART III

POLICY PRESCRIPTION

[16]

The Analytics of a Substitution Account *

Peter B. Kenen

Introduction

In 1979 and 1980, the Interim Committee of the International Monetary Fund considered a series of reports from the Executive Board of the Fund concerned with the creation of a substitution account, a facility in which member countries might deposit some of their foreign-currency reserves in exchange for claims denominated in Special Drawing Rights (SDR). These new claims would be transferable on the books of the account and would thus function as reserves. The account was intended to advance the long-term objective enshrined in the Articles of Agreement of the Fund — to make the SDR "the principal reserve asset in the international monetary system" (Art. VIII, Sec. 7), but it was also meant to serve immediate objectives. Member countries could diversify their reserve holdings without disturbing foreign-exchange markets, and the availability of this opportunity could help to arrest the drift toward a multiple reserve-currency system — a movement that was gathering momentum with the weakness of the U.S. dollar and the growth of reserve balances in Deutschemark, Swiss Franc, and Yen.

In October 1979, at its meeting in Belgrade, the Interim Committee concluded that "such an account, if properly designed, could contribute to an improvement of the international monetary system" and set out some principles to guide the Executive Board in its attempt to design an account:

> In order for the account to achieve widespread participation on a voluntary basis and on a large scale, among other things, it should satisfy the needs of depositing members, both developed and developing, its costs and benefits

* I am grateful to Charles Averill and Olga Jonas, who wrote the computer programs used for the simulations in this paper, to the Research Department of the International Monetary Fund, for supplying some of the interest-rate and exchange-rate data, and to the International Finance Section, Princeton University, for research support. The views expressed in this paper are my own and should not be ascribed to the International Finance Section or to any other institution.

should be fairly shared among all parties concerned, and it should contain satisfactory provisions with respect to the liquidity of the claims, their rate of interest, and the preservation of their capital value.

The Executive Board made progess in resolving a number of issues but was unable to reach agreement on the way to preserve the capital value of the SDR claim, and it referred the matter back to the Interim Committee, which met at Hamburg in April 1980. There has been no official account of the discussion at that meeting, but the communiqué suggests that the question of capital value, rechristened as the question of financial balance, was the main obstacle to agreement:

> The Committee commended the Executive Board for the progress it had made in designing a plan for a substitution account along the lines requested by the Committee in its communiqué issued in Belgrade. The Committee noted that the Board had reached ... provisional agreement on a wide range of features of such an account. The Committee also noted that some issues remained to be solved, including arrangements for the maintenance of financial balance in the account. The Committee, after a discussion of these issues, expressed its intention to continue its work on this subject.

The matter was not referred again to the Executive Board. It was set aside.

There is no way to know when the subject will come up again or the form in which it will arise. But the problem of financial balance will have to be solved by any successful proposal, and that is the problem examined in this paper. It presents a series of simulations showing that the problem of financial balance derives from the way that exchange rates interact with interest rates during the life of an account, defining the size of the problem under various plans, and measuring the costs of various solutions.The simulations pretend that a substitution account was set up at the beginning of 1964 and examine the balance sheet of the account in each of the next fifteen years. They are thus based on actual exchange rates and interest rates in 1964-1978.

I started to conduct these simulations in 1979, when discussions of various plans got under way, and repeated them several times, as new plans were brought forward. The simulations reproduced in this paper deal with the small group of proposals that survived discussions in the Fund and with some variants that should perhaps have been discussed. All of these simulations have been rerun for publication, to make them fully comparable. While most of the plans considered in this paper resemble in general design those that were discussed in the Fund, they are not faithful reproductions of their official counterparts. As a participant in several groups that examined the case for a substitution account, including a study group on reserve assets established by the Group of Thirty,[1] I made the acquaintance of the proposals that had been examined in the Fund, but the documents containing the details were not available to me when I designed my simulations.

This paper has three main parts. In the first, I make a brief excursion into history, recalling that the first plan for a substitution account was advanced in the *Report* of the Committee of Twenty,[2] and that the discussions of that plan raised many of the issues considered in 1979-1980. I point out, however, that the plans advanced in 1979-1980 addressed themselves to different aims and go on to list the main problems involved in designing a substitution account along the lines laid down in the Belgrade communiqué. In the second part, I present my simulations, which deal with a subset of those problems, and show how various interest-rate arrangements, interacting with exchange-rate behavior, would have affected the financial balance of an account created in 1964. I look at ways of solving the problem of financial balance, including a guarantee by the United States, a guarantee provided jointly by the United States and the depositors, and the use of gold held by the IMF to make good an imbalance in the account. These arrangements are compared by measuring their impact on financial benefits and costs, viewed first from the standpoint of the depositors and then from the standpoint of the United States. Finally, in the third part, I comment briefly on some plans that have been put forth recently and offer some suggestions of my own.

Origins and Issues

The Committee of Twenty was established in 1972 to consider and report on proposals for reform of the international monetary system.[3] It sought to design a monetary system based on stable but adjustable par values and to make the new system more "symmetrical" than the earlier

---

[1] For the findings of this group, see *Towards a Less Unstable International Monetary System: Report of the Reserve Asset Study Group of the Group of Thirty,* Consultative Group on International Economic and Monetary Affairs, New York, 1980.

[2] COMMITTEE ON REFORM OF THE INTERNATIONAL MONETARY SYSTEM AND RELATED ISSUES, *International Monetary Reform: Documents of the Committee of Twenty,* International Monetary Fund, Washington, 1974, Outline of Reform, Annex 7.

[3] This discussion of the work of the Committee draws on ROBERT SOLOMON, *The International Monetary System, 1945-1976,* New York, 1977, JOHN WILLIAMSON, *The Failure of World Monetary Reform, 1971-1974,* New York, 1977, and my "Convertibility and Consolidation", reprinted in PETER B. KENEN, *Essays in International Economics*, Princeton, 1980, pt. III.

Bretton Woods System. It soon became apparent, however, that the leading governments disagreed about the meaning of symmetry. Europeans emphasized the need to reduce or eliminate the special role of the U.S. dollar, because that role permitted the United States to escape the "discipline" of reserve losses. They favored a new system of convertibility, based on mandatory asset settlement. The United States emphasized the need for surplus countries to take more responsibility for the functioning of the adjustment process and the need for ready recourse to exchange-rate changes. It proposed the use of an "objective indicator" to signal the need for policy changes in deficit and surplus countries alike.

The concerns of the two sides were complementary, in that the United States could accept European views about convertibility only if there were improvements in the adjustment process. It had to be sure that it would be able to eliminate the persistent deficit in the U.S. balance of payments. But another condition had to be fulfilled before the United States could contemplate mandatory asset settlement. Something had to be done about the large dollar balances already held by foreign official institutions. The United States had to be sure that these could not be presented for conversion into "primary" reserve assets, because they were several times larger than U.S. reserves.

Two ways of handling this "dollar overhang" were suggested in the course of the Committee's work: 1) Consolidation of the dollar balances into long-term U.S. government obligations. 2) Creation of a substitution account to exchange dollar balances for SDR. These proposals differed in two important ways. The consolidation of dollar balances into long-term U.S. debt would have removed them from reserves, reducing the total stock of reserves, whereas the substitution of SDR for dollars would have replaced the dollars with another reserve asset, leaving the stock of reserves unchanged. The consolidation of the balances, moreover, would impose on the United States, explicitly or implicitly, the task of amortizing its obligations, whereas the proposal for a substitution account left this question open.

This first plan for a substitution account left other questions open too.[4] Would substitution take place once, or could it be repeated? Would substitution go one way, or could it be reversed? Would substitution be mandatory or voluntary? This last question worried the

---

[4] Some of these questions are raised in COMMITTEE ON REFORM, *Documents*, Report of Technical Group on Global Liquidity and Consolidation, especially pp. 169-176.

developing countries, because they insist on complete freedom of choice in the management of their reserves. They were concerned, moreover, by the possibility that substitution would become the main way of issuing new SDR. They wanted SDR creation to increase the supply of reserves, not merely to alter the composition (and they hoped at that time to forge a "link" between SDR creation and development assistance).

The first proposal for a substitution account died with the Committee of Twenty itself, a victim of the economic ailments rampant at the time that made it impossible to contemplate an early return to par values. The proposal itself could not survive the move to floating exchange rates, because it was connected logically to the plan for mandatory asset settlement, and asset settlement has no clear-cut role to play under a floating-rate regime.

Yet floating rates had much to do with the revival of interest in a substitution account. They were the chief cause of the movement toward a multiple reserve-currency system that produced so much concern in 1978-1980. The diversification of reserves that began in earnest after 1976 was inspired by the expectation of exchange-rate fluctuations, exacerbated by the weakness of the U.S. dollar.

At the end of 1976, U.S. dollars accounted for 86.6 per cent of official foreign-exchange holdings; at the end of 1978, they accounted for only 82.1 per cent.[5] There is one sense in which these numbers overstate the shift from dollars into other reserve currencies; some part of the decline in the share of the dollar was due to the decline in its value. But there is another, more important sense in which the numbers understate the size of the shift; some of the dollars sold for other national currencies entered the reserves of the countries whose currencies were being bought. The full extent of diversification should therefore be measured by removing the currency reserves of the main reserve-currency countries.[6] Once this is done, the share of the dollar works out at about 80 per cent in 1976 and falls to only 70 per cent in 1978.

---

[5] INTERNATIONAL MONETARY FUND, *Annual Report 1980*, p. 64. The numbers for 1979 are harder to interpret, because that was the first year in which ECU were issued. If ECU are excluded (by treating those issued for dollars as though they were dollars and removing entirely those issued for gold), the share of the dollar works out at 77.8 per cent, substantially lower than in 1978. If ECU are included, by treating all of them as new foreign-currency reserves, the share of the dollar works out at 65.1 per cent.

[6] By subtracting the foreign-currency reserves of Germany, Japan, Switzerland, and the United Kingdom from global foreign-currency reserves and, on the limiting but plausible assumption that those reserves were dollars, subtracting them from global dollar reserves. This calculation cannot be repeated for 1979 without adjusting for the presence of ECU in German and U.K. reserves. Treating all ECU as foreign-currency reserves, one can subtract the foreign-currency reserves of the four major countries from global foreign-currency reserves, but one cannot subtract them from global dollar reserves without first removing ECU held by Germany and the United Kingdom. When this is done (approximately), the share of the dollar works out in the neighborhood of 53 per cent.

This trend was worrisome from several points of view. The United States, for example, was increasingly concerned to halt the depreciation of the dollar. On November 1, 1978, it undertook to intervene heavily in support of the dollar. Diversification interfered directly with this effort. Sales of dollars for Deutschemark and other strong currencies amounted to perverse intervention on the part of the central banks involved. And the indirect effects of diversification may have been bigger than its direct effects. Expectations of official sales may have caused private holders of dollars to step up their own sales, adding to the downward pressure on the dollar. Countries with strong currencies had symmetrical concerns. Diversification was making their currencies stronger, and it was also undermining their monetary policies, insofar as it was forcing them and the United States to intervene on a larger scale. But those countries had another worry. They were reluctant to become major reserve centers. Some, indeed, had tried to limit or discourage foreign official holdings of their currencies.[7]

There was the widespread belief, moreover, that a multiple reserve-currency system, the logical outcome of large-scale diversification, would prove to be "inherently" unstable. This view was defended by historical analogies. The bimetallic standard of the Nineteenth Century, based on gold and silver, was a multiple reserve-asset system, and it broke down eventually. The gold-exchange standards of the interwar and postwar periods, based on sterling and the dollar, were unstable too. But most analogies are imperfect, and so are these. The "inherent" instability of earlier reserve regimes derived from the authorities' attempts to peg the prices of the reserve assets despite changes in their relative scarcities. Those attempts invited self-aggravating speculation whenever it seemed possible that the authorities would exhaust their holdings of the scarce asset. Present arrangements may not invite this form of speculation, because the authorities do not try to peg the prices of the reserve assets. Exchange rates connecting the dollar, Deutschemark and other reserve currencies are managed, but management is very different from pegging in its implications for the stability of the reserve system. It does not invite self-aggravating speculation.

---

[7] These efforts were not successful, because they served merely to divert diversification into the Eurocurrency markets; much of the recent growth in official holdings of Deutschemark, Swiss Franc, and Yen, took place in those markets. For this reason, among others, the German and Swiss authorities altered their attitudes in 1980, and the Germans began to sell DM-denominated debt directly to Saudi Arabia when the German trade balance deteriorated. Countries' doubts about reserve-currency status usually give way when the need for balance-of-payments financing makes the short-term benefit seem large compared to the long-term cost.

Nevertheless, fears of instability were held widely, and they animated a new interest in reform of the reserve system. This interest turned quickly to consideration of a substitution account based on the SDR, because it could accommodate the demand for reserve diversification in a manner that would not compound the problems of the United States and other reserve-currency countries.

Because the SDR is a "basket" of currencies, a claim denominated in SDR is by itself a diversified asset, offering protection against exchange-rate fluctuations. Because claims denominated in SDR would be issued directly to official institutions, diversification through a substitution account would not affect the foreign-exchange markets and could relieve the pressure on Germany and other countries to permit wider use of their currencies as reserve assets.

Participation in a substitution account would be voluntary. That was understood early on and was stated as a premise, not a principle, in the Belgrade communiqué. Furthermore, the new account would be managed by the IMF but would have to be segregated from the books of the Fund.[8] This was also understood, because any other approach would require an amendment to the Articles of Agreement, a time-consuming process, and many observers recommended rapid action to divert diversification from foreign-exchange markets and block the development of a multiple reserve-currency system.

The creation of a separate substitution account, however, posed special problems, and the solution of those problems was greatly complicated by the need to attract participation on a voluntary basis and on a scale large enough to make the exercise worthwhile. The account would be able to issue claims denominated in SDR, but it could not issue the SDR defined in the Articles of Agreement. In consequence, those claims would not assume automatically the attributes of the SDR. The transferability (liquidity) of the SDR is guaranteed within limits, because the Fund can "designate" a member to receive SDR in exchange for that member's own currency (Art. XIX, Sec. 5). The redemption of the SDR is guaranteed by the provisions of the Articles pertaining to the liquidation of the SDR Department (Art. XXV and Sched. I). The transferability of the new asset, its interest rate, and ways

---

[8] The present Articles allow the Fund to manage an account of this sort if participation by members is voluntary. Under Art. V, Sec. 2 (b).

    If requested, the Fund may decide to perform financial and technical services, including the administration of resources contributed by members, that are consistent with the purposes of the Fund. Operations involved in the performance of such financial services shall not be on the account of the Fund. Services under this subsection shall not impose any obligation on a member without its consent.

to guarantee its value in the event of liquidation — the problem of financial balance — had to be negotiated, and these issues were connected in complicated ways.

Holders of claims on the account would be able to transfer them freely among themselves. But potential holders wanted to be sure that they would find buyers whenever necessary. It was therefore suggested that holders should have the right to cash in their claims (i.e., that the account itself should serve as buyer of last resort). Some said that this right should be unconditional, but others said that it should be circumscribed, to be exercised only as a last resort, and that penalties should be imposed to make the option costly.[9]

There were, of course, proposals for "designation" patterned on the plan adopted for the SDR itself. But reliance on this mechanism, it was said, might discourage participation in the substitution account. Countries with strong currencies and large reserves, whose participation would be important for success, might be unwilling to make big deposits, because these would expose them lo large-scale "designation" (i.e., the obligation to grant large amounts of credit to countries in balance-of-payments need). There was some discussion of marketability as the ultimate solution to the problem of liquidity, but marketability looked to be a long way off. It would be necessary first to foster private use of the SDR claim and to develop active markets in which official sellers could count on finding private buyers.[10]

What rate of interest should the new claim pay? There had to be a sensible relationship between liquidity and yield, but two other relationships had to be considered — the relationship between the interest rate on the new claim and the rate paid on the SDR itself, and the relationship between the rate on the new claim and the rate that would be paid by the United States on the dollar holdings of the account.

In 1979-1980, when the matter was examined, the interest rate on the SDR was set at 80 per cent of the so-called full combined rate, a weighted average of five national interest rates, including most importantly the U.S. Treasury Bill rate, which was the rate that many countries earned on their dollars. If the interest rate on the new claim was to be no higher than the SDR rate, it would be lower than most market rates, including those available on dollar, Deutschemark, and other currency

---

[9] There are no encashments in my simulations; once SDR claims are created, they remain in existence until liquidation of the substitution account.

[10] Marketability is discussed extensively in the report of the study group established by the GROUP OF THIRTY, *Towards a Less Unstable International Monetary System*.

reserves. This could discourage participation in the account. Furthermore, a low rate on the SDR claim would make it less attractive to private purchasers if and when it was decided to permit private holdings and thus to foster marketability as the long-run solution to the problem of liquidity. If the interest rate were higher than the SDR rate, however, the SDR would be less attractive as a reserve asset, and some feared that this would diminish enthusiasm for new allocations of SDR, a matter of continuing concern to the less-developed countries. This issue was not resolved completely, but it is not especially important now, because the Executive Board has unified the relevant interest rates; the rate on the SDR has been raised to 100 per cent of the full combined rate. (It is for this reason that all of my simulations use the full combined rate as the one at which depositors earn interest on their SDR claims.)

The relationship between the rate on the new claim and the rate to be paid by the United States was important for the problem of financial balance. That problem has two dimensions. There is first the problem of flow balance, by which I mean the relationship between the interest income of the account and its interest payments to depositors. If all interest payments were made in U.S. dollars, one of the possibilities examined in the Fund and in my simulations, dollars would leak out of the account when its interest income from the United States was larger than its interest payments to depositors. This could happen if the interest rate paid by the United States was lower than the interest rate paid to depositors. It could also happen, however, if the dollar depreciated against the SDR, because of the manner in which interest payments would be calculated. Interest payments by the United States would normally be calculated in U.S. dollars, being payments made on the dollars held by the account. Interest payments to depositors would normally be calculated in SDR, being payments made on the SDR claims issued by the account. A depreciation of the dollar against the SDR would raise the dollar value of the interest payments calculated in SDR and would thus raise the dollar payments made by the account without also raising its receipts.

The problem of flow balance translates itself eventually into a problem of stock balance. If large numbers of dollars leak out of the account, those that remain may not suffice to pay off the depositors in the event of liquidation. But a depreciation of the dollar can jeopardize stock balance or solvency even if there is no problem of flow balance. This is made quite clear by my simulations, and it leads in turn to a consideration of the ways in which financial balance can be secured – by guarantees, by deficiency payments, or by using gold held by the IMF.

Rather than examining these problems abstractly, I have tried to quantify them and to measure the costs of solving them. That is the main aim of my simulations.[11]

The Simulations

All of my simulations start at the beginning of 1964 and close at the end of 1978. There was no SDR in 1964, however, which posed the first question that had to be answered before I could run my simulations: What numbers should be used to represent the dollar value of the SDR?

In the First Amendment to the Articles of Agreement, creating the SDR, the value of the SDR was tied to gold, at SDR 35 per ounce, so that one SDR was worth $ 1.00. (With the devaluations of the dollar in 1971 and 1973, the dollar value of the SDR rose automatically to $ 1.0857, then to $ 1.0263.) In mid-1974, however, the valuation of the SDR was redefined in terms of a "basket" of sixteen currencies and thus came to fluctuate vis-à-vis the dollar. In some of my early simulations (and some done elsewhere), these were the valuations used (with the old parity in terms of the dollar carried back to 1964). Here, by contrast, I carry back the "basket" valuation. At the beginning of each simulation, then, the value of the SDR is $ 1.1016, and it rises to $ 1.3028 at the end. In other words, the dollar depreciates by 18.3 per cent in terms of the SDR. Had I carried back the old dollar parity, the depreciation would have been much bigger, at 30.3 per cent. But the one obtained by my method is large historically, because of the period covered by my

---

[11] In a world of the sort that economists like to contemplate, populated by risk-neutral speculators with "rational" expectations, the problems of flow and stock balance would be solved automatically. Expectations of currency depreciation would be accurate over time and would be reflected accurately by interest-rate differences. Therefore, a depreciation of the dollar in terms of the other currencies entering the SDR "basket" would be matched by an increase of U.S. interest rates relative to interest rates on assets denominated in those currencies. There would be an increase in U.S. interest payments large enough to offset the flow and stock effects of the depreciation. This does not happen in my simulations, and there are two explanations. First, the SDR "basket" contained the currencies of sixteen countries, but the full combined rate was based on a five-country average. Second and much more important, interest-rate differences did not reflect accurately the changes in exchange rates affecting the dollar value of the SDR in 1964-1978. The discrepancies were large, and there were many causes. Exchange rates were not freely flexible, even after 1973. Interest rates were not freely flexible either, but were influenced heavily by monetary policies. And the world is not populated by risk-neutral speculators with "rational" expectations.

simulations. At the end of 1980, for example, the dollar value of the SDR was $ 1.2754, and depreciation of the dollar was reduced to 15.8 per cent. Therefore, my simulations produce pessimistic measures of the problem of financial balance and of the costs of dealing with it.

Some of the other questions raised in this paper had also to be answered. Should substitution take place once, or should the account remain open to new deposits? What interest rates should be paid by the account and by the United States? How should the interest payments be made?

The first of these questions came up in connection with the proposal by the Committee of Twenty and again in 1979-1980. My simulations answer it by opening the account at the start of 1964 and holding it open for five years. At the start of each year, depositors acquire SDR 10 billion of new claims, so that the stock of claims rises to SDR 50 billion at the beginning of 1968 and remains at that level thereafter (unless interest payments are made in additional SDR claims). Each year's claims are issued, of course, at the then-current dollar price of the SDR, so that the number of dollars deposited varies from year to year.

What interest rate is paid on the new claims and what form do the payments take? The full combined rate is employed in all my simulations, for the reason given earlier, but the form of payment varies. In some simulations, payments are made in U.S. dollars; in others, they are made in additional SDR claims.[12]

What interest rate is paid on dollars held by the account, and what form do these payments take? I work with five interest rates:

(1) The ninety-day U.S. Treasury Bill rate.

(2) A floating fifteen-year U.S. Government Bond rate (which is an average of the ten-year and twenty-year rates).

(3) A fixed fifteen-year U.S. Government Bond rate (which is the average level of the floating rate for 1964-1978).

---

[12] One other possibility was discussed and was examined by my simulations. Interest payments might be made in SDR. For this to be done, however, the United States would have to make its interest payments in SDR, and this might not be possible. In one of my simulations, the United States was given SDR 4 billion initially (an amount roughly equal to actual allocations through 1980) and received an additional SDR 750 million per year through new allocations (slightly less than its actual allocation in 1980). It made only half of its interest payments in SDR. Nevertheless, it ran out of SDR long before the end of the fifteen-year simulation. Accordingly, the simulations present in this paper deal only with the options mentioned in the text — payments in U.S. dollars and payments in new SDR claims created by the account.

(4) The full combined rate.

(5) The full combined rate plus a premium of one percentage point.

All payments, however, are made in U.S. dollars.

Annual results for one simulation are shown in Table 1. This is the one in which depositors earn interest in U.S. dollars, and the United States pays the Treasury Bill rate. At the start of 1964, depositors acquire SDR 10 billion of claims on the account by turning in $ 11.016 billion of U.S. dollars. (Recall that the dollar value of the SDR was $ 1.1016 under my method of valuation.) At the end of 1964, however, the account holds only $ 10.899 billion of U.S. dollars, because the problem of flow balance arises right away. The account pays $0.508 billion to the depositors (an amount obtained by applying the full combined rate to the SDR 10 billion of depositors' claims and converting the result into U.S. dollars). But the account earns only $ 0.391 billion from the United States (an amount obtained by applying the U.S. Treasury Bill rate to

TABLE 1

U.S. PAYS TREASURY BILL RATE: ALL INTEREST PAID IN U.S. DOLLARS

End Year	SDR Claims Outstanding	Dollar Holdings	SDR Value of (3)	Interest Earned		Interest Paid by U.S. in $
				SDR Claims	$	
1964	10.000	10.899	9.885	0.000	0.508	0.391
1965	20.000	21.746	19.739	0.000	1.044	0.866
1966	30.000	32.571	29.621	0.000	1.791	1.599
1967	40.000	43.397	40.182	0.000	2.056	1.886
1968	50.000	54.060	50.111	0.000	3.037	2.900
1969	50.000	53.909	50.013	0.000	3.767	3.617
1970	50.000	53.327	49.194	0.000	4.054	3.472
1971	50.000	52.594	46.347	0.000	3.047	2.314
1972	50.000	52.069	45.715	0.000	2.665	2.141
1973	50.000	50.712	42.543	0.000	5.018	3.660
1974	50.000	48.746	39.812	0.000	5.957	3.991
1975	50.000	47.538	40.607	0.000	4.045	2.837
1976	50.000	46.309	39.859	0.000	3.602	2.372
1977	50.000	45.172	37.188	0.000	3.577	2.440
1978	50.000	44.303	34.006	0.000	4.130	3.261

Status at liquidation: shortfall of 15.994 billion SDR (20.837 billion dollars)

Total interest paid by the United States: 37.748 billion dollars

Total interest earned by participants : 48.299 billion dollars the $ 11.016 billion of U.S. dollars held by the account before the completion of interest payments). There is thus a shortfall of $ 0.117 billion (which equals the difference between the initial deposits of $ 11.016 billion and the balance of $ 10.899 billion at the end of the year). The problem of stock balance arises too, because the SDR value of the dollars dips below SDR 10 billion.

The problem of flow balance does not go away. In fact, the account loses dollars year after year, with the loss reaching a peak of $ 1.966 billion in 1974 and totalling $ 10.551 billion at the close of the fifteen-year period. (Interest payments to depositors total $ 48.299 billion, and interest payments by the United States total only $ 37.748 billion.) The problem of stock balance is resolved temporarily in 1967, when the devaluation of the pound causes the dollar to appreciate in terms of the SDR, but reappears in 1970 and grows thereafter. At the end of the simulation, the shortfall is SDR 15.994 billion, which translates into $ 20.837 billion and is twice as large as the loss of dollars resulting from the problem of flow balance.

There is a simple way to solve the problem of flow balance. The account can pay interest in additional SDR claims and thus store up all of the dollars received from the United States. That is what happens in Table 2, which shows that this solution to the problem of flow balance greatly exacerbates the problem of stock balance. Claims on the account grow to SDR 112.469 billion by the end of 1978, and dollar holding grow to $ 112.553 billion, but the latter are worth only SDR 86.393 billion, leaving a shortfall of SDR 26.077 billion, equivalent to $ 33.973 billion. The crediting of interest in SDR claims defers the problem of financial balance, but the size of the problem rises with the size of the account.

To compare these simulations more systematically, I have discounted back to 1964 all of the relevant payments and receipts. In this and every other instance, I use the U.S. Treasury Bill rate as the discount rate. I assume, in effect, that this is the rate at which the U.S. Government can borrow, and that it is the rate that foreign central banks and governments earn on their dollar balances.

The discounted values for the simulations are shown in Table 3. If the account were liquidated after fifteen years and the whole cost of liquidation (making good shortfall) were borne by the United States, depositors would get back the full dollar value of their claims on the account (SDR 50 billion or $ 65.140 billion in the first simulation, and SDR 112.469 billion or $ 146.526 billion in the second simulation). The discounted values of these payments are listed on the first line of

TABLE 2

U.S. PAYS TREASURY BILL RATE: ALL INTEREST PAID IN SDR CLAIMS

End Year	SDR Claims Outstanding	Dollar Holdings	SDR Value of (3)	Interest Earned SDR Claims	Interest Earned $	Interest Paid by U.S. in $
1964	10.461	11.407	10.346	0.461	0.000	0.391
1965	21.431	23.319	21.167	0.970	0.000	0.886
1966	33.138	36.012	32.750	1.707	0.000	1.676
1967	45.191	49.043	45.410	2.053	0.000	2.035
1968	58.298	63.045	58.440	3.107	0.000	3.202
1969	62.373	67.262	62.401	4.075	0.000	4.218
1970	67.039	71.594	66.046	4.666	0.000	4.332
1971	70.639	74.701	65.828	3.600	0.000	3.107
1972	73.944	77.742	68.254	3.306	0.000	3.040
1973	80.171	83.207	69.804	6.226	0.000	5.465
1974	87.971	89.755	73.305	7.801	0.000	6.548
1975	94.050	94.979	81.130	6.079	0.000	5.224
1976	99.881	99.718	85.831	5.831	0.000	4.739
1977	105.764	104.974	86.419	5.883	0.000	5.255
1978	112.469	112.553	86.393	6.705	0.000	7.579

Status at liquidation: shortfall of 26.077 billion SDR (33.973 billion dollars)
Total interest paid by the United States: 57.698 billion dollars
Total interest earned by participants : 73.069 billion dollars

Table 3. When all interest income accumulates inside the account, as in the second simulation, this number measures the gross benefit of participation. When interest income is paid out in dollars, as in the first simulation, it is an understatement of the gross benefit. One must add in the discounted value of the interest income (and of interest earned on that interest income, because that income is added to the depositors' dollar reserves and, therefore, invested at the Treasury Bill rate). This is the number listed on the second line of Table 3, and the sum of the two numbers is the measure of gross benefit. It is, of course, larger in the second simulation, because interest income inside the account is valued in SDR, whereas interest income outside the account is valued in U.S. dollars, and the dollar depreciates in terms of the SDR during the period I examine.

The benefits of one arrangement, however, must always be compared with those of an alternative, and that done on the fourth line of Table 3. The alternative that I select may not be the one that some countries would have chosen, but is the one whose benefits are easiest to

TABLE 3

DISCOUNTED VALUES FOR SIMULATIONS IN WHICH U.S.
PAYS TREASURY BILL RATE
(All Values in Billions of U.S. Dollars)

Item	Interest Paid in	
	Dollars	SDR Claims
I. United States Pays Whole Cost of Liquidation:		
Value of depositors claims on account	29.406	66.145
Value of interest earned in dollars	30.809	—
Gross benefit of participation	60.215	66.145
Value of dollars reserves in account	50.809	50.809
Net benefit of participation	9.406	15.336
Cost of interest payment	35.572	35.572
Cost of liquidation payments	9.406	15.336
Gross cost of obligation	44.978	50.908
Cost of interest on dollar reserves	35.572	35.572
Net cost of obligation	9.406	15.336
II. United States Pays Half of Cost of Liquidation:		
Gross benefit of participation	55.512	58.477
Net benefit of participation	4.703	7.668
Gross cost of obligation	40.275	43.240
Net cost of obligation	4.703	7.668

calculate. If there had been support in 1964 for the creation of a substitution account, there might also have been interest on the part of some countries in diversifying their currency reserves, and they might have put together "baskets" of their currencies with rates of return higher than the one on the U.S. dollar (or, for that matter, higher than the one on the claim issued by the substitution account). Throughout this paper, however, I assume that all reserves are held in dollars if they are not deposited with the account, and they earn interest at the Treasury Bill rate. Therefore, I calculate the discounted value of the dollars put into the account (and of the interest income that would have been earned on those dollars), and I use it to compute the *net* benefit of participation in the account. Net benefit is positive in every single simulation, which says that participation would have been advantageous from the depositors' standpoint, compared with the retention of dollar reserves, even though it was not necessarily the most advantageous course of action.

The next five lines of Table 3 examine the costs of the obligation borne by the United States. The first line measures the discounted stream of interest payments made by the United States, including interest payments made directly to depositors when they invest their interest income from the account in additional dollar balances. The second line discounts back to 1964 the total shortfall at the time of liquidation, because I am assuming temporarily that the United States makes good the whole shortfall. The third line is the sum of the first two, and it measures the gross cost of the obligation borne by the United States. Finally, I invoke the assumption made above, that the alternative to participation was the retention of dollar reserves, and calculate the interest payments on those reserves. The discounted value of those payments is, of course, the saving conferred on the United States by the creation of the account, and it is therefore subtracted from the gross cost to measure the *net* cost of the obligation borne by the United States.

In the two simulations summarized by Table 3, the net benefit to the depositors equals exactly the net cost of the obligation borne by the United States. This is because the Treasury Bill rate has been used to calculate interest payments on the dollars held by the depositors and on the dollars held by the account itself. Total interest payments made by the United States are the same in the two simulations. Furthermore, the total interest payments made by the United States equal exactly the interest payments saved by the reduction in dollar reserves. Putting the point in different terms, the use of the Treasury Bill rate to calculate all interest payments made by the United States has the effect of isolating the liquidation payment as the only net benefit to the depositors and the only net cost to the United States. The account serves merely to confer an SDR guarantee on the depositors' dollar reserves. In subsequent simulations, where other interest rates are used to calculate interest payments by the United States, net benefits and costs will differ, and it will not be possible to identify net benefit or costs with the size of the liquidation payment.

At the start of this paper, I quoted the communiqué issued by the Interim Committee at its Belgrade meeting. It said that "costs and benefits should be fairly shared among all parties concerned ..." The calculations in the first part of Table 3 violate that principle, because the whole cost of liquidation is borne by the United States. We do not know how this principle would have been implemented, but I have applied it by splitting the liquidation costs evenly between the United States and the depositors. In the lower part of Table 3, half of the discounted cost of liquidation is transferred from the United States to the depositors, reducing the gross and net benefits of participation and reducing by the same amounts the gross and net costs of the obligation borne by the United States. In the first simulation, the benefits and costs are cut by half of $ 9.406 billion, and in the second simulation, they are cut by half of $ 15.336 billion. Note that the net benefit is still positive, and this is true in every simulation.

Before moving on to other interest-rate arrangements and other ways of dealing with the problem of financial balance, one more point should be made about my calculations. All of them assume that liquidation takes place at the end of fifteen years, so that the costs of liquidation are certain costs, just like the costs of interest payments. If liquidation were a possibility rather than a certainty, one would want to use the expected cost of liquidation in the fifteenth year (i.e., to multiply the cost of liquidation by the probability). But this procedure would be wrong if done for only one year. It would be necessary to construct a distribution of probabilities, one for each year in which liquidation might take place, and compute the benefits and costs of the account using the whole distribution.

Simulations were conducted using other interest rates. The United States was made to pay the floating bond rate, the fixed bond rate, the full combined rate, and the full combined rate plus a premium of one percentage point. The effects of these interest-rate arrangements are summarized in Table 4.

When the United States pays the long-term bond rate, the problem of flow balance is virtually solved. When the United States pays the full combined rate, the size of the problem is reduced substantially but not as dramatically. (Although the same interest rate is used to calculate the interest payments made by the account and by the United States, the depreciation of the dollar raises the dollar payments made by the account.) Because the problem of flow balance is reduced by all of these new arrangements, the shortfalls are smaller when the account is liquidated. When the United States paid the Treasury Bill rate, the shortfall was $ 20.837 billion; when it pays a floating fifteen-year U.S. Government Bond rate, the shortfall is cut to $ 11.386 billion; and when it pays the full combined rate plus a premium of one percentage point, the shortfall is cut to $ 1.501 billion. But these reductions in the shortfall do not reduce the net costs of the obligation borne by the United States — not when it bears the whole cost of liquidation nor when that cost is

TABLE 4

SUMMARY STATISTICS FOR SIMULATIONS IN WHICH ALL INTEREST IS PAID IN U.S. DOLLARS, WITH VARIOUS INTEREST RATES PAID BY THE UNITED STATES
(All Entries in Billions of U.S. Dollars)

Item	Interest Rate Paid by United States				
	Treasury Bill	Floating Bond	Fixed Bond	Full Combined	Full Combined Plus Premium [a]
Shortfall (−) at liquidation [b] ...	−20.837	−11.386	−11.667	−13.105	− 1.501
I. United States Pays Whole Cost of Liquidation:					
Cost of interest payments	35.572	40.962	41.873	40.370	47.563
Cost of liquidation payment ..	9.406	5.140	5.267	5.916	0.678
Gross cost of obligation	44.978	46.102	47.140	46.286	48.241
Net cost of obligation	9.406	10.530	11.568	10.714	12.669
II. United States Pays Half of Cost of Liquidation:					
Net benefit of participation ..	4.703	6.886	6.773	6.448	9.067
Net cost of obligation	4.703	7.960	8.934	7.756	12.330

[a] Premium set at one percentage point.

[b] This entry is measured in current dollars at the end of 1978; all other entries are discounted back to the start of 1964.

shared with the depositors. The increase in the cost of interest payments is always larger than the decrease in the cost of the liquidation payment. (This result reflects the fact that interest payments are made yearly, whereas the liquidation payment is made at the end, so that the liquidation payment is discounted more heavily.)

When the United States pays the whole cost of liquidation, interest-rate arrangements do not affect the gross or net benefits of participation, because depositors receive the full value of their claims. When liquidation costs are shared, however, gross and net benefits are affected by the size of the shortfall. The effect is shown in the second part of Table 4, where net benefits are higher under all of the new interest-rate arrangements. When, in fact, the shortfall is reduced to $ 1.501 billion, the net benefit of participation is almost as high as it is when the United States is made to bear the whole cost of liquidation; the cost of the depositors' share of the liquidation payment falls to only $ 0.339 billion.

There is no way to say that one of these arrangements is better than the rest. It depends on your point of view. Suppose that the United

States were pledged to pay the whole cost of liquidation and that the depositors were sure that it would do so, regardless of the size of the shortfall. The net benefit to the depositors would not be affected by the interest-rate arrangements, and they would have no reason to be worried about large dollar losses or large gaps on the books of the account. Accordingly, they would have no reason to insist that the United States pay a high interest rate. The United States, of course, would want to pay a low rate, such as the Treasury Bill rate, in order to replace (current) interest costs with (deferred) liquidation costs. In two other circumstances, however, the depositors might insist that the United States pay a high interest rate — if they had doubts about the willingness of the United States to honor its commitment or had themselves to bear some of the liquidation cost. They would then want to minimize the size of the shortfall in the account, because a shortfall would reduce the net benefit expected from participation. In these same circumstances, moreover, high interest rates have the largest effects on the costs of the account viewed from the standpoint of the United States. Look at the last two lines of Table 4, which deal with the case in which liquidation costs are shared, and concentrate on the effect of adding one percentage point to the full combined rate paid by the United States. The net benefit to the depositors rises by $ 2.619 billion, but the net cost to the United States rises by $ 4.574 billion. When the depositors have the strongest reasons for favoring the use of a high interest rate, the United States has the strongest reasons for resisting a high rate.

No one has suggested that the United States would default on its obligation to the account, but some countries were concerned at the prospect of large gaps on the books of the accounts. Their concerns produced two more proposals:

(1) That the parties make maintenance-of-value payments to limit the gaps (i.e., that they pay currently some fraction of their share of the liquidation payment implied by any gap).

(2) That some of the gold held by the IMF be sold for the benefit of the account.[13]

---

[13] There were two variants of the gold proposal: (a) that gold be sold at the outset and the net proceeds invested in dollars, giving the account some "equity" and additional interest income; (b) that gold be sold when necessary to make good an imbalance in the account. In both cases, the account would receive the net proceeds or profits from gold sales, defined as the difference between the market price of gold and the bookkeeping price used by the IMF. I do not deal with the first variant, because it is difficult to simulate historically. Had gold been sold at the start of 1964, there would have been no profit for the use of the account. The market price of gold was about the same as the relevant bookkeeping price.

To show how these schemes would work in the context of my simulations, I call for a "deficiency payment" or gold sale at the end of any year in which claims on the account exceed by more than five percent the value of the dollars held by the account. The payment or sale brings the gap back down to five per cent rather than closing it completely. The results are illustrated by Table 5, and additional results are summarized by Table 6. (If the "deficiency payments" shown in these tables had been made by the United States or shared by the depositors, one would want to discount them back to 1964 and use them in the benefit and cost calculations. I have not done so in Table 6, because the call for "deficiency payments" was replaced quite speedily by the plan to use the profits from gold sales, and I treat them as gold sales in the discussion that follows.)

TABLE 5

U.S. PAYS TREASURY BILL RATE: ALL INTEREST PAID IN U.S. DOLLARS
EFFECTS OF PROVISION FOR DEFICIENCY (GOLD) PAYMENTS

End Year	SDR Claims Outstanding	Dollar Holdings	SDR Value of (3)	Interest Earned		Interest Paid by U.S. in $	Deficiency Payment
				SDR Claims	$		
1964	10.000	10.899	9.885	0.000	0.508	0.391	0.000
1965	20.000	21.746	19.739	0.000	1.044	0.866	0.000
1966	30.000	32.571	29.621	0.000	1.791	1.599	0.000
1967	40.000	43.397	40.182	0.000	2.056	1.886	0.000
1968	50.000	54.060	50.111	0.000	3.037	2.900	0.000
1969	50.000	53.909	50.013	0.000	3.767	3.617	0.000
1970	50.000	53.327	49.194	0.000	4.054	3.472	0.000
1971	50.000	53.903	47.500	0.000	3.047	2.314	1.309
1972	50.000	54.102	47.500	0.000	2.665	2.194	0.671
1973	50.000	56.620	47.500	0.000	5.018	3.803	3.732
1974	50.000	58.159	47.500	0.000	5.957	4.456	3.040
1975	50.000	57.499	49.115	0.000	4.045	3.385	0.000
1976	50.000	56.767	48.861	0.000	3.602	2.869	0.000
1977	50.000	57.698	47.500	0.000	3.577	2.992	1.517
1978	50.000	61.883	47.500	0.000	4.130	4.166	4.149

Status at liquidation: shortfall of 2.500 billion SDR (3.257 billion dollars)
Total interest paid by the United States: 40.909 billion dollars
Total interest earned by participants: 48.299 billion dollars
Total deficiency (gold) payment: 14.418 billion dollars

When the United States is made to bear all of the liquidation cost, the addition of gold sales to the simulations has no effect on gross or net benefits of participation. The depositors receive the full value of their claims, and the benefits remain at the levels given in Table 3. The costs to the United States are reduced, however, and the reductions are quite large in the simulation that uses the Treasury Bill rate. There is, of course, some increase in the interest cost, because the United States has to pay interest on all dollars held by the account, including those obtained from gold sales, but this increase is smaller than the decrease in the cost of liquidation resulting from the cut in the size of the shortfall. When the liquidation costs are shared, the addition of gold

TABLE 6

EFFECTS OF PROVISION FOR DEFICIENCY (GOLD) PAYMENTS
SUMMARY STATISTICS FOR SELECTED SIMULATIONS IN WHICH
ALL INTEREST IS PAID IN U.S. DOLLARS
(All Entries in Billions of U.S. Dollars, Except as Noted)

Item	Interest Rate Paid by United States		
	Treasury Bill	Floating Bond	Full Combined
Shortfall (−) at liquidation [a]	−3.257	−3.257	−3.257
I. United States Pays Whole Cost of Liquidation:			
Cost of interest payments	37.179	42.108	41.077
Cost of liquidation payment	1.470	1.470	1.470
Gross cost of obligation	38.649	43.578	42.547
Net cost of obligation	3.077	8.006	6.975
II. United States Pays Half of Cost of Liquidation:			
Net benefit of participation	8.671	8.761	8.671
Net cost of obligation	2.342	7.271	6.240
Sum of deficiency payments	14.418	5.830	8.446
Gold sales implied by payments (millions of ounces) [b]	471	59	68

[a] This entry is measured in current dollars at the end of 1978; all entries in Parts I and II are discounted back to the start of 1964.

[b] Obtained by dividing an end-year profit rate on gold sales into the deficiency payment for that year. The profit rate is the difference between the dollar price of gold in London and the dollar equivalent of the official price (SDR 35 per ounce). The dollar equivalent is calculated with the "basket" valuation of the SDR used throughout these simulations.

sales adds to the benefits of participation, because it reduces the liquidation cost borne by the depositors. This effect is shown in the second part of Table 6, and it is largest when, without the sales, there was a large shortfall at liquidation. But the final section of the table is the most important, because it shows the sizes of the sales needed to make the requisite deficiency payments.[14]

The plan to use Fund gold in support of the account was flawed for three reasons. First, it antagonized less-developed countries, who argued that the Fund's gold should be used for their benefit.[15] Second, it attracted too much support from countries that wanted to limit their own obligations and argued that gold sales could substitute for governmental guarantees. Third and most important, gold sales could exhaust the Fund's gold holdings. In one of my simulations, the Fund has to sell 471 million ounces, more than the Fund held at any point in time.[16] In the other simulations, it must sell some 60-70 million ounces, which is more than half of what it held when the gold proposal was being considered.

Conclusion

The simulations summarized in this paper dealt with years in which the dollar depreciated sharply in terms of the SDR. There were thus substantial benefits to the depositors and large costs to the United States under all of the interest-rate arrangements examined, even when the liquidation costs were "fairly shared" between the depositors and the United States. The use of gold held by the IMF reduced the liquidation costs but ate up a large fraction of that gold. If the simulations had been run for another period, the benefits and costs would have been different. If they had started, for example, at the end of 1971, following

---

[14] To calculate the number of ounces sold, I have divided each year's deficiency payment by a "profit rate" (the London gold price at the end of the year in question *less* the dollar equivalent of the bookkeeping price used by the IMF).

[15] The Fund sold off some 50 million ounces of gold in 1976-1980. Half of this gold was sold directly to Fund members, at the old official price; the rest was sold at public auction, with the profits going to a Trust Fund established for the benefit of the less-developed countries. (Profits were defined in the manner described by the previous footnote.)

[16] The large gold sales in this simulation reflect the need to make gold sales in 1971 and 1972, when the "profit rates" on sales were quite low (market prices were not far from the old official price). But the sales required in subsequent years, when "profit rates" were higher, total about 100 million ounces.

the first devaluation of the dollar, and ended in 1980, after the dollar began to appreciate in terms of the SDR, the benefits and costs would have been somewhat smaller. To look ahead, moreover, one would have to take account of the recent changes in the attributes of the SDR — the reduction from sixteen to five in the number of currencies entering the valuation "basket" and the change in the definition of the full combined rate. These might have mixed effects on costs and benefits.[17]

The decision to create a substitution account, however, should not be based primarily on financial benefits and costs, even if one could calculate them accurately. Much weight should be given to the implications for the monetary system. I have argued that a multiple reserve-currency system is not "inherently" unstable, but it can add to the instability of exchange rates and can complicate the task of monetary management in countries whose currencies are used as reserves. One should give some weight, moreover, to the way that an account might widen the role of the SDR and enhance the role of the IMF itself. There are, in brief, important systemic effects that cannot be quantified.

There is never a good time to negotiate major changes in the international monetary system. One U.S. official put it well. When the dollar is weak, he suggested, the United States cannot obtain acceptable terms. When the dollar is strong, no one else is interested. This is all the more reason, however, to start talking soon again about a substitution account. To wait until cyclical forces weaken the dollar may be worse than trying to reach agreement at a time when holders of dollars have no wish to part with them.

New suggestions have been made, and they need to be considered. One participant in the last round of discussions has suggested that the next round should look at the integration of a substitution account with the IMF itself.[18] This would require an amendment to the Articles of Agreement, and that would take time, but there was perhaps excessive emphasis on haste in 1979-1980. An amendment would permit the exchange of currencies for SDR, not for a claim designed expressly for the purpose, which means that the problems of liquidity and yield could be solved by making appropriate changes in the attributes of the SDR, and the problem of financial balance might figure less prominently in

---

[17] Some of these effects have been studied in the Fund; see GEORGE M. VON FURSTENBERG, "Simulated Reserve Currency Performance Indicates Investment Qualities of the SDR", *IMF Survey*, January 26, 1981.

[18] See the remarks of J.J. POLAK at the Georgetown University Bankers Forum, summarized in the *IMF Survey*, October 27, 1980.

the negotiations. Governments might want to change some of the relevant Articles, and there would no doubt be bargaining on other issues too; but this process might serve to raise the numbers of countries and dollars involved in substitution.

Some participants in the last round have suggested a connection between substitution and recycling.[19] This is an interesting possibility, but it raises difficult issues. Substitution is intended to replace one reserve asset with another. The nature and success of the enterprise could perhaps be jeopardized by attempting to engage simultaneously in large-scale maturity transformation. Furthermore, the quality of the new reserve asset might be seen to depend on the creditworthiness of long-term borrowers, and this could limit the demand for the new asset. Finally, an attempt to connect the two endeavors might raise questions concerning the locus of control over Fund policies regarding the use of its resources — policies relating to eligibility and conditionality.

The role of gold in substitution and in the monetary system presents an interesting challenge. It was not wrong in principle but was perhaps unwise in practice to propose the use of IMF gold holdings as "backing" for the substitution account. If gold is to have a role in substitution, it should be quite different. Participants in a substitution account might be asked to deposit gold along with reserve currencies, and the United States might be asked to do so too. Valuation gains due to an increase in the market price of gold could be "monetized" in part, as in the European Monetary System, or used entirely to protect the financial balance of the substitution account.[20]

The first attempt to reach agreement, in 1979-1980, was inspired by belief that the system was in trouble — that it was moving rapidly in the wrong direction and had to be deflected. The next attempt, I have suggested, should be more leisurely, inspired by the need for a better reserve system rather than the fear of a worse one. But the need to take a long look at the problem is the strongest reason for starting right away.

Princeton

PETER B. KENEN

---

[19] See, for example, the address.by H. Johannes Witteveen at the Second International Monetary Conference in Philadelphia, November 13, 1980.

[20] Interest in this way of using gold was, of course, awakened by the creation of the EMS, but the idea has been around for many years. In 1969, for example, I recommended that "all central banks deposit all their gold, dollars and other reserve assets with the IMF, obtaining in exchange a new composite reserve asset backed by all the gold and other assets that had been held separately". ("The International Position of the Dollar in a Changing World", reprinted in KENEN, *Essays*, pt. III, p. 332).

Use of the SDR to Supplement or Substitute for Other Means of Finance

PETER B. KENEN*

The international economy does not stand still, and as it changes the international monetary system changes with it. Most of us have said this frequently. We cite as examples the decline in the role of the U.S. dollar as an international currency that reflected the decline in the global dominance of the U.S. economy and the earlier decline in the role of sterling that reflected the decline in the dominance of the U.K. economy. Two errors, however, creep into our analyses.

On the one hand, we pay insufficient attention to differences in the timing and extent of changes. The decline in the role of the dollar, for instance, began later than the decline in the dominance of the U.S. economy and has been much smaller (Kenen (1982)). On the other hand, we tend to concentrate on discontinuous changes in the monetary system, even though they may merely dramatize or ratify processes that started earlier. The closing of the U.S. gold window on August 15, 1971, was a dramatic event, but it should be viewed as the last act in a long process that transformed the gold-dollar standard into a pure dollar standard. The Jamaica Agreement of 1976, which led to the Second Amendment of the Articles of Agreement of the Fund, was a landmark in the history of the monetary system, but it served

*I am grateful to Richard Cooper, George von Furstenberg, Jeffrey Goldstein, Mohsin Khan, Jacques Polak, Ellen Seiler, and John Williamson for comments on the first draft of this paper. I am particularly grateful to John Williamson for his answer to a student's question at a Princeton seminar. Asked why governments should want to hold the SDR in lieu of a tailor-made basket of currencies, he pointed out that the "optimality" of a basket depends on the costs of buying and selling it. If the SDR were easier to transfer, it could be bought and sold cheaply, and governments might find it more attractive than a tailor-made basket. His answer led me to think about making the SDR more usable as a means of payment and thus to develop one main theme of this paper.

mainly to ratify changes in exchange rate arrangements that started even earlier than 1973, when rates began to float.

It is very hard to locate precisely the dates of innovations in the monetary system, even with the benefit of hindsight. It may be impossible to know when we are living through one. Nevertheless, I am becoming convinced that we passed through one such date in the last two years—that there has been another major change in the monetary system. If I am right, moreover, this conference is well timed, because the latest change in the monetary system will force us to pay more attention to reserve supplies and thus more attention to the special drawing right (SDR) as a reserve asset.

In the first part of this paper, I give reasons for believing that there has been such a change and that the SDR may have a more important role to play. In the second and third parts, I warn against being excessively ambitious. There is no point in trying to make the SDR the "principal reserve asset in the international monetary system" as envisaged in the Second Amendment of the Articles of Agreement of the Fund and no good way to do so without drastic changes in the system as a whole. In the fourth part of the paper, I list the steps that must be taken to make the SDR a more important reserve asset. In the fifth, I look at ways of making it more usable. In the sixth, I look at ways of making it more prominent. In the final section, I look at ways of making the supply more flexible.

I. WHERE WE MAY BE GOING

The changes in the monetary system that took place in the 1970s reduced the importance of reserves and the attention paid to them. The demand for reserves was surprisingly stable, according to conventional econometric estimates. But that demand was satisfied rather differently than it was in the 1960s. Furthermore, governments that had to finance balance of payments deficits did not rely primarily on the use of reserves.

Demand for Reserves

Although I was one of the first to estimate a demand function for reserves, I am somewhat skeptical of the whole approach. I have no problem with the basic premise. Governments hold reserves to bridge gaps between demand and supply in the foreign exchange market; when the demand for foreign currency exceeds the supply, a government can use its reserves to keep its exchange rate from changing. If governments anticipate large gaps, they will hold large reserves, given the costs of closing the gaps by changing or switching expenditure and the opportunity cost of investing in reserves. On this same premise, however, it should be hard to estimate a demand function for reserves; actual holdings at any time can be expected to differ appreciably from optimal holdings.

This objection has been raised before, and efforts have been made to meet it.[1] But it seems to have more force in principle than in practice. There does appear to be a demand function for reserves, although there is debate about some of its finer properties. More to the point, the demand functions estimated recently resemble closely those that were estimated earlier. The time-series estimates of Heller and Khan (1978) show that demand functions shifted in 1972 or 1973. So do the cross-country estimates of Frenkel (1980). But the shifts were smaller than one might have predicted, knowing what has happened to exchange rate arrangements and to other aspects of the monetary system.[2]

Supply of Reserves

The important innovations took place on the supply side, and they are often deemed to cast doubt on the need to make the SDR a more important reserve asset.

In the 1960s, the United States was the main supplier of reserves. It ran balance of payments deficits for most of the decade, and other countries financed them by building up their dollar holdings. In other words, the United States engaged in "liability financing" many years before that term was coined, but did so in a special way: it issued debt denominated in domestic currency. The amounts seem small in retrospect—$2 billion or $3 billion a year—but looked large at the time, and there was widespread agreement on the need to end the process. That is why the SDR was put in place, and the first allocation would not have occurred in 1969 if the United States had not incurred a balance of payments surplus in 1968-69, owing to a capital inflow induced by a tightening of monetary policy, which caused a sharp decline in other countries' reserves (see Solomon (1982, Chapter VIII)).

No country can run a balance of payments deficit unless some other country runs a balance of payments surplus. It is therefore simplistic to say that the stock of reserves was "supply determined" in the 1960s.[3] The term is useful, however, as a way to summarize three features of the situation.

First, major exchange rates were pegged. Changes in exchange rates

[1] For more on this issue, see Black (to be published in 1984). The method used most frequently to deal with the issue is the estimation of a long-run demand function with a fixed speed-of-adjustment coefficient. But theory argues that the speed of adjustment is determined jointly with the optimal quantity of reserves, which means that the speed-of-adjustment coefficient should not be fixed. I know of only one empirical paper (Bilson and Frenkel (1979)) in which the speed of adjustment is endogenous.

[2] Research on the use of reserves supports this conclusion. Reserve use did not decline in the early 1970s, despite the change in the exchange rate regime. See Suss (1976) and Williamson (1976). On factors affecting the demand for reserves under the present exchange rate regime, see von Furstenberg (1982).

[3] Some said that the stock of reserves was "demand determined" in the 1960s, because the surplus countries wanted more reserves and thus followed policies that drove the United States into deficit; see, for example, Kindleberger (1965).

could take place from time to time, but they were exceptional in law and practice. Therefore, intervention was more or less mandatory. Second, the dollar was the main intervention currency and was by far the most important reserve currency. Therefore, intervention led to increases in dollar holdings, and most countries were willing to retain those holdings. Finally, the deficits of the United States were the main cause for intervention. Looking at matters from the standpoint of a single country, intervention was required because its currency was strong; looking at matters from a global standpoint, however, intervention was required because the dollar was weak.

It is likewise simplistic but quite useful to say that the stock of reserves was "demand determined" in the 1970s. Intervention was not mandatory, not even for countries that were pegging their exchange rates. The dollar continued to be the main intervention currency, but it was not the only major reserve currency. And the payments deficits of the United States were not the main cause for intervention. (There was, indeed, a sense in which its measured deficits reflected the desire or willingness of others to increase their dollar holdings. The U.S. authorities did not intervene on a large scale before 1978. Therefore, measured deficits could come into being only insofar as other governments and central banks acquired dollars willingly.) In brief, there was no single source of reserves, and more important, there was no clear way to decide whether there was a shortage or surfeit of reserves.

The "Nonsystem" as a System

None of this was changed by the Second Amendment of the Fund's Articles of Agreement. Even after it took effect, some said that we were living with a nonsystem rather than a system. There were too few rules, and they were too weak.[4] But others argued that we were building a new system and should take some pride in it. Its rules were not written down. They were set by markets. But they might be more effective for that very reason.[5]

How does a market-based system work? International financial markets set the terms on which governments must choose between financing and adjustment. Foreign exchange markets set the terms on which governments must choose between types of adjustment and also force them to make realistic use of their freedom to select their own exchange rate arrangements. Governments are made to behave like ordinary economic actors—large ones to be sure—in credit and currency markets alike.

Even those who had strong reservations about the sufficiency of these

[4] See, for example, de Vries (1976) and Williamson (1977).
[5] See Corden (1981) and his paper, "Is There an Important Role for an International Reserve Asset Such as the SDR?," which is Chapter 5 in this volume.

implicit rules and the consistency with which markets would apply them saw that there had been fundamental changes in the monetary system, in addition to the changes in exchange rate arrangements. The successful "recycling" of the surpluses of the oil exporting countries had demonstrated that liability financing was an option open to most governments—not only to reserve centers—and its availability could markedly reduce the need for reserves to finance balance of payments deficits. When reserves were needed, moreover, they could be created by borrowing, as well as by official intervention in the foreign exchange markets. There would thus be no need for organized reserve creation of the kind envisaged a decade ago, when the First Amendment of the Fund's Articles made way for the creation of SDRs.

Now that recycling has ended, however, we can see why so many countries were able to engage in liability financing—why recycling was successful. There were three special reasons:

(1) In the 1960s, many developing countries adopted "outward-looking" development strategies; they abandoned import substitution in favor of export promotion. One would expect this policy change to raise rates of return in export-oriented industries (and those related to them), and that is what seems to have happened. The countries that adopted outward-looking policies in the 1960s were, of course, the newly industrializing countries of the 1970s, and they were large borrowers when recycling started. This is, I believe, the explanation for the relationship that Sachs (1981) has discovered: capital formation continued at high rates in many developing countries by comparison with rates in developed countries, and the current account deficits of those countries were therefore associated with high levels of investment rather than "excessive" levels of consumption.

(2) Most of those same countries entered the 1970s with rather light debt-service burdens. There was some concern about those burdens in the 1960s. Yet Bacha and Díaz-Alejandro (1982) remind us that debt-service ratios were quite low by historical standards. Furthermore, it looked as though most countries could borrow large amounts without greatly increasing their debt-service burdens. At the start of each burst of borrowing, in 1974 and in 1979, nominal interest rates were low and real rates were even lower.

(3) The concentration of current account surpluses was unique, and so was its disposition. A handful of oil exporting countries were building up huge claims on the outside world, and they chose for various reasons to hold those claims in liquid forms. Thus, banks had large sums to lend just when they were wanted.

This set of circumstances would be hard to reproduce—and it did not last. In fact, it fell apart completely. A recession, increased resort to protection, and other events in the developed countries conspired to reduce rates of return in the developing countries. The policies that caused the recession, moreover, led to a sharp increase in debt-service burdens. Finally, the decline in the demand for oil induced by price increases and by the recession ended the concentration of current account surpluses.

In 1976-78, the years between the oil price increases, the developing countries built up their reserves. Total reserves (excluding gold) of the non-oil developing countries rose from SDR 28.4 billion at the end of 1975 to SDR 57.5 billion at the end of 1978. Broadly speaking, moreover, the buildup was deliberate: governments chose to borrow more than they needed to finance their countries' current account deficits. There is a fairly strong cross-country correlation between reserves and debts, and it easy to adduce good reasons for it. (See, for example, Eaton and Gersovitz (1981).) But events were soon to prove the truth of Robertson's remark that "owned reserves are no use unless you use them and borrowed reserves are no use if you *do* have to use them" (Robertson (1956, p. 111)). When the new market-based monetary system started to show signs of strain in 1981–82, the banks began to gobble up the reserves that they had furnished.

In the 1970s, the banks were part of the solution. In the 1980s, they are part of the problem. Governments must still choose between financing and adjustment on terms set by credit markets, but those terms have changed abruptly. Some governments continue to believe that market forces should determine their exchange rates, but there is growing discontent with the rates that markets choose. Changes in exchange rates are part of the solution, but they can be part of the problem as well.

Need for a Little Less Endogeneity

Looking back on the events of the last ten years, I arrive at one very general conclusion. We may have built too much endogeneity into the international monetary system. Movements in real exchange rates have been too large, because of the big medium-term swings in nominal exchange rates. Credit flows have been too large and now threaten to be too small. The supply of reserves may be too elastic—in both directions. It is, I believe, important to impart a bit more "viscosity" to the monetary system—to reduce the amplitude of exchange rate changes, to stabilize credit flows, and to keep reserve supplies from behaving perversely.

The need for a more stable stock of reserves has not attracted much attention. It may be less important than the need for more stable exchange rates or for more stable credit flows. It may attract attention too tardily, however, only after reserves have contracted sharply. We should therefore start work on the problem immediately, using to the fullest extent possible the powers and facilities of the Fund. It is the only agency that can create a reserve asset whose quantity and quality can be controlled precisely—an attribute that we may come to value highly in an increasingly uncertain world.

II. WHERE WE SHOULD BE GOING

The objective just set forth—to make the stock of reserves more stable by raising or reducing the supply of SDRs to offset in whole or part sharp fluctuations in supplies of other reserve assets—can be achieved without a change in existing law or practice. It is thoroughly consistent with the language of Article XVIII, Section 1(*a*):

> In all its decisions with respect to the allocation and cancellation of special drawing rights the Fund shall seek to meet the long-term global need, as and when it arises, to supplement existing reserve assets in such a manner as will promote the attainment of its purposes and will avoid economic stagnation and deflation as well as excess demand and inflation in the world.

If reserves begin to fall and the members of the Fund become concerned, the Managing Director can propose an SDR allocation, even in the midst of a "basic period" for which no allocation was voted initially (see Article XVIII, Section 3).[6]

The stabilization of reserves is, in fact, a modest aim compared with the avoidance of deflation and inflation, and very much more modest than the long-term objective "of making the special drawing right the principal reserve asset in the international monetary system," set forth in Article XXII.

Under present circumstances, however, stabilization is feasible only if there is a tendency for the supply of reserves to contract. The Fund can allocate additional SDRs. Stabilization is not feasible if there is a tendency for reserves to expand. The Fund can cancel existing SDRs, but there are too few to matter. That is why a large part of this paper will be concerned with ways of introducing SDRs into the system without necessarily increasing reserves and with ways of stimulating the demand for them by making the SDR more attractive. Before turning to these issues, however, let us look more closely at the long-term aim embodied in Article XXII.

Why the SDR Might Be Made the Principal Reserve Asset

Why would one want to make the SDR the principal reserve asset in the international monetary system? Two main reasons have been given:

The first has to do with economic stability. Unless the SDR becomes the principal reserve asset, it will be impossible to control the supply of reserves,

---

[6] Such an allocation should probably be voted in conjunction with the current round of increases in quotas. I return to this matter at the end of my paper.

and firm control is necessary in order to avoid the twin evils of deflation and inflation.

The second has to do with systemic stability. Unless the SDR becomes the principal reserve asset, it will be impossible to consolidate the stock of reserves, and consolidation is necessary in order to avoid the "inherent instability" of a multiple reserve asset system.

I am not greatly impressed by either of these arguments. A sharp contraction in the supply of reserves would be costly. That is why I stress the need for stabilization. I do not believe, however, that the world can avoid deflation and inflation merely by controlling the supply of international reserves. It is not sufficient or efficient for that purpose. Sudden shifts between reserve assets could be costly too, because they can exacerbate exchange rate instability. That is one of my reasons for favoring substitution, and I will return to this subject. I do not believe, however, that a multiple reserve asset system is a threat to systemic stability.

The Case for Control

There is by now abundant statistical evidence that reserves can "cause" inflation. But one must look behind this statistical relationship, especially in light of the finding by Khan (1979) for industrial countries that inflation "caused" reserves in the 1970s. In the years before the breakdown of the Bretton Woods system, most of the growth in reserves was due to the U.S. payments deficit, and much of it was monetized. In other words, reserve growth was part of the process by which U.S. monetary growth was transformed into global monetary growth. The evidence should not be read to say that reserve growth per se causes inflation.

I can make my point more strongly. Many say that money is the main cause of inflation, and some put the argument in global terms—most recently McKinnon (1982). But no one has been able to convince me that there is a close and stable relationship between money and reserves—for any single country or the world as a whole. When reserve creation takes place because of nonsterilized intervention, there will be an increase in the supply of money. When it is accomplished by bookkeeping alone, as is the case with an SDR allocation, it has no direct effect on the supply of money.

But what about the need for discipline? Is it not self-evident that governments are cowardly and irresponsible and will therefore produce inflations whenever they confront unpleasant choices? Is it not essential to constrain them externally by limiting the stock of reserves?

Governments do produce inflations. No one else can—for long. But external constraints cannot stop them. Governments violate those constraints whenever they get in the way. In fact, the case for imposing external constraints is based on quixotic logic. If governments are responsible enough to abide by external constraints, the constraints will be redundant. If governments are irresponsible enough to opt for inflation when they face hard choices, external constraints will not work. Governments will violate them—as they have before.[7]

Furthermore, reserve constraints are inefficient. They cannot have much influence on policies in countries that have floating exchange rates, and those are the countries that matter most for global stability. They can induce a country with a pegged exchange rate to deal quickly with a balance of payments deficit—but only if the country cannot borrow and must draw on its reserves. Even in these instances, moreover, they cannot control the quality of the adjustment process. They cannot force a country to choose sensible policies.

The Case for Consolidation

At the end of 1975, the U.S. dollar accounted for 79.4 percent of official foreign exchange holdings; at the end of 1981, it accounted for 70.6 percent. Its share in the reserves of industrial countries fell from 87.3 percent to 78.9 percent; its share in the reserves of developing countries fell faster and more sharply, from 70.8 percent to 61.7 percent.[8] The decline in the relative importance of the dollar as a reserve asset was matched by an increase in the relative (and absolute) importance of the deutsche mark, the Japanese yen, and the Swiss franc. The share of the deutsche mark in total foreign exchange reserves rose from 6.3 percent in 1975 to 12.5 percent in 1981. In brief, the world moved much closer to a multiple reserve asset system.

Many central banks and governments have engaged in reserve diversification. Their reasons are listed and discussed elsewhere (see Group of Thirty (1982)). The governments of the new reserve centers were at first

---

[7] Cooper (1982, p. 45) makes a similar point with reference to *all* monetary rules. He asks

...why one should think that experts are more clever at devising operational, nondiscretionary monetary regimes than they are at monetary management within a discretionary regime. If the desire for a nondiscretionary regime is really simply another way ... of assigning priority above all others to the objective of price stability in the management of monetary policy, that can be done directly by instructing the Federal Reserve unambiguously to take whatever action is necessary to ensure price stability. If collectively we are ambivalent about that priority, that is the principal source of the problem, not the nature of the regime.

Note that there would be something uniquely quixotic about an attempt to impose an SDR reserve constraint. If governments were determined to produce inflations, they would need merely to vote large allocations. They would control the reserve constraint.

[8] International Monetary Fund (1982, p. 65). These figures exclude European Currency Units (ECUs); those ECUs that were issued against dollars are treated as if they were dollars, and those issued against gold are omitted. When ECUs are treated as foreign exchange reserves, the share of the dollar in global foreign exchange holdings falls to 58.4 percent at the end of 1981, and its share in the holdings of industrial countries falls to 55.9 percent.

reluctant to accept more important roles for their currencies, but they have become increasingly comfortable with them (see the papers by Rieke and Leutwiler and Kästli in Roosa and others (1982)). There is no need to say much more about those matters here. It is important, however, to look at the consequences of these developments.

Two strong views obtain. Some say that a multiple reserve asset system is "inherently unstable" (see, e.g., Group of Thirty (1980)). Others have suggested, however, that it may contribute to stability by subjecting a larger number of important countries to more monetary discipline (see, e.g., Leutwiler and Kästli in Roosa and others (1982)).

The first of these two views is based on an invalid analogy. I have discussed it elsewhere (Kenen (1981, p. 408)):

> The bimetallic standard of the Nineteenth Century, based on gold and silver, was a multiple reserve-asset system, and it broke down eventually. The gold-exchange standards of the interwar and postwar periods, based on sterling and the dollar, were unstable too. But most analogies are imperfect, and so are these. The "inherent" instability of earlier reserve regimes derived from the authorities' attempts to peg the prices of the reserve assets despite changes in their relative scarcities. Those attempts invited self-aggravating speculation whenever it seemed possible that the authorities would exhaust their holdings of the scarce asset. Present arrangements may not invite this form of speculation, because the authorities do not try to peg the prices of the reserve assets. Exchange rates connecting the dollar, Deutschemark and other reserve currencies are managed, but management is very different from pegging in its implications for the stability of the reserve system. It does not invite self-aggravating speculation.

Flexible exchange rates cannot repeal Gresham's Law but can protect the reserve system from its worst effect—a "run" on the supply of one reserve asset that can exhaust official holdings and thus undermine the system.

What about the other view, that a multiple reserve asset system can impose an appropriate discipline on the reserve centers? The usual objections hold. The very feature that maintains stability in a multiple reserve asset system—exchange rate flexibility—also reduces the power of any external constraint to improve policy, and I have expressed other doubts about the efficiency of any such constraint (Kenen (1981)). But two additional objections apply to this particular version of the case for discipline.

Recent experience warns that we can suffer a surplus of discipline rather than a shortage. A shift of funds from one reserve currency to another, from the deutsche mark to the dollar, for example, can be produced by an excessively restrictive monetary policy on the part of the United States rather than an excessively lax policy on the part of the Federal Republic of Germany. The shift is then apt to foster a competitive tightening of monetary policies.

The argument, moreover, appears to be founded on an inconsistency. It tells us that governments cannot be trusted to make good policies—that they have to be disciplined by market forces. At the same time, it says that governments and central banks will manage their reserves in ways that will force others to improve their policies. If the government of country X cannot be trusted to keep its own house in order, why should it be trusted to manage its reserves in a manner that will force the governments of the United States, the Federal Republic of Germany, and Japan, to keep *their* houses in order?

Conceivably, a government or central bank will act prudently when managing its currency reserves even though it acts imprudently when managing its economy. To rely on this possibility, however, is to place great confidence indeed in the optimality of profitable speculation—and in the ability of governments and central banks to engage in profitable speculation. Some central banks have lost money (Group of Thirty (1982, p. 6)), and central banks as a group have tended to destabilize exchange rates when switching from one currency to another (Bergsten and Williamson (1983)). I do not have much confidence in their ability to optimize the policies of the reserve currency countries.

A More Modest Case for Consolidation

Nevertheless, there is a case for consolidation. It is based on the threat to exchange rate stability, not any threat to systemic stability, posed by the possibility of large switches between reserve assets.

I have already cited recent work by Bergsten and Williamson (1983), which covers seven currencies and examines separately behavior by developed and developing countries. Bergsten and Williamson are careful to point out that their methods are not perfect; an outright shift from one reserve asset to another is hard to segregate from a change in asset shares due to a change in total reserves, and they have used trend values of exchange rates to define "equilibrating" speculation. But theirs is the most careful study I have seen, and this is their conclusion:

> The results suggest rather strongly that reserve shifts were in general destabilizing. In only four [of fourteen] cases is there evidence of an overall stabilizing pattern, and one of those results is very weak.... For example, the largest shift (as measured) by the industrial countries into the dollar occurred in 1976:4, almost simultaneously with the dollar's peak, while the largest shifts out occurred during the weakness of 1978-79.... They moved into the DM when it first began to weaken in 1975:3 ... but afterwards shifted out all through the period of DM weakness, only to shift back in as the DM strengthened in 1978. The shifts of the nonindustrial countries are less dramatically destabilizing, but the net effect was qualitatively similar.

No sensible observer would claim that these shifts by central banks and governments were the main reason for exchange rate fluctuations. Too many sensible people tend to disregard them, however, or belittle their importance in the past and the damage they can do in the future.

There is another reason for favoring consolidation, and it is more important for the main theme of this paper. It may be the fastest way to increase the quantity of SDRs in the reserve system and therefore to give the Fund significant symmetrical influence over the supply of reserves—the ability to cancel SDRs on a significant scale when and if it is appropriate to do so, as well as the ability to create them.

III. INTERDEPENDENCE OF INSTITUTIONAL ARRANGEMENTS

There are two ways in which the SDR could be made the principal reserve asset in the monetary system:

(1) By introducing a system of fractional reserve requirements based on the SDR.

(2) By moving in one step to a monetary system in which the SDR is the only reserve asset.

The first method could give the Fund partial control over the quantity of reserves—the power to keep reserves from rising, if not from falling. But it would be an awkward way to achieve control, and it would not insulate exchange rates from the effects of switches between other reserve assets, because it would not take them out of the system. The second method would require mandatory substitution—an exchange of newly issued SDRs for all other reserve assets. But that would not be enough. Mandatory substitution would have to be accompanied by mandatory asset settlement or by major changes in the functioning of currency and credit markets. I will give the reasons shortly.

Making the SDR the Primary Reserve Asset

A system of fractional reserve requirements was proposed by H. Johannes Witteveen when he was Managing Director of the Fund. Under his proposal, the SDR would become the principal reserve asset by becoming the "primary" reserve asset. National currencies would be treated as "secondary" reserve assets, and there would be "holding limits" on those secondary assets. They could not be larger than some multiple (or fraction) of a country's holdings of primary assets. By controlling the supply of primary assets, the Fund would limit its members' ability to hold secondary assets and could therefore control the growth of global reserve holdings.

There are fundamental difficulties with this plan. Here is what I said about it in another paper (Kenen (1977, p. 216)):

> Consider the plight of a country that has reached its holding limit. If it is unable to obtain additional SDRs, its holding limit is transformed into an absolute injunction against intervention to prevent appreciation of the country's currency. As such, it is exposed to all of my complaints about reserve-based rules to regulate intervention—and to the additional complaint that an injunction against intervention could be imposed by the compo-

sition as well as the level of a country's reserves, an accident of history that can have little bearing on the desirability of intervention.

There are, of course, two ways in which a country can acquire additional SDRs: it can buy them or can borrow them. No country, however, is entitled automatically to buy SDRs from another.... The Second Amendment does allow countries to deal more freely in SDRs than they could before; voluntary transfers, presumably including loans or sales subject to repurchase, can be agreed between two countries without specific IMF approval. But the removal of restrictions on transfers not mandated by "designation" is no guarantee that a country will find a voluntary seller or lender, and the likehood of finding a supplier is itself inversely related to the effectiveness of a holding limit.

It would, of course, be possible to give each member of the Fund the right to purchase SDRs from some other member when it came into possession of the other member's currency. But this solution would impose a form of mandatory asset settlement that would function in a strangely asymmetrical manner. The same problem arises in conjunction with the other way to make the SDR the principal reserve asset, and I will discuss it in that connection.[9]

Making the SDR the Only Reserve Asset

Suppose that the members of the Fund decide that the SDR should be the *only* reserve asset. They agree to exchange all other reserve assets for new SDRs and never again to hold those other reserve assets. Let us set aside the transitional problems and those that have to do with the final disposition of the other reserve assets. They will have a chance to plague us later. Let us focus on the problems that members of the Fund must solve after the exchange of assets has been completed.

Once the SDR becomes the only reserve asset, a government or central bank that acquires dollars by intervening in the foreign exchange market cannot hold those dollars as reserves. It has to exchange them for SDRs. Therefore, someone must stand ready to swap SDRs for dollars, and there are two candidates—the Fund and the United States. But both of them should be reluctant to take on that obligation.

If the Fund agreed to create SDRs whenever its members wanted to sell dollars, it would be seen as giving open-ended support to the currency and policies of a single member. The United States would continue to possess the "exorbitant privilege" of being a reserve currency country even though

[9] There are practical problems as well. Governments have many ways of hiding reserve assets; they can place them with commercial banks and nonmonetary institutions. It would be impossible for the Fund to monitor reserves comprehensively in order to make sure that members were obeying the fractional reserve requirement. Similar problems arise in connection with the proposal discussed below, under which the SDR would be the only reserve asset. It would be hard for the Fund to make sure that members were holding only SDRs (and even harder to make sure that the SDR was used in all official transactions that could affect reserves).

the dollar had ceased to be a reserve asset. In fact, it would possess a more potent privilege than ever before, because it could finance its "deficits" by running the Fund's printing press. (No matter that those "deficits" would be, as noted earlier, by-products of discretionary intervention on the part of other countries. They would say what they have always said—that U.S. policies forced them to intervene.)

If the United States agreed to sell SDRs for dollars, even at a market price that could change from day to day, it would be subject to a form of mandatory asset settlement, and that would be ironic. Mandatory settlement has no proper place in the present monetary system.

In the days of the Committee of Twenty, mandatory asset settlement was seen as a way of making the monetary system more symmetrical—of imposing a conventional reserve constraint on the United States. In present circumstances, mandatory settlement would make the monetary system *less* symmetrical. The vast majority of Fund members would continue to control their own reserve positions and be free to choose between financing and adjustment in the light of those positions. The United States and other key-currency countries would lose control of their positions and would thus be less free to choose between financing and adjustment. In fact, the key-currency countries might have to adjust precisely because other countries wanted to finance—to build up their reserves by purchasing dollars, deutsche mark, or Japanese yen and selling them for SDRs.

I have argued elsewhere (Kenen (1980)) that there is just one way out. If governments and central banks cannot hold national currencies as reserve assets, they cannot be allowed to use them. They must use the SDR instead. The SDR can become the only reserve asset in the international monetary system only when it has become the instrument of choice for *all* official operations that affect reserves—for intervention, borrowing, and so on. Otherwise, asymmetries will creep into the system.

The SDR cannot become the instrument of choice, however, until it is widely used in currency and credit markets. Central banks cannot begin to intervene in SDRs until the SDR is traded in the foreign exchange markets. Governments cannot begin to borrow SDRs until banks and other private institutions are capable of lending them.[10] The monetary system is a complicated organism. It can change by itself, rapidly at times. It can be

---

[10] It might indeed be necessary to alter commercial arrangements as well as financial arrangements. Many primary products, including oil, are sold for dollars, and some of the dollars find their way into the hands of central banks, more or less directly. There are several ways of preventing this from happening. Exports could be sold for dollars, but exporters could be required to go to the foreign exchange market to sell their dollars for SDR deposits at commercial banks. Exports could be sold for domestic currency, which means that importers would be required to go to the foreign exchange market to buy it. Exports could be sold directly for SDR deposits.

changed by governments, but it has to be changed carefully. It is hard to modify one of its main features without also modifying many other features.

IV. HOW TO MAKE THE SDR A MORE IMPORTANT RESERVE ASSET

If I am right about the interdependence of institutional arrangements and its implications for reform of the international monetary system, there is little point in dwelling longer on ways to make the SDR the principal reserve asset. It cannot be done without making many other institutional changes. If I am also right, however, in saying that the monetary system will work differently in the 1980s than it did in the 1970s, reserves will play a larger role in the years ahead, and more attention should be paid to the supply of reserves. Therefore, an attempt should be made to stabilize the stock or growth rate of reserves, and that can be done by altering the supply of SDRs to offset unanticipated increases and decreases in supplies of other reserve assets—especially to offset decreases brought about by abrupt withdrawals of borrowed reserves.

The supply of SDRs can, of course, be increased by resuming allocations. Experience suggests, however, that this method will add only slowly to the stock of SDRs. The major industrial countries must consent to any allocation, and they have little direct interest in increasing or stabilizing global reserves. They have their own credit facilities—the swaps, the European Monetary Cooperation Fund, and so on—and can still count on borrowing if that should be necessary. Furthermore, too many of their governments continue to believe that they must fortify their "credibility" and are thus prone to seize every opportunity, sensible or silly, to display their horror of inflation. Finally, other issues tend to "crowd out" allocations. If forced to choose between an increase of Fund quotas and an allocation of SDRs, I would have done just what the Managing Director did—devote most of my time and even more of my political capital to the increase of Fund quotas.

If time and capital are to be invested in the SDR, they should be used in these three ways:

—To make the SDR more attractive by making it more usable as a means of payment.

—To make the SDR more prominent by trying once again to induce voluntary substitution.

—To find ways in which the Fund can alter the supply of SDRs without having to allocate or cancel them formally.

These three objectives should be pursued simultaneously, but I attach particular importance to the first. Unless the SDR is made more attractive, it cannot be made more plentiful.

V. MAKING THE SDR MORE USABLE

In early discussions of the SDR, it was sometimes described as "paper gold" and did indeed resemble gold. Its value was defined in terms of gold; its interest rate was very low; and it was transferable between official institutions, not between official and private institutions.[11]

There were, of course, important differences between the SDR and gold, mainly with regard to transferability. No country could run down its holdings of SDRs unless it had a "balance of payments need" to use them, even if some other country wanted to accept them, and when a country used them for balance of payments purposes, it still had to "reconstitute" some of them eventually. No country was required to accept SDRs, even under "designation" by the Fund, if its holdings were already three times as large as its allocations.[12] Nevertheless, the two assets were more similar than different, because the SDR was deliberately designed to serve the same basic monetary function as gold—to make official settlements.

There have been many changes in the attributes of the SDR. Its value is defined today in terms of a basket of five currencies; its interest rate is based on short-term market rates in the five countries whose currencies go into the basket; and some of the restrictions on its use have been eliminated. (Voluntary transfers are permitted freely between official institutions, and the "reconstitution" requirement has been abolished.) The SDR has become a more attractive store of value and, to that extent, a more attractive reserve asset.

The changes in the attributes of the SDR, however, have not caught up with one fundamental change in the monetary system—the virtual elimination of official settlements. Governments continue to hold reserves for financing balance of payments deficits. When they use reserves, however,

[11] Gold was transferable between official and private institutions before March 1968 by way of the "gold pool" established in 1960. Once that arrangement was abandoned, however, and the free-market price of gold was allowed to rise, two gold stocks came into being—gold held officially and gold held privately—and they were strictly separated for several years. Note that the SDR as defined initially could have been used in much the way that gold was used in the nineteenth century—to maintain fixed exchange rates without active intervention. Suppose that the SDR had become the "pivot" for parities, and each government had posted prices for its currency in terms of the SDR—a buying price and selling price. Arbitrage in SDRs would have kept exchange rates within the margins corresponding to the posted prices. It would not have been necessary to permit private holdings of SDRs, only to issue transferable drafts on official holdings.

[12] For details and subsequent developments, see the background paper by the staff of the Fund, "The Evolving Role of the SDR in the International Monetary System," which is Chapter 11 in this volume.

they typically transfer them to private institutions rather than official institutions, through the foreign exchange market. Those official settlements that do take place today are mainly between governments and the Fund— and they are the ones that use the SDR most frequently.

To make the SDR much more attractive as a reserve asset, it must be made more usable as a means of payment. It must be made transferable to private institutions.

Transferability can be achieved by permitting private institutions to hold official SDRs, but this direct approach has three disadvantages: (1) it would require an amendment to the Articles of Agreement; (2) it would add hugely to the volume of transactions crossing the books of the Fund; and (3) it would complicate decision making in the Fund, because decisions affecting the supply of official SDRs would be seen to affect the liquidity of the private sector and thus to impinge directly on the powers and responsibilities of national central banks. I will soon show, however, that transferability can be achieved without permitting private holdings of official SDRs.

The Private Life of the SDR

Private use of the SDR has developed rapidly in the last two years, spurred by the simplification of the currency basket at the beginning of 1981. It is used as a unit of account in credit and bond markets, and a number of banks accept deposits denominated in it. Furthermore, official institutions have been involved importantly in these innovations. In fact, the bulk of borrowing in SDRs has been by governments and state-owned enterprises, and official institutions are said to hold some of the SDR deposits.[13] The SDR, however, is used in private markets *only* as a unit of account, not as a means of payment. Loan proceeds are transferred in national currencies (usually in dollars), and repayments are also made in currencies.

One could probably arrange to transfer an SDR deposit to pay for an SDR bond, even for one issued by an official institution. But this could be done only on an ad hoc basis, and it would be difficult, because the SDR in which the bond is denominated can differ in small but significant ways from the one in which the deposit is denominated. There are "open" and "closed" baskets and other definitions as well (see Coats (1982, p. 428)). Furthermore, an official institution that took in SDR deposits by borrowing or floating a bond issue could not add them to its balance with the Fund; it could not transform them into official SDRs.

---

[13] These developments are discussed by Sobol (1981) and in the background paper by the staff of the Fund, "Evolution of the SDR Outside the Fund," which is Chapter 13 in this volume.

The staff of the Fund has looked at ways of reducing the differences among private SDRs, with a view to broadening the private use of the SDR in international financial markets (see the background paper, "Possible Further Improvements in the Existing SDR," which is Chapter 12 in this volume). Coats (1982) develops one proposal in detail—the use of the Fund as a clearinghouse and of the official SDR as the instrument for making the private SDR an efficient means of payment. He is on the right track, but he does not emphasize sufficiently the most important advantages of his proposal, and his scheme is unnecessarily radical.

The Need for a Clearinghouse

If the official SDR were used to clear private payments, the small but tricky differences in private SDRs would begin to disappear. The official SDR would gradually become the standard SDR. This sort of standardization must take place if the SDR is to be used eventually in foreign exchange trading, and that has to happen before the SDR can be used for official intervention. Furthermore, use of the official SDR to clear private payments would link it directly to the private SDR, and this linkage must take place to make the official SDR a useful reserve asset—to catch up with the main change in the monetary system to which I referred earlier. Governments that borrow in SDRs should be able to add the proceeds to their SDR balances with the Fund, and they should also be able to use those balances to repay their debts. Governments that finance their balance of payments deficits by intervention in the foreign exchange market should be able to transfer SDRs to foreign exchange traders.

Under the plan proposed by Coats, members of the Fund would authorize their central banks to open SDR accounts for their own commercial banks. Such accounts could be used to clear transactions between banks in a single country. They could be used jointly with accounts at the Fund— official SDRs—to clear transactions between banks in different countries. Under this particular plan, however, governments would have to give up control over their own holdings of official SDRs. Whenever a French bank made an SDR payment to a British bank, official SDRs would be transferred automatically from the Bank of France to the Bank of England.

Under that same plan, moreover, it would be necessary to abolish immediately the "acceptance limit" on official holdings, along with the requirement of "balance of payments need," and the viability of "designation" may still depend on the survival of those two provisions. If the official SDR were freely transferable to private holders and thus fully usable for balance of payments purposes, there would be no need for "designation" and for the provisions that make it acceptable. But those provisions cannot be abolished in order to begin a process that renders them redundant only at the end.

These difficulties can be overcome, however, by inserting a clearing-house between the central banks and the commercial banks. Transactions between commercial banks would take place on the books of the clearing-house, even those involving banks in different countries, and there would be no need for transfers of official SDRs. But transfers of official SDRs would take place whenever central banks (or governments) had dealings with commercial banks—whenever official institutions wanted to "trans-form" private SDRs into official SDRs or to go the other way—by borrow-ing, repaying debt, or intervening in the foreign exchange market.

Table 1 traces the transactions involved in setting up a clearinghouse. If Lloyds Bank wanted to join it, it would use its (sterling) balance at the Bank of England to buy official SDRs and pay them over to the clearing-house. In this example, its subscription is SDR 100 million. The accounts of the Bank of England show a 100 million reduction in official SDRs held by the Bank of England and in its (sterling) deposit obligation to Lloyds Bank. The accounts of Lloyds Bank show the same reduction in the bank's (sterling) balance at the Bank of England. It is offset by the bank's SDR deposit with the clearinghouse. The accounts of the clearinghouse show an SDR deposit with the Fund and an SDR deposit obligation to Lloyds Bank.[14]

Table 2 traces a transaction between two commercial banks and shows that it has no effect on the SDR holdings of any central bank. In this exam-ple, Lloyds Bank uses SDR 75 million to buy yen from the Bank of Tokyo, and the SDR transfer is made on the books of the clearinghouse. (I omit the balance sheet of the Bank of Tokyo, as I do not need it to make my point.) The accounts of Lloyds Bank show its additional holdings of yen and the reduction in its SDR balance at the clearinghouse. The accounts of

---

[14] In consequence of the transactions shown in Table 1, the Bank of England is a net user of official SDRs and loses interest income; the clearinghouse is a net holder and earns interest income. In this particular example, the clearinghouse holds official SDRs and must therefore be given quasi-official status so as to qualify as a holder under Article XVII, Section 3. But other arrangements are easy to devise. The clearinghouse could be private but have an official sponsor, such as the Bank for International Settlements. Its sponsor would hold the official SDRs transferred to the clearinghouse; the clearinghouse would hold SDR certificates issued by its sponsor and backed fully by those holdings. Subsequent transactions involving official SDRs, such as the one in Table 3 below, would be handled by issuing or canceling certificates. I owe this suggestion to Jacques Polak, although he made it in a somewhat different context. (Note that there is no need to allocate new SDRs to the clearinghouse when SDRs are allo-cated to official holders. At some point, however, the commercial banks might have to make supplementary subscriptions, which means that central banks would have to make additional transfers of official SDRs. To this limited extent, official holders would still give up control over their own SDR holdings.)

the clearinghouse show the SDR transfer from Lloyds Bank to the Bank of Tokyo.

Table 3 traces the effects of intervention by the Bank of England. In this example, it uses sterling to purchase SDR 50 million from Lloyds Bank. (Lloyds Bank could be replaced by a foreign bank without changing the story in any significant way.) The accounts of the three institutions change in much the same way that they did in Table 1, but the signs of the entries are reversed. The Bank of England acquires SDRs from the clearinghouse, and they are official SDRs. Lloyds Bank acquires sterling from the Bank of England. The books of the clearinghouse reflect the "transformation" of private SDRs into official SDRs.[15]

The transactions shown in Table 3 are similar to those that would take place on account of borrowing by the Fund itself. The Fund would be able to issue debt to private institutions and take payment in official SDRs. If someone holding an SDR deposit with Lloyds Bank lent SDR 50 million to the Fund, the books of the bank would show reductions of 50 million in its deposit liabilities and in its balance with the clearinghouse. The books of the clearinghouse would show what they do now—reductions of 50 million in its deposit obligations and in its balance with the Fund. The books of the Bank of England would not be affected. The General Resources Account of the Fund would show a 50 million increase in debt and a 50 million increase in holdings of SDRs (a claim on the Special Drawing Rights Department of the Fund). If the Fund were authorized to borrow in private markets, it could denominate the debt it issues in SDRs until a clearinghouse was established. However, it could not take payment of the proceeds in official SDRs. It would, instead, have to take payment in national currencies or in private SDRs.

Whenever a central bank or the Fund itself is involved in a transaction with a private institution, there is a change in the ownership of official SDRs. Transactions between private institutions, by contrast, affect the ownership of claims on the clearinghouse but do not affect the ownership of official SDRs.

---

[15] One reader of my first draft pointed out that the transactions in Tables 2 and 3, taken together, pose a problem for Lloyds Bank. It winds up with a debit balance in its account at the clearinghouse. Lloyds Bank would have to buy SDRs in the foreign exchange market or borrow them from other participating banks. The creation of a clearinghouse would probably give rise to an interbank market in SDR balances—the SDR counterpart of the federal funds market in the United States. (If all banks ran short of balances with the clearinghouse, because of large-scale official purchases, they would have to buy SDRs from their central banks to make supplementary subscriptions to the clearinghouse.) Note that intervention by the Bank of England has the usual effect on the money supply in the United Kingdom; the increase in the sterling balance held by Lloyds Bank constitutes an increase in the monetary base. If the effects of intervention are to be sterilized, it must be done deliberately. (Transactions between commercial banks, by contrast, do not affect the monetary base.)

TABLE 1. SETTING UP THE CLEARINGHOUSE

(In millions of SDRs and SDR equivalents of sterling)

Bank of England

Assets	Liabilities
SDR balance with International Monetary Fund . . . . −100	Sterling deposit obligation to Lloyds Bank . . . . −100

Lloyds Bank

Assets	Liabilities
Sterling deposit with Bank of England . . . . −100	
SDR deposit with clearinghouse . . +100	

Clearinghouse

Assets	Liabilities
SDR deposit with International Monetary Fund . . . . +100	SDR deposit obligation to Lloyds Bank . . . . +100

TABLE 2. AN INTERBANK TRANSACTION

(In millions of SDRs and SDR equivalents of yen)

Lloyds Bank

Assets	Liabilities
Yen deposit with Bank of Tokyo . . +75	
SDR deposit with clearinghouse . . −75	

Clearinghouse

Assets	Liabilities
	SDR deposit obligation to Lloyds Bank . . . . −75
	SDR deposit obligation to Bank of Tokyo . . . . +75

TABLE 3. INTERVENTION BY BANK OF ENGLAND

(In millions of SDRs and SDR equivalents of sterling)

Bank of England

Assets		Liabilities	
SDR balance with International Monetary Fund	+50	Sterling deposit obligation to Lloyds Bank................	+50

Lloyds Bank

Assets		Liabilities	
Sterling deposit with Bank of England	+50		
SDR deposit with clearinghouse ..	−50		

Clearinghouse

Assets		Liabilities	
SDR deposit with International Monetary Fund	−50	SDR deposit obligation to Lloyds Bank................	−50

Other Innovations

In the long run, of course, the need for "designation" should die away. It should perhaps be kept on the books of the Fund to guarantee the transferability of the official SDR, but the provisions that support it—the acceptance limit and the requirement of balance of payments need—stand in the way of transferability and should be repealed as quickly as possible. In the interim, additional steps might be taken to stimulate the demand for the SDR.

When the Fund's holdings of a member's currency fall below 75 percent of quota, the Fund should offer to sell SDRs to that member in exchange for its currency. The exchange would not affect the volume of reserves. The member would give up a claim on the General Resources Account, which is itself a reserve asset, for a claim on the Special Drawing Rights Department, which is another reserve asset. I have not been able to find any legal obstacle to an initiative of this sort—only the obvious practical obstacle that the General Resources Account cannot sell SDRs unless it has them. It has a large quantity now, however, and would be well-endowed with SDRs on a regular basis under a proposal made later in this paper.

An offer of this sort would be mildly attractive from the member's standpoint. The rate of remuneration paid on a reserve position is four fifths of the interest rate paid on the SDR. The offer could be made much more attractive by allowing the Fund to tack on a premium of, say, 1 percent (i.e., to sell SDRs at a discount). The Fund might go further. Whenever a member draws on the Fund, it should be encouraged to purchase SDRs rather than national currencies. Therefore, the Fund might impose an additional service charge of, say, ½ of 1 percent on purchases of currencies and no such charge on purchases of SDRs. There may be legal obstacles to these innovations, but I have found no clear-cut prohibitions.[16]

Finally, the Fund might pay an interest rate premium on SDR holdings larger than some multiple of a member's allocation (and might charge a penalty on holdings smaller than a fraction of a member's allocation). In other words, it might replace the present uniform interest rate with a graduated schedule of rates, paving the way for repeal of the acceptance limit and increasing the attractiveness of an offer by the Fund to buy a member's currency in exchange for SDRs. This particular proposal cannot be implemented without amending the Articles of Agreement, which state that the same interest rate must be paid to all holders of SDRs and that the rate of charges must equal the rate of interest (Article XX, Sections 1-3). Therefore, the proposal should be introduced as part of a third amendment of the Articles of Agreement—the one that would repeal the acceptance limit and the requirement of balance of payments need and, what is more important, would make way for the larger innovations suggested in the next two sections of this paper.

VI. SUBSTITUTION ONCE AGAIN

If measures of the type proposed above succeed in increasing the demand for SDRs by official holders, it would not be hard to increase the supply. Substitution is an attractive approach. It does not add to the stock of reserves and is therefore immune to the main objection that governments might raise with regard to large allocations and other methods considered below.

[16] An increased use of SDRs in ordinary drawings can affect reserves. When Brazil draws SDRs and uses them to buy dollars from the United States, it increases the gross reserves of the United States. When Brazil draws dollars instead, it can increase the gross reserves of the United States to the same extent, but only if the Fund's holdings of dollars are not larger initially than 75 percent of the U.S. quota. At first, I thought of proposing that the Fund impose an additional service charge on repurchases made with SDRs (and no charge on repurchases made with currencies), to keep SDRs from coming back into the Fund. But my main aim is wide use of the SDR, including its use in transactions with the Fund, and a charge on repurchases made with SDRs would have the opposite effect. Furthermore, such a charge would remove an important incentive for members to accumulate SDRs. From this standpoint, it might be more sensible to place a service charge on repurchases made with currencies (i.e., to penalize currency sales to the Fund as well as currency purchases), in order to encourage the use of SDRs in *all* transactions with the Fund. Note, finally, that this entire proposal would be rendered obsolete if the Fund adopted the more ambitious plan proposed in the final section of this paper—if all transactions with the Fund were made in SDRs.

350   PETER B. KENEN

Some History

The first official discussion of substitution took place ten years ago in
the Committee of Twenty, when substitution was suggested as a way to
reduce the reserve currency role of the dollar and thus to facilitate the introduction of mandatory asset settlement (see International Monetary Fund
(1974, pp. 162–82), and Williamson (1977, pp. 151–54)). That discussion
ended inconclusively, when it became clear that mandatory settlement
would not be introduced. The second discussion took place in 1979–80,
when substitution was suggested as a way to divert the diversification of currency reserves and thus to prevent the emergence of a multiple reserve currency system (see Kenen (1981, pp. 407–12) and Solomon (1982, pp. 285–
93)). That discussion also ended inconclusively, partly because governments could not reach agreement on the best way to maintain "financial
balance" in the proposed substitution account and partly because the
dollar began to strengthen, reducing the incentive for diversification.

Although the first discussion took place long ago and was based on views
about the monetary system different from those held today, it is perhaps
more relevant than the second. It was concerned with long-run reform of
the system and dealt with substitution through the Fund, using the SDR.
The second discussion was strongly influenced by short-run concerns—the
effects of diversification on foreign exchange markets—and stressed the
need for rapid action. In consequence, it dealt with substitution through a
separate facility, managed by the Fund but segregated from it, and thus
with use of an SDR-denominated claim but not the SDR itself. This ad hoc
approach proved to be self-defeating (Kenen (1981, pp. 409–10)):

> The creation of a separate substitution account ... posed special problems, and the
> solution of those problems was greatly complicated by the need to attract participation
> on a voluntary basis and on a scale large enough to make the exercise worthwhile. The
> account would be able to issue claims denominated in SDR, but it could not issue the
> SDR defined in the Articles of Agreement. In consequence, those claims would not
> assume automatically the attributes of the SDR. The transferability (liquidity) of the
> SDR is guaranteed within limits.... The redemption of the SDR is guaranteed by
> the provisions of the Articles pertaining to the liquidation of the SDR Department....
> The transferability of the new asset, its interest rate, and ways to guarantee its value in
> the event of liquidation—the problem of financial balance—had to be negotiated, and
> these issues were connected in complicated ways.
> Holders of claims on the account would be able to transfer them freely among them-
> selves. But potential holders wanted to be sure that they would find buyers whenever
> necessary. It was therefore suggested that holders should have the right to cash in their
> claims.... Some said that this right should be unconditional, but others said that it
> should be circumscribed, to be exercised only as a last resort, and that penalties should
> be imposed to make the option costly.
> There were, of course, proposals for "designation" patterned on the plan for the SDR
> itself. But reliance on this mechanism, it was said, might discourage participation in the
> substitution account. Countries with strong currencies and large reserves, whose partici-

pation would be important for success, might be unwilling to make big deposits, because these would expose them to large-scale "designation" (i.e., the obligation to grant large amounts of credit to countries in balance-of-payments need)....

What rate of interest should the new claim pay? There had to be a sensible relationship between liquidity and yield, but two other relationships had to be considered—the relationship between the interest rate on the new claim and the rate paid on the SDR itself, and the relationship between the rate on the new claim and the rate that would be paid by the United States on the dollar holdings of the account.

The interest rate relationships were important for "financial balance" and the long-run solvency of the substitution account. Its solvency could be impaired if its income was smaller than its payments to depositors. This could happen if the interest rate paid by the United States was lower than the interest rate paid to the depositors. It could also happen, however, if the dollar depreciated against the SDR. Interest payments by the United States would be calculated in dollars, being payments on the dollars held by the account, but interest payments to depositors would be calculated in SDRs, being payments on the SDR-denominated claims held by the depositors. Therefore, a depreciation of the dollar would raise the interest payments made by the account relative to its receipts. What is more important, a depreciation of the dollar could impair the solvency of the account directly. The SDR value of its dollar holdings could fall below the value of its obligations to its depositors, and this possibility was particularly worrisome to governments that were concerned about the transferability of their claims on the account and that consequently wanted substitution to be reversible.[17]

If substitution were conducted through the Fund itself, using the SDR, some of these problems would be eliminated and others would be simplified. There would be no need to worry about transferability—which would be greatly enhanced by establishing a clearinghouse.[18] In consequence, there would be much less need to provide for reversibility and less need to worry about the problem of solvency. The account would not have to be self-balancing from year to year. In fact, there would be no separate

---

[17] For simulations showing the importance of interest rate relationships and their interaction with exchange rate fluctuations, see the simulations in Kenen (1981). When depositors received the SDR interest rate and the United States paid the treasury bill rate, there was a $20.8 billion shortfall in the account at the end of 15 years; when the United States paid the SDR interest rate, the shortfall was reduced to $13.1 billion. (The shortfall was not eliminated, because the dollar depreciated during the period under study, and the depreciation acted directly to reduce the SDR value of the dollar claims held by the account.)

[18] A study group established by the Group of Thirty looked to marketability as the long-run solution to the problem of transferability (see Group of Thirty (1980, pp. 12–15)). It made no mention, however, of the need for a clearinghouse to link official SDRs with private SDRs. The importance of that link was perhaps obscured because the study group based its own proposal on the one that was being discussed in official circles—the use of an SDR-denominated claim rather than the SDR itself.

account. Liquidation would take place only in conjunction with the liquidation of the Special Drawing Rights Department—for which provision is already made in the Articles of Agreement. There might still be hard bargaining about the interest rate payable on currency balances held by the Fund, but this issue would be simplified, because the rate payable to depositors would be the one payable on the SDR.

Nevertheless, three issues would remain: (1) Should substitution be mandatory or voluntary? (2) Should substitution take place once or twice, or should it be an open-ended option? (3) What should be done with the currencies deposited with the Fund in the course of substitution? These are the questions on which I will concentrate.[19]

Why Substitution Should Be Voluntary

A large increase in demand for the SDR might make it possible for governments to reach agreement on mandatory substitution. Each one would deposit a fraction of its currency reserves in a newly established account at the Fund and receive in exchange new SDRs.[20] They would not have to *hold* that fraction of reserves in SDRs; they would be free to add to their currency reserves. Mandatory substitution need not be accompanied by regulated reserve composition or used to tie total holdings of reserves to the supply of SDRs.

This approach, however, has one major defect. The amount of substitution could be governed by the views of the least-willing governments, as it would require an amendment of the Articles of Agreement of the Fund and, therefore, approval by three fifths of the members having 85 percent

[19] Questions can be raised about interest payments too, but they are less important in the present context than in earlier discussions, because the problem of solvency is less important. Members whose currencies were acquired by the Fund could pay interest in those currencies. Members holding SDRs issued in the process of substitution could earn interest in SDRs. In other words, interest payments could be transferred by supplementary substitution. (For this purpose, however, SDRs issued in the process of substitution would have to be excluded from cumulative allocations, regardless of their treatment in connection with the issues raised in the next note.)

[20] If the acceptance limit was not repealed before or concurrently with the introduction of mandatory substitution, members of the Fund would have to decide whether SDRs issued in the course of substitution should be treated as allocations and counted in actual holdings when calculating the acceptance limits (see Article XIX, Section 4). If included in cumulative allocations (and therefore the base on which acceptance limits are computed), they should be counted in actual holdings. If excluded from cumulative allocations, they should not be counted in actual holdings. A decision on this point would not be too difficult with mandatory substitution, because all members of the Fund would be affected uniformly, but would be quite difficult with voluntary substitution. A member of the Fund that swapped a large amount of currency reserves for SDRs would expose itself to large-scale "designation" if SDRs issued in the course of substitution were treated as allocations, even if they were counted in actual holdings as well.

of the votes. If a few large countries wanted to turn in only a small fraction of their currency reserves, they could hold the others back, and the exercise would not accomplish very much. It may therefore be best to plan for voluntary substitution, even though it might likewise require an amendment if it were conducted through the Fund itself. Some important governments would probably agree to put in place a framework for voluntary substitution if it did not bind them to participate fully.

When Substitution Should Take Place

There are many ways to deal with the problem of timing, but they are bounded by two possibilities. (1) Substitution could take place on a single day, in amounts negotiated in advance, or left to the participants' decisions on that day. (2) It could be an open-ended option, with regard to timing and amounts. As usual, the best course lies somewhere in between.

If substitution had to take place on a single day, the extent of substitution would be far too sensitive to short-term views about the outlook for exchange rates, the balance of payments prospects of the participants, and the progress made to date in improving the quality of the SDR as a reserve asset, especially in making it more usable in currency and credit markets. The outcome of the exercise might be disappointing, and an initial disappointment could make it very difficult for the Fund to organize a second round.

If substitution were open ended in timing and amount, the Fund would be in difficulty—the same sort of difficulty it would encounter if it were to serve as the residual buyer of dollars in an SDR-based reserve system.[21] It would be issuing SDRs whenever its members wanted to get rid of currency reserves and could be accused of giving unconditional balance of payments support to reserve currency countries. An open-ended approach could meet with one more objection. The United States and other reserve currency countries would have to reach agreement with the Fund concerning the currencies acquired by the Fund—one having to do with maintenance of value, currency use on the part of the Fund, and even amortization. I shall discuss some of these matters later. They are relevant here, however, because no government can be expected to sign an agreement with the Fund unless it knows how much of its country's currency might be acquired by the Fund.

I am thus led to conclude that the opportunity for substitution should be strictly limited in time and amount. Members of the Fund might agree, for example, to open up the option for a five-year period but to put a ceiling on its use by any member—a limit on the number of SDRs that a member can

[21] See Section III.

obtain by selling reserve currencies to the Fund. Such ceilings might be based on gross reserves at the start of the five-year period (or on quotas in the Fund) but would not have to be absolutely uniform. Members could request higher or lower ceilings. Each member should perhaps be asked to use the first 25 percent of the allotment corresponding to its ceiling at the very start of the five-year period, so as to get substitution under way (and to discourage applications for huge ceilings that would remain unused). A member could use the rest of its allotment and thus move to its ceiling at any time within the five-year period.

Rules for revising the initial agreement—extending the five-year period or altering the ceilings—could be included in the agreement itself or in the amendment of the Articles of Agreement that would be required to permit the Fund to issue SDRs in exchange for currencies.[22] No country, however, should be obliged to accept an increase or decrease in its ceiling during the first five-year period.

What Might Be Done with the Currencies

When substitution was discussed by the Committee of Twenty, much attention was paid to the disposition of the reserve currencies (International Monetary Fund (1974, p. 174)):

> There was strong support for the view that the currency balances surrendered to a Substitution Account should be eliminated gradually over time by amortization payments by the issuers of the currencies. Mention was made of amortization periods of from 10 to 30 years.... It was agreed that some flexibility to vary the rate of amortization in relation to the balance of payments situation of a reserve center would be appropriate, although there were differences as to the degree of flexibility to be permitted and the direction in which it should operate. The United States favored flexibility for reserve centers to speed up or slow down the rate of amortization in response to balance of payments developments. Some participants favored a facility to speed up payments, but no facility to slow down.

In the second discussion of substitution, less attention was paid to this possibility. The participants had come to understand that currency balances could remain indefinitely in a substitution account, and those who favored reversibility wanted them to stay there to guarantee the liquidity of the claims issued by the account. That is why the problem of financial bal-

---

[22] It might not be absolutely necessary to amend the Articles of Agreement. Members of the Fund could vote to allocate SDRs, agree to turn their allocations back to the General Resources Account, and then buy them back with reserve currencies. But this cumbersome procedure might have to be executed on a one-time basis, and it would work only if all members of the Fund agreed to participate in substitution to the full extent of their allocations. It might break down if any member asked itself the obvious question: Why give my SDRs back to the Fund merely to buy them back again with currency reserves? It might then decide to keep its SDRs and not participate in substitution.

ance became so important. If large numbers of dollars and other reserve currencies are to lie dormant for decades, there is bound to be concern about maintenance of value in terms of the SDR, even though no one expects to take the currencies out again. Provisions for limited use or amortization could therefore allay concerns about maintenance of value and make it easier to reach agreement on large-scale substitution.

Several possibilities come to mind, and they could be combined. The Fund might be allowed to use the currencies for purchases of SDR-denominated debt issued by the World Bank and other development institutions. This would forge the missing link between SDR creation and development assistance, and it would promote the use of the SDR as a unit of account in long-term capital transactions. The Fund itself might borrow currencies to finance drawings by its members, in much the same way that it has borrowed currencies from members during the last several years. In this instance, however, the Fund would not make repayments; it would be regarded as borrowing from itself rather than borrowing from the countries issuing the currencies.[23]

Finally, currency balances acquired by the Fund could be amortized indirectly by transferring them gradually to the General Resources Account, even if they were not needed currently to finance drawings on the Fund. Such transfers would reduce the reserve positions of the countries issuing the currencies—which is why the transfers would amortize the balances—and could take place in accordance with a schedule negotiated with those countries to reduce the balances at an agreed rate. The transfers would take place whenever the methods proposed above—lending to the World Bank and borrowing by the Fund itself—had not reduced the balances at the agreed rate, but they would not take place if the issuing country did not have a positive reserve position with which to amortize them.[24]

---

[23] In other words, this sort of borrowing should not affect the rights of the member issuing the currency (e.g., its right to appoint an Executive Director under Article XII, Section 3, and the number of votes it can cast under Article XII, Section 5). Such borrowing would, of course, reduce the member's obligation to pay interest to the Fund. Within the Fund itself, the Special Drawing Rights Department would obtain an SDR-denominated claim on the General Resources Account and would hold it indefinitely.

[24] An illustration will perhaps clarify matters. Suppose that dollars worth SDR 80 billion are deposited with the Fund in consequence of substitution, that the United States agrees to amortize them over 20 years (i.e., at SDR 4 billion a year), and that the Fund uses dollars worth SDR 1.5 billion during the second year to buy bonds from the World Bank. Dollars worth SDR 2.5 billion remain to be amortized by the end of the second year, and they would be transferred to the General Resources Account if, at the end of that year, the U.S. reserve position in the Fund was no smaller than SDR 2.5 billion. (If its reserve position was, say, SDR 1.0 billion, dollars worth only SDR 1.0 billion would be transferred. The rest of the dollars, equivalent to SDR 1.5 billion, would be added to third-year amortization or to the end of the 20-year schedule.)

VII. AN INTERNATIONAL MONETARY FUND BASED ALMOST FULLY ON THE SDR

If Keynes had won his great debate with White, the Fund would have functioned from the start as a fledgling central bank. It would have created credit instead of selling currencies when one of its members needed balance of payments support. The First Amendment of the Articles of Agreement, which introduced the SDR, took the first formal step required to transform the Fund into a central bank.

It is not time to take the next steps formally, because they would be big steps. But it may be possible to move informally in the right direction by allowing the Fund to make more extensive use of the SDR in transactions with its members and reducing in the process the need to increase quotas in order to enlarge the resources of the Fund.

A Short Look at the Long Run

The Fund has done much more, of course, than manage a pool of currencies. Keynes and White might be surprised by what has happened to it. Quoting Polak (1979, p. 5):

> The attempt to view transactions through which the Fund made resources available to members in payments difficulties as a mere exchange of one currency for another never took hold. Fund transactions (beyond the reserve tranche) are now generally regarded as the extension of balance of payments *credit*. This view is reflected, for example, in the adoption of the concept of "credit tranches" and the widespread use of the term "repayment" as both more general and more meaningful than "repurchase."

Polak goes on to point out that ordinary drawings on the Fund usually create reserves, although the Fund is passive in this particular process. They do so whenever the sale of a member's currency adds to the member's reserve position. Reserve positions, moreover, are close substitutes for SDR holdings, which leads Polak to make his main recommendation. The Fund should be based fully on the SDR by eliminating completely the distinction between the General Resources Account and the Special Drawing Rights Department and allowing the Fund to finance its credit operations by issuing SDRs.

But something more must happen once that starts to happen. The supply of SDRs cannot be permitted to depend too heavily on countries' balance of payments needs. The supply must conform to the need for reserves, to the extent that one can judge it. Therefore, the Executive Board of the Fund has eventually to function as an open-market committee for the international monetary system—to increase or decrease the supply of

SDRs on its own initiative.[25] That is why it is not time to take the next steps formally. Members are not ready to allow the Fund to create SDRs in a flexible manner, even to meet members' balance of payments needs. They are far from ready to go the rest of the way and allow the Fund to conduct open-market operations, even within guidelines set by its members.

Important progress can be made in that direction, however, without reorganizing the Fund formally. Until the Articles of Agreement are amended, the Fund cannot be empowered to create SDRs when meeting its members' balance of payments needs. By interpreting the Articles elastically, however, the Fund can be supplied with SDRs in amounts appropriate to meet those needs.

What Can Be Done in the Short Run

The proposal I make here ties in with those I made above designed to encourage members of the Fund to take SDRs when drawing on the General Resources Account. It is closely related to Polak's proposal, but it can be adopted right away without another amendment of the Articles of Agreement.

Let us look five years ahead to the next increase in quotas. Normally, a member would pay in one fourth of the increase in SDRs and the rest in its national currency. This procedure is cumbersome, to say the least. Quotas affect voting rights, drawing rights, and contributions of resources. Therefore, decisions regarding the size and distribution of a quota increase run into conflicting objectives—from the standpoint of each member and among the members. Furthermore, the Fund itself acquires "resources" it cannot use—currencies that members do not want to draw. Finally, some members encounter political problems because they must obtain legislative approval to transfer their currencies to the Fund.

Matters could be simplified and the SDR given a much larger role in the Fund itself by combining an increase in quotas with an allocation of SDRs large enough to pay in the *whole* quota increase in newly issued SDRs—or at least a fraction larger than one fourth of the increase, if an allocation equal to the increase was thought to be excessive, given the requirements of

---

[25] Reserve supplies could perhaps be regulated by allocations and cancellations rather than open-market operations. Lending and repayments, however, could cause large fluctuations in the stock of SDRs that would be hard to offset by adjusting allocations. They might have to be offset by open-market operations. The need for open-market operations was mentioned by Triffin (1960, p. 115), but Polak does not make provision for them in his plan for unifying the departments of the Fund. For more on open-market operations by the Fund, see the paper by Fischer (Chapter 4 in this volume), which makes a point germane to a main theme of this paper: the macroeconomic effects of those operations will be increased if the SDR is widely used as a unit of account and means of payment.

Article XVIII, Section 1(*a*) that govern allocations. Each member would obtain an increase in its reserve position equal to the increase in its quota; that is the form in which it would experience the increase in reserves produced by the SDR allocation. The General Resources Account would acquire SDRs that the Fund could use to finance subsequent drawings. No member of the Fund could be required to turn over the whole increase in its SDR holdings—only an amount equal to one fourth of the increase in its quota—but no great damage would be done if some of the smaller members kept most of their SDRs.[26]

There is, of course, one danger. Some governments object to allocations, which add to owned reserves; they object less strongly to increases in quotas, which add instead to the supply of conditional balance of payments credit. If the two were tied together, those who object to allocations might also object to increases in quotas. But the proposal made above is meant mainly to demonstrate that the operations of the Fund can be based more fully on the SDR without amending the Articles of Agreement. It does not say that *every* quota increase must be financed by issuing new SDRs. It does not say that allocations must take place *only* in conjunction with increases in quotas. In my view, allocations should resume right now, not on the occasion of the next quota increase, in order to combat the damaging effects of stagnation or decline in the stock of reserves.

REFERENCES

Bacha, Edmar Lisboa, and Carlos F. Díaz-Alejandro, *International Financial Intermediation: A Long and Tropical View*, Essays in International Finance, No. 147 (Princeton, New Jersey: International Finance Section, Princeton University, 1982).

Bergsten, C. Fred, and John Williamson, *The Multiple Reserve Currency System: Evolution, Consequences, and Alternatives* (Washington: Institute for International Economics, 1983).

Bilson, John F.O., and Jacob A. Frenkel, "International Reserves: Adjustment Dynamics," *Economics Letters*, Vol. 4 (1979), pp. 267–70.

Black, Stanley, "International Money and International Monetary Arrangements," Chapter 23 in *Handbook of International Economics*, ed. by Ronald W. Jones and Peter B. Kenen (Amsterdam: North-Holland, to be published in 1984).

[26] Defections would not be as serious as in the case of substitution (see footnote 22), where countries that kept their SDR allocations instead of turning them back to the Fund would be increasing their reserves, whereas those that turned them back and repurchased them with currencies would merely be changing the composition of their reserves.

Coats, Warren L., Jr., "The SDR as a Means of Payment," International Monetary Fund, *Staff Papers*, Vol. 29 (September 1982), pp. 422-36.

Cooper, Richard N., "The Gold Standard: Historical Facts and Future Prospects," *Brookings Papers on Economic Activity: 1* (1982), pp. 1-45.

Corden, W. Max, "The Logic of the International Monetary Non-System" (Canberra: Center for Economic Policy Research, Australian National University, Discussion Paper No. 24, March 1981).

de Vries, Tom, "Jamaica, Or the Non-Reform of the International Monetary System," *Foreign Affairs*, Vol. 54 (April 1976), pp. 577-605.

Eaton, Jonathan, and Mark Gersovitz, *Poor-Country Borrowing in Private Financial Markets and the Repudiation Issue*, Studies in International Finance, No. 47 (Princeton, New Jersey: International Finance Section, Princeton University, 1981).

Frenkel, Jacob A., "The Demand for International Reserves under Pegged and Flexible Exchange Rate Regimes and Aspects of the Economics of Managed Float," Chapter 7 in *The Functioning of Floating Exchange Rates: Theory, Evidence, and Policy Implications*, ed. by David Bigman and Teizo Taya (Cambridge, Massachusetts: Ballinger, 1980), pp. 169-95.

Group of Thirty, Reserve Assets Study Group, *Towards a Less Unstable International Monetary System* (New York, 1980).

_____, *How Central Banks Manage Their Reserves* (New York, 1982).

Heller, H. Robert, and Mohsin S. Khan, "The Demand for International Reserves Under Fixed and Floating Exchange Rates," International Monetary Fund, *Staff Papers*, Vol. 25 (December 1978), pp. 623-49.

International Monetary Fund, *International Monetary Reform: Documents of the Committee of Twenty* (Washington, 1974).

_____, *Annual Report 1982* (Washington, 1982).

Kenen, Peter B., "Techniques to Control International Reserves," in *The New International Monetary System*, ed. by Robert A. Mundell and Jacques J. Polak (New York: Columbia University Press, 1977), pp. 202-22.

_____, "Changing Views About the SDR and Implications for Its Attributes" (paper prepared for the Secretariat of the United Nations Conference on Trade and Development; International Finance Section, Princeton University, 1980).

_____, "The Analytics of a Substitution Account," Banca Nazionale del Lavoro, *Quarterly Review*, Vol. 34 (December 1981), pp. 403-26.

_____, "The Role of the U.S. Dollar as an International Currency" (paper presented at the annual meetings of the American Economic Association, December 1982; International Finance Section, Princeton University, 1982).

Khan, Mohsin S., "Inflation and International Reserves: A Time-Series Analysis," International Monetary Fund, *Staff Papers*, Vol. 26 (December 1979), pp. 699-724.

Kindleberger, Charles P., *Balance of Payments Deficits and the International Market for Liquidity*, Essays in International Finance, No. 46 (Princeton, New Jersey: International Finance Section, Princeton University, 1965).

McKinnon, Ronald I., "Currency Substitution and Instability in the World Dollar Market," *American Economic Review*, Vol. 72 (June 1982), pp. 320–33.

Polak, J.J., *Thoughts on an International Monetary Fund Based Fully on the SDR*, International Monetary Fund, Pamphlet Series, No. 28 (Washington, 1979).

Robertson, Dennis H., *Economic Commentaries* (London: Staples Press Limited, 1956).

Roosa, Robert V., and others, *Reserve Currencies in Transition* (New York: Group of Thirty, 1982).

Sachs, Jeffrey D., "The Current Account and Macroeconomic Adjustment in the 1970s," *Brookings Papers on Economic Activity: 1* (1981), pp. 201–68.

Sobol, Dorothy M., "The SDR in Private International Finance," Federal Reserve Bank of New York, *Quarterly Review*, Vol. 6 (Winter 1981–82), pp. 29–41.

Solomon, Robert, *The International Monetary System, 1945–1981* (New York: Harper and Row, 1982).

Suss, Esther C., "A Note on Reserve Use Under Alternative Exchange Rate Regimes," International Monetary Fund, *Staff Papers*, Vol. 23 (July 1976), pp. 387–94.

Triffin, Robert, *Gold and the Dollar Crisis: The Future of Convertibility* (New Haven: Yale University Press, 1960).

von Furstenberg, George M., "New Estimates of the Demand for Non-Gold Reserves under Floating Exchange Rates," *Journal of International Money and Finance*, Vol. 1 (1982), pp. 81–95.

Williamson, John H., "Exchange Rate Flexibility and Reserve Use," *Scandinavian Journal of Economics*, Vol. 78 (1976), pp. 327–39.

_____, *The Failure of World Monetary Reform, 1971–1974* (New York: New York University Press, 1977).

[18]

World Development, Vol. 15, No. 12, pp. 1445–1456, 1987.
Printed in Great Britain.

0305–750X/87 $3.00 + 0.00
© 1987 Pergamon Journals Ltd.

What Role for IMF Surveillance?

PETER B. KENEN*
Princeton University, New Jersey

Summary. — This paper reviews two recent reports on the international monetary system, one by the Group of 10 (industrial countries) and the other by the Group of 24 (developing countries). It contrasts their recommendations for improving policy surveillance by the International Monetary Fund. Its own recommendations include the strengthening of "enhanced surveillance" to make it more formal without making it more onerous, the introduction of "shadow conditionality" to give guidance to governments about their eligibility to draw on the Fund, and the further development of multilateral surveillance along lines proposed at the Tokyo Summit. It would broaden that process, however, by shifting the focus from policy compatibility, defined with reference to exchange-rate behavior, to policy quality, defined with reference to the behavior of global aggregates such as the growth rate of world trade. The paper examines the use of target zones to manage exchange rates and argues that it would not weaken the case for multilateral surveillance, which is needed not only in setting the zones but also to make sure that policies adopted by participating countries do not impart an inflationary or deflationary bias to the international economy.

1. INTRODUCTION

Can the International Monetary Fund (IMF) bring significant influence to bear on its members' macroeconomic policies?

The question is most easily answered for members that seek to draw on the Fund, although there is much debate about the way that the Fund should exercise its influence — whether it should concern itself with internal targets, such as the inflation rate, or restrict itself to external targets, such as the balance of payments, and whether it should measure its members' compliance with reference to policy targets or to policy instruments.[1] Even in those instances, moreover, it is hard to quantify the Fund's influence. Members may elect to draw on the Fund only when they have decided on their own to follow policies that will meet the Fund's approval, and they may likewise decide to abandon those policies, foregoing further recourse to the Fund, when the costs become too large. Furthermore, economists have found it hard to show that members' adherence to Fund-approved policies has affected the actual performance of their economies.[2]

The question becomes much harder when discussion turns from the principles and practice of conditionality to the broader problem of surveillance. Can the Fund be expected to influence the policies of members that do not seek to use its resources? Can it influence the policies of surplus as well as deficit countries? Of creditors as well as debtors? Of large as well as small countries?

What principles should govern the Fund's practices? Should it concern itself primarily with exchange-rate and balance-of-payments behavior, or should it look within each national economy, at its growth rate, inflation rate, and other target variables? If the Fund should take a broad view, should it examine internal performance comprehensively or confine its attention to the international ramifications of national policies — the macroeconomic manifestations of interdependence? What roles should be played by the management and staff, the Board and the Interim Committee? Should the Fund restrict itself to confidential discussions with governments or should it "go public" in certain circumstances and thus try to mobilize public opinion within and across countries?

These questions have attracted much attention recently, for a variety of reasons. First, the onset of debt problems a few years ago underscored the responsibility of the major industrial countries for global economic conditions — for the environment in which developing countries must manage their affairs. The sharp increase of real and nominal interest rates after 1979 and the deep recession of 1981–82 illustrated vividly the extent to which developing countries depend on prosperity and stability in the developed countries, and the various scenarios constructed thereafter stressed the importance of global con-

*Walker Professor of Economics and International Finance and Director of the International Finance Section, Princeton University.

ditions for an early solution to the debt problem.[3] Second, the behavior of the dollar in foreign-exchange markets focused international attention on the domestic policies of the United States, and criticism of US budget deficits led in turn to close examination of other countries' fiscal policies, especially West German and Japanese policies. Some economists, such as McKinnon (1984), continue to believe that exchange-rate stability can be achieved by coordinating monetary policies, but this may be very hard without a concurrent coordination of fiscal policies. Finally, governments have begun to display an interest in active exchange-rate management. They have come to realize that the pursuit of similar monetary policies is necessary but not sufficient to maintain exchange-rate stability. The change in the position of the US government has been most marked and most remarked upon. Washington has retreated from the view, articulated forcefully a few years ago, that exchange rates will take care of themselves when governments take care of their national economies.

2. THE G-10 AND G-24 REPORTS

Two recent reports on the monetary system deal at length with the Fund's surveillance of national policies — one by the Deputies of the Group of 10 (1985), representing the views of developed countries, the other by the Deputies of the Group of 24 (1985), representing the views of developing countries. The two reports are remarkably similar in coverage, and they give the same answers to many of the questions posed above. Both of them examine the two types of surveillance — the formal bilateral process mandated by Article IV of the Fund Agreement, involving an annual consultation between the Fund and each member government, and the newer, less formal multilateral process, which includes a semiannual discussion of *The World Economic Outlook (WEO)* by the Fund's Interim Committee, and ministerial meetings of the G-5 (France, West Germany, Japan, the United Kingdom, and the United States) in which the Fund's Managing Director participates.[4] Both reports stress the need for strengthening the multilateral process, partly by linking it more closely to the bilateral process. But the two reports differ in emphasis and in the urgency that they attach to various improvements and reforms.

(a) *Symmetry and scope*

Both reports reiterate an old complaint, that

the international monetary system does not operate symmetrically *vis-à-vis* deficit and surplus countries. In the words of the G-10 Report:

> Surveillance has not been sufficiently effective in inducing policy changes in countries which have adequate access to external financing and do not require an IMF-supported adjustment program. These countries appear to have been able on occasion to sustain policy courses not fully compatible with the goals of international adjustment and financial stability.

The Deputies also note that

> . . . in the implementation of surveillance the focus has tended to be on a country-specific approach, with less attention being given to the interaction of national policies and economic structures.

The G-24 Report uses similar language but frames the issue mainly in North–South terms:

> . . . Fund surveillance has to date been largely ineffective over the major industrial countries whose actions have substantial spillover effects on the world economy. These countries have been able to pursue domestic policies without taking into account their impact on the international economy. In some cases, the subordination of international responsibilities to domestic priorities has been quite explicit. . . . On the other hand, the influence of the Fund has been effectively felt by the users of its resources, mostly developing countries. Even if a formal distinction is made between Article IV consultations and adjustment programs associated with the use of Fund resources, the effect of Fund surveillance on inducing policy changes is much larger on developing countries than on major industrial countries, which have adequate access to external financing and do not require an IMF-supported adjustment program.

Both reports define surveillance broadly but stop short of suggesting that the Fund concern itself with domestic matters except insofar as they impinge on a member's external position and the adjustment process. Nevertheless, both reports see the need for important departures from completely uniform treatment. In the words of the G-10 Report:

> Countries should be treated in the same manner irrespective of their size, exchange rate regime, or financial position. However, equal treatment cannot mean uniformity of prescriptions. Policy advice must take account not only of different situations, economic structures, and institutional settings but also of the impact of individual countries on the world economy.

It even recommends a significant departure from uniform procedure in the conduct of bilateral consultations:

For industrial and developing countries whose policies and performance are of greatest concern for the world economy, a confidential exchange of views between the Managing Director and the Finance Minister should be envisaged at the end of the consultation process.

But the G-24 Report goes farther, proposing a distinction between the *objectives* of surveillance, even in the bilateral setting:

In the case of major industrial countries, the consultations should concentrate on a thorough assessment of their national economic policies, including the exchange rate policies, their domestic and international impact, and also their effect on the adjustment efforts of other countries. . . .

In the case of developing countries, by contrast, the G-24 Report says that policy recommendations should be made to promote adjustment "as a part of economic development," that "underlying needs of finance for such adjustment should be assessed," and that the bilateral consultations should seek to identify "the part that exogenous factors play in the adjustment efforts of these countries and also the effects of the actions of other countries, in particular the major industrial countries." The point is driven home by a long description of structural and other limitations on the ability of developing countries to use exchange-rate changes for balance-of-payments adjustment.

(b) *Process and publicity*

To achieve its objectives in respect of the major industrial countries, the G-24 Report would forge more formal links between bilateral and multilateral surveillance. They would become "two stages of the surveillance process, rather than two parallel operations." The first stage would involve regular multilateral discussions and negotiations aimed at achieving a mutually consistent set of objectives and choosing a suitable set of policies. "The aim might be to search for a set of outcomes or 'objective indicators' or 'targets' that appear to be sustainable in the medium term and desirable to all parties." The second stage would involve a comparison between actual outcomes and targets, and the discussion of remedial measures when the two diverge. This second stage "might most efficiently be conducted on a bilateral basis," as part of the regular consultation process.

In April 1986, the Fund's Interim Committee gave very tentative endorsement to the use of objective indicators, as an approach "worth exploring" in the search for ways of improving multilateral surveillance. In May 1986, however, the seven Summit countries went farther, asking their finance ministers to "review their individual economic objectives and forecasts collectively at least once a year . . . with a particular view to examining their mutual compatibility." They commended the use of indicators such as growth rates, inflation rates, interest rates, unemployment rates, fiscal deficit ratios, current account and trade balances, monetary growth rates, reserves and exchange rates. Furthermore, they urged the officials involved in multilateral surveillance "to make their best efforts to reach an understanding on appropriate remedial measures whenever there are significant deviations from an intended course. . . ."

There is one major difference between the recommendation made by the G-24 Report and the approach adopted by the Summit countries. The G-24 Report envisaged a two-stage process, with the choice of targets and indicators taking place in a multilateral context and the assessment of actual performance taking place in a bilateral context. By implication, it assigned a larger role to the Fund, which would conduct a separate assessment with each participating country. The Summit countries, by contrast, assigned the whole process to their own officials, though the Fund's Managing Director would continue to participate in their dicussions.

The Summit countries may be right, for analytical as well as political reasons. Differences between outcomes and targets may not be due exclusively to one country's policies. It would thus be appropriate analytically and fruitful politically to pursue the second stage in a multilateral framework. The Fund might still monitor national policies and compare them to targets in its bilateral consultations. When policy adjustments are needed, however, a new round of multilateral discussions may be necessary, in order to re-examine the targets themselves and decide on the sharing of policy changes. Governments must be able to show that they have "won" policy changes from others in exchange for the changes that they have made, and this can best be done in a multilateral framework.

Both of the reports on the monetary system would use the *WEO* in the multilateral process, but both of them propose improvements. The G-10 Deputies suggest that the *WEO* include a separate chapter analyzing the international repercussions of G-10 policies and providing an analytical framework for policy discussions. The main conclusions should be reviewed by the G-10 countries at the ministerial level. As usual, the G-24 Deputies want the Fund to go farther in dealing with the major industrial countries. The

WEO should not only analyze the international repercussions of those countries' policies but should make specific policy proposals. These should be considered by the Fund Board, "to recommend a set of policies and the likely outcomes or performance indicators."[5]

As the *WEO* is published eventually, this recommendation constitutes a peculiarly prominent exception to the general injunction against publicity with which the G-24 Deputies conclude their discussions of surveillance:

> The underlying confidentiality of the exchange of information and discussions between the members and the Fund should be preserved. As such, no publicity should be given to the conclusions of the consultations either through release of a statement or through release of reports.

Some G-10 Deputies, by contrast, envisage a limited role for publicity in the bilateral context as well as the multilateral:

> The Deputies agree that the basic confidentiality of the exchange of information between the IMF and its members should be preserved. The view has been expressed, however, that giving some publicity to consultation conclusions could help make them more influential. In particular, it has been suggested that a public statement might be made by the Managing Director, on his own authority and without Executive Board approval, at the end of the consultation process; the statement, which could be based on his own summing-up of the Executive Board discussions, would give a brief assessment of a country's policies and prospects and would indicate the broad direction of suggested policy changes.

Some Deputies also proposed that the G-10 Chairman issue a statement after the G-10 Ministers have reviewed the *WEO*, summarizing the Group's views about its members' policies.

(c) *Surveillance and exchange-rate stabilization*

Both reports devote long sections to the functioning and improvement of exchange-rate arrangements, and though that subject lies beyond the purview of this paper, something must be said about it. Surveillance cannot be conducted without reference to exchange rates, even if it is not meant to stabilize exchange rates, and some of the plans for reforming exchange-rate arrangements, such as those for target zones, would use surveillance chiefly for exchange-rate management.

Both reports express concern about exchange-rate volatility and large medium-term swings in real exchange rates. But the G-10 Report is ambivalent about them. It recognizes tht some such variability is "inherent" in a floating-rate regime:

> Since trade flows tend to adjust more slowly than financial flows, the impact of changes in current conditions is first reflected in financial and foreign exchange markets. Furthermore, in an uncertain environment the difficulty of assessing policy stances and underlying economic fundamentals may lead markets initially to overreact to unexpected developments.

It also warns against expecting policy convergence to stabilize exchange rates:

> A stable international environment certainly requires sound and consistent policies that promote convergence of economic performance. But even if there were widespread and persistent application of non-inflationary policies, exchange rates and exchange rate expectations would be influenced by a number of factors, including the international configuration of fiscal policies, monetary policies, structural rigidities, domestic savings and investment patterns, and political uncertainties. More generally, different policy responses to exogenous disturbances can exert an impact on exchange rates.

Nevertheless, the G-10 Report says that exchange-rate variability is due mainly to "inadequate and inconsistent policies that have led to divergent economic performance," expectations that such policies "might not be quickly corrected," and the problems of market participants trying to find an anchor for their expectations. Thus, the system itself can be faulted only for failing to prevent inadequate policies and divergent economic performances.

Some G-10 Deputies favored the introduction of target zones, believing that convergent policies and performance may not be sufficient to bring about exchange-rate stability, and that "credible commitments to target zones would contribute to stabilizing market expectations and would promote greater international policy consistency by reinforcing multilateral surveillance." But most of the Deputies opposed target zones, raising five objections: (1) it would be hard to reach agreement on the relevant exchange rates; (2) the zones would have to be too wide to serve as an anchor for expectations; (3) it would still be necessary to allocate the burden of policy adjustment among the participating countries; (4) markets would inevitably test the zones, adding to exchange-rates instability; and (5) the constraints imposed on domestic policies might actually undermine efforts to pursue sound and stable policies in a medium-term framework. (The last point should probably be read to represent the West German view that the pursuit of exchange-rate stability might force countries with strong currencies and low inflation rates to accept too much inflation.)

The G-24 Report is more sympathetic but not optimistic about early action:

> Adoption of target zones for the exchange rates of major currencies could help achieve the objective of exchange rate stability and a sustainable pattern of payments balances. The proposal needs to be further studied and pursued to gain general acceptance. In the meantime, a mechanism has to be devised to enforce policy coordination among the developed, especially the key currency, countries. . . .
>
> Policy coordination in this context implies that monetary policy for exchange rate stability should complement the use of fiscal policy to counter inflationary and deflationary pressures as well as the use of other policy instruments. Intervention, for instance, could be used on a meaningful scale, without confining it to "leaning against the wind," towards the end of exchange rate stability, as a complementary measure to other policies, and sometimes in coordination with other countries.

The G-24 Report goes on to suggest that the Fund adopt a mechanism to trigger consultations among the countries concerned and with the Fund itself whenever available indicators suggest that an "excessive" exchange-rate movement is taking place or that a major currency is seriously misaligned or becoming misaligned.

3. IMPROVEMENTS IN BILATERAL SURVEILLANCE

The two reports reviewed above do not recommend any major change in the conduct of bilateral surveillance. Yet recent events suggest that some change is needed.

(a) *The Fund and the Baker Initiative*

At the start of the debt crisis, many countries sought to draw on the Fund and had therefore to submit Letters of Intent, describing the policies they would pursue to solve their balance-of-payments problems, and those letters served several purposes. Once the Fund had set its "seal of approval" on a country's policies, commercial banks were willing to reschedule the country's debts and to grant new credits in many cases. Furthermore, the Fund's seal of approval was required for a country to reschedule its debts *vis-à-vis* official creditors — to open the doors of the Paris Club — and for access to structural adjustment loans from the World Bank.

Commercial banks, official creditors, and the World Bank continue to require the Fund's seal of approval, but governments are far more reluc-

tant to request it. They have less need for balance-of-payments credit of the sort provided by the Fund, and they find it expensive politically to seek the Fund's approval — and thus to court the disapproval that normally follows when a country fails to achieve its targets.[6]

This reluctance helps to explain why little progress has been made toward the goals embodied in the Baker Initiative. At the 1985 Fund-Bank Meeting in Seoul, the US Secretary of the Treasury, James Baker, called on the World Bank and Inter-American Development Bank to raise their disbursements to the principal debtor countries by 50% (from about $6 billion annually) by making more policy-related loans, and he called on the commercial banks to lend an additional $20 billion over the next three years. He urged debtor countries to adopt growth-oriented policies, including tax reform, market-oriented pricing, trade liberalization, and the removal of barriers to foreign investment.

Baker warned that this emphasis on growth-oriented policies must not be made an excuse for reducing the role of the IMF. But he appears to have anticipated the debtors' reluctance to seek the Fund's approval by submitting to full-fledged conditionality. He suggested that the Fund should find new ways to continue its involvement in the policymaking process.

(b) *Enhanced surveillance*

One new method, enhanced surveillance, was developed by Mexico and its commercial-bank creditors in connection with the multi-year rescheduling agreement approved in 1985. Mexico undertook to formulate and quantify its macroeconomic objectives, year by year, for review by the IMF staff during the annual Article IV consultation. The staff would summarize that review in its usual report to the Executive Board, commenting specifically on the consistency of Mexico's objectives and targets and their compatibility with Mexico's external obligations. The staff would also conduct a mid-year review of Mexican performance, with particular reference to Mexico's own targets. The results of this additional review would likewise be reported to the Board. Under the terms of the rescheduling agreement, Mexico would transmit the Fund's reports to its commercial-bank creditors, who would decide for themselves whether Mexico's program and progress were compatible with its obligations under the agreement. (An adverse finding would constitute grounds for declaring Mexico in default.)

A second experiment took placed in 1986,

when Brazil was negotiating to reschedule some of its external debt. Brazil was not willing to draw on the Fund or submit to enhanced surveillance. But Brazil announced dramatic policy changes early in 1986, including the introduction of a new currency pegged to the US dollar, a freeze on prices and wages, and an end to pervasive indexation, and the Managing Director of the Fund gave these policies his personal endorsement. This was, of course, a face-saving device. Brazil got something like a seal of approval from the Fund without having to ask for it, and the banks could say they had not rescheduled the country's debts without the Fund's approval of the debtor's policies.

This may prove to be an unfortunate precedent. Other debtors are likely to ask for similar treatment, to avoid a more formal review of their policies, but the banks will want the Fund to involve itself more fully. They have noted repeatedly that official creditors refuse to settle for any arrangement short of full-fledged conditionality, not even enhanced surveillance. Furthermore, the Fund should not be asked to endorse a country's policies on a take-it-or-leave-it basis, without an opportunity to examine the assumptions and projections on which they are based and a clear understanding with the government concerned that the Fund can rescind its approval if subsequent review in the framework of surveillance raises doubts about the government's policies.

The problem is to make enhanced surveillance more attractive from the standpoint of creditors that want the Fund's advice about a country's policies without making it too onerous for the country concerned. The Fund should be involved in the policymaking process, which is what happens when a member is drafting a Letter of Intent, not asked to endorse or comment on policies after they are put in place, which is what happens with enhanced surveillance. But staff involvement should be sufficient for this purpose; there is no need for formal action by the Executive Board.[7] Thereafter, the staff can review the country's progress semiannually, as in the Mexican case, and report to the Executive Board.

When reviewing a country's policies, however, the staff should draw a distinction that is not always drawn sharply enough when the Fund reviews a government's compliance with performance criteria contained in a formal Letter of Intent. When a country does not meet its policy targets, the staff should try to acertain the reasons — whether the government has failed to implement its policies with sufficient vigor or was unduly optimistic about the evolution of the world economy and other events beyond its control.[8]

I have argued (Kenen, 1986) that countries subjected to external shocks should not be treated differently than those that have made major policy errors. Submission to conditionality is not an admission of culpability. When measuring the quality of policies, however, it is necessary and proper to distinguish between shortfalls in performance that reflect unanticipated shocks and those that reflect an inadequate effort by the government. The distinction is not easy to draw, because governments do not have complete control over their policy instruments. Budget deficits are partly endogenous, which means that public-sector borrowing is also partly endogenous. In developing countries, moveover, the behavior of the money supply depends strongly on the volume of public-sector borrowing. But the staff of the Fund should do its best (and should seek to draw the same distinction when assessing a country's compliance with full-fledged conditionality).

It may be appropriate to recommend that a country redouble its efforts when it has failed to meet its targets, regardless of the reason, and the case for making up lost ground is particularly strong when the country has drawn on the Fund, because the Fund must be repaid. But judgments about progress in meeting targets are necessarily invidious, and governments might be more willing to submit to them in the context of surveillance if they could be sure than the Fund would try to identify the reasons for gaps between outcomes and targets.

One more procedural change could help. Countries might find it easier to submit to enhanced surveillance if it was not an exceptional procedure but one that was normal for countries with balance-of-payments problems, whether or not related to the servicing of debt. Therefore, enhanced surveillance might be linked to a suggestion I have made for dealing with a different problem — the tendency for governments to wait too long before seeking the Fund's advice:[9]

> When the staff of the Fund believes that a member is facing a serious problem, the staff should solicit a "provisional" letter of intent, describing the policies that the member proposes to follow in order to deal with its surplus or deficit. . . .
>
> If the staff of the Fund does not object to these plans, the member should have the right to expect that the staff would recommend approval if the plans were embodied in a formal letter of intent submitted in conjunction with a request for a drawing. If the staff believes that a member's plans will not deal adequately with its problems, it should request revision of the provisional letter of intent.
>
> A provisional letter of intent should be appended to the report that the staff submits to the executive board of the Fund, summarizing the results of its consultation. If the staff is not satisfied with the letter, even after it has been revised, the staff

should give its reasons to the board, and the board may then choose to pursue the matter. . . .

If the executive board concludes that a member's plans are inadequate, it may decide to make representations to the member, either formally, in its own name, or informally through the managing director and staff. In the case of a member thought likely to draw on the Fund, the executive board should indicate its dissatisfaction explicitly and give its reasons, so that the member will know that it cannot expect to draw on the Fund unless it changes its plans.

Whether it is joined to this procedure or conducted separately, enhanced surveillance should be molded to the needs of each country and those of the creditors that seek the Fund's advice concerning the country's policies — commercial banks, the Paris Club, the World Bank, and so on.

When conducting enhanced surveillance, however, the staff of the Fund should decline to make broad judgments about a member's efforts. It should survey the country's experience and problem and should draw the appropriate distinctions, but it should leave to the commercial banks and other "consumers" of enhanced surveillance the difficult task of grading a government's performance. That task necessarily involves an assessment of political constraints and priorities, and it may involve precedent-setting comparative judgments affecting the consumers' relations with other governments. The Fund cannot avoid making such judgments when it reviews the experience of a member that is using the Fund's resources and must therefore satisfy performance criteria. The question of eligibility arises here. But it does not arise in the context of enhanced surveillance.

4. IMPROVEMENTS IN MULTILATERAL SURVEILLANCE

Everyone wants to improve multilateral surveillance, but there is less agreement about purposes and methods. Some proponents focus on the need for *consistency* in national policies, measured with reference to their impact on exchange rates or current-account balances. Others are concerned with the *quality* of national policies, measured with reference to their influence on world trade, output, and other global aggregates.

The two goals are not mutually exclusive. If national policies are inconsistent, they are likely to produce low-quality outcomes.[10] If quality is given too little attention, consistency may be much harder to achieve, and the consequences of inconsistencies may be more serious. But the two

approaches have rather different implications for the conduct of multilateral surveillance.

(a) *Goals for multilateral surveillance*

Much of the new interest in multilateral surveillance reflects dissatisfaction with the performance of floating exchange rates — the short-run volatility of nominal and real rates and the longer-lasting misalignments that have caused large swings in current-account balances. The change in the attitude of the US government, mentioned earlier, was due to one such misalignment — the appreciation of the dollar — that has altered the industrial and political landscape of the United States in ways which will last for a long time.

There is no significant support among governments for a shift to pegged exchange rates, partly because the advocates of such a shift have been very candid about the requirements. Governments have come to understand that the defense of pegged exchange rates calls for a big change in the targeting of policies, especially the targeting of monetary policies, or for interference with capital movements — changes that governments are not prepared to make. There is much admiration for the European Monetary System (EMS), even among advocates of floating rates. The EMS has been far more cohesive than its critics expected. But most of its admirers, as well as its critics, ascribe its success to its political sponsorship. Without the link to the European Community, the EMS would not have been born and might not continue to command adequate allegiance.

Governments are looking for ways of improving exchange-rate behavior without reforming exchange-rate arrangements and have therefore returned to policy coordination. They used to say that they could not control exchange rates, because that would be trying to defy the fundamentals. Today, they concede that they control some of those same fundamentals, their own monetary and fiscal policies, and can therefore attempt to manage exchange rates. They look to multilateral surveillance as the framework for achieving the necessary changes in national policies.

But some who want to strengthen multilateral surveillance have a more ambitious goal. They seek to improve the quality of national policies, taken collectively, not merely to remove cross-country inconsistencies that generate large movements in exchange rates. In their view, multilateral surveillance should concern itself with the growth rates of global output, employment, trade, average inflation rates and interest rates, and other variables that define the international environment. This aim was endorsed implicitly by the G-24 Report, which wanted multilateral surveillance to focus on the ways that large countries' policies affect smaller countries' adjustment efforts.

Although the G-10 countries have emphasized consistency, because of their new interest in exchange-rate stability, they seem at times to be concerned with quality as well. The communiqué following the Tokyo Summit said that "the purposes of improved coordination should explicitly include promoting noninflationary economic growth, strengthening market-oriented incentives for employment and productive investment, opening the international trading and investment system and fostering greater stability in exchange rates." Here, as in the list of "indicators" mentioned earlier, global aggregates are put before exchange rates. And though the operative paragraph of the communiqué emphasized the "mutual compatibility" of policies, it defined compatibility with reference to the whole list of indicators, not to exchange-rate stability alone. That puts the Summit countries in the quality-improving camp.

Doubts have been expressed about the standing of the Fund to deal with the quality of national policies, because its authority in all such matters derives from its obligation to "exercise firm surveillance over the exchange rate policies of members," and the authors of that phrase had a fairly narrow aim — to make sure that governments do not conduct their policies in ways that infringe on the rights of other governments or manipulate their own exchange rates "to prevent effective balance of payments adjustment or to gain an unfair competitive advantage over other members. . . ."[11] But the Fund has taken a far broader view, and its members are not known to object (except perhaps when one of them is singled out for criticism — a matter to which we must return eventually). Its *Annual Report*, for example, begins by reviewing "Developments in the World Economy," before looking at exchange rates and related matters, and the *WEO* takes a similar tack. It is therefore appropriate to contemplate a policy-improving role for the Fund, even though this means that multilateral surveillance will not focus mainly on exchange-rate behavior.[12]

(b) *Target zones and multilateral surveillance*

Would there be any need for multilateral surveillance if target zones were put in place to stabilize exchange rates? The answer appears to depend in part on the way that the zones are defined and on the way that governments are supposed to respond when market rates approach the boundaries of those zones.

Under McKinnon's proposal for the dollar, mark, and yen (McKinnon, 1984, pp. 69–74), target zones would be defined in terms of bilateral exchange rates, and both of the governments directly concerned would modify their monetary policies whenever the bilateral exchange rate for their currencies reached one of its boundaries, even if the other bilateral rate was still well within its zone.

Consultations would be needed to initiate this system. In McKinnon's world, the quality of policies is measured by the long-run growth rate of the "global" money supply (actually, a weighted sum of the growth rates of the US, West German, and Japanese money supplies), and it must be chosen collectively with a view to preserving price stability. Furthermore, the target zones must be chosen multilaterally, even when defined bilaterally. This is because the setting of the dollar-mark and dollar-yen zones also sets the mark-yen zone. But there would be no need for consultations once the system was set up, unless questions arose about the appropriate growth rate for the global money supply or about the target zones themselves. The symmetrical character of McKinnon's system would produce consistency and would maintain quality in McKinnon's world.[13]

Under Williamson's proposal (Williamson, 1985, pp. 62–72), each country's target zone would be defined in relation to a "fundamental equilibrium exchange rate" (FEER) for its currency, and its obligations would thus be determined by its effective exchange rate, not by any single bilateral rate.[14] This proposal appears to leave to each participating government the calculation of its own FEER and, therefore, the setting of its target zone, as well as the right to make crucial policy decisions after its zone has been put in place — whether to intervene or modify its policies in order to keep its currency from straying from its zone, or to shift the zone itself (i.e., to devalue or revalue its currency in relation to the currencies that define its effective exchange rate). But some of this autonomy proves to be illusory. There is a problem of consistency, which can be solved only by choosing the FEERs collectively, and a problem of symmetry, which can be solved only by continuous surveillance over national policies.

Williamson acknowledges the problem of consistency and assigns multilateral surveillance to solving it:[15]

Suppose that each individual country were to. . . estimate its FEER, adopt a target zone bounded by soft margins around that rate, and intervene (while in general not fully sterilizing) to discourage the market rate from straying beyond the target zone. Would this produce a viable and consistent *system* of exchange rates for the world economy?

There is one obvious but essential condition that would need to be satisfied to give an affirmative answer to that question. That condition is that the FEERs be mutually consistent. If that condition were not approximately satisfied, the system would become an engine of inflation or deflation. Suppose, for example, that countries in general wished for more depreciated FEERs than was consistent with the choices being made by their partners. . . . Then each country would be driven to a more expansionary monetary policy in the attempt to achieve its exchange rate target. . . .

It is therefore a matter of importance that the estimates of FEERs, which provide the central rates for target zones, be mutually consistent. One would obviously need some international mechanism to check for such consistency and to negotiate changes in target zones when it is lacking. The obvious organization to take on this task is the IMF, which would at last achieve a focus for its responsibilities for the surveillance of exchange rate policies that has been sadly lacking up to now.

But consistency would not be easy to achieve[16] and would not be sufficient to prevent the system from producing low-quality policy outcomes.

When target zones are defined in terms of effective exchange rates, which is what Williamson wants, one currency can reach the lower limit of its zone without some other currency going to its upper limit, and policies may change sequentially rather than reciprocally. Policy changes may not balance out when effective exchange rates do not move symmetrically, even in relation to target zones that have been defined consistently. Continuing surveillance is needed to guard against imbalances of this sort — deflationary pressures, for example, stemming from the actions of one country trying to keep its effective exchange rate from passing through its lower limit when no other country is obliged to keep its rate from passing through its upper limit.[17]

(c) A quality-improving approach to surveillance

How should multilateral surveillance be conducted? I have tried to show why it must be separate from bilateral surveillance. Bargains must be struck at every stage, and each of the participants must be allowed to show that it has "won" concessions from the others — concessions that the Fund cannot make on their behalf. I have argued

that it should not aim at managing exchange rates, even though that is why many governments are interested. It should aim at the improvement of national policies over the medium term, measured in terms of their impact on key global aggregates.

I seem to be saying — to my surprise — that the Summit countries have got it right. But the Fund should be involved, through its Managing Director, in both stages of the process.

The first stage should articulate and quantify composite policy objectives for the major industrial countries, relating to growth rates, inflation rates, and other variables. These should be framed as medium-term targets, but they should be updated and extended periodically. No attempt should be made to "fine tune" the world, but the major industrial countries should not be allowed to pretend that they have no influence on — or responsibility for — the evolution of the world economy.

The second stage should translate the composite targets into operational commitments on the part of each participating government. Each country's obligations must be framed to take account of that country's special problems, but they should be consistent in two senses: (1) they should be adequate, taken together, to achieve the composite policy objectives; and (2) they should not involve larger changes in exchange rates than any other set of policy commitments capable of reaching the same objectives. Implementation of the policy commitments should be monitored collectively, not by the Fund bilaterally, in order to facilitate reciprocal adjustments whenever the need becomes apparent.

At the first stage, the Fund should represent the interests of all other countries. It should seek to prevent the participating countries from defining their objectives too modestly or narrowly — which is what they started to do at the Tokyo Summit, when they promised to review their *own* targets and forecasts to make sure of their mutual compatibility. The Fund should try to make them raise their sights and take account not only of their own interactions but their impact on the rest of the world as well.

At the second stage, the Fund should be prepared to propose explicit distributions of policy commitments among the participating countries. These should meet the two *desiderata* proposed above, and they should be published in the *WEO*, along with global economic projections showing what they are expected to achieve. This is where the Fund can get itself in trouble, because it will be forced to say that some of its most influential members should shoulder additional responsibilities and take risks that make their governments uncomfortable. This leads me to my final procedural suggestion.

The Fund should establish its own council of economic advisers. The members should be chosen by the Executive Board on the recommendation of the Managing Director; they should serve for fixed but staggered terms that would not be renewable. The council would draft an additional chapter for the *WEO*, in which it would propose specific distributions of policy commitments for consideration by the governments concerned. (It should perhaps propose more than one such distribution and compare the merits of competing plans.) A draft of the new chapter would be discussed by the Board, just like other chapters, but the council could not be instructed to revise or withdraw it. It would be

published as the council's own advice, not that of the Board or the staff of the Fund. Furthermore, the council should be required to comment frankly on the performance of individual governments — to say that some have fallen short and praise those that have done well. This would publicize the process of surveillance and put some more "peer pressure" on participating governments without forcing them to criticize each other. From time to time, moreover, the Board might comment on the process, basing its assessments on the council's comments. It could do so publicly in its *Annual Report* but might make more pointed observations, when required, by communicating confidentially with the governments concerned.

NOTES

1. On these issues, see Williamson (1983), especially the comments by Cooper and Diaz-Alejandro and the concluding chapter by Williamson; also Dell (1981); Nowzad (1981); and Spraos (1984).

2. See Khan and Knight (1985) and the papers by Connors, Donovan, Gylfason, Kelly, and Reichman and Stillson, cited there.

3. For a recent review of these issues, see Dornbusch (1985), who goes farther than most other analysts in distinguishing clearly between the cash-flow and welfare implications of various scenarios and in drawing attention to differences among developing countries in their sensitivity to external shocks; see also Sachs and McKibbin (1985), whose work suggests that policy coordination among developed countries may be more beneficial to the developing countries than to the developed countries directly involved in the process.

4. These processes are described in Johnson (1985) and in other articles cited there.

5. The two reports are equally unclear about the extent to which their recommendations regarding the *WEO* contemplate departures from current practices. At present, the *WEO* is reviewed by the Executive Board and discussed by the Interim Committee. These deliberations are not publicized, although the communiqué of the Interim Committee may convey some highlights. The *WEO* itself is published shortly after the Interim Committee meeting. The G-10 Report suggests that the G-10 countries should discuss the new chapter of the *WEO*. The G-24 Report says that the Fund Board should make explicit policy recommendations based on an expanded version of the *WEO*. Both reports are silent on the role of the Interim Committee and the question of publication. Both reports are likewise silent on a technical matter. The *WEO* contains detailed quantitative projections, but these are based mainly on iterative consultations within the Fund,

rather than a large econometric model. This sort of consensus forecasting may not lend itself to the detailed analysis of national policies that both reports want to include in the *WEO*. To have much confidence in that sort of policy analysis, one would want to see the model that lies behind it or, at least, formal sensitivity analyses showing how each country's policies are deemed to function and how national economies are linked. There may thus be need for major changes in the technology used to prepare the *WEO* before it can be made to do new work. (The 1986 *WEO* responded to the suggestion in the G-10 Report with a new chapter on "Policy Interactions in Industrial Countries," and it was based partly on a small econometric model, as well as simulations conducted by other institutions, using larger models. That experimental chapter, however, focused on one problem, the global implications of the fiscal contraction required by the Gramm-Rudman-Hollings Act, and the analysis was not fully integrated with the projections and analyses in other chapters. For that same reason, it is somewhat hard to judge the usefulness of this response to the G-10 suggestion. The budget cuts required by the Gramm-Rudman-Hollings Act are uniquely large and well-defined, relative to run-of-the-mill policy changes, giving the analysis sharper focus than one might anticipate year after year.)

6. These disapprovals were far too frequent in 1983–84, which raised the political costs of exposure to them and damaged the credibility of the Fund itself. Anxious to contain the debt crisis, governments and the IMF staff agreed to ambitious policy targets that proved to be unrealistic in the short run. Some countries, such as Brazil, were able to make large improvements in their trade balances but did not make comparable progress internally in reducing budget deficits and cutting inflation rates.

7. Strictly speaking, the Board does not approve the policies outlined in a Letter of Intent (and does not

withdraw approval when a member fails to meet its performance criteria). It indicates approval by agreeing to a stand-by arrangement (and indicates disapproval by deciding that a member is ineligible to make further drawings).

8. Spraos (1984) makes a similar suggestion but would go much farther. He would have the Fund focus exclusively on "ultimate" policy targets, not monitor policy instruments as well, and concentrate primarily on a balance-of-payments target, not concern itself with inflation and other domestic phenomena. But when the Fund is asked to assess a government's performance, it must look at policy instruments; otherwise, it cannot distinguish between the effects of exogenous shocks and of inadequate efforts. The question of accountability is central here, and governments should be held accountable only for those variables they can control. The same point is made by Cooper (in Williamson, 1983, p. 572).

9. Kenen (1986), pp. 70–71.

10. On the way that inconsistent policy targets can lead to low-quality policy outcomes, see Eichengreen (1984).

11. Article IV, Section 3(b), and Article IV, Section 1. The same language is used in the statement of principles for the conduct of surveillance adopted by the Executive Board in 1977, which goes on to list developments that might call for discussions between the Fund and a member. These include "protracted large-scale intervention in one direction in the exchange market; an unsustainable level of official or quasi-official borrowing. . . for balance of payments purposes," and the use of direct controls over current or capital transactions that may reflect an effort to manipulate the exchange rate.

12. Although the statement of principle cited above takes a narrow approach, it says that the Fund's surveillance of exchange-rate policies ". . . shall be made within the framework of a comprehensive analysis of the general economic situation and economic policy strategy of the member, and shall recognize that domestic as well as external policies can contribute to timely adjustment of the balance of payments. The appraisal shall take into account the extent to which the policies of the member, including its exchange rate policies, serve the objectives of the continuing development of the orderly underlying conditions that are necessary for financial stability, the promotion of sustained sound economic growth, and reasonable levels of employment." Thus, it affirms the Fund's concern with the quality of policies, not merely with consistency or convergence.

13. I hasten to add, however, that McKinnon's world is not mine; I am not persuaded by his argument or evidence concerning the role of the "global" money supply, his views on "indirect" currency substitution, or his treatment of fiscal policies. I use his framework merely to illustrate my point that surveillance would not be needed under certain target-zone proposals. (It would be possible to transfer McKinnon's proposals to a more realistic macroeconomic model. In that case, surveillance might not be needed to stabilize exchange rates. That could still be done by symmetrical changes in monetary policies. But one would want surveillance in order to decide whether this was the *best* way to stabilize exchange rates — to deal with the quality of economic policies.)

14. Williamson (1985), pp. 72–73.

15. The FEER is the real exchange rate required to elicit the current-account surplus (deficit) that matches the "underlying" capital outflow (inflow) for the country concerned; it is therefore the one that reflects "productivity" and "thrift" (and the cyclically-adjusted budget deficit). On the conceptual and practical problems involved in applying these notions, see Artus and Knight (1984), pp. 18–28.

16. Consistency could best be achieved by obtaining agreement initially concerning the character of the "underlying" capital flow among the participating countries and thus the appropriate pattern of current-account balances, then computing from a common model the set of real exchange rates needed to achieve those balances. When the task is described this way, however, its magnitude becomes fully apparent. It would be necessary to reach agreement about prospective fiscal policies and many other variables in order to reach agreement about the pattern of capital flows, and to reach agreement about the outlook for real growth rates in order to determine the real exchange rates required to achieve the current-account balances that match the capital flows. Furthermore, the calculations would have to be made for many countries, including some that would not be involved in the target-zone arrangements, because of their importance for the capital and trade flows of certain key countries. (Canada and Mexico would have to be included in all calculations involving the United States, even though they play a minor role in the transactions of other countries and might not choose to participate in the target-zone arrangements.)

17. The problem is similar to one that crops up in the EMS, where each member's exchange-rate obligations are defined in terms of bilateral exchange rates but its more general policy obligations are defined by the divergence indicator, which is in turn based on an effective exchange rate (i.e., the value of the member's currency in terms of the ECU). The divergence indicator can tell an EMS member to tighten its monetary policy without telling any other member to move in the opposite direction.

REFERENCES

Artus, J., and M. D. Knight, *Issues in the assessment of the exchange rates of industrial countries*, Occasional Paper 29 (Washington, DC: International Monetary Fund, 1984).

Dell, S., *On Being Grandmotherly: The Evolution of IMF Conditionality*, Essays in International Finance 144 (Princeton: International Finance Section, Princeton University, 1981).

Deputies of the Group of Ten, *Report on the Functioning of the International Monetary System*, reprinted in *IMF Survey* (Washington, DC: International Monetary Fund, supplement, July 1985); cited as G-10 Report.

Deputies of the Intergovernmental Group of 24, *International Monetary Affairs: The Functioning and Improvement of the International Monetary System*, reprinted in *IMF Survey* (Washington, DC: International Monetary Fund, supplement, September 1985); cited as G-24 Report.

Dornbusch, R., "Policy and performance links between LDC debtors and industrial nations," *Brookings Papers on Economic Activity*, Vol. 2 (1985), pp. 303–356.

Eichengreen, B., "International policy coordination in historical perspective: A view from the interwar years," in W. H. Buiter and R. C. Marston (Eds.), *International Economic Policy Coordination* (Cambridge: Cambridge University Press, 1984), pp. 139–178.

Johnson, G. G., "Enhancing the effectiveness of surveillance," *Finance and Development*, Vol. 22, No. 4 (December 1985), pp. 2–6.

Kenen, P. B., *Financing, Adjustment, and the International Monetary Fund*, Studies in International Economics (Washington, DC: The Brookings Institution, 1986).

Khan, M. S., and M. D. Knight, *Fund-supported adjustment programs and economic growth*, Occasional Paper 41 (Washington, DC: International Monetary Fund, 1985).

McKinnon, R. I., *An International Standard for Monetary Stabilization*, Policy Analyses in International Economics 8 (Washington, DC: Institute for International Economics, 1984).

Nowzad, B., *The IMF and Its Critics*, Essays in International Finance 146 (Princeton: International Finance Section, Princeton University, 1981).

Sachs, J., and W. McKibbon, "Macroeconomic policies in the OECD and LDC external adjustment," Discussion Paper 56 (London: Centre for Economic Policy Research, 1985).

Spraos, J., "IMF conditionality — A better way," Banca Nazionale del Lavoro, *Quarterly Review* (December 1984), pp. 411–421.

Williamson, J. (Ed.), *IMF Conditionality* (Washington, DC: Institute for International Economics, 1983).

Williamson, J., *The Exchange Rate System*, Policy Analyses in International Economics 5 (Washington, DC: Institute for International Economics, 1985).

[19]

REFORMING THE INTERNATIONAL MONETARY SYSTEM[†]

Exchange Rate Management: What Role for Intervention?

By Peter B. Kenen*

Economists are fond of stylized facts—those most striking features of a situation that require explanation, or perhaps those features we can model easily. I will start with some stylized opinions about the costs and benefits of exchange rate management.

In the years right after the shift to floating exchange rates, we heard much talk about monetary autonomy. Floating rates, it was said, would allow each government to control its own money supply and use it to pursue its own policy objectives. Under the Bretton Woods regime, by contrast, there had been two constraints on monetary autonomy.

A normative constraint was imposed by the need to keep inflation rates and interest rates in line with those of the United States, to avoid a persistent deficit or surplus in the balance of payments, and an eventual exchange rate change. A mechanical constraint was imposed by the need to intervene in the foreign-exchange market to keep exchange rates pegged. An official purchase of foreign currency raises the money supply, just like an open market purchase of domestic bonds, and a sale of foreign currency reduces it.

Most central banks tried to sterilize their interventions—to offset the money-supply effects by open market operations. But capital mobility was high, even then, and limited the effectiveness of sterilization; an open market sale of domestic bonds attracted a capital inflow, forcing the central bank to buy more foreign currency. Economists disagreed about the net effect, rep-

resented by the size of the offset coefficient, which compared the capital inflow to the open market sale and thus measured the additional intervention induced by any attempt to sterilize previous intervention. We continue to debate that issue but cast in different terms—the degree of substitutability between assets denominated in different currencies or, equivalently, the size and stability of the so-called risk premium.

At that early stage, then, the shift to floating rates was seen to reflect other governments' dissatisfaction with their subservience to U.S. monetary policy, as well as the first stirrings of official interest in monetary targeting. The first wave of discontent with floating rates was also related to monetary policies, but this time to the side effects of having more autonomy. Floating rates were blamed for vicious circles, in which depreciation caused inflation that produced additional depreciation, preventing a change in the nominal exchange rate from having a long-lasting effect on the real rate.

It is now commonly acknowledged that vicious circles cannot spiral on unless they are accommodated by monetary policy, and they may not even start in the absence of inflationary expectations. This brings us up to date. Now that inflationary forces have abated, floating exchange rates are criticized for having excessive effects on real exchange rates, not the deficient effects that were the focus of earlier concern. This was the main complaint about the appreciation of the dollar from 1981 through 1985, which impaired the competitiveness of U.S. industry and contributed to the buildup of protectionist pressures. Those pressures, in turn, were the chief reason for the Plaza Communique of September 1985, in which the G-5 countries sought to talk the dollar down but backed

[†]*Discussants*: Allan H. Meltzer, Carnegie-Mellon University; Maurice Obstfeld, Columbia University.

*Walker Professor of Economics and International Finance and Director of the International Finance Section, Princeton University, Princeton, NJ 08544.

their talk by threating to sell it down by concerted intervention.

Proponents of exchange rate management hailed the Plaza Agreement as the start of a new era in international monetary cooperation, and some have since said that the Plaza Agreement is dead because it disappointed them. Rather than inaugurating close cooperation, it has been followed by disputes about appropriate exchange rates, interest rates, and budget deficits.

The Plaza Agreement marked a sharp change in the attitude of the United States or, more accurately, a change in leadership at the U.S. Treasury. Nevertheless, it should be viewed as an instance of *ad hoc* cooperation undertaken to prevent existing institutions, the GATT system in this case, from crumbling under pressure. Although different in form, it resembled in nature the brief period of close cooperation after the onset of the debt crisis in 1982, inspired by the threat of a banking crisis. This sort of regime-preserving cooperation is gratifying, but a single episode such as the Plaza Agreement cannot be taken to signal a basic change in governments' habits.

The first wave of dissatisfaction with floating exchange rates, when changes in nominal rates were seen to have too little influence on real rates, was not as strong as the second, when changes in nominal rates were seen to be too influential. I venture to suggest a simple reason, in keeping with the spirit of this stylized history. At the time of the first wave of criticism, few officials or economists believed in the feasibility of managing exchange rates, let alone returning to pegged rates. Central banks did not enjoy the credibility they have bought back since. The second wave of criticism has been more effective in mobilizing support for reform of the system because central banks are deemed to have the credibility required to influence market expectations.

Yet there is an odd aspect to this stylized history. Exchange rate management has gained favor recently but intervention has not.

In an early version of his plan for managing the dollar-mark-yen relationship, Ronald McKinnon (1984) wanted to rely primarily on nonsterilized intervention to stabilize exchange rates. In a recent paper, by contrast, he calls for the establishment of target zones but says that central banks should "agree to mutual and symmetrical monetary adjustment to achieve these exchange rate targets" (1986, p. 16). The country with the overvalued currency should reduce the growth rate of its money supply; the one with the undervalued currency should raise its growth rate. McKinnon does not mention intervention. In most presentations of his target-zone proposal, John Williamson assigns a limited role to intervention: Monetary policy should be the principal instrument for keeping rates within their target zones, "reinforced by exchange rate intervention" (1986, p. 166).

What about official views? The Versailles Summit of 1982 created a Working Group to study the effectiveness of intervention. Its conclusions were negotiated carefully and formulated cautiously. It said that intervention has been effective in dealing with disorderly market conditions, by narrowing bid-offer spreads and day-to-day fluctuations. But the Working Group was rather skeptical about the use of intervention for more ambitious purposes—not only the ability of sterilized intervention to alter exchange rates by changing supplies of assets, but even its influence on expectations. From time to time, governments had intervened "when they judged that market participants had not taken full account of fundamental factors…or had lost confidence in the policies of some of the major countries." On occasion, such intervention bought time for market participants to revise their views and showed the authorities' determination to restore confidence. But it was "useless or even counterproductive in the absence of appropriate policy changes" (Working Group, paras. 40, 47–48).

The views of the Working Group were echoed by the Plaza Communique, when it declared that "recent shifts in fundamental economic conditions…, together with policy commitments for the future, have not been reflected fully in exchange markets" and concluded that "in view of the present and prospective changes in fundamentals, some further orderly appreciation of the main non-dollar currencies...is desirable" (paras. 5, 18).

There was much intervention right after the Plaza Agreement, and official accounts gave it more importance than earlier views might have led us to expect. But they gave even more importance to the announcement effects of the Agreement itself and to subsequent policy changes:

> [The] dollar dropped sharply on the day following the G-5 announcement...[It] had already fallen against major foreign currencies by the time the Bundesbank stepped in.... Later the same day, the U.S. authorities conducted their first operation during the period, selling dollars...in a visible manner to resist a rise of the dollar from the lower levels.
>
> During the next few days, there was some skepticism in the market that the lower dollar levels would be maintained.... The Bank of Japan responded with massive dollar sales... [Market] participants came to believe that the authorities were firmly committed to the joint effort....
>
> Late in October the Bank of Japan allowed Japanese money market interest rates to drift higher. It was then that the dollar began to decline particularly sharply against the yen. Many market observers viewed the Japanese actions on interest rates as possibly representing the first of a series of steps to be taken by the G-5 countries....
>
> [Interim Report, 1985, pp. 46–47]

Academic assessments of recent experience have been equally skeptical (Martin Feldstein, 1986).

My stylized history has mentioned three ways of using intervention for exchange rate management.

1) It might be used to peg an exchange rate or modify its path. The monetary authorities would purchase all of the foreign or domestic currency that the market was unwilling to absorb. This is sometimes called brute-force intervention.

2) It might be used to alter asset-market equilibrium by changing money supplies or supplies of nonmonetary assets in various currencies. It would be nonsterilized in the first case and sterilized in the second.

3) It might be used to alter expectations by underscoring the authorities' commitment to a particular policy, signalling a future policy change, or making the market more or less confident about its own projections.

We are so accustomed to warning against excessive reliance on intervention that we tend to forget the obvious. A brute-force policy can put the exchange rate wherever the authorities want it, for as long as they are capable of intervening. That is what they did under the Bretton Woods system and what they go on doing under the European Monetary System (EMS). Furthermore, they may actually enhance their ability to peg or move the rate by announcing their intentions. Once they do so, however, their credibility is at stake. That is why governments were so loathe to make exchange rate changes under the Bretton Woods system, when they were committed to pegging rates.

Problems arise when the market comes to believe that the authorities will back off— voluntarily because they have decided that the exchange rate should change, or involuntarily because they are going to run out of reserves. The result is a speculative crisis of the sort modeled by Paul Krugman (1979). The authorities adopt a rigid monetary policy that causes a gradual loss of reserves. Once the nature of that policy is known, because it is announced or readily observable, a speculative attack is inevitable. It will occur as soon as holders of domestic currency realize that the collective effect of their individual actions is certain to exhaust the authorities' reserves or drive them below some minimal level, forcing the authorities to abandon their defense of the exchange rate.

Maurice Obstfeld (1986) has extended Krugman's model to show that there can be a speculative crisis even when it is not fore-ordained by current policies; it can be produced by self-fulfilling expectations about the policy response to a future crisis. Robert Flood and Peter Garber (1984) have made the money supply wander stochastically around its trend, so that the market cannot predict the path of reserves exactly and the model cannot tell us the date of the crisis. But no one has shown why the authorities should behave so foolishly. If they know what the market knows, that their monetary policy will produce a crisis eventually, why don't they devalue or float the currency before they embark on that policy? To make the crisis model meaningful, we should attach reputational costs to changing the exchange rate and make the authorities weigh them, day by day, against the benefits of continuing to pursue a crisis-inducing monetary policy.

A brute-force policy is usually modeled as continuing flow intervention to keep market forces from changing the exchange rate. Intervention to affect asset-market equilibrium is usually studied by looking at a single act of intervention—an exchange of foreign-currency assets between the central bank and private asset holders.

It is easy to show that a single act of nonsterilized intervention can alter the exchange rate permanently. It affects the fundamentals by changing the money supply. In fact, a nonsterilized purchase of foreign currency has a larger short-run effect on the exchange rate than an open market purchase of domestic securities having the same impact on the money supply (my 1982 paper). By implication, monetary policy should be conducted by purchases and sales of foreign exchange, rather than open market operations in domestic securities, if it is assigned to exchange-rate management, as McKinnon (1986) and Williamson propose. That would buy the biggest bang for a buck.

The effect of sterilized intervention is more controversial. It depends on the degree of substitutability between assets denominated in different currencies. If foreign and domestic bonds were perfect substitutes, sterilized intervention would be futile, because it can merely replace one bond with the other, and this would not matter to asset holders. Even if they are imperfect substitutes, moreover, sterilized intervention has less effect on the exchange rate than an equal amount of non-sterilized intervention (my earlier paper). In some circumstances, however, the authorities may want to alter the exchange rate without affecting the money supply, which raises the crucial quantitative question. Is sterilized intervention powerful enough to be useful?

Simulations by Obstfeld (1983) and others said that it is not, but recent empirical work makes me wonder whether the models they used could capture its whole influence. Wing Woo (1984) has shown that we may understate or miss completely the effects of imperfect substitutability if we do not make sufficient allowance for speculative bubbles. Furthermore, recent attempts to model directly the influence of sterilized intervention say that is may be effective (see, for example Karen Lewis, 1986, and work cited there).

Going back to basics, careful econometric work decisively rejects the joint hypothesis that the forward exchange rate can be taken to predict the rationally expected future spot rate. If expectations were truly rational, we could therefore reject risk neutrality, and bonds denominated in different currencies would not be perfect substitutes. But we have to assimilate two other findings. First, it has been hard to account for the behavior of the risk premium when it is measured in the usual way, by invoking the rational expectations hypothesis. Second, that hypothesis is challenged directly by new work with survey data on exchange rate expectations (Jeffrey Frankel and Kenneth Froot, 1986, and Kathryn Dominguez, 1986). It may be time to measure the risk premium differently —to replace the rational expectations hypothesis with other suppositions about the formation of expectations or to use the survey data. This much seems clear: the use of realized exchange rates to represent expected rates produces a noisy measure of the risk premium (Dominguez and Lewis). In brief, the jury is still out on the size and behavior of the risk premium, and it is not yet possible to decide whether sterilized intervention is a reliable way to alter asset-market equilibrium.

I turn now to the of intervention as a way of changing expectations. Consider first the view most commonly advanced that intervention can be used to let the market know about future policies. This is, of course, a special case of the more general view that governments are justified in trying to alter market prices when they are better informed than the market—in this case, better informed about their own intentions. For the argument to hold in this instance, however, the market must have rational expectations; otherwise, it cannot be expected to draw the appropriate inference about future policies from the exchange rate changes induced by intervention. But other restrictive conditions must hold as well.

First, the authorities must have no other reason for intervening; otherwise, the market cannot know whether the authorities are trying to convey information or trying to achieve some other exchange rate objective. Second, intervention must have a distinct advantage over other ways of conveying information; it must be more persuasive than a simple announcement or a way of avoiding the bureaucratic obstacles to making an announcement. Third, there must be a one-to-one correspondence between the exchange rate change induced by intervention and the future policy it is meant to forecast. This would be true in a simple monetary model, where the exchange rate does not respond to any future policy other than a change in the money supply. It is not true in realistic models. What were the U.S. authorities trying to signal after the Plaza Agreement—a future tightening of fiscal policy or future easing of monetary policy? Because these requirements are so stringent, intervention cannot be a very useful way to provide information about future policies, and I am inclined to emphasize more strongly the other ways of using it to alter expectations.

Intervention can be used for underscoring the authorities' commitment to current policies or for trying to persuade the market that the prevailing exchange rate is inconsistent with the fundamentals—the case of the Plaza Agreement. Whatever the authorities' reason for wanting the market to revise its views, the market is more likely to take heed when the authorities intervene and thus back their words with money. The market will take losses if it bets against them and the authorities prove to be right. Dean Taylor (1982) has tried to show that the authorities have been wrong—that the market has made

profits by betting against them—but his calculations have been sharply challenged; they are exceedingly sensitive to the exchange rate chosen for valuing reserves at the end of the period.

Intervention can also be used to change the market's confidence in its own projections, and this may be its most appropriate role. In most theoretical models, especially those in which expectations are rational, all agents hold identical views. In fact, expectations are heterogeneous and held with varying degrees of confidence. This is recognized implicitly in recent work on speculative bubbles, including so-called rational bubbles— instances in which the market has fallen off the saddle path. When expectations are heterogeneous and especially when a bubble appears to be building, intervention may be quite effective. It need not be conducted in brute-force fashion, but rather with the aim of making market participants reassess their views about the likelihood that they will have time to cover their positions before the bubble bursts.

To influence expectations, however, governments must be willing to stand by their views. They should not start to intervene unless they are prepared to persist, which means that they must hold very large reserves or have ample access to short-term credit—a key feature of the EMS that is often ignored but was stressed by the Working Group (para. 52). Furthermore, they should not intervene without saying why. They need not necessarily commit themselves to a target rate or zone. They should be prepared to say that current rates are out of line if they hold that view, and they should not intervene unless they hold that view. They should not lean against the wind unless exchange rates are being blown far off course.

REFERENCES

Dominguez, Kathryn M., "Are Foreign Exchange Forecasts Rational? New Evidence from Survey Data," International Finance Discussion Paper No. 281, Board of Governors of the Federal Reserve System, 1986.

Feldstein, Martin, "New Evidence on the Effects of Exchange Rate Intervention," NBER Working Paper No. 2052, 1986.

Flood, Robert P. and Garber, Peter M., "Collapsing Exchange-Rate Regimes: Some Linear Examples," *Journal of International Economics*, August 1984, *17*, 1–13.

Frankel, Jeffrey A. and Froot, Kenneth, "Three Essays Using Survey Data on Exchange Rate Expectations," Working Paper No. 8614, Department of Economics, University of California-Berkeley, 1986.

Kenen, Peter B., "Effects of Intervention and Sterilization in the Short Run and the Long Run," in R. N. Cooper et al., eds., *The International Monetary System under Flexible Exchange Rate*, Cambridge: Ballinger, 1982.

Krugman, Paul, "A Model of Balance-of-Payments Crises," *Journal of Money, Credit and Banking*, August 1979, *11*, 311–25.

Lewis, Karen K., "Testing for the Effectiveness of Sterilized Foreign Exchange Market Intervention Using a Structural Multi-lateral Asset Market Approach," Working Paper No. 372, Salomon Brothers Center for the Study of Financial Institutions, New York University, 1986.

McKinnon, Ronald I., *An International Standard for Monetary Stabilization*, Policy Analyses in International Economics 8, Washington: Institute for International Economics, 1984.

_____, "Monetary and Exchange Rate Policies for International Financial Stability: A Proposal," unpublished, September 1986.

Obstfeld, Maurice, "Exchange Rates, Inflation and the Sterilization Problem: Germany, 1975–1981," *European Economic Review*, March-April 1983, 21, 161–89.

_____, "Rational and Self-Fulfilling Balance-of-Payments Crises," *American Economic Review*, March 1986, *76*, 72–81.

Taylor, Dean, "Official Intervention in the Foreign Exchange Market, or, Bet Against the Central Bank," *Journal of Political Economy*, April 1982, *90*, 356–68.

Williamson, John, "Target Zones and the Management of the Dollar," *Brookings Papers on Economic Activity*, 1:1986, 165–74.

Woo, Wing T., "Speculative Bubbles in the Foreign Exchange Markets," *Brookings Discussion Papers in International Economics*, No. 13, 1984.

Interim Report on Treasury and Federal Reserve Foreign Exchange Operations, August–October 1985, Federal Reserve Bank of New York, *Quarterly Review*, Winter 1985–86.

Plaza Communique, *Group of 5 Statement, September 22, 1985*; reprinted in *IMF Survey*, October 7, 1985.

Working Group, *Report of the Working Group on Exchange Market Intervention*, March, 1983.

20

Chapter 2

The Use of IMF Credit

Peter B. Kenen

The International Monetary Fund changed greatly in form and function during the 1970s and 1980s. Designed originally to meet the needs of industrial countries and to maintain orderly relations among their currencies, the Fund has become increasingly concerned with the needs and problems of developing countries—the only users of Fund credit in the 1980s.

A number of events combined to bring about these changes. The shift to floating exchange rates in 1973 was decisively important; it weakened the major countries' obligations to the Fund and reduced their need to use its resources. The oil shocks of the 1970s, the rapid growth in lending by commercial banks, and the debt crisis of the 1980s changed the Fund in other ways. It had been designed to function as a credit union: Each member would contribute to the Fund's resources, and each could then draw on them to meet its balance-of-payments needs.[1] Faced with huge demands for balance-of-payments credit in the wake of the two oil shocks, and even larger demands at the start of the debt crisis, the Fund began to function as a financial intermediary, borrowing resources from one group of countries to meet the needs of others.

The changes in the Fund's role as a financial institution were accompanied by changes in its policies and practices. These had been designed to safeguard members' rights by protecting the liquidity of the Fund itself, but they began to take on broader purposes. The improvement of national policies became a goal in itself, and the Fund encouraged its members to use Fund credit as soon as they ran into balance-of-payments problems, to expose them to the Fund's advice and policy conditions. For this same reason, however, the Fund was increasingly criticized for being paternalistic. In the 1980s, moreover, the Fund was widely seen as a debt collector for creditor governments and banks because it would not disburse Fund credit to any member that was not up to date in its interest payments. Finally, the Fund began to be part of the debt problem rather than part of the solution as it started to draw net resources away from the debtor countries instead of making more money available to them.

The Fund will need to change further in the 1990s to keep pace with the evolution of the monetary system and to help its members deal with new problems. Changes will be needed in all aspects of its work, including the surveillance of national policies and the provision of financing. This chapter concentrates on the Fund's financial activities, while its policy role is examined in other chapters. It focuses primarily on two requirements. First, the Fund must help reduce and consolidate the debts of developing countries, including the $33 billion owed to the Fund itself, and it must modify its policies to make that task easier. Second, the Fund must involve itself in the process of exchange rate management initiated by the Louvre Accord of 1987 and the further reform of exchange rate arrangements that must take place eventually.

The Breakdown of the Bretton Woods Bargain

The Bretton Woods Agreement of 1944 was a neatly balanced bargain. On the one hand, participating governments acknowledged that exchange rates are shared variables, not to be chosen or altered unilaterally; that decisions about exchange rates would not be taken without the consent of the Fund. On the other hand, governments were promised that they could use Fund resources to deal with balance-of-payments problems; they would not have to sacrifice important domestic objectives to maintain exchange rate stability.

The bargain was balanced in another way. When one country purchased a second country's currency from the pool held by the Fund, the second country's drawing rights would rise automatically. The second country could thus expect to purchase the first country's currency when it began to run a balance-of-payments deficit. The Fund's resources would revolve automatically if balance-of-payments deficits rotated regularly. As that might not happen, however, the Bretton Woods bargain contained two provisions to protect its members' rights by protecting the liquidity of the Fund. The first was the Scarce Currency Clause, which allowed the Fund to declare that a particular currency was scarce, ration its own holdings of that currency, and authorize its members to control commercial uses of that currency. This clause has never been invoked. The second provision authorized the Fund to adopt rules and policies designed to guarantee that members would repay their drawings on the Fund rather than become permanent debtors.

At first, the Fund relied on a complicated formula that held that part of any increase in a member's own reserves must be used to pay back drawings. It also relied on assurances by the Fund's staff that a member wanting to use Fund credit was taking steps to solve its balance-of-payments problem. The formula proved to be cumbersome, however, and the Fund soon moved instead to fixed-term use of its resources and more elaborate forms of conditionality.[2] Ordinary credit-tranche drawings had to be repaid in three to five years, and a member wanting to use Fund credit beyond the first credit tranche had to submit a "letter of intent" describing the policies it would follow to solve its balance-of-payments problem and proposing precise "performance criteria" by which the Fund might monitor its progress.[3] If it failed to meet those self-imposed objectives—by letting its money supply grow too fast, for example, or by reducing its budget deficit too slowly—and could not offer satisfactory reasons for its failure, the Fund would not allow it to draw down the rest of the stand-by credit established in response to its initial application.

The Bretton Woods bargain seemed to be working fairly well at the start of the 1970s, and there was reason to hope that the Fund would exceed its founders' expectations. In 1969, the First Amendment to the Fund's Articles of Agreement addressed an important issue neglected by the original bargain—the management of international liquidity. The Fund was given the power to create its own reserve asset, the Special Drawing Right (SDR), to supplement supplies of other assets, and 9.3 billion of SDRs were created within the next three years.

But much was wrong with the monetary system in 1970. The Fund did not have the power to propose exchange rate changes, and the exchange rate system had become too rigid:

> From the vantage point of today it takes an effort to realize the extent to which parity changes were resisted. . . . Maintenance of a constant parity was treated as tantamount to maintenance of stable social arrangements, and the contemplation of parity changes as the equivalent of 'thinking the unthinkable.'[4]

It is worth recalling, however, that the initial breakdown of fixed parities in August 1971 was engineered by the United States to achieve a realignment of pegged exchange rates—not to replace them with floating rates—and that the Fund played a role in the process. The Fund helped to produce the Smithsonian Agreement, which defined the new set of exchange rates. That agreement, moreover, led to the creation of the Committee of Twenty, charged with proposing long-run reforms of the monetary system, and its *Outline of Reform* favored an exchange rate regime "based on stable but adjustable par values."[5]

Fund credit was not used heavily, but it was used widely. In 1968–72, the five years preceding the first oil shock, eleven industrial countries drew on the Fund, including the United States and five other Group of Seven (G-7) countries (Japan was the exception); their drawings totaled SDR 7.8 billion. But only two of those countries (France and the United Kingdom) made credit-tranche drawings, and all drawings had been repaid by the end of 1972. Drawings by developing countries were more numerous but still fairly small, and their use of Fund credit was even more modest; thirty-three developing countries used Fund credit in that five-year period, but when their drawings peaked in 1968, they came to only 23 per cent of the total quotas of developing countries.[6] At the end of 1988, in contrast, the use of Fund credit by developing countries amounted to 73 per cent of their total quotas, and thirty-five developing countries were using amounts larger than their quotas.

The effects of the shift to floating exchange rates—the weakening of obligations to the Fund and reduced reliance on Fund credit by the industrial countries—did not show up immediately. The float was considered temporary, and the balance-of-payments effects of the first oil shock led to large drawings by developed as well as developing countries. Drawings by the U.K. and Italy totaled SDR 7.5 billion, amounting to 39 per cent of total drawings in 1974–77, and the use of Fund credit by developed countries exceeded 32 per cent of their total quotas at the end of 1977.

But the size of the imbalances caused by the first oil shock and differences in national responses to it appeared to rule out an early return to pegged exchange rates, and the Fund's Articles of Agreement were amended in 1978 to make law conform to fact and legitimize floating exchange rates. The Fund was to "exercise firm surveillance over the exchange rate policies of members" and to formulate guidelines for that purpose (Article IV, Section 3), but each government was free to peg or float its own exchange rate. The basic obligation of the Bretton Woods bargain was transformed by the migration of a single word: the commitment to a system of stable exchange rates became instead a commitment to "a stable system of exchange rates" (Article IV, Section 1). Thereafter, none of the G-10 countries used Fund credit.[7] In 1979, moreover, when the European Community (EC) countries established the European Monetary System (EMS), they set up their own credit facilities, allowing them to stabilize the exchange rates among their currencies without drawing on the Fund; the credit lines are open-ended in the short run and backed by the longer-term credit facilities of the European Monetary Cooperation Fund (EMCF).[8]

The Fund as a Financial Intermediary

The large drawings that took place after the first oil shock represented a turning point in the Fund's own history. At that point the Fund began to function as a financial intermediary, rather than a credit union, by using money borrowed from some members to make loans to others.

The Fund had borrowed before. In 1962, the Group of Ten (G-10) countries entered into a standing agreement with the Fund, the General Arrangements to Borrow (GAB), promising to lend their currencies to the Fund "when supplementary resources are needed to forestall or cope with an impairment of the international monetary system," but only when one of the participating countries was about to make a drawing. In effect, the G-10 countries took on obligations to each other by undertaking to assure that the Fund would have the particular currencies needed to facilitate their own drawings.[9]

In the 1970s, however, the Fund began borrowing to supplement ordinary drawings rather than to facilitate an ordinary drawing by relieving an impending shortage of a particular currency. In 1974 and 1975, it borrowed SDR 6.9 billion from sixteen industrial and oil-producing countries to set up two oil facilities.[10] In 1977, the Interim Committee found "grounds for believing that the Fund's role as a *financial intermediary* could contribute significantly to promotion of international adjustment" and endorsed the creation of supplementary arrangements for members that "will face payments imbalances that are large in relation to their economies."[11] Accordingly, the Fund established the Supplementary Financing Facility (SFF) in 1979, under which it would borrow an additional SDR 7.8 billion from fourteen countries.

The SFF was supposed to be temporary and was due to expire in 1982, but its resources were fully committed in 1981, and the need for large drawings was expected to continue. Therefore, the Fund embarked on a third exercise in intermediation to finance what it called the policy of Enlarged Access to Resources (EAR). The policy and borrowings associated with it were meant to bridge the gap between the expiration of the SFF and an increase in Fund quotas (which was not due to take place until 1984, but was completed in 1983 because of the outbreak of the debt crisis). The EAR remains in place, however, although it is a ghost of its former self, and total lending under the EAR amounted to SDR 13.1 billion by the end of 1988 (of which SDR 8.6 billion was still outstanding). Saudi Arabia was the largest lender of resources for the EAR (and the Fund owes it about SDR 6 billion for its contributions to the SFF and the EAR). The Fund's position as financial intermediary is summarized in Table 1.

Table 1. Scheduled Repayments of Borrowings from and by the Fund (millions SDRs, fiscal years ending April 30)

Payable by End of Fiscal Year	Owed to the Fund	Owed by the Fund
1989	3,741	3,690
1990	2,849	2,907
1991	2,176	1,159
1992	1,396	590
1993	902	350
1994	607	300
1995	319	75
Total	11,990	9,070

Source: International Monetary Fund, *Annual Report 1988,* pp. 180–81. (Detail may not add up to total because of rounding.)

At the start of the 1970s, the rules governing access to Fund credit were quite simple. Drawings on the first credit tranche were not subject to formal conditionality; a member merely had to demonstrate that it was making reasonable efforts to deal with its problems. Drawings on the higher credit tranches were reviewed more rigorously and usually conditioned on performance criteria. Drawings on the Compensatory Financing Facility (CFF), established in 1963, were meant to offset fluctuations in a member's exports arising from causes beyond its control. Therefore their size depended on the size of the export shortfall. But cumulative drawings on the CFF could not exceed a member's quota, and when they reached 50 per cent of quota, the Fund had to be satisfied that the member was cooperating with the Fund "to find, where required, appropriate solutions for its balance of payments difficulties."[12] But CFF drawings were not subject to any other form of conditionality at that time, although they were subject to the same fixed-term repayment rule as ordinary credit-tranche drawings.

Access to the Extended Fund Facility (EFF), created in 1974, was governed by somewhat different conditions. The EFF was designed to help countries adopting "comprehensive" adjustment programs, including policies to correct "structural imbalances in production, trade, and prices," as well as macroeconomic policies. As structural adjustments take time to implement and even longer to affect economic behavior, EFF drawings may take three years, amount to 140 per cent of quota, and be amortized over a six-year period starting four years after each year's drawing. By its very nature, however, the EFF is highly conditional; compliance is monitored by performance criteria, and programs are reviewed annually, before the next year's drawings can be made.

Access to the two oil facilities was subject to certain limitations relating to the increase in the member's oil-import bill, quota, and reserves, but not to the usual forms of conditionality. Drawings on the SFF, however, were tied mechanically to credit-tranche drawings, and similar rules were used for the EAR. Under both arrangements, the size of each drawing was decided first, in light of the member's needs, but its character was governed by so-called mixing rules. A member drawing on the first credit tranche would draw an additional 12.5 per cent of quota from the Fund's borrowed resources; and when it went on to the higher credit tranches, it would draw an additional 30 per cent with each tranche. In consequence, a member's drawing could be as large as 202.5 per cent of quota, with 100 per cent coming from the credit tranches and 102.5 per cent coming from the Fund's borrowed resources. Under the EAR, moreover, a member might be authorized to draw more than this amount, within certain annual and cumulative limits, and would thus use more borrowed money. In brief, the SFF and EAR made much more credit available, just when it was needed, but on stricter terms than those that governed access to the oil facilities. Amounts of Fund credit outstanding from these and other facilities are shown in Table 2.

Soon after putting these facilities in place, however, the Fund began to tighten access to them and to other forms of Fund credit. The tightening started in 1983, when the Fund reduced the ceiling on cumulative use of the CFF from 100 per cent to 83 per cent of quota, preventing the automatic increase in access that would have been produced by the general quota increase of that year, and it made the terms of access to the upper 33 per cent virtually the same as those that apply to the higher credit tranches. And similar rules were adopted in 1988, when the CFF was replaced by the Compensatory and Contingency Financing Facility (CCFF). The CCFF is more liberal than the CFF because it covers additional contingencies, such as an increase in debt service payments resulting from higher world interest rates. But this additional insurance is available only to those members that have other

Table 2. Fund Credit Outstanding from Principal Facilities (billions of SDRs, January 31, 1989)

Facility	Amount
Ordinary Resources:	
Credit-tranche drawings	5,810
Compensatory Financing Facility (CFF)	3,833
Extended Fund Facility (EFF)	5,208
Borrowed and Other Resources:	
Supplementary Financing Facility (SFF)	1,334
Enlarged Access to Resources (EAR)	8,363
Structural Adjustment Facilities (SAF and ESAF)	1,005
Total	25,552

Source: International Monetary Fund, *International Financial Statistics*, March 1989. (Detail may not add up to total because of rounding).

highly conditional credit arrangements with the Fund.[13] During and after 1984, moreover, the Fund cut the annual and cumulative limits on drawings under the EAR. The annual use of Fund credit cannot exceed 110 per cent of quota, and cumulative use cannot exceed 440 per cent. These ceilings cover all credit-tranche and EFF drawings, as well as drawings on borrowed resources.

The Fund continues to create new facilities, however, as it seeks to deal with new problems. The Structural Adjustment Facility (SAF) was established in 1986 to provide long-term concessional credit to low-income countries; it was part of the Fund's response to the 1985 Baker Initiative, which sought to combine adjustment with growth in heavily indebted countries. The Enhanced Structural Adjustment Facility (ESAF) was established in 1988 and dedicated formally to the same objective, but it had a more immediate purpose: to refinance low-income countries' obligations to the Fund.

Thus the Fund acted speedily and flexibly to meet new problems in the 1970s and 1980s, but its own flexibility and credibility were damaged in the process—especially by the Fund's involvement in the debt crisis. To contribute effectively to the solution of that problem and to play a central role in the further evolution of the international monetary system, the Fund must modify some of its policies and consolidate its own financial operations.

The Fund and the Debt Crisis

The shift from low to high conditionality that occurred when the SFF replaced the oil facilities was followed by a tightening of conditionality itself. Some trace this policy change to the advent of the Reagan administration; others trace it to the judgment made earlier by many governments that there had been too much financing and too little adjustment after the first oil shock, and that a tougher stance was needed to deal with the second shock.[14] Nevertheless, there was little difference between the amounts of Fund credit used by developing countries following those shocks. Net drawings totaled SDR 6.6 billion in 1979–81, compared with SDR 5.8 billion in 1974–76. And the stock of Fund credit rose hugely with the start of the debt crisis, as a large number of countries resorted heavily to Fund credit (see Table 3).[15]

Table 3. Numbers of Countries Using Fund Credit in Amounts Larger than their Quotas, 1982–88

Level of Use	1982	1985	1988
From 100 to 200 per cent of quota	14	20	22
From 200 to 300 per cent of quota	14	22	11
Larger than 300 per cent of quota	10	7	2
Total	38	49	35

Source: International Monetary Fund, *International Financial Statistics*, February 1989; data for end of each calendar year.

The Fund's involvement in the debt crisis is discussed extensively elsewhere in this book and need not be examined comprehensively here. Three comments will suffice:

1. Although the terms of access to Fund credit had hardened before the crisis and conditionality was being tightened, the Fund should not be blamed for the painful measures that debtor countries had to take. They had to reduce their current account deficits when bank lending ceased, and expenditure-reducing measures were the fastest way to do so.

2. The Fund *can* be faulted for putting its seal of approval on unrealistic policy packages. But ultimate responsibility for this error resides with the governments of the creditor countries. They wanted the Fund to deliver those packages quickly, so that commercial banks could be persuaded to provide new money and reschedule the debtors' obligations.[16]

3. The Fund was chronically optimistic about the prospects for growth and inflation in the debtor countries, and the evolution of debt burdens, which is perhaps to say that it put too much trust in the technical and political feasibility of the policy packages it endorsed.[17]

The Changing Debt Strategy

At the start of the debt crisis, debtor and creditor governments were virtually unanimous in adopting the "liquidity" view of the problem and in their concern to prevent a crisis of confidence in the banking system—a concern quite different from solicitude for the banks themselves.[18] The debtors were deemed to face a short-term problem reflecting the unusual combination of worldwide recession and high interest rates brought on by the shift in the policy stance of the major industrial countries. On this view, it was eminently sensible for the debtors to take on more debt temporarily to service their existing debts and preserve their creditworthiness.

When the problem proved to be more obdurate, the case for short-term borrowing weakened, and there was less justification for using Fund credit. The Baker Initiative of 1985 recognized this tacitly when stressing the need for long-term, growth-oriented lending by the multi-lateral development banks rather than balance-of-payments lending by the Fund. By 1988, moreover, it was becoming clear that the most heavily indebted countries could not be expected to grow out of their debt problems, even with the help of long-term lending, and the official community began considering ways to reduce the stock of debt.

At the Toronto summit, the major industrial countries agreed to grant debt relief to the low-income debtors, but pointedly excluded the middle-income debtors. At the 1988 IMF-World Bank Annual Meeting in Berlin, however, the Interim Committee went further, agreeing that the "menu" of methods for dealing with debt problems should be broadened to include "voluntary market-based techniques which increase financial flows and which reduce the stock of debt without transferring risk from private lenders to official creditors."[19] In March 1989, moreover, U.S. Secretary of the Treasury Nicholas Brady called for a three-year waiver of the clauses in existing loan agreements that stand in the way of debt reduction "to accelerate sharply the pace of debt reduction and pass the benefits directly to the debtor nations" and suggested that the Fund and World Bank could contribute to the process.

> A portion of their policy based loans could be used to finance specific debt reduction plans. These funds could support collateralized debt for bond exchanges involving a significant discount on out-

standing debt. They could also be used to replenish reserves following a cash buyback. Moreover, both institutions could offer new, additional financial support to collateralize a portion of interest payments for debt or debt service reduction transactions.[20]

The Executive Board of the Fund responded in May 1989 by adopting guidelines for the Fund's support of debt and debt service reductions. Such support, it said, will be linked to medium-term adjustment programs and to programs involving appropriate flows of new money, and it will be governed by these rules:

(1) In appropriate cases, part of a member's access under an extended or a stand-by arrangement could be set aside to support operations involving principal reduction, such as debt buybacks or exchanges. The exact size of the set aside would be determined on a case-by-case basis, but would involve a figure of about 25 per cent of the arrangement, determined on the basis of existing access policy. . . .

(2) In appropriate cases, the Fund would be prepared to approve requests for additional resources of up to 40 per cent of a member's quota, where such support would be decisive in facilitating further cost-effective operations. . . . The additional resources from the Fund are to be used for interest support in connection with debt reduction or debt-service reduction operations. . . .

(3) Recognizing the need for cautious adaptation of its policy . . ., the Fund may, on a case-by-case basis, approve an arrangement outright before the conclusion of an appropriate package is agreed between the member and commercial bank creditors. . . .[21]

The Board went on to warn that an accumulation of arrears to banks may sometimes be tolerated, but repeated its refusal to tolerate arrears to official creditors. Immediately after adopting these guidelines, the Fund approved drawings by Costa Rica, the Philippines, and Mexico, each involving a set-aside for debt reduction.

There is an impeccable case for debt reduction. In certain special circumstances, partial debt forgiveness can benefit a debtor and its creditors by raising the debtor's ability to service its remaining debt.[22] In a much larger class of cases, reductions in debt or debt service payments can benefit both parties if they are accompanied by measures that raise the quality of the remaining debt. A debt buyback does this by replacing the remaining debt with other assets, but the debtor may not gain if the assets it uses or borrows to buy back debt could be devoted to other productive purposes.[23] Other methods for reducing debt or debt service payments do this by reducing the riskiness of the remaining debt. This can be accomplished by posting other assets as collateral to guarantee the principal or interest payments or by obtaining a third-party guarantee.

Yet there are risks and problems here. The amounts of financing available from the Fund and the World Bank may be too small to support large amounts of debt reduction, and large amounts are needed to generate significant improvements in the debtor countries' policies and prospects. (The figure commonly quoted—a 20-per-cent cut in annual debt service payments resulting from reductions in interest rates or principal—would be far too small even if combined with new lending by the banks, and debtors have asked for much larger cuts.) The opportunity cost of debt reduction may be very high if debtors must borrow what they need to buy back debt or post collateral for interest payments. And the speed with which Fund credit must be repaid, even on EFF or ESAF terms, calls into question the wisdom of using it for debt-reducing purposes. A debtor's cash flow problem may get worse if it must use medium-term credit to buy back or collateralize long-term debt.

The Case for a Quota Increase

The Fund can continue to provide some of the money required for debt reduction, along with the World Bank and other multilateral institutions. But the Fund must not encourage the belief that it can be the principal provider and must not base the case for an increase in its own resources on that unrealistic premise. The amounts of money required for meaningful debt relief are larger than those that the Fund can be expected to supply without concentrating its efforts and resources far too narrowly on the particular countries involved, and the terms on which Fund credit is normally provided are inappropriate for the purpose. If the scale and character of debt reduction come to be conditioned on the quantity of credit available from the Fund and World Bank, there will be too little debt relief and an excessive concentration of the corresponding risks on those two institutions.

It will be hard enough for the Fund to prevent the debtors' cash flow problems from getting worse in the next few years, as its claims on those countries fall due. It must find ways to roll over those claims, and it must liberalize access to the CCFF to help the debtors deal with unforeseen contingencies.[24] To keep its own claims from contracting, however, the Fund must confront the consequences of having relied on borrowed money to finance the SFF and EAR, and it may have to modify the conduct of conditionality.

A small but growing number of countries, including Peru and Sudan, have failed to repay their obligations to the Fund, and it has declared formally that they are ineligible for more Fund credit. But this stance is symbolic, and the Fund is rightly reluctant to take the next step: expelling a member completely. Indeed, it has engaged whenever possible in its own oblique form of debt rescheduling: A member that cannot repay its old drawings submits a new letter of intent, containing a fresh set of performance criteria, draws once again on the Fund, and uses the proceeds, in whole or in part, to meet its old obligations. In consequence, some twenty countries have been continuous users of Fund credit for more than a dozen years. This sort of refinancing has not been available to Peru and the other countries that have fallen far behind in their payments to the Fund; they have been unwilling or unable to produce acceptable letters of intent. In other cases, however, the Fund has accepted letters of intent that it might have rejected in ordinary circumstances. In effect, it has been forced to choose between two unpalatable practices: declaring that some of its members cannot continue to draw on the Fund or papering over the problem by accepting letters of intent that are not very credible and thus tarnishing the Fund's own seal of approval.[25]

The nature of the problem facing the Fund and its link with the Fund's own borrowing are illustrated by the position of Mexico, the largest user of Fund credit (and the second largest user relative to quota). Its obligations to the Fund are shown in Table 4.[26] The credit-tranche drawings are recent and not yet due to be repaid; the EFF drawings were made some time ago, and Mexico is starting to repay them. But that distinction is less important than another. Much of Mexico's debt to the Fund is matched by the Fund's own debt to Saudi Arabia, the Fund's main creditor. The Fund cannot roll over its claims on Mexico unless it can roll over its own debts or use its own resources to pay them off.

It would not be impossible for the Fund to refinance its debt. Saudi Arabia may not want to renew its lending, given its own situation, but Japan and other surplus countries might be willing to replace it. (The Fund already has a medium-term credit arrangement with Japan.) Over the long run, however, the Fund should rely less heavily on borrowing, apart from temporary borrowing under the GAB to meet a shortfall of liquidity or the need for particular currencies. Borrowing made sense when OPEC surpluses were very large, and the world might be better off today if the Fund had played a larger role in recycling them. Borrowing makes less sense, however, when current account surpluses are less sharply concentrated or when, as now, surplus countries pile up private sector claims rather than reserves at the disposal of their governments. Finally, reliance on borrowing may gradually reduce the Fund's ability to mobilize support for increases in quotas, and that in turn would increase its reliance on borrowing, as well as its vulnerability to the views and circumstances of the surplus countries. The influence of individual governments on the Fund's decisions was meant to depend on vot-

Table 4. Fund Credit Outstanding to Mexico, December 1988

Type	Millions of SDRs	Percentage of quota
Ordinary Resources:		
Credit-tranche drawings	674	57.8
Extended facility	998	85.6
Borrowed Resources (EAR):		
Credit-tranche drawings	1,017	87.2
Extended facility	881	75.5
Total	3,570	306.1

Source: International Monetary Fund, *International Financial Statistics*, February 1989.

ing power, which depends on quotas, and the distribution of quotas is renegotiated periodically. The distribution of influence over the Fund's decisions should not change haphazardly because of a change in the distribution of surpluses and deficits or the state of the Fund's own liquidity.

It is therefore more sensible for the Fund to pay off its debts with some of its own assets. It has, in fact, been doing this (which is why Table 1 shows that the Fund is owed more than it owes), and it can go on doing so. The Fund's total debts amounted to about SDR 9 billion at the end of the most recent fiscal year. Its holdings of usable currencies amounted to about SDR 41 billion.[27] The Fund must be ready to meet its members' needs, but it has additional sources of liquidity: Its drawing rights under the GAB amount to SDR 18.5 billion, and it holds 103 million ounces of gold, worth more than SDR 3.6 billion at the Fund's accounting price but close to SDR 31 billion at the current market price. (It could not sell that gold in the open market without depressing the market price, but it could borrow against it at market-related prices.)

If the Fund ceased to rely on borrowed resources, however, it would have to recast its policies regarding the use of its own resources. Credit-tranche drawings do not normally exceed 100 per cent of quota, and drawings under the Extended Fund Facility (EFF) do not normally exceed 140 per cent of quota. Yet Mexico's total drawings already are greater than 300 per cent of quota, and those of several other middle-income debtor countries exceed 200 per cent of quota.

The Fund can deal with this difficulty by waiving its own rules on a case-by-case basis or by liberalizing access with an increase in Fund quotas. The second method is far better than the first.

When the Fund set up the EFF and SFF, it agreed in principle to waive the quota-based ceiling on the use of its resources, and it did this again for drawings under the EAR. Hence waivers were granted routinely to individual members that were qualified to use those facilities. For the Fund to do so on an ad hoc basis, however, to refinance its claims on large, chronic users of Fund credit, would come close to violating its Articles of Agreement. The Articles state that the Fund may grant such waivers at its discretion but "on terms which safeguard its interests" and "especially in the case of members with a record of *avoiding* large or continuous use of the Fund's general resources."[28]

It would thus be more prudent to rationalize the situation by raising quotas, which would safeguard the Fund's liquidity as well as its integrity. Three steps might be taken:

(1) A 50-per-cent increase in quotas, partly to provide the Fund with the additional resources it will need eventually, but mainly to raise drawing rights.

(2) An increase in the ceiling for EFF drawings from 140 to, say, 180 per cent of quota.

(3) An increase in the ceiling for all CCFF drawings to 150 per cent of quota, with a cumulative ceiling on the use of Fund credit at, say, 250 per cent of quota.

If these proposals were adopted, Mexico's quota would rise from SDR 1,166 million to SDR 1,749 million, and the upper limit for an EFF drawing would rise to SDR 3,148 million. Mexico could refinance most of its debt to the Fund; it would have to pay back only SDR 400 million (about $520 million) net. And it could still enter into contingency arrangements amounting to 70 per cent of its quota (250 per cent *less* 180 per cent) or SDR 1,224 billion.

The numbers in this example are meant to be illustrative, not definitive. In fact, they would not cover Mexico completely, although they would cover most of the other middle-income debtors.[29] Countries with obligations smaller than 150 per cent of their present quotas would be covered by the credit-tranche ceiling; those with obligations smaller than 270 per cent of quota would be covered by the new EFF ceiling (if they qualify for EFF drawings in all other relevant respects).[30] And all of them would still have room to enter into CCFF arrangements to protect them from unforeseen shocks.

A quota increase of less than 50 per cent on average would make no sense at all. Too much time and trouble would have to be invested. A somewhat bigger increase, averaging 75 per cent, will probably be needed if the Fund is to make a large financial contribution to the debt reduction process—and that is the widespread expectation, even though it is not entirely appropriate.

Making Conditionality Less Intrusive

Some heavily indebted countries pose problems more complicated than those of Mexico. The Fund and Mexico have been able to agree on a new stand-by arrangement and a new policy package to go with it. It would be far harder for the Fund to reach similar agreements with many other debtor countries. Their political situations would prevent them from making the appropriate policy commitments, while their economic prospects could prevent the Fund from endorsing the very best sets of policies that their political situations would permit them to produce. To keep the supply of Fund credit from shrinking, conditionality must be made more palatable without damaging the Fund's own credibility.

The Fund is frequently described as the scapegoat for decisions that governments must take but do not have enough political support to take by themselves. Furthermore, governments are not monolithic, and officials concerned with balance-of-payments and debt problems do not always win their bureaucratic battles because they do not have powerful political constituencies. The Fund can strengthen their bargaining positions. These arguments make sense when the Fund can provide financing for a country that confronts a short-term problem and can protect its creditworthiness by dealing boldly with it. They make less sense under present circumstances because they are myopic. A government that hides behind the Fund will be accused of failing to defend its independence from foreign interference and will find it increasingly hard to return to the Fund to refinance its obligations. It would be helpful, however, for the Fund to devise less intrusive forms of conditionality—to make "going to the Fund" less traumatic and "staying with the Fund" less embarrassing.

The Fund must continue to ask for policy commitments, including, where appropriate, commitments aimed at long-term structural adjustment as well as those concerning monetary and fiscal policies. Whenever possible, moreover, governments should be encouraged to change their policies *before* they apply for Fund credit. They should be seen as seeking the Fund's endorsement, not its tutelage.[31] The Fund should offer its advice during the annual consultation that it holds with each member, not in the negotiations that precede a drawing.

The Fund must continue to monitor implementation, but it should not pay so much attention to the short-term evolution of financial or fiscal variables such as the growth rate of domestic credit or the level of public sector borrowing. It should focus instead on the evolution of the external situation by monitoring trade flows, reserves, and the path of the real exchange rate. If these are behaving badly compared to projections made in the member's letter of intent, the Fund should ask for an explanation. In some cases, external circumstances will be to blame, and the member may need help from the CCFF. In other cases, domestic policies will be to blame, and the member should be asked to intensify its efforts by adhering more faithfully to its policy commitments or revising them. Under multiyear EFF programs, of course, a member's situation and policies should be reviewed at the end of each year, and it should be asked to modify commitments made for the coming year if it has not made satisfactory progress.

The Fund has begun to move in this direction. The transformation of the CFF into the CCFF will force the Fund to make balance-of-payments projections and monitor subsequent developments closely, because it may have to decide whether a member has been adversely affected by external circumstances. Furthermore, the Fund appears to be putting less emphasis on short-term movements in domestic indicators. But it should go further. Domestic trends are very important for the sustainability of a country's external position. An increase in the budget deficit is likely to worsen the current account balance, and inflation is bound to affect competitiveness. A country with a high inflation rate, however, should be expected to adjust its nominal exchange rate frequently, not necessarily to reduce its inflation rate quickly.

In brief, the Fund should administer conditionality in keeping with its own obligations and purposes. It should try not to complicate the problems of the heavily indebted countries while striving to make sure that those countries' problems do not complicate its own, and it should not allow creditor governments and commercial banks to use the institution for their own purposes.

The Fund and the Developed Countries

Industrial countries have not used the Fund's resources for many years, but they may need them in the future. Exchange rate arrangements are changing, and reserve arrangements will have to change with them.

At the start of the 1980s, the governments of the major industrial countries were mildly schizophrenic about the exchange rate regime. On the one hand, they appeared to believe that it was desirable and possible to peg exchange rates within Europe and to defend them by official intervention. On the other hand, they favored freely floating rates for the key currencies and doubted the wisdom or feasibility of large-scale intervention.[32]

A few years later, however, they were trying to manage exchange rates intensively. In the Plaza Communiqué of September 1985, governments chided foreign exchange markets for failing to take account of changes in national policies and other "fundamentals" affecting exchange rates. They called on markets to bring down the dollar and warned that they would intervene when and if that would be helpful. In the Louvre Accord of February 1987, they went much further. In 1985, they had agreed on the "wrongness" of current exchange rates, which was not very difficult in light of the large U.S. trade deficit and the protectionist pressures it was producing. In 1987, they agreed on the "rightness" of current rates—that the dollar had fallen far enough—and intervened heavily to stabilize them. In fact, foreign official purchases of dollars financed most of the U.S. current account deficit in 1987. In early 1988, moreover, skillfully executed intervention helped to halt the depreciation of the dollar triggered three months earlier by the stock market crash.

The Louvre Accord marked a major change in the international monetary system, and it has been widely criticized. Some critics say that it is wrong in principle and bound to fail in practice—that governments should not try to second-guess markets and will not be willing to coordinate their policies, most notably their monetary policies, closely enough to stabilize exchange rates effectively.[33] Other critics believe that present arrangements are not tight or transparent enough. They want governments to commit themselves explicitly to exchange rate targets, although they disagree about the most appropriate methods of choosing and defending them. Some of them favor wide, soft bands, which would be defended by coordinating interest rate policies; others favor narrower and harder bands, which would have to be defended by intervention as well as by interest rate coordination.[34]

This is not the appropriate place to argue the case for exchange rate management. It is fitting, however, to ask what role the Fund should play in a highly managed system, and the answer has two parts. The first relates to its role in policy coordination, which is necessary for successful exchange rate management; this issue was examined by Jacques J. Polak in Chapter 1. The second relates to the financing of official intervention, which is the issue addressed in the balance of this chapter.

Economists continue to debate the role of official intervention in exchange rate management.[35] But one lesson taught by recent experience has importance for the future of the Fund. Intervention is most effective when conducted jointly:

> When governments give the appearance of being united and of holding their views firmly, while market participants are divided and uncertain, official pronouncements about exchange rates can have large effects, especially when backed by intervention or the threat of intervention, and intervention can be effective even when markets are skeptical about the governments' pronouncements.[36]

But the ability of the United States to intervene jointly with other countries is rather limited, because it does not have large foreign currency reserves. It has ample access to short-term reserve credit but not to longer-term financing. There are many ways to rectify this situation, and some of them involve the Fund.

The Fund might be asked to manage a substitution account that would make the monetary system more symmetrical by raising the readily usable reserves of the United States and reducing the exchange rate risks borne by other governments.Under arrangements proposed in 1979, when the subject was last discussed in the Fund, governments and central banks holding dollar balances would have deposited some of them with the Fund in exchange for SDR-denominated claims. They could not have used those claims for intervention, because foreign exchange markets do not deal in SDRs, but they could have sold them to other governments in exchange for those governments' currencies. It was agreed in principle that the costs and benefits of the arrangement would be shared by the United States and the depositors, and Washington interpreted this understanding to mean that the depositors would bear some of any losses.[37] But other countries did not buy this interpretation, and discussions of the subject ended in 1980, when the United States shifted its own position, proposing that all losses be borne by the Fund, which would set aside some of its gold for the purpose. In fact, the whole proposal became less attractive when the dollar began to appreciate.

The 1979 proposal would have reduced the exchange rate risks borne by the holders of dollar reserves but would not have raised U.S. reserves. A variant of the proposal would do both, however, and would reduce the risk of loss. The United States would deposit gold. Other governments would deposit dollars. Both would obtain an SDR-denominated claim to be used as a reserve asset.[38]

The creation of a substitution account would serve an additional purpose: making the SDR a more important reserve asset. A change in the functioning of the Fund itself would serve that same purpose and prepare the Fund for a larger role in a more highly managed monetary system. Under present arrangements, governments hold two reserve assets with the Fund, their reserve positions in the General Department and their SDR balances in the SDR Department, and they obtain Fund credit from the General Department. To complicate matters, allocations of SDRs are made on the recommendation of the Managing Director, using explicit criteria set out in the Fund's Articles of Agreement (Article XVIII, Section 1), while reserve positions are reviewed automatically whenever Fund quotas are reviewed, but without reference to explicit criteria (Article III, Section 2).

These arrangements are cumbersome and blur the functional distinction between the two departments of the Fund. One department is involved in providing Fund credit, but both departments are involved in creating reserve assets. Furthermore, these arrangements blur the nature of each member's rights and obligations: Its rights are defined with respect to its SDR holdings, reserve position, and access to Fund credit. Its obligations are defined with respect to the acceptance of SDRs and by the size of its quota (currency subscription). Finally, basic decisions about the creation of Fund-related reserve assets are not adequately integrated. Governments are not required to look at the size of the Fund as a whole in relation to global reserve needs and supplies from other sources.

The Fund's structure should be altered eventually to consolidate its reserve-creating activities and simplify its members' obligations to provide financing through the Fund.[39] Decisions affecting the size of the Fund should be taken on the basis of consistent criteria relating to the need for balance-of-payments financing, global supplies of reserves and reserve credit, and the appropriate division of Fund-related financing between reserve creation and extensions of Fund credit. These aims can be advanced by shifting the boundary between the two departments of the Fund. These basic organizational issues should be addressed in conjunction with the Tenth General Review of Quotas, due to take place in the mid-1990s.

Conclusion

In the late 1970s, some observers wondered whether the Fund had a future. Its members' obligations had been weakened by the shift to floating exchange rates, and the rapid growth of international bank lending was seen as likely to reduce the importance of the Fund as a source of reserve credit. The debt crisis gave the Fund new responsibilities, and it has a role to play in solving the problem. Nevertheless, the international community must rely less heavily on the use of Fund resources to deal with debt and on the use of the Fund as tutor to the debtor countries. At the same time, the industrial countries must come to rely more heavily on the Fund's resources and advice as they move toward a more managed monetary system.

Notes

[1] On the Fund as a credit union, see Peter B. Kenen, *Financing, Adjustment, and the International Monetary Fund,* Studies in International Economics (Washington, D.C.: The Brookings Institution, 1986), pp. 2–6.

[2] For contrasting views on the origins and purposes of conditionality, see Sidney Dell, *On Being Grandmotherly: The Evolution of IMF Conditionality,* Essays in International Finance, 144 (Princeton, N.J.: International Finance Section, Princeton University, 1981), and C. David Finch, *The International Monetary Fund: The Record and the Prospect,* Essays in International Finance, 175 (Princeton, N.J.: International Finance Section, Princeton University, 1989); see also John Williamson, ed., *IMF Conditionality* (Washington, D.C.: Institute for International Economics, 1983), Chapters 1–3, 7.

[3] Most readers will be familiar with Fund terminology, but repetition may be helpful. Every member's quota serves four purposes: (1) It determines the member's voting power; (2) It determines the member's contribution to the Fund. One quarter of each member's quota was payable in gold under the original Articles of Agreement and is currently payable in Special Drawing Rights (SDRs); the rest is payable in the member's own currency; (3) It determines the member's share in any allocation of new SDRs; (4) It determines the member's access to Fund credit. Access is defined by five tranches—each equal to one quarter of the member's quota. One is the reserve tranche, which the member is entitled to treat as an ordinary reserve asset; it can be drawn down and reconstituted at the member's discretion. The other four are credit tranches, which cannot be used without the Fund's approval. Drawings on the first credit tranche are approved rather routinely; drawings on the higher credit tranches are subject to close scrutiny and, as indicated in the text, various sorts of conditionality. All credit-tranche drawings must be repaid in full.

[4] Michael Artis and Sylvia Ostry, *International Economic Policy Coordination,* Chatham House Papers, No. 30 (London: Royal Institute of International Affairs and Routledge & Kegan Paul, 1986), p. 33.

[5] On the engineering of the 1971 crisis and subsequent events, see Robert Solomon, *The International Monetary System, 1945–1981,* expanded edition (New York: Harper and Row, 1982), Chapters xi–xiv.

[6] The credit-tranche drawings listed above include drawings on the Compensatory Financing Facility (CFF) as well as ordinary credit-tranche drawings. There were no other Fund facilities at that time, apart from the small Buffer Stock Facility. (Unless otherwise indicated, all figures in this chapter relating to the Fund come from its *Annual Reports* or from *International Financial Statistics.*)

[7] The United States drew on the Fund in November 1978, when it also borrowed from other G-10 countries to mobilize reserves for halting a depreciation of the dollar. But this was a reserve-tranche drawing that did not involve the use of Fund credit.

[8] For details, see Francesco Giavazzi and Alberto Giovannini, *Limiting Exchange Rate Flexibility: The European Monetary System* (Cambridge, Mass: MIT Press, 1989), Chapter 2. Initially, the EC countries planned to convert the EMCF into a European Monetary Fund, but that has not happened. The existence of these credit facilities does not rule out recourse to the IMF, which could indeed be necessary if the EMS countries wanted to combat a depreciation of their currencies against outside currencies such as the dollar and yen, but the size of their reserves makes this unlikely. The United States is more likely to need Fund credit, because its foreign currency reserves are small.

[9] The GAB was put in place to furnish the currencies the Fund would need to finance a drawing by the United States, because U.S. drawing rights were very large compared to the Fund's holdings of the other countries' currencies. The GAB was revised in 1983 to allow the Fund to use it when the participants' currencies are needed for drawings by nonparticipants. This change, however, came much later in the process by which the Fund became a financial intermediary.

[10] A total of fifty-five countries borrowed from the oil facilities, including the two largest users of Fund credit, the U.K. and Italy; these borrowings were repaid in full by 1983 (so references to problems arising from the use of borrowed resources relate entirely to subsequent borrowings).

[11] Press Communiqué, April 29, 1977, in International Monetary Fund, *Annual Report 1977,* p. 115. Emphasis added.

[12] International Monetary Fund, *Annual Report 1980,* p. 137.

[13] Complicated ceilings and sub-ceilings apply to the various forms of contingency financing; some are tied to the member's quota and some to the size of the other credit arrangement.

[14] For the first interpretation, see John Williamson, "The Lending Policies of the International Monetary Fund," in Williamson, ed., op. cit., pp. 640–48; for the second, see Jacques J. Polak, "The Role of the Fund," in *The International Monetary System: Forty Years After Bretton Woods* (Boston: Federal Reserve Bank of Boston, 1984), p. 251.

[15] As Fund quotas rose by an average of 50 per cent during this period, the figures in Table 3 understate the increase in reliance on the Fund.

[16] See Joseph Kraft, *The Mexican Rescue* (New York: Group of Thirty, 1984).

[17] On the bias in the Fund's forecasts for growth and inflation, see Peter B. Kenen and Stephen B. Schwartz, "An Assessment of Macroeconomic Forecasts in the International Monetary Fund's World Economic Outlook," *Working Paper G–86–04* (Princeton, N.J.: International Finance Section, Princeton University, 1986), pp. 30–33. When forecasting the overall debt service ratio for all non-oil developing countries, the Fund was low for four years running (1983–1986) and high in 1987 (when Brazil's moratorium on debt service payments reduced the actual ratio).

[18] See Kraft, op. cit., who suggests that Mexican officials were even more worried about this aspect of the problem than some of their U.S. counterparts. (Otherwise, they might have taken a tougher stance in their early dealings with banks and creditor governments.)

[19] Press Communiqué, September 26, 1988, in *IMF Survey,* October 17, 1988, p. 325.

[20] U.S. Treasury Press Release, March 10, 1989.

[21] IMF Press Release 89/17, in *IMF Survey,* May 29, 1989, pp. 172–73.

[22] See, for example, Paul R. Krugman, "Market-Based Debt-Reduction Schemes," *Working Paper 2587* (Cambridge, Mass.: National Bureau of Economic Research, 1988).

[23] Jeremy Bulow and Kenneth Rogoff, "The Buyback Boondoggle," *Brookings Papers on Economic Activity,* 1988:2 (Washington, D.C.: The Brookings Institution).

[24] The low-income debtors present special problems, discussed in Louis Goreux's chapter in this volume, and the solution proposed below will not work for them. The Fund's claims on those countries must be replaced by concessional (ESAF) credits. But the problem facing the Fund in respect of the middle-income countries will arise eventually in respect of the low-income countries. They can use ESAF credits to repay their ordinary drawings on the Fund, in fact if not in form, but ESAF credits have to be repaid by 2002 (ten years after the final deadline for disbursement), and Goreux rightly asks what will happen then. Will ESAF be replenished by new loans (or the conversion of old loans into grants), allowing it to refinance its clients' debts, or will those countries have to draw on other Fund facilities to repay debts to ESAF?

[25] David Finch proposes one way out of this dilemma. Heavily indebted countries that are able to give "credible assurances that future debt servicing would be paid in full" should negotiate reductions in their debts to commercial banks and have access to a new, highly conditional Fund facility structured to provide them with additional credit. Countries that cannot offer such assurances should have access to another new facility with low conditionality, in order to refinance some of their obligations to the Fund, but they should repay the rest gradually. (C. David Finch, "An IMF Debt Plan," *The International Economy,* March/April 1989.) I have two difficulties with this approach. (1) Access to new Fund credit should not be made to depend on a country's ability to reach agreement with its commercial bank creditors. The ultimate success of a debt-reducing agreement may indeed depend on *prior* assurance that the debtor will have access to additional Fund credit. The Fund cannot be the main provider of the cash required to implement a debt reduction plan, but unused access to Fund credit may be an important assurance that the country will be able to meet its obligations to the banks. (2) There is something odd about an arrangement that imposes high conditionality on countries that are able to manage their affairs competently but low conditionality on countries that cannot do so—even though the arrangement offers additional Fund credit to the former and takes away some of it from the latter.

[26] These figures pertain to the situation before the 1989 agreement. Drawings under that agreement would add to Mexico's obligations, but repayments of old drawings would offset them partially. Use of the figures for Mexico should not be taken to imply that Mexico has failed to fulfill its obligations to the Fund. On the contrary, it has met its financial obligations fully and tried hard to carry out its policy commitments.

[27] International Monetary Fund, *Annual Report 1988,* p. 74.

[28] IMF Articles of Agreement Article V, Section 4.

[29] They might even be made to cover Mexico. Under present rules, a member may make an EFF drawing on top of an ordinary credit-tranche drawing if the two together do not exceed 165 per cent of quota. Mexico would be covered completely if this limit were raised to 200 per cent when the EFF limit was raised to 180 per cent. It should perhaps be emphasized that these revisions are meant mainly to facilitate the refinancing of mem-

bers' obligations, not to encourage larger drawings; in language used frequently in Fund decisions, the numbers are ceilings, not targets.

[30] This group includes Argentina, Brazil, Chile, Morocco, and the Philippines.

[31] The Managing Director of the Fund has stressed this point in recent statements; see, for example, *IMF Survey,* April 3, 1989, p. 99.

[32] It is not impossible to reconcile these two views. It can be argued, for example, that the EC is an "optimum currency area" within which exchange rates should be fixed, and that the whole world is not. Alternatively, it can be argued that the EMS is a Deutschemark zone, with one key currency, in which pegging is sensible and feasible. It can also be argued that capital controls have facilitated exchange rate management within the EMS. These issues are examined in Giavazzi and Giovanni, op. cit., Chapters 4–7, and in Peter B. Kenen, *Managing Exchange Rates* (New York: Council on Foreign Relations Press for the Royal Institute of International Affairs, 1988), Chapter 4.

[33] See, for example, Martin Feldstein, "The Case Against Trying to Stabilize the Dollar," *American Economic Review,* May 1989, pp. 36–40.

[34] For proposals of the first type, see John Williamson and Marcus H. Miller, *Targets and Indicators: A Blueprint for the International Coordination of Economic Policies* (Washington, D.C.: Institute for International Economics, 1987); their advocates appear to believe that foreign exchange markets are fairly well behaved, and that the main task is to influence monetary policies. For proposals of the second type, see Kenen, *Managing Exchange Rates,* op. cit., Chapters 3–4; their advocates tend to be critical of foreign exchange markets and believe that the main task is to influence the markets' expectations. The issues and evidence are reviewed skillfully in Paul R. Krugman, *Exchange-Rate Instability* (Cambridge, Mass.: MIT Press, 1988).

[35] Recent evidence and views are surveyed in Richard Marston, "Exchange Rate Coordination," in Martin Feldstein, ed., *International Economic Cooperation* (Chicago, Ill.: University of Chicago Press, 1988).

[36] Kenen, *Managing Exchange Rates,* op. cit., p. 26.

[37] Losses would occur if the dollar had depreciated in terms of the SDR over the lifetime of the account and the effects of the depreciation had not been offset by the net interest income of the account.

[38] A numerical illustration is given in Kenen, *Managing Exchange Rates,* op. cit., pp. 70–72; Jacques J. Polak's chapter in this volume suggests a different way of dealing with the problem of losses, but it would not increase U.S. reserves.

[39] For one such plan, see Kenen, *Financing, Adjustment, and the IMF,* op. cit., pp. 65–69.

21

Journal of Economic Perspectives — Volume 4, Number 1 — Winter 1990 — Pages 7–18

Organizing Debt Relief:
The Need for a New Institution

Peter B. Kenen

W hen Mexico suspended debt-service payments in August 1982, creditor countries, led by the United States, responded promptly. Animated by concern about confidence in the banking system, not mere solicitude for the banks, they extended large short-term credits to Mexico, then put pressure on the banks to reschedule Mexican debt and lend more to Mexico, once the International Monetary Fund had endorsed the policies that Mexico would follow to deal with its problems. This was the birth of the case-by-case approach to the debt problem. It was predicated implicitly on the belief that debtors faced a short-term problem arising from an unusual combination of worldwide recession and high interest rates brought on by a shift in the policy stance of the major industrial countries. On this view, it was eminently sensible for debtors to take on more debt temporarily in order to pay interest on their existing debts.[1]

The problem was still with us three years later, however, and the case-by-case approach was in trouble. The world economy was growing again and interest rates had fallen, but the debtor's export earnings were not growing, and their governments were increasingly reluctant to deal with the IMF, which was asking for more austerity but providing less Fund credit. The banks were willing to reschedule larger amounts of debt for longer intervals but would put up new money only for the largest debtors.

---

[1] This view is best represented in Cline (1984). The literature on debt is vast and space in this journal is precious, so I do not cite all of the relevant sources. Good bibliographies are found in Cohen (1989) and Dornbusch (1988), which also supplies a compact history of the debt problem; the theoretical literature is surveyed by Eaton, Gersovitz, and Stiglitz (1986).

■ *Peter B. Kenen is Walker Professor of Economics and International Finance and Director of the International Finance Section, Princeton University, Princeton, New Jersey.*

The Baker and Brady Plans

In October 1985, at the annual IMF-World Bank meeting in Seoul, the U.S. Secretary of the Treasury, James Baker, proposed a three-part "program for sustained growth" to deal with the debt problem:

> First and foremost, the adoption by principal debtor countries of comprehensive macroeconomic and structural policies, supported by the international financial institutions, to promote growth and balance of payments adjustment, and to reduce inflation.
>
> Second, a continued central role for the IMF, in conjunction with increased and more effective structural adjustment lending by the multilateral development banks ...
>
> Third, increased lending by the private banks in support of comprehensive economic adjustment programs.

Austerity would fight inflation and produce the trade surpluses needed by the debtors to make their debt-service payments. Structural reforms and new lending would generate the growth needed to reduce the burden of those payments. Secretary Baker went on to ask that the multilateral institutions and commercial banks adopt specific targets for new lending to the 15 highly indebted countries listed in Table 1.

The banks fell far short of those targets, however, and actually reduced their claims on some debtor countries. In mid-1987, moreover, major U.S. banks, led by Citicorp, set aside larger loan-loss reserves against their exposure to the debtor countries.[2] Secretary Baker came back to the banks in 1987, to ask that they develop a "menu" of new instruments and methods to step up their lending. But the whole debt strategy began to change in 1988, even as the banks were adopting the menu approach, most notably in a new agreement with Brazil.[3]

At the economic summit in Toronto, the seven major industrial countries had agreed to grant debt relief to low-income countries, mainly in Africa, but had pointedly excluded middle-income debtors, mainly in Latin America. At the IMF-World Bank meeting in Berlin, however, the IMF Interim Committee proposed that the menu approach be broadened to include "voluntary market-based techniques which ... reduce the stock of debt without transferring risk from private lenders to official creditors." The aim of the menu approach was shifted from raising to reducing debt: a late but fundamental change in the official interpretation of the debt problem.

In March 1989, the new U.S. Secretary of the Treasury, Nicholas Brady, endorsed the change in strategy, calling for a three-year waiver of clauses in existing loan agreements that stand in the way of debt reduction "to accelerate sharply the pace of debt reduction and pass the benefits directly to the debtor nations," and called on the IMF and World Bank to use some of their policy-based lending to aid the debt-reducing process; some of it could be used to collaterize debt-for-bond exchanges at significant discounts and replenish reserves following cash buybacks of debt, and

---

[2] For reasons and possible results, see Guttentag and Herring (1988).
[3] On the early evolution of the menu approach, see World Bank (1988); on the Brazilian agreement, see Lamdany (1988a).

Table 1
Discounts on the debts of fifteen heavily indebted countries

Argentina	$82\frac{1}{2}$	Ecuador	$86\frac{1}{2}$	Peru	97
Bolivia	89	Ivory Coast	94	Philippines	$50\frac{1}{2}$
Brazil	$70\frac{1}{2}$	Mexico	$58\frac{1}{2}$	Uruguay	45
Chile	$35\frac{1}{2}$	Morocco	$56\frac{1}{2}$	Venezuela	$62\frac{1}{4}$
Colombia	43	Nigeria	$76\frac{1}{2}$	Yugoslavia	49

Source: Salomon Brothers, July 1989; discounts are for cash bids.

some could be used to underwrite the interest payments on new or modified debt contracts.

Events moved rapidly thereafter. The IMF and World Bank adopted guidelines to implement the Brady plan, and the IMF extended new credits to Mexico, Costa Rica, and the Philippines in accordance with those guidelines. Japan agreed to provide $4.5 billion in supplementary lending (and has recently raised its pledge to $10 billion). Commercial banks began to negotiate an agreement with Mexico, which would reduce its interest payments to the banks by as much as 35 percent if every bank participated fully.[4]

Is there anything left to argue about? Unhappily, yes. Some economists, such as Bulow and Rogoff (1988, 1989), argue that debtors are wrong to use reserves or borrow to buy back debt, even at large discounts. Advocates of debt relief, such as Sachs (1989a) and myself, maintain that the Brady plan will not go far enough. It relies too heavily on debtors and creditors to strike mutually beneficial bargains; it does not provide enough resources to generate the deep debt reductions that debtors need to solve their problems; and it does not shift risk forthrightly enough from private lenders to official creditors. I would correct the defects of the Brady plan by creating a new international institution to manage and finance the debt-reducing process or assign the task to an existing institution but give it enough resources to get the job done.

[4] Under the agreement announced in July 1989, banks will have three main options: (1) To swap Mexican debt for new long-term bonds at a 35 percent discount; Mexico will buy zero-coupon U.S. Treasury securities to guarantee the principal. (2) To switch from floating-rate debt, paying about 10 percent when the agreement was announced, to new fixed-rate debt paying $6\frac{1}{4}$ percent, without any change in face value; the interest rate will rise after 1996 if higher oil prices raise Mexico's oil revenues in real terms. (3) To retain their present claims but make new loans to Mexico over the next four years by enough to raise those claims by 25 percent; they will thus capitalize some of Mexico's debt-service payments. Interest payments under the first two options will be covered by a rolling 18-month guarantee, backed by Mexican deposits in escrow accounts. The agreement has to be ratified by individual banks, and some time will pass before we know how much of Mexico's debt will be covered by each option. Bankers forecast that those holding about 60 percent of the debt will take the first option, with the rest divided evenly between the other two. In light of experience with earlier debt-for-bond swaps, cited later in this paper, the 60 percent figure seems high. Even if the forecast is accurate, however, the whole package will reduce the face value of the debt by just 16 percent (the 35 percent reduction in face value ×60 percent participation *less* the 25 percent increase in exposure ×20 percent participation), and it will reduce the present value of the debt by only 23 percent (if the interest rate cut on the other 20 percent is treated as being roughly equivalent to a 35 percent reduction in face value).

The Case for Debt Relief

Krugman (1989) argues that debt reduction can raise economic efficiency in a heavily indebted country, and thus raise the debtor's real income, reducing the probability of default. Therefore, a debt buyback can raise the present value of the remaining debt, and can raise it sufficiently to compensate creditors for selling debt on terms that benefit the debtor. Even outright debt forgiveness can benefit both parties.

A large debt overhang reduces economic efficiency in two ways. First, high debt-service payments require high tax rates that discourage capital formation and the repatriation of flight capital; see Krugman (1989) and Sachs (1988, 1989b). Second, the government is the main maker of debt-service payments in most of the heavily indebted countries, and its payments figure in its budget. Hence, they can prevent a devaluation from improving the trade balance, because a devaluation raises the domestic-currency cost of servicing foreign-currency debt, increasing the budget deficit, raising the growth of the money supply, and raising the inflation rate; see, e.g., Dornbusch (1988). Therefore, debtors must use less efficient methods to produce the trade surpluses required to make debt-service payments.

When these and other inefficiencies are powerful, creditors confront what Krugman calls the Debt Relief Laffer Curve—an apt but unfortunate name, because it should be taken more seriously than its namesake. If a debtor's obligations get very large, their expected value begins to fall. The income-depressing effects of the debt make it more likely that the debtor will default when an adverse shock arrives. By reducing that vulnerability, debt relief raises the expected value of the debt. The debtor is better off in "good states" because it keeps the incremental income produced by debt reduction, but creditors are better off in "bad states" because the debtor is more likely to meet its obligations.

Krugman believes that the small debtor countries are on the downward-sloping side of the Debt Relief Laffer Curve. He is less sure about large debtors. But he understates the strength and generality of the case for debt relief, which may apply most aptly to large debtors. Use of the conventional stochastic framework, with good and bad states, makes the shape of the Debt Relief Laffer Curve depend entirely on the strength of the inefficiencies associated with a big debt overhang. Use of a different framework frees it from that limitation.[5]

---

[5]The argument that follows is based on the model in Kenen (1989). A similar argument is made by Corden (1988a). The analysis depends crucially on one assumption. The penalties imposed when a debtor repudiates get weaker if they are delayed. Otherwise, the debtor would repudiate sooner rather than later. The use of the framework developed in the text also helps to answer the objections raised by Bulow and Rogoff (1988, 1989). Their case against debt buybacks is based on two premises: (1) Debtors and creditors hold identical views about the future, so that prices prevailing in the secondary market represent debtors' valuations of their obligations, as well as creditors' valuations of their claims. Under this assumption, a buyback at the market price cannot benefit a debtor unless the debtor can expect to raise its real income by reducing the inefficiencies associated with a large debt overhang. (2) If those inefficiencies reflect unexploited investment opportunities, a debtor would do better to use its scarce resources for capital formation than for debt reduction. In Kenen (1989), however, valuations by debtors and creditors differ, because the costs of repudiation borne by debtors do not directly raise the value of the creditors' claims, and I go on to show that a buyback at the market price can be mutually beneficial even under conditions resembling those embodied in the Bulow-Rogoff model. It can raise the debtor's income even when the opportunity costs of using scarce resources to buy back debt are larger at the margin than the costs of being in debt, including the income-depressing effects of a large debt overhang.

Consider the framework used by Eaton and Gersovitz (1981), where repudiation is voluntary and can benefit the debtor unambiguously. This is the most appropriate framework for analyzing the behavior of a sovereign debtor, which never faces insolvency in a strict balance-sheet sense but must weigh the costs of continuing to service its debt against the costs of repudiation.

When a country can look forward to borrowing and growing, it is apt to reject repudiation. When it cannot expect to borrow more, its decision will depend on the advantages of halting debt-service payments and the strength of the inefficiencies examined earlier, compared to the size of the penalties that creditors and their governments are likely to impose if the debtor repudiates. These may include the seizure of reserves, the penalty stressed in the current literature, but the debtor must also disguise its exports to keep creditors from seizing them and must pay for its imports with cash when trade-credit lines are cut. In effect, it can experience a deterioration in its terms of trade.

Repudiation will be beneficial to the debtor when its debt is large compared to the present value of the penalties. By implication, debt reduction can be mutually beneficial, because it reduces the debtor's obligations but raises the expected value of the creditors' claims by reducing the debtor's incentive to repudiate. The Debt Relief Laffer Curve comes into being, not because of the inefficiencies produced by a debt overhang but because debt reductions can tilt the debtor's cost-benefit calculation against repudiation.

There is no way to know *a priori* whether a particular country is on the downward-sloping side of the curve. That will depend in part on the nature of the penalties that creditors can be expected to impose. But these may not vary across countries in proportion to their debts, which means that large debtors are more likely to be on the downward-sloping side.

Unfortunately, large debtors are least likely to receive outright debt forgiveness. Their creditors are reluctant to accept the large accounting losses involved in reducing substantially the face value of their claims on Mexico, Brazil, and Argentina. And though they would have to reduce them by less than the amount of debt forgiveness, because it would raise the expected value of their remaining claims, it is hard to persuade accountants, regulators, and securities analysts that lower book values can mean larger economic values. When Citicorp and other U.S. banks set aside larger loan-loss reserves, their stock prices rose; investors were ready to reward the banks for being more realistic. But investors who were eager to accept the tax-policy implications of the original Laffer Curve are less eager to accept the more valid implications of the Debt Relief Laffer Curve.

The Mechanics of Debt Relief

There is a secondary market for sovereign debt in which it can be shifted from bank to bank or to other institutions. Most countries' debts sell there at large discounts, reflecting the creditors' belief that debtors will not meet their obligations fully. Representative discounts are shown in Table 1. When the Interim Committee endorsed voluntary, market-based debt reduction, it had in mind transactions based on these discounts.

Such transactions can involve purchases of debt with currently available resources or purchases with future resources made by exchanging new debt for old. The second method is known as defeasance (which sounds pejorative, but isn't). Their benefits and costs depend in part on the values that debtors and creditors attach to the existing debt—which need not coincide precisely with those represented by the discounts quoted in the secondary market.[6]

Purchases with currently available resources have taken two forms: buybacks with cash and debt-equity swaps, which may be deemed to represent an exchange of debt for an entrepreneurial opportunity. Buybacks with cash have been debated extensively, and I have already reviewed the main issues, but these transactions have been rare. Debtor countries do not have the cash needed to buy back their debts, even at deep discounts. The Bolivian example is cited frequently but was very special; the money was provided by official donors expressly for the purpose of debt reduction.[7]

Several debtor countries have experimented with debt-equity swaps, but Chile is the only one that encouraged them enthusiastically. Difficulties arise on three fronts. First, many debtor countries are ambivalent about foreign direct investment of any sort. Second, they wonder whether they are attracting additional investments or merely subsidizing what would take place anyway on normal commercial terms. Third, they worry about inflationary side effects, because external debt must be exchanged for domestic currency before it can be used for equity investment, and the domestic currency is usually supplied by the central bank, expanding the money supply, as the government is usually running a budget deficit and cannot put up the money.

This brings us to the use of future resources to buy back debt. What can be done by defeasance? A small number of governments have offered "exit bonds" to small

[6]There are at least two reasons for differences between the market's valuations and those at which debtors and creditors will do business with each other. (1) If creditors believe that they can seize the debtor's assets in the event of default or repudiation, the market price will reflect the present value of the gross debt *plus* the value of the assets that creditors can seize in the event of repudiation—and the debtor's assets do not change when creditors swap debt in the secondary market. But the debtor's assets fall when it uses some of its assets to buy back debt, and creditors will want to be compensated for the fall in the stock of assets that they can expect to seize if the debtor repudiates the rest of its debt; Froot (1989) and Kenen (1989). (2) The price at which the debtor can buy back debt for cash or trade it for new debt depends on both parties' expectations, whereas the market price depends on the creditors' expectations. All creditors do not have the same expectations, which is indeed one reason for the existence of a secondary market. Corden (1988b) studies the implications of differences between debtors' and creditors' expectations; Williamson (1989) examines the implications of heterogeneity in the creditors' expectations.

[7]Lamdany (1988b) points out, however, that some of the money was official aid earmarked for Bolivia, so the Bolivians had to act as though they were using their own resources. Sachs (1988) reports that banks agreed to a very large discount in the Bolivian case only under pressure from U.S. regulators. (It should perhaps be noted that Mexico may have to lay out some $7 billion to implement its new agreement with the banks—$3 billion for zero-coupon bonds to guarantee principal and $4 billion more to fund the escrow accounts that back up the rolling interest-payment guarantee. These figures reflect the assumption in Note 4 that banks holding 80 percent of Mexico's debt will take the debt-reducing options and thus cut the present value of their claims on Mexico by 35 percent. To buy back 80 percent of the debt at a 35 percent discount, Mexico would have to lay out some $28 billion. Buybacks are expensive.)

and medium-sized banks interested in opting out of debt reschedulings and concerted lending. The problem of subordination, discussed below, does not arise in connection with these issues; the bonds do not take precedence over other obligations but were thought to be potentially attractive because buyers would not have to increase their exposure. Hence, the holders of old debt would not be adversely affected financially, and were expected to benefit indirectly, because the creditors' coalition would become more compact and cohesive.

Yet experience has not been encouraging. Argentina tried to issue exit bonds in 1987, but the terms were not attractive. Mexico was somewhat more successful in 1988, but it used reserves to guarantee its promise to repay. It bought zero-coupon U.S. Treasury securities, which were used to back the principal of the Mexican bonds issued in exchange for Mexican debt. Yet Mexico's sales were smaller than expected, presumably because the interest payments were not guaranteed, and the promise to pay interest on the bonds was not more credible than the promise to pay interest on the debt. Exit bonds appeared in the menu of financial options listed in the 1988 agreement between Brazil and its bank creditors. Although they were not guaranteed, Brazil sold more than $1 billion to more than 100 banks (Rhodes, 1988), but it has not reached its $5 billion target.

It is sometimes suggested that debtors should subordinate old debt to new, to market the new debt successfully. But that cannot be done without the unanimous consent of those who hold the old debt, and this produces a paradox. If enough new debt is issued to retire much of the old debt, those who continue to hold the old debt may not accept subordination, even if the exercise sharply reduces the debtor's obligations and thus raises the expected value of the whole debt; the buyers of the new debt will be seen to appropriate most of the gain. But if the issue is cut back to reduce the redistribution of rights from holders of old debt to holders of new debt, the exercise will not reduce the debtor's obligations by enough to make subordination meaningful —to raise the value of the whole debt by enhancing the debtor's ability and willingness to service it.

When the problem of defeasance is viewed this way, the function of a new institution becomes very clear. It would guarantee new debt, whether by issuing its own obligations or backing new bonds issued by the debtor countries.

The Functioning of a New Institution

I suggested the creation of a new institution soon after the debt crisis erupted (Kenen, 1983).[8] An International Debt Discount Corporation (IDDC) would be established by the governments of the major industrial countries. It could be an

---

[8]The proposal was introduced earlier (Kenen, 1982), but so was its main rival. Felix Rohatyn published a similar plan early in 1983, but an early version appeared some months before (Rohatyn, 1982, 1983). Credit or blame may really belong to G. C. Rodney Leach, then General Manager of the Trade Development Bank in London, whose proposal appears in a letter circulated late in 1982, and his plan had some features that have come up again. Banks would be shareholders in his institution, as in the one proposed by Robinson (1988). A revised version of my own plan was circulated privately in 1985, and another revision was published in Kenen (1988); it is the one described in the text.

independent entity or an affiliate of the IMF or World Bank. Its capital would be subscribed by its sponsors and used exclusively to guarantee its own obligations. Subscriptions might be made in proportion to the sponsors' shares in the capital of the World Bank or quotas in the IMF. The IDDC would issue its own long-term obligations to commercial banks in exchange for their claims on developing countries. (The claims would be those issued or guaranteed by debtor governments, not those of private entities, and limited to those having an original maturity longer than one year.)

In 1983, when my plan appeared, there was no secondary market for sovereign debt. That is why I did not suggest that the IDDC might buy up debt at market prices. Nevertheless, that approach raises some serious problems. Market rates would begin to reflect expectations about IDDC operations even before it came into being, and they would cease to serve as independent benchmarks (Fischer, 1989). Furthermore, debtors should not be given incentives to threaten repudiation—explicitly or by following imprudent policies—to force down the prices at which the IDDC could buy up their debts in the market and thus raise the amounts of debt relief that it would pass on to them (Corden, 1988b). Hence, the IDDC should choose in advance the rate at which it will discount debt, say 40–50 percent. A case can be made for using several discount rates and letting each debtor choose the one for its own obligations. This would be particularly sensible if larger discounts were linked to tighter policy conditions.

Commercial banks would not be required to do business with the IDDC, but those that do would be subject to certain restrictions. First, banks should not be allowed to sell their claims on some debtors and keep their claims on others; a bank wanting to discount claims on any debtor country doing business with the IDDC should be required to discount a uniform fraction of its total claims on all such countries. Second, banks would have only a limited period, perhaps six months to a year, to decide whether they will turn to the IDDC.

Debtor countries would not have to deal with the IDDC, either, and it would deal only with those countries that agreed to enter into suitable arrangements with the IMF and World Bank concerning the debtors' policies. During the time that banks are deciding whether they will sell to the IDDC, the debtor governments would have to decide whether they will do business with the IDDC; the discount window would be opened at the end of that period.

Sponsoring governments would agree to make changes in their banking laws and regulations if such changes are required for their banks to deal with the IDDC. Furthermore, they would permit their banks to amortize gradually some of the losses incurred by discounting debt with the IDDC. Bonds issued by the IDDC might be amortized over a 30-year period, starting five years after issue, and bear an interest rate slightly higher than the then-current rate on long-term U.S. government bonds. The bonds should be marketable, and the IDDC should encourage the development of a secondary market for them. Furthermore, it should be empowered to redeem them by issuing new ones to holders of maturing bonds and in the open market.

Claims discounted by the IDDC would be converted into long-term debt at or slightly above the discounted value of those claims. The difference between the face value of the new debt and the discounted value of the old would yield a "profit" that the IDDC might hold as a reserve or use for selective interest-rate relief. Debt to the IDDC might be amortized over a 25-year period, after a 5-year grace period. It should bear an interest rate 50 basis points above the average rate on the IDDC's own bonds.

Many permutations of this plan have appeared recently. The boldest is by Robinson (1988), in which the new institution would issue consols. In that case, of course, it would be guaranteeing interest payments rather than principal, which would be eminently sensible. The present value of the institution's obligations would be the same whether its bonds were amortized or not, but its exposure to cash-flow problems would be reduced.

Another variant would use the new institution to guarantee bonds issued directly by the debtors, rather than its own.[9] This option has one disadvantage. It would produce a large number of new bonds, each with its own market, rather than one issue by the IDDC with a single market, and the latter would probably function more efficiently. Furthermore, the terms of existing debt contracts allow banks to block bond issues by debtors, but they could not be invoked as easily to block bond issues by the IDDC. The point is important because the success of the debt-conversion exercise will depend on the ability of the IDDC to make banks an offer they cannot refuse or block.

Answering the Critics

Critics of an international agency invoke a litany of difficulties—adverse selection, moral hazard, and the free-rider problem.

The first says that the IDDC will gather in the debt that is least likely to be honored. This problem is minimized by the requirement that banks sell baskets of debt to the IDDC, offering some or all of their claims on all participating debtor countries. The problem could be eliminated by requiring all debtors countries to participate, but that would be impractical and unfair. Some debtor countries, like Korea, have worked hard to preserve their creditworthiness; they should not have to damage it.

The moral hazard argument says that the scheme would invite debtor countries to pursue irresponsible policies and would lead eventually to a new round of overborrowing.

The first part of this assertion says that debtor governments would be less concerned to achieve domestic stability and promote economic growth if their debts were reduced. In other words, it rejects the main rationale for debt relief, that debtors have failed to achieve their policy objectives because the debt overhang prevents them

---

[9]The newest version of this variant comes from L. William Seidman, chairman of the Federal Deposit Insurance Corporation, who would elicit the required capital from the IMF, the World Bank, governments, and commercial banks, but would charge the banks an annual premium to insure their holdings of the debtor's bonds (*The New York Times*, July 10, 1989). An earlier version by Rotberg (1988) was designed initially to encourage new bank lending but could be adapted to insure bond issues by the debtors.

from doing so. (Alternatively, it may say that the debtors would take their obligations to the IDDC less seriously than their obligations to the commercial banks. That is unlikely. No country has kept up its debt-service payments to the banks but suspended its payments to the IMF or World Bank, but several have done the opposite.)

The second part of the assertion predicts that debt relief will cause another debt crisis by removing reminders of this one. There may be another debt crisis eventually, but its timing is less likely to reflect the manner of settling this one than the speed at which institutional memories fade. Many governments that strive today to meet their countries' obligations are not the ones that took them on, and they will not be around at the start of the next century to make new mistakes. Furthermore, the IDDC will not "bail out" the banks, though the banks are likely to do better than by letting the debt problem drag on.

The free-rider problem needs to be taken more seriously. If one bank believes that the rest will grant debt relief, bilaterally or through an IDDC, improving the debtor's ability to meet its remaining obligations, it has an incentive to hang back. The obvious solution, mandatory participation by the banks, is not politically feasible. It is hard enough to shift risk from private to official creditors, let alone to shift from voluntary to mandatory debt reduction. But the problem may be less serious than commonly supposed.

Although debt reduction will raise the debtors' ability to meet their remaining obligations, some of the benefits will accrue to the IDDC. In fact, banks that hang back may be hurt, because debtor governments may be less concerned to meet their obligations to those banks than to the IDDC, and the governments sponsoring the IDDC will not be particularly interested in upholding the claims of banks that decline to do business with it. In other words, it may be possible to subordinate old debt to new debt when the new debt is owed to the IDDC, not formally by abrogating existing debt contracts, but informally by casting doubt on the likelihood that those contracts will be honored.

Finally, the sponsors of the IDDC can limit the free-rider problem by offering incentives for banks to participate and penalizing those that don't. Participants can be allowed to amortize their losses, as proposed above. Nonparticipants can be required to mark remaining debt to market and thus acknowledge larger losses.[10] In short, the sponsors and debtors can make sure that the IDDC appropriates most of the increase in the value of the debt resulting from debt relief and thus reduce the value of the old debt still outstanding.

Critics have been slow to spot another problem. They endorse the view that participating debtors be subject to some form of conditionality—that they have a bargain with the IMF or take structural-adjustment loans from the World Bank. It may be very hard, however, to condition debt relief. IMF drawings and World Bank structural-adjustment loans are disbursed in tranches, not in a lump sum, and disbursements can be halted if policy commitments are not met. It is rather difficult to

---

[10]Corden (1988b) makes the same suggestion, and it is my reason for reversing the position I took in earlier presentations that banks should not be made to write down their remaining claims.

do this with debt relief. It would be foolish, indeed, to withdraw debt relief from governments that fail to meet their policy commitments, as that would merely make it harder for them to do so. It may make sense, however, for the IDDC to grant relief provisionally and modestly at first, so that debtors are made to meet their policy commitments to qualify for permanent, full-scale relief. This argues for providing provisional relief by reducing the interest rate payable to the IDDC, then moving to permanent relief by writing down the claims themselves by more than the counterpart of the initial interest-rate reduction.

Two questions remain: Would the creation of an IDDC interfere with the resumption of voluntary lending? Why should the U.S. taxpayer get involved?

The first is easily answered. Most of the numbers suggest that the heavily indebted countries are farther from returning to creditworthiness than they were at the start of the debt crisis. There has been no concerted lending to small debtors for some years, and the large debtors have continued to qualify only because banks have been reluctant to acknowledge the losses they would face if Argentina, Brazil, and Mexico could not borrow enough to keep on paying interest. If the IDDC can facilitate large-scale debt relief, the debtors will be able to manage their economies more effectively, and this will hasten, not delay, the return to creditworthiness.

The second question has two answers. First, the risks assumed by the sponsoring countries and their taxpayers are not large insofar as debtors lie on the downward-sloping side of the Debt Relief Laffer Curve. Debt relief reduces the risk by raising the value of the debt. Second, taxpayers are already involved. They take on risks directly whenever the World Bank makes another loan to one of the heavily indebted countries, and they take them on indirectly whenever the commercial banks engage in additional concerted lending. But there are larger issues. The taxpayers are involved because the debt problem impinges on foreign policy, the prospects for democracy in the debtor countries, and the outlook for reducing imbalances in the world economy. Much has been said about the need for the newly industrialized countries of Asia to liberalize their trade regimes and thus help to reduce the U.S. trade deficit. The debtor countries could make an equally important contribution if their foreign-exchange earnings were not eaten by their interest payments and their economies could grow more rapidly.

References

Bulow, Jeremy, and Kenneth Rogoff, "The Buyback Boondoggle," *Brookings Papers on Economic Activity*, 1988, *2*, 675–98.

Bulow, Jeremy, and Kenneth Rogoff, "Sovereign Debt Repurchases: No Cure for Overhang," Working Paper 2850. Cambridge: National Bureau of Economic Research, February 1989.

Cline, William R., *International Debt: Systemic Risk and Policy Response*. Washington: Institute for International Economics, 1984.

Cohen, Benjamin J., "LDC Debt: A Middle Way," *Essays in International Finance, 173*. Princeton: International Finance Section, Princeton University, 1989.

Corden, W. Max, "Debt Relief and Adjustment Incentives," *International Monetary Fund Staff Papers*, December 1988a, *35*, 628–43.

Corden, W. Max, "An International Debt Facility?," *International Monetary Fund Staff Papers*, September 1988b, *35*, 401–21.

Dornbusch, Rudiger, "Our LDC Debts," in Feldstein, Martin, ed., *The United States in the World Economy*. Chicago: University of Chicago Press for The National Bureau of Economic Research, 1988.

Eaton, Jonathan, and Mark Gersovitz, "Debt with Potential Repudiation," *Review of Economic Studies*, March 1981, *48*, 289–309.

Eaton, Jonathan, Mark Gersovitz, and Joseph E. Stiglitz, "The Pure Theory of Country Risk," *European Economic Review*, June 1986, *30*, 481–513.

Fischer, Stanley, "Resolving the International Debt Crisis," in Sachs, Jeffrey, ed., *Developing Country Debt and Economic Performance*. Chicago: University of Chicago Press, 1989.

Froot, Kenneth A., "Buybacks, Exit Bonds, and the Optimality of Debt and Liquidity Relief," *International Economic Review*, February 1989, *30*, 49–70.

Guttentag, Jack, and Richard Herring, "Provisioning, Charge-Offs, and the Willingness to Lend," *Essays in International Finance, 172*. Princeton: International Finance Section, Princeton University, 1988.

Kenen, Peter B., "National Economic Policy, International Adjustment, and Exchange Rates," *Foreign Exchange Service Conference Proceedings*. Philadelphia: Wharton Econometric Forecasting Associates, Fall 1982.

Kenen, Peter B., "Third-World Debt: Sharing the Burden. A Bailout Plan for the Banks," *The New York Times*, March 6, 1983.

Kenen, Peter B., "A Proposal for Reducing Debt Burdens for Developing Countries," in Denoon, David B. H., ed., *Changing Capital Markets and the Global Economy*. Philadelphia: Global Interdependence Center, 1988.

Kenen, Peter B., "Debt Buybacks and Forgiveness in a Model with Voluntary Repudiation," Working Paper 89-1. Princeton: International Finance Section, Princeton University, July 1989.

Krugman, Paul R., "Market-Based Debt-Reduction Schemes." In Frenkel, Jacob A., Michael P. Dooley, and Peter Wickham, eds., *Analytical Issues in Debt*. Washington D.C.: International Monetary Fund, 1989.

Lamdany, Ruben, "The Brazil Financing Package: Main Components and Lessons for the Future," unpublished manuscript, September 1988a.

Lamdany, Ruben, "Bolivia, Mexico, and Beyond...," unpublished manuscript, June 1988b.

Rhodes, William R., "An Insider's Reflection on the Brazilian Debt Package," *The Wall Street Journal*, October 14, 1988.

Robinson, James D., "A Comprehensive Agenda for LDC Debt and World Trade Growth," *Amex Bank Review Special Papers, 13*. London: American Express Bank, March 1988.

Rohatyn, Felix G., "The State of the Banks," *New York Review of Books*, November 4, 1982.

Rohatyn, Felix G., "A Plan for Stretching Out Global Debt," *Business Week*, February 28, 1983.

Rotberg, Eugene H., *Toward a Solution to the Debt Crisis*. New York: Merrill Lynch & Co., May 1988.

Sachs, Jeffrey, "Comprehensive Debt Retirement: The Bolivian Example," *Brookings Papers on Economic Activity*, 1988, *2*, 705–13.

Sachs, Jeffrey, "Making the Brady Plan Work," *Foreign Affairs*, Summer 1989a, *68*, 87–104.

Sachs, Jeffrey, "Conditionality, Debt Relief, and the Developing Country Debt Crisis," in Sachs, Jeffrey, ed., *Developing Country Debt and Economic Performance*. Chicago: University of Chicago Press, 1989b.

Williamson, John, "Voluntary Approaches to Debt Relief," *Policy Analyses in International Economics, 25*, Revised Edition. Washington D.C.: Institute for International Economics, 1989.

World Bank, *Market-Based Menu Approach*. Washington D.C.: World Bank Debt Management and Financial Advisory Services Department, September 1988.

22

IMF *Staff Papers*
Vol. 38, No. 2 (June 1991)
© 1991 International Monetary Fund

Transitional Arrangements for Trade and Payments Among the CMEA Countries

PETER B. KENEN*

The CMEA countries are starting to conduct their trade at world prices and in convertible currencies. These are crucial steps in economic reform but will worsen Eastern Europe's terms of trade and drive it into current account deficit with the U.S.S.R. Proposals have been made for a payments union, resembling the European Payments Union of 1950–58, to ease the transition. Such an arrangement would not function well if it included the U.S.S.R., which would be a persistent creditor. Other ways must be found to deal with the transition. [JEL F33, P33]

THE FRAMEWORK for trade in Eastern Europe has disintegrated. It was decisively rejected by the governments of Eastern Europe and by the U.S.S.R., for somewhat different reasons. All of the governments favor trading arrangements that emulate those in the rest of the world. Trade should take place between individual enterprises, not be monopolized by governmental entities. Trade should be conducted at world prices, and payments made in convertible currencies (which means that imbalances would normally be settled in those currencies). Agreement was reached in principle on these objectives in January 1990 at the Sofia meeting of the Council on Mutual Economic Assistance (CMEA), and the U.S.S.R.

* Peter B. Kenen is Walker Professor of Economics and International Finance and Director of the International Finance Section at Princeton University. He holds degrees from Columbia and Harvard Universities. This paper was prepared while he was a consultant in the European Department. He is indebted to colleagues in the European Department, especially to Thomas Wolf, for advice and comments, and to papers by Peter Bofinger (1990) and Constantine Michalopoulos (1990), which examine the same subject.

sought to implement the arrangements fully by the beginning of 1991. There is concern in Eastern Europe, however, and among Western observers, about the costs of moving quickly to the new regime.

A shift to trade at world prices will worsen Eastern Europe's terms of trade and drive it into current account deficit with the U.S.S.R. Under the new regime, moreover, a deficit with the U.S.S.R. will have to be settled in convertible currencies, which will be difficult. The countries of Eastern Europe cannot readily earn or borrow more in the West. In fact, they must spend more in the West to buy capital goods for economic modernization.

Some of the countries of Eastern Europe have made short-term bargains with the U.S.S.R. to finance their prospective current account deficits. Thus, Czechoslovakia and Hungary expect to draw down balances built up when they were running current account surpluses. The balances are denominated in transferable rubles (TR) but will be converted to U.S. dollars at exchange rates reported to approximate $0.90 = TR 1. (They will thus receive fewer dollars than they would have obtained at the official exchange rate prevailing when they acquired the balances but more than they would obtain at recent cross rates.)

Some observers believe, however, that longer-term arrangements are needed. These might be modeled on the European Payments Union (EPU), which helped Western Europe to move from bilateral trade before 1950 to current account convertibility in 1958. The suggestion has been made by a number of individuals and organizations, including the Economic Commission for Europe, in its *Economic Survey of Europe 1989–90.*[1]

The analogy is intriguing but may be deeply flawed. There are large differences between the postwar situation in Western Europe and the present situation in Eastern Europe. They are reviewed in this paper, which reaches the conclusion that an Eastern European Payments Union (EEPU) is not a good way to manage the transition to the new trading and payments regime.

An EEPU that excluded the U.S.S.R. might not be very useful, as there may be far less scope for trade expansion in Eastern Europe than there was in Western Europe after World War II. Trade and payments have been conducted bilaterally in the CMEA area, but that has not been the principal reason for the low level of trade among the countries involved. In Western Europe, by contrast, bilateral payments arrange-

---

[1] See also Ethier (1990), Hardt (1990), Lavigne (1990), Soros (1990), and van Brabant (1990).

ments depressed trade significantly in the late 1940s, and the multilateralization achieved through the EPU fostered liberalization, regionally and globally.

An EEPU that included the U.S.S.R. would not work well, because the U.S.S.R. would be a "structural creditor" in the years ahead and would have to lend to Eastern Europe through the EEPU. The EPU had structural creditors too, but Marshall Plan money was used to indemnify them for the dollars they sacrificed by lending to their partners. The same point can be made more vividly. Because the United States was not a member of the EPU, the "dollar shortage" faced by Western Europe was financed outside the EPU. If the U.S.S.R. were a member of an EEPU, the "ruble shortage" facing Eastern Europe would be financed automatically within the EEPU.

This paper has four parts. The first describes the old framework for trade and payments among the CMEA countries and the actual trade pattern. The next part reviews the main objections to that framework viewed from the perspectives of the U.S.S.R. and of the Eastern European countries—Bulgaria, Czechoslovakia, Hungary, Poland, and Romania—denoted here as the CMEA5. It also examines the outlook for CMEA trade, focusing on the effects of shifting to world prices and using convertible currencies. The third part of the paper describes the EPU and assesses its contribution. The final part shows how an EEPU might work, with and without the U.S.S.R. It is, on balance, critical of proposals to create an EEPU, but it stresses the need for balance of payments financing to help the CMEA5 adjust to the impending shift in their terms of trade and the switch to convertible currency payments.

I. The CMEA System

For more than forty years, most of the trade among the CMEA countries was conducted on a government-to-government basis. The framework for trade between each pair of countries was defined by five-year agreements, which were supplemented by annual protocols fixing the quantities and prices of the products to be traded.[2]

---

[2] For more on the CMEA system, see Wolf (1988), Schrenk (1990), and the sources cited in those works. The CMEA sponsored other forms of economic cooperation, but they lie beyond the scope of this paper.

PETER B. KENEN

Prices and Payments

The prices of primary commodities, most notably exports of oil and gas from the U.S.S.R., were based on world prices but tended to lag behind them; under the so-called Bucharest formula, adopted in 1975, a five-year moving average of world prices was used to obtain a dollar price, which was converted to TR at the official exchange rate (about $1.60 = TR 1). The prices of other goods were negotiated individually. Furthermore, the prices used in CMEA trade were not always linked very closely to home prices—the prices received by the producers of exports and those paid by the purchasers of imports. Trade flows were taxed or subsidized in opaque and complex ways. Home prices, however, did not reflect opportunity costs, and there is no way to know whether the implicit trade taxes and subsidies compounded or reduced distortions in real resource allocation.

After 1964 most of the payments between CMEA countries took place in TR, on the books of the International Bank for Economic Cooperation (IBEC) in Moscow. Exporters were paid in their countries' own currencies, and importers made their payments in their own currencies, but the corresponding payments between CMEA countries were made in TR, by crediting and debiting IBEC accounts. The transferable ruble, however, was not truly transferable, let alone convertible. If Poland built up a credit balance with IBEC by running a trade surplus with Hungary, it could not use the credit to finance a deficit with Bulgaria. For this and other reasons, each CMEA country sought to balance its trade bilaterally with each CMEA partner. This was, indeed, the normal expectation, even when a country had built up a credit balance. It could draw that balance down when it ran an *unexpected* deficit with its partner, but it could not always *plan* to run one.[3]

The transferable ruble was supposed to become transferable, as its name implies, and plans to make it so surfaced periodically, but they were never implemented. This failure raises an interesting question. Was the bilateral character of CMEA trade due to the nontransferability of the TR, or was it the reflection of more basic obstacles to the multilateralization of that trade? Without answering this question, it is hard to forecast

---

[3] Bilateral balancing was carried even further. Attempts were made to balance trade in certain types of goods to conserve scarce supplies for domestic use or for export to Western countries in exchange for convertible currencies. Furthermore, separate accounts and exchange rates were used for commercial and noncommercial transactions. For a detailed account of the CMEA payments system, see van Brabant (1987).

Table 1. *Openness, Income, and Size of Selected European Countries, 1988*

Country	Exports as Percentage of GDP	Income Per Capita (U.S. dollars)	Population Total in millions	Per square kilometer
Poland	22.8	1,860	37.9	121
Hungary	37.6	2,460	10.6	114
Portugal	33.5	3,650	10.3	113
Greece	24.2	4,800	10.0	76
Spain	19.5	7,740	39.0	77

Sources: International Monetary Fund (1990) and World Bank (1990a).

the short-run and long-run effects of changing the CMEA payments system. To answer it carefully, however, one must first examine the actual pattern of trade.

The Structure of CMEA Trade

Central planning tends to be biased against foreign trade. Planners crave certainty, and foreign trade, even between planned economies, involves uncertainty. It is hard to plan production, harder still to plan consumption, and very hard to plan the differences between them. To plan trade between two countries, moreover, the planners have to match the two countries' differences, imparting more uncertainty to each country's plan.

Nevertheless, the countries of Eastern Europe are heavily dependent on foreign trade. Numbers for Hungary and Poland are shown in Table 1, along with those for three other European countries. Hungary and Portugal are similar in size; so are Poland and Spain. But Hungarian exports are larger than Portuguese exports, relative to output, and Polish exports are larger than Spanish exports, although incomes are lower in Hungary and Poland—far lower in Hungary than Spain.[4] Comparable data are not available for the other CMEA countries, but imports per capita by Bulgaria and Czechoslovakia do not differ greatly from those

---

[4] The economic statistics of the CMEA countries are not as reliable as those of many other countries, because prices are not very meaningful. This caveat applies with particular force to the comparisons in Table 1 but must also be borne in mind when reading other tables in this paper. Trade data are extremely hard to compare, because the CMEA countries use different exchange rates between the TR and the dollar.

Table 2. *Trade Among the CMEA Countries, 1989*

Country	Exports		Imports	
	CMEA as percent of total	U.S.S.R. as percent of CMEA	CMEA as percent of total	U.S.S.R. as percent of CMEA
Bulgaria	57.3	84.9	42.4	80.4
Czechoslovakia	40.9	64.8	40.9	63.2
Hungary	35.8	70.7	33.9	66.9
Poland	39.7	67.9	33.4	65.5
Romania	19.9	68.3	30.5	68.7

Sources: Author's calculations using data in Economic Commission for Europe (1990a) and unpublished data provided by the Economic Commission for Europe.

Note: CMEA countries include the CMEA5 *plus* the U.S.S.R.; trade flows between CMEA countries are valued at a common exchange rate ($0.50/ruble).

of Hungary, and the figures for Romania and Poland are not very different either, although lower than the rest.[5]

Exports account for large shares of output in some of the countries' key industries. In Bulgaria, for instance, exports accounted for 60 percent of total machinery output in 1987 and for 30 percent of the output of manufactured consumer goods. In Poland, they accounted for 27 percent of machinery output and for 31 percent of the output of building materials.[6]

Nevertheless, the CMEA countries trade less with the outside world and more with each other than one might expect, given their small share of world trade (less than 4 percent of world exports in 1989). The distribution of their trade is shown in Table 2, and bilateral trade flows are shown in Table 3. Three features stand out immediately.

• The shares of intra-CMEA trade are quite high but differ from country to country, ranging from 57 percent of total Bulgarian exports and 42 percent of Bulgarian imports to just 20 percent of total Romanian exports and 30 percent of Romanian imports.[7]

[5] Trade data are from Economic Commission for Europe (1990a, chap. 2, p. 5); they are based on a common exchange rate ($0.50 per ruble) for the five countries. The actual figures are $845 for Bulgaria, $770 for Czechoslovakia, $850 for Hungary, $345 for Poland, and $250 for Romania. The figures for the other countries listed in Table 1 are much higher, at $1,715 for Portugal, $1,335 for Greece, and $1,735 for Spain (International Monetary Fund (1990)).

[6] Output and trade data from *PlanEcon Report,* Vol. V (1989, pp. 27–28, 36–37, and 42–43).

[7] The shares shown in Table 2 are smaller than those shown in several recent publications; see, for example, World Bank (1990b), where the 1988 figures range from 81 percent of total Bulgarian exports to 41 percent of total Polish exports. That is because those publications use official exchange rates and because they include trade with the German Democratic Republic.

Table 3. *Bilateral Trade in the CMEA Area, 1989*
(Percentage of total exports to CMEA5 and U.S.S.R.)

	Importer					
Exporter	Bulgaria	Czecho-slovakia	Hungary	Poland	Romania	U.S.S.R.
Bulgaria	—	5.7	1.8	4.7	2.6	85.2
Czechoslovakia	4.9	—	8.9	17.4	3.9	64.9
Hungary	2.0	14.8	—	8.1	4.1	71.0
Poland	4.8	17.7	5.5	—	3.4	68.6
Romania	5.0	9.6	8.2	8.8	—	68.4
U.S.S.R.	23.2	25.8	16.9	23.0	11.1	—

Source: See source note for Table 2.
Note: Entries are averages of percentages computed from the exporting countries' trade data and from the importing countries' data. Therefore, entries will
not agree exactly with those obtained from any single country's data.

• The U.S.S.R. dominates intra-CMEA trade. Its shares in its partners' trade are uniformly high, ranging from 85 percent of total Bulgarian
exports to the CMEA countries and 80 percent of Bulgarian imports
to 65 percent of Czechoslovak exports and 63 percent of Czechoslovak
imports.

• The other bilateral trade flows are small. The largest numbers in
Table 3 are for Polish and Hungarian exports to Czechoslovakia, which
account for 18 and 15 percent, respectively, of total Polish and Hungarian
exports to the CMEA countries, and for Czechoslovak exports to Poland,
which account for 17 percent of total Czechoslovak exports to its CMEA
partners. (One should remember, moreover, that Polish, Hungarian, and
Czechoslovak exports to the CMEA countries account for comparatively
small shares of those countries' total exports.)

Concerns have been expressed about the possibility of a sharp fall in the
volume of intra-CMEA trade, due to reductions in output in some CMEA
countries and impending shifts in demand to imports from the outside
world. These matters are discussed below. Note for now, however, that
apart from trade with the U.S.S.R., this trade is small.

There has also been discussion of prospects for expanding trade among
the CMEA5. The commodity composition of that trade, however, leads
one to doubt that it can grow rapidly. The economies of the CMEA5 are
complementary to the Soviet economy; they export machinery and other
manufactured goods and import primary products from the U.S.S.R. But
they are competitive with each other; they export similar goods and thus
export small amounts.

This is, of course, the answer to the question posed at the end of the previous section. The nontransferability of the TR was not the main reason for the bilateral pattern displayed by CMEA trade or the low level of trade within Eastern Europe. The pattern reflected the "socialist division of labor" imposed by the U.S.S.R. in the early years of the CMEA, which created the complementarities between Eastern Europe and the U.S.S.R., promoting bilateral trade with the U.S.S.R. but limiting specialization within Eastern Europe. Bilateral government-to-government bargaining also helped the U.S.S.R. exploit its monopoly power in the postwar period.[8] As a practical matter, moreover, it would have been hard to conduct multilateral bargaining on the product-by-product basis that typified dealings among CMEA countries.[9]

In brief, there was not much interest in making the TR transferable because bilateralism was deeply rooted in the industrial structure of the CMEA area and in its trade policies and practices, and there was little interest in multilateralism.

Tables 4a and 4b document some statements made above concerning the pattern of CMEA trade and the basic causes of bilateralism.[10] Note, first, that exports to socialist countries are much more sharply concentrated than exports to nonsocialist countries. In the case of Czechoslovakia, for instance, exports of machinery and transport equipment account for nearly 60 percent of total exports to socialist countries but for only 21 percent of exports to other countries. Conversely, exports of other manufactured goods account for only 29 percent of exports to socialist countries but for 42 percent of exports to other countries. Similarly, exports of investment goods account for a full 65 percent of total Bulgarian exports to socialist countries but for only 24 percent of exports to other countries.

The CMEA5 buy most of their oil and other fuel imports from the U.S.S.R., but most of their food and agricultural imports from nonsocialist countries. Their imports of machinery and other manufactures, how-

---

[8] The U.S.S.R. was not alone in using bilateral arrangements to maximize bargaining power. Kaplan and Schleiminger (1989, chaps. 3–4) note that the United Kingdom opposed the creation of the EPU partly because it wanted to promote the international use of sterling, but also because its bilateral payments arrangements gave it more bargaining power.

[9] It is worth remembering that the early rounds of tariff cuts under the General Agreement on Tariffs and Trade used bilateral bargaining on a product-by-product basis; "principal suppliers" of particular commodities swapped concessions with each other, then extended them to other countries *via* the most-favored-nation clause.

[10] Two tables are needed because Czechoslovakia, Hungary, and Poland use the Standard International Trade Classification (SITC) to organize their trade statistics, but Bulgaria and Romania have not yet shifted to it.

ever, come from both socialist and nonsocialist countries (and account for similar percentages of their total imports from each country group).

Detailed data for Hungary and Poland, shown in Table 5, say more about these patterns. Both countries export machinery and other manufactured goods to the U.S.S.R. and the rest of Eastern Europe, but they buy less of them from the U.S.S.R.; their manufactured imports from socialist countries come mainly from their partners in Eastern Europe.

Can the CMEA5 expand their trade with each other? Can they perhaps promote intra-industry trade in machinery and other manufactures? Hardt (1990) and Lavigne (1990), among others, are optimistic on this score—perhaps too optimistic. The Economic Commission for Europe (ECE) has tried to measure the technological intensity of trade in engineering goods, and some of its results are shown in Table 6. The exports and imports of Eastern Europe and of the U.S.S.R. are far lower in technological intensity than those of most other countries. These results suggest that they can meet their partners' needs—that each of them can export more low-tech goods. But they need goods of higher technological intensity to raise their productivity. Therefore, they must import less from their CMEA partners and more from the rest of the world.

There may be some scope for expanding trade within Eastern Europe, but not by more intensive intra-industry specialization in machinery. On the contrary, the CMEA5 should probably aim at making their trade with each other more like their trade with the outside world—more broadly diversified across product categories rather than more concentrated on the narrow range of goods that they have been trading with each other. This is the most sensible interpretation that can be attached to the view expressed by the ECE, which argues that "there are significant comparative advantages embodied in the resource endowments of the individual economies that, with the proper institutions and policies, could be exploited more fully to the benefit of welfare levels in the region and elsewhere" (ECE (1990b, p. 3–72)).

II. Objectives and Effects of Economic Reform

For reasons already mentioned, central planners tend to be strongly trade averse. Imports are a necessary evil—the source of last resort for basic raw materials and other inputs that cannot be produced at home in quantities sufficient to meet domestic needs. Exports are needed to pay for imports, but they are released reluctantly because of domestic shortages.

Western views are different. Trade is admired as an "engine of growth,"

Table 4a. *Commodity Composition of CMEA Trade*
(Percentage of total exports or imports)

Commodity Class (SITC Code)	Trade with Nonsocialist Countries			Trade with Socialist Countries		
	Czechoslovakia	Hungary	Poland	Czechoslovakia	Hungary	Poland
Exports						
Food, etc. (0,1,4)	10.7	17.7	15.9	1.5	17.6	3.2
Crude materials, excluding fuels (2)	6.1	6.4	9.4	2.1	4.1	2.7
Fuels (3)	9.1	5.7	11.7	2.7	3.2	8.5
Chemicals (5)	11.2	15.7	8.3	5.2	12.2	7.6
Machinery and transportation equipment (7)	20.9	22.5	15.7	59.5	35.9	53.6
Other manufactures, etc. (6,8,9)	41.9	31.9	39.0	28.9	27.0	24.4
Imports						
Food, etc. (0,1,4)	13.4	9.6	20.8	4.7	3.3	4.3
Crude materials, excluding fuels (2)	13.5	7.2	12.7	5.9	6.7	6.2
Fuels (3)	2.6	3.4	5.2	26.1	31.9	25.2
Chemicals (5)	16.5	20.1	15.9	5.0	8.1	5.8
Machinery and transportation equipment (7)	35.8	31.4	25.4	37.6	31.4	38.8
Other manufactures, etc. (6,8,9)	18.2	28.4	20.0	20.4	19.5	19.1

Source: National trade statistics.
Note: Czechoslovak data for 1989; Hungarian data for 1987; Polish data for 1988. Detail may not add to total because of rounding.

Table 4b. *Commodity Composition of CMEA Trade*
(Percentage of total exports or imports)

Commodity Class	Trade with Nonsocialist Countries		Trade with Socialist Countries	
	Bulgaria	Romania	Bulgaria	Romania
Exports				
Food and agricul- tural goods	17.1	4.3	13.3	5.7
Minerals and fuels	32.9	42.1	3.4	9.7
Other raw materials	7.8	5.5	. . .[a]	1.9
Chemicals	7.3	14.6	2.8	4.8
Investment goods	24.2	11.2	65.4	58.0
Consumer goods	7.6	18.6	11.7	17.4
Other	3.0	3.7	3.4	2.5
Imports				
Food and agricul- tural goods	12.4	4.1	2.3	3.4
Minerals and fuels	32.2	73.9	36.1	40.2
Other raw materials	12.1	5.8	3.0	4.2
Chemicals	9.8	7.8	3.4	5.2
Investment goods	25.2	5.6	48.5	34.4
Consumer goods	6.4	1.2	4.8	6.5
Other	2.0	1.6	1.9	6.1

Source: National trade statistics.
Note: Bulgarian data for 1989; Romanian data for 1988. Detail may not add to total because of rounding.
[a] Not shown separately.

and international competition is regarded as a powerful antidote to domestic inefficiency. The appeal of these views is so strong that protectionists have had to recast their arguments. Tariffs and other trade barriers, they say, should be used strategically to open other countries' markets—to promote rather than restrict competition—and to offset the "unfair" trade practices that others use to appropriate the gains from trade.

The Changing Role of Foreign Trade

Current views in Eastern Europe lie between these extremes, even in countries strongly committed to building market economies. The need for more imports is readily acknowledged. Imported capital goods embody the technologies that Eastern Europe needs to raise productivity; imported consumer goods widen workers' choices, raising real incomes

Table 5. *Commodity Composition of Hungarian and Polish Trade with CMEA Countries*

(Percentage of total exports or imports)

Commodity Class (SITC Code)	Hungary with		Poland with	
	U.S.S.R.	Other CMEA5	U.S.S.R.	Other CMEA5
Exports				
Food, etc. (0,1,4)	20.8	10.4	4.4	3.3
Crude materials, excluding fuels (2)	1.7	2.3	3.1	4.2
Fuels (3)	0.5	0.9	11.9	7.5
Chemicals (5)	8.3	10.7	10.7	3.7
Machinery and transportation equipment (7)	47.4	51.9	46.0	52.7
Other manufactures, etc. (6,8,9)	21.3	23.8	23.9	28.5
Imports				
Food, etc. (0,1,4)	1.2	5.8	1.3	5.1
Crude materials, excluding fuels (2)	8.4	3.1	9.4	2.7
Fuels (3)	50.7	6.3	59.7	2.2
Chemicals (5)	7.4	7.9	3.3	7.5
Machinery and transportation equipment (7)	18.8	49.4	17.4	58.3
Other manufactures, etc. (6,8,9)	13.5	27.5	8.9	24.2

Source: National trade statistics.
Note: All data for 1987. Detail may not add to total because of rounding.

and incentives. The need for more exports is also acknowledged, not only to pay for more imports but also to win large markets in which to exploit economies of scale. The domestic dimensions of reform, however, have attracted more attention than the external dimensions, although Poland and Hungary have acted boldly to liberalize their trade and payments.[11]

The domestic focus is understandable. The challenges are enormous and greatly complicated in most countries by huge macroeconomic problems. More attention to the external side, moreover, would require faster action on the macroeconomic side. Otherwise, the liberalization of trade and payments would allow excess domestic demand to produce current account deficits, and an attempt to limit them by devaluation would increase inflationary pressures at home.

It is, of course, essential to create the institutions that make a market

---

[11] Wolf (1990) examines the problems and progress of trade reform in the CMEA countries; Daviddi and Espa (1989) describe recent events in the U.S.S.R.

Table 6. *Exports and Imports of Engineering Goods
by Technological Intensity, 1987*

(Percentage of total exports or imports)

Country or Country Group	Technological Intensity			
	High	Advanced	Middle	Low
United States				
Exports	43.7	17.0	19.2	20.0
Imports	24.7	11.8	43.3	20.1
Japan				
Exports	25.5	12.3	40.6	21.5
Imports	41.1	19.6	15.3	24.0
Republic of Korea				
Exports	31.6	4.8	35.1	28.5
Imports	32.1	22.0	8.7	37.1
Taiwan Province of China				
Exports	34.9	11.7	17.0	36.4
Imports	33.6	17.4	10.8	38.2
Eastern Europe				
Exports	7.6	18.3	19.5	54.3
Imports	8.3	23.8	9.5	55.6
U.S.S.R.				
Exports	8.4	11.6	49.4	30.5
Imports	6.0	23.5	5.3	60.6

Source: Economic Commission for Europe (1990b, Tables 7.8 and 7.9).
Note: Figures do not always add to 100 percent because some goods in the totals have not been classified.

economy work. Property rights must be defined and liberalized to encourage the creation of new enterprises and permit them to function
effectively. It is especially important to promote wholesale trade, in order
to replace old methods for allocating inputs and bringing goods to market. It may be useful, however, to give more attention to the external side
when thinking about reform. Trade can be an engine of growth for the
small economies of Eastern Europe, just as it has been for those of East
Asia. Furthermore, domestic reform can be accelerated by "importing"
world markets and world prices. World markets for intermediate goods
can substitute in part for deficient domestic markets, and the use of world
prices for those goods would be more sensible than the laborious ratio-
nalization of domestic prices that appears to be contemplated in the
U.S.S.R. A two-step reform, moreover, involving a move to domestic
market prices, then to world prices, would be far more expensive than
an immediate move to world prices; it would require two sets of shifts in
resource allocation.

PETER B. KENEN

To import world markets wholeheartedly, the governments of Eastern
Europe will have to make large changes in their trade and payments systems. Purists would probably insist that they must move entirely to free
trade. Pragmatists would probably argue that they must achieve current
account convertibility and dismantle their quantitative trade controls,
including their import-licensing arrangements. This would be a "big
bang" indeed—bigger even than in Poland—and the governments of
Eastern Europe are not ready for it. They would probably say, with some
justification, what Lord Cherwell said when he was asked what would
happen if Britain made a "dash for convertibility" by allowing the pound
to float in the early 1950s:

> If a 6 percent Bank Rate, 1 million unemployed, and a 2/- loaf are not
> enough, there would have to be an 8 percent Bank Rate, 2 million unem-
> ployed, and a 3/- loaf. If workers, finding their food dearer, are inclined to
> demand higher wages, this will have to be stopped by increasing unemploy-
> ment until their bargaining power is destroyed. This is what comfortable
> phrases like 'letting the exchange rate take the strain' mean (Kaplan and
> Schleiminger (1989, p. 166)).

It can indeed be argued that the problems of Eastern Europe will be more
obdurate than those of Western Europe forty years ago, that the adjustment process will be more painful, and that the social tolerance for pain
may be lower.[12] The process will have to be gradual, and debate will
continue between those who would step on the accelerator to reap the
benefits sooner and those who would step on the brakes to reduce or defer
the costs.

Some Effects of Reforming CMEA Trade

Although governments in Eastern Europe have tended to focus on
domestic dimensions of reform, they have agreed in principle to move to
the use of world prices in CMEA trade and to convertible currency
payments. Some of them, moreover, are ready to let world prices influence domestic prices, which must be done to import world markets and
world prices. The U.S.S.R. is even more eager to move to world prices,
but for different reasons. Soviet reformers are more domestically ori-
ented than their counterparts in Eastern Europe, even those who want
to move quickly to a full-fledged market economy. They seem sometimes
to believe that a set of market-clearing prices can be made to rise from
the ruins of the planned economy, like the Phoenix from the ashes. But
the U.S.S.R. expects to gain commercially from a shift to world prices.

---

[12] For a well-balanced comparison between Western Europe in 1950 and Eastern Europe in 1990, see Economic Commission for Europe (1990b, pp. 1–9 ff).

A shift to world prices and to the use of convertible currencies will have two effects. First, it will raise the prices of fuels and other raw materials in CMEA trade. Second, it will cause a shift in demand from many manufactured goods produced by the CMEA countries to more attractive goods produced by other countries. If they must use convertible currencies to pay for imports from their partners, CMEA countries will have less incentive to buy from each other when they can get better goods elsewhere.

To estimate the effects of these developments, one has first to measure the differences between the prices presently imbedded in CMEA trade data and the corresponding world prices. This is quite difficult, even for fuels and other commodities with well-known world prices. Consider two ways to measure the relevant oil price.

First, if the Bucharest formula had been applied mechanically in 1989, the CMEA countries would have paid between TR 9.1 and TR 12.2 a barrel. (The low figure uses a three-year moving average of world oil prices, the high one uses a five-year moving average, and both use the official exchange rate between the TR and the dollar.) But the CMEA countries compile their trade data in a way that involves implicit use of the cross rate between the TR and the dollar. In the case of Poland, that rate was about $0.34 = TR 1 in 1989, which means that the dollar price of oil imbedded in Poland's trade data would have been between $3.10 and $4.15 a barrel. In the case of Czechoslovakia, however, the cross rate was $0.66 = TR 1, and the dollar price imbedded in its data would have been between $6.00 and $8.05 a barrel.

Second, an average oil price can be extracted directly from Poland's trade data; when converted from zloty into dollars at the commercial exchange rate, it works out at about $5.30 a barrel in 1989, which was roughly 30 percent of the world price. But Bulgarian figures for 1989 put its import price at 45 percent of the world price when Bulgaria's cross rate is used to convert it into dollars.

To complicate matters, some of the countries' trade data do not segregate oil from other fuels, and there is reason to believe that implicit import prices for coal and natural gas have been closer to world prices than the price of oil. Hence, the illustrative calculations described below assume that the shift to world prices would have raised implicit energy prices by an average of 150 percent in 1989.[13]

---

[13] The corresponding changes in domestic prices will differ from country to country. In Hungary, for example, petroleum products have been taxed to keep domestic prices close to world prices, and a higher price for imported oil is thus likely to result in tax cuts, not higher energy prices. (In that case, however, higher import prices will reduce tax revenues and magnify the budgetary problem.)

Information on other commodity prices is scarcer, but the use of the Bucharest formula in the manner described above for oil suggests that there would have been large increases in the prices of iron ore and nonferrous metals, because the import prices for those goods were lower, compared to world prices, than the price of oil. The prices of chemicals, by contrast, seem to have been closer to world prices. Accordingly, the calculations described below assume that the shift to world prices would have raised the prices of minerals by 200 percent and raised the prices of chemicals by 50 percent.

It is far harder to estimate the change in the prices of manufactures. It is widely believed that they are overpriced in CMEA trade and would have to fall sharply to offset the forthcoming shift in demand. Recent research on Hungarian prices, however, suggests that the prices of manufactured goods in CMEA trade may already be much lower than world prices of similar goods.

Marrese and Wittenberg (1990) have calculated dollar unit values for goods traded between Hungary and the West relative to forint unit values for goods traded between Hungary and the U.S.S.R.[14] Their figure for Hungarian exports of machinery is $0.0385 = Ft 1 in 1987, whereas the commercial exchange rate was $0.0213 = Ft 1. Suppose, then, that Western buyers had been free to purchase Hungarian goods at the forint prices paid by Soviet buyers. They should have been willing to pay about 80 percent more for the forint than the commercial rate, which says, in turn, that the forint prices of Hungarian goods sold to the U.S.S.R. were far lower than the forint prices of goods sold to the West.

For this and other reasons, the calculations summarized below do not make large adjustments in the prices of manufactured goods. They assume a 15 percent reduction in the prices of machinery and transport equipment had the shift to world prices occurred in 1989, but no changes in the prices of other manufactures. All of the foregoing suppositions are summarized below.

For Czechoslovakia, Hungary, and Poland, which use the Standard International Trade Classification (SITC):

---

[14] The Marrese-Wittenberg calculations can also be used to compare Hungary's terms of trade with the U.S.S.R. and Poland to its terms of trade with the market economies. In 1987, its terms of trade with the U.S.S.R. were 12.5 percent better than with the market economies, and its terms of trade with Poland were virtually the same as with the market economies. Since 1987, however, the forint has depreciated more sharply in terms of the dollar than in terms of the TR, and Hungary's terms of trade with the U.S.S.R. have probably improved relative to its terms of trade with the market economies.

Foods, beverages, fats and oils	No price change
Raw materials, except fuels	200 percent price increase
Fuels	150 percent price increase
Chemicals	50 percent price increase
Machinery and transport equipment	15 percent price decrease
Other manufactures and miscellaneous	No price change.

For Bulgaria and Romania, which use the CMEA classification:

Food and miscellaneous	No price change
Fuels, minerals, and metals	150 percent price increase
Chemicals	50 percent price increase
Machinery and transport equipment	15 percent price decrease
Industrial consumer goods	No price change.

These price changes were applied to the trade data shown in Tables 4a and 4b to generate the estimates in Tables 7 and 8.[15]

Every country under study would have suffered a large deterioration in its terms of trade with the CMEA area. It is largest for Hungary, at 37 percent, and smallest for Poland, at 23 percent. Each country would also have experienced a large deterioration in its trade balance with the CMEA area, ranging from $3.6 billion for Czechoslovakia to $1.5 billion for Poland.[16] Therefore, each country would have run a large current account deficit with the CMEA area, mainly with the U.S.S.R. These would have ranged from $2.8 billion for Czechoslovakia to $1.0 billion for Bulgaria.[17]

These are not forecasts for 1991, when the shift to world prices will be taking place. They ask how the shift would have affected each country's terms of trade and trade balance if it had taken place in 1989, and they

---

[15] Romania is omitted from Table 8 for want of the relevant current account data.

[16] The Czechoslovak figure may be too high. Czechoslovakia's cross rate between the TR and the dollar was higher in 1989 than those of some other countries. Hence, the dollar prices implicit in its trade statistics may have been closer to world prices and should be adjusted by smaller amounts than those used in this paper. If this is true, of course, the current account deficit in Table 8 is likewise too high.

[17] The figures in Tables 7 and 8 are not very sensitive to small changes in the assumptions about the prospective price changes. The computations were repeated on more pessimistic assumptions: that energy prices rise by 250 percent, the prices of other raw materials rise by 200 percent, and the prices of chemicals rise by 100 percent, while the prices of machinery and transport equipment fall

Table 7. *Estimated Effects of Shifting to World Prices on the 1989 Terms of Trade and Trade Balances*

Country	Change in Terms of Trade (in percent)	Change in Trade Balance (in millions of U.S. dollars)
Bulgaria	−24.0	−1,617
Czechoslovakia	−30.9	−3,585
Hungary	−36.7	−2,080
Poland	−22.6	−1,480
Romania	−31.4	−2,677

make no allowance for compensating changes in the quantities of exports and imports or for changes in earnings from services. Nor do they allow for many other factors that are likely to affect the underlying trade flows, including the output and exchange rate changes that occurred in 1990, the increase in the price of oil following the Kuwait crisis, and the worsening of economic conditions in the U.S.S.R., which may dominate the rest.[18]

Since the U.S.S.R. can expect to run current account surpluses with Eastern Europe, it has an obvious reason for wanting to use convertible currencies for settling CMEA payments; it wants to use its surpluses with the CMEA5 to cover its deficits with the rest of the world. That is why it was willing to countenance the demise of the TR. The interests and objectives of the CMEA5 are less clear. They want to *denominate* their payments in convertible currencies but not necessarily to make settlements in them. In other words, they were ready to replace the TR with a truly transferable means of payment but reluctant to shift immediately to a fully convertible means of payment.

The distinction between transferability and convertibility is a matter of degree. When a particular means of payment can be transferred freely to any entity in any country in exchange for goods or services, financial

---

by 30 percent, and the prices of other manufactures fall by 15 percent (rather than being unchanged). Here are the terms of trade and trade balance changes for the countries that report on the SITC basis:

	Czechoslovakia	Hungary	Poland
Terms of trade (percent)	−35.5	−39.3	−25.0
Trade balance (US$ billion)	−3.9	−2.2	−1.6

The terms of trade deteriorate more sharply and the trade balance effects are bigger, but the changes are not very different from those in Table 7.

[18] It should be noted, however, that cuts in Soviet oil exports of the sort that occurred in 1990 will not reduce the balance of payments problems of the CMEA5. Those countries have to buy more oil on the world market, and they are reporting reductions in their exports to the U.S.S.R., which has cut back its imports because of its own balance of payments problem.

Table 8. *Estimated Effects of Shifting to World Prices
on 1989 Current Account Balances*

(In millions of U.S. dollars)

Item	Bulgaria	Czechoslovakia	Hungary	Poland
		Actual		
Trade balance	507	−85	507	237
Services and				
transfers (net)	31	870	359	39
Current account	538	785	866	276
		Re-estimated		
Trade balance	−1,110	−3,670	−1,573	−1,243
Services and				
transfers (net)	31	870	359	39
Current account	−1,079	−2,800	−1,214	−1,204

Note: Data in TR converted to U.S. dollars at national cross rates.

assets, or another means of payment, it is fully convertible. Yet the difference of degree is crucial to the subject of this paper, which is concerned with the distinction between an external means of payment that can be transferred freely among the CMEA countries to pay for goods and services traded by those countries and one that can be swapped for fully convertible currencies and thus used for purchases from the outside world. (It is also important to distinguish between the use of a convertible currency for external settlements and convertibility of the domestic currency. Convertible currencies can be used for settlements without making the domestic currency convertible in any meaningful way. The countries of Western Europe made settlements in gold and dollars—among themselves and with other countries—long before making their own currencies convertible, even for current account transactions.)

Because the TR was not transferable, the CMEA countries could not make multilateral settlements, and bilateral balancing was inevitable. Insofar as the TR is replaced by a transferable means of payment, multilateral settlements will take place automatically and bilateral balancing will not be necessary. The CMEA countries will have no incentive to cut their exports to countries with which they have surpluses or raise them to countries with which they have deficits.[19] Nevertheless, they may

---

[19] Instances of this sort occurred in 1989; see Economic Commission for Europe (1990b, p. 3-70) and Lavigne (1990, p. 14). It should be noted that bilateralism can induce many forms of discrimination. A country that anticipates a surplus with one of its partners (or is a cumulative creditor under a bilateral payments arrangement) might seek to raise its imports rather than reduce its exports; conversely, a country that anticipates a deficit with one of its partners (or is a

have an incentive to export as little as possible to other CMEA countries and to import as much as possible from them, to keep goods at home for domestic consumption or sell them to outsiders for convertible currencies. Insofar as the TR is replaced by a fully convertible means of payment, by contrast, there will be no incentive to discriminate between trade with other CMEA countries and trade with the outside world.

The conventional assessment of postwar experience in Western Europe, reviewed in the next part of this paper, would lead one to recommend an immediate move to transferability. The bilateral balancing of trade in Western Europe was viewed as a major obstacle to economic recovery, and the multilateralization of trade that followed the advent of transferability under the aegis of the EPU was viewed at the time as making a major contribution to trade liberalization and thus to the growth of trade in the 1950s. Analogies are dangerous, however, and three caveats are in order.

First, the coverage of transferability was much larger in the case of Western Europe than it would be in the case of Eastern Europe. The EPU included the entire sterling area and the overseas dependencies of France, Belgium, and Portugal. Therefore, it covered most of Africa and Asia, as well as parts of the Western Hemisphere.[20] The metropolitan members, moreover, were much larger economically than the CMEA countries are today. They accounted for 35 percent of world exports in 1950, while the CMEA countries accounted for less than 4 percent in 1989.

Second, transferability by itself should eliminate discrimination in intra-CMEA trade, but it may not contribute greatly to trade liberalization. No CMEA country will want to run a current account surplus with the rest, even as a group, if it has a deficit with the outside world. By implication, the size and automaticity of future credit arrangements may have more influence on trade liberalization than the shift to transferability itself. The importance of this point is underscored by the EPU experience. The credit arrangements of the EPU were much harder to negotiate than the clearing arrangements, and it might have been impossible

---

cumulative debtor) might seek to reduce its imports rather than raise its exports. All of these possibilities distort trade, but some do not reduce it. The trade-reducing tendencies may dominate, however, when countries face excess domestic demand or current account deficits with the outside world. It is hard for deficit countries to increase their exports and thus hard for surplus countries to increase their imports.

[20] This point is stressed by Tew (1988), who describes the global economy of the 1950s as a "binary world" comprising the dollar area and the EPU area. (Japan did not belong to either but was not a major trading country in the early 1950s.)

to reach agreement if the United States had not used Marshall Plan money to make "side payments" to countries such as Belgium that expected to be creditors in the EPU.

Third, even if transferability leads to trade liberalization, there may not be a rapid increase in trade among the CMEA5. There are opportunities for trade expansion, along the lines mentioned earlier, but it may take a long time to exploit them. An extensive restructuring of output will be needed at a time when the countries of Eastern Europe are more urgently concerned with acquiring Western markets, for political as well as economic reasons.

It is also worth noting that Western Europe had well-functioning domestic markets in the 1950s and did not need to import them from the outside world. Hence, rapid progress toward current account convertibility was less urgent for Western Europe than it is for Eastern Europe.[21]

III. The European Payments Union

The currencies of Western Europe were not convertible in 1950, even for current account purposes, and transferability was strictly limited outside the sterling area and similar zones. Payments for trade in Western Europe took place through a network of bilateral agreements having built-in credit lines. Payments for imports were centralized at the central bank level and were cleared at the end of each month by netting credits against debits. Balances were settled bilaterally by building up a creditor and debtor position until the limit of each credit line was reached. After that, the deficit country had to pay gold or dollars to the surplus country. Attempts were made to multilateralize these arrangements in 1948 and 1949, using small amounts of Marshall Plan money, but were not very successful.[22]

Industrial production had recovered handsomely in Western Europe and was above its prewar level in 1950, except in Germany, but the growth of output was slowing down. Furthermore, the volume of trade was far below its prewar level, and trade liberalization was widely viewed as a precondition to the further growth of output. But trade could not be liberalized easily unless payments were liberalized too, which is why the EPU was organized.

---

[21] I owe this important point to John Williamson.
[22] See Kaplan and Schleiminger (1989) and Triffin (1957), the main sources used in this and the next section.

Structure and Functioning of the EPU

The design of the EPU was influenced by the bilateral arrangements it replaced. Importers of goods from other EPU countries continued to make payments in their own countries' currencies, and bilateral balances were built up at each country's central bank. At the end of each month, however, the Bank for International Settlements (BIS), which served as agent for the EPU, collected and consolidated those balances and converted them into a single number for each member country—its surplus or deficit for that month vis-à-vis the EPU. This multilateral clearing obviated the need for each country to make a bilateral settlement with every other country; it had merely to settle its surplus or deficit with the EPU.

The form of the monthly settlement depended on the country's balance for the current month and its cumulative position compared to its EPU quota. (A country's cumulative position was the sum of its monthly surpluses and deficits from the first month on, not what it had lent or borrowed in the course of settling them.) When a country had a cumulative deficit, it received or made gold payments, depending on the sign of its balance for the current month, in keeping with the schedule for cumulative deficits shown in Table 9, and settled the rest of its monthly balance by granting or receiving credit on the books of the EPU. When a country had a cumulative surplus, it received or made gold payments in keeping with the schedule for cumulative surpluses.

When a country had a cumulative deficit and went on running deficits, it had to make larger gold payments to the EPU and received less credit; when its cumulative deficit was equal to its EPU quota, it ran out of credit and had to settle completely in gold. The rules for countries with cumu-

Table 9. *Initial Schedule of Settlements in the EPU*

(Percent of current deficit or surplus)

Cumulative Surplus or Deficit (percentage of EPU quota)	Country with Cumulative Deficit		Country with Cumulative Surplus	
	Gold	Credit	Gold	Credit
From 0 to 20 percent	0	100	0	100
From 20 to 40 percent	20	80	50	50
From 40 to 60 percent	40	60	50	50
From 60 to 80 percent	60	40	50	50
From 80 to 100 percent	80	20	50	50
Overall percentage	40	60	40	60

lative surpluses were less clear. When a country's cumulative surplus was equal to its quota, it could not count on earning gold in an amount equal to its subsequent surplus, because it could be asked to give more credit to the EPU.

This open-ended obligation helped to protect the liquidity of the EPU. Nevertheless, the EPU could expect to experience gold losses from time to time because of asymmetries built into the system. It would experience a gold loss if the countries having deficits in the current month were at the low end of the schedule for cumulative deficits. Their gold payments would be small compared to the payments that the EPU would have to make to the corresponding surplus countries. The same thing could happen if the countries running deficits had large quotas and those running surpluses had small quotas (unless the surplus countries granted extra credits). To deal with these possibilities, the United States put $350 million of Marshall Plan money into the EPU, which proved to be sufficient.

The EPU agreement was renewed periodically, and major changes in the schedules were made on two occasions. In July 1954 the schedules for cumulative surpluses and deficits were unified, using a flat 50 percent gold ratio for all quota ranges; in August 1955 the uniform ratio was raised to 75 percent. These changes "hardened" EPU settlements; they reduced the gap between the terms for settling imbalances within Western Europe and the terms for settling them with the dollar area—the convertible currency countries of that era.

The operations of the EPU are summarized in Table 10, which shows the grand total of bilateral balances that were reported to the BIS, those that were settled multilaterally, those that were reversed as countries that

Table 10. *EPU Settlements, 1950–58*

(In billions of U.S. dollars)

Item	Amount
Total bilateral positions (deficits plus surpluses)	46.4
Compensations	
Multilateral	20.0
Through time	12.6
Special settlements and adjustments	0.4
Balance to be settled	13.4
Settled in gold and dollars	10.7
Settled in credit	2.7

Source: Kaplan and Schleiminger (1989, Table 10).

ran deficits offset them with surpluses, and those that had to be settled with the EPU itself, by gold and dollar payments and EPU credits. The credit figure is very small but understates the role of credit in the EPU system. It shows what was outstanding when the EPU was terminated, not what was extended from month to month or year to year. In 1951–52, for example, one of the more active years, net credits accounted for 44 percent of total settlements, compared with only 16 percent for the longer period covered by Table 10 (Triffin (1957, Table 26)).

Contribution of the EPU

Western Europe made remarkable progress during the EPU years. Trade was liberalized rapidly and expanded hugely. In 1950, 44 percent of private trade in Western Europe was subject to quantitative controls, along with 89 percent of trade between Western Europe and the dollar area; by 1959, the figures had fallen to 11 percent for trade in Western Europe and to 28 percent for trade with the dollar area.[23] Intra-European imports grew from $10.1 billion in 1950 to $23.3 billion in 1959, and imports from North America grew from $3.9 billion to $6.1 billion. (Data from Kaplan and Schleiminger (1989, Table 8).) In 1958, moreover, the major countries of Western Europe made their currencies convertible for current account purposes, and the EPU was terminated. It is hard, however, to assess precisely what the EPU contributed to these results.

The EPU did contribute to the multilateralization of settlements within Western Europe and to the conservation of official reserves. Under the interim arrangements of 1948 and 1949, bilateral balances totaled $4.4 billion, of which $1.3 billion was settled in gold and dollars, $3.0 billion was financed with bilateral credit, and only $0.1 billion was offset multilaterally (Triffin (1957, pp. 156–57)). In the first year of the EPU, by contrast, bilateral balances totaled $6.0 billion after applying Marshall Plan aid, of which only $0.8 billion was settled in gold and dollars, $2.2 billion was financed with EPU credit, and $3.0 billion was offset multilaterally (Triffin (1957, Table 26)).

---

[23] The liberalization of trade with the dollar area deserves particular attention. Most discussions of the EPU (for example, Triffin (1957, pp. 203 ff)) say that the United States accepted more discrimination against it as the price it was willing to pay for European integration—one of the main objectives of the Marshall Plan. An intensification of discrimination did occur in the early years of the EPU, when liberalization within Europe took place more rapidly than liberalization with the dollar area. The latter was more dramatic in the end, however, and reduced discrimination against the United States.

Furthermore, Kaplan and Schleiminger (1989) argue convincingly that the Managing Board of the EPU contributed importantly to the solution of major balance of payments problems, including the German crisis of 1951, which erupted right after the EPU began to operate. The Board made supplementary credit available to countries that had exhausted their EPU credit lines, and it monitored their domestic policies more closely than the International Monetary Fund (IMF) does today.[24]

Finally, the EPU helped to keep its member governments "on track" as they moved toward convertibility. The hardening of settlements within the EPU, described above, diminished the practical distinction between transferability and convertibility, because gold and dollars became more important in EPU settlements. Furthermore, discussions in the EPU Board helped the governments to formulate a common approach to convertibility.

The multilateralization of payments and the credit arrangements of the EPU were viewed at the time as preconditions for trade liberalization within Western Europe, and the hardening of EPU settlements probably encouraged liberalization with the dollar area. It is essential, however, to distinguish between necessary and sufficient preconditions. Trade liberalization was achieved during the life of the EPU, but it was monitored separately by the Organization for European Economic Cooperation. There was an agreed schedule for removing quantitative trade controls, and strong pressure was brought to bear on governments that fell behind. Liberalization was deemed to be part of the larger process of European integration, which was strongly supported in Washington as well as in Europe. If European governments had not been agreed on the need for liberalization per se and not been prodded by Washington when their own energies flagged, the payments arrangements of the EPU might not have done the job. The timid might have held back the rest, slowing the pace of liberalization.

One more point should be made. The circumstances and intellectual environment of the 1950s worked to rule out a "dash for convertibility" by Western Europe. The British thought briefly about floating the pound and making it convertible unilaterally, but Washington objected, partly because it opposed the delay of trade liberalization on which the plan was predicated (Kaplan and Schleiminger (1989, chap. 10)). Therefore, the

---

[24] The IMF itself did not have much influence on European policies in the early years of the EPU, partly because it had decided that countries receiving Marshall Plan aid should draw on the IMF only in "exceptional circumstances," so that its resources would be available intact after the Marshall Plan had ended. On relations between the IMF and the EPU, see de Vries (1969).

contributions of the EPU should be appraised as they were above, by
comparing the payments regime of the 1950s with the bilateral regime
that preceded it. A different frame of reference is needed, however, to
assess the potential contributions of an EEPU. The CMEA system has
disintegrated, and the TR is defunct. Hence, the contributions of an
EEPU should be appraised by comparison with the use of convertible
currencies for CMEA settlements.[25]

IV. An Eastern European Payments Union

A payments union for the CMEA countries could follow the basic
design of the EPU. Each country would have a quota, based on its trade
with the others, and its rights and obligations would be defined by its
cumulative surplus or deficit compared to its quota. The workings of an
EEPU can be illustrated by a simple numerical example. In this particular
example, 50 percent of each member's surplus or deficit is settled by
giving or getting credit, and the other 50 percent is settled in convertible
currency (the formula adopted by the EPU in 1954).

Functioning of an EEPU

Consider a hypothetical EEPU comprising four countries, Czechoslovakia, Hungary, Poland, and the U.S.S.R., and these bilateral balances,
as shown in Table 11.

Table 11. *Bilateral Balances to Be Settled in a Hypothetical EEPU*

(In millions of U.S. dollars)

Reporting Country	Partner Country				
	Czechoslovakia	Hungary	Poland	U.S.S.R.	Total
Czechoslovakia	—	+300	−50	−200	+50
Hungary	−300	—	+200	0	−100
Poland	+50	−200	—	−150	−300
U.S.S.R.	+200	0	+150	—	+350

The balances are expressed in millions of dollars, and the description that
follows assumes that payments and credits are likewise expressed in
dollars, but other convertible currencies could be used instead. (It would
also be possible to use the SDR or ECU as the unit of account.) Begin

[25] This point must be borne in mind when appraising proposals such as those
of Daviddi and Espa (1989) that were drafted before the Sofia meeting of the
CMEA.

with the case in which the countries' cumulative surpluses and deficits are smaller than their quotas, so the countries with surpluses during the current month will give credit to the EEPU, and the countries with deficits will get credit.

Under the old CMEA system, bilateral balances like those shown above would have appeared and remained on the books of IBEC (and would have been expressed in TR rather than dollars). Czechoslovakia would have built up its credit balance with Hungary or run down its debit balance, and so on. With settlements in convertible currencies, by contrast, Czechoslovakia would receive $300 million from Hungary but pay $50 million to Poland and $200 million to the U.S.S.R., so its total dollar holdings would rise by $50 million. With an EEPU, bilateral balances would be consolidated, so that Czechoslovakia would have a $50 million surplus. Hence, it would receive $25 million in dollars from the EEPU (half of its monthly surplus) and extend $25 million in credit to the EEPU. Poland, by contrast, would have a $300 million deficit, would pay $150 million to the EEPU, and would receive $150 million in credit.

This process would go on, month after month, until one of the members reached its credit ceiling. If that country had a cumulative surplus, its subsequent monthly surpluses would be settled entirely by dollar payments from the EEPU, and the EEPU could thus experience a net outflow of dollars; if it had a cumulative deficit, its subsequent deficits would be settled entirely by dollar payments to the EEPU, and the EEPU could experience a net inflow of dollars.

An EEPU might seem to be disadvantageous for Czechoslovakia and the U.S.S.R.—the surplus countries in this hypothetical example. If settlements were made entirely in convertible currencies, Czechoslovakia would earn $50 million from its partners, rather than $25 million from the EEPU, and could use the extra dollars to import more from the outside world. If it expected to run such surpluses steadily—to be a "structural creditor" in the EEPU—it might not want to join. If it did not join, however, its partners might have to cut down their imports from it, in order to reduce their dollar losses. Furthermore, surpluses do not always last. A country with a surplus this year may have a deficit next year, and the credit facilities of the EEPU would reduce the dollar losses resulting from that deficit.

Membership, Quotas, and Capital

Who would belong to an EEPU? How big should the quotas be? How much capital would be needed?

It would be extremely hard to include East Germany (formerly the

Table 12. *Hypothetical Quotas for an EEPU*

(In millions of U.S. dollars)

Country	Large EEPU	Small EEPU
Bulgaria	1,450	250
Czechoslovakia	2,035	730
Hungary	1,330	415
Poland	2,045	675
Romania	760	240
U.S.S.R.	5,370	—
Total	12,990	2,310

German Democratic Republic) in an EEPU, because it uses a convertible currency. There would be huge technical difficulties, as the trade and payments of East Germany would have to be segregated from those of Germany as a whole (and those of the rest of the European Community), in order to measure and settle its monthly balance with the CMEA countries. German unification may cause serious problems for some CMEA countries, and special remedies may be needed, including, perhaps, medium-term credits to avoid a sharp fall in German imports from the CMEA countries. It may be best to handle these matters bilaterally, however, between Germany as a whole, on the one hand, and the individual CMEA countries, on the other. Therefore, the discussion that follows, dealing with EEPU quotas and capital, will concentrate on two possibilities: a "large" EEPU comprising the CMEA5 and the U.S.S.R., and a "small" EEPU confined to the CMEA5.

When the EPU was being negotiated in 1950, a benchmark was needed to bargain about quotas. With two exceptions (Belgium and Switzerland), quotas were set at 15 percent of each member's visible and service trade (the sum of its exports and imports) with the rest of the EPU area in 1949. It is hard to apply this formula to an EEPU, because there are gaps in the data on trade in services. As an approximation, suppose that quotas were set at 20 percent of each member's visible trade with the others in 1989.[26] The quotas for a large EEPU, including the U.S.S.R., and for a small EEPU, excluding it, are shown in Table 12.

---

[26] In the case of Czechoslovakia, service exports to the whole CMEA area (including the German Democratic Republic) amounted to 14 percent of merchandise exports in 1988, and service imports amounted to 5 percent of merchandise imports. Thus, the 20 percent figure used instead of the 15 percent EPU figure may make an overly large allowance for omitting services. But the 20 percent figure makes no allowance for the effects of shifting trade to world prices. The underlying trade statistics are those that were used to construct Table 3.

What do these numbers say about the capitalization of an EEPU? How many dollars would it have to hold to honor its obligations fully? Its exposure to net dollar payments can be measured by asking what would happen if the member with the largest quota ran a long string of deficits, the one with the smallest quota ran a long string of surpluses, and no other country had a surplus or deficit. These imbalances would minimize the dollar receipts of the EEPU and maximize its dollar payments. A large EEPU would have to start out holding $2.3 billion (half of the difference between the quotas of the U.S.S.R. and Romania), an amount that would equal about 18 percent of total quotas. A small EEPU would have to start with only $245 million, an amount that would equal about 11 percent of total quotas. (Recall that the EPU began with $350 million, an amount equal to 9 percent of total quotas.) But the big figure for the large EEPU is based on an unrealistic supposition; the U.S.S.R. is likely to run surpluses, not deficits, which means that the EEPU would gain dollars rather than lose them.

The members of an EEPU might be willing to provide some of the capital, but most of it might have to come from Western governments or international institutions.

Benefits and Costs of an EEPU

What would an EEPU accomplish? If it had been introduced before 1990 to replace the bilateral arrangements based on the TR, it would have contributed to the multilateralization of CMEA payments and thus encouraged more efficient trade and specialization among the CMEA countries. But the shift to convertible currency settlements now taking place will do so too. In this sense, proposals for an EEPU represent solutions looking for a problem.

The case for an EEPU, then, must stand or fall on the contribution it might make to liberalizing trade and payments or, defensively, what it might do to keep trade from contracting in the face of impending balance of payments pressures. In other words, the credit facilities provided by an EEPU would be far more important than the clearing arrangements.

Two potential costs of an EEPU must be borne in mind, even though they cannot be quantified.

First, creation of an EEPU would probably interfere with the relaxation of exchange controls. A country participating in a payments union is obliged to centralize its payments to its partners; the central bank must record them on its books in order to report them to the agent for the union. That is, of course, the way in which the CMEA countries managed their accounts with IBEC. But some countries in Eastern Europe have already moved away from this sort of centralization. Exporters are paid in foreign currency and sell it to the central bank, unless they are authorized to retain and use it; importers buy foreign currency from the central bank, directly or by way of the foreign exchange market. (To this extent, of course, convertible currency settlements occur automatically; there is no need to arrange them on a government-to-government basis.) Creation of an EEPU, then, would involve a step backward—the recentralization of transactions with the other members.

Second, the creation of an EEPU might encourage the CMEA countries to liberalize their trade with each other at the expense of trade with the rest of the world, since EEPU credit could be used to finance imbalances within the CMEA area but not imbalances with the rest of the world. An intensification or prolongation of discrimination against the rest of the world would be unfortunate, because it would interfere with domestic reform. Recall the argument made earlier, that the CMEA countries should import world markets and world prices in order to accelerate the process of reform.

This second cost could be far higher than the first and much harder to control. Discrimination against goods from the outside world is, of course, the counterpart of preferential treatment for goods produced within Eastern Europe—the treatment that some experts recommend explicitly to prevent a contraction of trade in the CMEA area and the corresponding cuts in output and employment. There was an intensification of discrimination against the dollar area in the early years of the EPU, but it was reversed thereafter. The reversal, however, reflected the commitment to trade liberalization by the governments of Western Europe, as well as occasional prodding by the United States.

Participation in an EEPU would not require the CMEA countries to move together, in strict lockstep, to liberalize trade within Eastern Europe or with the outside world. The EPU countries did not do so in the 1950s. Market economies, moreover, have traded extensively with planned economies without planning or controlling their own trade heavily. The bilateral arrangement between Finland, a market economy, and the U.S.S.R., a planned economy, worked well for many years without forcing Finland to control the operations of Finnish firms trading with the U.S.S.R. (see Oblath and Pete (1985)). Yet a common approach to liberalization would perhaps be needed to keep an EEPU from discouraging trade with the outside world, and an attempt to formulate a common approach could conceivably retard trade reform in countries, such as Hungary and Poland, that have moved faster than the rest.

Turning from potential costs to potential benefits, a small EEPU would not be very powerful in promoting trade among its members. It would not be able to promise much financing, compared to the balance of payments needs of its members, since the level of EEPU lending would be tied mechanically to the level of imbalances among the CMEA5, and these are not likely to be large compared to prospective imbalances with the U.S.S.R. or the rest of the world. (The balance of payments effects of the "defection" of the German Democratic Republic may be much larger than the effects of liberalizing trade among the CMEA5.) Even if a small EEPU were successful in encouraging the CMEA5 to liberalize trade within Eastern Europe, the volume of trade might not grow very fast and would not lead to large imbalances within the area. Hence, the CMEA5 may be able to get along easily without an EEPU and should use convertible currencies to settle imbalances among themselves.

A large EEPU might be more effective. Its effectiveness in the short run, however, would reflect its contribution to the financing of prospective imbalances between the CMEA5 and the U.S.S.R. and would therefore depend on the willingness of the U.S.S.R. to lend to an EEPU. This possibility should not be ruled out. Participation would be costly for the U.S.S.R., which cannot readily forgo convertible currency earnings. Refusal would be costly too, however, because it would burden the countries of Eastern Europe with a serious balance of payments problem just when they are trying to stabilize and reform their economies. Furthermore, trade between the CMEA5 and the U.S.S.R. will continue to be mutually beneficial. Eastern Europe can provide manufactured goods that the U.S.S.R. will continue to require, and it would be expensive for the U.S.S.R. to divert its oil and other exports to more distant markets. The CMEA5 and the U.S.S.R. want to expand their trade with the West but should not want to disrupt their trade with each other.

It might be necessary to make "side payments" to the U.S.S.R. to induce it to participate in an EEPU, much like the payments made to Belgium in 1950, when it was reluctant to be a structural creditor in the EPU. In that case, however, the value of the exercise will come to depend on a judgment about the comparative merits of making balance of payments credit available to Eastern Europe through the U.S.S.R. and an EEPU and making that credit available directly, through the IMF and other institutions. A strong case can be made for following this second course (and thus attaching appropriate conditions to use of the credit), rather than setting up a new institution and compelling the governments of Eastern Europe to cooperate closely with the U.S.S.R. in monetary matters.

Debate about this issue, however, should not be allowed to obscure the fundamental problem posed by the impending shift to trade at world

PETER B. KENEN

prices. Eastern Europe will experience a significant deterioration in its terms of trade with the U.S.S.R. and is likely to run large balance of payments deficits that will have to be settled in convertible currencies. The magnitude of the problem will depend on the speed with which the shift takes place—whether it occurs rapidly in 1991 or is phased in gradually. The problem could be mitigated, moreover, if the U.S.S.R. could be persuaded to make modest amounts of medium-term credit available on an ad hoc basis, and it might be prepared to do that even if it was not willing to join a full-fledged payments union. Whatever the size and timing of the problem, however, the countries of Eastern Europe will need help to solve it.

REFERENCES

Bofinger, Peter, "A Multilateral Payments Union for Eastern Europe?" CEPR Discussion Paper No. 458 (London: Centre for Economic Policy Research, 1990).

Daviddi, Renzo, and Efisio Espa, "The Economics of Ruble Convertibility: New Scenarios for the Soviet Monetary Economy," *Banca Nazionale del Lavoro Quarterly Review,* No. 171 (December 1989).

de Vries, Margaret G., "The Fund and the EPU," in *The International Monetary Fund, 1945–1969; Volume II: Analysis,* ed. by Margaret G. de Vries and J. Keith Horsefield (Washington: International Monetary Fund, 1969).

Economic Commission for Europe (1990a), *Economic Bulletin for Europe,* Vol. 42 (Geneva: United Nations).

——— (1990b), *Economic Survey of Europe 1989–90* (Geneva: United Nations).

Ethier, Wilfred J., "Proposal for an Eastern European Payments Union" (unpublished; Philadelphia: University of Pennsylvania, May 1990).

Hardt, John P., "The Soviet Economy in Crisis and Transformation" (unpublished; Brussels: NATO Economic Colloquium, April 1990).

International Monetary Fund, *International Financial Statistics* (Washington: International Monetary Fund, various issues).

Kaplan, Jacob J., and Gunther Schleiminger, *The European Payments Union* (Oxford: Oxford University Press, 1989).

Lavigne, Marie, "Economic Relations Between Eastern Europe and the USSR: Bilateral Ties vs. Multilateral Cooperation" (unpublished; Brussels: NATO Economic Colloquium, April 1990).

Marrese, Michael, and Lauren Wittenberg, "Implicit Trade Subsidies within the CMEA: A Hungarian Perspective" (unpublished; Evanston, Illinois: Northwestern University, January 1990).

Michalopoulos, Constantine, "Payments Arrangements in Eastern Europe in the Post-CMEA Era" (unpublished; Washington: World Bank, 1990).

Oblath, G., and P. Pete, "Trade with the Soviet Union: The Finnish Case," *Acta Oeconomica,* Vol. 35 (1985), pp. 165–94.

Schrenk, Martin, "The CMEA System of Trade and Payments: Today and Tomorrow," Discussion Paper No. 5, World Bank Strategic Planning and Review Department (Washington: World Bank, 1990).

Soros, George, *Opening the Soviet System* (London: Weidenfeld and Nicolson, 1990).

Tew, Brian, *The Evolution of the International Monetary System, 1945–88* (London: Hutchinson, 1988).

Triffin, Robert, *Europe and the Money Muddle* (New Haven: Yale University Press, 1957).

van Brabant, Joseph M., *Adjustment, Structural Change and Economic Efficiency: Aspects of Monetary Cooperation in Eastern Europe* (Cambridge: Cambridge University Press, 1987).

————, "Convertibility in Eastern Europe Through a Payments Union" (unpublished; Washington: Institute for International Economics, September 1990).

Wolf, Thomas A., *Foreign Trade in the Centrally Planned Economy* (New York: Harwood, 1988).

————, "Market-Oriented Reform of Foreign Trade in Planned Economies," IMF Working Paper WP/90/28 (Washington: International Monetary Fund, 1990).

World Bank (1990a), *World Development Report 1990* (Washington: World Bank).

———— (1990b), *Socialist Economies in Transition* (Washington: World Bank, April).

[23]

The European Central Bank and

monetary policy in stage three of

EMU

PETER B. KENEN

If all goes according to the plan adopted at the Maastricht summit, the European Community will have a single central bank before the end of the century and a single currency soon thereafter. How will the European Central Bank (ECB) be organized? What powers and duties will it have? How will it conduct monetary policy? Peter Kenen proposes answers to those questions by drawing on the text of the treaty approved at Maastricht and filling some of the gaps on the basis of experience in the United States, where the Federal Reserve System has had to solve some of the same problems that will confront the ECB. He starts by reviewing the recommendations of the Delors report, on which the treaty is based, then turns to the treaty itself before taking up some operational problems that the treaty poses but does not solve.

The Delors report

In June 1988, the Hanover summit reaffirmed the Community's commitment to the 'progressive realization of economic and monetary union' and appointed a committee, chaired by Jacques Delors, president of the EC Commission, to develop 'concrete stages' aimed at that objective. The committee was asked to report to the Madrid summit in June 1989.

The Delors report began by listing the three basic attributes of monetary union: full currency convertibility, complete integration of financial markets and irrevocable locking of exchange rates. As the first and second already obtain in Europe, it has to focus on the third. But Europe should go further:

The adoption of a *single currency*, while not strictly necessary for the creation of a monetary union, might be seen ... as a natural and desirable further development of the monetary union. A single currency would clearly demonstrate the irreversibility of the ... monetary union, considerably facilitate the monetary management of the Community and avoid the transactions costs of converting currencies ... The replacement of national currencies by a single currency should therefore take place as soon as possible after the locking of parities. (para. 23)[1]

[1] The quotations in this section are taken from the *Report of the Committee for the Study of Economic and Monetary Union* (Delors report, Luxembourg: Office for Official Publications of the European Communities, 1989). Paragraph numbers are given in parentheses; italics are in original text.

Peter B. Kenen

The creation of a monetary union, however, would have far-reaching implications for monetary policy:

> Once permanently fixed exchange rates had been adopted, there would be a *need for a common monetary policy*, which would be carried out through new operating procedures. The coordination of...national monetary policies...would not be sufficient. The responsibility for the single monetary policy would have to be vested in a new institution, in which centralized and collective decisions would be taken on the supply of money and credit as well as on other instruments of monetary policy, including interest rates. This shift from national monetary policies to a single monetary policy is an inescapable consequence of monetary union and constitutes one of the principal institutional changes. (para. 24)

These observations led the committee to recommend that the EC establish a European System of Central Banks (ESCB), comprising a central institution and the national central banks. The ESCB would design and implement monetary policy for the Community and manage its exchange rate policy *vis-à-vis* third currencies. The national central banks would be entrusted with implementation. The ESCB would have a fourfold mandate:

> The System would be committed to the objective of price stability;

> Subject to the foregoing, the System should support the general economic policy set at the Community level by the competent bodies;

> The System would be responsible for the formulation and implementation of monetary policy, exchange rate and reserve management, and the maintenance of a properly functioning payment system.

> The System would participate in the coordination of banking supervision policies of the supervisory authorities. (para. 32)

Most of these recommendations found their way to Maastricht, along with the committee's recommendations regarding the organization and powers of the ESCB.

The committee proposed a three-stage process for reaching EMU. Stage one would see completion of the internal market, enlargement of the structural funds to reduce regional disparities in the EC and introduction of a comprehensive framework for policy surveillance and coordination. Fiscal coordination would be based on 'precise quantitative guidelines' and provide for 'concerted budgetary action' (para. 51). Stage one would also see the intensification of monetary coordination, and all of the EC currencies would join the exchange rate mechanism of the European Monetary System (EMS). Exchange rate realignments might still occur, but efforts would be made to improve other adjustment mechanisms.

In stage two, policy surveillance would be strengthened, limits would be imposed on national budget deficits (but would not be binding until stage three) and the Community *per se* would begin to participate in international

The ECB and stage three of EMU

discussions on exchange rate management and policy coordination. The ECB would be established, take over the tasks of the European Monetary Cooperation Fund (EMCF), which administers the credit arrangements of the EMS, and begin to move from the coordination of national monetary policies to the design of a common monetary policy. Realignments would take place only in exceptional circumstances.

Stage three would begin with the irrevocable locking of exchange rates: the ESCB would assume full control over monetary policy. Eventually, a single currency would be issued to replace the members' national currencies. Official reserves would be transferred to the ESCB, which would take responsibility for intervention *vis-à-vis* third currencies.

In June 1989, the Madrid summit received the Delors report and decided that stage one should start in July 1990. In December 1989, the Strasbourg summit decided to convene an intergovernmental conference (IGC) to work on the subsequent stages. In June 1990, the Dublin summit agreed to convene *two* conferences—one on economic and monetary union and the other on political union—and asked them to finish their work in time for the ratification of amendments to the Treaty of Rome by the end of 1992, the deadline for completing the internal market.

These decisions would seem to reflect widespread acceptance of the Delors report, but basic disagreements developed immediately. Some governments wanted to complete EMU quickly; they believed that rapid institutional change would induce the necessary adaptations in economic policies and performance. Other governments wanted economic convergence to take place before the creation of the ECB; they believed that this would protect the ECB against political pressures from countries that had failed to reduce their inflation rates and might want the ECB to pursue a monetary policy less stringent than required to achieve price stability. The first view, held by France and Italy, endorsed the recommendation in the Delors report that the ECB should be created in stage two: an ECB in being would help to maintain political momentum. The second view, held by Germany and the Netherlands, questioned that recommendation: institutional change might outstrip economic convergence, and ECB involvement in the conduct of monetary policy would be inconsistent with the indivisibility of operational responsibility.[2]

The United Kingdom raised fundamental questions about the ultimate aims of EMU. It supported the completion of the internal market but not the creation of a ECB at some fixed date in the future or the introduction of a single currency. It agreed to the beginning of stage one but favoured an 'evolutionary approach' thereafter.[3] Later, it introduced its own proposal, involving the creation of a European Monetary Fund to issue a 'hard ECU' in exchange for national currencies. The hard ECU could not be devalued against

---

[2] See A. Crockett, 'The role of stage II', paper presented at the Estoril Conference on the Transition to Economic and Monetary Union in Europe, 1991.

[3] See HM Treasury, *An evolutionary approach to economic and monetary union* (London: HMSO, 1989).

Peter B. Kenen

any other EC currency and would compete with them in the private sector. If successful in this competition, it would gradually become the common currency of the Community and might even become the single currency in the long run.[4]

These issues were debated at the Rome summit in October 1990, where eleven EC governments agreed to start stage two in January 1994 and listed the steps to be taken in stage three. Exchange rates would be locked, there would be a single currency, and a new institution would take over the conduct of monetary policy, with price stability as its primary aim. But the governments refrained from endorsing any transfer of responsibility in stage two; during this period the new institution would merely coordinate national policies, develop the instruments needed in stage three to conduct a single policy and oversee development of the ECU. The starting date for stage three would depend on the degree of convergence achieved in previous stages. The United Kingdom was the lone dissenter. It was willing to move beyond stage one by creating a new institution and a common currency, but 'common' rather than 'single' was meant to endorse the hard ECU rather than the strategy favoured by its partners.

The transition to stage three

Early in its work, the IGC decided to create *two* new institutions: the European Monetary Institute (EMI), to be established in January 1994, at the start of stage two, to coordinate national monetary policies and manage the transition to monetary union; and the ECB itself, to be established just before stage three begins. Furthermore, strict convergence criteria were adopted, not merely to decide if and when stage three should start, but also to determine which countries could participate. These decisions were embodied in a draft of the treaty prepared by the Netherlands presidency of the IGC. Although that draft was not fully acceptable to any EC government, it can be taken to describe the direction in which the IGC was moving six weeks before Maastricht.[5]

The transitional provisions instructed the Commission and the EMI to report to the Council of Ministers by the end of 1996 on the progress made by member states in meeting their obligations with regard to EMU and achieving a 'high degree of sustainable convergence' measured by specific quantitative criteria.[6] The Council would then decide which countries 'fulfil the necessary conditions for the adoption of a single currency' and recommend its findings to the European Council, which would determine whether it was appropriate to begin stage three and, if so, on what date. If it could not agree on a date, the

---

[4] See HM Treasury, *Economic and monetary union—beyond stage I: possible treaty provisions and statute for a European Monetary Fund* (London: HMSO, 1991); A. Crockett, 'Monetary integration in Europe', in J. A. Frenkel and M. Goldstein, eds, *International financial policy: essays in honor of Jacques J. Polak* (Washington DC: International Monetary Fund, 1991).

[5] Several such drafts were prepared for the IGC, but the draft dated 28 Oct. 1991 was the only one published.

[6] The criteria resemble those actually adopted at Maastricht, which appear in article 109j of the treaty and in a protocol attached to it.

The ECB and stage three of EMU

whole process would be repeated periodically. Those countries not ready to participate by the date agreed, because they had failed to meet the convergence criteria, would be granted derogations from their obligations under the relevant provisions of the treaty. No country would be forced to participate in stage three, however, if its parliament did not approve. It would be granted an 'exemption' with effects similar to a derogation.

These elaborate procedures were endorsed initially by those countries wanting to be sure that stage three would not start unless there was convergence; but others were unhappy with them, because they could postpone stage three indefinitely. Pessimists warned, moreover, that Britain might not be alone in wanting an exemption; Germany might want one too, and EMU without Germany would not be viable.[7]

Seeking to make sure that stage three could not be postponed indefinitely, France made a new proposal in the final hours of the IGC, and this was accepted at Maastricht. The procedures adopted at Maastricht differ from the Netherlands draft in a crucial respect: 'If by the end of 1997 the date for the beginning of the third stage has not been set, the third stage shall start on 1 January 1999.' No ifs, buts, or maybes. It will still be necessary to decide which countries are ready for stage three, so that the others can be granted derogations, but stage three will start automatically, even if the number of participants is small. Furthermore, there is no opt-out clause. Instead, two protocols are attached to the treaty allowing Britain and Denmark, but not others, to abstain from participating in stage three.[8] Although the ECB will not be established at the beginning of stage two to work for the early arrival of stage three, there is no way to keep stage three from starting in 1999 unless the EC countries agree unanimously to amend the treaty.[9]

As soon as the starting date has been set, but no later than July 1998, three steps will be taken.

(1) The executive board of the ECB will be appointed—the president, vice-president, and four other members. They will be chosen by 'common accord' of the EC governments participating in stage three, on the recommendation of the Council of Ministers, after consulting the European Parliament and the governing council of the ECB. Their terms will last eight years and not be renewable. (On this first round, however, the vice-president will serve for four years and the four other members for five to eight years, so that membership will rotate thereafter.)

---

[7] This concern may explain why Germany itself backed away from the idea even before the German press began to attack EMU. (Shortly before Maastricht, *Bild Zeitung* ran a banner headline, 'The mark to be abolished', and continued in this vein for several days, citing opinion polls opposed to EMU: see *Financial Times*, 6, 12 Dec. 1991.)

[8] The UK protocol says that 'the United Kingdom shall not be obliged or committed to move to the third stage of Economic and Monetary Union without a separate decision to do so by its government and Parliament' and lists the provisions of the treaty and ESCB statute that will not apply to the United Kingdom. The Danish protocol notes that a referendum may be needed before Denmark can participate in stage three and grants it an exemption if it cannot participate.

[9] The wording of the Maastricht text, however, may allow one other way to postpone stage three: by deciding before 1998 to start stage three on a date later than 1 Jan. 1999.

Peter B. Kenen

(2) The ECB will be established as soon as the executive board has been appointed and will exercise its powers from the first day of stage three. The EMI will be liquidated when the ECB is established.

(3) The Council of Ministers will adopt the legislation required by various articles of the ESCB statute. These pertain, *inter alia*, to the terms on which the ECB may issue regulations, impose reserve requirements and call up foreign exchange reserves from the national central banks.

On the first day of stage three, the Council of Ministers will adopt the irrevocably fixed exchange rates for the participating countries' currencies and the rates at which the ECU will replace them, 'and the ECU will become a currency in its own right'. It will take a while to substitute the ECU for the participants' national currencies. Every coin-using machine must be modified, all sorts of menus must be rewritten and thousands of computer programs must be amended.[10] But fewer changes will be needed at the 'wholesale' level. The ECB could keep its books in ECU from the first day of stage three, and the national central banks could shift to it too. Commercial banks would have to move in tandem with them in respect of their transactions with the central banks and one another, but not with the general public. This shift would make it easy to keep exchange rates fixed without intervening on foreign exchange markets.

The constitution of the ESCB

A draft of the ESCB statute was prepared by the Committee of Central Bank Governors, whose members had served on the Delors committee, and the IGC did not make many changes. The version adopted at Maastricht is remarkably similar to the governors' draft.[11]

The objectives of the ESCB are set out in Article 2 of the ESCB statute. It will have as its 'primary objective' the maintenance of price stability. Without prejudice to that objective, however, it shall support 'the general economic policies in the Community' to contribute to the realization of the policy objectives laid down in the treaty.[12] These objectives include 'sustainable and

---

[10] Introduction of the ECU will be complicated by the fact that no EC currency is equal in value to a convenient multiple or fraction of the ECU, and it is impossible to round up or down without changing exchange rates significantly; see A. Giovannini, 'The currency reform as the last stage of economic and monetary union', CEPR Discussion Paper 591 (London: Centre for Economic Policy Research, 1991); C. A. E. Goodhart, 'The ESCB after Maastricht' (London: London School of Economics, 1992).

[11] Portions of the ESCB statute are replicated in articles 105–8 of the treaty; for brevity, however, the statute alone is cited here. Elsewhere in this paper, I follow common practice and refer to the ECB when discussing monetary policy in stage three, but the rest of this section follows the statute and refers to the ESCB whenever the statute does so.

[12] There is a small but important difference between this phrasing and that of the governors' draft, which referred to the economic policy 'of' the Community. Apparently, 'of' was seen to invite the ESCB to disregard the policies of individual EC countries and seemed also to invite the Community to adopt a wide range of common policies. Article 103 of the treaty provides for the setting of guidelines but in somewhat weaker language.

The ECB and stage three of EMU

non-inflationary growth' and 'a high level of employment' (article 2 of the treaty). In other words, the ESCB must pay attention to growth and employment whenever it can do so without endangering price stability.

The tasks of the ESCB are set out in Article 3 of the statute:

to define and implement the monetary policy of the Community;

to conduct foreign exchange operations consistent with the provisions of Article 109 of this Treaty;

to hold and manage the official foreign reserves of the Member States;

to promote the smooth operation of payment systems.

In addition, the ESCB 'shall contribute to the smooth conduct of policies pursued by the competent authorities relating to the prudential supervision of credit institutions and the stability of the financial system'.

There are two important differences between this list and the one in the governors' draft—one half hidden and the other all too clear.

First, article 109 of the treaty, pertaining to exchange rate policy, contains provisions different from those the governors contemplated when they wrote their draft. Under certain circumstances, described below, the ESCB might have to intervene on foreign exchange markets even when this would be inconsistent with maintaining price stability.

Second, the governors' draft gave the ECB a much larger role in prudential supervision. It would have participated in 'the formulation, coordination and execution of policies relating to prudential supervision and the stability of the financial system', not merely 'contribute to the smooth functioning' of policies designed and pursued by others. But the governors left to the IGC the method by which the ECB would be so designated, and the IGC weakened the governors' draft in two vital ways. Under article 25 of the statute, the ECB 'may' offer advice and be consulted, which is weaker than the governors' 'is entitled to', and under article 105 of the treaty 'the Council may, acting unanimously on a proposal from the Commission and after consulting the ECB and after receiving the assent of the European Parliament, confer upon the ECB specific tasks concerning policies relating to the prudential supervision of credit institutions and other financial institutions with the exception of insurance undertakings'. No one could have built a higher set of hurdles.[13]

The Community's second banking directive creates a single market for banking services; the banks of every EC country will be free to establish branches or subsidiaries in all other EC countries. Under the principle of 'mutual recognition', they will be subject to home-country (consolidated) supervision but will have to conform to common capital adequacy standards. These rules by themselves, however, will not be adequate to protect the

---

[13] This reduction in the role of the ECB took place late in the IGC. In the Netherlands draft of 28 Oct., the wording of article 25 was closer to the governors' draft and there were fewer hurdles in the treaty; the Council was to act by qualified majority, and the assent of the Parliament was not required.

Peter B. Kenen

financial system from systemic risk; central banks must be involved. They need not assume complete responsibility for prudential supervision, which they share with other agencies in several EC countries. But the ECB must play a role, not only as lender of last resort, but also in every decision to close or restructure an individual bank.

Why the ECB and not the national central banks? They can and must be involved—and some will continue to supervise their own countries' banks. But serious conflicts could arise if one of them undertook to act as lender of last resort to domestic banks having severe liquidity problems and its lending were seen by the ECB as threatening the stance of monetary policy.

Begg *et al.* discount this possibility. They believe that this sort of lending can be offset completely by open market operations and thus need not interfere with price stability. But Chiappori *et al.* take a grimmer view, as do Folkerts-Landau and Garber.[14] Highly developed financial systems are very vulnerable to liquidity crises, which can disrupt the payments system or lead to large price changes on financial markets. To serve as lenders of last resort in these circumstances, central banks may have to operate aggressively in ways they cannot offset by open market operations. In fact, they may have to *use* open market operations to make enough credit available.

The ESCB will consist of the ECB and the national central banks, and it will be governed by the decision-making bodies of the ECB. The national central banks will be the only shareholders in the ECB, and their shares in its capital will reflect their countries' shares in the total population and GDP of the Community.

The ECB will have an executive board and governing council. The six board members will be voting members of the governing council, along with the governors of the national central banks. Certain financial decisions must be made by weighted voting, but all other decisions by the executive board and governing council will be taken by simple majority voting, with the president able to cast a tie-breaking vote.

The responsibilities of the two decision-making bodies are described in article 12 of the ESCB statute, which reads in part:

The Governing Council shall adopt the guidelines and take the decisions necessary to ensure the performance of the tasks entrusted to the ESCB under this Treaty and this Statute. The Governing Council shall formulate the monetary policy of the Community including, as appropriate, decisions relating to intermediate monetary objectives, key interest rates and the supply of reserves in the ESCB, and shall establish the necessary guidelines for their implementation.

The Executive Board shall implement monetary policy in accordance with the guidelines and decisions laid down by the Governing Council. In doing so the Executive Board shall give the necessary instructions to national central banks...

[14] D. Begg, F. Giavazzi, L. Spaventa and C. Wyplosz, 'European monetary union—the macro issues', and P. A. Chiappori, C. Mayer, D. Neven and X. Vives, 'The microeconomics of monetary union', both in *Monitoring European integration: the making of monetary union* (London: Centre for Economic Policy Research, 1991); D. Folkerts-Landau and P. M. Garber, 'The ECB: a bank or a monetary policy rule', paper presented at the Georgetown Conference on Establishing a Central Bank, 1991.

The ECB and stage three of EMU

To the extent deemed possible and appropriate...the ECB shall have recourse to the national central banks to carry out operations which form part of the tasks of the ESCB.

Note that the text is silent on one question: which body will decide when it is 'possible and appropriate' for the ECB to 'have recourse to' the national central banks? Will it be done by the governing council, when adopting 'guidelines' for implementing monetary policy, or by the board, when giving 'instructions' to the national central banks?

Although the ECB must make use of the national central banks when 'possible and appropriate', it may conduct open market and credit operations on its own account. Furthermore, the ESCB as a whole has wide powers in the monetary field.

The governing council will have the exclusive right to authorize the issue of bank notes in the ESCB countries, although the notes themselves may be issued by the ECB or by the national central banks; these will be the only notes with legal-tender status in the ESCB countries.

The ECB and national central banks may buy and sell securities and other claims, spot or forward, outright or for repurchase, and in EC or foreign currencies, and may borrow and lend securities. They may also conduct credit operations with banks and other institutions, but these must be based on adequate collateral.[15] The ECB may require banks to hold minimum reserves in accounts with the ECB or national central banks and may levy penalties for non-compliance.

Although the ECB and national central banks may not lend to governments or buy securities directly from them, they may act as fiscal agents.[16] They may also supply facilities—and the ECB may issue regulations—to 'ensure sufficient and sound clearing and payment systems' within the EC and with other countries.

By the start of stage three, foreign exchange holdings and other reserve assets held by the participating governments must be shifted to their central banks, and they in turn must transfer some of their reserves to the ECB. The use of reserves retained by the national central banks may be regulated by the ECB to ensure consistency with the Community's exchange rate and monetary policies.

But the powers of the ECB are likewise limited, because article 109 of the treaty divides responsibility for exchange rate policy between the Council of Ministers and the ECB. It has two major parts. First, the Council, acting unanimously, may conclude agreements on an exchange rate system for the ECU in relation to non-Community currencies. It must consult the ECB in an effort to achieve a 'consensus' consistent with price stability, but the

---

[15] The collateral requirement may call into question the ability of the ECB to act as lender of last resort. Credit institutions able to post adequate collateral can usually borrow commercially—unless financial markets are hit by a systemic crisis. The institutions needing central bank credit are those that might have trouble providing collateral.

[16] C. A. E. Goodhart, 'The ESCB after Maastricht' (London: London School of Economics, 1992), points out, however, that the prohibition of 'monetary financing' may force EC governments to establish commercial bank credit lines, which may lead them to shift other functions to private-sector institutions, and the national central banks may cease to serve as fiscal agents.

Peter B. Kenen

agreements made by the Council will be binding on the ECB, which must implement them even if they interfere with price stability. Second, the Council, acting by qualified majority, the Council may adopt 'general orientations' for exchange rate policy in relation to non-Community currencies; but these may not conflict with price stability. Until the Council takes one of these steps, the ECB is apparently free to decide whether to intervene on foreign exchange markets. Once the Council acts, however, the autonomy of the ECB will be circumscribed, not only with regard to exchange rate management but also in the conduct of monetary policy, because intervention on foreign exchange markets can affect the money supply.

Several provisions in the treaty and statute bear on the independence of the ECB. The most important is article 107 of the treaty, which applies to the ECB and to the national central banks:

When exercising the powers and carrying out the tasks and duties conferred upon them by this Treaty and the Statute of the ESCB, neither the ECB, nor a national central bank, nor any member of their decision-making bodies, shall seek or take instructions from Community institutions or bodies, from any Government of a Member State or from any other body. The Community institutions and bodies and the governments of the Member States undertake to respect this principle and not to seek to influence the members of the decision-making bodies of the ECB or of the national central banks in the performance of their tasks.

This injunction is reinforced by a prohibition cited earlier. As members of the executive board cannot be reappointed, they will have no incentive to please politicians—neither those of member governments nor those of the Community.[17] Under article 14 of the statute, moreover, the term of a national central bank governor can be no shorter than five years (though reappointment is not ruled out). Other articles protect the executive board and governors of national central banks from being dismissed arbitrarily. However, the president of the Council of Ministers and a member of the Commission may participate without vote in the governing council of the ECB, and the president of the Council may submit a motion for it to consider.

The fiscal provisions of the treaty are also meant to protect the independence of the ESCB, but may not be very effective in doing so. The prohibition of 'monetary financing' will prevent any government from forcing the ECB or its own national central bank to print high-powered money. Suppose, however, that a large EC country runs a big fiscal deficit. Even if it is not 'excessive' by the criteria in the treaty, the deficit may be big enough to pose a difficult problem for the ECB, much like that faced by the US Federal Reserve System in the early 1980s, when the United States began to run huge budget deficits. If the ECB does not alter its monetary policy, EC interest rates may rise, 'crowding out' domestic investment, and an inflow of foreign capital may

---

[17] B. Eichengreen, 'Toward a European central bank' (Berkeley: University of California Press, 1992), points out, however, that board members may try to please politicians precisely because their terms are non-renewable; they will need new jobs after eight years on the board. For more on this issue, see M. J. M. Neumann, 'Central bank independence as a prerequisite of price stability', in *The economics of EMU*, special issue of *European Economy*, 1, 1991.

The ECB and stage three of EMU

cause the ECU to appreciate on foreign exchange markets, 'crowding out' the domestic production of tradable goods. The ECB may have to engage in indirect 'monetary financing' by intervening on domestic financial markets to keep interest rates from rising, or intervening on foreign exchange markets to keep the ECU from rising.[18]

In what ways will the ESCB be accountable for its actions? It will publish quarterly reports and make an annual report to the Council, Commission, European Council and European Parliament, and the president of the ECB will present the report to the Council and the Parliament, which may debate it. Furthermore, the president and other members of the board may be heard by the appropriate committees of the Parliament, at the request of the Parliament or at their initiative. In one basic sense, however, the ESCB will be more independent than any other central bank—even the Bundesbank—and thus less accountable. The powers of the European Parliament *vis-à-vis* the ESCB are smaller than those of the Bundestag *vis-à-vis* the Bundesbank or those of the US Congress *vis-à-vis* the Federal Reserve System. Those two legislatures can amend the laws defining the powers and duties of their central banks and can even abolish the central banks by rescinding the relevant laws. But the ESCB statute is part of the treaty, and an amendment to the treaty must be ratified by every EC country.[19]

Monetary policy in stage three

Discussions of European monetary union often draw an analogy between the federal structure of the ESCB and that of the Federal Reserve System in the United States. The analogy is quite appropriate for some purposes but utterly inappropriate for others.

The analogy is appropriate and helpful for understanding how the ESCB can keep exchange rates irrevocably locked at the outset of stage three, before the ECU replaces the national currencies. No one worries about the credibility of the commitment made by each Federal Reserve Bank to exchange its own dollar bills for bills issued by the other Federal Reserve Banks, and the implementation of the commitment to fix the 'exchange rates' between those dollar bills takes place routinely by transfers on the books of the Federal Reserve Banks (and those of the Interdistrict Settlement Fund). When central bankers

---

[18] This point has been made many times: see, e.g., W. H. Buiter and K. M. Kletzer, 'Reflections on the fiscal implications of a common currency', CEPR Discussion Paper 418 (London: Centre for Economic Policy Research, 1990), and A. Giovannini and L. Spaventa, 'Fiscal rules in the European monetary union: a no-entry clause', CEPR Discussion Paper 516 (London: Centre for Economic Policy Research, 1991). The problem is not solved by forbidding the ECB to make open market purchases of government securities, as proposed by Neumann in 'Central bank independence'; the ECB could still buy private debt to keep interest rates from rising. The provisions of the treaty designed to prevent governments from running excessive budget deficits are also intended to protect the independence of the ECB; see P. B. Kenen, *EMU after Maastricht* (Washington DC: Group of Thirty, 1992), ch. IV.

[19] Under article 106 of the treaty, some articles of the ESCB statute may be amended by the Council of Ministers, acting by a qualified majority and with the assent of the Parliament. But the articles in question relate mainly to administrative and financial matters and the scope of ECB operations, not to the objectives or tasks of the ESCB, its constitution, or its independence.

Peter B. Kenen

in Europe begin to think seriously about monetary mechanics in stage three, they will realize that the locking of exchange rates between ESCB currencies does not require intervention on foreign exchange markets or the holding of large currency reserves. It requires book-keeping entries on the books of the national central banks and those of the ECB, which will play a role resembling that of the Interdistrict Settlement Fund.[20] They may then cease to worry about the effects of an exchange rate realignment in stage two on the viability of stage three—concern that is totally misplaced and can do much damage by precluding realignments in stage two, when they may be needed.

Analogies with the Federal Reserve System are less appropriate, however, when looking at the conduct of monetary policy by the ESCB. The Federal Reserve System is not truly federal in the policy domain. It is strongly centralized. Decisions about monetary policy are made by the Open Market Committee, consisting of the seven members of the board of governors and five of the twelve Federal Reserve Bank presidents.[21] Furthermore, open market operations are conducted by the Federal Reserve Bank of New York on instructions from the Open Market Committee. The other Federal Reserve Banks play no role at all. But the monetary policy of the ECB will be formulated by the governing council, comprising the six board members and all twelve of the national central bank governors. Furthermore, the ECB is expected to use the national central banks to implement its monetary policy. There are various ways in which the ECB can do this, involving different degrees of decentralization. Most of them, however, will require the national central banks to pursue the same policy targets and use the same techniques to conduct open market and credit operations. How much change will this standardization require?

There are significant differences in the operating procedures of EC central banks. But many appear to reflect cross-country differences in the structures of national financial markets and the asset holdings of credit institutions, and the central banks' procedures have become more similar as those differences have diminished.[22] In fact, the four largest central banks—the Bundesbank, Banque de France, Banca d'Italia, and Bank of England—use the same basic methods in their day-to-day operations.

Each of the first three has established a 'corridor' for short-term interest rates. The corridor is bounded from below by the interest rate at which the central bank supplies liquidity on its own initiative by open market operations and bounded from above by the interest rate at which it supplies liquidity at the initiative of the banking system. There are differences, however, in the ways that these and other central banks conduct their open market operations, and some use more than one technique. Furthermore, the EC central banks have

---

[20] See Kenen, *EMU after Maastricht*, ch. IV.

[21] The president of the Federal Reserve Bank of New York is a permanent member (and vice chairman) of the Open Market Committee; the other presidents serve in rotation.

[22] See J. T. Kneeshaw and P. Van de Bergh, *Changes in central bank money market operating procedures in the 1980s*, BIS Economic Papers 23 (Basle: Bank for International Settlements, 1989), and D. S. Batten, M. P. Blackwell, I. S. Kim, S. E. Nocera and Y. Ozeki, *The conduct of monetary policy in major industrial countries*, Occasional Paper 70 (Washington DC: International Monetary Fund, 1990).

different ways of lending to their banking systems, and some, including the Bundesbank, have more than one credit facility.

The French, German, and Italian central banks deal directly with domestic banks. The Bank of England, by contrast, deals primarily with the London discount houses. Furthermore, the upper limit of its interest rate corridor is not defined as sharply as in France or Germany, because the Bank of England does not have a fixed lending rate. But these differences are not fundamental. The liquidity provided by the Bank of England, through open market operations and lending to the discount houses, flows on to the clearing banks as they sell bills to the discount houses or call in their loans.

The ECB can be expected to adopt techniques similar to those used currently by the four largest central banks. Nevertheless, changes will have to be made in the practices and balance sheets of the national central banks, and the size of the changes will depend on the way in which the ECB interprets the requirement that it use the national central banks to carry out its policies.

There are several ways to use the national central banks for open market operations. Discussion has focused on three possibilities: a *centralized model* in which the size and terms of an open market purchase would be decided by the ECB, bids would be collected by the national central banks from their domestic credit institutions and the ECB would make the allotments; a *distributive model* in which the ECB would decide the size and terms but the total amount would be distributed among the national central banks, which would conduct their own tenders; and a *decentralized model* in which each national central bank would undertake its own open market operations but would operate within two bands set by the ECB—one for its interest rate instrument and one for its balance with the ECB. Note that all three models assume that each national central bank will continue to deal with its own domestic credit institutions.

Before looking at the problems raised by the first two models, consider the main problem raised by the third. It appears to assume that there will continue to be some separation of national financial markets, even in stage three. If there is instead a single, well functioning interbank market, arbitrage within that market will eradicate incipient interest rate difference produced by the central banks' open market operations. The decentralized model will serve merely to produce large movements in the central banks' cash balances with the ECB. Those balances will change, moreover, whenever there are net payments from one country to another, forcing the national central banks to fine-tune their open market operations to keep their cash balances within the bands set by the ECB. The decentralized model would thus introduce unnecessary noise into the financial system, making it harder for market participants to read signals sent by the ECB.

This objection can be put more broadly. The decentralized model necessarily attaches normative importance to the central banks' balances with the ECB. But changes in those balances should be ignored in a monetary union. They are mere clearing balances, not reserve balances, and no one should pay attention to them. If the operating rules of the ESCB say that the central banks' balances

Peter B. Kenen

should not fluctuate widely (or should be balanced at the end of the day), fluctuations should be offset by transferring securities between the ECB and the national central banks, not by open market operations.

If the decentralized model goes in the wrong direction, what must be done to go in the right direction? Should the ECB try to move directly to the centralized model? Or should it begin by moving to the distributive model and perhaps move later to the centralized model?

In the early years of the US Federal Reserve System, individual Reserve Banks conducted their own open market operations, mainly to acquire income-producing assets. It took many years to coordinate those operations fully and many more years before they displaced discount-window lending as the main instrument of monetary policy.[23] The ECB will not have this problem. Its statute gives it full control of monetary policy and of the instruments required to conduct it. The governors of the national central banks, however, will have more influence in the ECB than the presidents of the Federal Reserve Banks in the United States; they will be voting members of the governing council, where they will outnumber the members of the board. And they will surely oppose any arrangement that gives some of the national central banks more prominence than others or favours the use of some countries' markets. Hence, the ECB is less likely to adopt a centralized model than a distributive model and quite unlikely to adopt an arrangement like that in the United States, where the Federal Reserve Bank of New York acts for the whole Federal Reserve System.

Furthermore, the distributive model may be better suited to the conditions prevailing early in stage three. It cannot give way to a centralized model until certain conditions are fulfilled. One of those conditions was mentioned earlier: there must be a unified interbank market where banks can lend and borrow ECU-denominated balances held at the national central banks. But two other conditions must also be met: there must be a well integrated market in ECU-denominated bills and bonds and banks must have in their portfolios adequate supplies of the various securities traded on the integrated market. If these conditions are not met, the effects of open market operations will not spread speedily or evenly across the ESCB countries.

It may be possible to satisfy the first condition quickly by adopting the recommendation that the ECB and national central banks should denominate their balance sheets in ECU as soon as stage three begins. The integration of financial markets would likewise be accelerated if government securities were redenominated in ECU. But it may be hard to meet the third condition quickly. Some countries' banks will not hold the securities most likely to be traded on integrated markets and used by the main central banks in open market operations. Hence, the ECB may have to distribute its open market operations among the national central banks at the beginning of stage three and allow them to use somewhat different methods in order to accommodate cross-country differences in the portfolios of credit institutions.

---

[23] See B. Eichengreen, 'Designing a central bank for Europe: a cautionary tale from the early years of the Federal Reserve System', paper presented at the Georgetown Conference on Establishing a Central Bank, 1991.

The ECB and stage three of EMU

From the very start, however, the ECB could tilt the distribution of its open market operation in favour of centralization. By giving disproportionately large allocations to the central banks in the main financial centres, it can encourage other countries' credit institutions to use those major centres and adapt their own portfolios accordingly. To this end, however, it must insist from the outset that all credit institutions be free to participate on equal terms in the tenders conducted by the national central banks.[24]

To carry standardization further, the ECB could foster competition among the national central banks. If banks could participate on equal terms in tenders conducted outside their own countries, they would take their business to the most efficient centres, and that would have two consequences. First, banks would have more incentive to adapt their own portfolios—to build up their holdings of the securities used in the most efficient centres. Second, banks would make less use of the more expensive tenders. Business would come to be concentrated at the national central banks having the most attractive methods, and the ECB, in turn, could shift the distribution of its open market operations in favour of those central banks. It could raise the shares of the central banks whose tenders were, on average, most heavily oversubscribed.

Some central banks that lost out in this competition might not be able to do much about it, but others might alter their methods. If intermediation by the discount market made it more expensive for banks to sell bills in London, the Bank of England would lose business to other central banks; it might then decide to open its tenders directly to banks, rather than conduct them through the discount houses. The discount houses would have to find new work, but adaptation forced by competition would be easier to justify than adaptation forced by fiat.

Although central banks in Europe use similar techniques to manage money market conditions and thus influence interest rates, they differ in another way. Reserve requirements are used in France, Germany, Italy, and several other EC countries but not in the United Kingdom. Those who were taught that the money supply depends on the stock of bank reserves and the deposit multiplier, which depends on the reserve requirement, find it hard to believe that the money supply can behave in a non-explosive way unless it is constrained by reserve requirements. But it does not behave much differently in Britain than in other countries. The existence of a stable deposit multiplier does not depend on the use of reserve requirements. It is sufficient to have a stable relationship between the demand for currency and the total money stock, so that part of any increase in the banks' cash balances at the central bank will leak into currency holdings by the public.

Most central banks acknowledge that reserve requirements are not necessary for short-term monetary management—not even for long-term control over the money supply. Reserve requirements can even reduce their control of the

---

[24] This rule would also give effect to article 2 of the ESCB statute, which requires that the ESCB 'act in accordance with the principle of an open market economy with free competition' and would attack the restrictive practices of some countries' banks. Each national central bank might retain the right to judge the creditworthiness of the institutions seeking to do business with it, but could not discriminate by nationality.

Peter B. Kenen

money supply by driving domestic deposits offshore. Nevertheless, they appear to believe that reserve requirements give them more leverage and allow them to control monetary conditions without conducting massive open market operations. Accordingly, the central banks that use reserve requirements are likely to press for their adoption by the ECB rather than agree to abandon them.

If the ECB uses reserve requirements, it will have to impose them uniformly. It will also have to decide whether to impose them on a host-country or home-country basis. At present, central banks typically impose reserve requirements on domestic currency deposits at domestic branches of domestic and foreign banks. They exempt domestic currency deposits at the foreign branches of domestic banks, as well as all foreign currency deposits. This treatment is consistent with the principle embodied in the Basle Concordat and the second banking directive. With the advent of a single currency, however, there may be reason to reconsider. The distinction between domestic and foreign currencies will vanish in respect of EC currencies, so that most of the present foreign currency deposits will be subject automatically to reserve requirements. But the jurisdictional question will crop up differently. German banks will have to hold reserves against the ECU deposit liabilities of their French branches. Should they hold them with the Banque de France or with the Bundesbank? If all of the major EC countries participate in the monetary union, it will not make much difference, and administrative convenience might dictate a shift to home country reserve accounting. That is the practice in the United States; a bank with branches in two or more Federal Reserve districts holds its required reserves with the Reserve Bank for the district in which it has its headquarters. But matters are more complicated if some EC countries do not participate.

Suppose that Britain does not participate. Under host-country reserve accounting, banks in ESCB countries would have an incentive to book ECU deposits in London, as they would not have to hold reserves against them and would not be handicapped *vis-à-vis* British banks in competing for them. But UK banks would have no incentive to attract ECU deposits by opening branches in ESCB countries, as those deposits would be subject to reserve requirements. The ECB's control over the volume of ECU deposits would thus be limited by a large offshore market in London, but there would be no limitation on its control over the volume of ECU deposits at banks in ESCB countries. Under home-country reserve accounting, by contrast, banks in ESCB countries would have no incentive to book ECU deposits in London, and the offshore markets would probably be smaller. But UK banks would have an incentive to compete for ECU deposits in ESCB countries, as they would not have to hold reserves against them. Hence, home-country accounting might limit the ECB's control over the volume of ECU deposits in ESCB countries, and this limitation might be more serious than the one produced by a larger offshore market.

If reserves earned interest at a market rate, the problem would vanish. But the central banks most likely to insist that the ECB use reserve requirements are the ones most likely to resist that innovation. It may thus be imprudent for the

The ECB and stage three of EMU

ESCB to switch from host-country to home-country reserve accounting, even though the latter would be less cumbersome.

The problem of non-participation

The possibility of non-participation raises other problems. Countries that do not participate immediately in stage three will be affected nonetheless by the policies of the ECB. Will they be able to influence those policies?

Some EC governments, especially those that are worried about entering stage three immediately, wanted all of the national central bank governors to be involved in the work of the governing council, even if they were not allowed to vote on decisions about monetary policy. Other governments wanted to exclude them completely. A compromise was struck in the IGC, and the treaty provides for the creation of a general council as the third decision-making body of the ECB. The president and vice-president of the ECB and all of the central bank governors will be voting members of the general council, and the president will chair it. (Other board members may participate in its meetings but may not vote.) The general council will 'contribute' to the work of the ECB in various areas (e.g. collecting statistical information and setting personnel policies) but will have no role in making monetary policy. It will be 'informed' about decisions of the governing council and can no doubt discuss them. But it has no right to be informed about matters *pending* before the governing council.

What about policy coordination? What about the management of exchange rates between the ECU and the non-participants' currencies? The treaty and ESCB statute do not answer these questions. They say that the general council will 'take over those tasks of the EMI which ... have still to be performed in the third stage' (articles 44 and 47 of the statute) but do not say that the general council will inherit the *powers* of the EMI—the right to make recommendations to individual countries and be consulted in advance about future monetary policies.[25] Furthermore, the general council is not well designed for coordinating monetary and exchange rate policies. Suppose that Canada, Mexico and the United States set up a committee for that purpose. Surely the governors of the Bank of Canada and Banco de Mexico would expect to meet with the chairman of the board of governors of the Federal Reserve System, not sit with the presidents of the twelve Federal Reserve Banks and have the chairman of the board of governors preside at the opposite end of the table. If Canada and Mexico asked to join the Federal Reserve System, their governors would become the presidents of the thirteenth and fourteenth Federal Reserve Banks, but that is a different story.

The practical importance of these organizational matters will depend on the

[25] Article 44 of the ESCB statute, which transfers residual tasks from the EMI to the ECB, was presumably designed to transfer the EMI's responsibilities for managing the EMS credit facilities. Furthermore, articles 4 and 5 of the EMI statute, which give the EMI the rights listed above, are drafted with reference to the 'national' monetary authorities; they cannot easily be construed as giving the general council the right to make recommendations to the ECB.

Peter B. Kenen

number and size of the countries that do not participate in stage three. If they are few and small, there will be little need for consultations about monetary and exchange rate policies. The non-participants will have to adapt their policies to those of the ECB and peg their currencies to the ECU if they wish to qualify for eventual participation. If they are numerous and some of them are large, policy coordination may matter, not only to them but also to the ESCB countries. And questions remain about the way in which exchange rates should be pegged.[26] The non-participants could peg their currencies unilaterally to the ECU and take responsibility for keeping their exchange rates inside predetermined bands. They would use their own reserves for intervention and set their own national interest rates at the levels required to maintain exchange rate stability. They would probably intervene in ECU and thus hold some of their reserves with the ECB. If asked to assume these responsibilities, however, they might also insist on the right to change their exchange rates whenever they saw fit, without the consent of the ECB or the Community as a whole. Alternatively, decisions and obligations could be shared between the ECB and the non-participants' central banks, under a residual version of the EMS. Central rates would be chosen collectively, the ECB would have to intervene whenever the ECU reached the limit of its band, and it might be expected to adjust its interest rates whenever that was needed for exchange rate stability. There would be short-term credit facilities like those of the EMS.

It may be objected that participation by the ECB in a residual EMS arrangement could impair its ability to pursue price stability. But unilateral pegging would have the same effect if the non-participants intervened in ECU and thus held reserves with the ECB; sales of ECU by a non-participant's central bank would increase the liquidity of credit institutions in the ESCB countries, just like ECU sales by the ECB itself under a cooperative currency arrangement. Unilateral pegging, moreover, could impose heavy burdens on the non-participants. Consider the plight of a country that had failed to meet the exchange rate criterion for participation. Should it be expected to do better on its own, without the benefit of the credibility conferred by a collective exchange rate arrangement, the obligation of the ECB to intervene, and large credit lines? The case for a cooperative arrangement is even stronger if several EC countries do not participate in stage three and some of them are large. Intervention could have bigger effects on the liquidity of credit institutions in the ESCB countries, and decisions about realignments could not be left to the non-participants acting unilaterally, because of their effects on the ESCB countries.

These issues will take on great importance if, as now seems likely, the Community admits a number of new members before 1999.

---

[26] The treaty is nearly silent on this matter. Article 109m calls on EC countries to treat their exchange rates as matters of common interest in stage two and 'take account of the experience acquired' in the EMS. These obligations will apply 'by analogy' in stage three to countries with derogations. But the treaty does not impose any reciprocal obligation on the ECB regarding exchange rates between the ECU and the non-participants' currencies. Its silence can perhaps be read as an endorsement of unilateral pegging by the non-participants.

[24]

Financial Opening and the Exchange Rate Regime

by Peter B. Kenen

Introduction

The first half of this paper examines the exchange rate effects of moving to capital account convertibility. When developing countries dismantle their capital controls, they often experience large capitals inflows that cause the domestic currency to appreciate in real terms. The nominal rate appreciates when it is flexible; the price level rises when the nominal rate is pegged. The real appreciation causes the trade balance to deteriorate, which impairs confidence in the sustainability of the liberalisation; capital inflows give way to capital outflows, and governments sometimes respond by reversing the liberalisation[1]. A portfolio-balance model is used to tell this story and show what might be done to make the ending happier.

The second half of the paper examines some longer-run implications of capital account convertibility. The elimination of capital controls has two major consequences for exchange rate policy. Capital movements become more sensitive to domestic monetary policy, but they also become more sensitive to other events, domestic and foreign, expected and actual. The first effect strengthens the case for exchange rate flexibility — unless, of course, one holds the view that monetary independence will be abused and should be limited by pegging the exchange rate. The second effect weakens the case for exchange rate flexibility, as volatile capital movements can do greater damage to the real economy when they affect the exchange rate than when they affect the money supply.

It should be noted that I have been asked to address the effects of a "credible" move to capital account convertibility by a developing country. I take this to mean that the country will not reimpose controls because it has achieved three basic objectives.

First, it has achieved a reasonable degree of macro economic stability. The budget deficit is small and is financed for the most part by issuing debt to the public, not borrowing from the banking system. The inflation rate is low and stable, so that nominal and real interest rates are not very far apart. As a practical matter, the country may be some way from reaching these objectives when it starts to liberalise the capital account. But I will assume that it has reached them fully. Otherwise, we would have to disentangle the effects of liberalisation from the effects of stabilization. Stabilization, for example, may

237

stimulate domestic capital formation and produce a sharp rise in domestic asset prices.

Second, the country has taken the steps required to strengthen domestic financial institutions and to broaden and deepen domestic financial markets. Furthermore, it has assembled the rules and people needed to conduct strict prudential supervision. It is not sufficient to write down or take over the banks' bad loans and to make them build up their capital. These once-for-all measures are useful only insofar as they provide a clean base for subsequent supervision. Again, liberalisation may begin before these steps have been completed, and it can help with some of them. The liberalisation of trade in domestic securities can broaden and deepen domestic financial markets; the entry of foreign banks can force local banks to function more efficiently. We should have learned by now, however, not to confuse financial liberalisation with indiscriminate deregulation. Viable liberalisation may indeed require more intensive supervision. Those who continue to equate liberalisation with deregulation, deliberately or carelessly, are seeking a quick fix by favouring those who seek a quick buck. They are likely to cause a big crash.

Finally, the country has sought to tie its own hands by dismantling the bureaucracy involved in administering capital controls and the trade controls associated with them. This can be done by a "big bang" that abolishes all such controls together. If that is not possible or prudent, the job should be done by abolishing groups of controls completely, sector by sector, not by relaxing all of them gradually, and transferring responsibility for those that remain to other government agencies. One might begin, for example, by abolishing all controls on households and non-financial businesses, to get rid of the trade controls that go with them and the big bureaucracy needed to administer them. Controls on direct investment could be retained, if needed for political or other reasons; they do not require a large bureaucracy. Controls on domestic and foreign financial institutions could be administered temporarily by the agencies involved in prudential supervision[2].

Exchange rate policy during liberalisation

Research on the effectiveness of capital controls suggests that they are leaky and uneven in their incidence[3]. Individuals and businesses engaged in foreign trade can evade them easily. But controls on financial institutions are usually effective in preventing or reducing domestic participation in foreign financial markets and foreign participation in domestic markets, and controls on foreign direct investment tend to reduce capital inflows — though that is rarely their main purpose. Furthermore, evasion can be costly. The costs can range from outright bribery to implicit price concessions made to foreigners for help in underinvoicing exports, overinvoicing exports, and managing assets sequestered abroad. In the absence of these costs, it would be hard to explain why the abolition of capital controls often leads to the repatriation of domestic assets.

Taxing the option of re-exporting capital

This last point is easily illustrated by treating the cost of evading controls as a tax on exporting capital and examining the options open to an investor who has already paid the tax and thus holds foreign assets. Using subscripts

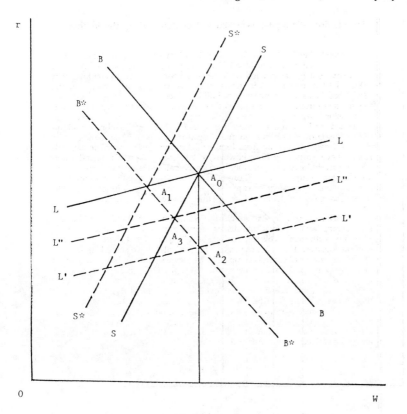

Figure 1

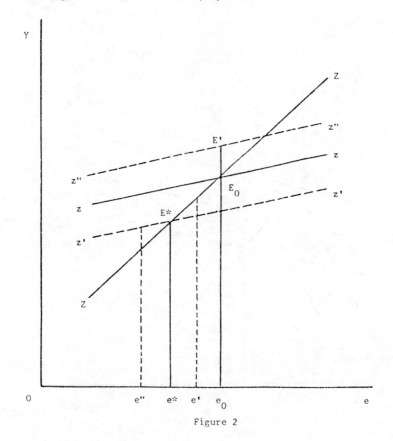

Figure 2

to denote time periods and asterisks to denote foreign rates of return, we can define the four options available in a two-period framework:

1) Earning $(1 + r_1^*)(1 + r_2^*)$ by investing abroad in both periods;

2) Earning $(1 + r_1^*)(1 + r_2)$ by investing abroad in the first and at home in the second;

3) Earning $(1 + r_1)(1 + r_2^*)$ by investing at home in the first and abroad in the second;

4) Earning $(1 + r_1)(1 + r_2)$ by investing at home in both periods.

When $r_1 = r_1^*$ but $r_2^* > r_2$, the investor will prefer (1) to (2) or (4) but be indifferent between (1) and (3)[4]. With capital controls, however, the third option becomes:

3a) Earning $(1 + r_1)(1 - t)(1 + r_2^*)$ by investing at home in the first and paying the tax equivalent of evading controls to invest abroad in the second.

Clearly, the investor will prefer (1) to (3a) unless $(r_1 - r_1^*) > (1 + r_1)t$, which cannot be true when $r_1 = r_1^*$ and $t > 0$. In general terms, controls on capital outflows reduce the incentive to repatriate capital now by taxing the option of re-exporting capital later.

A portfolio-balance model

To model the effects of removing capital controls, I will use a simple version of the portfolio-balance model set out in Allen and Kenen (1980) and used in Kenen (1981) to analyse closely related issues. The model is frankly old-fashioned in two important ways. First, expectations are static, so that actual and expected exchange rates are equal, as are real and nominal interest rates. Second, short-run price stickiness is represented by complete price rigidity, so that changes in aggregate demand affect output and employment. It is better to start this way, however, and accommodate more realistic outcomes informally, than to start at the opposite extreme, with rational expectations and complete price flexibility, which rule out real effects entirely and force us to make other simplifications merely to obtain well-behaved solutions.

Table 1. Equations of the Portfolio-Balance Model

(1)	$W = L^h + B^h + eF^h$
(2)	$L^h = L(r,r^*,W)$, $L_r, L_{r^*} < 0, L_w > 0$
(3)	$B^h = B(r,r^*,W)$, $B_r > 0, B_{r^*} < 0, B_w > 0$
(4)	$L = B^b + eR - W^b = L^h$
(5)	$B = B^h + B^b$
(6)	$N = N(Y,e)$, $N_Y < 0, N_e > 0$
(7)	$N = S-I+T-G$
(8)	$S = S(Y,r,r^*,W)$, $S_Y, S_r, S_{r^*} > 0, S_w < 0$

Table 1 lists the equations of the model. The variables are denominated in home currency, except for foreign securities held by domestic residents and the foreign exchange reserves held by the banking system, which are measured in foreign currency. The nominal exchange rate, e, is measured in units of domestic currency per unit of foreign currency.

Households have three assets, domestic money, L^h, domestic bonds, B^h, and foreign bonds, F^h. Their wealth, W, is defined by Equation (1). Their demands for money and domestic bonds are given by Equations (2) and (3), where r and r^* are the interest rates on the domestic and foreign bond; their demand for foreign bonds is implied by Equations (1) through (3), taken together. Equations (4) and (5) are the market-clearing equations for money and domestic bonds. The money supply, L, equals the sum of the domestic bonds, B^b, and foreign exchange reserves, R, held by the banking system[5]. The supply of domestic bonds, B, is exogenous and equals the sum of the quantities held by households and banks. The fixity of B reflects the assumption made below that the government's budget is always balanced. The banks' bond holdings are policy determined; they change only in response to open market operations by the central bank. The banks' foreign exchange holdings are completely fixed when the exchange rate floats but vary endogenously when it is pegged.

The home currency price of the domestic good is set at unity, as is the foreign currency price of the foreign good[6]. Therefore, the current account balance, N, is given by Equation (6), and the national income identity is given by Equation (7). But the government's budget is balanced continuously (G = T), and there is no investment (I = 0), so that S = N. Finally, Equation (8) describes the behaviour of saving, which is positively related to income, Y, and to the two interest rates, but negatively related to wealth. Income equals output, which is demand determined[7].

The economy begins in a stationary state, where S = 0. When displaced by a disturbance or policy change, it returns to a stationary state, driven by the influence of saving on wealth and the influence of wealth on saving.

Figures 1 and 2 summarise the model. In Figure 1, the BB and LL curves list the combinations of wealth and the domestic interest rate that clear the bond and money markets, given the supplies of bonds and money and the foreign interest rate. (If the domestic and foreign bonds were perfect substitutes, r would equal r^*, and BB would be horizontal.) Under a floating exchange rate, the LL curve cannot shift unless the banking system buys or sells bonds. With a floating rate wealth can change instantaneously; an appreciation of the domestic currency reduces wealth by reducing the home-currency value of the households' foreign bonds. Under a pegged exchange rate, the LL curve shifts whenever the economy runs a balance-of-payments surplus or deficit; a surplus raises the foreign exchange reserves held by the banking system, increasing the money supply, and the LL curve shifts downward. Here wealth cannot change instantaneously.

The BB and LL curves describe market clearing requirements and thus hold continuously. The SS curve holds only in the stationary state. It describes the relationship between wealth and the domestic interest rate that obtains when S = 0, given the initial level of income. By implication, points above SS identify conditions in which households want to save at that initial income level, and points below it identify conditions in which they want to dissave. Furthermore, a shift in the SS curve denotes a permanent change in income from one stationary state to another. If income falls permanently, the SS curve shifts upward; a permanent fall in income must be offset by a higher interest rate or lower level of wealth to keep S = 0 in the new stationary state.

In Figure 2, the ZZ curve shows the combinations of income and the (real) exchange rate that balance the current account, which says that it holds only in the stationary state (where N = S = 0). As imports rise with income, a real depreciation is needed to keep N = 0. The ZZ curve does not shift unless the economy experiences a permanent goods market shock. The zz curve shows the corresponding short-run relationship. As S can be positive or negative in the short run, N can also be positive or negative, and an increase in income need not be fully offset by a real depreciation[9].

The position of the zz curve depends on the location of the equilibrium point in Figure 1. When asset market equilibrium occurs at A_0, where BB, LL, and SS meet, goods market equilibrium must occur at E_0, where zz and ZZ meet (and S = N = 0). When it moves to a point above the SS curve, there is saving and a current account surplus, and the zz curve shifts downward. Accordingly, vertical distances between zz and ZZ measure N and S. When zz is below ZZ for a given e, then N = S > 0, and the short-run income level is lower than the corresponding long-run level; when zz is above ZZ, then N = S < 0, and the short-run income level is higher than the long-run level. The nature of the subsequent adjustment process, however, depends on the exchange rate regime. It is described below.

Representing the capital inflow

A permanent dismantling of capital controls has two effects. First, it flattens the BB curve, because households can switch freely between domestic and foreign bonds. (In what follows, I assume that the BB curve in Figure 1 is the new, flatter curve.) Second, it shifts the BB curve downward to B*B*. As households can buy foreign bonds in the future without incurring the cost of evading controls, they will demand more domestic bonds now, and the domestic interest rate must fall to clear the bond market because the supply of bonds is fixed. But the nature of the new asset market equilibrium will depend on the exchange rate regime.

The floating rate case

Under a floating exchange rate, the LL curve does not shift unless the central bank modifies its monetary policy. But wealth changes instantaneously with any change in the exchange rate. In Figure 1, then, the equilibrium point moves to A_1. The interest rate rises, and the currency appreciates, reducing wealth. The size of the appreciation, however, depends on F^h, the quantity of foreign bonds held initially. The smaller is F^h initially, the larger is the appreciation required to produce the necessary fall in wealth. But capital controls have tended to hold down F^h. Therefore, I assume hereafter that there is a "large" appreciation.

Before examining the goods market counterparts of these results, note two more points. (1) As A_1 lies above the SS curve when, as here, LL is flatter than SS, households start to save at the new levels of r and W and the initial level of income. (2) The money-market curve cannot shift again unless there is another change in households' portfolio preferences, a change in the foreign interest rate, or a change in the supply of bonds, and the money market curve cannot shift at all unless there is a change in monetary policy. Therefore, A_1 must represent not only the new short-run equilibrium but also the new long-run equilibrium. Accordingly, the SS curve must shift to S*S*, to pass through A_1, which means, in turn, that there must be a permanent reduction in income.

The implications of these findings are reflected in Figure 2. The short-run goods market curve shifts downward to z'z'. The vertical distance between z'z' and ZZ at the initial exchange rate measures the current account surplus that would emerge without an exchange rate change. Furthermore, z'z' and ZZ intersect at E*, which says that there must be a permanent appreciation of the domestic currency and, as we have seen, a permanent reduction in income. But the size of the short-run exchange rate change depends on the size of F^h. When F^h is large, the domestic currency will appreciate to some such level as e' (where N = S > 0), and more appreciation will be needed to reach e* in the long run. When F^h is small, the domestic currency will appreciate to some such level as e" (where N = S < 0), and some depreciation will be needed to reach e* in the long run. This second outcome replicates the experience of those developing countries that have abolished capital controls, experienced capital inflows, and run current account deficits after liberalisation[9].

Under a floating exchange rate, then, the dismantling of capital controls tends to be deflationary. In this particular model, with rigid prices, real income falls. In a model with price flexibility, prices would fall and real income would rise on the way to the new long-run equilibrium. (The dynamics would be complicated, however, as falling prices would affect the real values of bonds and money, the real exchange rate, and the real interest rate.)

One more possibility needs attention. When the exchange rate "overshoots" initially because F^h is small, the credibility of the liberalisation may be impaired by the resulting current-account deficit and subsequent depreciation of the domestic currency. If these are mistaken for symptoms of fundamental deterioration in the country's competitive position, asset holders may come to expect a reversal of liberalisation and will shift back to foreign assets.

The pegged-rate case

Under a pegged exchange rate, wealth does not change instantaneously, but the LL curve shifts endogenously in response to nonsterilised intervention. Therefore, the shift of the bond market curve to B*B* displaces asset market equilibrium to A₂ in Figure 1, and the LL curve shifts to L'L'. The central bank buys foreign currency to keep the domestic currency from appreciating, and the increase in reserves raises the money supply.

Hence, the pegged rate case differs from the floating rate case in two major ways. (1) As A₂ lies below the SS curve, the zz curve must shift upward to z"z" in Figure 2, shifting goods market equilibrium to E'. Income rises in the short run, but households start to dissave, driving the current account into deficit. (2) Because the exchange rate cannot change, there cannot be a permanent change in income, so z"z" must return to zz. Without any permanent income change, moreover, the SS curve cannot shift. In Figure 1, then, asset market equilibrium must move eventually to A₃, where B*B* and SS intersect, and the money market curve must move upward to L"L", which implies a gradual loss of reserves. The cumulative loss of reserves, however, cannot be as large as the initial gain, as L"L" must lie below LL[10].

Under a pegged exchange rate, then, the dismantling of controls tends to be inflationary. There is an increase of aggregate demand, which raises income when prices are rigid and raises prices when they are flexible. Furthermore, "overshooting" is inevitable here. Reserves must rise initially, then fall gradually. (With a floating rate, by contrast, the exchange rate overshoots its long-run level only when F^h is small relative to wealth.) There are two threats to credibility here. First, the once-for-all increase in prices, along with the initial increase in the money supply, may be taken as the harbingers of future inflation. Second, the current account deficit and gradual loss of reserves may be mistakenly viewed as signs of basic weakness in the external situation, and asset holders may come to expect a reversal of liberalisation.

The case for sterilised intervention

When prices are downwardly rigid and upwardly flexible, a capital inflow resulting from liberalisation led to real appreciation in both cases studied here. Under a floating exchange rate, the foreign exchange market responded by producing a nominal appreciation. Under a pegged exchange rate, the goods market responded by raising domestic prices. The basic cause resides, however, in the failure of the monetary authorities to supply the appropriate mix of assets. The authorities did nothing in the floating rate case; they issued money in exchange for foreign assets in the pegged rate case. They should have issued bonds instead, by engaging in sterilised intervention.

Suppose they had swapped money for reserves to peg the exchange rate and then swapped bonds for money to peg the interest rate. The BB and LL curves would not have shifted, and there would have been no change in the exchange rate or domestic interest rate. The economy would have stayed at A_0 in Figure 1 and at E_0 in Figure 2. The dismantling of capital controls would not have affected income, the price level, or the current account balance.

The practical problems are large. Fischer and Reisen (1992) point out, for example, that households and others are likely to demand a wide range of domestic assets when they repatriate their funds — a range far wider than the one held by the monetary authorities. If households want to hold domestic bonds and money, the policy rule suggested above — pegging the exchange rate and domestic interest rate — will meet their requirements automatically. If they want to hold equities, real estate, and so on, it cannot work as well.

Furthermore, the monetary authorities may not want to give the appearance of pegging the interest rate when they are also trying to impart more flexibility to domestic financial markets. Sterilised intervention, moreover, prevents the government from enjoying a reduction in its debt service burden by preventing the fall in the domestic interest rate that typically accompanies a capital inflow[11]. Finally, the monetary authorities may not hold domestic assets in quantities sufficient to satisfy the increase in demand for them. But all of these are second-order objections to what is, in principle, the first-best policy, and ways have been found to deal with most of them[12].

There is a more basic objection to using sterilised intervention. It is utterly ineffective when foreign and domestic assets are perfect substitutes (i.e., when open interest parity obtains). But the evidence on this score is far from conclusive, even for the major currencies and countries[13]. In the present case, moreover, it would be wrong analytically to treat foreign and domestic assets as perfect substitutes. When the abolition of capital controls produces a capital inflow, it must be deemed to reveal a repressed preference for domestic assets that can and should be offset by sterilised intervention. The policy problem is harder thereafter, because credible liberalisation will flatten the BB curve and make it more difficult to manage the exchange rate.

Exchange rate policy after liberalisation

An increase of capital mobility resulting from liberalisation makes it harder to peg the exchange rate while pursuing an independent monetary policy. With perfect capital mobility, indeed, a small country loses all control over its money supply. An open market purchase of domestic assets aimed at raising the money supply causes an immediate loss of reserves equal in size to the open market purchase[14]. Looking at the matter from a different standpoint, perfect capital mobility precludes the use of sterilised intervention to peg the exchange rate. When the central bank buys foreign currency, raising the money supply, it cannot cut back the money supply by selling domestic bonds; households will sell foreign bonds to take up the domestic bonds, and the households' sales of foreign bonds will prolong the capital inflow, forcing the central bank to buy more foreign currency.

Perfect capital mobility, however, is a limiting case useful for solving intractable models and describing **tendencies** in the real world. It is unlikely to obtain in any developing country, even after a credible move to capital account convertibility. The elimination of capital controls will remove the most important barriers to international capital flows but will not convert risk-averse investors into risk-neutral investors, and risk-averse investors will not treat foreign and domestic bonds as perfect substitutes unless the exchange rate is fixed completely and immutably. When the rate can fluctuate within a band around its peg, and when the peg itself is not immutable, the central bank will have room for manoeuvre, not only to affect the money supply but also to sterilise intervention in the foreign exchange market.

Under these same circumstances, however, capital flows will become more sensitive to changes in exchange rate expectations. Any apparent inconsistency between the existing exchange rate peg and the domestic policy stance is apt to generate capital flows that will speedily exhaust the authorities' holdings of foreign or domestic assets. A capital outflow will strip them of foreign assets, making it impossible to defend the exchange rate; an inflow will strip them of domestic assets, making it impossible to pursue an interest rate or money supply target.

These considerations have led Corden (1990) to argue that the abolition of capital controls calls for more agility in policy formation. Conflicts between the exchange rate and policy stance must be resolved speedily, whether by changing the rate or the stance. Furthermore, high capital mobility may reduce the temptation to use trade restrictions for dealing with balance-of-payments problems. The effects of trade controls are too small and tardy to offset the capital flows produced by obvious conflicts between the exchange rate and policy stance.

Other economists argue, however, that the abolition of capital controls calls for much more than agility. It calls for resort to floating exchange rates, which are said to confer three sorts of autonomy. First, they give the central bank full control of the money supply. Second, they allow a country to follow sensible policies even when the rest of the world does not. Third, they minimise the real costs of following foolish policies, as the nominal exchange rate can adjust automatically to prevent domestic inflation from changing the real exchange rate.

The first statement is incontrovertible. The other two are controversial, because they assume that the foreign exchange market pays close attention to the so-called fundamentals, especially those that influence inflation rates. Most of us said so a few years ago, but some have started to suspect that the foreign exchange market is more capricious than judicious. Mussa (1990) puts it nicely:

> *"I have long been sympathetic to the view that the behavior of asset prices, including exchange rates, is afflicted by some degree of craziness. Many aspects of human behavior impress me as being not entirely sane, and I see no reason why the behavior of asset prices should be a virtually unique exception (p. 7)."*

Mussa blames economists for some of this craziness, as we have not produced a theory of exchange rate determination capable of helping the foreign exchange market to process the relevant information. But others who have studied the foreign exchange market say that it has little interest in the fundamentals and has turned to black-box methods for exchange rate forecasting; see, e.g., Frankel and Froot (1986) and Taylor and Allen (1992). It is thus possible for floating exchange rates to lead lives of their own, completely detached from the fundamentals, and thus to affect the real economy in unpredictable ways. This conclusion does not argue for fixing exchange rates rigidly and defending them tenaciously. It argues instead for managing them closely, by making explicit commitments to keeping rates within broad bands, intervening when rates move to the limits of those bands, and shifting the positions of the bands themselves by small and timely changes rather than by big and tardy changes[15].

Corden (1990) would not like this formulation, because it relies rather heavily on governments, not market forces, to prevent large changes in the real exchange rates. But he and I agree that stable real rates are needed[16]. More controversially, he and I agree that the nominal exchange rate should be used directly for that task, not for achieving price stability. Our view was not controversial a few years ago, but it has been abandoned by large numbers of economists, who want exchange rate pegging to promote price stability and thus to stabilize the real rate indirectly.

There are several versions of the case for using the exchange rate as a nominal anchor. Some seek to make monetary policy more credible by replacing tarnished commitments to domestic price stability with bright new commitments to exchange rate stability. Some seek to make monetary policy more potent by relying on goods market arbitrage to stabilize the prices of traded goods. And some seek to make monetary policy less fallible by relying on capital flows to maintain equilibrium in the money market.

Belief that an exchange rate peg can make monetary policy more credible has been the main theme of the recent literature on the European Monetary System (EMS)[17], and it was influential in transforming the EMS from a system of adjustably pegged exchange rates into the system of virtually fixed rates that prevailed from 1987 until the EMS crisis in September 1992. Why should a commitment to a pegged exchange rate be more credible than a straightforward commitment to price stability? It is, of course, more transparent and easier to monitor. The exchange rate can fluctuate within the band around its peg, but a change in the peg itself is easily detected; it is far harder to detect a change in the commitment to combat inflation[18]. It is also easier to fix responsibility for a change in the exchange rate. The actual rate is endogenous, but the peg is policy determined; the inflation rate, by contrast, is totally endogenous. But these points bear on accountability, not on credibility. A commitment to a pegged exchange rate will not be more credible than a commitment to price stability unless it is more costly to abandon a pegged rate than abandon an effort to combat inflation rate. Cooper (1971) found that devaluation under the Bretton Woods System shortened the political life expectancy of a finance minister. But that may not be true today, because of the freedom governments enjoy to choose, change, and customise their exchange rate arrangements[19]. Pegging to acquire credibility, however, is a high-risk strategy. When a government ties down the exchange rate, it deprives itself of recourse to the instrument most useful for offsetting the effects of previous inflation and, more importantly, offsetting the additional increase in prices that typically occurs before exchange rate pegging can impart credibility to monetary policy and thus help to stabilize the price level. Worse yet, a government may cling to a pegged exchange rate even when it has failed to impart credibility. That is why Corden (1992) believes that policy commitments to price stability "must be direct, rather than brought about via an exchange rate commitment."

The second version of the case for using the exchange rate as a nominal anchor argues that goods market arbitrage can slow down inflation by tying domestic prices to world prices. This argument has been advanced in two quite different contexts. (1) The "heterodox" approach to stabilization in Latin America said that high inflation rates could be reduced abruptly by freezing prices and wages temporarily and tying domestic prices to world prices by pegging the exchange rate[20]. (2) Recent writers on reform in Central and Eastern Europe have favoured a quick move to current account convertibility *cum* exchange rate pegging as an expeditious way of attaching sensible prices to domestic goods and factors[21].

Advocates of "heterodox" stabilization concede that price controls and pegged exchange rates cannot halt inflation permanently. But they can affect expectations temporarily, buying the time required for strict monetary and fiscal policies to have their "orthodox" effects on inflation. Once this point is acknowledged, however, something more must be conceded. Although a pegged exchange rate can help goods market arbitrage to hold down the domestic prices of traded goods, it cannot stabilize the whole price level or hold down money wages. The prices of nontraded goods can go on rising, and the resulting real appreciation can cause the current account to deteriorate. Matters are made worse when wages rise as well. This brings us back to a point made earlier. The use of an exchange rate peg for domestic stabilization makes it hard to change the exchange rate later and offset the price increases that occur *en route* to stabilization. A colleague put it nicely: no sensible sailor throws out an anchor before the boat stops moving.

The third version of the case for exchange rate pegging to improve the quality of monetary policy would combine asset market arbitrage with goods market arbitrage to neutralise the errors made by central bankers.

This is proposed pragmatically by those who believe that many central banks lack the skills and instruments to manage money properly, especially when economic and financial conditions are changing rapidly. Rather than pursue an interest rate or money supply target and thus try to offset shifts in the demand for money, such central banks should target the exchange rate and make no attempt to sterilise the money supply effects of their operations in the foreign exchange market. The same proposal is made more dogmatically by those who believe that central banks must be constrained — or must constrain themselves — to minimise the damage done by their own fallibility, as well as to protect them from profligate governments. Thus, Bofinger (1991) maintains that exchange rate pegging should be combined with full convertibility in order to facilitate asset market arbitrage along with goods market arbitrage. And because he associates asset market arbitrage with the maintenance of open interest parity, one can interpret his recommendation as an attempt to prevent sterilised intervention and thus to keep the central bank from doing anything whatsoever, apart from pegging the exchange rate.

The exchange rate arrangements of developing countries

The new case for pegged exchange rates appears to have had some effect on the exchange rate arrangements of the developing countries. It influenced the heterodox stabilization programs adopted by Argentina in 1985 and Brazil in 1986 and the more orthodox Argentine program adopted in 1991. Its influence can likewise be detected in several other countries, most notably in 1986-87, when several developing countries moved temporarily from flexible to pegged exchange rates.

The exchange rate arrangements of developing countries are summarised in Table 2, which employs the classification used by the International Monetary Fund[22]. The table invites two generalisations.

Table 2. Classification of Developing Countries' Exchange Rate Arrangements
(Ends of calendar years)

Arrangement	Small countries		Large countries	
	1982	1991	1982	1991
Pegged to single currency	19	18	34	21
Pegged to SDR	5	1	9	5
Pegged to other composite	7	9	11	14
Flexibility limited in terms of single currency	5	3	5	1
Adjusted according to set of indicators	0	0	4	4
Other managed floating	1	4	14	17
Independently floating	0	2	4	19
Total	37	37	81	81

Source: International Monetary Fund, *International Financial Statistics* (various issues); for lists of small and large countries, see Tables A-1 and A-2.

First, small developing countries (those with populations no larger than 2 million) have tended to peg their exchange rates — a finding consistent with McKinnon's (1963) basic contribution to the theory of optimum currency areas. All but one of those small countries had pegged rate arrangements at the end of 1982, when the Fund began to use the present classification, and all but six still had them at the end of 1991[23].

Second, the larger developing countries have migrated in great numbers to more flexible exchange rates. Of the 81 countries in this group, only 22 had flexible rate arrangements in 1982, but 40 countries had them in 1991. Note further that the number of countries with independently floating rates rose from four in 1982 to 19 in 1991. Table 3 examines this migration in detail.

In 1983-85, ten "large" developing countries switched from pegged rate to flexible rate arrangements (and six went all the way to independent floating). Only two countries went the other way. Furthermore, four of the seven that moved between pegged rate arrangements adopted their own baskets, and two of the three that moved between flexible rate arrangements went to independent floating. In 1986-88, by contrast, seven countries switched from pegged-rate to flexible-rate arrangements, but six countries went the other way, including four that had moved to greater flexibility in the previous three-year period. But the migration to flexibility picked up again in 1989-91, with 12 countries going in that direction, including five that had switched back to pegged rates during the previous three-year period.

Table 3. Changes in Exchange Rate Arrangements by the
Large Developing Countries, 1983-91

Nature of change	1983-85	1986-88	1989-91
Between pegged rate arrangements	7	4	2
To other composite	4	1	2
From flexible rate to pegged rate	2	6	3
From pegged rate to flexible rate	10	7	12
To independent floating	6	1	7
Between flexible rate arrangements	3	4	1
To independent floating	2	1	1
Reversing arrangements within period	0	1	3

Source: Appendix Tables A-3 through A-5.

Can anything be said about the characteristics of the three groups of countries covered here — those that stayed with pegged rate arrangements, those that stayed with flexible rate arrangements, and those that moved from one to the other or went back and forth? Aghevli *et al.* (1991) find large differences between the inflation rates of countries with pegged and flexible rates, and that point can be carried further. Countries that stayed with pegged exchange rates had the lowest inflation rates; those that stayed with flexible rates had higher inflation rates; and those that changed their exchange rate arrangements had the highest inflation rates. This ranking holds uniformly, moreover, at the start and the end of the period[24].

At first glance, these results would appear to support the new case for exchange rate pegging, but I do not read them that way, partly because the rankings hold at both ends of the period. The countries that had low inflation rates initially and continued to pegged their exchange rates thereafter may have found exchange rate pegging helpful in holding down inflation. But those that moved to more flexible rates had the highest inflation rates initially. That some of them moved back and forth, moreover, suggests that exchange rate pegging was not very helpful to them; those switched to pegged exchange rates were forced to abandon them in order to offset the real appreciations produced by chronic inflation.

Conclusion

Summing up a recent conference on exchange rate arrangements for small industrial countries, Jacques Polak (1990) contrasted two ways of looking at the choice between managed exchange rates on the one hand and fixed or fully flexible rates on the other. One stresses optimality, the other credibility. A managed float allows the authorities to choose the change in the nominal rate most appropriate for each shock. Governments seeking credibility, however, may want to foreclose options, and nondiscretionary regimes — both fixed rates and clean floats — are better from that standpoint. But Polak's conclusion may not carry over fully to the developing countries, even to those that may be ready for credible liberalisation of the capital account. A floating exchange rate may be too volatile, particularly during the transition, and a pegged rate by itself is unlikely to confer enough credibility on domestic policies to keep the real exchange rate from appreciating sharply. It may be wise to keep all options open, not foreclose them quickly.

Notes

1. Fischer and Reisen (1992) and Mathieson and Rojas-Suarez (1992) provide illustrations.

2. Recent experience in Argentina and Colombia indicates, however, that domestic banks should be allowed and even encouraged to invest abroad when they acquire foreign exchange from businesses and households who are bringing home their assets; otherwise, the increase in bank liquidity may trigger a huge increase of domestic lending; see Rodriguez (1992).

3. See Mathieson and Rojas-Suarez (1992) and the sources cited there.

4. The investor will likewise be indifferent between (2) and (4), but both are dominated by (1) and (3).

5. The net-worth term W^b in Equation (4) is needed to offset capital gains and losses on R resulting from exchange rate changes; otherwise, those gains and losses would affect the money supply.

6. The model works equally well when both goods are tradable (so that e is the relative price of the foreign good) and when the foreign good is tradable but the domestic good is nontradable (so that e is the relative price of the tradable good).

7. Allen and Kenen (1980) provide assumptions sufficient to wash interest income terms out of the model. The positive effect of interest rates on saving substitutes for their negative effect on investment; in its absence, monetary policy would have no influence on aggregate demand.

8. Under a floating exchange rate, however, some real depreciation must occur, as an increase in income leads to saving, which has to be offset by a current account surplus, and an increase of income alone would produce a current account deficit.

9. With a small initial appreciation, the further appreciation offsets the saving that occurs on the way to long-run equilibrium. With a large initial appreciation, the partial depreciation offsets the dissaving that occurs on the way to long-run equilibrium. In both cases, wealth remains constant at the level given by A_1 in Figure 1.

10. In the pegged rate case, wealth falls gradually under the influence of dissaving, and the interest rate rises under the influence of the resulting decline in the demand for the domestic bond. The fall in wealth and increase in the interest rate drive the z"z" curve back gradually to zz.

11. Fischer and Reisen (1992) make this point but imprecisely, by saying that sterilisation raises domestic interest rates; see also Calvo (1991).

12. Fischer and Reisen (1992) mention the Indonesian case, in which the central bank dealt with a shortage of government paper by issuing obligations of its own. Furthermore, an increase of reserve requirements can compel the commercial banks to disgorge domestic assets and thus supplement or substitute for open market sales by the central bank itself.

13. For two views of this evidence, contrast Obstfeld (1988) with Dominguez and Frankel (1990).

14. In Figure 1, the BB curve becomes horizontal and does not shift down on account of an open market purchase. Therefore, the purchase cannot displace asset market equilibrium. The LL curve is shifted downward momentarily but snaps back to its initial position immediately.

15. I develop this view fully in Kenen (1988), drawing on the experience of the EMS countries but making a case for wider bands, in order to accommodate realignments without forcing changes in actual exchange rates.

16. There are, of course, occasions on which the real rate must change, and much of the recent literature stresses the costs of failing to recognise them; see Montiel and Ostry (1991) and the references there.

17. A useful survey is provided by Haldane (1991).

18. Corden (1990) points out that a single currency peg may be better for this purpose than a basket peg. But a single currency peg is hard to sustain when other rates are changing. Poland pegged the zloty to the dollar in 1990 but switched to a basket peg in 1991, when the dollar was appreciating against the Deutsche mark, dragging the zloty with it and hurting Poland's competitive position in European markets. Many developing countries have also switched from single currency to basket pegs.

19. The pegged rate arrangements of the EMS are unique in this respect. In fact, they represent an exchange rate constraint stronger than the one imposed by the original Bretton Woods System. A realignment of EMS exchange rates can be initiated by a single country but requires collective consent. Giavazzi and Giovannini (1988) point out, moreover, that EMS membership attaches to EC membership, so that EMS commitments are EC commitments, and failure to honour them is bound to weaken a member's standing in the Community. A pegged rate adopted unilaterally may be much less credible.

20. Dornbusch (1986) provides a concise statement of the "heterodox" view; Kiguel and Liviatan (1992) provide a retrospective critique.

21. See the papers by Kenen, Polak, and Williamson in Williamson (1991).

22. The classification is discussed and assessed in Kenen (1992). Brief explanatory notes are appended to this paper.

23. Countries with "flexibility limited in terms of a single currency" are treated here as having pegged exchange rates; those that adjust their rates according to a set of indicators are treated here as having flexible rates. This convention is consistent with the general finding that the nominal rates of countries in the first group are not much more volatile in the short run than the rates of countries with strictly pegged rates, while the nominal rates of countries in the second group are no less volatile than those of countries with floating or other managed rates.

24. I used consumer prices to measure inflation rates (because they are readily available for most of the countries concerned) and computed average inflation rates for 1981-83 and 1988-90. These are my results for the three groups of countries (the numbers of countries are given in parentheses):

	1981-83	1988-90
Staying with pegged rate arrangements (24)	10.2	9.3
Staying with flexible rate arrangements (14)	30.5	143.3
Changing exchange rate arrangements (25)	40.5	283.5

When Brazil is dropped from the second group and Argentina and Peru from the third, because they had extremely high inflation rates, the differences get smaller but do not vanish. The averages for the second group fall to 24 and 28.5 per cent; the averages for the third fall to 31.5 and 57.7 per cent. The first group includes countries that moved between pegged rate arrangements; the second includes countries that moved between flexible rate arrangements. Countries omitted from each group are those that were missing inflation rate data for one or more of the years studied.

The tables in this appendix are based on the tabulations of exchange rate arrangements published by the International Monetary Fund in *International Financial Statistics*. Kenen (1992) provides a critical examination of those tabulations. The tables cover the 118 developing countries that were listed continuously in the Fund's tabulations from end-1982 through end-1991 (but Hungary, Laos, Romania, and Viet Nam have been omitted).

Four conventions were used to prepare Tables A-3 through A-5, which deal with changes in exchange rate arrangements:

1) Countries with limited exchange rate flexibility are treated as having pegged exchange rates.

2) Countries that moved between pegged rate arrangements but also moved to flexible rates within a particular period are listed as moving to flexible rates (but the tables also record the prior moves between pegged rate arrangements and any subsequent moves between flexible-rate arrangements).

3) Countries that moved between flexible rate arrangements but also moved to pegged rates within a particular period are listed as moving to pegged rates (but the tables also record the prior moves between flexible rate arrangements and any subsequent moves between pegged rate arrangements).

4) The changes themselves were identified by comparing successive end-year tables in *International Financial Statistics*. Hence, they omit exchange rate arrangements that lasted for less than a year (including some short-lived attempts at exchange rate pegging). But a quarter-by-quarter study of 1990 and 1991 turned up only two such cases.

Appendix

255

Table A-1. **Exchange Rate Arrangements of "Small" Developing Countries, End 1991**
(Those with populations not larger than two million)

Pegged to single foreign currency or the SDR
or flexibility limited in terms of single currency

Antigua & Barbuda	Granada
Bahamas	Lesotho
Bahrain	Oman
Barbados	Qatar
Belize	St Lucia
Bhutan	St Vincent
Comoros	Seychelles
Djibouti	Suriname
Dominica	Swaziland
Equatorial Guinea	Trinidad & Tobago
Gabon	United Arab Emirates

Pegged to other composite

Botswana	Mauritius*
Cape Verde	Solomon Islands
Cyprus	Vanuatu*
Fiji	Western Samoa*
Malta	

Other managed or independent float

Gambia*	Maldives*
Guinea Bissau*	Mauritania*
Guyana*	Sao Tome & Principe*

Change in exchange rate arrangement after 1982.

Table A-2. **Exchange Rate Arrangements of "Large" Developing Countries, End 1991**
(Those with populations larger than two million)

Pegged to single foreign currency or the SDR
or flexibility limited in terms of single currency

Argentina*	Ethiopia	Panama
Benin	Iran	Rwanda*
Burkina Faso	Iraq	Saudi Arabia
Burundi*	Liberia	Senegal
Cameroon	Libya*	Sudan*
Cent African Republic	Mali	Syria
Chad	Myanmar	Togo
Congo	Nicaragua*	Yemen
Cote d'Ivoire	Niger	Yugoslavia*

Pegged to other composite

Algeria	Malawi*	Tanzania
Bangladesh	Malaysia	Thailand*
Jordan*	Morocco*	Uganda*
Kenya*	Nepal*	Zimbabwe
Kuwait	Papua New Guinea	

Adjusted according to indicator
other managed, or independent float

Afghanistan*	Haiti*	Peru*
Bolivia*	Honduras*	Philippines*
Brazil*	India	Sierra Leone*
Chile	Indonesia*	Singapore*
China*	Israel*	Somalia*
Colombia	Jamaica*	South Africa
Costa Rica	Korea	Sri Lanka
Dominican Republic*	Lebanon	Tunisia*
Ecuador*	Madagascar*	Turkey
Egypt*	Mexico	Uruguay
El Salvador*	Nigeria*	Venezuela*
Ghana*	Pakistan	Zaire*
Guatemala*	Paraguay*	Zambia*
Guinea*		

*   Change in exchange rate arrangement after 1982

257

Table A-3. **Changes in Exchange Rate Arrangements, 1983-85**

Between pegged-rate arrangements:

Burundi [US$ to SDR, 1983; none thereafter]
Ghana [FL to US$, 1985]
Malawi [SDR to OC, 1984; none thereafter]
Nepal [US$ to OC, 1983; none thereafter]
Rwanda [US$ to SDR, 1983; none thereafter]
Sudan [US$ to OC, 1985]
Thailand [FL to OC, 1984; none thereafter]

To pegged rate arrangements:

Peru [AAI to OM, 1983; OM to AAI, 1984; AAI to $, 1985]
Sierra Leone [OM to US$, 1983; US$ to SDR, 1985]

To flexible-rate arrangements:

Bolivia [US$ to IF, 1985; none thereafter]
Dominican Republic [US$ to IF, 1985]
Ecuador [US$ to OM, 1983]
El Salvador [US$ to OM, 1985]
Guinea [SDR to IF, 1985]
Indonesia [FL to OM, 1983; none thereafter]
Jamaica [US$ to OM, 1983; OM to IF, 1984]
Somalia [SDR to AAI, 1983]
Zaire [SDR to OM, 1983; OM to IF, 1984; none thereafter]
Zambia [SDR to OC, 1983; OC to IF, 1985]

Between flexible rate arrangements:

Philippines [OM to IF, 1984; none thereafter]
Israel [IF to OM, 1984]
Uganda [OM to IF, 1985]

Table A-4. **Changes in Exchange Rate Arrangements, 1986-88**

Between pegged rate arrangements:

    Afghanistan [FL to US$, 1987]
    Kenya [SDR to OC, 1987; none thereafter]
    Libya [US$ to SDR, 1986; none thereafter]
    Sudan [OC to US$, 1987; none thereafter]

To pegged rate arrangements:

    Ecuador [OM to US$, 1988]
    El Salvador [OM to US$, 1986]
    Israel [OM to OC, 1987]
    Somalia [AAI to US$, 1987; US$ to OC, 1988]
    Uganda [IF to OM, 1986; OM to US$, 1987]
    Zambia [IF to US$, 1987; US$ to SDR, 1988]

To flexible rate arrangements:

    China [OC to OM, 1986; none thereafter]
    Egypt [US$ to OM, 1987; none thereafter]
    Ghana [FL to IF, 1986; none thereafter]
    Madagascar [OC to AAI, 1986; none thereafter]
    Mauritania [OC to OM, 1987; none thereafter]
    Singapore [OC to OM, 1987; none thereafter]
    Tunisia [OC to OM, 1987; none thereafter]

Between flexible rate arrangements:

    Dominican Republic [IF to OM, 1988]
    Guinea [IF to OM, 1988; none thereafter]
    Jamaica [IF to OM, 1986]
    Nigeria [OM to IF, 1986; none thereafter]

Reversal within period:

    Sierra Leone [SDR to IF, 1986; IF to US$, 1987]

Table A-5. **Changes in Exchange Rate Arrangements, 1989-91**

Between pegged rate arrangements:

   Jordan [SDR to OC, 1989]
   Uganda [US$ to OC, 1989]

To pegged rate arrangements:

   Argentina [OM to IF, 1989; IF to US$ 1991]
   Morocco [OM to OC, 1990]
   Yugoslavia [OM to DM, 1990]

To flexible rate arrangements:

   Afghanistan [US$ to IF, 1991]
   Ecuador [US$ to OM, 1989]
   El Salvador [US$ to OM, 1989; OM to IF, 1990]
   Haiti [US$ to IF, 1991]
   Honduras [US$ to OM, 1990]
   Israel [OC to OM, 1991]
   Paraguay [US$ to IF, 1989]
   Peru [US$ to IF, 1990]
   Sierra Leone [US$ to IF, 1990]
   Somalia [OC to OM, 1990]
   Venezuela [US$ to IF, 1989]
   Zambia [SDR to AAI, 1990]

Between flexible rate arrangements:

   Brazil [AAI to IF, 1990]

Reversal within period:

   Dominican Republic [OM to US$, 1990; US$ to IF, 1991]
   Jamaica [OM to US$, 1989; US$ to IF, 1990]
   Nicaragua [US$ to OM, 1990; OM to US$, 1991]

AGHEVLI, B.B., M.S. KHAN and P.J. MONTIEL (1991), *Exchange Rate Policy in Developing Countries: Some Analytical Issues*, Occasional Paper 78, International Monetary Fund, Washington, D.C.

ALLEN, P.R. and P.B. KENEN (1980), *Asset Markets, Exchange Rates, and Economic Integration*, Cambridge University Press, Cambridge, London and New York.

CALVO, G.A. (1991), "The Perils of Sterilization," *IMF Staff Papers* 38, Washington, D.C.

COOPER, R.N. (1971), *Currency Devaluation in Developing Countries*, Essays in International Finance 86, International Finance Section, Princeton University, Princeton.

CORDEN, W.M. (1990), "Exchange Rate Policy in Developing Countries," Country Economic Department Working Paper 412, World Bank, Washington, D.C.

------ (1992), "Integration and Trade Policy Issues in the Ex-Soviet Union" (processed).

DOMINGUEZ, K.M. and J.A. Frankel (1990), "Does Foreign Exchange Intervention Matter: Disentangling the Portfolio and Expectation Effects for the Mark," NBER Working Paper 3299, National Bureau of Economic Research, Cambridge.

DORNBUSCH, R. (1986), *Inflation, Exchange Rates, and Stabilization*, Essays in International Finance 165, International Finance Section, Princeton University, Princeton.

FISCHER, B. and H. REISEN (1992), *Toward Capital Account Convertibility*, OECD Development Centre Policy Brief 4, Organisation for Economic Co-operation and Development, Paris.

FRANKEL, J.A. and K.A. FROOT (1986), "Understanding the Dollar in the 1980s: The Expectations of Chartists and Fundamentalists," *Economic Record*, Supplement.

GIAVAZZI, F. and A. GIOVANNINI (1988), "Can the European Monetary System Be Copied Outside Europe" NBER Working Paper 2786, National Bureau of Economic Research, Cambridge.

HALDANE, A.G. (1991), "The Exchange Rate Mechanism of the European Monetary System," *Bank of England Quarterly Bulletin*.

KENEN, P.B. (1981), "Intervention and Sterilization in the Short Run and the Long Run," in *The International Monetary System Under Flexible Exchange Rates*, R.N. Cooper, et al., eds., Ballinger, Cambridge.

------ (1988), *Managing Exchange Rates*, Royal Institute of International Affairs, London, and Council on Foreign Relations, New York.

------ (1992), "Floating Exchange Rates Reconsidered: The Influence of New Ideas, Priorities, and Problems," paper prepared for the Rinaldo Ossola Memorial Conference sponsored by the Banca d'Italia (processed).

KIGUEL, M.A. and N. LIVIATAN (1992), "When Do Heterodox Stabilization Programs Work," *World Bank Research Observer* 7.

MATHIESON, D.J. and L. ROJAS-SUAREZ (1992), "Liberalization of the Capital Account: Experiences and Issues," International Monetary Fund, Washington, D.C. (processed).

MCKINNON, R.I. (1963), "Optimum Currency Areas," *American Economic Review* 53.

MONTIEL, P.J. and J.D. OSTRY (1991), "Macroeconomic Consequences of Real Exchange Rate Targeting in Developing Countries," *IMF Staff Papers* 38, Washington D.C.

MUSSA, M.L. (1990), *Exchange Rates in Theory and Reality*, Essays in International Finance 179, International Finance Section, Princeton University, Princeton.

OBSTFELD, M. (1988), "The Effectiveness of Foreign exchange Intervention: Recent Experience," NBER Working Paper 2796, National Bureau of Economic Research, Cambridge.

POLAK, J.J. (1990), "Summary," in *Choosing an Exchange Rate Regime: The Challenge for Smaller Industrial Countries*, V. Argy and P. De Grauwe, eds., International Monetary Fund, Washington, D.C.

RODRIQUEZ, C.A. (1992), "Money and Credit under Currency Substitution" (processed)

TAYLOR, M.P. and H.L. ALLEN (1992), "The Use of Technical Analysis in the Foreign Exchange Market," *Journal of International Money and Finance* 11.

WILLIAMSON, J., ed. (1991), *Currency Convertibility in Eastern Europe*, Institute for International Economics, Washington, D.C.

Name Index

Khan, M. 298, 299, 350, 389, 391, 396, 432, 540
Kiguel, M. 543
Kim, I. 520
Kindleberger, C. 141, 391
Kletzer, K. 519
Kneeshaw, J. 520
Knight, M. 284, 432, 433
Kohlhagen, S. 348, 350
Korteweg, P. 284, 288
Kouri, P.J.K. 39, 88
Kraft, J. 462
Kravis, I. 281
Kreinin, H. 280
Krugman, P. 123, 141, 142, 143, 173, 175, 180, 181, 188, 329, 355, 356, 437, 462, 463, 467
Kwack, S.Y. 249

Lamdany, R. 465, 469
Laskar, D. 169
Lau, L. 298
Laursen, S. 65
Lavigne, M. 477, 484, 494
Lawrence, R. 236
Leach, G. 470
Leahy, J. 356
Lerner, A.P. 59
Leutwiler, F. 398
Levine, P. 142
Lewis, K. 438
Lewis, M. 94
Lindbeck, A. 47
Lipsey, R. 281
Liviatan, N. 543
Lopez-Claros, A. 354, 355
Love, J.P. 122
Lowrey, B. 278, 283
Lucas, R.E. 101, 284

MacBean, A. 236, 237, 238, 240, 242, 244, 245, 246, 247
Macedo, J. de 23, 203
Machlup, F. 42, 59, 65, 227
Magee, S. 294, 298, 329, 330
Maizels, A. 236
Makin, J. 330, 339
Markowitz, H.M. 87
Marrese, M. 491
Marris, S. 142
Marshall, A. 59
Marston, R. 96, 142, 463
Massell, B. 236, 238
Masson, P. 123
Mastropasqua, C. 360, 361

Mathieson, D. 103, 356, 542
Mayer, C. 516
Mayer, T. 354, 355
MaCafferty, S. 94, 95
McCallum, B. 96
McCormick, F. 95
McKibbin, W. 114, 432
McKinnon, R.I. 4, 6, 7, 12, 42, 50, 73, 74, 85, 87, 111, 132, 141, 142, 304, 396, 424, 430, 433, 436, 438, 539
McQuirk, A. 281
Meade, J.E. 3, 8, 42, 48, 49, 50, 52, 53, 58, 64, 72, 73, 76, 111, 141
Metzler, J.E. 26, 42, 52, 56, 65, 76, 88
Michalopoulos, C. 476
Micossi, S. 360, 361
Miller, M.H. 111, 112–13, 123, 131, 132, 141, 142, 143, 463
Miller, N.C. 88
Mintz, N. 236
Montiel, P. 540, 543
Morgan, J.P. 122
Mundell, R.A. 3, 4, 5, 6, 7, 8, 9, 10, 11, 13, 15, 16, 49, 52, 68, 73, 74, 76, 85, 88, 101, 258
Mussa, M. 23, 24, 25, 36, 39, 42, 89, 537

Negishi, T. 59
Neumann, M. 518, 519
Neven, D. 516
Nocera, S. 520
Nowzad, B. 432
Nurkse, R. 44, 45, 46, 72, 73

Oates, W.E. 85, 87
Oblath, G. 505
Obstfeld, M. 355, 437, 438, 542
Officer, L. 299
Ohlin, B. 56
Okun, A. 286
Orcutt, G.H. 73, 239
Orey, V. d' 142, 169
Ostry, S. 141, 461, 543
Oudiz, G. 124, 141
Ozeki, Y. 520

Pack, C. 279, 293
Page, S.A.B. 330, 336
Patinkin, D. 85
Patrick, J.D. 69, 258
Perron, P. 353
Pete, P. 505
Pierce, D. 358
Ploeg, F. van der 187, 206

Economists of the Twentieth Century

Monetarism and Macroeconomic Policy
Thomas Mayer

Studies in Fiscal Federalism
Wallace E. Oates

The World Economy in Perspective
Essays in International Trade and European Integration
Herbert Giersch

Towards a New Economics
Critical Essays on Ecology, Distribution and Other Themes
Kenneth E. Boulding

Studies in Positive and Normative Economics
Martin J. Bailey

The Collected Essays of Richard E. Quandt (2 volumes)
Richard E. Quandt

International Trade Theory and Policy
Selected Essays of W. Max Corden
W. Max Corden

Organization and Technology in Capitalist Development
William Lazonick

Studies in Human Capital
Collected Essays of Jacob Mincer, Volume 1
Jacob Mincer

Studies in Labor Supply
Collected Essays of Jacob Mincer, Volume 2
Jacob Mincer

Macroeconomics and Economic Policy
The Selected Essays of Assar Lindbeck, Volume I
Assar Lindbeck

The Welfare State
The Selected Essays of Assar Lindbeck, Volume II
Assar Lindbeck

Classical Economics, Public Expenditure and Growth
Walter Eltis

Money, Interest Rates and Inflation
Frederic S. Mishkin

The Public Choice Approach to Politics
Dennis C. Mueller

The Liberal Economic Order
Volume I Essays on International Economics
Volume II Money, Cycles and Related Themes
Gottfried Haberler
Edited by Anthony Y.C. Koo

Economic Growth and Business Cycles
Prices and the Process of Cyclical Development
Paolo Sylos Labini

International Adjustment, Money and Trade
Theory and Measurement for Economic Policy, Volume I
Herbert G. Grubel

International Capital and Service Flows
Theory and Measurement for Economic Policy, Volume II
Herbert G. Grubel

Unintended Effects of Government Policies
Theory and Measurement for Economic Policy, Volume III
Herbert G. Grubel

The Economics of Competitive Enterprise
Selected Essays of P.W.S. Andrews
Edited by Frederic S. Lee and Peter E. Earl

The Repressed Economy
Causes, Consequences, Reform
Deepak Lal

Economic Theory and Market Socialism
Selected Essays of Oskar Lange
Edited by Tadeusz Kowalik

Trade, Development and Political Economy
Selected Essays of Ronald Findlay
Ronald Findlay

General Equilibrium Theory
The Collected Essays of Takashi Negishi, Volume I
Takashi Negishi

The History of Economics
The Collected Essays of Takashi Negishi, Volume II
Takashi Negishi

Studies in Econometric Theory
The Collected Essays of Takeshi Amemiya
Takeshi Amemiya

Exchange Rates and the Monetary System
Selected Essays of Peter B. Kenen
Peter B. Kenen

Econometric Methods and Applications (2 volumes)
G.S. Maddala

National Accounting and Economic Theory
The Collected Papers of Dan Usher, Volume I
Dan Usher

Welfare Economics and Public Finance
The Collected Papers of Dan Usher, Volume II
Dan Usher